Georg

Arcana Coelestia

THE

HEAVENLY ARCANA

CONTAINED IN THE HOLY SCRIPTURE OR WORD OF THE LORD

UNFOLDED

BEGINNING WITH THE BOOK OF GENESIS

TOGETHER WITH WONDERFUL THINGS SEEN IN THE WORLD OF
SPIRITS AND IN THE HEAVEN OF ANGELS

TRANSLATED FROM THE LATIN OF

EMANUEL SWEDENBORG

THOROUGHLY REVISED AND EDITED BY THE
REV. JOHN FAULKNER POTTS, B.A. LOND.

VOLUME III.

STANDARD EDITION

NEW YORK
THE AMERICAN SWEDENBORG PRINTING AND PUBLISHING
SOCIETY
3 WEST TWENTY-NINTH STREET
1915

Published by The American Swedenborg Printing and Publishing Society, organized for the business and objects solely of printing, publishing and circulating the Theological Works and Writings of Emanuel Swedenborg for charitable and missionary purposes. Incorporated in the State of New York, A.D. 1850.

have made Thee this day a defenced city," means that it was from eternity. Of the Lord nothing else than what is eternal can be predicated. [3] In *Moses :*—

Ye are standing this day all of you before Jehovah your God, to enter into the covenant of Jehovah thy God, and into His oath, which Jehovah thy God maketh with thee this day, that He may establish thee this day unto Himself for a people ; and He will be a God unto thee ; and not with you only, but with them who stand here with us this day before Jehovah our God, and with them who are not with us this day (*Deut.* xxix. 10, 12–14).

In the sense of the letter here "this day" is the time present when Moses spoke to the people ; but that it nevertheless involves the time to come and what is perpetual, is evident ; for to make a covenant with any one, and with those who were there, and not there, involves perpetuity, and the perpetuity itself is what is meant in the internal sense. [4] That "daily" and "this day" signify what is perpetual, is also evident from the sacrifice which was made every day. This, on account of the signification of "day," "daily," and "this day," was called the continual or perpetual sacrifice (*Num.* xxviii. 3, 23 ; *Deut.* viii. 13 ; xi. 31 ; xii. 11). This is still more plainly evident from the manna which rained from heaven, of which it is thus said in *Moses :*—

Behold I will rain bread from heaven ; and the people shall go out and gather a portion day by day ; and let no man leave of it till the morning. What they left till the morning bred worms, and putrefied, except what was kept the day before the Sabbath (*Exod.* xvi. 4, 19, 20, 23).

This was because the manna signified the Lord's Divine Human (*John* vi. 31, 32, 49, 50, 58). And because it signified the Lord's Divine Human, it signified heavenly food, which is nothing else than love and charity together with the goods and truths of faith. This food is given by the Lord in the heavens to the angels every moment, and thus perpetually and to eternity (see n. 2493). This also is what is meant in the Lord's Prayer by "Give us this day our daily bread" (*Matt.* vi. 11 ; *Luke* xi. 3) ; that is, every instant to eternity.

2839. *In the mountain Jehovah will see.* That this signifies charity, by means of which it is provided by the Lord that they should be saved, namely, the spiritual, is evident from the signification of a "mountain," as being love and charity (see n. 795, 796, 1430). That "Jehovah will see" denotes the Lord's providence, or what is provided by the Lord, was said just above (n. 2836). Here charity is spoken of, and not love, on account of the difference between charity and love (see n. 2023). That the spiritual are saved by charity, and not by faith separate from charity, is evident from many passages in the Word. With charity and with faith the case is this : charity without faith is not genuine charity, and faith without charity is not faith. That there may be charity, there must be faith; and that there may be faith, there must be charity; but the essential itself is charity; for in no other ground can the seed which is faith be implanted. From the conjunction of the two mutually and reciprocally is the heavenly marriage, that is, the Lord's kingdom. Unless faith is implanted in charity it is mere memory-knowledge; for it goes no further than the memory; there is no affection of the heart which receives it; but when it is implanted in charity, that is, in the life, it becomes intelligence and wisdom. Charity without faith, such as is with children and with upright Gentiles, is only ground in which faith is implanted—if not in the life of the body, still in the other life (see n. 1802, 2280, 2290–2309, 2419, 2589–2604).

2840. Verses 15, 16. *And the angel of Jehovah called unto Abraham a second time out of heaven, and said, By Myself have I sworn, saith Jehovah, because thou hast done this thing, and hast not withheld thy son, thine only one.* "The angel of Jehovah called unto Abraham a second time out of heaven," signifies still greater consolation of the Lord from the Divine; "and said, By Myself have I sworn, saith Jehovah," signifies irrevocable confirmation from the Divine; "because thou hast done this thing," signifies the thing accomplished; "and hast not kept back thy son, thine only one," signifies the unition of the Human with the Divine by the utmost of temptation.

2841. *The Angel of Jehovah called unto Abraham a second time out of heaven.* That this signifies still greater consolation of the Lord, is evident from the signification of "calling out of heaven," as being to console; and from the signification of the "angel of Jehovah," as being the Lord's Divine Itself (see above, n. 2821, where the same words occur). This is said a "second time," because there is greater consolation. The first consolation is contained in verses 12, 13, and 14, where the subject is the Lord's providence that those from the human race who are called the spiritual should be adopted. The second consolation, which is greater, is contained in the verses that follow (17, 18, etc., to the end), namely, that the spiritual should be multiplied as the stars of the heavens, and as the sand upon the sea shore; and that not they only should be saved, but also all who are in good. These were things of the Lord's love, and therefore He had consolation from them. No one has consolation except from the things which are of his love.

2842. *And said, By Myself have I sworn, saith Jehovah.* That this signifies irrevocable confirmation from the Divine, namely, concerning the things which follow, is evident from the signification of "saying by Myself have I sworn," and of "saith Jehovah;" all which involve confirmation, and indeed from the Divine, that is, from Himself. The Divine cannot confirm from any other source than from Itself; and what it confirms is irrevocable, because it is eternal truth. Whatever Jehovah or the Lord speaks is eternal truth (*Matt.* xxiv. 35), for it comes from the very being of truth. But His confirming it as it were by an oath (as here and elsewhere in the Word) is not for the reason that it may be more true, but for the reason that it is said to such as do not receive truth Divine unless it is so confirmed; for they have no other idea of Jehovah or the Lord than as of a man, who can say, and change, as we frequently read in the Word; but in the internal sense it is very different. Every one may know that Jehovah or the Lord never confirms anything by an oath; but when the Divine truth itself, and its confirmation, passes down to a man of such nature, it is turned into the semblance of an oath. The case herein is as it was with the devouring fire and smoke that appeared upon Mount Sinai before the eyes of the people, when Jehovah or the Lord came down (*Exod.* xix. 18; *Deut.* iv. 11, 12; v. 19–21): His glory in heaven, even mercy itself, appeared in this manner before the people there, who were in evil and falsity (see n. 1861); and the case is the same with many things called the sayings and doings of Jehovah that are spoken of in the Word. It may be seen from this that the expression, " by Myself have I sworn, saith Jehovah," is significative of irrevocable confirmation from the Divine. [2] That to "swear," when predicated of Jehovah, signifies to confirm with a man who is of such nature, may be seen from many other passages in the Word; as in *David* :—

Jehovah remembered His covenant forever, the word which He commanded to a thousand generations ; which He made with Abraham, and His oath unto Isaac (*Ps.* cv. 8, 9).

The case is the same with a covenant as with an oath, in that Jehovah or the Lord does not make a covenant with man, but when conjunction by love and charity is treated of, this is set forth in act as a covenant (see n. 1864). In the same :—

Jehovah hath sworn, and will not repent, Thou art a Priest forever, after the manner of Melchizedek* (*Ps.* cx. 4).

This is said concerning the Lord, and " Jehovah hath sworn" denotes irrevocable confirmation from the Divine, that is, that it is eternal truth. [3] In the same :—

I have made a covenant with My chosen, I have sworn unto David My servant, Thy seed will I establish forever, and build up thy throne to generation and generation (*Ps.* lxxxix. 3, 4).

This also is concerning the Lord : to " make a covenant with the chosen," and to "swear unto David," denote irrevocable confirmation or eternal truth ; "David" denotes the Lord (n. 1888); to "make a covenant" regards the Divine good; to "swear," the Divine truth. In the same :—

My covenant will I not profane nor alter the thing that is gone out of My lips ; once have I sworn by My holiness, I will not lie unto David (*Ps.* lxxxix. 34, 35) ;

where also "David" denotes the Lord; the "covenant" here likewise has regard to the Divine good; and the "thing that has gone out of My lips," to the Divine truth, and this on account of the marriage of good and truth which is in everything in the Word (see n. 683, 793, 801, 2516, 2712). [4] In the same :—

Poenituit . . . juxta verbum meum, Malchizedech ; but *poenitebit . . . juxta modum Malchizedechi,* n. 6148. [*Rotch ed.*]

Jehovah hath sworn unto David in truth, He will not turn from it, Of the fruit of thy body will I set upon thy throne, if thy sons will keep My covenant, and My testimony that I shall teach them (*Ps.* cxxxii. 11, 12) ;

" Jehovah hath sworn unto David in truth" manifestly denotes the confirmation of eternal truth; and therefore it is said, " He will not turn from it;" that by David is meant the Lord has been stated already; the oath was still " to David," because he was of such a character that he believed that the confirmation was concerning himself and his posterity; for David was in the love of himself and of his posterity, and hence believed that it was concerning him; that is, as said above, that his seed should be established forever, and his throne to generation and generation; but this was said of the Lord.   [5] In *Isaiah* :—

This is as the waters of Noah unto Me ; for as I have sworn that the waters of Noah should no more go over the earth, so have I sworn that I would not be wroth with thee (liv. 9) ;

where to " swear" denotes making a covenant and confirming it by an oath.   That it was a covenant, and not an oath, may be seen in *Genesis* ix. 11.   In the same :—

Jehovah hath sworn, saying, Surely as I have thought, so shall it come to pass (xiv. 24).

In the same :—

Jehovah hath sworn by His right hand, and by the arm of His strength (lxii. 8).

In *Jeremiah* :—

Hear ye the word of Jehovah, all Judah, that dwell in the land of Egypt; behold I have sworn by My great name, saith Jehovah, that My name shall no more be named in the mouth of any man of Judah, saying, As the Lord Jehovih liveth, in all the land of Egypt (xliv. 26).

In the same :—

By Myself have I sworn, saith Jehovah, that Bozrah shall become a desolation (xlix. 13).

In the same :—

Jehovah Zebaoth hath sworn by His soul, Surely I will fill thee with men as with the locust (li. 14).

In *Amos*:—

The Lord Jehovih hath sworn by His holiness, that behold the days shall come (iv. 2).

In the same :—

Jehovah hath sworn by the excellency of Jacob, Surely I will never forget any of their deeds (viii. 7).

[6] In these passages, "Jehovah swearing by His right hand," by His "great name," by "Himself," by His "soul," by His "holiness," by the "excellency of Jacob," signifies the confirmation there is in Jehovah or the Lord. A confirmation by Jehovah can be given only from Himself. The "right hand of Jehovah," the "great name of Jehovah," the "soul of Jehovah," the "holiness of Jehovah," the "excellency of Jacob," signify the Lord's Divine Human : "swearing" thereby was confirmation. [7] Jehovah or the Lord "swearing" to give the land to Abraham, Isaac, and Jacob, or to their posterity, signifies in the internal sense the confirmation that He would give the heavenly kingdom to those who are in love to Him and faith in Him. It is they who are meant in the internal sense of the Word by the sons and the posterity of Abraham, Isaac, and Jacob, or of the fathers; which was also actually represented by the fact that the land of Canaan was given to their posterity, and that the church at that time with them represented the Lord's heavenly kingdom, as the land itself also did. (That "land" and the "land of Canaan" in the internal sense is the Lord's kingdom, may be seen above, n. 1413, 1437, 1607.) It is from this that it is said in *Moses* :—

That ye may prolong your days upon the ground which Jehovah sware unto your fathers, to give unto them, and to their seed, a land flowing with milk and honey ; that your days may be multiplied, and the days of your children, upon the ground which Jehovah sware unto your fathers, to give them, as the days of the heavens upon the earth (*Deut.* xi. 9, 21).

From these passages it must now be evident that Jehovah's "swearing" was representative of confirmation, and indeed of an irrevocable one. This is still more plainly manifest in *Isaiah* :—

By Myself have I sworn, the word of righteousness is gone forth from My mouth, and shall not return, that to Me every knee shall bow, every tongue shall swear (xlv. 23).

[8] Moreover it was enjoined upon those who were of the representative Jewish Church, that when they confirmed covenants by an oath, and likewise vows, also promises, and sureties, they should "swear by the name of Jehovah." The reason why this was enjoined upon them, although it was only permitted, was that the confirmation of the internal man also would thus be represented; so that oaths at that time in the name of Jehovah, were as other things were, namely, representative. That it was enjoined, that is, permitted, is evident in *Moses* :—

Thou shalt fear Jehovah thy God, and Him shalt thou serve, and shalt swear by His name ; ye shall not go after other gods (*Deut.* vi. 13, 14).

Again in the same :—

Thou shalt fear Jehovah thy God, Him shalt thou serve and to Him shalt thou cleave, and shalt swear by His name (*Deut.* x. 20).

In *Isaiah* :—

He who blesseth himself in the earth shall bless himself in the God of truth, and he that sweareth in the earth shall swear by the God of truth (lxv. 16).

In *Jeremiah* :—

If thou wilt return, O Israel, saith Jehovah, unto Me shalt thou return ; and if thou wilt put away thine abominations from before Me, waver not ; and thou shalt swear, Jehovah liveth, in truth, in judgment, and in righteousness (iv. 1, 2).

In the same :—

If learning they will learn the ways of My people, to swear by My name, then they shall be built up in the midst of My people (xii. 16).

That they also swore " by the name of Jehovah," or swore "to Jehovah," may be seen in *Isaiah* :—

Hear ye this, O house of Jacob, that are called by the name of Israel, and are come forth out of the waters of Judah, that swear by the name of Jehovah, and have made mention of the God of Israel, not in truth, and not in righteousness (xlviii. 1).

In the same :—

In that day there shall be five cities in the land of Egypt that speak the language of Canaan, and swear to Jehovah Zebaoth (xix. 18).

In *Joshua :—*

The princes of the congregation sware to the Gibeonites by Jehovah the God of Israel (ix. 18, 19).

[9] From this it is evident that they were permitted to swear by the name of Jehovah, or by Jehovah; yet it is evident that this was nothing else than a representative of the confirmation of the internal man. But it is known that internal men, that is, those who have conscience, have no need to confirm anything by an oath; and that they do not thus confirm. To them oaths are a cause of shame. They can indeed say with some asseveration that a thing is so, and can also confirm the truth by reasons; but to swear that it is so, they cannot. They have an internal bond by which they are bound, namely, that of conscience. To superadd to this an external bond, which is an oath, is like imputing to them that they are not upright in heart. The internal man is also of such a character that he loves to speak and act from freedom, but not from compulsion; for with them the internal compels the external, but not the reverse. On this account they who have conscience do not swear; still less do they who have perception of good and truth, that is, celestial men. These do not even confirm themselves or one another by reasons, but merely say that a thing is so, or is not so (n. 202, 337, 2718); wherefore they are still further removed from taking an oath. [10] For these reasons, and because oaths were among the representatives which were to be abrogated, the Lord taught that we are not to swear at all, in these words in *Matthew :—*

Ye have heard that it has been said, Thou shalt not forswear thyself; but shalt perform unto the Lord thine oaths. But I say unto you, Swear not at all; neither by the heaven, for it is God's throne; nor by the earth, for it is His footstool; nor by Jerusalem, for it is the city of the great king; neither shalt thou swear by thy head, for thou canst not make one hair white or black. But let your speech be, Yea, yea; nay, nay; for whatsoever is more than these cometh of evil (v. 33–37).

By these words is meant that we are not to swear at all by Jehovah, nor by anything which is of Jehovah or the Lord.

2843. *Because thou hast done this thing.* That this signifies the thing accomplished, is evident without explication.

2844. *And hast not withheld thy son, thine only one.* That this signifies the unition of the Human with the Divine by the utmost of temptation, is evident from what was said above (n. 2827), where the same words occur, except that we do not here read "from Me," by which is signified that there will be a still further unition. That there was always a further unition of the Lord's Human Essence with His Divine Essence, even to a plenary unition, may be seen above (n. 1864, 2033).

2845. Verse 17. *That in blessing I will bless thee, and in multiplying I will multiply thy seed, as the stars of the heavens, and as the sand which is upon the sea shore ; and thy seed shall inherit the gate of thine enemies.* "That in blessing I will bless thee," signifies fructification from the affection of truth; "and in multiplying I will multiply," signifies derivations of truth therefrom ; "thy seed," signifies the spiritual, who being in the good of faith are saved by the Lord's Divine Human ; "as the stars of the heavens," signifies the multitude of the knowledges of good and truth ; "and as the sand which is upon the sea shore," signifies the multitude of corresponding memory-knowledges ; "and thy seed shall inherit the gate of thine enemies," signifies that charity and faith shall come into the place where evil and falsity were before.

2846. *That in blessing I will bless thee.* That this signifies fructification from the affection of truth, is evident from the signification of "being blessed," as meaning to be enriched with celestial and spiritual good (see n. 981, 1096, 1420, 1422); here, to be made fruitful from the good of faith, or what is the same, from the affection of truth, because the spiritual are treated of. It is here said by Jehovah to Abraham, "in blessing I will bless thee," and by Abraham is represented the Lord as to His Divine Human, as before in this chapter; and yet the Lord Himself could not be blessed, because He is blessing itself; but He is said to be blessed, when in accordance with His love those abound who are saved ; and therefore in the internal sense these are here signified, as is also evident from what immediately follows. Fructification is here spoken of, because this is predicated of affection ; but multiplication, as next follows, is predicated of the truths which are therefrom.

2847. *In multiplying I will multiply.* That this signifies the derivations of truth therefrom, is evident from the predication of "being multiplied," as being concerning truth; here therefore as meaning the derivations of truth from affection, as was said just above. (That being "fructified" is predicated of good, and being "multiplied," of truth, may be seen above, n. 43, 55, 913, 983.)

2848. *Thy seed.* That this signifies the spiritual who are saved in the good of faith by the Lord's Divine Human, is evident from the signification of "seed," as being the faith of charity (concerning which see n. 1025, 1447, 1610, 1941); or what is the same, those of the human race who are in the faith of charity, that is, who are spiritual. They are also called by the Lord the "seed," and the "sons of the kingdom," in *Matthew :—*

He who soweth the good seed is the Son of man, but the seed are the sons of the kingdom (xiii. 37, 38).

2849. *As the stars of the heavens.* That this signifies the multitude of the knowledges of good and truth, is evident from the signification of the "stars," as being the knowledges of good and truth (see n. 1808, 2495). The spiritual are they who in the Word are in various places compared to the stars, and this owing to the knowledges of good and truth which they have; but the celestial are not so compared, because they have not knowledges but perceptions; moreover the stars illumine the night, and the spiritual have a light of night (as from the moon and stars) in comparison with the light of day in which the celestial are. (That the spiritual have comparative obscurity may be seen above, n. 1043, 2708 at the beginning, 2715.)

2850. *And as the sand which is upon the sea shore.* That this signifies the multitude of corresponding memory-knowledges, is evident from the signification of the "sea," as being memory-knowledges in general, or a gathering of them (see n. 28, 2120); and from the signification of "sand," as being memory-knowledges specifically or in particular. Memory-knowledges are compared to "sand," because the little stones of which sand is made, in the internal sense signify memory-knowledges (n. 643, 1298). It is here said that they shall be multiplied "as the stars of the heavens," and also "as the sand of the sea shore," because the stars or knowledges have relation to the rational, but the sand of the sea shore or memory-knowledges to the natural. When the things of the rational man, namely, the goods and truths of knowledges, agree with those of the natural man, namely, with memory-knowledges, so that they make a one, or mutually confirm each other, they then correspond. To this correspondence the Lord reduces the rational and natural things of man when he regenerates him, or makes him spiritual. From this cause it is that both the stars of the heavens and the sand of the sea shore are here mentioned; otherwise one would have been sufficient.

2851. *And thy seed shall inherit the gate of thine enemies.* That this signifies that charity and faith shall succeed in the place where evil and falsity were before, is evident from the signification of "inheriting," as being to receive the Lord's life (see n. 2658); here, to succeed in the place, because when charity and faith are in the place where evil and falsity were before, then the Lord's life succeeds there; from the signification of "seed," as being charity and faith (see n. 1025, 1447, 1610, 1941); from the signification of a "gate" (explained in what follows); and from the signification of "enemies," as being evils and falsities, or what is the same, those who are in evil and falsity: in the internal sense of the Word these are signified by "enemies" and "foes." [2] As regards the signification of a "gate," there are in general two gates with every man; the one opens toward hell, and is opened to the evils and falsities therefrom; in this gate are infernal genii and spirits; the other gate opens toward heaven, and is opened to good and the truths therefrom; in this gate are angels. There is thus a gate which leads to hell, and a gate which leads to heaven. The gate of hell is opened to those who are in evil and falsity, and only through chinks round about above does anything of the light from heaven enter, by means of which they are able to think and reason; but the gate of heaven is opened to those who are in good and the truth therefrom. [3] For there are two ways which lead into man's rational mind—a higher or internal one, through which good and truth from the Lord enter, and a lower or external one, through which evil and falsity come up from hell. The rational mind itself is in the middle, and to it these ways tend. That mind, from the goods and truths which are in it, is compared in the Word to a city, and is called a "city." And because it is compared to a city, and is called a "city," gates are attributed to it, and it is often described as being besieged and stormed by enemies, that is, by evil genii and spirits; and as being defended by angels from the Lord, that is by the Lord. The infernal genii and spirits, with their evils and falsities, cannot come further than to the lower or outer gate, and in no case into the city. If they could get into the city, or into the rational mind, all would be over with the man. But when they come so far as to seem to themselves to have taken that city by storm, it is then closed, so that good and truth no longer flow into it from heaven except as was said some little through chinks round about. From this it is that such persons no longer have anything of charity or anything of faith, but make good consist in evil, and truth in falsity. From this also it is that they are no longer truly rational, although they seem to themselves to be so (n. 1914, 1944). And it is from this that they are called dead men, although they believe that they are more alive than others (n. 81, 290 at the end). These things are so because the gate of heaven is closed to them. That it is closed to them manifestly appears and is perceived in the other life; as also on the other hand that the gate of heaven is open to those who are in good and truth. [4] As regards the "gate of enemies" in particular, which is treated of in this verse, it is with man in his natural mind. When man is wholly natural, or not regenerate, evils and falsities occupy the gate; or what is the same, evil genii and spirits flow into it with cupidities of evil and persuasions of falsity (see n. 687, 697, 1692); but when man becomes spiritual, or is being regenerated, then the evils and falsities, or what is the same, the evil genii and spirits, are driven away from the gate, or from the mind; then goods and truths, or charity and faith, take their place; which things are signified by its being said, "thy seed shall inherit the gate of thine enemies." This takes place in particular with every man when he is being regenerated; and in like manner in the other life with those who come into the Lord's kingdom; and it also takes place in the general body, or in the church, which is composed of many. [5] This was represented by the sons of Israel expelling the nations from the land of Canaan. The latter is meant in the literal sense where it is said, "thy seed shall inherit the gate of thine enemies;" but in the internal sense are signified the things which have been told. Hence in ancient times it became customary to speak thus when blessing those who were entering into marriage; as is also manifest from the benediction of Laban to his sister Rebekah, when she was going away betrothed to Isaac :—

Our sister, be thou thousands of ten thousands, and let thy seed inherit the gate of those that hate thee (*Gen.* xxiv. 60).

[6] That such things are signified in the Word by the "gate of enemies" or of "those that hate," may be seen from the following passages. In *Isaiah :*—

I will kill thy root with famine, and I will slay them that remain of thee. Howl, O gate ; cry, O city ; thou art melted away O Philistia all of thee, for there cometh a smoke out of the north (xiv. 30, 31) ;

to "kill the root with famine, and to slay them that remain," denotes to take away the goods and truths which had been stored up interiorly by the Lord. That "they that remain" mean these, may be seen above (n. 468, 530, 560–562, 661, 798, 1050, 1738, 1906, 2284). The "gate" denotes access to the interiors, or to the rational mind; the "city," that mind, or what is the same, the goods and truths in it (n. 402, 2268, 2450, 2451, 2712); "Philistia" denotes the memory-knowledge of the knowledges of faith, or what is the same, those who are in the memory-knowledge of them, but not in the goods of faith (n. 1197, 1198); "a smoke out of the north" signifies that there is falsity from hell (that "smoke" is falsity from evil, may be seen above, n. 1861). [7] In the same :—

The city of emptiness shall be broken down, every house shall be shut up that no one may come in ; there is a crying in the streets because of the wine ; all gladness shall be desolated, the joy of the land shall be exiled, that which is left in the city shall be desolation, and the gate shall be smitten with devastation, for thus shall it be in the midst of the earth, among the people (xxiv. 10–13) ;

the "city of emptiness which shall be broken down" denotes
the human mind as being deprived of truth; that "every
house shall be shut up," denotes being without good (that a
"house" is good, may be seen above, n. 2233, 2234); the "crying in the streets because of the wine" denotes a state of falsity (that a "cry" is predicated of falsities, may be seen
above, n. 2240; also that "wine" is truth, of which the cry is
that there is none, n. 1071, 1798; that "streets" are what
lead to truths, n. 2336); "gladness which is desolated" is
predicated of truth; the "joy of the land which is exiled" is
predicated of good; hence it is manifest what is signified by
"that which is left in the city shall be desolation," and by
"the gate shall be smitten with devastation;" the gate is said
to be "devastated" when nothing but evils and falsities reign.
[8] In *Jeremiah* :—

The ways of Zion do mourn, because none come to the appointed
feast ; all her gates are desolate, her priests do sigh, her virgins are afflicted, and she herself is in bitterness ; her adversaries have become the
head, her enemies are secure, because Jehovah hath afflicted her for the
multitude of her transgressions ; her children are gone into captivity before the adversary (*Lam.* i. 4, 5) ;

"the ways of Zion mourning" denotes there being no longer
truths from good (that "ways" are truths, may be seen above,
n. 189, 627, 2333); "all the gates being desolated" denotes
that all the approaches are occupied by falsities; "the enemies having become the head" denotes that evils reign. [9] In
the same :—

Jehovah hath made the rampart and the wall of the daughter of Zion
to lament ; they languish together ; her gates are sunk into the earth ;
He hath destroyed and broken her bars ; her king and her princes are
among the nations ; the law is not ; yea her prophets found no vision
from Jehovah ; all thine enemies have opened their mouth against thee ;
they hissed and gnashed the teeth ; they said, We have swallowed her
up ; surely this is the day that we looked for ; we have found, we have
seen it (*Lam.* ii. 8, 9, 16) ;

"the gates sunk down into the earth" denotes the natural
mind occupied by evils and falsities; "her king and her
princes being among the nations" denotes that truths are immersed in evils (that a "king" is truth in general, may be seen
above, n. 1672, 1728, 2015, 2069; also that "princes" are

primary truths, n. 1482, 1089; and that "nations" are evils, n. 1259, 1260, 1849, 1868, 2588). **[10]** In *Moses :*—

A nation from far, from the end of the earth, shall straiten thee in all thy gates, in all thy land; thus shall thine enemy straiten thee (*Deut.* xxviii. 49, 52, 53).

This is among the curses which Moses foretold to the people if they should not remain in the precepts and statutes : a "nation from far from the end of the earth," in the internal sense, denotes evils and falsities, or those who are in evil and falsity ; to "besiege in all the gates" denotes cutting off all access to good and truth.   **[11]** In *Nahum :*—

Behold, thy people in the midst of thee are women, the gates of thy land are set wide open to thine enemies, the fire hath devoured thy bars ; draw thee water for the siege ; strengthen thy fortresses ; go into the clay and tread the mortar, make strong the brickkiln (iii. 13, 14) ;

"the gates of thy land being set wide open to thine enemies" denotes that evils occupy the place where there should be goods.   In the book of *Judges :*—

The highways ceased, and they walked through byways, they went through crooked ways, the villages ceased in Israel.   He chose new gods ; then was war against the gates ; was there a shield seen or a spear in forty thousands of Israel ? (v. 6–8) ;

the prophecy of Deborah and Barak ; there being "war against the gates" denotes against goods and truths.   **[12]** In *David :*—

They that dwell in the gate plot against me, they that drink strong drink sing songs (*Ps.* lxix. 12) ;

"they that dwell in the gate" denotes evils and falsities, and also the infernals.   In *Ezekiel :*—

In the visions of God he brought me to the door of the inner gate that looketh toward the north.   (He there saw the great abominations of the house of Israel.)   He also brought me to the door of the gate of the house of Jehovah that looketh toward the north ; (he there also saw abominations) (viii. 6, 14, 15) ;

"the door of the inner gate that looketh toward the north" denotes the place where interior falsities are; "the door of the gate of the house of Jehovah toward the north" denotes the place where interior evils are (that the falsities and evils are interior ones, and that it is an interior sphere in which such

spirits and genii are, may be seen above, n. 2121–2124). [13]
In *David* :—

Lo, sons are a possession of Jehovah, and the fruit of the womb is His
reward ; as arrows in the hand of a mighty man, so are sons of the youth.
Happy is the man that hath filled his quiver with them ; they shall not
be ashamed, for they shall speak with the enemies in the gate (*Ps.*
cxxvii. 3–5) ;

"to speak with the enemies in the gate" denotes to have no
fear of evils and falsities, and thus not of hell. In *Isaiah* :—

In that day shall Jehovah Zebaoth be for a spirit of judgment to him
that sitteth in judgment, and for strength to them that turn back the
battle to the gate ; and these also are insane through wine, and through
strong drink are gone astray (xxviii. 5–7).

In the same :—

They shall be cut off that make men to sin by a word, and lay a snare
for him that reproveth in the gate ; and make the just to turn aside to a
thing of nought (xxix. 20, 21).

In the same :—

Elam bare the quiver in a chariot of a man, and horsemen ; Kir un-
covered the shield ; and the choice of thy valleys was full of chariots and
horsemen ; placing they placed themselves at the gate, and he looked in
that day to the armory of the house of the forest (xxii. 6–8).

In *Jeremiah* :—

Judah hath mourned, and the gates thereof languished ; they have
mourned to the earth, and the cry of Jerusalem is gone up ; their nobles
have sent their little ones to the waters ; they came to the pits, they found
no waters (xiv. 2, 3).

In the same :—

The elders have ceased from the gate, the young men from their music
(*Lam.* v. 14).

[14] It may be seen from these passages what is signified by
the "gate of enemies," namely, that it is hell, or infernal
spirits, who are continually attacking goods and truths. Their
seat with man as before said is in his natural mind. But
when a man is of such a character as to admit goods and
truths, and thus angels, the infernal spirits are then driven
away by the Lord from that seat ; and on their being driven
away, the gate of heaven or heaven itself is opened. This gate
is also mentioned in the Word in various places ; as in *Isaiah* :—

A song in the land of Judah : We have a strong city, salvation will He appoint for walls and bulwarks ; open ye the gates, and the righteous nation that keepeth fidelities shall enter in (xxvi. 1, 2).

In the same :—

Thus said Jehovah to His anointed, to Cyrus, whose right hand I have holden, to subdue nations before him ; and I will loose the loins of kings, to open the doors before him, and the gates shall not be shut ; I will go before thee, and will make the crooked places straight, and I will break in pieces the doors of brass, and cut in sunder the bars of iron (xlv. 1, 2).

In the same :—

The sons of the stranger shall build up thy walls, and their kings shall minister unto thee ; they shall open thy gates continually, they shall not be shut day nor night ; violence shall no more be heard in thy land, wasting and destruction within thy borders ; and thou shalt call thy walls salvation, and thy gates praise (lx. 10, 11, 18).

In the same :—

Go through, go through the gates ; prepare ye the way for the people, level, make level the highway ; say ye to the daughter of Zion, Behold thy salvation cometh (lxii. 10–12).

In *Micah* :—

They shall pass through the gate, and shall go out thereat, and their king shall pass on before them, and Jehovah in their beginning (ii. 13).

In *David* :—

Lift up your heads, O ye gates ; and be ye lifted up, ye everlasting doors ; and the King of glory shall come in.   Who is this King of glory ? Jehovah strong and mighty, Jehovah mighty in battle.   Lift up your heads, O ye gates ; lift them up, ye everlasting doors (*Ps.* xxiv. 7–10).

In the same :—

Praise Jehovah, O Jerusalem ; praise thy God, O Zion : for He hath strengthened the bars of thy gates, He hath blessed thy children within thee (*Ps.* cxlvii. 12, 13).

[15] From these passages it is manifest that the " gate of heaven" is where angels are with man, that is, where there is an influx of good and truth from the Lord; and thus that as before said there are two gates.   Concerning these two gates the Lord speaks thus in *Matthew* :—

Enter ye in by the strait gate ; for wide is the gate and broad is the way that leadeth to destruction, and many there be that go in thereat ;

because strait is the gate and narrow is the way that leadeth unto life, and few there be that find it (vii. 12–14; *Luke* xiii. 23, 24).

Moreover the gates to the New Jerusalem and the gates to the new temple are much treated of in *Ezekiel*, and also by John in the *Apocalypse*, by which nothing else is meant than the entrances to heaven (see *Ezek.* xl. 6–49; xliii. 1, 2, 4; xliv. 1–3; xlvi. 1–9, 12; xlviii. 31–34; *Rev.* xxi. 12, 13, 21, 25; xxii. 14; *Isa.* liv. 11, 12). Hence Jerusalem is called the "gate of the people" (*Micah* i. 9; *Obad.* verse 13).

2852. Verse 18. *And in thy seed shall all the nations of the earth be blessed, because thou hast hearkened to My voice.* "In thy seed shall all the nations of the earth be blessed," signifies the salvation of all who are in good; "because thou hast hearkened to My voice," signifies by the union of His Human Essence with His Divine Essence.

2853. *In thy seed shall all the nations of the earth be blessed.* That this signifies the salvation of all who are in good, is evident from the signification of "being blessed," as being to be enriched with celestial and spiritual good (see n. 981, 1096, 1420, 1422); here, to be saved, because spoken of those who are saved (that "to be blessed" has a comprehensive meaning is well known); from the signification of "seed," as being the faith of charity (see n. 1025, 1447, 1610); and from the signification of the "nations of the earth," as being those who are in good (see n. 1159, 1258–1260, 1416, 1849). [2] Moreover in these words there is contained the following arcanum: that through the church (which is here the "earth," n. 662, 1066, 1067, 1262) those are saved who are out of the church; for as just stated, "thy seed" denotes the faith of charity; and no others are in the faith of charity than those within the church, for the faith of charity is truth of doctrine adjoined to good of life. The case is this: The Lord's kingdom on earth consists of all those who are in good, who though scattered over the whole earth, are still one, and as members constitute one body. Such is the Lord's kingdom in the heavens, where the whole heaven represents one man, which is therefore also called the Grand Man (n. 684, 1276); and what is wonderful and hitherto unknown, all parts of the human body correspond to societies in heaven. And therefore it is sometimes said that some societies belong to the province of the head, some to the province of the eye, others to that of the chest, and so on, which correspondence will of the Lord's Divine mercy be spoken of by itself. [3] The case is the same with the Lord's church on earth, where the church is like the heart and lungs; while those outside the church answer to the parts of the body which are supported and live from the heart and lungs. Hence it is manifest that without a church somewhere on the earth the human race could not subsist, as the body could not without the heart and lungs (see n. 468, 637, 931, 2054). From this cause it is that whenever any church is consummated, that is, becomes no church because there is no longer any charity, a new one is of the Lord's providence always raised up; as when the Most Ancient Church called "Man" perished, a new one was created by the Lord, which was called "Noah," and was the Ancient Church that was after the flood; and when this degenerated and became none, the Jewish and Israelitish representative Church was instituted; and when this became altogether extinct, the Lord then came into the world, and set up again a new one; and this for the purpose that there might be conjunction of heaven with the human race through the church. This is also what is signified by "in thy seed shall all the nations of the earth be blessed."

2854. *Because thou hast hearkened to My voice.* That this signifies by the union of the Lord's Human Essence with His Divine Essence, is evident from all that precedes, of which this is the conclusion. To "hearken to the voice" signifies that He underwent the utmost of temptation, and thus united His Human Essence to His Divine Essence. That the Lord united His Human to His Divine and His Divine to His Human by continual temptations and victories, may be seen above (n. 1737, 1813); and that by this union He saved the human race (n. 1676 at the end, 1990, 2016, 2025). From this the human race has all its salvation. It is the common opinion that the Father sent the Son to suffer the hardest things even to the death of the cross; and thus that by looking upon the passion and merit of the Son, He has mercy upon the human race. But every one can know that Jehovah does not have mercy by any looking upon the Son, for He is mercy itself; but that the arcanum of the Lord's coming into the world is that He united in Himself the Divine to the Human and the Human to the Divine; which could not be done except through the most grievous things of temptations; and thus that by that union it became possible for salvation to reach the human race, in which no celestial and spiritual, or even natural good, any longer remained; and it is this union which saves those who are in the faith of charity. It is the Lord Himself who shows the mercy.

2855. Verse 19. *And Abraham returned unto his boys; and they rose up, and went together to Beer-sheba; and Abraham dwelt in Beer-sheba.* " Abraham returned unto his boys," signifies conjunction again with His former rational; "and they rose up," signifies a greater degree of elevation; "and went together to Beer-sheba," signifies advancement in the doctrine of charity and faith, which is Divine, and to which human rational things were adjoined; "and Abraham dwelt in Beer-sheba," signifies that the Lord is that doctrine itself.

2856. *Abraham returned unto his boys.* That this signifies conjunction again with the former rational, is evident from the signification of the " boys," as being the former or merely human rational which was to serve the Divine rational (see above n. 2782, 2792); and from the signification of " returning to them," as being to be conjoined (see also above, n. 2795). That the Lord separated the merely human rational from Himself when He underwent the most grievous temptations, is evident from the explication of verse 5 (n. 2791–2793, 2795); and that after the temptations He again conjoined Himself with that rational is evident from what has been said before (n. 2795), and from these things in this verse.

2857. *And they rose up.* That this signifies a greater degree of elevation, is evident from the signification of " rising up," as, when mentioned in the Word, being some elevation which is signified (n. 2401); here, the elevation of the rational after temptation; for after temptations the rational was always elevated, and this takes place also with man. Every temptation in which a man overcomes, elevates his mind and the things which belong to his mind; for it confirms his goods and truths and superadds new ones (n. 1692, 1717, 1740, 2272).

2858. *And they went together to Beer-sheba.* That this signifies advancement in the doctrine of charity and faith, which is Divine and to which human rational things were adjoined, is evident from the signification of "Beer-sheba," as being the doctrine of charity and faith which was Divine and to which human rational things were adjoined (see n. 2614, 2723). The human rational things are signified by the "boys" (n. 2782, 2792, 2856); and that the doctrine to which they were adjoined was Divine, is signified by their going together with Abraham (see n. 2767).

2859. *And Abraham dwelt in Beer-sheba.* That this signifies that the Lord is that doctrine itself, is evident from the signification of "dwelling;" from the representation of Abraham; from the signification of "Beer-sheba" (explained before); and at the same time from the things which just precede. To "dwell in Beer-sheba" is to be in doctrine, but when predicated of the Lord it is to be doctrine; just as to dwell in heaven, which is also said of the Lord, signifies not only that He is in heaven, but also that He Himself is heaven; for He is the all of heaven (n. 551, 552). That the Lord is the Word is known, and therefore the Lord is doctrine (n. 2531), for all doctrine is from the Word. The all of doctrine in the Word is from the Lord, and is concerning the Lord. In the internal sense of the Word nothing but the Lord and His kingdom is treated of, as has been shown many times. It is the Lord's Divine Human of which the internal sense of the Word especially treats; and the all of doctrine in the Word as regards man is to worship Him and love Him.

2860. Verses 20, 21, 22, 23. *And it came to pass after these words that it was told Abraham, saying, Behold, Milcah, she also hath borne children unto Nahor thy brother. Uz his first-born, and Buz his brother, and Kemuel the father of Aram. And Chesed, and Hazo, and Pildash, and Jidlaph, and Bethuel. And Bethuel begat Rebekah: these eight did Milcah bear to Nahor Abraham's brother.* "It came to pass after these words," signifies the things done relating to those who are within the church; "that it was told Abraham, saying," signifies the Lord's perception; " Behold, Milcah, she also hath borne children unto Nahor thy brother," signifies those out of the church who are in brotherhood from good: " Uz his first-born, and Buz his brother, and Kemuel the father of Aram; and Chesed, and Hazo, and Pildash, and Jidlaph, and Be-thuel," signify various religions and their modes of worship; " Bethuel begat Rebekah," signifies from good the affection of truth; " these eight did Milcah bear to Nahor Abraham's brother," signifies a second class of those who are saved.

2861. *It came to pass after these words.* That this signifies the things done relating to those who are within the church, is evident from the signification of " words," as being actual things. In the original language things are called " words;" and thus " after these words" means after the things done. In what precedes, from verse 13 to this verse, the salvation of the spiritual by the Lord's Divine Human is treated of, and indeed those who are in good within the church. These are they who can be truly spiritual, because they have the Word, and thus the truths of faith. By truths of doctrine conjoined with good of life, man becomes spiritual. All spiritual qual-ity is from this. But the nations without the church, because they have not the Word, and thus not the truths of faith, so long as they live in the world, although in the good of charity, are still not truly spiritual until they have been instructed in the truths of faith. And as most of these nations cannot be in-structed in the world, those who have lived in mutual charity and in obedience are of the Lord's providence and mercy in-structed in the other life, and then receive the truths of faith easily, and become spiritual. (That the state and lot of these nations is such in the other life, may be seen above, n. 2589–2604.) [2] As those within the church who are saved by the Lord's Divine Human are treated of in what precedes, in the things which follow to the end of this chapter those out of the church who are saved are treated of, and are signified by those who were born to Nahor, Abraham's brother, from Mil-cah his wife and Reumah his concubine: this also follows in the series. He who has not become acquainted with the in-ternal sense of the Word would suppose that these things re-late merely to the genealogy of the house of Terah, being

given on account of Rebekah who became Isaac's wife, and
also on account of Bethuel, whose two granddaughters, Leah
and Rachel, became Jacob's wives. But as has been very
often said and shown, all the names in the Word signify actual
things (n. 1224, 1264, 1876, 1888); and unless they signified
such things, the Word would not be Divine, but worldly.
From this it is also evident that these things which follow relate in series to the Lord's spiritual church, but to that which
is among the Gentiles; and this through Nahor, Abraham's
brother, in order that those who are in brotherhood from good
may be signified (as follows, n. 2863).

2862. *And it was told Abraham, saying.* That this signifies
the Lord's perception, is evident from the signification of
"telling," as being to think and reflect; and of "saying," as
being to perceive—explained often before. The Lord's reflecting and perceiving, treated of in the internal sense of the Word,
cannot be expressed in the historical form in any other way
than by "telling and saying." In itself also reflection and
perception is an internal telling and saying.

2863. *Behold, Milcah, she also hath borne children unto
Nahor thy brother.* That this signifies those out of the church
who are in brotherhood from good, is also evident from what
was said before respecting Milcah and Nahor (n. 1363, 1369,
1370). For Terah had three sons,—Abraham, Nahor, and
Haran; and that they worshiped other gods may be seen above
(n 1356). Milcah was the daughter of Haran, who became
Nahor's wife (n. 2369). And Haran died upon the faces of
Terah in Ur of the Chaldees (n. 1365–1368). Hence it is evident what is signified by "Milcah" and "Nahor," namely, by
"Milcah" the truth of those nations, and by "Nahor" their
good. [2] That there were truths among the Gentiles is evident from many things, for it is known that formerly there
was wisdom and intelligence among the nations, as that they
acknowledged one God, and wrote concerning Him in a holy
manner; also that they acknowledged the immortality of the
soul, and the life after death, and also the happiness of the
good and the unhappiness of the evil; and further that they
had for their law the precepts of the decalogue, namely, that
God is to be worshiped, that parents are to be honored, that

men must not kill, steal, commit adultery, nor covet the property of others; nor were they content to be of this character
in externals, but were so in internals.   [3] It is the same at
this day; the better behaved Gentiles from all parts of the
earth sometimes speak better on such subjects than Christians
do; nor do they merely speak better things, but also live according to them.   These and many other truths are among the
Gentiles, and conjoin themselves with the good which they
have from the Lord, from the conjunction of which they are
in a state to receive still more truths, because one truth recog-
nizes another, and truths easily consociate themselves together,
for they are connected with and related to each other.   Hence
it is that they who have been in good in the world easily receive the truths of faith in the other life.   The falsities that
are with them do not conjoin themselves with their good, but
only apply themselves to it in such manner as to be separable
from it.   The falsities which have been conjoined remain, but
those which have been merely applied are separated; and they
are separated at the time when the men learn the truths of
faith and imbue themselves with them.   Every truth of faith
removes and separates what is false, so that at length the man
is averse to it and shuns it.   From all this we can see what
kind of persons are signified by the sons whom Milcah bare to
Nahor Abraham's brother, namely, those out of the church who
are in brotherhood from good.

   2864. *Uz his firstborn, and Buz his brother, and Kemuel
the father of Aram; and Chesed and Hazo, and Pildash, and
Jidlaph, and Bethuel.*   That these signify various religions
and their modes of worship, is evident from the fact that as before said names signify actual things.   The things which these
names signify are religions and their modes of worship, as also
are signified by the names which are found in *Genesis* v. and
xi.   But what each name and each son here signifies, cannot
so well be told, as they are merely named.   Uz and Buz are
also named in *Jeremiah* (xxv. 20, 23), but among several other
names.   Uz is also found in *Lamentations* iv. 21; *Job* i. 1;
(concerning whom see *Genesis* x. 23, n. 1233, 1234).

   2865. *And Bethuel begat Rebekah.*   That this signifies from
good their affection of truth, is evident from the representation

of Bethuel and of Rebekah, treated of in chapter xxiv., which follows.

2866. *These eight did Milcah bear to Nahor, Abraham's brother.* That this signifies a second class of those who are saved, is evident from the signification of "eight;" and from its being again said that "Milcah bare to Nahor, Abraham's brother." Because the eighth day is the first day of the following week, therefore "eight" signifies something that is distinct from what has gone before (see n. 2044); here therefore it denotes another class, and the number was added for the sake of this signification. Milcah's "bearing them to Nahor, Abraham's brother," signifies those out of the church who are in brotherhood from good (as shown above, n. 2863, 2865). Here, being the conclusion, it signifies the same, and in addition the fact that they are saved.

2867. Verse 24. *And his concubine, whose name was Reumah ; she also bare Tebah, and Gaham, and Tahash, and Maacah.* "His concubine whose name was Reumah," signifies Gentiles who are in idolatrous worship and in good; "she also bare Tebah, and Gaham, and Tahash, and Maacah," signifies their various religions : these constitute a third class of the spiritual who are saved.

2868. *His concubine, whose name was Reumah.* That this signifies Gentiles who are in idolatrous worship and in good, is evident from the things which precede; for in the former place are the Gentiles who are signified by the sons who were born to Nahor from his wife, and in this place are the Gentiles signified by those born from his concubine. By those from the wife were signified (as before shown) the Gentiles out of the church who are in brotherhood from good (n. 2863); those now signified are those out of the church who are in idolatrous worship and in good; thus these are not from so legitimate a stock as the former. Nevertheless they are as if legitimate; for at that time children who were born of maidservants were adopted as legitimate (as is evident from the sons of Jacob who were born of the maidservants Bilhah and Zilpah, *Gen.* xxx. 4-12; from whom tribes were derived equally as from those who were born of Leah and Rachel, and indeed without any difference). But that still there was a difference is evident from *Genesis* xxxiii. 1, 2, 6, 7. The maidservants who were at that time given to the husband by the wife for the sake of procreating children were called concubines; as is manifest from Bilhah, Rachel's maidservant, who is also called Jacob's concubine (*Gen.* xxxv. 22). That men should procreate children from maidservants or concubines was tolerated at that time, in order that those who are out of the church might thus be represented, and also those who are in a lower degree within the church. The name of this concubine being said to be "Reumah" involves her quality (n. 1896, 2009); which here is exaltation, this being the meaning of the word "Reumah." (Concerning the state and lot of the nations and peoples who are out of the church, see above, n. 593, 932, 1032, 1059, 1327, 1328, 1366, 2049, 2051, 2284, 2589–2604.)

2869. *She also bare Tebah, and Gaham, and Tahash, and Maacah.* That this signifies their various religions and the kinds of worship from them; and that these constitute a third class of the spiritual who are saved, is evident from what was said above (n. 2864, 2866, 2868).

CONCERNING MAN'S FREEDOM.

2870. Few know what freedom is, and what non-freedom is. All that which is of any love and its delight appears to be freedom, and that which is contrary to these, non-freedom. What is of the love of self and the love of the world, and of their cupidities, appears to man as freedom, but it is infernal freedom; while what is of love to the Lord and of love toward the neighbor, consequently of the love of good and truth, is freedom itself, and is heavenly freedom.

2871. Infernal spirits do not know that there is any other freedom than that which is of the love of self and the love of the world; that is, of the cupidities of commanding, of persecuting and hating all who do not serve them, of tormenting every one, of destroying the universe if they could for the sake of self; of taking away and claiming to themselves what-

ever is another's.   When they are in these and similar things,
they are in their freedom, because they are in their delight.
Their life consists in this freedom to such a degree that if it
were taken away from them, nothing more of life would remain to them than that of a new-born infant.   This was also
shown by living experience.   A certain evil spirit was in the
persuasion that such things could be taken away from him,
and that in this way he could come into heaven; consequently
that his life could be miraculously changed into heavenly life;
on which account those loves together with their cupidities
were taken away from him (which is done in the other life by
dissociation), and he then appeared like an infant paddling
with his hands, which he could scarcely move; and he was at
the same time in such a state as to be less able to think than
any infant, and unable to speak anything at all, or to know
anything.   But he was soon restored to his delight, and thus
to his freedom.   From this it is manifest that it is impossible
for any one to come into heaven who has procured a life for
himself from the love of self and the world, and consequently
who is in the freedom of these loves; for if that life were
taken away from such a person, he would not have anything
of thought and will remaining.

2872. But heavenly freedom is that which is from the
Lord, and in it are all the angels in the heavens.   As before
said this is the freedom of love to the Lord and mutual love,
and thus of the affection of good and truth.   The quality of this
freedom may be seen from the fact that every one who is in it
communicates his blessedness and happiness to another from
inmost affection, and that it is a blessedness and happiness to
him that he is able to communicate it.   And because the universal heaven is such, it follows that every one is a center of
all forms of blessedness and happiness, and that all these belong at the same time to each angel.   The communication
itself is effected by the Lord, by wonderful inflowings in an
incomprehensible form, which is the form of heaven.   This
shows what heavenly freedom is, and that it is from the Lord
alone.

2873. How far distant heavenly freedom (which is from
the affection of good and truth) is from infernal freedom

(which is from the affection of evil and falsity), is evident
from the fact that when the angels in heaven merely think
about such freedom as is from the affection of evil and falsity,
or what is the same, from the cupidities of the love of self and
the world, they are immediately seized with internal pain;
and on the other hand, when evil spirits merely think about
the freedom which is from the affection of good and truth, or
what is the same, from the desires of mutual love, they at
once come into anguish; and what is wonderful, so opposite is
the one freedom to the other, that the freedom of the love of
self and the world is hell to good spirits; and on the other
hand, the freedom of love to the Lord and mutual love is hell
to evil spirits. Hence all in the other life are distinct according to their kinds of freedom, or what is the same, according
to their loves and affections, consequently according to the delights of their life, which is the same as according to their
lives; for lives are nothing else than delights, and these are
nothing else than affections which are of the loves.

2874. From this it is now evident what freedom is, namely,
that it is to think and will from affection, and that the freedom is such as is the affection; also that the one freedom is
infernal, and the other freedom heavenly, and that infernal
freedom is from hell, whereas heavenly freedom is from the
Lord. It is also evident that they who are in infernal freedom cannot come into heavenly freedom (which would be coming from hell into heaven) unless the whole of their life is
taken away from them; also that no one can come into heavenly freedom except by reformation from the Lord; and that
he is then introduced into it by the affection of good and
truth, that is, by the good of life in which the truth of doctrine is being implanted.

2875. The good of life, or the affection of good, is insinuated by the Lord by an internal way, without man's knowing
anything about it; but the truth of doctrine, or faith, by an
external way, into the memory, whence it is called forth by
the Lord in His own time and according to His own order,
and is conjoined with the affection of good. This is done in
man's freedom; for as before said man's freedom is from affection. Such is the insemination and inrooting of faith.

Whatever is done in freedom is conjoined, but that which is done under compulsion is not conjoined; as may be seen from considering that by no possibility can anything be conjoined except that by which we are affected: affection is the very thing that receives; to receive anything contrary to the affection is to receive it contrary to the life. Hence it is manifest that truth of doctrine, or faith, cannot be received except by the affection of it. But such as is the affection, such is the reception. It is only the affection of truth and good that receives the truth of faith; for they agree, and because they agree, they conjoin themselves together.

2876. As no one can be reformed except in freedom, therefore freedom is never taken away from a man, in so far as the appearance is concerned; for it is an eternal law that every one should be in freedom as to his interiors, that is, as to his affections and thoughts, in order that the affection of good and truth may be implanted in him.

2877. Whenever the affection of truth and the affection of good are insinuated by the Lord, which is done without man's knowledge, he then imbues himself with truth and does good in freedom, because from affection; for when anything is done from affection, then as before said there is freedom; and the truth of faith conjoins itself with the good of charity. Unless a man had freedom in everything he thinks and wills, the freedom of thinking truth and of willing good could never be insinuated by the Lord into any one; for in order that a man may be reformed he must think truth as of himself, and do good as of himself; and what is done as of one's self is done in freedom. Unless this were so, there would never be any reformation or regeneration.

2878. There are innumerable causes from which and on account of which a man loves to learn truth and to will good (very many from the world, and also very many from the body); and sometimes these things are not done for the sake of heaven, and still less for the sake of the Lord. A man is thus introduced by the Lord into truth and good by affections, and one man altogether differently from another, each one according to his disposition, innate and acquired. And as he is continually being introduced into truth and good by affections, and thus continually by freedom, and at length into the affections of spiritual truth and spiritual good, the Lord alone knows the times and the states, and He alone arranges and governs them in application to each one's genius and life. This shows why man has freedom.

2879. The Lord flows in through man's inmost with good, and there conjoins truth with it: their root must be in the inmost. Unless a man is in freedom interiorly as to all his affections and as to all his thoughts, he can never be so disposed that good and truth may take any root.

2880. Nothing else appears to a man as his (or what is the same, as his own) except that which flows from freedom. The reason is that all affection which is of love is his veriest life; and to act from affection is to act from life, that is, from himself, and thus from what is his, or what is the same, from his own. In order therefore that man may receive an Own that is heavenly, such as have the angels in heaven, he is kept in freedom, and through freedom he is introduced into it, in the way already stated. It may be known to every one that to worship the Lord from freedom appears as if it were from one's self, or from one's own; but that to worship Him under compulsion is not from one's self, but from a force from without, or from some other source, compelling him to do it; thus that worship from freedom is worship itself, and that worship under compulsion is no worship.

2881. If man could have been reformed by compulsion, there would not be any man in the universe who would not be saved; for nothing would be easier for the Lord than to compel man to fear Him, to worship Him, and indeed as it were to love Him; the means being innumerable. But as that which is done under compulsion is not conjoined, and thus is not appropriated, it is therefore the furthest possible from the Lord to compel any one. So long as a man is in combats, or is one of the church militant, it appears as if the Lord compels the man, and thus that he has no freedom; for he is then continually combating against the love of self and of the world, thus against the freedom into which he was born and into which he has grown up; hence comes the appearance just referred to. But that in the combats in which he overcomes, the freedom is stronger than when out of combats (a freedom not from himself, but from the Lord, and still appearing as his), may be seen above (n. 1937, 1947).

2882. Most of all does man believe that he has no freedom from the fact that he has learned that he cannot do good and think truth of himself.   But let him not believe that any one ever has or ever had any freedom of thinking truth and doing good of himself, not even the man who, from the state of perfection in which he was, was called a "likeness and image of God;" for the freedom of thinking the truth of faith, and of doing the good of charity, all flows in from the Lord.   The Lord is Good itself and Truth itself; and is hence their fountain.   All the angels are in such freedom, and indeed in the very perception that what we have just stated is the truth. The inmost angels perceive how much is from the Lord, and how much from themselves; and so far as it is from the Lord, they are in happiness; but so far as it is from themselves, they are not in what is happy.

2883. In order therefore that a man may receive an Own that is heavenly, he must do good of himself, and think truth of himself; but still must know, and when reformed must think and believe, that all the good and all the truth are from the Lord, even as to the very least of all (and this because it is so); while its being given to man to think that it is from himself, is in order that the good and truth may become as his own.

2884. The freedom of the love of self and of the world, and of their cupidities, is anything but freedom, being complete slavery; but still it is called freedom, just as love, affection, and delight are so called in both senses; and yet the love of self and of the world is anything but love, being hatred; and so are its affection and delight.   They are named according to what they appear; not according to what they are.

2885. No one can know what slavery is and what freedom is, unless he knows the origin of them (which no one can know except from the Word), and unless he knows how the case is with man in regard to his affections which are of his will, and his thoughts which are of his understanding.

2886. As to man's affections and thoughts, the case is this: No one, whoever he may be, whether man, spirit, or angel, can will and think from himself; but from others; nor can these others will and think from themselves, but all again from others, and so on; and thus each one from the First of life, which is the Lord. That which is unconnected has no existence. Evils and falsities have connection with the hells; from the hells come the willing and thinking of those who are in evils and falsities; and also their love, affection, and delight, consequently their freedom. But goods and truths have connection with heaven, and the willing and thinking of those who are in them is from heaven, and so also are their love, affection, and delight, and therefore their freedom. From this we may see whence comes the one freedom, and whence the other. That the case is really so is most fully known in the other life, but is at this day altogether unknown in the world.

2887. With man there are evil spirits constantly, and also angels; by the spirits he communicates with the hells, and by the angels with the heavens. If these spirits and angels were to be taken away from him, he would in a moment be devoid of willing and thinking, thus of life. That this is so may seem a paradox; and yet it is most true. But concerning the spirits and angels who are with man, of the Lord's Divine mercy elsewhere.

2888. The truth is that the life of every one, both of man, of spirit, and also of angel, flows in solely from the Lord, who is life itself; and diffuses itself through the whole heaven and also through hell, thus into every one; and this in an order and series incomprehensible: but the life which flows in is received by each one according to his disposition. Good and truth are received as good and truth by the good; but good and truth are received as evil and falsity by the evil, and are also turned into evil and falsity in them. The case with this is comparatively like the light of the sun, which diffuses itself into all the objects of the earth, but is received according to the quality of each object, and becomes of a beautiful color in beautiful forms, and of a disagreeable color in disagreeable forms. In the world this is an arcanum, but nothing is better known in the other life. That I might know that influx is of such a nature, it has been given me to speak with the spirits and angels who were with me, and also to feel and perceive their influx; and this so often that I cannot number the times. But I know that the fallacy will prevail, the fallacy that is to say, that men will believe that they will from themselves, and think from themselves, and thus have life from themselves; whereas nothing is further from the truth.

2889. Evil spirits cannot possibly apprehend that they do not live from themselves, and that they are only organs of life; still less that there is no life except that which is from good and truth; and still less that they do not begin to live until the life of the cupidities of evil and of the persuasions of falsity, in which they are, is extinguished. They believe that if they were deprived of these there could be nothing of life remaining; whereas the truth is that when they have lost the life of the cupidities of evil and of the persuasions of falsity, they then first begin to live; and that the Lord, together with the good and truth in which life solely consists, is not till then received; and that intelligence and wisdom, and thus the veriest life, then flow in, and are afterwards immensely increased; and this with delight, blessedness, and happiness, and thus with inmost joy, and with ineffable variety, to eternity.

2890. The evil spirits who are with man, through whom he communicates with hell, regard him no otherwise than as a vile slave; for they infuse into him their cupidities and their persuasions, and thus lead him whithersoever they will. But the angels through whom man communicates with heaven, regard him as a brother, and insinuate into him affections of good and truth, and thus lead him by freedom, not whither they will, but whither it pleases the Lord. From this we can see of what kind the one freedom is, and of what kind the other; and that it is slavery to be led by the devil, and freedom to be led by the Lord.

2891. Spirits fresh from this world severely torment themselves by trying to comprehend how no one can do good of himself, or think truth of himself, except from the Lord; believing that thus they would be like machines, having no control of anything; and that if this is really so they should let their hands hang down, and suffer themselves to be acted upon. But they were told that they ought by all means to think, to will, and to do good of themselves; and that in no other way could they have an Own that is heavenly, and heavenly freedom; but that still they should acknowledge that the good and truth are not from them, but from the Lord: and they are instructed that all the angels are in such an acknowledgment, nay, in the perception that it is so; and the more exquisitely they perceive that they are led by the Lord, and thus are in the Lord, the more are they in freedom.

2892. He who lives in good, and believes that the Lord governs the universe, and that all the good which is of love and charity, and all the truth which is of faith, are from the Lord alone; nay, that life is from Him, and thus that from Him we live, move, and have our being, is in such a state that he can be gifted with heavenly freedom, and together with it with peace; for he then trusts solely in the Lord and has no care for other things, and is certain that all things are tending to his good, his blessedness, and his happiness to eternity.   But he who believes that he governs himself is continually disquieted, being borne along into cupidities, and into solicitude respecting future things, and thus into manifold anxieties; and because he so believes, the cupidities of evil and the persuasions of falsity also adhere to him.

2893. Good spirits wondered exceedingly that the man of the church at this day does not believe that all the evils and falsities within him flow in from hell, and all the goods and truths from the Lord; when yet he has learned this from the Word, and also from the doctrine of faith; and, when any one has done a grievous evil, everybody says that he has suffered himself to be led by the devil; and when any one has done good, that he has suffered himself to be led by the Lord.

END OF VOL. III.

THEOLOGICAL WORKS OF EMANUEL SWEDENBORG

ENGLISH EDITIONS

LATIN-ENGLISH EDITIONS

Latin and corresponding English on opposite pages.   *Post-*
paid

HEAVEN AND HELL	$1.00
DIVINE LOVE AND WISDOM	1.00
DIVINE PROVIDENCE	1.00
APOCALYPSE EXPLAINED, twelve volumes, per volume	1.00
SUMMARIES OF THE INTERNAL SENSE OF THE PROPHETS AND PSALMS	1.00
THE CREED OF ATHANASIUS, paper	.25

LATIN EDITIONS

APOCALYPSIS REVELATA, two volumes, per volume	$1.00
DE CAELO ET INFERNO	1.00
VERA CHRISTIANA RELIGIO, two volumes, per volume	1.00
DE AMORE CONJUGIALI	1.00
DE DIVINO AMORE ET DE DIVINA SAPIENTIA ET DE DIVINA PROVIDENTIA	1.00
QUATUOR DOCTRINAE ET ULTIMO JUDICIO	1.00
OPERA MINORA	1.00
APOCALYPSIS EXPLICATA, six volumes, per volume	1.00
PSALMI EX LINGUA ORIGINALI IN LATINAM AB EMANUELE SWEDENBORGIO	.75

SPANISH EDITION

EL CIELO Y SUS MARAVILLAS Y EL INFIERNO (Heaven and Hell) paper	$0.50
DE LA PENITENCIA (Repentance), from True Christian Religion, paper	.10

OTHER FOREIGN LANGUAGES.   ..

DUTCH—VAN HET NIEUWE JERUSALEM EN ZIJNE HEMELSCHE LEER (The New Jerusalem and its Heavenly Doctrine), pp. 75, paper	$0.10
ICELANDIC—UM HINE NYU JERUSALEM OG HENNAR HIMNESKU KENNINGU (The New Jerusalem and its Heavenly Doctrine), with a Life of Swedenborg, pp. 74, paper	.10
UM KAERLEIKANN (Charity), pp. 66, paper	.10

PUBLISHED BY

THE AMERICAN SWEDENBORG PRINTING AND PUBLISHING SOCIETY

3 West 29th Street   New York, N. Y.

TABLE OF CONTENTS OF VOLUME III.*

The Heavenly Arcana which have been unfolded in the Holy Scripture or Word of the Lord are contained in the Explication, which is the INTERNAL SENSE of the Word.

Prefixed and subjoined to the several chapters are the following:—

* Compiled by the Reviser.

NOTE.—The figures between brackets in the text of the long paragraphs indicate the subdivisions arranged for the *Swedenborg Concordance*.

THE
BOOK OF GENESIS

PREFACE TO THE EIGHTEENTH CHAPTER.

At the end of the preceding chapter, the subject of the Last Judgment was treated of, and it was shown what is signified thereby, namely, not the destruction of the world, but the last time of the church. When this is at hand, the Lord says that He "will come in the clouds of the heavens, with power and glory" (*Matt.* xxiv. 30; *Mark* xiii. 26; *Luke* xxi. 27). Hitherto no one has known what is meant by the "clouds of the heavens." But it has been disclosed to me that nothing else is meant than the literal sense of the Word; and by "power and glory" the internal sense of the Word, for in the internal sense of the Word there is glory, since whatever is there is concerning the Lord and His kingdom (see in Part First, n. 1769–1772). [2] Similar is the signification of the "cloud" which encompassed Peter, James, and John, when the Lord appeared to them in glory; of which it is said in *Luke:*—

A voice came out of the cloud, saying, This is My beloved Son, hear ye Him; but when the voice had passed, Jesus was found alone (ix. 35, 36),

where by "Moses and Elias" who spake with the Lord, was represented the Word of the Old Testament, which is also called "Moses and the Prophets" (by "Moses," his books together with the other historical books, and by "Elias" the prophet, all the books of the Prophets); but by "Peter, James, and John," as in all other places where they are named in the books of the Evangelists, were represented faith, charity, and the good of charity. That they only were present signifies that no others can see the glory of the Lord which is in His

Word than those who are in faith, in its charity, and in the
good of charity.   Others are indeed able to see, but still do
not see, because they do not believe.   This is the internal
sense in regard to the foregoing two passages; and in various
places in the Prophets also, a "cloud" signifies the Word in its
letter, and "glory" the Word in its life.   [3] The nature and
quality of the internal sense of the Word has already been fre-
qently stated, and has been shown in the explication word by
word.   It was those skilled in the Law in the Lord's time who
least of all believed that there was anything written in the
Word concerning the Lord.   At the present day, those skilled
in the Law know indeed, but it may be that they will believe
least of all that there is any other glory in the Word than
that which appears in the letter; when yet this is the cloud
in which is the glory.

CHAPTER THE EIGHTEENTH.

2135. From this chapter we may see, in an especial manner, what is the nature of the internal sense of the Word, and how the angels perceive it when it is being read by man. From the historical sense of the letter we can understand nothing else than that Jehovah appeared to Abraham under the form of three men; and that Sarah, Abraham, and his lad prepared food for them, namely, cakes made of the meal of fine flour, a "son of an ox," and also butter and milk; which things, though they are true historicals describing what really took place, are still not so perceived by the angels; but the things which they represent and signify are what are perceived, altogether abstractedly from the letter, in accordance with the explication given in the CONTENTS. Thus, instead of the things historically related in this chapter, the angels perceive the state of the Lord's perception in the Human, and the communication with the Divine at that time, before the perfect union of His Divine Essence with the Human Essence, and of the Human Essence with the Divine Essence, which state is also that concerning which the Lord thus speaks :—

No one hath seen God at any time; the Only-begotten Son, who is in the bosom of the Father, He hath set Him forth (*John* i. 18).

[2] And by the various kinds of food here mentioned, the angels perceive nothing but celestial and spiritual goods, concerning which see the explication. Moreover by what is afterwards said concerning the son that Sarah should bear at the set time of another year, they perceive nothing else than that the Lord's human rational should be made Divine. Lastly, by the things which Abraham spake with Jehovah concerning the overthrow of Sodom and Gomorrah, the angels perceive nothing else than the Lord's intercession for the human race; and by fifty, forty-five, forty, thirty, twenty, and ten, they perceive His intercession for those with whom truths should be adjoined to goods, and who should have goods by means of temptations and combats, or by means of other states. So it is with all other things in the Word, as may be more

clearly seen from the explication word by word, where it is shown that in each word similar things are involved in the Word, both Historic and Prophetic. [**3**] That there is such an internal sense everywhere in the Word, which treats solely of the Lord, of His kingdom in the heavens, of His church on earth and in particular with every man, thus treating of the goods of love and truths of faith, may also be seen by every one from the passages cited by the Evangelists from the Old Testament. As in *Matthew*:—

The Lord said unto my Lord, Sit thou on My right hand, until I make thine enemies thy footstool (xxii. 44; compare *Ps.* cx. 1).

That these words treat of the Lord, cannot be apparent in the literal sense of the passage cited, as found in David; but yet that no other than the Lord is meant, He Himself here teaches in *Matthew*. [**4**] Again:—

Thou Bethlehem, the land of Judah, art in no wise least among the leaders of Judah; for out of thee shall come forth a Leader, who shall feed My people Israel (ii. 6; compare *Micah* v. 1).

They who abide in the literal sense, as do the Jews, know indeed from this passage that the Lord should be born there; but as they are expecting a leader and a king who will bring them back into the land of Canaan, they therefore explain the words found here according to the letter; that is, by the " land of Judah" they understand the land of Canaan; by " Israel" they understand Israel, although they know not where Israel now is; and by a " Leader" they still understand their Messiah; when yet other things are meant by " Judah" and " Israel;" namely, by " Judah" those who are celestial, by " Israel," those who are spiritual, in heaven and on earth; and by the " Leader" the Lord. [**5**] Again in the same:—

A voice was heard in Ramah, lamentation, a cry, and great wailing; Rachel weeping for her children, and she would not be comforted, because they are not (ii. 18; compare *Jer.* xxxi. 15).

They who abide in the literal sense of these words cannot possibly gather from it what is the internal sense; and yet that there is an internal sense is evident in the Evangelist. Again:—

Out of Egypt have I called My Son (*Matt.* ii. 15; compare *Hos.* xi. 1).

In *Hosea* it is said :—

When Israel was a child, then I loved him, and called My son out of Egypt. They called them, so they went from their faces, and I made Ephraim to go (xi. 1–3).

They who know not that there is an internal sense, cannot know otherwise than that Jacob is here meant when he entered into Egypt, and his posterity when they went out from it, and that by Ephraim is meant the tribe of Ephraim, thus the same things that are in the historicals of the Word ; nevertheless it is evident from the Word of the Evangelist that they signify the Lord. But what the several particulars signify could not possibly be known unless it were disclosed by means of the internal sense.

CHAPTER XVIII.

1. And Jehovah appeared unto him in the oak-groves of Mamre, and he was sitting at the door of the tent, as the day was growing hot.

2. And he lifted up his eyes and saw, and behold three men standing over him ; and he saw, and ran to meet them from the door of the tent, and bowed himself toward the earth.

3. And he said, My Lord, if I pray I have found grace in thine eyes, pass not I pray from over thy servant.

4. Let I pray a little water be taken, and wash ye your feet, and lie down under the tree.

5. And I will take a piece of bread, and support ye your heart; afterwards ye may pass on; for therefore have ye passed over unto your servant. And they said, So do as thou hast spoken.

6. And Abraham hastened toward the tent unto Sarah, and said, Make ready quickly three measures of meal of fine flour, knead, and make cakes.

7. And Abraham ran unto the herd and took a son of an ox, tender and good, and gave it to the lad, and he hasted to make it.

8. And he took butter and milk, and the son of an ox that he had made, and set before them; and he stood before them under the tree, and they did eat.

9. And they said unto him, Where is Sarah thy wife? And he said, Behold in the tent.

10. And he said, Returning I will return unto thee about this time of life, and behold Sarah thy wife shall have a son. And Sarah heard at the door of the tent, and it was behind him.

11. And Abraham and Sarah were old, entering into days; it had ceased to be with Sarah in the way as of women.

12. And Sarah laughed within herself, saying, After I am grown old shall I have pleasure? and my lord old?

13. And Jehovah said unto Abraham, Wherefore did Sarah laugh, saying, Shall I indeed truly bear, and I am become old?

14. Shall anything be wonderful for Jehovah? At the set time I will return unto thee, about this time of life, and Sarah shall have a son.

15. And Sarah denied, saying, I laughed not; for she was afraid. And He said, Nay, for thou didst laugh.

16. And the men rose up thence, and looked toward the faces of Sodom; and Abraham went with them, to send them away.

17. And Jehovah said, Shall I hide from Abraham that which I do?

18. And Abraham shall surely be for a nation great and numerous, and all the nations of the earth shall be blessed in him.

19. For I know him, because he will command his sons, and his house after him, and they will keep the way of Jehovah, to do righteousness and judgment; that Jehovah may bring upon Abraham that which He hath spoken concerning him.

20. And Jehovah said, Because the cry of Sodom and Gomorrah has become great, and because their sin has become very grievous.

21. I will go down I pray, and I will see whether they have made a consummation according to the cry thereof which is come unto Me, and if not I will know.

22. And the men looked forth thence, and went toward Sodom; and Abraham as yet he was standing before Jehovah.

23. And Abraham drew near, and said, Wilt Thou also destroy the righteous with the wicked?

24. Peradventure there be fifty righteous in the midst of the city; wilt Thou also destroy and not spare the place for the sake of the fifty righteous that are in the midst of it?

25. Be it far from Thee to do according to this thing, to cause the righteous to die with the wicked, that so the righteous be as the wicked; be it far from Thee; shall not the Judge of all the earth do judgment?

26. And Jehovah said, If I find in Sodom fifty righteous in the midst of the city, I will spare all the place for their sake.

27. And Abraham answered and said, Behold I pray I have taken upon me to speak unto my Lord, and I am dust and ashes.

28. Peradventure there shall lack five of the fifty righteous; wilt Thou destroy all the city for five? and He said, I will not destroy it, if I find there forty and five.

29. And he added yet to speak unto Him, and said, Peradventure forty shall be found there; and He said, I will not do it for forty's sake.

30. And he said, Oh let not my Lord be angry, and I will speak: peradventure thirty shall be found there; and He said, I will not do it if I find thirty there.

31. And he said, Behold I pray I have taken upon me to speak unto my Lord: peradventure twenty shall be found there; and He said, I will not destroy it for twenty's sake.

32. And he said, Oh let not my Lord be angry, and I will speak but this once: peradventure ten shall be found there; and He said, I will not destroy it for ten's sake.

33. And Jehovah went when He had completed His speaking unto Abraham; and Abraham returned unto his place.

THE CONTENTS.

2136. In the *first* place, this chapter treats concerning the Lord's state of perception in the Human and concerning the communication with the Divine at that time, before the perfect union of His Human Essence with the Divine Essence, which state is also that in regard to which the Lord says, "No one hath seen God at any time, the Only-begotten Son who is in the bosom of the Father" (*John* i. 18).

2137. The Lord's state of perception in the Human at that time is signified by the "oak-groves of Mamre" (verse 1); and that in this state He perceived the Divine which was manifesting itself before His Human (verse 2); at which He rejoiced (verse 3); and desired that the Divine should draw nearer to His Human by putting on something natural (verse 4), and His Human nearer to the Divine by putting on the celestial (verse 5). The celestial and the derivative spiritual, which He put on, are signified by the "three measures of meal of fine flour" of which the cakes were made (verse 6); and that He also put on a conforming natural, is signified by the "son of an ox" (verse 7); the result being conformation, and a communication of the Divine with the Human, and of the Human with the Divine (verse 8).

2138. In the *second* place, this chapter treats concerning the Lord's perception in that state respecting the rational with Him, in that it would put off the Human, and be made Divine.

2139. That the rational would be made Divine, is signified by the "son" whom Sarah was to bear (verse 9). That the human rational truth that was with the Lord did not perceive this, and thus did not believe it, is signified by Sarah's "laughing" at the door of the tent that was behind him (verses 10 to 13, 15). It is confirmed that the Lord would put off this also, and would put on in its place truth Divine (verse 14).

2140. In the *third* place, the chapter treats concerning the Lord's grief and anxiety over the human race, because men were so greatly imbued with the love of self, and from this with the cupidity of exercising command over others from what is evil and false, for whom in that state He interceded, and obtained that those should be saved with whom there should be goods and truths; and who these are, is recounted in order.

2141. The Lord's perception concerning the human race, that it was in evil and falsity, "Sodom" being the love of self and the derivative cupidity of exercising command from what is evil, and "Gomorrah" being the same from what is false (verses 16, 20). That this could not be concealed from the Lord in that state, because by Him and from Him is all salvation (verses 17 to 19); that is to say, they were to be visited when their wickedness reached its height (verses 20, 21). That when He was in this perception (verse 22), He interceded for them; first for those with whom there should be truths, and these truths full of goods, who are signified by the "fifty" (verses 23 to 26); also for those with whom there should be less of good, but this good nevertheless conjoined with truths, who are signified by the "forty-five" (verses 27, 28); next for those who have been in temptations, who are signified by the "forty" (verse 29); as likewise for those who have been in some combats against evils, who are signified by the "thirty" (verse 30); afterwards for those with whom there should be states of the affection of good from any other source, who are signified by the "twenty" (verse 31); lastly for those with whom there should be states of the affection of truth, who are signified by the "ten" (verse 32); and the constant answer was that they should be saved (verses 26, 28 to 32). These things being accomplished, the Lord returned into His former state of perception (verse 33). These are the arcana contained in the internal sense of this chapter, which are not manifest from the letter.

THE INTERNAL SENSE.

2142. Verse 1. *And Jehovah appeared unto him in the oak-groves of Mamre, and he was sitting at the door of the tent, as the day was growing hot.* "Jehovah appeared unto him," signifies the Lord's perception; "in the oak-groves of Mamre," signifies the quality of the perception; " he was sitting at the door of the tent," signifies the holiness which at that time appertained to Him; " as the day was growing hot," signifies from love.

2143. *Jehovah appeared unto him.* That this signifies the Lord's perception, may be seen from the fact that the historicals of the Word are merely representative, and the words therein significative, of those things which are in the internal sense. In the internal sense of the passage before us the subject treated of is the Lord and His perception, which perception was represented by the appearing to Abraham of Jehovah; for such is the representative nature in the historicals of the Word of every appearing, of every discourse, and of every deed. But what they represent does not appear unless the historicals are attended to simply as objects, like those of sight, from which there is given the occasion and the opportunity for thinking about things more lofty; for instance, from gardens, as we behold them, for thinking about fruits, their uses, and also the derivative delight of life, and, still more loftily, about paradisal or heavenly happiness. When such things are thought of, the several objects of the garden are indeed seen, but so slightly that they are not attended to. The case is the very same with the historicals of the Word, for when the celestial and spiritual things that are in the internal sense of these historicals are thought of, these, together with the words themselves, are attended to just as little.

2144. *In the oak-groves of Mamre.* That this signifies the quality of the perception, is evident from the representation and signification of " oak-groves," and also from the representation and signification of " Mamre." What " oak-groves " represented and signified in general, was shown in Part First (n. 1442, 1443); and what " the oak-groves of Mamre" represented and signified specifically (n. 1616), namely, perceptions, but such as are human from memory-knowledges (*scientifica*), and from the first rational things thence derived. [2] What perception is, is at this day utterly unknown, because at this day no one has perception like that of the ancients, especially like that of the most ancients; for these latter knew from perception whether a thing was good, and consequently whether it was true. There was an influx into their rational from the Lord through heaven, whereby, when they thought about any holy thing, they instantly perceived whether it was so, or was not so. Such perception afterwards perished with man, when he began to be no longer in heavenly ideas, but solely in worldly and corporeal ones; and in place of it there succeeded conscience, which also is a kind of perception; for to act contrary to conscience and according to conscience is nothing else than to perceive from it whether a thing is so or is not so, or whether it is to be done. [3] But the perception of conscience is not from good that flows in, but it is from the truth that from infancy has been implanted in the rational of men in accordance with the holy of their worship, and which has afterwards been confirmed, for this alone do they in such case believe to be good. Hence it is that conscience is a kind of perception, but from such truth; and when charity and innocence are insinuated into this truth by the Lord, there comes into existence the good of this conscience. From these few observations we can see what perception is. But between perception and conscience there is much difference. (See what is said about perception in Part First, n. 104, 125, 371, 483, 495, 503, 521, 536, 597, 607, 784, 865, 895, 1121, 1616; about the perception of spirits and angels, n. 202, 203, 1008, 1383, 1384, 1390–1392, 1394, 1397, 1504; and that the learned do not know what perception is, n. 1387.) [4] As regards the Lord when He lived in the world, all His thought was from Divine perception, because He alone was a Divine and Celestial Man; for He was the only one in whom was Jehovah Himself, from whom was His perception (as to which see also in Part First, n. 1616, 1791). His perceptions were more and more interior in proportion as He approached more nearly to union with Jehovah. Of what quality His perception was at the time here treated of, may be seen from what has been said about the oak-groves of Mamre in Part First (n. 1616); and of what quality it became when He perceived the things that are contained in this chapter, is described in what now follows.

2145. *He was sitting at the door of the tent.* That this signifies the holy which at that time appertained to Him, namely, the holy of love,—which is signified by the day growing hot,

as explained in what follows,—is evident from the signification
of a "tent," as being what is holy (see n. 414, 1102, 1566,
where also the reason of this signification of "tents" is explained). As the Lord was then in the perception which is
signified by the oak-groves of Mamre, which is a lower rational
perception, but yet is a perception more internal than that
which is signified by the oak-grove of Moreh (concerning
which see n. 1442, 1443), it is here represented and therefore
signified by His sitting at the door of the tent, that is, at the
entrance to what is holy. How the case is with perceptions,
as being less or more interior, may be illustrated by the perceptions of the most ancient people, from whom I have heard
that the more they were in memory-knowledges from the things
which are objects of hearing and sight, the lower were their
perceptions; but that the more they were uplifted above them to
the celestial things of charity and love, the more interior their
perceptions were, because they were then nearer to the Lord.

2146. *As the day was growing hot.* That this signifies from
love, is evident from the signification of "heat," as being in
the internal sense love; and since heat belongs either to the
day or to the year, love is represented either by the heat of
the day or by the heat of the year, according to what is related
in the historicals. That "heat" signifies love may be seen from
the fact that love is called spiritual heat, and that growing
warm is predicated of all affection, even in common speech;
and further from the fact that love and its affections, in man's
interiors, as also in his exteriors, and even in his very cor-
poreals, make themselves manifest under the guise of heat;
in fact heat has no other origin in connection with man when
it flows forth from his interiors. Such however as is the love,
such is the heat. Celestial love and spiritual love are what
give genuine heat. All other heat, namely, that which is from
the loves of self and of the world, and also from other filthy
loves, is unclean, and in the other life sinks into what is ex-
crementitious (see n. 1773). Be it known moreover that holiness is never predicated except of love and charity; not of
faith except in so far as love and charity are in the truths of
faith. Except from this the truths of faith are not holy.
(See what was said before, n. 2049.)

2147. Verse 2. *And he lifted up his eyes, and saw, and behold three men standing over him ; and he saw them, and ran to meet them from the door of the tent, and bowed himself toward the earth.* " He lifted up his eyes," signifies that He saw within Himself; " and behold three men standing over him," signifies the Divine Itself, the Divine Human, and the Holy proceeding; " and he saw them," signifies when He observed this; " and ran to meet them," signifies that in thought He approached nearer to the things that were being perceived; " from the door of the tent," signifies from the holy which at that time appertained to the Lord; " and bowed himself toward the earth," signifies the effect of humiliation, from the consequent joy.

2148. *He lifted up his eyes.* That this signifies that the Lord saw within Himself, is evident from the signification of " lifting up the eyes." By " eyes" in the Word is signified the interior sight, or the understanding, as may be seen from the passages cited above (n. 212). Hence to " lift up the eyes" means to see and perceive things which are above self. Things that are interior are expressed in the Word by those which are higher, as " looking upward," " lifting up the eyes to heaven," " thinking high things," the reason of which is that man supposes heaven to be on high, or above himself; when yet it is not on high, but is in things internal—as when a man is in the celestial things of love, his heaven is then within him (see n. 450). From this it follows that to " lift up the eyes" signifies to see within one's self.

2149. *Behold three men standing over him.* That this signifies the Divine Itself, the Divine Human, and the Holy proceeding, may be seen without explication; for it is known to every one that there is a Trine, and that this Trine is a One.* That it is a One is plainly evident in this chapter, to wit, in verse 3, where it is said, " He said, My Lord, if I pray I have found grace in Thine eyes, pass Thou not, I pray," which words were addressed to the three men. And further, in verse 10, " And he said, Returning I will return unto thee." In verse 13, " And Jehovah said unto Abraham." In verse 15, " He said, Nay, but thou didst laugh." In verse 17, " And Jehovah said, Shall I hide from Abraham that which I do ?" In verse

---

* That is, a complex whole which constitutes a unity. [REVISER.]

19, "Because I have known him." In verse 20, "And Jehovah said." In verse 21, "I will go down, and I will see whether they have made a consummation according to the cry thereof which is come unto Me; and if not, I will know." In verse 23, Abraham said, "Wilt Thou also destroy the righteous with the wicked?" In verse 25, "Be it far from Thee to do according to this thing; be it far from Thee." In verse 26, "And Jehovah said, If I find fifty righteous I will spare the whole place for their sake." In verse 27, "I have taken upon me to speak unto my Lord." In verse 28, "Wilt Thou destroy the whole city for five? And He said, I will not destroy it, if I find there forty and five." In verse 29, "He added yet to speak unto Him; He said, I will not do it for forty's sake." In verse 30, "Let not my Lord be angry; He said, I will not do it if I find thirty there." In verse 31, "He said, I have taken upon me to speak unto my Lord; He said, I will not destroy it for twenty's sake." In verse 32, "Let not I pray my Lord be angry; and He said, I will not destroy it for ten's sake." And in verse 33, "And Jehovah went when He had left off speaking to Abraham." From all this it may be seen that by the three men who appeared to Abraham was signified the Divine Itself, the Divine Human, and the Holy proceeding; and that this Trine is in itself a One. In the internal sense the subject here treated of is Jehovah, in that He appeared to the Lord, and that the Lord perceived this; but not by an appearing such as there was to Abraham; for it is historically true that three men were seen by Abraham, but this represents the Divine perception, or the perception from the Divine which the Lord had when in the Human, which perception is treated of in what follows.

2150. *And he saw them.* That this signifies when the Lord observed this, is evident from the signification of "seeing" in the internal sense, as being to understand and observe, and also to be illuminated (see n. 1584). Nothing is more common in the Word than for "seeing" to have this signification. The signification here is that the Lord observed a perception from the Divine to be present, as just stated.

2151. *And Abraham ran to meet them.* That this signifies that the Lord approached nearer to the things which were perceived, is evident from the series of things in the internal sense; for the preceding verse treats of the Lord's perception, in which He then was; this verse treats of His observing the perception to be from the Divine, and here now His approaching nearer to it is represented and thus signified by his running to meet them.

2152. *From the door of the tent.* That this signifies from the holy which then appertained to the Lord, is evident from the signification of a "tent," as being what is holy, and from the signification of the "door," as being the entrance into what is holy (explained above, n. 2145).

2153. *And bowed himself toward the earth.* That this signifies the effect of the humiliation from the consequent joy, is evident from the signification of "bowing himself," as being to humble. Just as all interior affections have gestures corresponding to them in outward or bodily motions, which gestures are the effects of the affections as their effecting causes, so the affection of humbling one's self has humiliation and also prostration. That this prostration was from joy is evident, because He observed, as before said, the perception to be from the Divine. The state of the Lord's humiliation when He was in the Human, has already been treated of in various places, and of the Lord's Divine mercy shall be further treated of in this chapter.

2154. Verse 3. *And he said, My Lord, if I pray I have found grace in Thine eyes, pass not I pray from Thy servant.* "And he said," signifies that the Lord so thought; "My Lord," signifies the Trine in a One; "if I pray I have found grace in Thine eyes," signifies the deference of the Lord's state when He noticed that perception; "pass not I pray from Thy servant," signifies that He intensely desired that what He began to perceive should not pass away. The "servant" is the human that appertained to the Lord before it was made Divine.

2155. *He said.* That this signifies that the Lord so thought, is evident from the signification of "saying," when found in the historical sense, as being to perceive (see n. 1898, 1919, 2080).

2156. *My Lord.* That this signifies the Trine in a One, namely, the Divine Itself, the Divine Human, and the Holy proceeding, which Trine is in a One, is evident from its being here said "Lord," in the singular number. So too in verses 27, 31, "Behold I pray I have taken upon me to speak unto my Lord," and in verses 30, 32, "Let not I pray my Lord be angry." The three men are also called "Jehovah," in verse 13, "Jehovah said unto Abraham;" in verse 14, "Shall anything be wonderful for Jehovah?" in verse 22, "Abraham was yet standing before Jehovah;" and in verse 33, "And Jehovah went when He left off speaking to Abraham." Hence it is evident that the three men (that is, the Divine Itself, the Divine Human, and the Holy proceeding), are the same as the Lord, and the Lord the same as Jehovah. In the Christian Faith, called the Creed, the same is acknowledged, where it is said in plain words, "There are not three Uncreate, nor three Infinite, nor three Eternal, nor three Almighty, nor three Lords, but One." There are none who separate this Trine which is in a One except those who say that they acknowledge one Supreme Existence (*Ens*), the Creator of the Universe; which is forgiven those who are outside of the church. But they who are within the church, and say this, although they say it and sometimes think it, do not in fact acknowledge any God; still less do they acknowledge the Lord.

2157. *If I pray I have found grace in Thine eyes.* That this signifies the deference of the Lord's state when He observed that perception, may be seen from the affection of humiliation which there is in these very words; and also in those which directly follow—"Pass not I pray from over Thy servant"—in which likewise there is humiliation. In every particular in the Word there are both affection and subject matter. The celestial angels perceive the Word such as it is in the internal sense as to the affection; but the spiritual angels perceive it such as it is in the internal sense as to the matter. Those who perceive the Word in the internal sense as to the affection, pay no attention to the words which belong to the matter, but form for themselves ideas from the affection and its series, and this with endless variety. Here for example at the words, "If I pray I have found grace in Thine eyes, pass not I pray from over Thy servant," they perceive the Lord's state of humiliation in the Human, but only the affection of the humiliation.   From this, in a manner, variety, and abundance inexpressible, they form for themselves celestial ideas, which can scarcely be called ideas, but rather so many lights of affections and perceptions, which follow in a continuous series, in accordance with the series of the affection of the things contained in the Word that is being read.   [2] This shows that the perception, thought, and speech of the celestial angels are more ineffable and much richer than the perception, thought, and speech of the spiritual angels, the latter being simply determined to the subject matter (*rem*), in accordance with the series of the expressions.   (That the speech of the celestial angels is of this nature, may be seen in Part First, n. 1647.)   Hence it is that these words, " If I pray I have found grace in Thine eyes," in the celestial sense signify the deference of the Lord's state when He observed that perception.   Moreover to " find grace in thine eyes" was a customary mode of speech for every expression of deference ; as may be seen from Laban's deference to Jacob :—

Laban said unto him, If I pray I have found grace in thine eyes (*Gen.* xxx. 27) ;

also from Jacob's deference to Esau :—

Jacob said, Nay, I pray, if I pray I have found grace in thine eyes (*Gen.* xxxiii. 10) ;

and in like manner elsewhere in the Word.

2158. *Pass not I pray from over Thy servant.*   That this signifies that He intensely desired, appears from what has just been said, the case being much the same, namely, that here also there is deference, which is expressed in this way, and at the same time the affection of desire that what He began to perceive should not pass away.

2159. That the " servant" denotes the human that appertained to the Lord, before it was made Divine, may be seen from many passages in the Prophets.   The reason is—as already shown several times— that until He had put it off and made it Divine the human that appertained to the Lord was merely a servant.   The human that appertained to Him was from the mother, thus was infirm, having with it from the mother an hereditary which by means of the combats of tempta-

tions He overcame and utterly expelled, insomuch that nothing
was left of that which was infirm and hereditary from the
mother, nay, at last there remained not anything whatever
from the mother. Thus He entirely put off all that was from
the mother, and therefore was no longer her son, as also He
himself says in *Mark* :—

They said unto Him, Behold Thy mother and Thy brethren without
seek for Thee : and He answered them, saying, Who is My mother, or My
brethren ? And looking round on them that sat about Him, He said,
Behold My mother and My brethren ; for whosoever shall do the will of
God, the same is My brother, and My sister, and My mother (iii. 32–35 ;
Matt. xii. 46–49 ; *Luke* viii. 20, 21).

[2] And when He had put off this human, he put on the Divine Human, from which He called Himself the "Son of
man," as we find many times in the Word of the New Testament ; and also the "Son of God ;" and by the "Son of man"
He meant the truth itself, and by the "Son of God" the good
itself, which belonged to His Human Essence when this was
made Divine. The former state was that of the Lord's humiliation, but the latter that of His glorification (treated of
before, n. 1999), [3] In the former state, namely, that of
humiliation, when as yet He had appertaining to Him an infirm
human, He adored Jehovah as one other than Himself; and
indeed like a servant ; for relatively to the Divine the human
is nothing else, on which account in the Word the term "servant" is predicated of that human, as in *Isaiah* :—

I will defend this city to save it, for Mine own sake, and for My servant David's sake (xxxvii. 35),

where the Assyrians are treated of, in whose camp a hundred
and eighty-five thousand were smitten by an angel. "David"
denotes the Lord, who, as He was to come, in respect to the
human is called a "servant." (That in the Word "David"
denotes the Lord, may be seen above, n. 1888.) [4] In the
same Prophet :—

Behold My servant upon whom I will lean ; My chosen, My soul is well
pleased. I have put My spirit upon him ; he shall bring forth judgment
unto the nations (xlii. 1),

manifestly concerning the Lord, of whom, when He was in
the human, the terms "servant" and "chosen" are predicated.

Again:—

Who is blind but My servant? and deaf, as the angel I will send? who is blind as the perfect one, and blind as the servant of Jehovah? (xlii. 19),

where also the Lord is spoken of; and of whom in like manner the terms "servant" and "angel" are predicated when He was in the human. [5] Again :—

Ye are My witnesses, saith Jehovah, and My servant whom I have chosen ; that ye may know and believe Me, and understand that I am He (xliii. 10).

Again :—

Said Jehovah, My Former from the womb to be His servant ; to bring Jacob again unto Him, and that Israel be gathered unto Him ; and He said, Thou art a slight thing that thou shouldest be My servant, to set up the tribes of Jacob ; I have given thee for a light of the nations to be My salvation unto the extremity of the earth (xlix. 5, 6),

where also the Lord and His human are manifestly treated of before He was made the "light of the nations," and "salvation unto the extremity of the earth." Again:—

Who is among you that feareth Jehovah, that heareth the voice of His servant, who walketh in darkness, and hath no brightness ? let him trust in the name of Jehovah, and lean upon His God (l. 10).

"Servant" here also denotes the human that appertained to the Lord; and that He was in this human and taught the way of truth, is the "voice of the servant of Jehovah." [6] Again :—

Jehovah goeth before you, and the God of Israel gathereth you. Behold, My servant shall act prudently, he shall be lifted up, and shall be exalted, and shall be raised up exceedingly (lii. 12, 13).

It is evident that "servant" is here predicated of the Lord when He was in the human; for it is said of Him that He "shall be lifted up, exalted, and raised up." Again :—

He hath no form and no honor ; we saw him, but there was no appearance ; He was despised, a man of sorrows, acquainted with disease. Jehovah willed to bruise him ; He made him infirm ; if he shall make his soul guilt, he shall see seed, he shall prolong days, and the will of Jehovah shall prosper by his hand ; he shall see of the labor of his soul, he shall be satisfied ; by his knowledge shall My righteous servant justify many ; and he himself hath carried their iniquities (liii. 2, 3, 10, 11).

Here, as in the whole of this chapter, the Lord's state of humiliation is openly treated of; and it is also said that He was then in an infirm human, namely, that He was a "man of sorrows, acquainted with disease, infirm, was in the labor of His soul," besides a number of other statements, in which state He is called "servant."

2160. Verse 4. *Let I pray a little water be taken, and wash ye your feet, and lie down under the tree.* "Let I pray a little water be taken," signifies that they should draw near, and let themselves down from things Divine nearer to His intellectual things; "and wash ye your feet," signifies that they should put on something natural, in order that in the state in which He then was, He might the better perceive; "and lie down under the tree," signifies near to the perception of His state in which He was; "tree" is perception.

2161. *Let I pray a little water be taken.* That this signifies that they should draw near, and let themselves down from things Divine nearer to His intellectual things, cannot be so evident from these words alone—that they should take a little water—but it is evident from the series of things in this verse, and from their connection with those which go before and those which follow. From what is said in this verse no one would ever know that the words "Let I pray a little water be taken, and wash ye your feet, and lie down under the tree" signify that the Divine should let itself down nearer to the state of perception in which the Lord then was, and should put on something natural in order that He might the better perceive; for not a trace of this arcanum is manifest in the words as understood historically; but that nevertheless such in the internal sense is their signification, and that the angels so perceive them, I know for certain. [2] This shows what great and deep arcana lie hidden in the Word. Moreover that such is the signification, may be seen from the signification in the internal sense of the several words, namely, from the signification of "water" as being intellectual things, from the signification of "feet" as being natural things, and from the signification of a "tree" as being perception. When these things are understood, the signification in the internal sense (to wit, that which has been stated) can be seen from the series of things, and from their connection with those which precede and those which follow. (That "waters" signify memory-knowledges and rational things, consequently the things of the understanding, has been shown in Part First, n. 28, 680, and may be seen from very many other passages in the Word that it would be too tedious to bring forward.)

2162. *Wash ye your feet.* That this signifies that [the Divine] should put on something natural, in order that, in the state in which the Lord then was, He might the better perceive, may be seen from the signification of "feet," as being natural things, and also likewise from the series of things. That arcana here lie hidden may to some extent be seen from the fact that Abraham prayed the three men to take a little water and wash their feet, and to recline under a tree; when yet he knew that it was the Lord or Jehovah; and also from the fact that otherwise such things would not have been mentioned. [2] That "feet" signify natural things, is evident from the representatives in the other life, and from the derivative representatives among the most ancient people, and thus in the Word. Celestial and spiritual things are represented by the head and its belongings; rational things and their belongings, by the breast and its belongings; natural things and their belongings, by the feet and their belongings. Hence it is that the "sole" and the "heel" of the foot signify the lowest natural things (concerning which see n. 259); and a "shoe" the lowest things of all, which are unclean (concerning which see n. 1748). [3] Similar things are signified by the representations in the dreams and visions in the Prophets—as by the statue seen by Nebuchadnezzar,

The head of which was good gold, the breast and arms of silver, the belly and thighs of brass, the legs of iron, the feet part of iron and part of clay (*Dan.* ii. 32, 33),

where the "head" signifies celestial things, which are inmost, and are "gold" (as shown, n. 113, 1551, 1552); the "breast and arms" spiritual or rational things, which are "silver" (as shown, n. 1551); but the "feet" are the lower things, which are natural, the truths of which are signified by "iron," and the goods by "clay" (*argillum seu lutum*). That "iron" denotes truth, may be seen above (n. 425, 426); also that "clay" denotes good (n. 1300); in the present case both being natural. Such is the order of succession in the Lord's kingdom in the heavens, and in the church which is the Lord's kingdom on earth, and also in every one who is a kingdom of the Lord. [4] The case is similar with the vision that Daniel saw, of which it is said:—

I lifted up mine eyes, and saw, and behold a man clothed in linen, and his loins were girded with gold of Uphaz; his body also was like the beryl (Tarshish), and his face as the appearance of lightning, and his eyes as lamps of fire, and his arms and his feet like the brightness of burnished brass (x. 5, 6).

Specifically, by these words are signified the interiors of the Word as to goods and truths; the "arms" and "feet" are its exteriors, which are the sense of the letter, because natural things are therein, for the exterior things of the Word are taken from natural things. What each part signifies besides, namely, the loins, body, face, eyes, and the many other things of man, is evident from the representatives in the other life, concerning which, of the Lord's Divine mercy more will be said when we come to treat of the Grand Man, which is the Lord's heaven, and of the derivative representatives in the world of spirits. [5] That which we read concerning Moses, Aaron, Nadab, Abihu, and the seventy elders—that "they saw the God of Israel, under whose feet there was as it were a work of sapphire stone, and as it were the substance of heaven as to purity" (*Exod.* xxiv. 9, 10), signifies that they saw only the externals of the church represented in natural things; and also the literal sense of the Word, in which likewise external things are represented by natural things—as before said— which are the "feet under which was as it were a work of sapphire stone, and as it were the substance of heaven." That it was the Lord who was seen by them, but only in those lower or natural things, is evident, for He is called "the God of Israel," whom all things of the church represented, and all things of the Word in the internal sense signified. For the Lord is presented to view in accordance with the things which are at the time signified—in John, as a Man upon a white horse, when He signified the Word, as is plainly said (*Rev.* xix. 11, 13). [6] The animals seen by Ezekiel, which were cherubs, are described as to celestial and spiritual things—among other representatives—by their faces and wings, but as to natural things, as follows :—

Their feet, a straight foot ; and the sole of their feet as the sole of a calf's foot ; and they glittered like the brightness of burnished brass (*Ezek.* i. 7).

The feet (that is, the natural things) are said to have "glittered like burnished brass," for the reason that "brass" signifies natural good (n. 425, 1551). It was much the same with the Lord's appearance to John as the "Son of man :"—

Whose eyes were as a flame of fire, and His feet like unto burnished brass (*Rev.* i. 14, 15 ; ii. 18).

[7] That the "feet" signify natural things, may be further evident from the passages that now follow. In *John :*—

I saw a strong angel coming down out of heaven, encompassed with a cloud, and a rainbow about his head, and his face as the sun, and his feet as pillars of fire ; and he had in his hand a little book open ; and he set his right foot upon the sea, and his left upon the earth (*Rev.* x. 1, 2).

By this angel there is in like manner signified the Word; the quality of which in the internal sense is signified by the "rainbow about his head," and by "his face being as the sun ;" but the external sense, or that of the letter, by the "feet." The "sea" denotes natural truths, the "earth" natural goods, which shows what is signified by his putting "his right foot upon the sea, and his left upon the earth." [8] A "footstool" is mentioned in various passages of the Word; but it is not known what it signifies in the internal sense. As in *Isaiah :*—

Jehovah said, The heavens are My throne, and the earth is My footstool. Where is that house which ye will build unto Me ? and where is that place of My rest ? (lxvi. 1).

The "heavens" are the celestial and spiritual things (thus the inmost things) of both the Lord's kingdom in the heavens, and of the Lord's kingdom on the earth, that is, in the church, and also in every man who is a kingdom of the Lord or a church; thus they also denote celestial and spiritual things as regarded in themselves, which are those of love and charity and of the derivative faith ; and thus are all things which are of internal worship, and in like manner all things which are

of the internal sense of the Word : these are the " heavens,"
and are called the Lord's "throne." But the "earth" is all
lower things that correspond to these—as the lower rational
and natural things, whereof also things celestial and spiritual
are predicated from correspondence; such as are the things
which are in the lower heavens, also those in the church and
in external worship, and in the literal sense of the Word; in
short, all such things as proceed from things internal and are
presented in things external—these, being natural things, are
called the " earth" and the Lord's " footstool." (What "heaven
and earth" denote in the internal sense, may be seen above, n.
82, 1733; also what the " new heaven and the· new earth" denote, n. 2117, 2118 end; and that man is a little heaven, n.
911, 978, 1900.)   [9] In like manner in *Jeremiah* :—

The Lord covereth the daughter of Zion with a cloud in His anger ;
He hath cast down from the heavens unto the earth the beauty of Israel,
and hath not remembered His footstool in the day of His anger (*Lam.*
ii. 1).

Also in *David* :—

Exalt ye Jehovah our God, and bow yourselves down at His footstool,
Holy is He (*Ps.* xcix. 5).

And again :—

We will enter into His tabernacles, we will bow down at His footstool
(*Ps.* cxxxii. 7).

In the Representative Church—thus among the Jews—it was
supposed that the house of God and the temple were His footstool, for they knew not that external representative worship
was signified by the house of God and the temple; and what
the internals of the church were (which were signified by
" heaven," or God's "throne"), they were utterly ignorant of.
[10] Again :—

The saying of Jehovah unto my Lord : Sit Thou at My right hand,
until I make Thine enemies Thy footstool (*Ps.* cx. 1 ; *Matt.* xxii. 42–45 ;
Mark xii. 36 ; *Luke* xx. 42, 43).

Here in like manner a " footstool" signifies natural things
both those which are sensuous, and those of memory-knowledge, and the derivative rational things of man, which are
called " enemies" when they pervert worship, and do this from

the literal sense of the Word, so that there is worship solely in externals, and either no internal worship, or else that which is filthy (see n. 1094, 1175, 1182). When things natural and rational are thus perverted and defiled, they are called " ene-mies ;" but because, regarded in themselves, they have reference to internal worship—when this is restored, they become as before said a " footstool," whether they are things of external worship, or of the literal sense of the Word. [11] In *Isaiah :—*

The glory of Lebanon shall come unto thee, the fir-tree, the pine, and the box together, to beautify the place of My sanctuary, and I will make the place of My feet honorable (lx. 13),

where the subject is the Lord's kingdom and church, the celes-tial spiritual things of which are the " glory of Lebanon" (that is, the cedars), and its celestial natural things are the " fir-tree, the pine, and the box" (as also in the Word else-where), and thus the things which are of external worship ; of which it is said, " I will make the place of My feet honorable ;" and this cannot be made honorable by the fir, the pine, and the box, but by the things which they signify. [12] That the " feet" signify these things, is evident also from the represent-atives in the Jewish Church—as from Aaron and his sons washing their hands and their feet before entering into the tabernacle (*Exod.* xxx. 19, 20 ; xl. 31, 32). No one can fail to see that arcana were thus represented, for what is the washing of the hands and feet but an external affair which is of no avail unless the internal is clean and pure ? Nor can the in-ternal be cleaned and purified by such a washing. But as all the rites of that church were significative of internal things, which are celestial and spiritual, such is the case here also : it is cleanness of external worship that is here signified, and external worship is clean when there is internal worship within it. Hence their lavers were of brass, and also that great laver that was called the brazen sea, and the ten smaller lavers of brass around the temple of Solomon (1 *Kings* vii. 23, 38) ; be-cause " brass" represented the good of external worship, which is the same as natural good (concerning which signification of " brass," see n. 425, 1551). [13] In like manner it was a rep-resentative that,

A man of the seed of Aaron in whom there was a fracture of the foot, or a fracture of the hand, should not approach to offer the offerings made by fire to Jehovah (*Lev.* xxi. 19, 21).

By those who had a "fracture" in the feet or hands were represented such as are in perverted external worship. [14] That "feet" signify natural things, is further evident in other passages that occur in the Prophets, as in these propheticals in *Moses* :—

Blessed be Asher above sons ; let him be accepted of his brethren, and let him dip his foot in oil ; the iron and brass of thy shoe (*Deut.* xxxiii. 24, 25).

No one can understand these words unless it is known what " oil," the " foot," " iron," " brass," and a " shoe" signify in the internal sense. That " foot" is the natural, and " shoe" the still lower natural, such as is the corporeal sensual, may be seen above (n. 1748) ; also that " oil" is the celestial (n. 886), " iron" natural truth (n. 425, 426), and " brass" natural good (n. 425, 1551), which shows what these words involve. [15] In *Nahum* :—

The way of Jehovah is in the storm and tempest, and the clouds are the dust of His feet (i. 3),

where the " dust of the feet" signifies the natural and corporeal things with man, whence come the " clouds." The same also is signified by these words in *David* :—

Jehovah bowed the heavens, and came down, and thick darkness was under His feet (*Ps.* xviii. 9).

[16] When the goods and truths of faith are perverted by means of natural light, as it is called, this is described in the Word by the " feet" and " hoofs" of a beast, whereby waters are disturbed, and food is trampled upon. As in *Ezekiel* :—

Thou hast come forth into the rivers, and hast troubled the waters with thy feet ; and trampled the streams thereof. I will destroy every beast thereof from off many waters ; and the foot of man shall not trouble them any more, nor the hoof of beast (xxxii. 2, 13).

Egypt is here treated of, by which are signified memory-knowledges (*scientiae*) (as has been shown, n. 1164, 1165, 1462) ; so that by the " feet" and " hoofs" by which the streams and waters are troubled, are signified memory-knowledges (*scien-*

tifica) derived from sensuous and natural things, from which they reason about the arcana of faith; nor do they believe until these arcana are comprehended by means of such knowledges; and this is not to believe at all, for the more such persons reason, the less do they believe (see n. 128–130, 215, 232, 233, 1072, 1385). From all this it is now evident that by "feet" in the Word are signified natural things; but what more is signified, is evident from the series of things.

2163. *And lie down under the tree.* That this signifies near to the perception of His state in which He then was, is evident from the signification of a "tree," as being perception (see n. 103); bearing which in mind the series of things shows that the above is the real sense of the words. That "trees" signified perceptions, originated in the fact that the celestial man was compared and likened to Paradise, or the garden in Eden; from which the perceptions of celestial things with him were likened to the trees therein.

2164. Verse 5. *And I will take a piece of bread, and support ye your heart; afterwards ye may pass on; for therefore have ye passed over unto your servant. And they said, So do as thou hast spoken.* "I will take a piece of bread," signifies something celestial adjoined; "support ye your heart," signifies as much as is meet; "afterwards ye may pass on," signifies that when He had left off perceiving He would be content therewith; "for therefore have ye passed over unto your servant," signifies that they came for this purpose; "and they said, So do as thou hast spoken," signifies that it should be so done.

2165. *I will take a piece of bread.* That this signifies something celestial adjoined, is evident from the signification of "bread," as being what is celestial (explained before, n. 276, 680, 681, 1798). That "bread" signifies what is celestial, is because "bread" means all food in general, and thus in the internal sense all celestial food. What celestial food is, has been stated in Part First (n. 56–58, 680, 681, 1480, 1695). That "bread" means all food in general, is evident from the following passages of the Word. We read of Joseph that,

He said to him who was over his house, that he should bring the men
—his brethren—home, and should slay what was to be slain, and should

make ready; and afterwards, when they had made ready, and were to eat, he said, Set on bread (*Gen.* xliii. 16, 31);

meaning that they should make ready the table; "bread" thus denoting all kinds of food.   We read concerning Jethro that,

Aaron came, and all the elders of Israel to eat bread with Moses' father-in-law before God (*Exod.* xviii. 12),

where also "bread" denotes all kinds of food.   Concerning Manoah, in the Book of *Judges :*—

Manoah said unto the Angel of Jehovah, Let us I pray detain thee, and let us make ready before thee a kid of the goats.   And the Angel of Jehovah said unto Manoah, Though thou detain me, I will not eat of thy bread (xiii. 15, 16),

where "bread" denotes a kid of the goats.   When Jonathan ate of the honey-comb, they told him that Saul had adjured the people, saying :—

Cursed be the man that shall eat bread this day (1 *Sam.* xiv. 27, 28),

where "bread" denotes all food.   Again, concerning Saul :—

When Saul sat down to eat bread, he said unto Jonathan, Wherefore cometh not the son of Jesse to bread either yesterday or to-day ? (1 *Sam.* xx. 24, 27),

meaning to the table, where were all kinds of food.   We read concerning David that he said to Mephibosheth the son of Jonathan :—

Thou shalt eat bread on my table continually (2 *Sam.* ix. 7, 10).

So too concerning Evil-merodach, who said that,

Jehoiachin king of Judah should eat bread before him continually, all the days of his life (2 *Kings* xxv. 29).

Concerning Solomon also :—

Solomon's bread for each day was thirty cors of fine flour, and sixty cors of meal, ten fat oxen, and twenty oxen of the pastures, and a hundred sheep, besides the hart and the wild she-goat, and the antelope, and fatted fowl (1 *Kings* iv. 22, 23),

where "bread" plainly denotes all of these things.   [2] Now as "bread" means all kinds of food in general, it therefore signifies in the internal sense all those things which are called celestial foods, as may be still more evident from the burnt-offerings and sacrifices that were made of lambs, sheep, she-goats, kids, he-goats, heifers, and oxen, which were called in one word the "bread of the offering made by fire unto Jehovah," as is clearly evident from the following passages in *Moses*, where the various sacrifices are treated of, of which it is said that,

The priest should burn them upon the altar, the bread of the offering made by fire unto Jehovah, for an odor of rest (*Lev.* iii. 11, 16),

all those sacrifices and burnt-offerings being so called. Again:—

The sons of Aaron shall be holy unto their God, neither shall they profane the name of their God ; because the offerings to Jehovah made by fire, the bread of their God, they do offer. Thou shalt sanctify him, because he offereth the bread of thy God. A man of the seed of Aaron in whom there shall be a blemish, shall not come nigh to offer the bread of his God (*Lev.* xxi. 6, 8, 17, 21),

where also sacrifices and burnt-offerings are the "bread." The same is true of *Leviticus* xxii. 25. Again:—

Command the sons of Israel, and say unto them, My oblation, My bread for offerings made by fire, of an odor of rest, shall ye observe, to offer unto Me at their appointed time (*Num.* xxviii. 2).

Here also "bread" denotes all the sacrifices which are there enumerated. In *Malachi:*—

Offering polluted bread upon Mine altar (i. 7),

where also the sacrifices are spoken of. The hallowed things of the sacrifices, which they ate, were also called "bread," as is evident from these words in *Moses:*—

He that toucheth an unclean thing shall not eat of the hallowed things, but he shall wash his flesh in water, and when the sun is down, he shall be clean ; and afterwards he shall eat of the hallowed things, because this is his bread (*Lev.* xxii. 6, 7).

[3] The burnt-offerings and sacrifices in the Jewish Church represented nothing else than the celestial things of the Lord's kingdom in the heavens, and of the Lord's kingdom on earth (that is, in the church), also of the Lord's kingdom or church with each person, and in general all those things which are of love and charity, for these are things celestial; and each kind of sacrifice represented something special and peculiar. All these were at that time called BREAD, and therefore when sacrifices were abolished, and other things succeeded in their place

for external worship, it was commanded that bread and wine should be made use of. [4] From all this we may now see what the "bread" [in the Holy Supper] signifies, namely, all the things represented by the sacrifices, thus in the internal sense the Lord Himself. And because the "bread" signifies the Lord Himself, it signifies love itself toward the universal human race, and what belongs to love; as also man's reciprocal love to the Lord and toward the neighbor. The "bread" thus signifies all celestial things, and in the same way the "wine" signifies all spiritual things, as the Lord also teaches in plain words in *John*. They said,

Our fathers did eat the manna in the wilderness; as it is written, He gave them bread from heaven to eat. Jesus said unto them, Verily, verily I say unto you, Moses gave you not that bread from heaven, but My Father giveth you the true bread from heaven; for the bread of God is He that cometh down from heaven, and giveth life unto the world. They said unto Him, Lord, evermore give us this bread. Jesus said unto them, I am the bread of life; he that cometh to Me shall never hunger, and he that believeth on Me shall never thirst (vi. 31–35).

And again :—

Verily I say unto you, he that believeth on Me hath eternal life. I am the bread of life. Your fathers did eat the manna in the wilderness, and are dead; this is the bread that cometh down from heaven, that one may eat thereof and not die. I am the living bread that came down from heaven; if any one eat of this bread, he shall live to eternity (vi. 47–51).

[5] Now because the "bread" is the Lord, it belongs to the celestial things which are of love, which are the Lord's; for the Lord is the celestial itself, because He is love itself, that is, mercy itself; and because this is so, "bread" means all the celestial, that is, all the love and charity with man, for these are from the Lord; and therefore they who are not in love and charity have not the Lord with them, and thus are not gifted with the good and happy things that in the internal sense are signified by "bread." This outward symbol was commanded because the greatest part of the human race are in external worship, and therefore without some outward symbol there would be scarcely anything holy with them. And therefore when they live in love to the Lord and in charity toward the neighbor, they nevertheless have appertaining to them what is internal, although they do not know that this love and

charity is the veriest internal of worship. Thus in their external worship they are confirmed in the goods which are signified by the " bread." [6] In the Prophets also the celestial things of love are signified by "bread" (as in *Isa.* iii. 1, 7; xxx. 23; xxxiii. 15, 16; lv. 2; lviii. 7, 8; *Lam.* v. 9; *Ezek.* iv. 16, 17; v. 16; xiv. 13; *Amos* iv. 6; viii. 11; *Ps.* cv. 16), in like manner by the "bread of faces" upon the table (mentioned *Lev.* xxiv. 5–9; *Exod.* xxv. 30; xl. 23; *Num.* iv. 7; 1 *Kings* vii. 48).

2166. *Support ye your heart.* That this signifies as much as is meet, cannot be so evident from the proximate signification of the words in the internal sense, but yet it is evident from the series of things, for the subject treated of is the Divine perception—that this might draw nearer to the perception of the human which then appertained to the Lord, and that it might let itself down to His intellectual things, by putting on something natural and also something celestial adjoined to it, as much as was meet—which is to "support the heart." In the proximate sense, to "support the heart by bread" is to be refreshed, and thus to enjoy what little of the celestial is meet.

2167. *Afterwards ye may pass on.* That this signifies that when He had left off perceiving He would be content therewith, is in like manner evident from the series.

2168. *For therefore have ye passed over unto your servant.* That this signifies that they came for this purpose, is also evident without explication.

2169. *And they said, So do as thou hast spoken.* That this signifies that it would be so done, likewise needs no explication.

2170. Verse 6. *And Abraham hastened toward the tent unto Sarah, and said, Make ready quickly three measures of meal of fine flour, knead, and make cakes.* " Abraham hastened toward the tent unto Sarah," signifies the Lord's rational good conjoined with His truth; " Abraham" is here the Lord in that state as to good; " Sarah," as to truth; the " tent," as to the holy of love: " and said," signifies the state of perception relatively at that time; " make ready quickly three measures of meal of fine flour, knead, and make cakes," signifies the celestial of His love in that state; "three" denotes what is holy; "meal of fine flour," is the spiritual and the celestial of the rational which were then with the Lord; "cakes" denote the same when both are conjoined.

2171. *Abraham hastened toward the tent unto Sarah.* That this signifies the Lord's rational good conjoined with His truth, is evident from the representation of "Abraham," and also of "Sarah," and from the signification of·a "tent," concerning which presently. As each and all things bear relation to the subject treated of in the internal sense, so do these words bear relation to the Divine perception into which the Lord came when He was in the perception of the human. But those who do not know what perception is, cannot know either how the case is with it, still less that there exists a perception that is more and more interior, namely, natural perception, then rational perception, and finally internal perception, which is Divine, and which the Lord alone had. They who are in perception, as are the angels, know very well in which perception they are; whether in natural, in rational, or in a still more interior perception which to them is Divine. What then must have been the case with the Lord, who had a perception from the Supreme and Infinite Divine (concerning which see n. 1616 at the end, 1791), in which no angels ever are, for perception flows into them from the Lord's Supreme or Infinite Divine through His Human Essence. [2] The reason why the Lord's perception is described, is that when He was in the human, it was thus made known to Him how the Divine Itself, the Divine Human, and the Holy proceeding were to be united in Him; then, how His rational was to be made Divine; and finally what was the quality of the human race—that it was to be saved by Him, that is, by the union of the Human Essence with the Divine Essence in Him; which are the subjects treated of in this chapter. On these accounts the Lord's perception is first described, as also on account of the union itself which was to be effected.

2172. That "Abraham" is here the Lord in that state as to good, is evident from the representation of Abraham. When he is speaking with Jehovah, as here, Abraham represents the Lord in the Human (as also before, n. 1989, where he represented the

Lord in the state and at the age there described, because then also he spoke with Jehovah). In other cases Abraham represents the Lord's Divine good, and Sarah His Divine truth; hence Abraham now represents the Lord's rational good.

2173. That "Sarah" is here the Lord as to truth, is evident from the representation of Sarah, as being intellectual truth adjoined to good ; here, as being rational truth, for the same reason as just now stated in regard to Abraham. (That Sarah represents truth may be seen above, n. 1468, 1901, 2063, 2065). In the historicals of the Word good and truth cannot be represented otherwise than by a marriage, for this is really the case with them, for there is a Divine marriage between things celestial and spiritual, or what is the same, between those which are of love and those which are of faith, or again what is the same, between those of the will and those of the understanding. The former are of good, the latter are of truth. There is such a marriage in the Lord's kingdom in the heavens; such also in the Lord's kingdom on the earth (that is, in the church); such a marriage in every man, in every single thing of him, nay, in the veriest singulars of all. That which is not in such a marriage does not live. Nay, from that Divine marriage there is such a marriage in universal nature, and in every particular of it, but under other form and appearance, otherwise nothing whatever would there subsist. Because there is such marriage in everything, therefore with the Prophets every matter is expressed in a twofold manner, especially in *Isaiah*—one expression referring to what is celestial, or to good, and the other to what is spiritual, or to truth (see n. 683, 793, 801). That in everything there is a resemblance of a marriage, may be seen above (n. 718, 747, 917, 1432). Hence it is that the Lord's good is represented by Abraham, and His truth by Sarah.

2174. That a "tent" is the Lord as to the holy of love, is evident from the signification of a "tent," as being what is holy (explained before, n. 414, 1102, 1566, 2145).

2175. *And he said.* That this signifies the state of the perception relatively at that time, is evident from the signification in the historical sense of "saying" as being to perceive (explained before, n. 1898, 1919, 2080).

Vol. III.—3

2176. *Make ready quickly three measures of meal of fine flour, knead, and make cakes.* That this signifies the celestial of His love in that state, is evident from the signification of "meal," "fine flour," and "cakes," which will be treated of in what next follows. That such things are involved, no one can believe who keeps his mind intent on the literal sense, or that of the words, still less if on the historical things described by them; for he is thinking not only about this preparation, but also about the men who came to Abraham, and not about these matters involving more secret things. This is the reason why he can still less believe that the historicals of the Word in every detail store up within them such arcana equally as do the propheticals; for the historicals draw the mind strongly to themselves, and darken the interiors. Nevertheless that there really are arcana deeply hidden in these historicals is evident from the mere fact that it is the Word of the Lord, written not only for man, but at the same time also for heaven; and this in such a manner, that when a man is reading it, the angels have heavenly ideas therefrom; so that in this way heaven is conjoined with the human race by means of the Word. What is meant in the internal sense by "meal," "fine flour," and "cakes," will now be shown.

2177. That the "meal of fine flour" denotes the spiritual and the celestial which were then with the Lord, and that "cakes" denote the same when both are conjoined, is very evident from the sacrifices of the Representative Church, and from the meat-offering then made use of, which consisted of fine flour mingled with oil and made into cakes. The chief part of representative worship consisted in burnt-offerings and sacrifices. What these represented has already been stated, where bread is treated of (n. 2165), namely, the celestial things of the Lord's kingdom in the heavens and of the Lord's kingdom on the earth (that is, in the church), and also those of the Lord's kingdom or church with each person; and in general all the things of love and charity, because these are celestial. All these offerings and sacrifices were at that time called "bread," and to them was adjoined the meat-offering also, which, as already said, consisted of fine flour mingled with oil, to which frankincense was likewise added, as well as a

libation of wine. [2] What these represented is also evident,
namely, similar things as the sacrifices, but in a less degree,
thus the things which are of the spiritual church, and likewise those of the external church. Every one can see that
such things would never have been commanded unless they
had represented Divine things, and also that each one represents something special and peculiar, for unless they had represented Divine things, they would not have differed from similar things in use among the Gentiles, among whom also there
were sacrifices—meat-offerings, libations, frankincense, perpetual fires, and many other things, derived to them from the
Ancient Church, and especially from the Hebrew Church. But
as internal things (that is, the Divine things that were represented) were separated from these Gentile rites, they were
merely idolatrous, as also they became with the Jews, who for
this reason fell into all kinds of idolatry. From what has
been said every one can see that there were heavenly arcana
in every rite, especially in the sacrifices and all their particulars. [3] As regards the meat-offering, the nature of it and
how it was to be prepared into cakes, is described in a whole
chapter in *Moses* (*Lev.* ii.; also in *Num.* xv., and elsewhere).
The law of the meat-offering is described in *Leviticus* in these
words:—

Fire shall be kept burning upon the altar continually, it shall not go
out. And this is the law of the meat-offering : the sons of Aaron shall
bring it before Jehovah to the faces of the altar ; and he shall take therefrom his handful of the fine flour of the meat-offering, and of the oil
thereof, and all the frankincense which is upon the meat-offering, and
shall burn it upon the altar, an odor of rest, for a memorial unto Jehovah ; and the residue thereof Aaron and his sons shall eat ; unleavened
shall they be eaten in a holy place ; in the court of the tent of meeting
shall they eat it. It shall not be baked leavened ; I have given it as their
portion of My offerings made by fire ; it is a holy of holies (vi. 13–17).

[4] The fire which must be kept burning upon the altar continually, represented the love, that is, the mercy of the Lord,
perpetual and eternal. That in the Word " fire" signifies love,
see n. 934; hence " offerings made by fire for an odor of rest"
signify the Lord's pleasure in the things which are of love
and charity. (That " odor" denotes what is well-pleasing,
that is, what is grateful, see n. 925, 1519.) Their " taking

a handful" represented that they should love with all the
strength, or with all the soul; for the hand, or the palm of the
hand, signifies power (as shown n. 878), from which "handful" also signifies power. The fine flour, with the oil and the
frankincense, represented all things of charity—the fine flour
the spiritual, and the oil the celestial of charity, the frankincense what was in this manner grateful. (That fine flour represents what is spiritual, is evident from what has just been
said, and from what follows; that oil represents what is
celestial, or the good of charity, may be seen above, n. 886;
and also that frankincense, from its odor, represents what is
grateful and acceptable, n. 925.)   [5] Its being "unleavened,"
or not fermented, signifies that it should be sincere, and thus
from a sincere heart, and free from uncleanness.   That Aaron
and his sons should eat the residue, represented man's reciprocality and his appropriation, thus conjunction through love
and charity; on which account it was commanded that they
should eat it in a holy place.   Hence it is called a "holy of
holies."   These were the things that were represented by the
meat-offering; and the representatives themselves were so perceived in heaven; and when the man of the church so apprehended them, he was then in an idea similar to the perception
of the angels, thus he was in the Lord's kingdom itself in the
heavens although he was on earth.   [6] The meat-offering is
further treated of, as regards what it ought to be in connection with each kind of sacrifice, and how it should be baked
into cakes, also what kind should be offered by those who were
being cleansed, and what on other occasions; to mention and
explain all of which would be too tedious; but concerning all
these matters see *Exod.* xxix. 39–41; *Lev.* v. 11–13; vi. 14–23;
x. 12, 13; xxiii. 10–13, 16, 17; *Num.* v. 15, etc.; vi. 15–17,
19, 20; chapter vii., in several places; xxviii. 5, 7, 9, 12, 13,
20, 21, 28, 29; xxix. 3, 4, 9, 10, 14, 15, 18, 21, 24, 27, 30, 33,
37.   [7] Fine flour made into cakes in general represented
the same as bread, namely, the celestial of love, and meal the
spiritual of it, as is evident from the passages cited above.
The "breads" (or loaves) that were called the "bread of faces,"
or the "show bread" (*panis propositionis*), were made of fine
flour, which was prepared in cakes and placed upon the table,

for a perpetual representation of the love, that is, the mercy, of the Lord toward the universal human race, and the reciprocality of man. Concerning these loaves we read as follows in *Moses* :—

> Thou shalt take fine flour and shalt bake it into twelve cakes ; of two tenths shall one cake be ; and thou shalt set them in two rows, six in a row, upon the clean table, before Jehovah ; and thou shalt put pure frankincense upon each row, and it shall be to the breads for a memorial, an offering made by fire unto Jehovah. On every Sabbath day he shall set it in order before Jehovah continually, from the sons of Israel in a covenant of eternity. And it shall be for Aaron and his sons, and they shall eat it in a holy place, for it is a holy of holies unto him, of the offerings made by fire unto Jehovah by a statute of eternity (*Lev.* xxiv. 5–9).

Every particular in this description and all the smallest details represented the holy of love and of charity, the " fine flour" the same as the " meal of fine flour," namely, the celestial and its spiritual, and the " cake" the two conjoined. [8] Hence it is evident what is the holiness of the Word to those who are in heavenly ideas, nay, what holiness there was in this very representative rite, on account of which it is called a holiness of holinesses ; and on the contrary, how void of holiness it is to those who suppose that there is nothing heavenly in these things, and who abide solely in the externals ; as do they who perceive the meal here merely as meal, the fine flour as fine flour, and the cake as a cake, and who suppose these things to have been stated without each particular involving something of the Divine. These do in like manner as do those who think the bread and wine of the Holy Supper to be nothing but a certain rite, containing nothing holy within ; whereas there is such holiness that human minds are by that Supper conjoined with heavenly minds, when from internal affection they are thinking that the bread and wine signify the Lord's love and the reciprocality of man, and are thus in holiness from interior thought and feeling. [9] The like was involved in that the sons of Israel on their coming into the land of Canaan were to offer a cake of the first of their dough, as a heave-offering unto Jehovah (*Num.* xv. 20). That such things are signified is also evident in the Prophets, from which we may at present adduce only this from *Ezekiel* :—

Thou wast decked with gold and silver; and thy raiment was fine linen and silk, and broidered work ; thou didst eat fine flour, honey, and oil, and thou wast become beautiful very exceedingly, and thou wast prospered unto a kingdom (xvi. 13) ;

where the subject treated of is Jerusalem, by which is signified the church, that was so decked in its earliest time—that is, the Ancient Church—and which is described by the garments and other ornaments ; as also its affections of truth and good by the fine flour, honey, and oil. Every one can see that all these things have a very different meaning in the internal sense from that in the sense of the letter. And so have these words which Abraham said to Sarah: "Make ready quickly three measures of the meal of fine flour, knead, and make cakes." (That "three" signifies holy things has been shown before, n. 720, 901.)

2178. Verse 7. *And Abraham ran unto the herd, and took a son of an ox tender and good, and gave it to the lad, and he hasted to make it.* "Abraham ran unto the herd," signifies natural good; "and took a son of an ox tender and good," signifies the celestial natural which is conformable, and which the rational associated to itself in order that it might conjoin itself with the perception from the Divine; "and gave it to the lad, and he hasted to make it," signifies the conjunction of this good with rational good; "the lad" is here the natural man.

2179. *Abraham ran unto the herd.* That this signifies natural good, is evident from the signification of the oxen and bullocks of the herd—to be explained presently. That the beasts of the herd and of the flock signify such things as are in man, is evident from what has been shown in Part First (n. 45, 46, 142, 143, 246, 714, 715, 719, 776), and also from what was said concerning the beasts used in the sacrifices (n. 1823). It may seem surprising that the animals named in the Word, and also those offered in the sacrifices, should signify goods and truths, or what is the same, things celestial and spiritual, but the reason of this may be briefly stated. [2] In the world of spirits various representatives are presented to view, and withal animals are often presented before the eyes of the spirits there, such as horses variously caparisoned, oxen, sheep, lambs, with other animals of various kinds, sometimes such as are never seen on the earth, but are only representative. Such animals were also seen by the prophets, as described in the Word, and were from the same source. The animals that appear in the world of spirits are representative of affections of good and truth, and also of evil and falsity. Good spirits know perfectly well what they signify, and thus also gather from them what the angels are conversing about; for the speech of angels, passing down into the world of spirits, is sometimes presented in this way. For example, when horses appear, they know that the speech of the angels is about the things of the understanding; when oxen and bullocks, that it is about natural goods; when sheep, that it is about rational goods, and probity; when lambs, that it is about goods still more internal and about innocence; and so on. [3] As the men of the Most Ancient Church had communication with spirits and angels, and constantly had visions and also dreams such as the prophets had, the consequence was that whenever they saw any beast, there occurred to them the idea of what it signified. Representatives and significatives originated in this way, and remained long after their times; and at length became so venerated from their antiquity that men wrote by mere representatives; books not so written being held in no esteem; and those written within the church being of no sanctity. From this and other hidden causes, concerning which of the Lord's Divine mercy elsewhere, the books of the Word also were so written.

2180. *And took a son of an ox tender and good.* That this signifies the celestial natural which the rational associated to itself, in order that it might conjoin itself with the perception from the Divine, is evident from the signification in the Word of a "bullock" or "son of an ox," as being natural good. And as the Lord's rational is treated of, it is called "tender" from the celestial spiritual, or the truth of good; and "good" from the celestial itself, or good itself. In the genuine rational there is the affection of truth and the affection of good; but its chief thing (*primarium*) is the affection of truth (as before shown, n. 2072). Hence it is first called "tender," and yet is called both "tender and good," according to the usual practice in the Word, to indicate the marriage of good and truth (spoken of above, n. 2173). [2] That a "bullock," or "son of an ox," signifies the celestial natural, or what is the same, natural good, is especially evident from the sacrifices, which were the principal representatives of worship in the Hebrew Church, and afterwards in the Jewish. Their sacrifices were made either from the herd or from the flock, thus from animals of various kinds that were clean, such as oxen, bullocks, he-goats, sheep, rams, she-goats, kids, and lambs; besides turtle-doves and young pigeons, all of which animals signified internal things of worship, that is, things celestial and spiritual (n. 2165, 2177); the animals taken from the herd signifying celestial natural things, and those from the flock celestial rational things; and as both the natural and the rational things are more and more interior, and are various, therefore so many kinds and species of those animals were made use of in the sacrifices; as is also evident from its being prescribed what animals should be offered—in the burnt-offerings; in the sacrifices of various kinds, as in those that were daily, those of the Sabbaths and festivals, those that were voluntary, those for thanksgiving and vows, those expiatory of guilt and sin, those of purifying and cleansing, and those of inauguration—and also from their being expressly named, and how many of them should be used in each kind of sacrifice; which would never have been done unless each had signified some special thing. This is very evident from those passages where the sacrifices are treated of (as *Exod.* xxix.; *Lev.* i., iii., iv., ix., xvi., xxiii.; *Num.* vii., viii., xv., xxix.). But this is not the place to set forth what each one signified. The case is similar in the Prophets where these animals are named, and from them it is evident that "bullocks" signified celestial natural things. [3] That no other than heavenly things were signified, is also evident from the cherubs seen by Ezekiel, and from the animals before the throne seen by John. Concerning the cherubs the Prophet says :—

The likeness of their faces was the face of a man, and they four had the face of a lion on the right side, and they four had the face of an ox on the left side, and they four had the face of an eagle (*Ezek.* i. 10).

Concerning the four animals before the throne John says :—

Around the throne were four animals ; the first animal was like a lion, the second animal like a young bullock, the third animal had a face like a man, the fourth animal was like a flying eagle ; saying, Holy, holy, holy, Lord God Almighty, who was, and who is, and who is to come (*Rev.* iv. 6–8).

Every one can see that holy things were represented by the cherubs and by these animals, and also by the oxen and young bullocks in the sacrifices.   In like manner in the prophecy of Moses concerning Joseph :—

Let it come upon the head of Joseph, and upon the crown of the head of him that was a Nazirite from his brethren.   The firstling of his ox, honor is his ; and his horns are the horns of the unicorn, with them he shall push the peoples together, to the ends of the earth (*Deut.* xxxiii. 16, 17).

None can understand these things unless it is known what an ox, a unicorn, horns, and other things signify in the internal sense.   [4] As regards sacrifices in general, they were indeed enjoined through Moses on the people of Israel, but the Most Ancient Church, that existed before the flood, knew nothing whatever about sacrifices ; nor did it even come into their minds to worship the Lord by slaughtering animals.   The Ancient Church, that existed after the flood, was likewise unacquainted with sacrifices.   This church was indeed in representatives, but not in sacrifices.   In fact sacrifices were first instituted in the following church, which was called the Hebrew Church, and from this spread to the nations, and from the same source they came to Abraham, Isaac, and Jacob, and thus to the descendants of Jacob.   That the nations were in a worship of sacrifices, was shown above (n. 1343); and that so were Jacob's posterity before they went out of Egypt, thus before sacrifices were commanded by Moses upon Mount Sinai, is evident from what is said in *Exodus* (chapter v. 3; x. 25, 27 ; xviii. 12; xxiv. 4, 5) ; and especially from their idolatrous worship before the golden calf, [5] thus described in *Moses :*—

Aaron built an altar before the calf, and Aaron made proclamation and said, To-morrow is the feast of Jehovah.   And they rose up early on the morrow, and offered burnt-offerings, and brought peace-offerings ; and the people sat down to eat, and to drink, and rose up to play (*Exod.* xxxii. 5, 6).

This was done while Moses was upon Mount Sinai, and thus before the command concerning the altar and the sacrifices came to them. The command came on this account—that the worship of sacrifices had become idolatrous with them, as it had with the Gentiles, and from this worship they could not be withdrawn, because they regarded it as the chief holy thing. For what has once been implanted from infancy as holy, especially if by fathers, and thus inrooted, the Lord never breaks, but bends, unless it is contrary to order itself. This is the reason why it was directed that sacrifices should be instituted in the way described in the books of *Moses.* [6] That sacrifices were by no means acceptable to Jehovah, thus were merely permitted and tolerated for the reason just stated, is very evident in the Prophets, as we read in *Jeremiah* :—

Thus saith Jehovah Zebaoth the God of Israel, Add your burnt-offerings to your sacrifices, and eat flesh. I spake not unto your fathers, and I commanded them not in the day that I brought them out of the land of Egypt, concerning burnt-offering and sacrifice ; but this word I commanded them, saying, Obey My voice, and I will be your God (vii. 21–23).

In *David* :—

O Jehovah, sacrifice and offering Thou hast not willed, burnt-offering and sin-offering Thou hast not required. I have desired to do Thy will, O my God (*Ps.* xl. 6, 8).

In the same :—

Thou delightest not in sacrifice, that I should give it ; burnt-offering Thou dost not accept. The sacrifices of God are a broken * spirit (*Ps.* li. 16, 17).

In the same :—

I will take no bullock out of thy house, nor he-goats out of thy folds ; sacrifice to God confession (*Ps.* l. 9, 13, 14 ; cvii. 21, 22 ; cxvi. 17 ; *Deut.* xxiii. 19).

In *Hosea* :—

I will mercy, and not sacrifice, and the knowledge of God more than burnt-offerings (vi. 6).

Samuel said to Saul :—

Hath Jehovah pleasure in burnt-offerings and sacrifices ? Behold, to obey is better than sacrifice, to hearken than the fat of rams (1 *Sam.* xv. 22).

* *Contritus ;* but *infractus* n. 9818.

In *Micah* :—

> Wherewith shall I come before Jehovah, and bow myself to the high God ? Shall I come before Him with burnt-offerings, with calves of a year old ? will Jehovah be pleased with thousands of rams, with ten thousands of rivers of oil ? He hath showed thee, O man, what is good ; and what doth Jehovah require of thee, but to do judgment, and to love mercy, and to humble thyself in walking with thy God (vi. 6–8).

[7] From all this it is now evident that sacrifices were not commanded, but permitted ; also that nothing else was regarded in the sacrifices than what is internal ; and that it was the internal, not the external, that was acceptable. On this account also, the Lord abrogated them, as was likewise foretold by *Daniel* in these words :—

> In the midst of the week shall He cause the sacrifice and the oblation to cease (ix. 27),

where the Lord's advent is treated of. (See what is said concerning sacrifices in Part First, n. 922, 923, 1128, 1823.) As regards the " son of an ox" which Abraham "made" or prepared for the three men, the case is the same as with that animal in the sacrifices. That it had a like signification is evident also from his telling Sarah to take three measures of fine flour. Concerning the fine flour to a bullock, we read in *Moses* :—

> When ye be come into the land ; when thou shalt make a son of an ox a burnt-offering or a sacrifice, in pronouncing publicly a vow, or peace-offerings unto Jehovah, thou shalt offer upon the son of an ox a meat-offering of three tenths of fine flour, mingled with oil (*Num.* xv. 8, 9),

where it is in like manner " three," here " three tenths," and above, " three measures ;" but to a ram there were to be only two tenths, and to a lamb one tenth (*Num.* xv. 4–6).

2181. *And gave it to the lad, and he hasted to make it.* That this signifies the conjunction of this good with rational good, and that the "lad" is the natural man, is evident from the signification of a " lad" as being one who ministers and administers ; and that which is ministered or done is to make—to wit, the son of an ox, by which is signified natural good, as already shown. That it may be better perceived how this is, be it known that there exist with every man an internal, a rational which is intermediate, and a natural; also that these are distinct from each other (see n. 1889, 1940), and are to be made to conform, in order that they may make a one—thus rational good with natural good—and that without conformation and thereby conjunction there can be no Divine perception. As in these words the Lord's Divine perception is treated of, they signify in the internal sense the conformation and conjunction of these two kinds of good.

2182. Verse 8. *And he took butter and milk, and the son of an ox that he had made, and set before them ; and he stood before them under the tree, and they did eat.* "He took butter and milk, and the son of an ox that he had made," signifies all those things thus conjoined together; "butter" is the celestial of the rational, "milk" is the derivative spiritual, a "son of an ox" is the corresponding natural; "and set before them," signifies that He so prepared Himself to receive; "and he stood before them under the tree," signifies derivative perception (the "tree," as before, is perception) ; "and they did eat," signifies communication in this manner.

2183. *He took butter and milk, and the son of an ox that he had made.* That this signifies all those things thus conjoined together, is evident from the signification of "butter," of "milk," and of a "son of an ox," to be explained presently. In the verses which precede, the subject was the Lord's rational in that it was instructed in the celestial and the derivative spiritual, which are signified by the "meal of fine flour made into a cake" (n. 2176, 2177); and it also was the celestial natural, which is signified by the "son of an ox" (n. 2180). The same things are now expressed by other words, namely, by "butter," "milk," and also a "son of an ox," by which are signified all those things conjoined together. [2] But these things can with difficulty be described to the ordinary understanding, because to most people it is unknown that every man has an internal, a rational, and a natural, and that these are most distinct from each other, nay, so distinct, that one of them may be dissident from another; to wit, that the rational, which is called the rational man, may be dissident from the natural, which is the natural man ; nay, that the rational man can even see and perceive the evil which is in the natural man

and, if it is a genuine rational, may chastise it (see n. 1904).
Before these two have been conjoined together, the man cannot
be an entire (or perfect) man, nor can he be in the tranquillity
of peace, for the one fights with the other. For the angels who
are with the man rule his rational, but the evil spirits who are
with him, his natural, and hence comes combat. [3] If the
rational then conquers, the natural is subjugated, and the man
is thus gifted with conscience; but if the natural conquers, he
can then receive nothing of conscience. If the rational conquers, his natural then becomes as if it also was rational; but
if the natural conquers, the rational becomes as if it also was
natural. And further, if the rational conquers, the angels
then draw nearer into the man, and insinuate to him charity
(which is the celestial that comes from the Lord through the
angels), and the evil spirits remove themselves to a distance;
but if the natural conquers, the angels then remove themselves
further away (that is, more toward the man's interiors), while
the evil spirits draw nearer toward the rational, and continually
attack it, and fill the lower parts of his mind with hatreds, revenges, deceits, and the like. If the rational conquers, the
man then comes into the tranquillity of peace, and in the other
life into the peace of heaven; but if the natural conquers, then,
while the man lives he appears as if he were in tranquillity,
but in the other life he comes into the unrest and torment of
hell. [4] In this way may be known what is the quality of a
man's state as to his rational, and as to his natural; so that
there is nothing else that can make a man blessed and happy
but that his natural be conformed to his rational, and both
be conjoined together. This is effected solely by means of
charity, and charity is solely from the Lord.

2184. That "butter" is the celestial of the rational; that
"milk" is the derivative spiritual; and that a "son of an ox"
is the corresponding natural, is evident from the signification
of "butter," of "milk," and of a "son of an ox." As regards
butter, it signifies in the Word what is celestial, and this from
its fatness. (That fat denotes what is celestial was shown in
Part First, n. 353; and that "oil," because fat, is the celestial
itself, n. 886.) That "butter" also is the celestial, is evident
in *Isaiah:*—

Behold, a virgin beareth a son, and shall call His name Immanuel, Butter and honey shall He eat, that He may know to refuse what is evil, and choose what is good (vii. 14, 15),

where the Lord (who is "Immanuel") is treated of; and any one can see that butter is not signified by "butter," nor honey by "honey;" but that by "butter" is signified His celestial, and by "honey" that which is from the celestial.   [2] In the same :—

And it shall come to pass, for the multitude of the making of milk He shall eat butter ; for butter and honey shall every one eat that is left in the midst of the land (vii. 22),

where the Lord's kingdom is treated of, and those on earth who are in the Lord's kingdom.   "Milk" here denotes spiritual good, "butter" celestial good, and "honey" the derivative happiness.   [3] In *Moses :*—

Jehovah alone leadeth him, and there is no strange god with him. He maketh him to ride upon the high places of the earth, and to eat the produce of the fields, and He maketh him to suck honey out of the rock, and oil out of the flint of the rock ; butter of the herd, and milk of the flock, with the fat of lambs, and of rams the sons of Bashan, and of he-goats, with the fat of the kidneys of wheat ; and of the blood of the grape shalt thou drink unmixed wine (*merum*) (*Deut.* xxxii. 12–14).

No one can understand what these things denote unless he knows the internal sense of each one.   It appears like a heap of expressions such as are used by the eloquent among the wise ones of the world, and yet every expression signifies the celestial and its spiritual, and also the derivative blessedness and happiness, and all these in a well-ordered series.   "Butter of the herd" is the celestial natural, "milk of the flock" is the celestial spiritual of the rational.   [4] But as regards milk, as before said, this signifies the spiritual from the celestial, that is, the celestial spiritual.   (What the celestial spiritual is may be seen in Part First, n. 1577, 1824, and occasionally elsewhere.)   That "milk" is the spiritual which is from the celestial, comes from the fact that "water" signifies what is spiritual (n. 680, 739); but "milk," as there is fat in it, signifies the celestial spiritual, or what is the same, the truth of good; or what is the same, the faith of love or of charity; or what is also the same, the intellectual of the good of the will; and again the same, the affection of truth in which there is inwardly the affection of good; and yet again the same, the affection of knowledges (*cognitiones et scientiae*) from the affection of charity toward the neighbor, such as exists with those who love the neighbor, and confirm themselves in this love from the knowledges of faith, and also from memory-knowledges, which they love on this account. All these things are the same as the Celestial-spiritual, and are predicated according to the subject treated of. [5] That this is signified, is evident also from the Word, as in *Isaiah :*—

Every one that thirsteth, come ye to the waters, and he that hath no silver, come ye, buy, and eat; yea come, buy wine and milk without silver, and without price. Wherefore do ye weigh silver for that which is not bread? (lv. 1, 2),

where "wine" denotes the spiritual which is of faith, and "milk" the spiritual which is of love. In *Moses :*—

He hath washed his garment in wine, and his clothing in the blood of grapes; his eyes are redder than wine, and his teeth are whiter than milk (*Gen.* xlix. 11, 12),

which is the prophecy of Jacob, then Israel, concerning Judah; and by Judah the Lord is here described, and by his "teeth being whiter than milk," is signified the celestial spiritual that pertained to His natural. [6] In *Joel :*—

It shall be in that day that the mountains shall drop new wine, and the hills shall flow with milk; and all the brooks of Judah shall flow with waters (iii. 18),

speaking of the Lord's kingdom; "milk" denotes the celestial spiritual. In the Word the land of Canaan also (by which the Lord's kingdom is represented and signified) is called a "land flowing with milk and honey" (as in *Num.* xiii. 27; xiv. 8; *Deut.* xxvi. 9, 15; xxvii. 3; *Jer.* xi. 5; xxxii. 22; *Ezek.* xx. 6, 15), and in these passages nothing else is meant by "milk" than an abundance of celestial spiritual things, and by "honey" an abundance of the derivative happinesses; the "land" is the celestial itself of the kingdom, from which those things come. [7] As regards the "son of an ox," it was shown just above that thereby is signified the celestial natural (n. 2180), the celestial natural being the same as natural good, or good in the natural. The natural of man, like his rational, has its good and its truth; for there is everywhere the marriage of good and truth (as said above, n. 2173). The good of the natural is the delight which is perceived from charity, or from the friendship which is of charity; from which delight there comes forth a pleasure which is properly of the body. The truth of the natural is the memory-knowledge (*scientificum*) which favors that delight. Hence it is evident what the celestial natural is.

2185. *And set before them.* That this signifies that He thus prepared Himself to receive, is evident from the signification in the internal sense of " setting before them," when the subject treated of is the preparation of the rational to receive perception from the Divine, thus without further explication.

2186. *And he stood before them under the tree.* That this signifies the derivative perception, follows from the signification of a " tree," as being perception (see n. 103, 2163). It has been already stated (verse 4), that the three men who came to Abraham lay down under a tree, by which was signified that the Divine approached the perception of that state in which the Lord then was. But it is here said that Abraham stood under the tree, by which is signified that the Lord approached Divine perception, after He had prepared Himself; and this is the reciprocality. Every one can see that it is not without a cause, that mention is made of the three men and of Abraham standing under a tree, consequently that it was said for the sake of the arcana which lie hidden in these things.

2187. *And they did eat.* That this signifies communication in this manner, is evident from the signification of " eating," as being to be communicated and to be conjoined; as is also evident from the Word. The fact that Aaron, his sons, the Levites, and also the people, ate the hallowed things of the sacrifices in the holy place, signified nothing else than communication, conjunction, and appropriation, as above said at the explication of the passage from *Leviticus* vi. 9, 10 (see n. 2177), for it was celestial and spiritual food that was signified by the hallowed things which they ate, consequently the appropriation of it. The hallowed things were the parts of the sacrifices which were not burned upon the altar, and were eaten either by the priests, or by the people that made the offering; as is evident from many passages where the sacrifices are treated of (what should be eaten by the priests, *Exod.* xxix. 32, 33; *Lev.* vi. 9, 16, 18, 26; vii. 6, 15, 16, 18; viii. 31; x. 12, 13; *Num.* xviii. 9–11; what should be eaten by the people, *Lev.* xix. 5, 6; *Deut.* xii. 27; xxvii. 7; and elsewhere; and that the unclean should not eat of them, *Lev.* vii. 19–21; xxii. 4–7). These feastings were made in a holy place near the altar, either at the door, or in the court of the tabernacle; and they signified nothing else than the communication, conjunction, and appropriation of celestial goods; for by them were represented celestial foods (concerning which food see n. 56, 57, 58, 680, 681, 1480, 1695), and they were all called "bread," the signification of which may be seen above (n. 2165). The like was represented by Aaron and his sons eating the showbread or "bread of faces," in a holy place (*Lev.* xxiv. 9). [2] The law given for the Nazirite—that in the days of his Naziriteship he should not eat of anything from the grape, whence wine is made, from the seeds even to the skin (*Num.* vi. 4)—was because the Nazirite represented the celestial man, and the celestial man is such that he is not willing even to mention spiritual things (as may be seen in Part First, n. 202, 337, 880 at the end, 1647); and as wine and the grape, and also whatever is from the grape, signified what is spiritual, it was therefore forbidden the Nazirite to eat of them; that is, to have communication with them, to conjoin himself with them, and to appropriate them to himself. [3] The like is meant by "eating" in *Isaiah :*—

Every one that thirsteth, come ye to the waters, and he that hath no silver, come ye, buy, and eat; yea come, buy wine and milk without silver and without price. Wherefore do ye weigh silver for that which is not bread? and your labor for that which satisfieth not? Hearken diligently unto Me, and eat ye that which is good, and your soul shall be deliciated in fatness (lv. 1, 2).

As also in *John :*—

To him that overcometh I will give to eat of the tree of life, which is in the midst of the paradise of God (*Rev.* ii. 7).

The "tree of life" is the celestial itself, and in the supreme sense is the Lord Himself, because from Him is all the celestial, that is, all love and charity. Thus to "eat of the tree of life" is the same as to eat the Lord, and to eat the Lord is to be gifted with love and charity, and thus with those things which are of heavenly life. This the Lord Himself says in *John* :—

I am the living bread that came down from heaven, if any one eat of this bread, he shall live to eternity ; he that eateth Me shall live by Me (vi. 51, 57). But they said, This is a hard saying. And Jesus said, The words that I speak unto you are spirit, and are life (verses 60, 63).

[4] Hence it is manifest what is meant by eating in the Holy Supper (*Matt.* xxvi. 26–28 ; *Mark* xiv. 22, 23 ; *Luke* xxii. 19, 20) ; namely, to have communication, to be conjoined, and to appropriate to one's self. Hence also it is clear what is meant by the Lord's saying that :—

Many shall come from the east and the west, and shall recline with Abraham, Isaac, and Jacob (*Matt.* viii. 11),

not that they are to eat with them in the kingdom of God, but that they will enjoy the celestial goods which are signified by " Abraham, Isaac, and Jacob," namely, the celestial things of love ; not only the inmost, which are " Abraham," but also the lower that are intermediate, as are those of the rational, which are " Isaac ;" and the still lower, which are the celestial natural, such as are in the first heaven, and which are meant by " Jacob." Such is the internal sense of these words. (That these things are meant by " Abraham, Isaac, and Jacob," may be seen in n. 1893, and wherever else they are treated of.) For whether we speak of enjoying those celestial things, or of enjoying the Lord, who is represented by those men, it is the same thing ; for all those things are from the Lord, and the Lord is the all in all of them.

2188. Verse 9. *And they said unto him, Where is Sarah thy wife? And he said, Behold, in the tent.* " They said to him, Where is Sarah thy wife ?" signifies rational truth, which did not then appear because it was in rational good ; "and he said, Behold, in the tent," signifies that it was in what is holy.

2189. *They said unto him, Where is Sarah thy wife?* That this signifies rational truth, which did not then appear because it was in rational good, is evident from the representation here

of Sarah, as being rational truth (spoken of above, n. 2173).
How the case is with these things, as also with those which
follow, where the state of the rational with the Lord is treated
of, which is represented by Sarah, cannot be so well explained
to the understanding unless it is known what in general is
the state of the rational as to good and as to truth; and with
the Lord, as to the Divine and as to the Human in which He
then was. [2] The primary thing of the rational with man
is truth (as before said, n. 2072), consequently it is the affection of truth, to the end that man may be reformed, and so
regenerated. This is effected by means of knowledges (*cognitiones et scientifica*) that are of truth, which are continually
being implanted in good, that is, in charity, that so the man
may receive the life of charity. It is on this account that the
affection of truth in man is predominant in his rational. For
it is the case with the life of charity (which is the heavenly life
itself) that with those who are being reformed and regenerated
it is continually being born and growing up and receiving in-
crements, and this by means of truths; therefore the more of
truth there is insinuated, the more is the life of charity perfected; wherefore *according to the quality and quantity of
truth, so is the charity with a man.* [3] From all this it may
in some measure be evident how the case is with man's rational.
In truth, however, there is no life, but in good. Truth is only
a recipient of life, that is, of good. Truth is as the clothing
or garment of good; therefore also truths are called in the
Word "clothing," and also "garments." But when good constitutes the rational, truth disappears and becomes as if it were
good. Good then shines through the truth, in the same way
as takes place with the angels, for when they appear clothed,
it is a brightness inducing the appearance of raiment, as was
the case also when angels appeared before the prophets. [4]
This then is what is meant by rational truth not then appearing because it was in rational good, and which is signified by
their saying to him, "Where is Sarah thy wife?" But as the
Lord's rational good was then Divine, such as it can be with
no angel, it cannot be described otherwise than by comparison,
and thus by illustration from something similar, and which is
not the same.

2190. *And he said, Behold, in the tent.* That this signifies that it was in what is holy, is evident from the signification of a "tent," as being what is holy (explained n. 414, 1102, 1566, 2145). It is said in what is holy, because it was in good. All good is called holy from the fact that it is of love and charity, which are solely from the Lord. But such as are the goods, such are the holinesses. Goods are formed, that is, are born and grow up, by means of the truths of faith, and their quality and quantity are therefore determined by those of the truth of faith implanted in charity (as just said, n. 2189), from which it follows that goods or the holinesses differ with every one; and although in the external form they may appear to be alike, yet in the internal forms they are unlike; and this both with those who are out of the church and with those who are within the church. There are more things in the good of charity with a man than man can possibly believe. All the things of his faith are in it, and consequently they are in the holiness of his worship. The quality of the holiness of his worship appears to the angels as in clear day, although the man knows nothing beyond the fact that he is in a certain holy state. Myriads of myriads of his thoughts concerning the goods and truths of faith and of the derivative affections, are in the holiness of his state. But as to the holiness of worship, what it is in general, of the Lord's Divine mercy elsewhere.

2191. Verse 10. *And He said, Returning I will return unto thee about this time of life; and behold Sarah thy wife shall have a son. And Sarah heard at the door of the tent, and it was behind him.* "And He said," signifies perception; "Returning I will return unto thee about this time of life," signifies the conjunction of the Divine with the Lord's Human; "and behold Sarah thy wife shall have a son," signifies the rational that was to be Divine; "and Sarah heard at the door of the tent," signifies rational truth then near what is holy; "and it was behind him," signifies near the good in which the rational then was, and thus separated from it in so far as anything of the human was in it.

2192. *And He said.* That this signifies perception, is evident from the signification in the historical sense of "saying," as being perceiving (explained before, n. 1898, 1919, 2080).

2193. *Returning I will return unto thee, about this time of life.* That this signifies the conjunction of the Divine with the Human, is evident from the fact that the coming of Jehovah to Abraham represented the Divine perception, for receiving which the Lord prepared Himself, consequently it represented conjunction, as shown above; thus by "returning He would return to him," there is signified the like, namely, the conjunction of the Divine with the Human. "At this time of life," means at the same time of the following year.

2194. *Behold, Sarah thy wife shall have a son.* That this signifies the rational that was to be Divine, is evident from the signification of a "son" and of "Sarah," and also of "Isaac" who should be born to her. Both "son" and "Sarah," and also "Isaac," signify that which is of the Lord's rational. (That a "son" is truth may be seen above, n. 489, 491, 533, 1147; also that "Sarah" signifies rational truth, n. 2173; and that "Isaac" signifies the Divine rational, n. 1893, 2066, 2083.) The human with every man begins in the inmost of his rational (as before said, n. 2106); and so also the Lord's Human: that which was above it was Jehovah Himself, differently from any other man whatever. As the human begins in the inmost of the rational, and as the Lord made all the Human that was with Himself Divine, He first made the rational itself so from its inmost, which, when made Divine, is represented and signified (as before said) by "Isaac."

2195. *And Sarah heard at the door of the tent.* That this signifies that rational truth was then near what is holy, is evident from the representation of Sarah, as being rational truth (see n. 2173, 2194); and from the signification of a "tent," as being what is holy (see n. 414, 1102, 1566, 2145); and thus from the signification of the "door of the tent," as being the entrance to what is holy, thus near what is holy (see above, n. 2145). How the case is with these things now follows.

2196. *And it was behind him.* That this signifies near the good in which the rational then was, and separated from it in so far as anything of the human was in it, is evident from the fact that it is said of the door where Sarah was that it was "behind him." To be "behind him" signifies not to be conjoined, but at his back. That which is separated from any one is represented by a kind of rejection as it were to the back, as is evident from the representatives in the other life (concerning which from experience, n. 1393, 1875). This is here expressed by its being said that the door where Sarah was, was "behind him." [2] As regards the merely human rational truth which was then with the Lord being separated from Him when He conjoined Himself with the Divine, the case is this. Human rational truth does not apprehend Divine things, because these are above the sphere of its understanding, for this truth communicates with the memory-knowledges which are in the natural man, and in so far as it looks from these at the things which are above itself, so far it does not acknowledge them. For this truth is in appearances, which it is not able to put off; and appearances are born from sensuous things, which induce a belief as if Divine things themselves also were of a like nature, when yet these are exempt from all appearances, and when they are stated, this rational truth cannot possibly believe them, because it cannot apprehend them. [3] If for example it is stated that man has no life except what is from the Lord, the rational supposes from appearances that in that case man cannot live as of himself; whereas he for the first time truly lives when he perceives that he does so from the Lord. [4] The rational supposes from appearances that the good which man does is from himself, and yet there is nothing of good from self, but all is from the Lord. [5] From appearances the rational supposes that man merits salvation when he does what is good; whereas of himself man can merit nothing, but all merit is the Lord's. [6] From appearances man supposes that when he is withheld from evil and is kept in good by the Lord, there is nothing with him but what is good and just, nay, holy; whereas there is nothing in man but what is evil, unjust, and profane. [7] From appearances man supposes that when he does what is good from charity, he does it from his will; whereas it is not from his will part, but from his intellectual part, in which charity has been implanted. [8] From appearances man supposes that there can be no glory without the glory of the world; whereas in the glory of heaven there is not a particle of the world's glory. [9] From appearances man supposes that no one can love his neighbor more than himself, but that all love begins from self; when yet in heavenly love there is nothing of the love of self. [10] From appearances man supposes that there can be no light but that which is from the light of the world; whereas in the heavens there is not one whit of the light of the world, and yet the light is so great that it surpasses the world's noon day light a thousand times. [11] From appearances man supposes that the Lord cannot shine before the universal heaven as a sun; when yet all the light of heaven is from Him. [12] From appearances man cannot apprehend that in the other life there are motions forward; whereas those who are there appear to themselves to move forward just as do men on earth—in their dwellings, courts, and paradises; and still less can he apprehend if it is said that these movings forward are changes of state, which so appear. [13] Nor can man from appearances apprehend that spirits and angels, who are invisible before our eyes, can be seen; nor that they can speak with man; when yet they appear to the internal sight, or that of the spirit, more manifestly than man does to man on earth; and their voices are heard as distinctly; besides thousands of thousands of such things, which man's rational, from its own light, born from things of sense, and thereby darkened, cannot possibly believe. Nay, the rational is blinded in natural things themselves, not being able to apprehend, for instance, how those who dwell on the opposite side of the globe can stand on their feet and walk; and it is the same with very many other things. How blind then must the rational not be in spiritual and heavenly things, which are far above natural things? [14] As the human rational is of such a character, it is here said of it that it was separated when the Lord in Divine perception was united to the Divine, which is signified by the standing of Sarah (who is here such rational truth) at the door of the tent, and by this being behind him.

2197. Verse 11. *And Abraham and Sarah were old, entering into days; it had ceased to be with Sarah in the way as of women.* "Abraham and Sarah were old," signifies the Human with the Lord, that it should be put off; "entering into days," signifies that the time was come; "it had ceased to be with

Sarah in the way as of women," signifies the state of rational truth, that it could no longer remain so.

2198. *Abraham and Sarah were old.* That this signifies the Human with the Lord, that it should be put off, is evident from the representation of Abraham and of Sarah; as also from the signification of the "old," or of "old age." Abraham here represents the Lord as to rational good, and Sarah represents the Lord as to rational truth, as has been said repeatedly in this chapter; thus each here represents the Human with the Lord, for the reason, as before said, that Jehovah was now present and spake with Abraham; and Jehovah was the Lord's Divine itself, not separate from Him, although it is presented as separate in the historical representatives, for by means of historical things it cannot be represented otherwise. But as regards its being said that "Abraham and Sarah were old," signifying that that human should be put off—"old age" involves nothing else than the last time. "Old age" is mentioned in various places in the Word, as also that men "died;" but in the internal sense no old age, or death, such as those of the body, are ever perceived; but something else that is evident from the series of things; for in the other life old age and death are unknown. What is here meant is evident, as before said, from the series of things, namely, that the Lord was to put off the human.

2199. *Entering into days.* That this signifies that the time was come, now follows from what has been said. A "day," in the Word, as also a "year," and indeed time in general, signifies state (as shown n. 23, 487, 488, 493, 893). Thus here, to "enter into days" signifies in the internal sense to enter into that state in which He should put off the Human; thus that the time was come.

2200. *It had ceased to be with Sarah in the way as of women.* That this signifies that it could no longer so remain, is evident from what has been now said; thus without explication.

2201. Verse 12. *And Sarah laughed within herself, saying, After I am grown old, shall I have pleasure? and my lord old?* "Sarah laughed within herself," signifies the affection of that rational truth in regard to its being so done; "saying, After I am grown old, shall I have pleasure?" signifies that it was not of the affection of that truth that it should change its state; "and my lord old," signifies that the affection of truth wondered that the rational good to which truth was adjoined should also put off the human.

2202. *Sarah laughed within herself.* That this signifies the affection of that rational truth in regard to its being so done, is evident from the signification of "laughing" or of "laughter," as being the affection of truth (spoken of before, n. 2072). What these things involve now follows.

2203. *Saying, After I am grown old, shall I have pleasure?* That this signifies that it was not of the affection of that truth that it should change its state, is evident from the signification of "growing old," as being to put off the human, and thus to change the state (as explained above, n. 2198); and from the signification of "shall I have pleasure?" as being not to desire; thus that this was not its affection. How the case is with these things is evident from what was said of Sarah above (n. 2196), that she stood at the door of the tent, and it was behind him; that is, that the human rational as to truth is of such a nature that it cannot understand what the Divine is, for the reason that that truth is in appearances; and therefore that which it cannot understand, it does not believe; and by that which it does not believe it is not affected. The appearances in which the rational is, are such as to affect it, for there is delight in the appearances themselves; and therefore if it is deprived of appearances, it supposes that there is nothing of delight left; whereas heavenly affection is not in appearances, but in good and truth itself. As rational truth is of this nature, this is pardoned, and it is permitted to be in appearances, and to have delight in them. Such truth as was in appearances is represented by Sarah, when the Lord had conjoined Himself with the Divine, and therefore it is said that she "stood at the door," and that she "laughed and said, After I am grown old, shall I have pleasure?" by which is signified that it was not of its affection that it should change its state.

2204. *And my lord old?* That this signifies that the affection of truth wondered that the rational good to which truth was adjoined should also put off the human, is evident from the representation of Abraham, who is here "my lord," as here

denoting rational good (spoken of above, n. 2198, and elsewhere) ; also from the signification of "growing old," as being
to put off the human (also spoken of n. 2198). Human rational good is such as to have in itself much from worldly
delights, for it is formed not only from truths, but also from
the delights of sensuous things, and from many of the delights
that are in the world. Into these delights (when the man is
being reformed and regenerated) spiritual good is insinuated
by the Lord; and thereby what is worldly is then tempered,
and thus afterwards has its happiness therein. But the Lord
utterly expelled from the rational all that was worldly, and so
made it Divine; which is what the rational truth meant by
"Sarah" wondered at.

2205. Verse 13. *And Jehovah said unto Abraham, Wherefore did Sarah laugh, saying, Shall I indeed truly bear, and I
am become old?* "Jehovah said unto Abraham," signifies the
Lord's perception from the Divine; "Wherefore did Sarah
laugh?" signifies the thought of rational truth from the affection of it; "saying, Shall I indeed truly bear?" signifies that
it wondered that the rational should become Divine; "and I
am become old," signifies after it should be no longer of such
a nature.

2206. *Jehovah said unto Abraham.* That this signifies the
Lord's perception from the Divine, is evident from the signification of "saying" as being to perceive (explained before, n.
1898, 1919, 2080); and from the words "Jehovah said," as
being to perceive from the Divine, for as already often shown,
the Lord's internal itself was Jehovah.

2207. *Wherefore did Sarah laugh?* That this signifies the
thought of rational truth from its affection, is evident from the
signification of "laughing," or of "laughter," as being the affection which is of truth (spoken of above, n. 2072); and from
the representation of Sarah as being rational truth (concerning
which several times before in this chapter). This interrogation
involves that the Lord perceived that in His rational there was
still what was human.

2208. *Shall I indeed truly bear?* That this signifies that
it wondered that the rational was to become Divine, is evident
from the signification here in the internal sense of "bearing," to

wit, that as the Lord's Divine rational is represented by Isaac (as before said, and as will be evident from what follows), so to "bear" here signifies Isaac, that is, the rational in that it should be made Divine; which the rational truth represented by Sarah could not comprehend.

2209. *And I am become old.* That this signifies after it should no longer be of such a nature, namely, not Divine but human, and that this latter should be put off, is evident from the signification of "becoming old," as being to put off the human (spoken of above, n. 2198, 2203). As regards the rational in general, when it thinks about Divine things, especially from its own truth, it cannot possibly believe that there are such things; both because it does not apprehend them, and because there adhere to it the appearances born from the fallacies of the senses by which and from which it thinks; as is evident from the examples adduced above (n. 2196); to which the following may be added for the sake of illustration. [2] If the rational be consulted, can it believe that the Word has an internal sense, and this so remote from the literal sense as has been shown? and thus that the Word is that which conjoins heaven with earth, that is, the Lord's kingdom in the heavens with the Lord's kingdom on earth? Can the rational believe that souls after death speak with each other most distinctly, without the speech of words, and yet so fully as to express more in a minute than a man does by his speech in an hour? and that the angels do the same, but in a speech still more perfect, and one that is not perceivable by spirits? also, that on coming into the other life all souls know how to speak in this way, although they receive no instruction in so speaking? Can the rational believe that in one affection of man, nay, in one sigh, there are such numberless things as can never be described, and yet are perceived by angels? and that every affection of man, nay, every idea of his thought, is an image of him, being such as to contain within it in a wonderful manner all the things of his life? not to mention thousands upon thousands of such things. [3] The rational, which is wise from sensuous things, and is imbued with their fallacies, when thinking of such things, does not believe that they can be so, because it is unable to form to itself any idea except from such things as it perceives by some sense either external or internal; and what then must be the case when it thinks about Divine celestial and spiritual things, which are still higher? For there must always be some appearances from sensuous things, upon which the thought must lean, and when these appearances are withdrawn, the idea perishes, as has also been evident to me from novitiate spirits, who take the greatest delight in the appearances which they have brought with them from the world, saying that if these should be taken away from them, they did not know whether they could think. Such is the rational as regarded in itself.

2210. Verse 14. *Shall anything be wonderful for Jehovah? At the set time I will return unto thee, about this time of life, and Sarah shall have a son.* "Shall anything be wonderful for Jehovah?" signifies that everything is possible for Jehovah; "at the set time I will return unto thee," signifies a state that was to come; "about this time of life, and Sarah shall have a son," signifies that the Lord would then put off the human rational, and put on the Divine rational.

2211. *Shall anything be wonderful for Jehovah?* That this signifies that everything is possible to Jehovah, is evident without explication.

2212. *At the set time I will return unto thee.* That this signifies a state that was to come, is evident from the signification of "time," as being state (see above, n. 2199). It is here said that Jehovah would "return at the set time," and then "at this time of life," or what is the same, at the present time of the following year. Each expression involves something peculiar, to wit, the "set time" involves the general of that state which is signified by "this time of life," and the general is that it was about to come; but *how* it was to be is signified by "this time of life." It is usual in the Word, especially in the Prophets, to describe states by double expressions seemingly alike; when yet the one involves the general, and the other something determinate in the general.

2213. *About this time of life, and Sarah shall have a son.* That this signifies that the Lord would then put off the human rational, and put on the Divine rational, is evident from the signification of "returning at this time of life," or at this present time of the following year, as being the conjunction of the Lord's Divine with His Human (spoken of above, n. 2193); and from the signification of Sarah's "son," as being the rational about to be Divine (also spoken of above, n. 2194). This time of life, or the present time of the following year, denotes the time when Abraham should enter upon his hundredth year, by which year is signified the unition of the Lord's Human with His Divine and of His Divine with His Human (as shown above, n. 1988). There then intervened a year, because by a "year" in the Word is not signified a year, but an entire time, and thus a whole period, whether it be of a thousand years, or of a hundred, or of ten, or of hours (as was also shown before, n. 482, 487, 488, 493, 893; and also by a "week," see above, n. 2044).

2214. Verse 15. *And Sarah denied, saying, I laughed not, for she was afraid. And He said, Nay, for thou didst laugh.* "And Sarah denied, saying, I laughed not, for she was afraid," signifies that human rational truth wished to excuse itself, because it observed that it was not such as it ought to be. "And He said, Nay, for thou didst laugh," signifies that nevertheless it was such.

2215. *Sarah denied, saying, I laughed not, for she was afraid.* That this signifies that human rational truth wished to excuse itself, because it observed that it was not such as it ought to be, is evident without explication.

2216. *He said, Nay, for thou didst laugh.* That this signifies that nevertheless it was such, is also evident without explication. How the case is with these things is evident from what is said above (n. 2072) concerning the signification of "laughing," or of "laughter," that it is an affection of the rational, and indeed the affection of truth or of falsity, in the rational, that is the source of all laughter. So long as there is in the rational such an affection as displays itself in laughter, so long there is in it something corporeal or worldly, and thus merely human. Celestial good and spiritual good do not laugh, but express their delight and cheerfulness in the face, the speech, and the gesture, in another way; for there are very many things in laughter, for the most part something of contempt, which, even if it does not appear, nevertheless lies concealed; and laughter is easily distinguished from cheerfulness of the mind, which also produces something similar to it. The state of the human rational with the Lord is described by Sarah's "laughing;" and thereby is signified with what kind of affection the truth of the rational, at that time separated from good, regarded what was said : that it should be put off, and the Divine put on; not that the Lord laughed, but that He perceived from the Divine what the rational still was, and how much of the human there still was in it, and which was to be expelled. In the internal sense this is what is signified by Sarah's "laughing."

2217. Verse 16. *And the men rose up thence, and looked toward the faces of Sodom, and Abraham went with them to send them away.* "The men rose up thence," signifies that that perception came to an end; "and looked toward the faces of Sodom," signifies the state of the human race; "Sodom" is all evil from the love of self; "and Abraham went with them," signifies that the Lord still remained with them in perception, but concerning the human race; "to send them away," signifies that He willed to withdraw from that perception.

2218. *The men rose up.* That this signifies that that perception came to an end, is evident from the signification of "rising up," as being to go away; and from that of the "men," described above. By the coming of the three men, or of Jehovah, to Abraham, was represented the Lord's Divine perception, as shown above. The Lord's perception from the Divine at that time was first concerning the Divine Trine, which is the Divine Itself, the Divine Human, and the Proceeding. Afterwards it was concerning His Human, that it should put on the Divine. Now follows a perception from the Divine concerning the human race, as regards its quality. These three things are what are treated of in this chapter, and they follow in order, namely, that the Divine assumed the Human, and made this Divine, in order that it might save the human race. Concerning the former two it is said that the perception came to an end, which is meant in the internal sense by the "men rising up;" but the perception concerning the human race, as regards its quality, is signified in the internal sense by their "looking to the faces of Sodom, and by Abraham going with them;" and that the Lord did not will to remain in that perception, is signified by Abraham "going with them to send them away." How the case is with these things can be better seen from the Contents which were premised, as also from the explication of what follows.

2219. *They looked toward the faces of Sodom.* That this signifies the state of the human race, is evident from the signification of "looking to the faces," here, to the faces of Sodom. By "faces" are signified all man's interiors, both good and evil, for the reason that they shine forth from the face (as shown in Part First, n. 358). Here therefore "faces," because predicated of Sodom, signify interior evils, which are those of the love of self, and which evils in general are meant by "Sodom," as will be evident from what now follows. That the worst evils of all originate from the love of self, is because the love of self is destructive of human society (as shown above, n. 2045), and of heavenly society (n. 2057); and since the perversity of the human race is thence known, by the "faces of Sodom" is here signified the state of the human race. [2] Moreover it has been shown in Part First, in various places, what the nature of the love of self is, namely, that it is diametrically contrary to the order into which man was created. Man is distinguished above beasts by having a rational given him, to the end that every one may will well and do well to others, as in general so in particular. This is the order into which man has been created, consequently it is love to God and love toward the neighbor that should be man's life, and by which he should be distinguished from brute animals. This is also the order of heaven, in which it was intended man should be while he lives in the world; thus in the Lord's kingdom; and into this kingdom he would pass when he had put off the body that had been of service to him upon the earth, and there he would rise into a state continually advancing in heavenly perfection. [3] But the love of self is the primary and indeed the only thing that destroys all this; and not so much so the love of the world, for this is indeed opposite to the spiritual things of faith, but the love of self is diametrically opposite to the celestial things of love; for he

who loves himself loves no others, but endeavors to destroy
all persons whatever that do not pay reverence to him; nor
does he will well and do well to any one, except to him who is
a part of himself, or can be captivated so as to be a part of
himself, like something inoculated as it were with his cupidities and phantasies. Hence it is evident that from the love
of self there gush forth all hatreds, all revenges and cruelties,
as also all infamous simulations and deceits, and thus all
heinous things against the order of human society and against
the order of heavenly society. [4] Nay, so heinous is the love
of self, that when its bonds are relaxed, that is, when opportunity of free range is given it, even with those who are in the
lowest condition, it so rushes on, that it not only wills to exercise dominion over neighbors and those near at hand, but
also over the universe, and even over the Supreme Divine Itself.
Of this the man is indeed ignorant, because he is kept in bonds
not well known to him, but in so far as these bonds are slack-
ened (as before said), so far he rushes on; and this it has been
given me to know from much experience in the other life. As
these things lie hidden in the love of self, they who are in the
love of self, and are not endowed with the bonds of conscience,
above all others hold the Lord in hatred, consequently all the
truths of faith, for these are the very laws of order in the
Lord's kingdom, and these they reject so as to abominate
them, which also shows itself openly in the other life. This
love is also the "serpent's head," which the "Seed of the
woman" (that is, the Lord) "treads down" (concerning which
see Part First, n. 257). [5] But the love of self is not always
that which appears in the outward form as pride and haughti-
ness, for sometimes such persons are able to hold the neighbor
in charity, for with some such an external is born, and with
some it is contracted in early life, but is afterwards subjugated, the external still remaining. But those are in the love
of self who despise others and make them of no account in
comparison with themselves, and who care nothing for the
common good, unless it is for them, and they themselves, as it
were, are it, especially those who hate all by whom they are
not favored and served, persecuting them, and so far as they
are able depriving them of their possessions, honor, reputation,

and even life.. Let those who breathe such things in intention know that they are pre-eminently in the love of self.

2220. That " Sodom" is all evil from the love of self, is evident from the signification of " Sodom" in the Word. Although in the following chapter it appears as if the evil of the worst adultery was signified by " Sodom," nevertheless in the internal sense nothing else than evil from the love of self is signified by it. In the Word also the abominations that well forth from the love of self are represented by adulteries of various kinds. That " Sodom" signifies in general all evil from the love of self, and " Gomorrah" all falsity therefrom, has been shown in Part First (n. 1212, 1663, 1682, 1689), and is further evident from the following passages in the Word. In *Jeremiah :*—

A sword upon the Chaldeans, and upon the inhabitants of Babel, as when God overthrew Sodom and Gomorrah, and the neighbor cities thereof, saith Jehovah, there shall not a man dwell there, and there shall not a son of man sojourn therein (l. 35, 40).

This passage treats of those signified by the Chaldeans, who are such as have profane falsity in their worship (see n. 1368) ; and of those signified by Babel, who are such as have profane evil in their worship (see n. 1182, 1326). Their condemnation is described by the " overthrow of Sodom," that is, of evil in general, and by the " overthrow of Gomorrah," that is, of falsity in general ; because they also have in their worship the evil of the love of self, and the derivative falsity. [2] In *Amos :*—

I have overthrown you as when God overthrew Sodom and Gomorrah ; and ye became as a brand plucked out of the burning (iv. 11),

where Samaria is treated of, by which is signified the perverted spiritual church, and which in respect to evils in general contrary to the goods of charity is called " Sodom," and in respect to falsities in general contrary to the truths of faith is called " Gomorrah ;" and in respect to both (here as previously) is called the " overthrowing of God." In *Zephaniah :*—

Moab shall be as Sodom, and the sons of Ammon as Gomorrah, a forsaken place of the nettle, and a pit of salt, and a desolation even to eternity ; this shall they have for their pride, because they have reproached and have enlarged upon the people of Jehovah Zebaoth (ii. 9, 10),

where " Sodom" denotes evil from the love of self, and " Gomorrah" the derivative falsity, of both of which " desolation" is

here predicated, as previously was "overthrow." "Pride" is
the love of self; to "reproach the people of Jehovah Zebaoth,"
is to bring evil upon truths; and to "enlarge upon the people,"
is to bring falsity upon them. [3] In *Ezekiel* :—

Thine elder sister is Samaria, that dwelleth at thy left hand, she and
her daughters; and thy younger sister, that dwelleth at thy right hand,
is Sodom and her daughters. Thy sister Sodom hath not done, she and
her daughters, as thou hast done, thou and thy daughters. Behold, this
was the iniquity of thy sister Sodom; pride, satiety of bread, and security
of ease, were in her and her daughters, and she did not strengthen the
hand of the wretched and needy; and they became haughty, and committed abomination before Me (xvi. 46–50),

where the abominations of Jerusalem are treated of, and are
described by " Samaria" and " Sodom ;" by " Samaria," instead
of Gomorrah, as to falsities, and by " Sodom" as to evils; and
it is stated what is specifically signified by " Sodom," for it is
said, " this was the iniquity of Sodom," to wit that it was the
love of self, which is there signified by " pride." That they
turned away from the goods of charity, is signified by the
" satiety of bread ;" that they had acquiesced in these things,
is signified by the " security of ease ;" that they had no mercy,
is described by their " not having strengthened the hand of the
poor and needy ;" and that all the cupidities thence derived are
imbued with the love of self, is signified by their " daughters
having become haughty ;" the " daughters" are cupidities. [4]
Hence it is manifestly evident what " Sodom" is, thus that it
is not according to the historic sense in the following chapter,
but that such things are there signified in the internal sense as
are described here by the prophet, namely, those which are of
the love of self. But Sodom is here described more mildly
because the abominations of Jerusalem are treated of as having
been greater than those of Sodom, as is also evident from the
Lord's words in *Matthew* :—

Verily I say unto you, it shall be more tolerable for the land of Sodom
and Gomorrah in the day of judgment, than for that city (x. 15 ; *Mark*
vi. 11 ; *Luke* x. 12).

In *John* :—

Their bodies shall lie upon the street of the great city which spiritually is called Sodom and Egypt (*Rev.* xi. 8),

where it is evident that by " Sodom" is not meant Sodom, nor
Egypt by " Egypt," for it is said that it is " spiritually called
Sodom and Egypt ;" " Sodom" denotes all evil from the love of
self, and " Egypt" (instead of Gomorrah) all derivative falsity.

2221. *Abraham went with them.* That this signifies that
the Lord still remained with them in perception, but concerning the human race, is evident from the series of things in the
internal sense ; for to " go with the three men" (that is, with
Jehovah) is to be still in perception.

2222. *To send them away.* That this signifies that He willed
to withdraw from that perception, is evident without explication. The reason is also manifest, namely, that the perception
from the Divine, and the thought therefrom concerning the human race that such was their quality, struck Him with horror,
for the Lord's love toward the human race was so great that
He willed to save all to eternity by the unition of His Human
Essence with the Divine, and of the Divine with the Human,
on which account, when He perceived that they were such, He
willed to withdraw from the perception and derivative thought,
which is signified by Abraham desiring to " send the men
away."

2223. Verse 17. *And Jehovah said, Shall I hide from Abraham that which I do?* " And Jehovah said," signifies perception ; " Shall I hide from Abraham that which I do ?" signifies
that nothing ought to be hidden before the Lord.

2224. *Jehovah said.* That this signifies perception, is evident from the signification of " saying," as being to perceive
(see n. 1898, 1919, 2080). Here, as it is Jehovah who " said,"
the meaning is that the Lord perceived from the Divine.

2225. *Shall I hide from Abraham that which I do?* That
this signifies that nothing ought to be hidden before the Lord,
is evident from the representation of Abraham, as being the
Lord in that state (as already explained several times in this
chapter). That the rest of the words signify that nothing
ought to be hidden, is evident. In this case the sense of the
letter is similar to the internal sense, as occasionally elsewhere,
especially where the essentials of faith are treated of, which,
being necessary to salvation, are stated in the letter such as
they are in the internal sense ; as for example in *Moses :—*

Jehovah our God is one Jehovah ; and thou shalt love Jehovah thy God with all thy heart, and with all thy soul, and with all thy strengths ; and these words shall be upon thy heart (*Deut.* vi. 4–6) ;

with other similar passages.

2226. Verse 18. *And Abraham shall surely be for a nation great and numerous ; and all the nations of the earth shall be blessed in him.* " Abraham shall surely be for a nation great and numerous," signifies that from the Lord will be all good and all the derivative truth ; " and in him shall all the nations of the earth be blessed," signifies that all who are in charity will be saved by Him.

2227. *Abraham shall surely be for a nation great and numerous.* That this signifies that all good and all the derivative truth will be from the Lord, is evident from the representation of Abraham, as being the Lord (often shown above), and also from the signification of a " nation," as being good (explained n. 1159, 1258–1260, 1416, 1849) ; here a " nation great and numerous," by which is signified good and the derivative truth. That " great" is predicated of good, and " numerous" of truth, appears from other places in the Word, but I must refrain from citing them here. The derivative truth, that is, truth from good, in the genuine sense is spiritual good. There are two kinds of good that are distinct from each other, namely, celestial good and spiritual good. Celestial good is that of love to the Lord, spiritual good is that of love toward the neighbor. From the former, or celestial good, comes the latter, or spiritual good ; for no one can love the Lord unless he also loves his neighbor. In love to the Lord is love toward the neighbor ; for love to the Lord is from the Lord, and thus is from love itself toward the universal human race. To be in love to the Lord is the same as to be in the Lord ; and he who is in the Lord cannot be otherwise than in His love ; which is toward the human race and thus toward the neighbor ; thus is he in both kinds of good, celestial and spiritual. The former is the veriest good itself ; but the latter is its truth, or the truth therefrom ; which truth is spiritual good, as said. The former is what is signified by " great," but the latter by " numerous."

2228. *All the nations of the earth shall be blessed in him.* That this signifies that all who are in charity will be saved by

Him, is evident from the signification of being "blessed," as being to be endowed with all goods which are from a heavenly origin (as explained n. 981, 1096, 1420, 1422). They who are endowed with goods from a heavenly origin, that is, with both celestial and spiritual goods (concerning which just above, n. 2177), are also endowed with eternal salvation, that is, are saved. By "all the nations of the earth" are meant in the internal sense those who are in the good of love and of charity, as is evident from the signification of a "nation," as being good (n. 1159, 1258–1260, 1416, 1849). That all men in the whole globe are not meant by "all the nations of the earth," is evident to every one, because there are very many among them who are not saved, but only those who are in charity, that is, who have attained the life of charity. [2] That none may be unaware how the case is with the salvation of men after their decease, it shall be briefly stated. There are many who say that man is saved by faith, or, in their words, if he only has faith; but for the most part they are those who do not know what faith is. Some suppose that it is mere thought; some that it is an acknowledgment of something to be believed; some that it is the whole doctrine of faith, which is to be believed; and others otherwise. Thus in the bare knowledge of what faith is they wander in error, consequently in the knowledge of what that is by which man is saved. Faith, however, is not mere thought, nor is it an acknowledgment of something to be believed, nor a knowledge of all things which belong to the doctrine of faith. By these no one can be saved; for they can take root no deeper than in the thought, and thought saves no one, but the life which the man has procured for himself in the world by means of the knowledges of faith. This life remains; whereas all thought which does not accord with the life perishes, even so as to become none at all. The heavenly consociations are according to lives; and by no means according to thoughts which are not of the life. Thoughts which are not of the life are counterfeit, and such are altogether rejected. [3] In general, life is twofold, being on the one hand infernal, on the other heavenly. Infernal life is acquired from all those ends, thoughts, and works which flow from the love of self, consequently from hatred against the neighbor; heavenly life, from all those ends, thoughts, and works which are of love toward the neighbor. The latter is the life to which all things that are called faith have regard, and which is procured by all things of faith. All this shows what faith is, namely, that it is charity, for to charity all things lead which are said to be of the doctrine, of faith; in it they are all contained, and from it they are all derived. The soul, after the life of the body, is such as its love is.

2229. Verse 19. *For I know him, because he will command his sons, and his house after him, and they will keep the way of Jehovah to do righteousness and judgment; that Jehovah may bring upon Abraham that which He hath spoken concerning him.* " For I know him," signifies that it is true; " because he will command his sons, and his house after him, and they will keep the way of Jehovah to do righteousness and judgment," signifies that all the doctrine of charity and faith is from Him; " sons" are they who are in truths, " house," they who are in goods, " way" is doctrine, " righteousness" has regard to good, " judgment" to truth; " that Jehovah may bring upon Abraham that which He hath spoken concerning him," signifies that the Human Essence will for this reason be adjoined to the Divine Essence.

2230. *For I know him.* That this signifies that it is true, is evident from the signification of " knowing." Properly speaking, to " know (*cognoscere*)" any one, is to know (*scire*) that he is of such and such a quality; and it is the same when the term is applied to any thing, or to anything else: to " know" it means to know that such is its quality; and therefore to " know (*nosse*)" has reference to that which is predicated, and it signifies that that which is meant in accordance with the series of things is so, or is true.

2231. *Because he will command his sons, and his house after him, and they will keep the way of Jehovah, to do righteousness and judgment.* That this signifies that all the doctrine of charity and faith is from Him, is evident from the signification of a " son," of a " house," of a " way," of " righteousness," and of " judgment;" which when summed up, or gathered into one sense, signify all the doctrine of charity and faith. For by " sons" are signified all who are in truths, by " house" all who are in goods, by a "way" the doctrine by which they are instructed, which doctrine in regard to good is signified by "righteousness," and in regard to truth by "judgment." Doctrine concerning good is the doctrine of charity, and doctrine concerning truth is the doctrine of faith. [2] In general, there is only one doctrine, namely, the doctrine of charity, for (as before said, n. 2228) all things of faith look to charity. Between charity and faith there is no other difference than that between willing what is good and thinking what is good (for he who wills what is good also thinks what is good), thus than that between the will and the understanding. They who reflect, know that the will is one thing and the understanding another. This is also known in the learned world, and it plainly appears with those who will evil and yet from thought speak well; from all which it is evident to every one that the will is one thing, and the understanding another; and thus that the human mind is distinguished into two parts, which do not make a one. Yet man was so created that these two parts should constitute one mind; nor should there be any other distinction (to speak by comparison) than such as there is between a flame and the light from it (love to the Lord and charity toward the neighbor being like the flame, and all perception and thought being like the light from it); thus love and charity should be the all of the perception and thought, that is should be in each and all things of them. Perception or thought concerning the quality of love and charity is that which is called faith. [3] But as the human race began to will what is evil, to hate the neighbor, and to exercise revenges and cruelties, insomuch that that part of the mind which is called the will was altogether destroyed, men began to make a distinction between charity and faith, and to refer to faith all the doctrinal matters that were of their religion, and call them by the single term faith; and at length they went so far as to say that they could be saved by faith alone—by which they meant their doctrinal things—provided they merely believed these, no matter how they might live. Thus was charity separated from faith, which is then nothing else whatever (to speak by comparison) than a kind of light without flame, such as is wont to be the light of the sun in time of winter, which is cold and icy, insomuch that the vegetation of the earth grows torpid and dies; whereas faith from charity is like the light in the time of spring and summer, by which all things germinate and bloom. ˙[4] This may also be known from the fact that love and charity are celestial flame, and that faith is the spiritual light therefrom. In this manner also do they present themselves to perception and sight in the other life; for there the Lord's celestial manifests itself before the angels by a flaming radiance like that of the sun, and the Lord's spiritual by the light from this radiance, by which also angels and spirits are affected as to their interiors, in accordance with the life of love and charity that appertains to them. This is the source in the other life of joys and happinesses with all their varieties. And all this shows how the case is with the statement that faith alone saves.

2232. That "sons" are those who are in truths, is evident from the signification of a "son" in the Word as being truth (see n. 489, 491, 533, 1147). By "sons" in the abstract sense are signified truths; but as applied to man, "sons" denote all those who are in truths.

2233. That a "house" denotes those who are in goods, is evident from the signification of a "house," as being good (see n. 710, 1708, 2048). By a "house," or those born in the house, in the abstract sense goods are in like manner signified, but as applied to man they denote all who are in good.

2234. That a "way" denotes doctrine, is evident from the signification of a "way." A "way" in the Word is predicated of truths, because truths lead to good and proceed from good (as is evident from the passages adduced in Part First, n. 627); and as a "way" is predicated of truths, it denotes doctrine, because doctrine comprises in one complex all the things which lead to good, that is, to charity.

2235. That "righteousness" has regard to good, and "judgment" to truth, is evident from the signification of "righteousness," and from the signification of "judgment." In the Word, "righteousness and judgment" are many times named together, but what they signify in the internal sense has not yet been known. In the proximate sense "righteousness" is predicated of what is righteous or just (*justus*), and "judgment" of what

is right (*rectus*). There is what is righteous when anything is
judged from good, and this according to conscience; but what
is right when anything is judged from the law, and thus from
the righteousness of the law, thus also according to conscience,
because it has the law for its rule. But in the internal sense
"righteousness" denotes that which is from good, and "judgment" that which is from truth. Good is all that which belongs to love and charity; truth is all that which belongs to
the derivative faith. Truth derives its essence from good, and
is called truth from good, just as faith derives its essence from
love, and in the same way judgment from righteousness. [2]
That such is the signification of "righteousness and judgment"
is evident from the following passages in the Word. In *Jeremiah* :—

> Thus saith Jehovah, Execute ye judgment and righteousness, and rescue
> the spoiled out of the hand of the oppressor. Woe to him that buildeth
> his house in that which is not righteousness and his chambers in that
> which is not judgment. Did not thy father eat and drink, and do judg-
> ment and righteousness ? then he had that which is good (xxii. 3, 13, 15),

where "judgment" denotes the things that are of truth, and
"righteousness" the things that are of good. In *Ezekiel* :—

> If the wicked shall return from his sin, and do judgment and right-
> eousness, all his sins that he hath sinned shall not be mentioned unto
> him; he hath done judgment and righteousness: he shall surely live.
> When the wicked turns himself from his wickedness, and does judgment
> and righteousness, for these he shall live (xxxiii. 14, 16, 19),

where in like manner "judgment" denotes truth, which is of
faith; and "righteousness" good, which is of charity. [3] So
in *Amos* :—

> Let judgment flow like waters, and righteousness like a mighty river
> (v. 24).

In *Isaiah* :—

> Thus saith Jehovah, Keep ye judgment, and do righteousness, for My
> salvation is near to come, and My righteousness to reveal itself (lvi. 1).

In the same :—

> To peace there shall be no end, upon the throne of David and upon
> his kingdom, to establish it, and to uphold it, with judgment and with
> righteousness, from henceforth and even to eternity (ix. 7),

denoting that they are in the truths of faith and in the goods of charity.   In the same :—

Jehovah is exalted, for He dwelleth on high ; He hath filled Zion with judgment and righteousness (xxxiii. 5),

where "judgment" denotes faith, "righteousness" love, and "Zion" the church.   "Judgment" stands first because love comes through faith; but when "righteousness" stands first, it is because the faith is from love, as in *Hosea :—*

I will betroth thee unto Me to eternity, and I will betroth thee unto Me in righteousness and judgment, and in mercy and in compassions ; and I will betroth thee unto Me in faith, and thou shalt know Jehovah (ii. 19, 20),

where "righteousness" stands first, as also " mercy," which are of love; and " judgment" follows, as also " compassions," which are of faith from love; both are called " faith" or " faithfulness."   [4] In *David :—*

Thy mercy, O Jehovah, is in the heavens, thy truth reacheth unto the skies (*aetheres*) ; Thy righteousness is like the mountains of God, Thy judgments are a great deep (*Ps.* xxxvi. 5, 6),

where both " mercy" and "righteousness" are in like manner of love, and " truth" and " judgments" are of faith.   In the same :—

Truth shall spring out of the earth, and righteousness shall look forth from heaven.   Yea, Jehovah shall give good, and our land shall yield its increase (*Ps.* lxxxv. 11, 12),

where " truth," which is of faith, denotes " judgment," and " righteousness" love or mercy.   In *Zechariah :—*

I will bring them, and they shall dwell in the midst of Jerusalem, and they shall be My people, and I will be their God in truth and in righteousness (viii. 8),

from which also it is evident that " judgment" denotes truth, and " righteousness" good; because " truth" is here used in place of " judgment."   In like manner in *David :—*

He that walketh perfect, and worketh righteousness, and speaketh truth (*Ps.* xv. 2).

[5] As faith is of charity, or as truth is of good, the truths of good are occasionally called the " judgments of righteousness ;"

and thus "judgments" signify almost the same as "precepts;" as in *Isaiah* :—

They will seek Me day by day, and desire to know My ways, as a nation that doeth righteousness and forsaketh not the judgment of their God ; they will ask of Me judgments of righteousness, they will desire to draw near to God (lviii. 2).

That "precepts" signify the same may be seen in *David* :—

Seven times a day have I praised Thee because of the judgments of Thy righteousness; all Thy precepts are righteousness (*Ps.* cxix. 164, 172).

It is especially said of the Lord that He "does judgment and righteousness," when He creates man anew ; as in *Jeremiah* :—

Let him that glorieth glory in this, that he understandeth and knoweth Me, that I am Jehovah that doeth mercy, judgment, and righteousness in the earth, for in these things I am well pleased (ix. 24),

where mercy, which is of love, is described by "judgment and righteousness." In the same :—

I will raise up unto David a righteous offshoot, and He shall reign as King, and shall act intelligently, and shall do judgment and righteousness in the earth (xxiii. 5 ; xxxiii. 15).

[6] Hence it is said in *John* :—

If I go away, I will send the Comforter unto you ; and when He is come, He will reprove the world of sin, of righteousness, and of judgment; of sin, because they believe not on Me ; of righteousness, because I go unto My father, and ye shall see Me no more ; of judgment, because the prince of this world is judged (xvi. 7–11).

" Sin" here denotes all unfaithfulness. His " reproving in regard to righteousness" means in regard to all that is against good, when yet the Lord united the Human to the Divine to save the world—which is the meaning of " I go unto My Father and ye shall see Me no more." His " reproving in regard to judgment" means in regard to all that is against truth, when yet evils were cast down into their hells so as no longer to be able to inflict injury—which is meant by the prince of the world being judged. In general, His " reproving in regard to sin, righteousness, and judgment," means that it was in regard to all unfaithfulness against good and truth; and thus that there was no charity and faith; for in ancient times by righteousness and judgment were understood, as regards the Lord, all mercy and grace ; and as regards man, all charity and faith.

2236. *That Jehovah may bring upon Abraham that which He hath spoken concerning him.* That this signifies that on this account the Human Essence will be adjoined to the Divine Essence, is not so evident from the signification of the words as from the fact that all things said in the Word involve the Lord's coming to unite the Human Essence to the Divine Essence, by which unition He should save the human race. These are the things signified in the internal sense by His " bringing upon Abraham that which He hath spoken concerning him."

2237. Verse 20. *And Jehovah said, Because the cry of Sodom and Gomorrah has become great, and because their sin has become very grievous.* " Jehovah said," signifies perception ; " because the cry of Sodom and Gomorrah has become great, and because their sin has become very grievous," signifies that the falsity and evil of the love of self have grown even to consummation. " Cry" is falsity, and " sin" is evil.

2238. *Jehovah said.* That this signifies perception, is evident from the signification, in the historical sense, of " saying," as being to perceive, as shown several times before. When the expression " Jehovah said" occurs in the historicals of the Word, it signifies a perception which is not altogether continuous with the previous one, but is a sequent one, and sometimes a new one (see also n. 2061).

2239. *Because the cry of Sodom and Gomorrah has become great, and because their sin has become very grievous.* That this signifies that the falsity and evil of the love of self have increased even to consummation, is evident from the signification of " Sodom," as being evil from the love of self ; and of " Gomorrah," as being the derivative falsity (shown above, n. 2220) ; also from the signification of a " cry," as being falsity ; and of " sin," as being evil (to be explained presently) ; from all which it is evident that the " cry having become great, and the sin having become very grievous," signifies that the falsity and evil had come to their height, or to consummation. This is better seen from what follows, where it is said that if ten were found there the city should be spared (verse 32) ; by which is signified, if there were still any remains, that is, anything of good and truth; for when there is no longer anything of good and truth within man, there is then wasteness and desolation, consequently consummation (concerning which in the following verse).

2240. That a "cry" denotes falsity, and "sin" evil, is evident from the signification in the Word of a "cry." That a "cry" signifies falsity, can be evident to no one unless he knows the internal sense of the Word. The word sometimes occurs in the Prophets, and when vastation and desolation are there treated of, it is said that men "howl and cry," by which is signified that goods and truths have been vastated; and a term is there made use of by which in the internal sense falsity is described; as in *Jeremiah :*—

A voice of the cry of the shepherds, and the howling of the powerful ones of the flock because Jehovah layeth waste their pasture (xxv. 36),

where the "cry of the shepherds" denotes that they are in falsity, from which there comes vastation. [2] In the same :—

Behold, waters rise up from the north, and shall become an overflowing stream, and shall overflow the land and the fullness thereof, the city and them that dwell therein ; and the men shall cry, and every inhabitant of the land shall howl, because of the day that cometh to lay waste (xlvii. 2, 4),

where the desolation of faith is treated of, which is brought about by falsities; the "overflowing stream" is falsity (as shown in Part First, n. 705, 790). [3] In *Zephaniah :*—

The voice of a cry from the fish gate, and a howling from the second, and a great shattering from the hills, and their wealth shall become a spoil, and their houses a desolation (i. 10, 13),

where also a "cry" is predicated of the falsities which lay waste. [4] In *Isaiah :*—

In the way of Horonaim they shall rouse up a cry of shattering, for the waters of Nimrim shall be desolations, for the grass has dried up, the herb is consumed, there is no green thing (xv. 5, 6 ; *Jer.* xlviii. 3),

where the desolation of faith and its consummation is described by a "cry." [5] In *Jeremiah :*—

Judah hath mourned, and her gates languish, they have been blackened upon the earth, and the cry of Jerusalem is gone up ; and their illustrious ones have sent their younger ones to the waters; they came to the pits, they found no waters, they returned with their vessels empty (xiv. 2, 3),

where the "cry of Jerusalem" denotes falsities; for by their "finding no waters" is signified that there were no knowledges of truth, which are "waters" (as shown in Part First, n. 28, 680, 739). [6] In *Isaiah :*—

I will exult in Jerusalem and be glad in My people, and the voice of weeping shall be no more heard in her, nor the voice of crying (lxv. 19),

where there "not being heard the voice of weeping" denotes that there shall not be evil; "nor the voice of crying" denotes that there shall not be falsity. Very many of these things cannot be understood from the sense of the letter, but only from the internal sense, and this is the case with a "cry." [7] In the same :—

Jehovah looked for judgment, but behold a scab; for righteousness, but behold a cry (v. 7),

where also the vastation of good and truth is treated of. There is in this passage a kind of reciprocation, such as is occasionally found in the Prophets, and which is of such a nature that in the place of truth there is found evil, which is meant by there being "a scab instead of judgment;" and falsity in place of good, which is meant by there being "a cry instead of righteousness" (for that "judgment" is truth, and "righteousness" good, was shown above, n. 2235). [8] There is a like reciprocation in *Moses*, where Sodom and Gomorrah are treated of :—

Of the vine of Sodom is their vine, and of the fields of Gomorrah are their grapes; they have grapes of gall, clusters of bitternesses (*Deut.* xxxii. 32),

where there is a similar mode of speaking; for the "vine" is predicated of truths and falsities, and the "fields" and "grapes," of goods and evils; so that "the vine of Sodom" is falsity from evil, and "the fields and grapes of Gomorrah" are evils from falsities; for there are two kinds of falsity (see Part First, n. 1212); and so also there are two kinds of evil. Both kinds of falsity and evil are signified in this verse by the "cry of Sodom and Gomorrah having become great, and their sin having become exceeding grievous;" as is evident from the fact that "cry" is named in the first place, and "sin" in the second; and yet

"Sodom," which is evil from the love of self, is mentioned first; and "Gomorrah," which is the derivative falsity, second.

2241. Verse 21. *I will go down, I pray, and I will see whether they have made a consummation according to the cry thereof which is come unto Me, and if not I will know.* "I will go down, I pray, and I will see," signifies visitation; "whether they have made a consummation according to the cry thereof which is come unto Me, and if not I will know," signifies whether the evil has arrived at its height.

2242. *I will go down, I pray, and I will see.* That this signifies visitation, is evident from the signification of "going down to see," as being Judgment (explained in Part First, n. 1311), consequently that it is visitation. The last time of the church in general, and that of every one in particular, is called in the Word "visitation," which precedes Judgment; thus a "visitation" is simply an exploration as to quality, that is, as to the quality of the church in general, or of a man in particular; and this exploration is expressed in the sense of the letter by Jehovah "going down and seeing." [2] This shows what is the nature of the sense of the letter, for Jehovah does not go down, since going down cannot be predicated of the Lord, because He is always in the highest; nor does Jehovah see whether a thing be so, for seeing whether it be so cannot be predicated of the Lord, because He knows all things from eternity both in general and in particular. Nevertheless it is so expressed because it appears to man as if it were so, for man is in things that are below, and when anything appears there, he does not think or even know how the case is with things that are above, thus neither how they flow in, for his thought goes no further than to what is nearest to him, and hence he cannot perceive otherwise than that there is some such thing as going down and seeing, and this the more because he imagines that no one knows what he is thinking; besides that he has no other idea than that there is a coming down from on high, and, when said of God, from the highest; whereas it is not from the highest, but from the inmost. [3] This shows what is the nature of the sense of the letter, namely, that it is according to appearances; and if it were not according to appearances, no one would understand and acknowledge the

Word; thus no one would receive it. But the angels are not in appearances in the way that man is, and therefore while the Word as to the sense of the letter is for man, as to the internal sense it is for the angels, as also for those men to whom of the Lord's Divine mercy it is given, while living in the world, to be like the angels. [4] "Visitation" is mentioned in various places in the Word, and by it is signified either vastation—whether of the church or of each man—or deliverance, and thus exploration as to quality. It denotes vastation in *Isaiah :*—

What will ye do in the day of visitation ? it shall come from far. To whom will ye flee for help ? and where will ye leave your glory ? (x. 3).

And again :—

The stars of the heavens and the constellations thereof shall not shine with their light, the sun shall be darkened in his going forth, and the moon shall not cause her light to shine, and I will visit evil upon the world, and upon the wicked their iniquity (xiii. 10, 11).

That by the stars and constellations which shall not shine, and the sun which shall be darkened, and the moon which shall not make her light to shine, is signified that there will be no love and no charity, may be seen above (n. 2120); and as this is vastation, it is the "day of visitation." [5] In *Jeremiah :*—

They shall fall among them that fall, and in the time of their visitation they shall stumble (viii. 12) ;

meaning the time when they have been vastated, or when there is no charity and faith. In *Ezekiel :*—

The visitations of the city have come near, and every man with his instrument of destruction in his hand (ix. 1).

Here also vastation is treated of; hence every man has an instrument of destruction. In *Hosea :*—

The days of visitation are come, the days of retribution are come (ix. 7).

In *Micah :*—

The day of thy watchmen, thy visitation, is come ; now shall be their perplexity (vii. 4),

also denoting vastated charity. In *Moses :*—

In the day of My visiting, and I will visit upon them their sin (*Exod.* xxxii. 34),

where the people in the wilderness are treated of, after they had
made for themselves the golden calf.   That deliverance is signified by "visitation" is plain from many passages (as *Exod.* iii.
16; iv. 31; *Jer.* xxvii. 22; xxix. 10; *Luke* i. 68, 78; xix. 41, 42).

2243. *Whether they have made a consummation according
to the cry of it which is come unto Me, and if not I will know.*
That this signifies whether evil has arrived at its height, is
evident from the signification of a "cry," as being falsity (explained just above, n. 2240).   As there said (near the end)
there are two kinds of falsity, namely, the falsity which is
from evil, and the falsity which produces evil.   The falsity
which is from evil is all that which a man thinks when he is
in evil, namely, all that favors his evil; as for example, when
he is in adultery, that which he then thinks about adultery :
that it is allowable, that it is becoming, that it is the delight of life, that the procreation of offspring is thereby pro-
moted, and so on; all these thoughts being falsities from evil.
[2] But the falsity which produces evil takes place when
from his religious belief a man conceives some principle, and
consequently believes that it is good or holy, when yet in
itself it is evil.   For example, he who believes from his religion that there is some man who can save, and therefore worships and adores him, does evil from that falsity; and the
same is true in regard to any other religious belief which in
itself is false.   As therefore falsity is from evil, and falsity
produces evil, the expression "cry" is here used, signifying,
as a kind of general expression, that which it involves, namely,
evil; as is also evident from its being said, "whether they
have made a consummation according to the cry of it which
is come unto Me;" where "its cry" is put in the singular
number, and "they have made a consummation," in the plural.
[3] What a "consummation" is, was shown in Part First (n.
1857); and what a consummation is further, may be comprehended from the churches.   The Most Ancient Church, which
was called "Man," was the most celestial of all.   This in process of time so far degenerated from the good of love, that at
length nothing celestial remained, and then was its consummation, which is described by the state of those just before
the flood.   [4] The Ancient Church (which was after the flood

and was called "Noah," and was less celestial) also in course
of time so departed from the good of charity, that nothing of
charity remained, for it was turned partly into magic, partly
into idolatry, and partly into a kind of dogmatic system separate from charity; and then was its consummation.   [5]
Another church succeeded, called the Hebrew Church, which
was still less celestial and spiritual, placing somewhat of holy
worship in external rites.   This in course of time was dis-
torted in various ways, and that external worship was turned
into idolatry; and then was its consummation.   [6] A fourth
church was then restored among the posterity of Jacob, which
had nothing celestial and spiritual, but only a representative
of it; and therefore that church was a church representative
of celestial and spiritual things, inasmuch as they did not
know what their rites represented and signified; but it was
instituted in order that there might still be some connection
between man and heaven, such as there is between the representatives of good and truth, and good and truth themselves.
This church at length so fell away into falsities and evils that
every rite became idolatrous; and then was its consummation.
Therefore, after the churches had thus successively declined—
when in the last one the connection between the human race
and heaven was altogether broken, insomuch that the human
race would have perished because there was no church by
which there could be a connection and a bond (see n. 468, 637,
931, 2054)—[7] the Lord then came into the world, and by
the unition of the Divine Essence with the Human Essence in
Himself, conjoined heaven with earth, and at the same time
He set up again a new church, called the Christian Church,
which at first was in the good of faith, and its members lived
in charity with one another as brethren.   But in process of
time this church has departed in divers ways, and at the present day has become such that its members do not even know
that the fundamental of faith is love to the Lord and charity
toward the neighbor; and although they say from doctrine
that the Lord is the Saviour of the human race, that they are
to rise again after death, and that there is a heaven and a hell,
yet few believe it.   As this church has become such, its consummation is not far off.   [8] All this shows what "consum-

mation" is, namely, that it is when evil has come to its height. The case is similar in particular, that is, with every man; but how the case is with consummation as regards each person in particular, will of the Lord's Divine mercy be told in what follows. Consummation is treated of in the Word in various places, and the state which precedes is described by "vastation" and "desolation," which is followed by "visitation."

2244. Verse 22. *And the men looked forth thence and went toward Sodom; and Abraham as yet he was standing before Jehovah.* "The men looked forth thence," signifies the Lord's thought from the Divine; "and went toward Sodom," signifies concerning the human race as being in such great evil; "and Abraham as yet he was standing before Jehovah," signifies the Lord's thought from the Human which was adjoined in the manner stated above.

2245. *The men looked forth thence.* That this signifies the Lord's thought from the Divine, is evident from the signification of "looking forth," as being to think (for to "see," in the internal sense, as in common discourse, is to understand, since understanding is internal sight, and in the same way to "look forth" is to think, which is of the internal sight, that is, of the understanding); and also from the signification of "the men," as being the Divine. In this chapter throughout mention is sometimes made of "the men," and sometimes of "Jehovah" instead of "the men:" when mention is made of "the men" there is signified a Trine, namely, the Divine Itself, the Divine Human, and the Proceeding. The Lord's thought from this Divine is signified by "the men looked forth thence." The thought was from the Human conjoined with the Divine, which conjunction was treated of at the beginning of this chapter; but the perception from which came the thought was from the Divine, therefore mention is now made in this same verse of "Jehovah"—that "Abraham was standing before Jehovah;" and when the Human was conjoined with the Divine, there was also together with them the Proceeding.

2246. *They went toward Sodom.* That this signifies thought concerning the human race as being in such great evil, is evident from the signification of "Sodom," as being evil from the love of self (see above, n. 2220); and of "looking forth toward the faces of Sodom," as being toward the state of the human race (n. 2219). That " Sodom" signifies the state of the human race as being in such great evil, is because by " Sodom" is not meant Sodom, but all those in the universal world who are in the love of self; and by the description of. Sodom is represented the state of all who are in that evil, as is evident from what follows. That the love of self is the fountain of all evils, thus evil itself, is evident from what was said and shown of it before (n. 2045, 2057, 2219), and therefore it is here said that they were in such great evil.

2247. *Abraham as yet he was standing before Jehovah.* That this signifies the Lord's thought from the Human which was adjoined in the manner stated above, is evident from the representation of Abraham in this chapter, as being the Lord as to the Human ; and from his " standing before Jehovah." Hence it follows without explication, that it was the thought from the Human which was adjoined in the manner stated at the beginning of this chapter, as also above (n. 2245).

2248. Verse 23. *And Abraham drew near, and said, Wilt Thou also destroy the righteous with the wicked?* " Abraham drew near, and said," signifies the Lord's thought from the Human, which thought adjoined itself more closely to the Divine; " wilt Thou also destroy the righteous with the wicked?" signifies the Lord's grief from love toward the human race, and His intercession, urging that possibly there might be what is good joined to them, although they were evil.

2249. *And Abraham drew near, and said.* That this signifies the Lord's thought from the Human, which thought adjoined itself more closely to the Divine, follows from the things that precede, where the Lord's thought concerning the human race is treated of : thus without explication. That in this chapter in the internal sense the state of the Lord's thought and perception is so fully described, and at the beginning the state of the conjunction of the Lord's Human with His Divine, will possibly appear to man as if it were not of so much importance. [2] And yet it is of the greatest moment; for before the angels, to whom the internal sense is the Word, these things are presented to the life, together with their representatives, in a most beautiful form ; besides numberless things that follow from them and bear their likeness, concerning the Lord's conjunction with heaven, and the reception of His Divine in their human; for the ideas of angels are such that they relish such things above all others, and perceive them as being most pleasant; and they are also enlightened and confirmed by them more and more in regard to the unition of the Lord's Human Essence with His Divine Essence; for the angels have been men, and when men they could not but think of the Lord as a man, and of the Lord as God, as also of the Divine Trinity, and form for themselves various ideas, although at that time they knew not of what quality these ideas were. [3] For heavenly arcana are of such a nature that although they surpass all apprehension, yet every one forms for himself some idea of them; for nothing can possibly be retained in the memory, still less enter into anything of thought, except by means of some idea formed in one way or another. And because their ideas could not be formed otherwise than from things in the world, or from things analogous to those in the world; and because fallacies then insinuated themselves from things not understood (which in the other life alienate the ideas of the thought—which are then more internal—from the truth and good of faith), [4] in order that such things may be dispersed, so much is said in this chapter, in its internal sense, about the conjunction of the Lord's Human with His Divine, and about His perception and thought; and accordingly when the Word is read, these things are so presented to the perception of the angels that their former ideas, formed from other sources and from scruples easily springing therefrom, are gradually dissipated, and new ideas are insinuated that are in conformity with the light of truth in which the angels are. This takes place more with the spiritual angels than with the celestial; for according to the purification of their ideas are they perfected for the reception of celestial things. It is known that heaven is not pure before the Lord; and it is a truth that the angels are continually being perfected.

2250. *Wilt Thou also destroy the righteous with the wicked?* That this signifies the Lord's grief from love toward the human race, and His intercession urging that possibly there might be what is good adjoined to them although they were evil, is evident from the zeal of love that here shines forth, and still more in the 25th verse just below, where it is said, " Be it far from Thee to do according to this thing, to cause the righteous to die with the wicked, that so the righteous be as the wicked ; be it far from Thee ; shall not the Judge of all the earth do judgment ?" The same is evident from the signification of " the righteous" as being good (see n. 612, 2235), and from the signification of "the wicked" as being opposite to "the righteous," that is, opposite to good, thus evil. It is likewise evident from these words, as also from the things that follow in this chapter, that there is intercession. The Lord's intercession for the human race existed at the time when He was in the world, and in fact when He was in a state of humiliation, for as before said, He then spoke with Jehovah as with another. But of course in His state of glorification, when the Human Essence has become united to the Divine Essence, and is itself also Jehovah, He does not intercede, but has mercy and affords aid from His Divine, and saves. It is Mercy itself which is the intercession, for such is its essence.

2251. Verse 24. *Peradventure there be fifty righteous in the midst of the city ; wilt Thou also destroy and not spare the place for the sake of the fifty righteous that are in the midst of it?* " Peradventure there be fifty righteous in the midst of the city," signifies that possibly the truths may be full of goods ; "wilt Thou also destroy and not spare the place for the sake of the fifty righteous that are in the midst of it ?" signifies intercession from love, that in such case they should not perish.

2252. *Peradventure there be fifty righteous in the midst of the city.* That this signifies that the truths may possibly be full of goods, is evident from the signification of " fifty," as being what is full ; from the signification of " righteous" as being good (see n. 612, 2235) ; from that of the " midst," as being what is within (n. 1074) ; and from that of " city," as being truth (n. 402). Thus " fifty righteous in the midst of the city," means in the internal sense that truths may possibly be full of goods within. That there is this meaning in these words cannot be seen from the letter, for the historicals of the literal sense lead the mind in quite a different direction, that is, to different thoughts ; and yet that these words are so perceived by those who are in the internal sense, I know of a certainty. The numbers themselves also, as here " fifty," and in what follows " forty-five," " forty," " thirty," " twenty," and " ten," are by no means perceived as numbers by those who are in the internal sense, but as real things or states (as is shown, n. 482, 487, 575, 647, 648, 755, 813, 1963, 2075). [2] For the ancients marked the states of their church—in one way—by numbers; and the nature of their computation in so doing is evident from the signification of the numbers in the places just referred to. They had the signification of numbers from the representatives which exist in the world of spirits, where, when anything appears as numbered, it does not signify anything that is determined by the numbers, but the thing or state itself; as is evident from the things that have been adduced (n. 2129, 2130, also n. 2089) concerning " twelve," as meaning all the things of faith. It is similar with the numbers which now follow. This shows what is the nature of the Word in the internal sense. [3] That " fifty" signifies what is full, comes from its following next after the product of seven into seven, or forty-nine, so that it is the impletion of this number, on which account there was in the Representative Church the festival of the Seven Sabbaths on the fiftieth day, and the Jubilee in the fiftieth year. As regards the festival of the seven sabbaths we read in *Moses:*—

Ye shall count unto you from the morrow of the sabbath, from the day that ye brought the sheaf of the wave-offering, seven entire sabbaths shall there be, even unto the morrow of the seventh sabbath shall ye count fifty days, and ye shall offer a new offering unto Jehovah (*Lev.* xxiii. 15).

And concerning the Jubilee :—

Thou shalt count for thee seven sabbaths of years, seven years seven times, and they shall be to thee seven sabbaths of years, nine and forty years, and ye shall hallow the fiftieth year, and proclaim liberty in the land to all the inhabitants thereof ; it shall be a jubilee unto you (*Lev.* xxv. 8, 10),

which shows that the fiftieth is what is full in relation to sabbaths. [4] Moreover, wherever " fifty" is mentioned in the Word, it signifies what is full; as when it is said that

The Levites were numbered from a son of thirty years and upward, even unto a son of fifty years (*Num.* iv. 23, 35, 39, 43, 47 ; viii. 25) ;

meaning the full or final state of discharging the ministry.

That a man lying with a damsel, a virgin, shall give unto the damsel's father fifty pieces of silver, and she should be to him for a wife, nor could he put her away (*Deut.* xxii. 29),

which denotes a full fine and full restitution.

David's giving to Araunah for the threshing-floor, where he built the altar to Jehovah, fifty shekels of silver (2 *Sam.* xxiv. 24),

denotes a full price and a full purchase.

Absalom's preparing for himself a chariot and horses, and having fifty men running before him (2 *Sam.* xv. 1),

and in like manner

Adonijah's having chariots and horsemen, and fifty men running before him (1 *Kings* i. 5),

denotes full excellence and greatness. For they had from the ancients certain representative and significative numbers, which they observed, and which were also commanded in their rites; but most of them did not know what they signified. [5] And in the same way, as " fifty" signifies what is full, and as this number was also representative—as already said—the same thing is signified by it in the Lord's parable of the steward, who said to him that owed the oil :—

How much owest thou unto my lord? and he said, a hundred baths of oil. And he said unto him, take thy bond, and sit down quickly, and write fifty (*Luke* xvi. 6) ;

" fifty" denoting full payment. As fifty is a number, it indeed appears to involve nothing beyond the number; whereas in the internal sense what is full is everywhere meant by it, as in *Haggai :*—

One came to the wine-press to draw out fifty out of the wine-press ; there were twenty (ii. 16),

that is, instead of fullness there was not much. " Fifty" would not have been mentioned here in the Prophet unless it had been significative.

2253. *Wilt thou also destroy and not spare the place for the sake of the fifty righteous that are in the midst of it?* That this signifies intercession from love—that they should not perish—is evident from the signification of "fifty," and of "righteous," as also of "the midst of it," that is, of the city (concerning which just above, n. 2252), all of which things involve intercession from love, and that they should not perish. (As regards the intercession, see above, n. 2250.) That it was from love is also manifest. With the Lord, when He was in the world, there was no other life than the life of love toward the universal human race, which He ardently desired to eternally save. This is the veriest celestial life, by which He united Himself to the Divine, and the Divine to Himself —for *Esse* itself, or Jehovah, is nothing else than Mercy, which is of love to the universal human race—and that life was one of pure love, which is never possible with any man. They who do not know what life is, and that the life is such as the love, do not comprehend this. This shows that in so far as any one loves his neighbor, in so far he partakes of the Lord's life.

2254. Verse 25. *Be it far from Thee to do according to this thing, to cause the righteous to die with the wicked, that so the righteous be as the wicked; be it far from Thee; shall not the Judge of all the earth do judgment?* "Be it far from Thee to do according to this thing," signifies the Lord's horror; "to cause the righteous to die with the wicked, that so the righteous be as the wicked," signifies that good cannot die, because evil can be separated from it; "be it far from Thee," signifies a greater degree of horror; "shall not the Judge of all the earth do judgment?" signifies that the Divine good cannot do this, after the manner of truth separated from good.

2255. *Be it far from Thee to do according to this thing.* That this signifies the Lord's horror, is evident without explication.

2256. *To cause the righteous to die with the wicked, that so the righteous be as the wicked.* That this signifies that good cannot die, because evil can be separated from it, is evident from the signification of "righteous," as being good, and of "wicked," as being evil (see above, n 2250). Hence to "cause the righteous to die with the wicked," is to make good die with evil. As this ought not to be done, and causes horror to think of, it is removed in the internal sense, and then there is presented this: that good cannot die, because evil can be separated from it. [2] How this matter stands, is known to few, if any. Be it known that all the good a man has thought and done from infancy even to the last of his life, remains; in like manner all the evil, so that not the least of it completely perishes. Both are inscribed on his book of life (that is, on each of his memories), and on his nature (that is, his native disposition and genius). From these he has formed for himself a life, and so to speak a soul, which after death is of a corresponding quality. But goods are never so commingled with evils, nor evils with goods, that they cannot be separated; for if they should be commingled, the man would eternally perish. In relation to this the Lord exercises His providence, and when a man comes into the other life, if he has lived in the good of love and of charity, the Lord then separates his evils, and by what is good with him elevates him into heaven. But if he has lived in evils, that is, in things contrary to love and charity, the Lord then separates from him what is good, and his evils bring him into hell. Such is the lot of every one after death; but it is a separation, and in no wise a complete removal. [3] Moreover, as the will of man, which is the one part of his life, has been utterly destroyed, the Lord separates this destroyed part from the other which is his intellectual part, and in those who are being regenerated, implants in this intellectual part the good of charity, and through this a new will; these are they who have conscience. Thus also, speaking generally, the Lord separates evil from good. These are the arcana which are meant in the internal sense by the statement that good cannot die, because evil can be separated from it.

2257. *Be it far from Thee.* That this signifies a greater degree of horror, is evident from the words being repeated; thus it also needs no explication.

2258. *Shall not the Judge of all the earth do judgment?* That this signifies that the Divine good cannot do this after the manner of truth separated from good, is evident from the signification of the " Judge of all the earth," as also from the signification of "judgment." The " Judge of all the earth," signifies in the internal sense the good itself from which comes truth; which also in the Representative Church was represented by the priests who were at the same time judges; for as priests they represented the Divine good, and as judges the

Divine truth; but the "Judge of all the earth" means both, and this from the signification of "earth," as explained in several places in Part First. But to prove these things now from the representatives of that church would be too tedious. "Judgment," however, signifies truth (as shown above, n. 2235). From these significations, and at the same time from the series of things in the internal sense, it is evident that "Shall not the Judge of all the earth do judgment?" signifies that the Divine good cannot do this after the manner of truth separated from good. [2] In order to the understanding of these things, be it known that there are two things which constitute the order of the universal heaven, and thence in the universe, namely, Good and Truth. Good is the essential of order, all the things of which are mercies. Truth is the secondary of order, all the things of which are truths. The Divine good adjudges all to heaven, but the Divine truth condemns all to hell; and therefore unless the Lord's Mercy, which is of good, were eternal, all men, however many, would be condemned. This is what is signified by the statement that the Divine good cannot do this after the manner of truth separated from good. (See also what is said concerning this in Part First, n. 1728.) [3] That the evil are nevertheless condemned to hell, is not because the Divine good is separated from the Divine truth, but because the man separates himself from the Divine good. For the Lord in no case sends any one down into hell, but the man sends himself, as has been already stated a number of times. In the following respect also the Divine good is conjoined with the Divine truth: that unless the evil were separated from the good, the evil would do harm to the good, and would be continually endeavoring to destroy order: thus that the good may not be harmed, is of Mercy. This stands just as in the kingdoms of the earth. If evils were not punished, the whole kingdom would be infected with evils, and so would perish; for which reason kings and judges show more mercy in punishing evils and in expelling from society those guilty of them, than by exercising in their behalf an unseasonable clemency.

2259. Verse 26. *And Jehovah said, If I find in Sodom fifty righteous in the midst of the city, I will spare all the place for* *their sake.* " Jehovah said," signifies perception; " If I find in Sodom fifty righteous in the midst of the city," signifies here as before, if truths are full of goods; " I will spare all the place for their sake," signifies that they will be saved.

2260. *Jehovah said.* That this signifies perception, is evident from the signification of " Jehovah's saying," in the historic Word, as being representative of the Lord's perception from the Divine, and something of thought following therefrom, and some reply. (Concerning the expression " Jehovah said," see above, n. 2238.)

2261. *If I find in Sodom fifty righteous in the midst of the city.* That this signifies if truths are full of goods, is evident from the signification of " fifty," as being what is full, and from the signification of " the midst of the city," as being within truth, or in truth (as explained above, n. 2252, where the same words occur). It may be supposed that a man cannot but be saved if truths are full of goods. But be it known that there are very few truths with man, and that if there are any, they have no life unless there are goods in them; and that if there are goods in them, he is saved, but from Mercy. For, as before said, the truths with man are very few; and the goods which are in them have their quality in accordance with the truths, and the man's life. [2] Regarded in themselves, truths do not give life. It is goods that give life. Truths are only recipients of life, that is, of good. And therefore no one can ever say that he can be saved by truths (or as the common expression is, by faith alone), unless there is good in the truths which are of faith, and this good that must be in the truths must be the good of charity; hence faith itself, in the internal sense, is nothing else than charity (as shown above, n. 2231). As regards people's saying that the acknowledgment of truth is the faith that saves, be it known that with those who live in things contrary to charity, there cannot possibly be any acknowledgment, but only persuasion, to which there has been adjoined the life of the love of self or of the world; thus in the acknowledgment they refer to there is not the life of faith, which is that of charity. The worst men of all—from the love of self or the world, that is, for the sake of being eminent above others in what is called intelligence and wisdom, and thus of winning honors, reputation, and gains—can learn the truths of faith, and confirm them by many things; but still with them these truths are dead. [3] The life of truth, and thus of faith, is solely from the Lord, who is life itself. The Lord's life is mercy, which is that of love toward the universal human race. In the Lord's life those can in no wise have part who although they profess the truths of faith despise others in comparison with themselves, and who, when their life of the love of self and of the world is touched, hold the neighbor in hatred, and take delight in his loss of wealth, of honor, of reputation, and of life. But the case with the truths of faith is that by means of them man is regenerated, for they are the veriest vessels recipient of good. Such therefore as are the truths, and such as are the goods in the truths, and such as is their conjunction and the consequent capability of being perfected in the other life, such is the state of blessedness and happiness after death.

2262. *I will spare all the place for their sake.* That this signifies that they will be saved, follows from the series as a conclusion, and thus without explication. " Place" signifies state (as shown above, n. 1273, 1378), and therefore it is here said the " place" instead of the " city," to signify that they who are in such a state would be saved.

2263. Verse 27. *And Abraham answered and said, Behold I pray I have taken upon me to speak unto my Lord, and I am dust and ashes.* " Abraham answered and said," signifies the Lord's thought from the human; " Behold I pray I have taken upon me to speak unto my Lord, and I am dust and ashes," signifies the humiliation of the human as to its relative quality.

2264. *Abraham answered and said.* That this signifies the Lord's thought from the human, is evident from the signification of " Abraham" in this chapter, as being the Lord in respect to the human, concerning which several times above.

2265. *Behold I pray I have taken upon me to speak unto my Lord, and I am dust and ashes.* That this signifies the humiliation of the human as to its relative quality, is evident. The Lord's state in the human (or His state of humiliation), and the Lord's state in the Divine (or His state of glorification), have been treated of several times before; and it has been shown that in His state of humiliation the Lord spoke with Jehovah as with another; but in His state of glorification, as with Himself (n. 1999). As in the present passage Abraham (as before said) represents the Lord in His human, it is said in that state that relatively to the Divine the human is dust and ashes; on which account that state is also called His state of humiliation. The humiliation results from the self-acknowledgment that one is relatively of such a character. By the human in this place is not meant the Divine Human, but the human which the Lord derived from the mother, and which He utterly expelled, and put on in its stead the Divine Human. It is the former human, namely, the maternal human, of which "dust and ashes" are here predicated. (See what has been said above at n. 2159.)

2266. Verse 28. *Peradventure there shall lack five of the fifty righteous ; wilt Thou destroy all the city for five? and He said, I will not destroy it if I find there forty and five.* "Peradventure there shall lack five of the fifty righteous," signifies if there should be somewhat less; "wilt thou destroy all the city for five?" signifies, shall man perish for the little which is wanting? "and He said, I will not destroy it if I find there forty and five," signifies that he should not perish if good and truth could be conjoined together.

2267. *Peradventure there shall lack five of the fifty righteous.* That this signifies if there should be somewhat less, is evident from the signification of "five," as being a little, or less (in regard to which signification of this number, see Part First, n. 649). What the "fifty righteous" signify, has been shown above (n. 2252).

2268. *Wilt Thou destroy all the city for five?* That this signifies shall man perish for the little which is wanting, is evident from the signification of "five," as being a little (as just stated) ; and from the signification of a "city," as being truth, also explained before. In regard to the truths in it the human mind is compared in the Word to a "city," and is also so called; and in regard to the goods which are in the truths, it is compared to the inhabitants of the city, and the goods are also so called; for the case as regards these is much the same. If the truths which are in man's memories, and in the thoughts of his mind, are devoid of goods, they are like a city without inhabitants, and are in the same way vacant and empty. Nay, even of the angels it may be declared that when a man lives in love to the Lord, and in charity toward the neighbor, they dwell as it were in his truths, and insinuate affections of good from the Lord; for they are delighted to dwell thus, that is, to live with such men. Very different is it with those who are in some truths, but in no goods of charity.

2269. *And He said, I will not destroy it if I find there forty and five.* That this signifies that man should not perish if good and truth could be conjoined together, is evident from the signification of the number forty-five, as being conjunction. It has been already shown that the simple numbers retain their signification even when they are multiplied; and that consequently the greater numbers have a signification similar to that of the less; and such is the case with forty-five, which number is compounded by the multiplication of five into nine; and as it has been compounded by the multiplication of five into nine, it has the same signification as have "five" and "nine." That "five" signifies a little, was shown above (n. 649), and that "nine" signifies conjunction, or what is conjoined (n. 2075); and thus the signification here is : If goods have in some measure been conjoined with truths. That in the Word numbers signify actual things, or states, is evident from what was said about fifty (n. 2252); also from what has been shown before concerning numbers (n. 482, 487, 575, 647, 648, 755, 813, 1963, 1988). [2] It is because "five" signifies a little, and "forty-five" conjunction, that the very setting forth of these numbers in this verse is of such a nature, for it is said, "Peradventure there shall lack five of the fifty righteous;" and by this is signified, If there should be somewhat less; and then it is said, "Wilt Thou destroy all the city for five?" by which is signified, Shall they perish for the little which is wanting? for as "five" signifies a little, this number is not employed again, but it is said, "I will not destroy it if I find there forty and five;" by which is signified that they would not perish if good and truth could be conjoined together. The

reason also of its being said here "forty and five," and not
"if there lack five of fifty," is because "five" not only signifies a little (as was shown, n. 649), but also signifies disjunction (as was likewise shown in Part First, n. 1686); and therefore in order that not disjunction, but conjunction, might be
signified, this number forty-five is named; for "forty-five" denotes some conjunction, as stated above; and thus in the internal sense all things follow on in a beautiful sequence of
their own. [3] As regards the conjunction of good with truth,
it is an arcanum which cannot be described so that it can be
grasped by the ordinary comprehension. It must be told in a
few words. The more genuine and pure the truth, the better
can the good which is from the Lord be adapted into it as its
recipient vessel; but the less genuine and pure the truth, the
less can the good which is from the Lord be adapted into it;
for they must correspond to each other, and the conjunction
of the two is effected according to the correspondence. Goods
cannot possibly be insinuated into falsities, nor evils into
truths, as their recipient vessels; for they are of a contrary
character and nature, the one casting out the other as its
enemy; nay, should they attempt to conjoin themselves together, the one would spew out the other, that is to say, good
would spew out evil as if it were poison, and evil would spew
out good as if it were an emetic. Such enmity between good
and evil has been provided by the Lord in order to prevent
the possibility of their being commingled, for if they were
commingled, the man would perish. In the deceitful and in
hypocrites they are not far from being conjoined together,
but still precautions are taken by the Lord in order to prevent
their being so conjoined. This is the reason why in the other
life those who are deceitful and those who are hypocrites suffer
things more direful than those which are suffered by any others.

2270. Verse 29. *And he added yet to speak unto Him, and
said, Peradventure forty shall be found there ; and He said, I
will not do it for forty's sake.* "He added yet to speak unto
Him," signifies thought; "and said, Peradventure forty shall
be found there," signifies those who have been in temptations;
"and He said, I will not do it for forty's sake," signifies that
they shall be saved.

2271. *He added yet to speak unto Him.* That this signifies thought, is evident from the signification in the internal sense of "speaking." To "speak" or "speaking" is nothing else than that which flows forth from the thought; and as internal things are signified by external things—like understanding by "seeing," the understanding by the "eye," obedience by the "ear," and so forth—so thinking is signified by "speaking."

2272. *And he said, Peradventure forty shall be found there.* That this signifies those who have been in temptation, is evident from the signification of the number forty, as being temptations (explained in Part First, n. 730). How these things follow on in a series may be seen from temptations. Temptations take place to the end not only that the man may be confirmed in truths, but also that truths may be more closely conjoined with goods; for man is then battling for truths against falsities, and as he is then in interior distress and in torment, the delights of the life of cupidities and their derivative pleasures come to a cessation; and then goods flow in from the Lord, the consequence of which is that evils are at the same time regarded as abominable, and the effect of this is new thoughts of a nature contrary to those possessed before, to which the man may afterwards be bent, thus from evils to goods, and these goods be conjoined with truths. And as the conjunction of good with truth is effected by means of temptations, and as it has been said in a former verse that those would be saved with whom goods can be conjoined with truths, therefore there follows what is here said; and indeed in such words as to signify that goods and truths can be conjoined by means of temptations. This is the connection of the subject matters for those who are in the internal sense.

2273. *And He said, I will not do it for forty's sake.* That this signifies that they will be saved, is evident without any unfolding of the meaning. As regards those who in the preceding verse are signified by "forty-five," it was said, "I will not destroy it if I find forty and five," and the signification was that they should not perish if goods were able to be conjoined with truths, and there here follows a statement concerning the forty: "I will not do it for forty's sake;" by which is not signified that they should be saved on account of temptations, for there are some who even undergo temptations and who yield in them; and therefore with these goods are not conjoined. I would even say that a man is not saved on account of temptations if he places anything of merit in them; for if he does this, it is from the love of self, in that he congratulates himself on their account, and believes that he has merited heaven more than others, and at the same time he is thinking of his own pre-eminence over others by despising others in comparison with himself; all of which things are contrary to mutual love, and therefore to heavenly blessedness. [2] The temptations in which a man overcomes are attended with a belief that all others are more worthy than himself, and that he is infernal rather than heavenly; for while in temptations such ideas are presented to him; and therefore when after temptations he comes into thoughts contrary to these, it is an indication that he has not overcome; for the thoughts which the man has had in temptations are those to which can be bent the thoughts which he has after the temptations; and if the latter cannot be bent to the former, the man has either yielded in the temptation, or he again comes into similar ones, and sometimes into more grievous ones, until he has been reduced to such sanity that he believes he has merited nothing. Hence it is evident that by "forty" are here signified those with whom by means of temptations goods have been conjoined with truths.

2274. Verse 30. *And he said, Oh let not my Lord be angry, and I will speak : peradventure thirty shall be found there ; and He said, I will not do it if I find thirty there.* " And he said, Oh let not my Lord be angry, and I will speak," signifies anxiety concerning the human race ; " peradventure thirty shall be found there," signifies somewhat of combat; "and He said, I will not do it if I find thirty there," signifies that these shall be saved.

2275. *And he said, Oh let not my Lord be angry, and I will speak.* That this signifies anxiety concerning the state of the human race, may be seen, not so much from the words, as from the affection that belongs to them. The internal sense of the Word contains within it two things, to wit, what is spiritual, and what is celestial. That which is spiritual consists in there being comprehended, abstractedly from the letter, actual things

to which the literal sense serves as an object, just as do those
things which the eye sees, when they serve as objects for sug-
gesting thought about matters of a more exalted nature. That
which is celestial consists in there being solely perceived the
affection that belongs to the actual things that are in the internal sense. In the former are the spiritual angels, in the
latter are the celestial angels. They who are in the latter,
that is, in the affection, perceive at once from the affection
alone what the letter involves when it is being read by man,
and from it they form for themselves celestial ideas, and this
with endless variety, and in an ineffable manner, in accordance
with the onflowing harmony of the celestial things of love that
are in the affection. From this we may see what the Word of
the Lord contains within its remote recesses. When therefore
these words are read: "Oh let not my Lord be angry, and I
will speak," the celestial angels at once perceive a certain
anxiety, and indeed the anxiety of love toward the human
race; and at the same time there are insinuated into them innumerable and ineffable things in regard to the anxiety of love
which the Lord felt when He thought about the state of the
human race.

2276. *Peradventure thirty shall be found.* That this signifies somewhat of combat, is evident from the signification of
the number thirty. That "thirty" signifies somewhat of combat, thus but a little of combat, comes from the fact that this
number is compounded by the multiplication of five (by which
is signified some little), and six (by which is signified labor or
combat, as was shown in Part First, n. 649, 720, 737, 900,
1709). [2] Hence also this number, wherever read in the
Word, signifies something that is relatively little; as in *Zechariah :—*

I said unto them, If it be good in your eyes, give me my hire ; and if
not, forbear ; and they weighed my hire, thirty pieces of silver. And
Jehovah said unto me, Cast it unto the potter, the goodly price * whereat
I was valued by them ; and I took the thirty silver pieces, and cast it to
the potter in the house of Jehovah (xi. 12, 13) ;

denoting that they valued so little the Lord's merit, and re-
demption and salvation by Him. The "potter" denotes refor-

* Literally, " the magnificence of the price." [REVISER.]

mation and regeneration. [3] Hence the same thirty silver pieces are spoken of in *Matthew :*—

They took the thirty pieces of silver, the price of Him whom they had bought from the sons of Israel, and gave them for the potter's field, as the Lord commanded me (xxvii. 9, 10) ;

from which it is plainly evident that "thirty" here denotes the price of what is but little valued. The valuation of a servant who was held as being of little account, was thirty shekels ; as is evident in *Moses :*—

If the ox gore a manservant, or a maidservant, he shall give unto their master thirty shekels of silver ; and the ox shall be stoned (*Exod.* xxi. 32).

Of how little account a servant was held, is evident in the same chapter (verses 20, 21). In the internal sense a "servant" denotes labor. [4] That the Levites were taken for the work of the ministerial office—which is described by the expression "one coming to exercise warfare, and to do the work in the tent"—from a "son of thirty years to one of fifty" (*Num.* iv. 3, 23, 30, 35, 39, 43), was because "thirty" signified those who were being initiated, and who therefore could as yet exercise but little warfare as understood in the spiritual sense. [5] So in other passages where "thirty" is named in the Word ; as that they should offer "upon a son of an ox a meat-offering of three tenths" (*Num.* xv. 9) ; which was because the sacrifice of an ox represented natural good (as shown above, n. 2180) ; and natural good is but little in comparison with spiritual good, which was represented by the sacrifice of a ram ; and still less in comparison with celestial good, which was represented by the sacrifice of a lamb ; in connection with which there was another rate of tenths for the meat-offering, as is evident in the same chapter (verses 4 to 6 ; also *Num.* xxviii. 12, 13, 20, 21, 28, 29 ; xxix. 3, 4, 9, 10, 14, 15) ; which rates of tenths, or which proportions, would never have been commanded, unless they had involved heavenly arcana. In *Mark* also "thirty" denotes a little :—

The seed which fell into good ground yielded fruit growing up and increasing, and brought forth, one thirty, and another sixty, and another a hundred (iv. 8), where "thirty" denotes a small growth, and that which has labored but little. These numbers would not have been marked out for use, unless they had contained within them the things which they signify.

2277. *He said, I will not do it if I find thirty there.* That this signifies that these shall be saved, is evident from the series or connection of things in the internal sense, without any unfolding of the meaning.

2278. Verse 31. *And he said, Behold I pray I have taken upon me to speak unto my Lord : peradventure twenty shall be found there ; and He said, I will not destroy it for twenty's sake.* " He said, Behold I pray I have taken upon me to speak unto my Lord," signifies here as before the humiliation of the human before the Divine ; " peradventure twenty shall be found there," signifies if there be not anything of combat, but still there be good ; "and He said, I will not destroy it for twenty's sake," signifies that they will be saved.

2279. *He said, Behold I pray I have taken upon me to speak unto my Lord.* That this signifies the humiliation of the human before the Divine, is evident from what was said above (n. 2265), where are the same words.

2280. *Peradventure twenty shall be found there.* That this signifies if there be not anything of combat, but still there be good, is evident from the signification of " twenty." As all the numbers that are mentioned in the Word signify actual things, and states (as before said and shown in many places, see n. 2252), so also does " twenty ;" and what it signifies can be seen from its derivation, namely, from twice ten. " Ten" in the Word, as also " tenths," signify remains, by which is meant everything good and true that the Lord insinuates into man from infancy even to the end of his life, and which are treated of in the following verse. Twice ten, or double tenths, that is, twenty, signify the same, but in a higher degree, namely, good. [2] Goods of three kinds are signified by remains, namely, the goods of infancy, the goods of ignorance, and the goods of intelligence. The goods of infancy are those which are insinuated into man from his very birth up to the age in which he is beginning to be instructed and to know something. The goods of ignorance are what are insinuated when he is being instructed and is beginning to know something. The goods of intelligence are what are insinuated when he is able to reflect upon what is good and what is true. The good of infancy exists from the man's infancy up to the tenth year of his age; the good of ignorance, from this age up to his twentieth year. From this year the man begins to become rational, and to have the faculty of reflecting upon good and truth, and to procure for himself the good of intelligence. [3] The good of ignorance is that which is signified by "twenty," because those who are in the good of ignorance do not come into any temptation; for no one is tempted before he is able to reflect, and in his own way to perceive the nature of good and truth. Those who have received goods by means of temptations have been treated of in the two immediately preceding verses; those who have not been in temptations, and yet have good, are now treated of in this verse. [4] As those who have this good, which is called the good of ignorance, are signified by "twenty," all those who went forth from Egypt were reckoned from "a son of twenty years" and upward; or as it is expressed, "every one going forth into the army," by whom are meant those who were no longer in the good of ignorance, concerning whom we read in *Numbers* (i. 20, 24, 26, 28, 30, 32, 34, 38, 40, 42, 45; xxvi. 4); and also that all those who were more than twenty years old died in the wilderness (xxxii. 10, 11), because evil could be imputed to them, and they represented those who yield in temptations; as well as that the valuing made of a male, from "a son of five years" to "a son of twenty years" was "twenty shekels" (*Lev.* xxvii. 5); and another valuing from "a son of twenty years" old to one of sixty was fifty shekels (verse 3). [5] As regards the before-mentioned goods, namely those of infancy, of ignorance, and of intelligence, the case is this. The good of intelligence is the best, for this is of wisdom; the good which precedes it, namely that of ignorance, is indeed good, but as there is but little of intelligence in it, it cannot be called the good of wisdom; and as for the good of infancy, it is indeed good in itself, but still it is less good than the other two; for as yet there is not any truth of intelligence adjoined to it, and thus it has not become any good of wisdom, but it is only a plane for being able to become so; for it is the knowledges of good and truth that cause a man to be wise as a man. Infancy itself, by which is signified innocence, does not belong to infancy, but to wisdom ; as can be better seen from what will be said about little children in the other life, at the end of this chapter. [6] By "twenty," in this verse, as has been said, there is signified no other good than the good of ignorance ; which good is not only declared to be with those who are under their twentieth year, as already said, but also with all who are in the good of charity and at the same time in ignorance of truth, as are those within the church who are in the good of charity, but from whatever cause, do not know what the truth of faith is ; as is the case with very many of those who think devoutly about God and kindly about the neighbor ; and as is also the case with all outside the church, who are called Gentiles, and who in like manner live in the good of charity. Both the latter and the former, although not in the truths of faith, yet being in good, are in the faculty of receiving the truths of faith in the other life equally as are little children ; for their understanding has not as yet been tainted with principles of falsity, nor their will so confirmed in a life of evil, because they are ignorant of its being falsity and evil ; and the life of charity is attended with this : that the falsity and evil of ignorance may be easily bent to truth and good. Not so is it with those who have confirmed themselves in things contrary to the truth, and at the same time have lived a life in things contrary to good. [7] In other cases by "two tenths" in the Word is signified good both celestial and spiritual, good celestial and thence spiritual by the two tenths of which every loaf of the showbread or bread of faces was prepared (*Lev.* xxiv. 5), and spiritual good by the two tenths of the meat-offering with the sacrifice of the ram (*Num.* xv. 6 ; xxviii. 12, 20, 28 ; xxix. 3, 9, 14), concerning which, of the Lord's Divine mercy elsewhere.

2281. *And He said I will not destroy it for twenty's sake.* That this signifies that they will be saved, is evident from the series of things in the internal sense, and thus without any unfolding of the meaning.

2282. Verse 32. *And he said, Oh let not my Lord be angry, and I will speak but this once : peradventure ten shall be found* *there ; and He said, I will not destroy it for ten's sake.* " He said, Oh let not my Lord be angry, and I will speak but this once," signifies anxiety still continued concerning the state of the human race; "peradventure ten shall be found there," signifies if there should still be remains; "and He said, I will not destroy it for ten's sake," signifies that they will be saved.

2283. *He said, Oh let not my Lord be angry, and I will speak but this once.* That this signifies anxiety still continued concerning the state of the human race, is evident from the affection of these words, as shown above (n. 2275), where the same words occur.

2284. *Peradventure ten shall be found there.* That this signifies if there should still be remains, is evident from the signification of the number "ten," as being remains (explained in Part First, n. 576, 1738). What remains are has been stated and shown before in various places (as in n. 468, 530, 560, 561, 660, 661, 1050, 1738, 1906), namely, that they are all the good and all the truth with man which lie stored up in his memories and in his life. [2] It is well known that there is nothing good and nothing true, except from the Lord; and also that what is good and true is continually inflowing from the Lord into man, but that it is received in various ways, and in fact in accordance with the life of evil, and in accordance with the principles of falsity in which the man has confirmed himself. These are what either quench, or stifle, or pervert the goods and truths that are continually flowing in from the Lord. Lest therefore goods should be commingled with evils, and truths with falsities (for if they were commingled the man would perish eternally), the Lord separates them, and stores up in his interior man the goods and truths which the man receives; whence He will never permit them to come forth so long as the man is in evil and falsity, but only at such a time as he is in a holy state, or in some anxiety, sickness, or other trouble. These things which the Lord has thus stored up with man are what are called "remains," of which very much mention is made in the Word; but it has not yet been known to any one that this is what they signify. [3] According to the quality and quantity of the remains—that is, of the good and truth with a man—does he enjoy bliss and happiness in the other life; for, as has been said, these remains are stored up in his interior man, and they are opened at the time when the man has left corporeal and worldly things behind. The Lord alone knows the quality and extent of the remains in a man; the man himself cannot possibly know this, for at the present day man is of such a character that he is able to counterfeit what is good, while within there is nothing but evil; and a man may also appear to be evil and yet have good within. On this account no man is ever allowed to judge concerning the quality of the spiritual life of another, for the Lord alone, as before said, knows this; but every one may judge of another in regard to the quality of his moral and civil life, for this concerns society.   [4] It is very common for those who have taken up an opinion respecting any truth of faith, to judge of others that they cannot be saved, unless they believe as *they* do—a judgment which the Lord has forbidden (*Matt.* vii. 1, 2). On the other hand, I have learned from much experience that men of every religion are saved, provided that by a life of charity they have received remains of good and of apparent truth.   This is what is meant by its being said that if ten were found, they should not be destroyed for the ten's sake; by which is signified that they would be saved if there were remains.   [5] The life of charity consists in thinking kindly of another, and in wishing him well; and in perceiving joy in one's self from the fact that others also are saved.   But those have not the life of charity who desire that none should be saved except those who believe as they do; and especially is this the case with those who are indignant that it is otherwise.   This may be seen from the mere fact that more from the Gentiles are saved than from Christians; for those Gentiles who have thought kindly of their neighbor and have wished well to him, receive the truths of faith in the other life better than those who are called Christians, and acknowledge the Lord more than Christians do.   For nothing is more delightful and blessed to the angels than to instruct those who come from the earth into the other life.

2285. *I will not destroy it for ten's sake.* That this signifies that they will be saved, is evident from the series of the things in the internal sense, and thus without any unfolding of the meaning.

2286. Verse 33. *And Jehovah went when He had completed His speaking unto Abraham ; and Abraham returned unto his place.* " Jehovah went when He had completed His speaking unto Abraham," signifies that this state of perception in which the Lord was, then ceased to be such ; " and Abraham returned unto his place," signifies that the Lord returned into the state in which He had been before He perceived these things.

2287. *Jehovah went when He had completed His speaking unto Abraham.* That this signifies that this state of perception in which the Lord was, then ceased to be such, is evident from the signification of " speaking," and from the representation of Abraham. " To speak," in the internal sense, signifies to think (as shown above, n. 2271) ; but here it signifies to perceive, because it is declared of Jehovah that He " had completed His speaking" to Abraham ; for the thought was from perception, as before said, and the perception was from the Lord's internal, which was Jehovah. But " Abraham" in this chapter represents the Lord in the human state, as often stated above. From this we can see that by its being said that " Jehovah went when He had completed His speaking unto Abraham," nothing else is signified in the internal sense than that the state of perception in which the Lord had been, then came to its close and completion. The reason why the Lord's perception and thought are so much treated of in this chapter in the internal sense, may be seen above (n. 2249).

2288. *Abraham returned to his place.* That this signifies that the Lord returned into the state in which He had been before He perceived these things, is evident from the representation of Abraham in this chapter, as being the Lord in the human state ; and from the signification of a " place," as being a state (as shown above, Part First, n. 1273, 1378) ; thus to " return to his place," in the internal sense, here signifies to return to the state in which He had been before. That while He lived in this world the Lord had two states, namely, a state of humiliation and a state of glorification, has been said and shown before. His state of humiliation was when He was in the human which He took by inheritance from the mother; His state of glorification was when He was in the Divine which He had from Jehovah His Father. The former state, namely, that of the human from the mother, the Lord altogether put off, and put on the Divine Human, when He passed out of the world, and returned to the Divine Itself, in which He was from eternity (*John* xvii. 5), together with the Human made Divine; from both of which comes the Holy which fills the universal heaven. Thus from the Divine Itself and the Divine Human, by means of the proceeding Holy, He directs the universe.

CONCERNING THE STATE OF LITTLE CHILDREN IN THE OTHER LIFE.

2289. I have been given to know with certainty that all little children in the wide world who die, are raised again by the Lord and are taken up into heaven, and there are brought up and instructed among angels who have the care of them, and that they also grow up in proportion to their advance in intelligence and wisdom. From this we can see how immense is the Lord's heaven from little children alone; for they are all instructed in the truths of faith and in the goods of mutual love, and become angels.

2290. They who know nothing about the state of the life after death may suppose that little children are in angelic intelligence and wisdom as soon as they come into the other life; but I have been instructed by much experience that such is not the case. Those who die not long after birth are of an infantile mind, almost as on earth, nor do they know anything more; for they possess only the faculty of knowing, and from this of understanding, and from this of being wise; which faculty is more perfect because they are not in the body, but are spirits. That they are so when they first come into heaven, has not merely been told, but has also been shown me; for of the Lord's Divine mercy little children have on several occasions been sent to me in choirs, and I have also been allowed to read to them the Lord's Prayer; and at the same time I have been given to perceive how the angels in whose company they were, insinuated into their tender and novitiate ideas the meaning of the things which are in this Prayer, and filled them, so far as the little ones were able to receive; and afterwards how the capacity was given the little ones of thinking such things as it were from themselves.

2291. The nature of their tender understanding was also shown me when I was praying the Lord's Prayer; and they then inflowed into the ideas of my thought from their own understanding, which was so tender that they understood scarcely anything beyond the sense of the words. Yet their ideas in that tenderness were capable of being opened even to the Lord, that is, even from the Lord, for the Lord inflows into the ideas of little children in especial, from the inmosts; for nothing has as yet closed their ideas, as is the case with adults : no principles of falsity against the understanding of truth, and no life of evil against the reception of good, and thus not against becoming wise.

2292. From all this we can see that little children do not come into the state of angels immediately after death; but that they are introduced successively, by means of the knowledges of good and truth, and this in accordance with all heavenly order; for the very least of all the things of their natural disposition are there most exquisitely perceived; and according to all the movements of their inclination both in general and in particular they are impelled to receive the truths of good and the goods of truth, and this under the Lord's constant oversight.

2293. Especially are they all the time initiated into knowing no other Father, and thereafter in acknowledging no other than the Lord alone, and that they have life from Him; for that they are lives, that is, truly human and angelic lives, is from the intelligence of truth and the wisdom of good, which they have solely from the Lord. Hence it is that they know no otherwise than that they have been born in heaven.

2294. Many times when children have been with me in choirs, they being as yet quite infantile, they have been heard as a tender something devoid of order, so that they did not as yet act as a one, as they do afterwards when they become older; and what surprised me, the spirits about me could not refrain from trying to lead them to think and to speak. Such a desire is innate in spirits. But I often noticed that the little children resisted, not being willing to think or speak in such a way. I have often observed this refusal and resistance attended with a kind of indignation, and when any ability to speak was granted them they merely said that *it was not so*. I have been instructed that such is the temptation of little children in the other life, to accustom and inaugurate them not only in the resisting of falsity and evil, but also in not allowing themselves to think, speak, and act from others, and thus in not suffering themselves to be led by any other than the Lord alone.

2295. When little children are not in that state, but in a more interior sphere, namely, the angelic sphere, they cannot possibly be infested by spirits; even if they are in the midst of them. Moreover the little children who are in the other life are sometimes sent by the Lord to little children on earth (although the little child on earth is quite unaware of it), and those little ones of heaven are in the highest degree delighted with these little ones of earth.

2296. The manner in which all things are insinuated into the little ones of the other life by means of delightful and pleasant things suited to their genius, has also been shown me; for I have been permitted to see the little children most beautifully clothed, having their bosoms and tender arms encircled with garlands of flowers that were resplendent with the most pleasing and heavenly colors. Once also I was permitted to see the little children with their maiden educatresses in a paradisal garden, that consisted not so much of trees, as of laurel espaliers and of bowers thus formed; beautifully laid out with paths that led toward the more interior parts; and I also saw the little children themselves, clothed as above described; and when they entered the garden the flower arch above the entrance shone most joyously. From this we can see the nature of their deliciousnesses, and also that by means of pleasant and delightful things they are introduced into the goods of innocence and charity, which are continually being insinuated by the Lord into those delightful and pleasant things.

2297. Moreover, as the little children are perfected, they are encompassed with atmospheres in accordance with the state of their perfection. (That in the other life there are atmospheres of endless variety and ineffable beauty, may be seen from experience in Part First, n. 1621.) Especially are there presented to them atmospheres as of sporting little children in least forms, not visible, but perceptible only by an inmost idea; from which they receive this heavenly idea: that everything around them is alive, and that they are in the Lord's life, and this idea affects their deepest being with happiness.

2298. It has been shown me by a method of communication that is familiar in the other life of what nature are the ideas of little children when they see any objects. They were as if everything was alive, so that they had life in every idea of their thought. I also perceived that little children on earth have very similar ideas when they are at play; for as yet they have not reflection, such as adults have, as regards that which is devoid of life.

2299. Especially are the little children instructed by means of representatives adapted to their various genius; and how beautiful these are, and at the same time how full of wisdom from within, no one can possibly believe. In this way there is by degrees insinuated into them an intelligence that draws its soul from good. I may here mention one representative only that I was permitted to see, from which the nature of the rest may be inferred. They represented the Lord rising out of the sepulchre, and at the same time the unition of His Human with the Divine; which was done in a manner so wise as to surpass all human wisdom, and at the same time in an innocent infantile manner. They presented also the idea of a sepulchre, but not at the same time the idea of the Lord, except so remotely that it was scarcely perceived that it was the Lord, except as it were from afar; for the reason that in the idea of a sepulchre there is something funereal, which they thus removed. They afterwards in the most discreet manner admitted into the sepulchre something of an atmospherical nature, yet appearing thinly aqueous, by which they signified, also with becoming remoteness, spiritual life in baptism. I afterwards saw represented by them the Lord's descent to the bound, and His ascent with the bound into heaven; and this with incomparable sagacity and piety. A child-like feature of the representation was that when they represented the Lord among the bound in the lower earth, they let down cords that were almost invisible, and that were very soft and tender, with which to lift the Lord in His ascent; with a constant holy fear lest anything in the representative should touch upon something in which there was not what is spiritual celestial. Besides other representatives wherein the little ones are, and by which, as well as by sports of infancy adapted to their various dispositions, they are brought into knowledges of truth and affections of good.

2300. Moreover little children are of diverse genius and of diverse natural disposition, and this from what they inherit from their parents, and by succession from grandparents and great-grandparents; for the actual life with parents, confirmed by habit, becomes a second nature, and is implanted hereditarily in the infants, and this is the source of their diverse tendencies.

2301. Speaking generally, little children are of a genius either celestial or spiritual. Those of a celestial genius are well distinguished from those of a spiritual genius. The former think, speak, and act more softly, so that hardly anything appears except a fluent something from the love of good to the Lord and toward other little children; but the latter do not think, speak, and act so softly, but something as it were winged and vibratile shows itself in all their doings; and is also evident from their indignation; besides other characteristic differences. Thus every little child has a natural disposition different from that of every other, and each is educated according to his natural disposition.

2302. There are certain and numerous societies of angels who have the care of little children; and which are chiefly from the female sex, who had loved them very tenderly in the life of the body. The little children who are more virtuous than others, by an established custom they offer to the Lord.

2303. Angelic spirits who were above in front spoke with me in angelic speech not distinguished into words, saying that their state was a state of the tranquillity of peace, and that there were also little children among them, and that they were conscious of blessedness from being in association with them; these spirits also were of the female sex. They said further concerning infants on earth, that directly after birth angels from the heaven of innocence are with them; in the succeeding age angels from the heaven of the tranquillity of peace; and afterwards those who are from the societies of charity; and then, as the innocence and charity with the young children decrease, other angels are with them; and at length, when they become older and enter into a life foreign to charity, angels are indeed present, but more remotely, and this in accordance with the ends of life, which the angels especially regulate by continually insinuating good ones, and turning aside evil ones; and they flow in more nearly or more remotely, in proportion as they can or cannot do this.

2304. Many may suppose that in the other life the little children remain such, and are as little children among the angels. They who do not know what an angel is, may have been confirmed in this opinion by the images that are common in churches and elsewhere, where angels are represented as little children. Very different however is the actual truth. It is intelligence and wisdom that make an angel, and so long as the little children have not these they are indeed with the angels, but are not angels. But when they have become intelligent and wise, then for the first time do they become angels; and it is a wonderful fact that they then do not appear as little children, but as adults; for they are then no longer of an infantile genius, but of a more adult angelic one. Intelligence and wisdom are attended with this result, for it is understanding and judgment, and a life according thereto, that cause every one to appear to himself and to others as an adult; as every one can see. [2] I have not only been informed by the angels that such is the case, but I have also spoken with a certain one who had died when an infant, and yet then appeared as an adult. The same also spoke with his brother who had died in adult age, and this from so much mutual brotherly love that his brother could not refrain from tears, saying that he perceived no otherwise than that it was love itself that was speaking. Besides other examples not necessary to mention.

2305. There are some who suppose that innocence is the same as infancy, for the reason that the Lord said of little children that of such is heaven; and that they who do not become as little children cannot enter into the kingdom of the heavens. But they who so imagine do not know the internal sense of the Word, nor therefore what is meant by "infancy." By "infancy" is meant the innocence of intelligence and wisdom, which is such that they acknowledge that they have life from the Lord alone, and that the Lord is their only Father; for that man is man is from the intelligence of truth and the wisdom of good, which he has solely from the Lord. Innocence itself, which in the Word is called "infancy," has no existence or abode except in wisdom; so much so that the wiser one is, the more innocent he is; on which account the Lord is innocence itself, because wisdom itself.

2306. As regards the innocence of little children, being as yet devoid of intelligence and wisdom it is only a kind of plane for receiving genuine innocence, which they receive by degrees as they become wise. The quality of the innocence of little children has been represented to me by a wooden something almost void of life, which is vivified in proportion as they are perfected by means of knowledges of truth and affections of good. The quality of genuine innocence was afterwards represented by a most beautiful little child, full of life, and naked; for the innocent themselves, who are in the inmost heaven, and thereby are nearest the Lord, appear before the eyes of other angels no otherwise than as little children, and indeed naked; for innocence is represented by the nakedness of which they are not ashamed, as we read of the first man and his wife in paradise. In a word, the wiser the angels are, the more innocent they are; and the more innocent they are, the more do they appear to themselves as little children. Hence it is that in the Word innocence is signified by "infancy." But concerning the state of innocence, of the Lord's Divine mercy hereafter.

2307. Concerning little children I have inquired of the angels whether they are pure from evils, seeing that they have no actual evil, as adults have. But I was told that they are equally in evil; nay, that they too are nothing but evil;

but that they, like all the angels, are withheld from evil and are kept in good by the Lord, insomuch that it appears to them as if they were in good from themselves. And therefore also the little children, after they have become adults in heaven, in order to prevent them from being of the false opinion regarding themselves that the good in them is from themselves, and not from the Lord, are sometimes remitted into their evils which they have received by inheritance, and are left in them until they know, acknowledge, and believe, that the truth is as has been said. A certain one also who had died when an infant, but had grown up in heaven, was of a similar opinion; and therefore he was remitted into the life of the evils inborn in him, and it was then given me to perceive from his sphere that he had a disposition to domineer over others, and that he esteemed lascivious things as of no account; which were evils that he had inherited from his parents. But after he had acknowledged that such was his nature, he was again received among the angels with whom he had been before.

2308. No one ever suffers punishment in the other life on account of hereditary evil, because it is not his, and therefore he is not to blame for being of such a nature; but every one suffers on account of the actual evil which is his own, and consequently for so much of the hereditary evil as he has appropriated to himself by actual life (as before said, n. 966). It is not therefore for the sake of punishment that the little children on becoming adult are remitted into the state of their hereditary evil; but that they may know that of themselves they are nothing but evil, and that it is of the Lord's mercy that they are taken away from the hell that is with them into heaven; and that they are not in heaven by their own merit, but of the Lord; and thereby to prevent them from boasting before others of the good that is in them; for this is contrary to the good of mutual love, as it is contrary to the truth of faith.

2309. From what has been adduced we can see what is the nature of the education of little children in heaven, namely, that by means of the intelligence of truth and the wisdom of good they are introduced into the angelic life, which is love to the Lord, and mutual love, in which loves there is innocence. But how contrary is the education of little children on earth, with many, has been evidenced from this one example. I was in the street of a great city, and saw little boys fighting with one another. A crowd gathered and looked on with much pleasure; and I was informed that the parents themselves urge on their little boys to such fights. The good spirits and angels who saw these things through my eyes were so averse to them that I perceived their horror, especially at the fact that the parents incite them to such things; saying that thus in their earliest age they extinguish all the mutual love and all the innocence which little children receive from the Lord, and initiate them into hatred and revenge; consequently that they deliberately shut out their children from heaven, where there is nothing but mutual love. Let parents therefore who wish well to their children beware of such things.

At the end of the preceding seventeenth chapter of *Genesis* the Last Judgment is treated of, and at the end of this eighteenth chapter the state of little children in the other life—in both cases from experience of things which have been seen and heard in the world of spirits and in the heaven of angels.

CHAPTER THE NINETEENTH.

2310. The Internal Sense of the Word has already been many times treated of; but I am aware that few can believe that there is such a sense in everything of the Word, not only in the prophetical, but also in the historical parts. That there is such a sense in the prophetical parts can more easily be believed, because in them there is not so connected a series of things, and there are also strange expressions in them, from which every one may conjecture that they contain within them some secret meaning. But that there is also such a sense in the historical parts, does not so easily appear, both because this has hitherto come into no one's mind, and because the historical parts are such as to keep the attention fixed on themselves, and thereby to draw away the mind from thinking that anything of a deeper nature is there stored up; and also because the historicals are truly such as related. [2] Nevertheless no one can fail to infer that within these parts of the Word also there is what is heavenly and Divine, and which does not shine forth; *first*, from the fact that the Word was sent down by the Lord through heaven to man, and therefore differs in its origin (and what the nature of this origin is, and that it is so different and distant from the literal sense as not even to be seen, and consequently not acknowledged, by those who are merely worldly, will be shown by many things in what follows); *secondly*, from the fact that the Word, being Divine, has not been written for man only, but also for the angels with man, in order that it might serve not only for use to the human race, but also for use to heaven; and that in this way the Word is a medium uniting heaven and earth. This union takes place by means of the church, and in fact by means of the Word in the church, which is for this reason such as it is, and is distinguished from all other writing. [3] As regards the historical parts specifically, unless they in like manner contained Divine and heavenly things in a sense abstracted from the letter, they could never be acknowledged by any one who thinks more deeply to be the inspired Word, even as to every jot. Would any one say that the abominable affair of Lot's daughters, treated of at the end of this chapter, would be related in a Divine Word? or Jacob's peeling rods and making the white appear, and placing them in the watering-troughs, that the flock might bear party-colored, speckled, and spotted young? besides many other things in the rest of the books of *Moses*, of *Joshua*, the *Judges*, *Samuel*, and the *Kings*, which would be of no importance, and in regard to which it would be a matter of indifference whether they were known or not known unless they enfolded deeply within them a secret Divine meaning. If it were not for this, they would differ in no respect from other historical narratives, which have sometimes been so written that they seem more effective. [4] As the learned world is unacquainted with the fact that Divine and heavenly things lie hidden even within the historical parts of the Word, were it not for the holy veneration for the books of the Word which has been impressed upon them from childhood, they would be quite ready to say in their hearts that the Word is not holy except solely from that fact; when yet it is not from that, but because there is within it an internal sense which is heavenly and Divine, and which causes it to unite heaven with earth, that is, angelic minds with human minds, and thereby these latter with the Lord.

2311. That the Word is of such a nature, and that it is in this way distinct from all other writing, may be seen also from the fact that not only do all the names signify actual things (as shown above, n. 1224, 1264, 1876, 1888), but all the words also have a spiritual sense; and they thus signify another thing in heaven from what they do on earth, and this most constantly, in both the prophetical and the historical parts. When these names and words are set forth in their heavenly sense in accordance with their constant signification in the whole Word, there comes forth an internal sense which is the angelic Word. This twofold sense of the Word is circumstanced as are the body and the soul; the literal sense is like the body, and the internal sense is like the soul; and as the body lives by means of the soul, so does the literal sense by means of the internal sense. Through the internal sense the Lord's life inflows into the literal sense, in accordance with the affection of him who is reading it. Hence it is evident how holy is the Word, although it does not appear so to worldly minds.

CHAPTER XIX.

1. And the two angels came to Sodom in the evening; and Lot was sitting in the gate of Sodom; and Lot saw, and rose up to meet them, and he bowed himself with his face to the earth.

2. And he said, Behold I pray my lords, turn aside, I pray, to the house of your servant, and pass the night, and wash your feet; and in the morning ye shall rise, and go on your

way; and they said, Nay, for we will pass the night in the street.

3. And he urged them exceedingly; and they turned aside unto him, and came to his house; and he made them a feast, and baked unleavened [bread]; and they did eat.

4. Scarcely yet were they lain down when the men of the city, the men of Sodom, compassed the house about, from·a boy even to an old man, all the people from the uttermost part.

5. And they cried unto Lot, and said unto him, Where are the men that came unto thee this night? Bring them out unto us, that we may know them.

6. And Lot went out unto them to the door and shut the door behind him.

7. And he said, I pray you, my brethren, do not wickedly.

8. Behold I pray I have two daughters, who have not known man; let me I pray bring them out unto you, and ye may do unto them as is good in your eyes; only unto these men do not anything; for therefore are they come under the shadow of my roof.

9. And they said, Come on. And they said, Is one come to sojourn, and shall he judge indeed? Now will we do worse to thee than to them. And they pressed upon the man, upon Lot, exceedingly; and drew near to break open the door.

10. And the men put forth their hand, and brought Lot into the house to them, and shut the door.

11. And the men who were at the door of the house they smote with blindness, from small even to great; and they labored to find the door.

12. And the men said unto Lot, Hast thou yet any one here? son-in-law, and thy sons, and thy daughters, and whomsoever thou hast in the city, bring them out of the place.

13. For we will destroy this place, because their cry is become great before Jehovah; and Jehovah hath sent us to destroy it.

14. And Lot went out, and spake to his sons-in-law that were to marry his daughters, and said, Up, get you out of this place, for Jehovah will destroy the city. And he was in the eyes of his sons-in-law as one that jested.

15. And when the dawn arose the angels pressed Lot to

hasten, saying, Arise, take thy wife, and thy two daughters that are found, lest thou be consumed in the iniquity of the city.

16. And he lingered; and the men laid hold of his hand, and of the hand of his wife, and of the hand of his two daughters, in the clemency of Jehovah upon him, and they led him forth, and set him without the city.

17. And it came to pass, when they were leading them forth abroad, that he said, Escape for thy life; look not back behind thee, and stay not in all the plain; escape to the mountain, lest thou be consumed.

18. And Lot said unto them, Nay I pray my lords.

19. Behold I pray thy servant hath found grace in thine eyes, and thou hast made thy mercy great, which thou hast done with me, to make alive my soul, and I cannot escape to the mountain, lest peradventure evil cleave to me, and I die.

20. Behold I pray this city is near to flee thither, and it is a little one; let me, I pray, escape thither—is it not a little one?—and my soul shall live.

21. And he said unto him, Behold I have accepted thy face as to this word also, that I will not overthrow the city of which thou hast spoken.

22. Hasten, escape thither, for I cannot do anything until thou be come thither. Therefore he called the name of the city Zoar.

23. The sun was gone forth upon the earth, and Lot came to Zoar.

24. And Jehovah caused it to rain upon Sodom and upon Gomorrah brimstone and fire from Jehovah out of heaven.

25. And He overthrew those cities, and all the plain, and all the inhabitants of the cities, and the growth of the ground.

26. And his wife looked back behind him, and became a pillar of salt.

27. And Abraham rose up early in the morning, unto the place where he had stood before Jehovah.

28. And he looked against the faces of Sodom and Gomorrah, and against all the faces of the land of the plain, and he saw and behold the smoke of the land went up, as the smoke of a furnace.

29. And it came to pass when God destroyed the cities of the plain, that God remembered Abraham, and sent Lot out of the midst of the overthrow, when He overthrew the cities in which Lot dwelt.

30. And Lot went up out of Zoar, and dwelt in the mountain, and his two daughters with him; for he feared to dwell in Zoar; and he dwelt in a cave, he and his two daughters.

31. And the firstborn said unto the younger, Our father is old, and there is no man in the earth to come unto us according to the way of all the earth.

32. Come, let us make our father drink wine, and let us lie with him, and let us quicken seed from our father.

33. And they made their father drink wine that night; and the firstborn went in, and lay with her father; and he knew not when she lay down, nor when she arose.

34. And it came to pass on the morrow, that the firstborn said unto the younger, Behold, I lay yesternight with my father; let us make him drink wine this night also, and go thou in and lie with him, and let us quicken seed from our father.

35. And they made their father drink wine that night also; and the younger arose, and lay with him; and he knew not when she lay down nor when she arose.

36. And the two daughters of Lot conceived by their father.

37. And the firstborn bare a son, and called his name Moab: he is the father of Moab even unto this day.

38. And the younger she also bare a son, and called his name Ben-ammi: he is the father of the sons of Ammon unto this day.

THE CONTENTS.

2312. In this chapter, in the internal sense, by "Lot" is described the state of the Spiritual Church which is in the good of charity but in external worship: how in course of time it declines.

2313. The *First* State of that church: that they are in the good of charity and acknowledge the Lord, and that from Him they are confirmed in good (verses 1 to 3); and are saved (verse 12). The *Second* State: that with them evils begin to act against goods, but they are powerfully withheld from evils and kept in goods by the Lord (verses 14 to 16). Their weakness is described (verse 17); that they are saved (verse 19). The *Third* State: that they no longer think and act from the affection of good, but from the affection of truth (verses 18 to 20); and that they are saved (verse 23). The *Fourth* State: that the affection of truth perishes, which is Lot's wife becoming a pillar of salt (verse 26). The *Fifth* State: that an impure good, or a good of falsity, succeeds, which is Lot in the cave of the mountain (verse 30). The *Sixth* State: that even this good is still more adulterated and falsified (verses 31 to 33); and the truth likewise (verses 34, 35). That therefrom there is conceived and born a certain semblance of a church whose good, so called, is "Moab," and whose truth, also so called, is the "son of Ammon" (verses 36 to 38).

2314. Further: in the internal sense, by the "inhabitants of Sodom" is described the state of those within the same church who are against the good of charity, and how in course of time evil and falsity increase with them until they have nothing but evil and falsity.

2315. Their *First* State: that they are against the good of charity and against the Lord (verses 4, 5). Their *Second* State: that although informed concerning the good of charity and concerning the delights of its affections which they should enjoy, they are obstinate and reject good (verses 6 to 8). That they also endeavor to destroy the very good of charity itself, but that the Lord protects it (verses 9, 10). The *Third* State: that at last they become such that they cannot even see truth and good, still less that truth leads to good (verse 11). That they are possessed by evil and falsity, so that they cannot but perish (verse 13). The *Fourth* State: their destruction (verse 24); and that all goods and truths are separated from them (verse 25).

2316. That the good are separated from the evil, and that the good are saved through the Lord's Human made Divine (verses 27 to 29).

THE INTERNAL SENSE

2317. Verse 1. *And the two angels came to Sodom in the evening; and Lot was sitting in the gate of Sodom; and Lot saw, and rose up to meet them, and bowed himself with his face to the earth.* " The two angels came to Sodom in the evening," signifies the visitation which precedes the Judgment; the "two angels" signify the Lord's Divine Human and Holy proceeding, to which Judgment belongs; "Sodom" signifies the evil, especially those within the church; "evening" is the time of visitation; "and Lot was sitting in the gate of Sodom," signifies those who are in the good of charity, but in external worship, who here are "Lot;" these are among the evil, but are separated from them, which is to "sit in the gate of Sodom;" "and Lot saw," signifies their conscience; "and rose up to meet them," signifies acknowledgment and a disposition of charity; "and bowed himself with his face to the earth," signifies humiliation.

2318. *The two angels came to Sodom in the evening.* That this signifies the visitation which precedes the Judgment, can be seen from the things said by the three men, or Jehovah, in the preceding chapter; and also from the things that follow in this chapter; and likewise from the signification of "evening." In the preceding chapter Jehovah said: "I will go down and see whether the inhabitants of Sodom and Gomorrah have made a consummation according to the cry which is come unto Me; and if not, I will know" (v. 20, 21), by which words, as has been there shown, is signified the visitation which precedes the Judgment. In this chapter there is described the act itself of visitation, and then the Judgment; as is evident from what follows. That "evening" signifies the time of visitation will be seen below. (What visitation is, and that visitation precedes Judgment, may be seen above, n. 2242.) The preceding chapter has treated of the perverted state of the human race, and of the Lord's grief and intercession for those who were in evil and yet in some good and truth; and therefore the present chapter treats, in continuance, of the salvation of those who are in some good and truth ; and it is these who are represented in this chapter by " Lot." At the same time also the destruction of those who are altogether in evil and falsity is treated of ; and it is these who are here signified by " Sodom and Gomorrah."

2319. "Two angels." That these signify the Lord's Divine Human and Holy proceeding, to which Judgment belongs, is evident both from the signification in the Word of " angels," and from its being here said that there were "two" angels. That in the Word "angels" signify some Divine essential in the Lord, and that what this is can be seen from the series, has been shown above (n. 1925). That they here signify the Lord's Divine Human and Holy proceeding, is evident from the fact that by the "three men" who were with Abraham was meant the Lord's Divine Itself, Divine Human, and Holy proceeding (n. 2149, 2156, 2288) ; from this and also from the fact that the angels are called " Jehovah" (verse 24), and also from the signification of " angels" (n. 1925), it is clear that by the " two angels" are here meant the Lord's Divine Human and Holy proceeding.

2320. Why there should here be only two angels, seeing that there were three men with Abraham, is an arcanum which cannot be set forth in few words. It can in some measure be seen from the fact that in this chapter Judgment is treated of, namely, the salvation of the faithful, and the condemnation of the unfaithful ; and it is evident from the Word that Judgment belongs to the Lord's Divine Human and Holy proceeding. That it belongs to the Divine Human see in *John :* " The Father judgeth not any one, but hath given all judgment unto the Son" (v. 22) ; by the " Son" is meant the Divine Human (see n. 2159). That Judgment belongs to the Holy that proceeds from the Lord's Divine Human, see also in *John :* " If I go away, I will send the Comforter unto you ; and when He is come, He shall reprove the world of sin, and of righteousness, and of judgment" (xvi. 7, 8) ; and that the Holy proceeds from the Lord, see in the same : " He shall not speak from Himself but shall take of Mine, and shall declare it" (xvi. 13, 15) ; and this when the Human was made Divine, that is, when the Lord had been glorified, see in the same : " The Holy Spirit was not yet, because Jesus was not yet glorified" (vii. 39).

2321. As regards the fact that Judgment pertains to the Lord's Divine Human and Holy proceeding, the case is this: The human race could no longer have been saved unless the Lord had come into the world and had united the Divine Essence to the Human Essence; for without the Lord's Human made Divine salvation could no longer have reached to man (n. 1990, 2016, 2034, 2035). The Holy Itself that proceeds from the Lord's Divine Human is that which separates the evil from the good; for the evil so fear and shudder at the Lord's Holy that they cannot approach it, but flee far away from it into their hells, each one according to the profaneness that is in him.

2322. That "Sodom" signifies the evil, especially those within the church, is evident from the signification of "Sodom," as being the evil of the love of self (see n. 2220, 2246); consequently as being those who are in that evil. They who apprehend the Word according to the sense of the letter alone, may suppose that by "Sodom" is meant a foulness that is contrary to the order of nature; but in the internal sense by "Sodom" is signified the evil of the love of self. Out of this evil all evils of every kind well forth; and all evils that thus spring from it are called in the Word "adulteries," and are described by the same, as will be evident from passages of the Word that will be adduced at the end of this chapter.

2323. That "evening" signifies the time of visitation, is evident from the signification of "evening." The states of the church are compared in the Word both to the seasons of the year and the times of the day; to the seasons of the year because to its summer, autumn, winter, and spring; to the times of the day because to its noon, evening, night, and morning; for the two things are similarly circumstanced. The state of the church which is called "evening," is when there is no longer any charity, consequently when there begins to be no faith, thus when the church is ceasing to be; this is the "evening" that is followed by the "night" (see n. 22). There is also an "evening" when charity shines forth, consequently when faith does so, and thus when a new church is rising up; this "evening" is the twilight before the morning (see n. 883). Thus "evening" has both significations, for it is provided by the Lord that when a church is ceasing to be, a new one is rising up, and this at the same time; for without a church somewhere on the globe the human race cannot subsist, because it would have no conjunction with heaven (as shown above in n. 468, 637, 931, 2054). [2] In the present chapter both states of the church are treated of, namely, the rising up of a new church, which is represented by "Lot," and the destruction of the old, which is signified by "Sodom and Gomorrah;" as can be seen from the Contents. This is why it is here said that the two angels came to Sodom "in the evening;" and why there is told what was done in the evening (verses 1 to 3), what in the night (verses 4 to 14), what in the morning or rising dawn (verses 15 to 22), and what after the sun had gone forth (verses 23 to 26). [3] As the "evening" signifies these states of the church, it also signifies the visitation which precedes Judgment; for when a Judgment is close at hand, that is, the salvation of the faithful and the condemnation of the unfaithful, then visitation precedes, or an exploration of what quality they are, that is, whether there is any charity and faith. This visitation takes place in the "evening;" and therefore the visitation itself is called "evening," as in *Zephaniah :*—

Woe to the inhabitants of the region of the sea, the nation of the Cherethites. The word of Jehovah is against you, O Canaan, the land of the Philistines ; and I will cause to destroy thee, till there shall be no inhabitant. The remnant of the house of Judah shall feed in the houses of Ashkelon, in the evening shall they lie down ; for Jehovah their God will visit them, and will bring back their captivity (ii. 5, 7).

2324. *And Lot was sitting in the gate of Sodom.* That this signifies those who are in the good of charity, but in external worship, who here are "Lot," and who are among the evil, but separate from them—which is to "sit in the gate of Sodom"— can be seen from the representation of "Lot," and from the signification of "gate," and also from that of "Sodom." From the representation of "Lot:" Lot when with Abraham represented the Lord's sensuous part, thus His external man (as shown in Part First, n. 1428, 1434, 1547). But here, when separated from Abraham, Lot no longer retains the representation of the Lord, but the representation of those who are

with the Lord, namely, the external man of the church, that
is, those who are in the good of charity, but in external worship; [2] nay, in this chapter Lot not only represents the
external man of the church, or what is the same, the external
church such as it is in the beginning, but also such as it is in
its progress, and also in its end. It is the end of that church
which is signified by "Moab" and the "son of Ammon," as of
the Lord's Divine mercy will appear from the series of the
things that follow. It is a common thing in the Word for one
person to represent a number of states that succeed each other,
and which are described by the successive acts of his life. [3]
From the signification of a "gate:" a gate is that through
which one enters into a city, and through which he goes out
of the city; consequently, to "sit in the gate" does indeed
here signify to be with the evil, but still to be separate from
them; as is wont to be the case with the men of the church
who are in the good of charity; these, although they are among
the wicked, are still separate from them; not as to civic society, but as to spiritual life. (That "Sodom" signifies evil in
general, or what is the same, the evil, especially within the
church, was said above, n. 2322.)

2325. *And Lot saw.* That this signifies the conscience,
namely, of those who are in the good of charity but in external worship, may be seen from the signification of to "see."
To "see," in the Word, signifies to understand (n. 897, 1584,
1806, 1807, 2150); but in the internal sense it signifies to
have faith, of which signification we shall speak, of the Lord's
Divine mercy, when we come to the 32d verse of chapter xxix.
That to "see" here signifies conscience, is because those who
have faith also have conscience. Faith is inseparable from
conscience, so inseparable indeed that whether you say faith
or conscience it is the same. By faith is meant the faith by
means of which there is charity, and which is from charity,
thus charity itself; for faith without charity is no faith; and as
faith is not possible without charity, so neither is conscience.

2326. *And he rose up to meet them.* That this signifies
acknowledgment, as also a disposition of charity, may be seen
from the fact that when they came Lot forthwith acknowledged that they were angels; but not so the men of Sodom,

of whom it is said : " They cried unto Lot, and said, Where are the men that came unto thee this night ?   Bring them out unto us, that we may know them" (verse 5).   In the internal sense these words signify that those within the church who are in the good of charity acknowledge the Lord's Divine Human and Holy proceeding (meant by the "two angels"), but not those who are not in the good of charity.   That the same words likewise involve a disposition of charity, is evident also from the fact that Lot, by whom are represented those who are in the good of charity, nay, by whom is signified the good of charity itself, invited them into his house.

2327. *He bowed himself with his face to the earth.*   That this signifies humiliation, may be seen without unfolding the meaning.   The reason that in former times, especially in the representative churches, they bowed themselves so low that they let down the face to the earth, was because the face signified man's interiors (n. 358, 1999); and the reason they let it down to the earth was that the dust of the earth signified what is profane and condemned (n. 278); consequently they thus represented that of themselves they were profane and condemned.   For the same reason they prostrated themselves, pressing the face to the earth, and even rolling themselves in dust and ashes, and also sprinkling dust and ashes upon their heads (as may be seen from *Lam.* ii. 10 ; *Ezek.* xxvii. 30 ; *Micah* i. 10 ; *Josh.* vii. 6 ; *Rev.* xviii. 19 ; and elsewhere).   [2] By all this they represented the state of true humiliation, which is possible to none unless they acknowledge that of themselves they are profane and condemned, and thus that they cannot of themselves look to the Lord, where there is nothing but what is Divine and Holy ; on which account, so far as a man is in self-acknowledgment, so far he can be in true humiliation, and in adoration when in worship.   For in all worship there must be humiliation ; and if this is separated therefrom, there is nothing of adoration, thus nothing of worship.   [3] That the state of humiliation is the essential state of worship itself, comes from the fact that so far as the heart is humbled, so far the love of self and all the evil therefrom ceases ; and so far as this ceases, so far good and truth, that is, charity and faith, flow in from the Lord ; for that which stands in the way of the reception of these is principally the love of self, in which there is contempt for others in comparison with one's self; hatred and revenge if self is not treated with honor; and also unmercifulness and cruelty; thus the worst evils of all; and into these good and truth can in no wise be introduced, for they are opposites.

2328. Verse 2. *And he said, Behold I pray my lords, turn aside I pray to the house of your servant, and pass the night, and wash your feet; and in the morning ye shall rise and go on your way; and they said, Nay, for we will pass the night in the street.* "And he said, Behold I pray my lords," signifies an interior acknowledgment and confession of the Lord's Divine Human and Holy proceeding; "turn aside I pray to the house of your servant, and pass the night," signifies an invitation to have an abode with him; "to the house of a servant," means in the good of charity; "and wash your feet," signifies application to his natural; "and in the morning ye shall rise and go on your way," signifies confirmation thereby in good and truth; "and they said, Nay," signifies a doubting, which is wont to attend temptation; "for we will pass the night in the street," signifies that He was as it were willing to judge from truth.

2329. *He said, Behold I pray my lords.* That this signifies an interior acknowledgment and confession of the Lord's Divine Human and Holy proceeding, is evident from the acknowledgment and humiliation spoken of just before; here confession immediately follows, for this is meant by Lot's saying, " Behold I pray my lords." Interior confession is of the heart and comes forth in humiliation, and at the same time in the affection of good; but exterior confession is of the lips, and may possibly come forth in a feigned humiliation and a feigned affection of good, which is none at all, being such as exists with those who confess the Lord for the sake of their own honor, or rather their own worship, and their own gain. That which these confess with the lips, they deny in the heart. [2] Its being said in the plural, " my lords," is for the same reason that in the preceding chapter it is said "three men;" for just as the "three" there signify the Divine Itself, the Divine Human, and the Holy proceeding, so here the "two" signify the Lord's Divine Human and Holy proceeding, as was said above. That these are one is known to every one within the church; and because they are one, they are also named in the singular in what follows, as in verse 17, "It came to pass when they had led them forth abroad, that He said, Escape for thy life;" verse 19, "Behold I pray thy servant hath found grace in thine eyes, and thou hast made thy mercy great which thou hast done with me;" verse 21, "And he said unto him, Behold I have accepted thy face as to this word also, that I will not overthrow the city;" and verse 22, "For I cannot do anything until thou be come thither." [3] That the Divine Itself, the Divine Human, and the Holy proceeding are Jehovah, is evident from the foregoing chapter, where the three men are called "Jehovah," as in verse 13, "Jehovah said unto Abraham;" verse 14, "Shall anything be too wonderful for Jehovah;" verse 22, "Abraham, he stood yet before Jehovah;" verse 33, "Jehovah went His way when He made an end of speaking with Abraham." Consequently the Divine Human and Holy proceeding are Jehovah, as also He is named in this chapter, verse 24, "And Jehovah caused it to rain upon Sodom and Gomorrah brimstone and fire from Jehovah out of heaven;" the internal sense of which words will be seen in what follows. (That the Lord is Jehovah Himself, who is so often named in the histories and prophecies of the Old Testament, may be seen above, n. 1736.) [4] They who are truly men of the church, that is, who are in love to the Lord and in charity toward the neighbor, are acquainted with and acknowledge a Trine; but still they humble themselves before the Lord and adore Him alone, for the reason that they know that there is no access to the Divine Itself which is called the "Father" except through the Son; and that all the Holy which is of the Holy Spirit proceeds from Him. When they are in this idea they adore no other than Him through whom and from whom all things are, thus One; [5] nor do they spread out their ideas among Three, as many within the church are wont to do, as can be seen from many in the other life, even the learned, who in the life of the body had supposed that they possessed the arcana of faith more than others. When these were ex-

plored in the other life as to what idea they had concerning
the one God—whether of Three Uncreates, Three Infinites,
Three Eternals, Three Almighties, Three Lords, it was plainly
perceived that they had the idea of Three (for there is a communication of ideas there), when yet it is part of the creed,
being stated in plain words, that there are not Three Uncreates, not Three Infinites, not Three Eternals, not Three Almighties, not Three Lords, but One; as also is the truth.
The result was that they confessed that with the mouth they
had indeed said that there is one God, yet still had thought,
and some had believed, that there are three, whom in idea they
could separate, but not join together, the reason of which is
that all arcana whatever, even the deepest, are attended with
an idea; for without an idea nothing can be thought of, nor
indeed can anything be kept in the memory. [6] Hence in
the other life it is manifest as in clear day what thought, and
thence what belief, each person has formed for himself concerning the One God. Indeed the Jews in the other life,
when they hear that the Lord is Jehovah and that there is
but One God, can say nothing. But when they perceive that
the ideas of Christians are divided among Three, they say that
they themselves worship One God, but Christians Three; and
this the more since none can join together the Three thus separated in idea, except those who are in the faith of charity;
for the Lord applies the minds of these to Himself.

2330. *Turn aside I pray to the house of your servant and
pass the night.* That this signifies an invitation for the Divine Human and Holy proceeding to have an abode with him,
is evident without unfolding the meaning.

2331. That "to the house of a servant" denotes in the
good of charity, is evident from the signification of a "house,"
as being celestial good, which is of love and charity alone (see
n. 2048, 2233).

2332. *Wash your feet.* That this signifies application to
his natural, is evident from what was said in the preceding
chapter (n. 2162), where are the same words. In former times,
when they saw an angel of Jehovah, they believed that they
were about to die (*Exod.* xix. 12, 21, 24; xx. 19; *Judges* vi. 22,
23; xiii. 22, 23), for the reason that when the Divine Holy

flows into the profane that is with man, its virtue is such as to cause it to be a devouring and consuming fire; and therefore when the Lord presents Himself to the view of any man, or even of any angel, He miraculously moderates and tempers the Holy that proceeds from Him, so that they may be able to endure it; or what is the same, He applies Himself to their natural. This then is what is signified in the internal sense by these words which Lot said to the angels: "Wash your feet." And this shows what is the nature of the internal sense, for that this is the signification cannot be seen from the sense of the letter.

2333. *And in the morning ye shall rise and go on your way.* That this signifies confirmation in good and truth, may be seen from the signification of "rising in the morning," and also from the signification of "going on the way." In the Word "morning" signifies the Lord's kingdom and whatever belongs to the Lord's kingdom, thus principally the good of love and of charity, as will be confirmed from the Word at verse 15; and a "way" signifies truth (see n. 627); for which reason it is said that after they had been in his house and had passed the night there (by which is signified that they had an abode in the good of charity that was with him), they should "rise in the morning and go on their way," by which is signified being thereby thus confirmed in good and truth. [2] From this, as from other passages, it is evident how remote from the sense of the letter, and consequently how much unseen, is the internal sense, especially in the historical parts of the Word; and that it does not come to view unless the meaning of every word is unfolded in accordance with its constant signification in the Word. On this account, when the ideas are kept in the sense of the letter, the internal sense appears no otherwise than as something obscure and dark; but on the other hand when the ideas are kept in the internal sense, the sense of the letter appears in like manner obscure, nay, to the angels as nothing. For the angels are no longer in worldly and corporeal things, like those of man, but in spiritual and celestial things, into which the words of the sense of the letter are wonderfully changed, when it ascends from a man who is reading the Word to the sphere in which

the angels are, that is, to heaven; and this from the correspondence of spiritual things with worldly, and of celestial
things with corporeal. This correspondence is most constant,
but its nature has not yet been disclosed until now in the unfolding of the meaning of the words, names, and numbers in
the Word, as to the internal sense. [3] That it may be known
what is the nature of this correspondence, or what is the
same, how worldly and corporeal ideas pass into corresponding
spiritual and celestial ideas when the former are elevated to
heaven, take as an example "morning" and "way." When
"morning" is read, as in the passage before us to "rise in the
morning," the angels do not get an idea of any morning of a
day, but an idea of morning in the spiritual sense; thus such
a one as is described in *Samuel:* "The Rock of Israel He is
as the light of the morning when the sun riseth, a morning
without clouds" (2 *Sam.* xxiii. 3, 4); and in *Daniel:* " The
holy one said unto me, Until evening, when morning comes,
two thousand three hundred" (viii. 14, 26). Thus instead of
"morning" the angels perceive the Lord, or His Kingdom, or
the heavenly things of love and charity; and these in fact with
variety according to the series of things in the Word which is
being read. [4] In like manner where "way" is read—as
here, to "go on your way"—they can have no idea of a way,
but another idea which is spiritual or celestial, namely, like
that in *John,* where the Lord said: "I am the way and the
truth" (xiv. 6); and as in *David:* "Make Thy ways known to
me, O Jehovah, lead my way in truth" (*Ps.* xxv. 4, 5); and in
Isaiah: "He made Him to know the way of understanding"
(xl. 14). Thus instead of "way" the angels perceive truth,
and this in both the historical and the prophetical parts of
the Word. For the angels no longer care for the historical
things, as these are altogether inadequate to their ideas; and
therefore in place of them they perceive such things as belong
to the Lord and His kingdom, and which also in the internal
sense follow on in a beautiful order and well-connected series.
For this reason, and also in order that the Word may be for
the angels, all the historical things therein are representative,
and each of the words is significative of such things; which
peculiarity the Word has above all other writing.

2334. *And they said, Nay.* That this signifies the doubting which is wont to attend temptation, may be seen from their declining and yet going into his house. In all temptation there is somewhat of doubt concerning the Lord's presence and mercy, and concerning salvation and the like things; for those who are in temptation are in interior anxiety, even to despair; in which they are for the most part kept, to the end that they may be at length confirmed in the fact that all things are of the Lord's mercy; that they are saved by Him alone; and that with themselves there is nothing but evil; in respect to which they are confirmed by means of conflicts in which they overcome. After the temptation there remain from it many states of truth and good to which their thoughts may afterwards be bent by the Lord, which would otherwise rush into insane things, and draw away the mind into opposition to what is true and good. [2] Since by "Lot" there is here treated of the first state of the church which is in the good of charity but in external worship, and since before a man comes into this state he is to be reformed, which is also done by a certain kind of temptation (but they who are in external worship undergo only a light temptation), therefore these things which involve something of temptation are said, namely, that the angels at first said they would pass the night in the street, and that Lot urged them, and so they turned aside to him, and came into his house.

2335. *For we will pass the night in the street.* That this signifies that he was as it were desirous to judge from truth, may be seen from the signification of a "street," and from the signification of "passing the night." A "street" is often named in the Word, and in the internal sense signifies the same as a "way," namely, truth—for a street is a way in a city—as will be evident from the passages that will soon follow. That "to pass the night" is here to judge, may be seen from the signification of "night." It was shown above (n. 2323) that "evening" signifies the state of the church before the last, when there begins to be no faith; and also the visitation which precedes the Judgment. From this it is evident that "night," which succeeds, is the last state, when there is no faith; also that it is the Judgment. It is clear from this

that to "pass the night in the street," in the internal sense
denotes to judge from truth. [2] As regards Judgment it is
twofold, namely, from good and from truth. The faithful are
judged from good, but the unfaithful from truth. That the faithful are judged from good, is plainly evident in *Matthew* (xxv.
34–40), and that the unfaithful are judged from truth (verses
41 to 46). To be judged from good is to be saved because they
have received it; but to be judged from truth is to be condemned because they have rejected good. Good is the Lord's,
and they who acknowledge this in life and faith are the Lord's,
and therefore are saved; but they who do not acknowledge it
in life, and consequently not in faith, cannot be the Lord's,
and therefore cannot be saved. They are therefore judged according to the acts of their life and according to their thoughts
and ends; and when they are judged according to these, they
cannot but be condemned; for it is a truth that of himself a
man does, thinks, and intends nothing but evil, and of himself rushes to hell in so far as he is not withheld therefrom
by the Lord. [3] But as regards judgment from truth the
case is this: The Lord never judges any one except from good;
for He desires to raise all into heaven, however many they
may be, and indeed, if it were possible, even to Himself; for
the Lord is mercy itself and good itself. Mercy itself and
good itself can never condemn any one; but it is the man who
condemns himself, because he rejects good. As in the life of
the body he had shunned good, so does he shun it in the other
life; consequently he shuns heaven and the Lord, for the Lord
cannot be in anything except good. He is likewise in truth,
but not in truth separated from good. That the Lord condemns no one, nor judges any to hell, He says in *John* :—

God sent not His Son into the world to judge the world, but that the
world through Him might be saved. This is the judgment, that the light
is come into the world, but men loved the darkness rather than the light,
because their works were evil (iii. 17, 19).

And in the same :—

If any one hear My words, and believe not, I judge him not; for I
came not to judge the world, but to save the world (xii. 47).

(See also what has been said on the subject before, n. 223, 245,
592, 696, 1093, 1683, 1874, 2258.) [4] Where Judgment was

treated of above (n. 2320, 2321), it was shown that all Judgment belongs to the Lord's Divine Human and Holy proceeding, according to His words in *John*:—

The Father judgeth not any one, but hath given all judgment unto the Son (v. 22) ;

and yet it is now said that the Lord does not judge by condemning any one.   From this it is evident what is the nature of the Word in the letter : that unless it were understood from another sense, namely, from the internal sense, it would not be comprehended.   From the internal sense alone is it manifest how the case is with Judgment.

2336. That a "street" signifies truth, may be seen from many passages in the Word, as in *John*, where the New Jerusalem is treated of :—

The twelve gates were twelve pearls, every gate was one pearl ; and the street of the city was pure gold, as it were transparent glass (*Rev.* xxi. 21).

[2] The "New Jerusalem" is the Lord's kingdom, which, being described as to good and truth, is described by "walls," "gates," and "streets."   By the "streets" are meant all things of truth which lead to good, or all things of faith which lead to love and charity ; and because truths then become of good, thus transparent from good, the street is said to be "gold, as it were transparent glass."   Again :

In the midst of the street of it and of the river, on this side and on that, was the tree of life, bearing twelve fruits (*Rev.* xxii. 2) ;

where also the New Jerusalem or the Lord's kingdom is treated of.   The "midst of the street" denotes the truth of faith, by means of which comes good, and which afterwards comes from good ; the "twelve fruits" are what are called the fruits of faith ; for "twelve" signifies all the things of faith (as shown above, n. 577, 2089, 2129, 2130).   [3] In *Daniel* :—

Know and perceive that from the going forth of the word to restore and to build Jerusalem, even unto Messiah the Leader, shall be seven weeks, and sixty and two weeks, and it shall be restored and built with street and moat (ix. 25),

where the Lord's advent is treated of ; "it shall be restored with street and moat," denotes that there will then be what is

true and good.   That Jerusalem was not then restored and
built is well known ; and that it is not to be restored and built
anew every one may also know provided he does not keep his
ideas fixed on a worldly kingdom, but on the heavenly kingdom that is meant by " Jerusalem" in the internal sense.   [4]
In *Luke :—*

The master of the house said to his servant, Go out quickly into the
streets and lanes of the city, and bring in hither the poor, the maimed,
the lame, and the blind (xiv. 21).

They who remain in the sense of the letter apprehend from
this nothing else than that the servant should go everywhere,
and that this is signified by the " streets and lanes ;" and that
he should bring in everybody, and that this is signified by the
" poor, maimed, lame, and blind."   But each of these words
contains deep secrets within it, for they are the Lord's words.
That he should " go into the streets and lanes," signifies that he
should seek everywhere for some genuine truth, or truth which
shines from good, or through which good shines.   That he
should " bring in the poor, the maimed, the lame, and the
blind," signifies such as were so called in the Ancient Church
and were such as to the faith, but were in the life of good,
who should thus be informed about the Lord's kingdom—thus
the nations which were not yet instructed.   [5] As " streets"
signified truths, it was a representative rite among the Jews to
teach in the streets (as appears in *Matt.* vi. 2, 5, and in *Luke*
xiii. 26, 27).   In the Prophets, " streets," wherever named,
signify in the internal sense either truths, or things contrary
to truths, as in *Isaiah :—*

Judgment is cast away backward, and righteousness standeth afar
off ; for truth hath stumbled in the street, and uprightness cannot enter
(lix. 14).

Again :—

Thy sons have fainted, and have lain at the head of all the streets
(li. 20).

In *Jeremiah :—*

Death is come up into our windows, it is entered into our palaces, to
cut off the child from the street, the young men from the roads (ix. 21).

[6] In *Ezekiel :—*

Nebuchadnezzar shall tread down all thy streets with the hoofs of his horses (xxvi. 11),

speaking of Tyre, by which are signified the knowledges of truth (n. 1201); the "hoofs of the horses" denote the memory-knowledges that pervert truth. In *Nahum :—*

The chariots rave in the streets, they run to and fro in the roads (ii. 4) ;

the "chariots" denote the doctrine of truth, which is said to "rave in the streets," when falsity is in the place of truth. In *Zechariah :—*

There shall yet old men and old women dwell in the streets of Jerusalem, and the streets of the city shall be full of boys and girls, playing in the streets (viii. 4, 5),

speaking of the affections of truth, and the consequent gladnesses and joys. (Besides other places, as *Isa.* xxiv. 11 ; *Jer.* v. 1; vii. 34; xlix. 26; *Lam.* ii. 11, 19; iv. 8, 14; *Zeph.* iii. 6).

2337. Verse 3. *And he urged them exceedingly, and they turned aside unto him, and came to his house; and he made them a feast, and baked unleavened [bread] ; and they did eat.* "He urged them exceedingly," signifies a state of temptation when one overcomes ; "and they turned aside unto him," signifies abode ; "and came to his house," signifies confirmation in good ; "and he made them a feast," signifies a dwelling together ; "and baked unleavened [bread]," signifies purification ; "and they did eat," signifies appropriation.

2338. *He urged them exceedingly.* That this signifies a state of temptation when one overcomes, cannot be seen except by those who have been in temptations. As before said, temptations are attended with doubt in regard to the Lord's presence and mercy, and also in regard to salvation. The evil spirits who are then with the man and induce the temptation strongly inspire negation, but the good spirits and angels from the Lord in every possible way dispel this state of doubt, and keep the man in a state of hope, and at last confirm him in what is affirmative. The result is that a man who is in temptation hangs between what is negative and what is affirmative.

One who yields in temptation remains in a state of doubt, and falls into what is negative; but one who overcomes is indeed in doubt, but still, if he suffers himself to be cheered by hope, he stands fast in what is affirmative. As during this conflict the man seems to urge the Lord, especially by prayers, to be present, to have mercy, to give aid, and to deliver from damnation, therefore where the temptation of those who are becoming men of the church is treated of, as in the passage before us, these things are described by the angels' first saying, " Nay," and that they would tarry all night in the street; and by Lot's then urging them exceedingly, so that they turned aside to him and came to his house.

2339. *And they turned aside unto him.* That this signifies abode, is evident from the signification of the same words above (n. 2330); thus without further explication.

2340. *And came to his house.* That this signifies confirmation in good, is evident from the signification of a " house," as being celestial good (see n. 2233, 2331); and from this, as well as from the series of things in the internal sense, it is evident that these words mean to be confirmed in good.

2341. *And he made them a feast.* That this signifies a dwelling together, is evident from the signification of a " feast." Feasts are often mentioned in the Word; and in the internal sense they signify a dwelling together; as in *Jeremiah :*—

The word of Jehovah to him : Thou shalt not go into the house of a feast, to sit with them, to eat and to drink (xvi. 8) ;

where several things are said to the prophet by which he should represent the fact that good should have no communication with evil, nor truth with falsity ; and among other things it is said that he should not enter into the house of a feast, by which was signified that good and truth should not dwell together with evil and falsity. [2] In *Isaiah :*—

In this mountain shall Jehovah Zebaoth make unto all people a feast of fat things, a feast of sweet wines, of fat things full of marrow, of wines well refined (xxv. 6) ;

where " mountain" denotes love to the Lord (n. 795, 1430). They who are in this love dwell with the Lord in good and truth, which is signified by the " feast." The " fat things full of marrow" are goods (n. 353); the "sweet" and the "refined wines" are the truths thereof (n. 1071). **[3]** The feasts made from the sanctified things in the Jewish Church, when they sacrificed, represented nothing else than the Lord's dwelling with man in the holy things of love signified by the sacrifices (n. 2187). The same was afterwards represented by the Holy Supper, which in the Primitive Church was called a Feast. **[4]** In the twenty-first chapter of *Genesis* it is related that Abraham made a great feast on the day that Isaac was weaned (verse 8); by which was represented, and thereby signified, the dwelling together and first conjunction of the Lord's Divine with His Human Rational. In the internal sense the same is also signified in other places by "feasts," as may also be inferred from the fact that feasts take place in a company of many who are in love and charity together, who mentally conjoin themselves together, and share with one another their glad feelings, which are emotions of love and charity.

2342. *And baked unleavened [bread].* That this signifies purification, is evident from the signification of "unleavened" or "unfermented." In the Word "bread" signifies in general all celestial and spiritual food, thus celestial and spiritual things in general (see n. 276, 680, 1798, 2165, 2177). That these should be free from everything impure was represented by bread without leaven; for "leaven" signifies that which is evil and false, by which celestial and spiritual things are rendered impure and profane. On account of this representation it was commanded those who were of the Representative Church that in their sacrifices they should not offer any other bread, that is, meat-offering, than that which was unfermented or unleavened; as is evident in *Moses :*—

No meat-offering which ye shall bring to Jehovah shall be made with leaven (*Lev.* ii. 11).

Again :—

Thou shalt not sacrifice the blood of My sacrifice with what is leavened (*Exod.* xxiii. 18 ; xxxiv. 25).

[2] And it was therefore also commanded, that on the seven days of the Passover they should not eat any other than unfermented or unleavened bread, as stated in *Moses :*—

Seven days shall ye eat unleavened [bread] ; even on the first day ye
shall cause leaven to cease from your houses ; for whosoever eateth what
is leavened, from the first day until the seventh day, that soul shall be
cut off from Israel. In the first month, on the fourteenth day of the
month, at even, ye shall eat unleavened [bread], until the one and twentieth day of the month at even ; seven days shall no leaven be found in
your houses ; for whosoever eateth what is leavened, that soul also shall
be cut off from the congregation of Israel, whether he be a sojourner or
born in the land (*Exod.* xii. 15, 18–20 ; and elsewhere, as *Exod.* xiii. 6,
7 ; xxiii. 15 ; xxxiv. 18 ; *Deut.* xvi. 3, 4).

Hence the Passover is called the "Feast of Unleavened
Bread" (*Lev.* xxiii. 6; *Num.* xxviii. 16, 17; *Matt.* xxvi. 17;
Luke xxii. 1, 7). [3] That the Passover represented the Lord's
glorification, and thereby the conjunction of the Divine with
.the human race, will of the Lord's Divine mercy be shown
elsewhere ; and as the Lord's conjunction with the human
race is effected through love and charity and the faith thence
derived, these celestial and spiritual things were represented
by the unleavened bread that they were to eat on the days
of the Passover; and lest these things should be contaminated by anything profane, that which was leavened was so
severely interdicted that whoever should eat of it was to be
cut off ; for whoever profanes celestial and spiritual things
cannot fail to perish. Every one can see that apart from this
secret meaning, this ceremonial, to which there was attached so
severe a penalty, would never have been given. [4] Everything that was commanded in that church represented some
secret thing, even the very cooking, as was the case with every
particular of what the sons of Israel did when they went forth
from Egypt; to wit :—

They shall eat on that night flesh roasted with fire, and unleavened
bread upon bitter herbs ; they shall not eat it raw, nor boiled in water ;
the head shall be on the legs ; they shall not leave of it until the morning, but shall burn the residue with fire (*Exod.* xii. 8–10).

These particulars, namely, that they should eat it by night,
the flesh roasted with fire, the unleavened bread upon bitter
herbs, the head on the legs, not raw, nor boiled in water, that
they should not leave of it until the morning, and that they
should burn the residue with fire, were representative. But
the arcana represented cannot possibly appear unless disclosed

by the internal sense; it is from this sense alone that it can be seen that all things are Divine.   [5] In like manner with the ritual in regard to the Nazirite :—

The priest shall take the boiled shoulder of a ram, and one unleavened cake out of a basket, and one unleavened wafer, and shall put them upon the palms of the Nazirite, after he has shaved his nazariteship (*Num.* vi. 19).

He who does not know that the Nazirite represented the celestial man himself, does not know that celestial things, thus arcana which do not appear in the letter, are enfolded within all these particulars, namely, the boiled shoulder of a ram, the unleavened cake, the unleavened wafer, and the shaving of the hair; which shows what kind of an opinion concerning the Word must be formed by those who do not believe that it contains an internal sense; for without what is internal these are particulars of no moment : whereas when the ceremonial or ritual is removed, everything there becomes Divine and holy. The same is the case with everything else, as here with the unleavened bread, which denotes the holy of love, or a holy of holies, as it is likewise called in *Moses :*—

The unleavened bread that is left shall be eaten by Aaron and his sons in a place of holiness, for it is a holy of holies (*Lev.* vi. 16, 17).

The " unleavened bread" therefore denotes pure love; and the " baking of what is unleavened" denotes purification.

2343. *And they did eat.*   That this signifies appropriation, is evident from the signification of " eating," which is to be communicated and conjoined, thus to be appropriated (see above, n. 2187).   From what has been already said and unfolded it can be seen how the things contained in the preceding verse, and in this, are circumstanced in the internal sense, and how in that sense they cohere together; from the fact that by the " angels" is signified the Lord's Divine Human and Holy proceeding; by " turning aside to him," having an abode; by " coming to his house," being confirmed in good; by " making a feast," dwelling together; by " baking unleavened bread," being purified; and by " eating," being appropriated.   From this it is evident what is the series and connection of things in the internal sense, although nothing whatever of it appears in the historical sense.   [2]

Such is the order and series in all of the things of the Word, both in general and particular. But the series itself such as it is in itself cannot be made to appear in an explication of the several words, for in that case everything appears in a disconnected form, and the continuity of the sense is dissipated. But when all things are viewed together in one idea, or are perceived in one mental view, as is the case with those who are in the internal sense and at the same time in heavenly light from the Lord, there is then presented to view in these words the entire process of the reformation and regeneration of those who are becoming men of the church (who are here represented by Lot), to wit, that at first they perceive something of temptation, but when they persist and overcome, the Lord has an abode with them, and confirms them in good, introduces them unto Himself in His kingdom, and dwells with them, and there purifies and perfects them, and at the same time appropriates good and happy things to them, and this by means of His Divine Human and Holy proceeding. [3] That all regeneration or new life, thus salvation, is from the Lord alone, is indeed known in the church, but is believed by few, for the reason that men are not in the good of charity. It is as impossible for those who are not in the good of charity to have this belief, as it is for a camel to go through the eye of a needle; for the good of charity is the very ground for the seeds of faith. Truth and good agree, but truth and evil never: they are of a contrary nature, and are averse one to the other. For this reason, so far as a man is in good, so far he can be in truth; or so far as he is in charity, so far he can be in faith; especially in this chief point of faith, that all salvation is from the Lord. [4] That this is the chief point of faith, is evident from many passages in the Word, as in *John* :—

God so loved the world, that He gave His only begotten Son, that whosoever believeth in Him should not perish, but have eternal life (iii. 16).

Again :—

He that believeth in the Son hath eternal life ; but he that believeth not the Son shall not see life ; but the wrath of God abideth on him (iii. 36).

Again :—

This is the work of God, that ye believe in Him whom the Father hath sent (vi. 29).

Again :—

This is the will of Him that sent Me, that every one that seeth the Son, and believeth in Him, should have eternal life ; and I will raise him up at the last day (vi. 40).

Again :—

Except ye believe that I am, ye shall die in your sins (viii. 24).

Again :—

I am the resurrection and the life ; he that believeth in Me, though he die, yet shall he live ; and whosoever liveth and believeth in Me shall never die (xi. 25, 26).

[5] That no one can believe in the Lord unless he is in good, that is, that no one can have faith unless he is in charity, is also evident in *John :—*

As many as received Him, to them gave He power to become children of God, to them that believe in His name ; who were born not of bloods, nor of the will of the flesh, nor of the will of man, but of God (i. 12, 13).

And again :—

I am the vine, ye are the branches ; he that abideth in Me, and I in him, the same beareth much fruit ; for without Me ye can do nothing. If one abide not in Me, he is cast forth as a branch, and is withered. As the Father hath loved Me, I also have loved you ; abide ye in My love. This is My commandment, that ye love one another as I have loved you (xv. 5, 6, 9, 12).

[6] From these passages it can be seen that love to the Lord and charity toward the neighbor are the life of faith. But that they who are in evil, that is, in a life of evil, cannot possibly believe that all salvation is from the Lord, has been made evident to me from those who had come into the other life from the Christian world ; and also from those who in the life of the body had confessed with the mouth and had even taught, according to the doctrinal tenet of faith, that without the Lord there is no salvation, and yet had led a life of evil. These, when the Lord was merely named, forthwith filled the sphere with endless difficulties (for in the other life that which spirits merely think is perceived, and diffuses from

itself a sphere, in which it becomes manifest in what kind of faith they are; see n. 1394). [**7**] Among the same, when love or charity was merely mentioned, there was perceived from them something as it were full of darkness and at the same time clotted from a kind of filthy love; which thing was of such a nature as to extinguish, suffocate, and pervert all perception of love to the Lord and of charity toward the neighbor. Such is the faith at this day, which they say saves without the good of charity. [**8**] The same also on being asked what faith they had (since they had not that which they had professed in the life of the body) said (for in the other life no one can conceal what he thinks) that they believed in God the Creator of the universe. But when they were examined in order to see whether it was so, it was found that they did not believe in any God, but thought that all things are of nature, and that all things that have been said about eternal life are empty and worthless. Such is the faith of all those within the Church who do not believe in the Lord, but say that they believe in God the Creator of the universe. For truth can flow in from no other source than the Lord; nor can truth be inseminated in anything except the good which is from the Lord. [**9**] That it is the Lord's Divine Human and Holy proceeding by means of which and from which come life and salvation, is very well known from the words of the Holy Supper : " This is My Body;" " this is My Blood;" which is the Lord's Divine Human; and it is evident that all the Holy is from this. Whether you say His Divine Human, or His Body, or His Flesh, or the Bread, or the Divine Love, it is the same; for the Lord's Divine Human is pure Love, and the Holy is of love alone, and from this is derived the Holy of faith.

2344. Verse 4. *Scarcely yet were they lain down when the men of the city, the men of Sodom, compassed the house about, from a boy even to an old man, all the people from the uttermost part.* " Scarcely yet were they lain down," signifies the first period of visitation; " the men of the city," signifies those who are in falsities; " the men of Sodom," signifies those who are in evils; " compassed the house about," signifies that they were against the good of charity; " from a boy even to an old man," signifies falsities and evils both recent and confirmed; "all the people from the uttermost part," signifies all and each of them.

2345. *Scarcely yet were they lain down.* That this signifies the first period of visitation, is evident from what was said above concerning "evening" and "night" (n. 2323, 2335), namely, that in the Word they signify visitation and Judgment. Here neither evening nor night is indeed mentioned, but it is said, "scarcely yet were they lain down," whereby there is implied the time of evening advancing to night, or of commencing night, consequently the first period of visitation upon the evil; as is also evident from what follows, for here commences an inquisition concerning the evil within the church who are meant by "Sodom."

2346. *The men of the city.* That this signifies those who are in falsities; and "the men of Sodom," those who are in evils, is evident from the signification of "city," and of "Sodom." That a "city" signifies truths, and also falsities or things contrary to truths, was shown before (n. 402); and that "Sodom" signifies evils of every kind (n. 2220, 2246). As there were both falsities and evils that were inquired into, or visited, it is said, "the men of the city, the men of Sodom." If both were not meant, it would only have been said, "the men of Sodom."

2347. *Compassed the house about.* That this signifies that they were against the good of charity, is evident from the signification of "house," as being celestial good, which is nothing else than the good of love and of charity (see n. 2048, 2233); and also from the signification of "compassing about," which is to be against that good, that is, to assail and attack it with hostile intent.

2348. *From a boy even to an old man.* That this signifies falsities and evils both recent and confirmed, can be seen from the signification of a "boy" and of an "old man," when predicated of falsities and evils; namely, that "boys" denote those not yet matured, thus recent ones; and "old men," those which have attained to considerable age, thus those confirmed. "Boy" and "old man" occur elsewhere in the Word in a similar sense, as in *Zechariah :—*

There shall yet old men and old women dwell in the streets of Jerusalem ; and the streets of the city shall be full of boys and girls playing in the streets (viii. 4, 5) ;

where " Jerusalem" denotes the Lord's kingdom and church (n. 402, 2117); the "streets," truths therein (n. 2336); thus "old men," confirmed truths; and "old women," confirmed goods; "boys playing in the streets," recent truths; and "girls," recent goods and their affections and the derivative gladnesses. It is evident from this how celestial and spiritual things are changed into things historic, in their descent into the worldly things of the sense of the letter, in which sense it scarcely appears otherwise than that old men, boys, women, and girls, are meant. [2] In *Jeremiah* :—

Pour out upon the child in the street of Jerusalem, and upon the assembly of young men in like manner ; for even the man with the woman shall be taken, the old man with him that is full of days (vi. 11) ;

here the " street of Jerusalem" denotes the falsities that reign in the church (n. 2336), of which the recent and the maturing are called the " child" and the " young men," and the old and the confirmed are called the " old man" and " him that is full of days." Again :—

I will scatter in thee the horse and his rider, and I will scatter in thee the chariot and him that is borne in it, and I will scatter in thee man and woman, and I will scatter in thee the old man and the boy (li. 21, 22) ;

where in like manner the " old man" and the " boy" denote confirmed truth and recent truth. [3] Again :—

Death is come up into our windows, it is entered into our palaces, to cut off the child in the street, the young men from the roads (ix. 21) ;

where the " child" denotes the truths which are first born, and which are cut off when death comes into the windows and palaces, that is, into the things of the intellect and of the will. (That " windows" denote things of the intellect, see above, n. 655, 658 ; and that " palaces," or " houses," denote things of the will, n. 710.)

2349. *All the people from the uttermost part.* That this signifies all and each of them, is evident from what precedes (that by " boys" and " old men" are signified falsities and evils both recent and confirmed), so that here the " people from the

uttermost part" signifies all and each of these. Moreover the
term "people" in general signifies falsities (see n. 1259, 1260).
[2] Here then there is described the first state of those within
the church who are against the good of charity, and consequently against the Lord, for the one involves the other, because no one can be conjoined with the Lord except through
love and charity. Love is spiritual conjunction itself, as can
be seen from the essence of love; and whoever cannot be conjoined with Him, also cannot acknowledge Him. That they
who are not in good cannot acknowledge the Lord, that is,
have faith in Him, is evident in *John* :—

> The light is come into the world, but men loved the darkness rather
> than the light, because their works were evil; for every one that doeth
> evil hateth the light, and cometh not to the light, lest his works should
> be reproved; but he that doeth the truth cometh to the light, that his
> works may be made manifest, because they have been wrought in God
> (iii. 19–21);

from which it is evident that they who are against the good of
charity are against the Lord; or what is the same, that they
who are in evil hate the light, and do not come to the light.
That the "light" is faith in the Lord, and is the Lord Himself,
is evident in *John* (i. 9, 10; xii. 35, 36, 46).   [3] In like manner in the same elsewhere :—

> The world cannot hate you, but Me it hateth, because I testify of it
> that its works are evil (vii. 7).

More plainly still in *Matthew* :—

> He shall say unto them on the left hand, Depart from Me, ye cursed;
> for I was hungry, and ye gave Me not to eat; I was thirsty, and ye gave
> Me not to drink; I was a stranger, and ye took Me not in; naked, and ye
> clothed Me not; sick, and in prison, and ye visited Me not. Verily I say
> unto you, Inasmuch as ye did it not to one of the least of these, ye did it
> not to Me (xxv. 41–43, 45).

[4] These words show in what manner those are against the
Lord who are against the good of charity; and also that every
one is judged according to the good of charity, and not according to the truth of faith when this is separated from good.
So also again in *Matthew* :—

> The Son of man shall come in the glory of His Father with His angels;
> and then shall He render to every one according to his deeds (xvi. 27);

"deeds" denote the goods which proceed from charity ; and the things which are of charity are also called the fruits of faith.

2350. Verse 5. *And they cried unto Lot, and said unto him, Where are the men that came unto thee this night? bring them out unto us that we may know them.* " They cried unto Lot, and said unto him," signifies falsity from evil becoming angry against good; " where are the men that came unto thee?" signifies the denial of the Lord's Divine Human and Holy proceeding; "this night," signifies the last time, when these are no longer acknowledged; "bring them out unto us, that we may know them," signifies that men then desire to show that it is false to acknowledge their existence.

2351. *They cried unto Lot and said unto him.* That this signifies falsity from evil becoming angry against good, can be seen from the signification of "crying," and also of "Lot," and thereby from the feeling that is expressed. That the term " crying" is predicated of falsity, was shown above (n. 2240); and that " Lot" represents the men of the church who are in good, thus good itself (n. 2324). From this and from the feeling of anger expressed in these words, it is evident that they signify falsity from evil becoming angry against good. That there are many kinds of falsity, but in general two, namely, the falsity which is produced from evil, and that which produces evil, may be seen above (n. 1188, 1212, 1295, 1679, 2243). [2] The falsity from evil, within the church, is especially that falsity which favors evils of life—such as that good, that is, charity, does not make a man of the church, but truth, that is, faith; and that a man is saved howsoever he may have lived in evils during the whole course of his life, provided that when corporeal things are lulled to sleep, as is usual a short time before death, he utters something of faith with apparent affection. This is the falsity which is especially angry against good, and is signified by their " crying to Lot." The cause of anger is all that which endeavors to destroy the delight of any love. It is called " anger" when evil attacks good, but " zeal" when good reproves evil.

2352. *Where are the men that came unto thee?* That this signifies a denial of the Lord's Divine Human and Holy proceeding, is evident from the signification of the " two men" (explained above, n. 2320); also from the feeling latent in the words expressive of this anger; and likewise from what immediately follows, where it is said, "Bring them out unto us, that we may know them;" all of which show that denial is involved. (That they who are against the good of charity are against the Lord and deny Him in heart, although they profess Him with the mouth for the sake of the love of self and of the world, may be seen above, n. 2343, 2349.)

2353. *This night.* That this signifies the last time, when these are no longer acknowledged, is evident from the signification of "night," as being a time of darkness, when the things of light are no longer seen. The angels did not come in the night, but in the evening; but as it is the men of Sodom who spoke and cried out, that is, those who are in falsity and evil, it is not said in the "evening," but in the "night." For in the Word "night" signifies the time and state when there is no longer any light of truth, but merely falsity and evil; [2] thus the last time when comes the Judgment; with which signification it is often found, as in *Micah:*—

Against the prophets that lead the people astray : It shall be night unto you that ye have no vision ; and it shall be dark unto you, that ye shall not divine, and the sun shall go down upon the prophets, and the day shall be black over them (iii. 5, 6).

"Prophets" here denote those who teach falsities; "night," the being "dark," the "going down of the sun," the "blackening day," denote falsities and evils. [3] In *John:*—

If any one walk in the day, he stumbleth not ; but if any one walk in the night he stumbleth, because the light is not in him (xi. 9, 10) ;

where "night" denotes falsity from evil; "light," truth from good; for as all the light of truth is from good, so all the night of falsity is from evil. [4] Again:—

I must work the works of Him that sent Me while it is day ; the night cometh when no one can work (ix. 4) ;

"day" denotes the time and state when there is what is good and true; but "night" when there is what is evil and false. [5] In *Luke:*—

I say unto you, in that night there shall be two upon one bed, the one shall be accepted, the other abandoned (xvii. 34) ;

here "night" denotes the last time, when there is no longer
any truth of faith.   [6] Inasmuch as when the sons of Israel
went out from Egypt there was represented in that country
the vastation of good and truth within the church, and that
there then reigned therein nothing but what was evil and
false, it was commanded that they should go out at midnight
(*Exod.* xi. 4); and it also came to pass that at midnight all
the firstborn of Egypt were slain (*Exod.* xii. 12, 29, 30).   And
inasmuch as they who are in what is good and true, who were
represented by the sons of Israel, are guarded when among
falsities and evils (as was Lot in Sodom), that night, in respect
to them, is called "a night of the guardings of Jehovah"
(verse 42).

2354. *Bring them out unto us, that we may know them.*
That this signifies that they desired to show that it is false
to acknowledge that these exist (namely, the Lord's Divine
Human and Holy proceeding), is evident from the signification
of the "two angels" (see n. 2320); as also from the angry feeling
with which these things were said, and in which there is what
is expressive of denial.   [2] There is here described the first
state of a vastated church; that is, the state when there begins
to be no faith because there is no charity; which state as before said is that because they are against the good of charity
they are also in no faith, and especially in no acknowledgment
of the Lord's Divine Human and Holy proceeding.   These are
at heart denied by all who are in a life of evil, that is, by all
who despise others in comparison with themselves, who hate
those who do not pay them respect, who feel a delight in being
revenged on them, who even feel delight in cruelty, and who
regard adulteries as matters of no moment.   The Pharisees of
old, who openly denied the Lord's Divinity, did better than is
the case with such men at the present day, who for the sake
of their own exaltation and sordid enrichment outwardly worship Him in a holy manner, but inwardly cherish that profane
state.   The successive development and doom of such as these
is described in what follows by the men of Sodom, and finally
by the overthrow of that city (verses 24, 25).   [3] The case
with man (as before stated several times) is that there are
with him evil spirits, and at the same time angels.   Through

the evil spirits he communicates with hell, and through the angels with heaven (n. 687, 697). In so far therefore as his life approximates to what is evil, so far hell flows in; but in so far as his life approximates to what is good, so far heaven flows in, and therefore the Lord. From this it is evident that they who are in a life of evil cannot acknowledge the Lord, but frame for themselves innumerable things against Him; because the phantasies of hell flow in and are received by them. But they who are in a life of good acknowledge the Lord, because heaven flows in, in which love and charity are the main thing; because heaven is the Lord's, from whom come all things of love and charity (see n. 537, 540, 547, 548, 551, 553, 685, 2130).

2355. Verses 6, 7. *And Lot went out unto them to the door* (janua), *and shut the door* (ostium) *behind him. And he said, I pray you my brethren do not wickedly.* " Lot went out unto them to the door," signifies that he applied himself prudently; " and shut the door behind him," signifies lest they should do violence to the good of charity, and also deny the Lord's Divine Human and Holy proceeding; "and he said," signifies exhortation; "I pray you my brethren do not wickedly," signifies that they should not do violence to them. He calls them " brethren," because it is from good that he exhorts them.

2356. *And Lot went out unto them to the door.* That this signifies that he applied himself prudently, is evident from the interior sense of the expression "door," and of "going out to the door." In the Word a "door" signifies that which introduces or gives admission either to truth, to good, or to the Lord. Hence it is that a "door" signifies truth itself, good itself, and also the Lord Himself; for truth leads to good, and good to the Lord. Such things were represented by the door and veils of the Tent, and also of the Temple (see n. 2145, 2152, 2576). [2] That this is the signification of a " door," is evident from the Lord's words in *John:*—

He that entereth not by the door into the sheepfold, but climbeth up some other way, the same is a thief and a robber; but he that entereth in by the door is the shepherd of the sheep; to him the porter openeth. I am the door of the sheep; by Me if any one enter in, he shall be saved (x. 1–3, 7, 9).

Here the "door" denotes truth and good, and therefore the
Lord, who is truth itself and good itself. From this it is evident what is signified by being admitted into heaven through
the door, and consequently what is signified by the keys with
which the door is opened. [3] But in the present case by the
"door" is signified some good adapted to the character of those
who beset the house; for the "door (*janua*)" is here distinguished from the "door (*ostium*)," and was at the front of the
house (as is evident from the fact that Lot went out and closed
the door behind him) and from what immediately follows it is
evident that the good in question was a blessedness of life by
which he would persuade those who were in falsity and evil;
for such do not suffer themselves to be persuaded by the veriest
good itself, but reject it. From all which it is evident that by
"going out to the door" is here signified that he applied himself prudently.

2357. *And shut the door behind him.* That this signifies
lest they should do violence to the good of charity and should
also deny the Lord's Divine Human and Holy proceeding, is
evident from what has been already said. In the present case
to "shut the door" denotes lest they should enter into the
good signified by the "house," and therefore to the Lord's
Divine and Holy. [2] These things involve still deeper arcana, into the sense and idea of which the angels come when
these words are being read, namely, that they who are in a life
of evil are admitted no further than to the knowledge of good
and of the Lord, but not into the veriest acknowledgment and
faith; for the reason that so long as they are in evil they cannot be at the same time in good. No one can at the same time
serve two masters. When a man who once acknowledges and
believes returns to a life of evil, he profanes what is good and
holy; but he who does not acknowledge and believe, cannot
profane. Care is therefore taken by the Lord's Divine Providence lest a man be admitted further into the very acknowledgment and faith of the heart than he can afterwards be
kept; and this on account of the punishment of profanation,
which is the most grievous in hell. [3] This is the reason
why at the present day it is vouchsafed to so few, to believe
from the heart that the good of love and charity are heaven

in man, and that all the Divine is in the Lord; for at the present day men are in a life of evil. This then is what is more interiorly signified by Lot's shutting the door behind him; for this door was an inner door, through which there was admission into the house itself where the angels were; that is, into the good in which is the Lord.

2358. *And he said.* That this signifies exhortation, is evident from what now follows, thus without further explication.

2359. *I pray you my brethren do not wickedly.* That this signifies that they should not do violence to them, namely, to the good of charity and the Lord's Divine Human and Holy proceeding, is evident from the signification of "doing wickedly," as being to do violence. From all this it is evident that those are treated of who are within the church, and that it is they who are meant by the "men of Sodom;" for no one can do violence to these holy things except one who is in possession of the Word. That these things are most holy can be seen from the fact that no one can be admitted into the Lord's kingdom (that is, into heaven) unless he is in the good of love and of charity; and no one can be in the good of love and of charity, unless he acknowledges the Lord's Divine and Holy; for this good flows in from Him alone, and indeed into the good itself which is from Him. The Divine cannot flow in except into the Divine, nor be communicated to man except through the Lord's Divine Human and His Holy thence derived. From this we can understand how it is that the Lord is the all in all of His kingdom; and also that nothing of the good that is with man is man's, but is the Lord's.

2360. That Lot calls them "brethren" because it is from good that he exhorts them, is evident from the signification of a "brother." In the Word "brother" signifies the same as "neighbor," for the reason that every one ought to love his neighbor as himself; thus brethren were so called from love; or what is the same, from good. This manner of naming and addressing the neighbor comes from the fact that in heaven the Lord is the Father of all and loves all as His children; and thus that love is spiritual conjunction. From this the universal heaven resembles as it were one family derived from love and charity (n. 685, 917). [2] Therefore as all the sons of Israel represented the Lord's heavenly kingdom, that is, the kingdom of love and charity; among each other they were called "brethren," and also "companions;" but the latter, that is, "companions," not from the good of love, but from the truth of faith; as in *Isaiah*:—

They help every man his companion, and he saith to his brother, Be of good courage (xli. 6).

In *Jeremiah*:—

Thus shall ye say every man to his companion, and every man to his brother, What hath Jehovah answered? and what hath Jehovah spoken? (xxiii. 35).

In *David*:—

For my brethren and companions' sakes I will say, Peace be within thee (*Ps.* cxxii. 8).

In *Moses*:—

He shall not press upon his companion or his brother, because the release of Jehovah hath been proclaimed (*Deut.* xv. 2, 3).

In *Isaiah*:—

I will confound Egypt with Egypt, and they shall fight every man against his brother, and every man against his companion (xix. 2).

In *Jeremiah*:—

Beware every man of his companion, and trust ye not in any brother; for every brother will utterly supplant, and every companion will slander (ix. 4).

[3] That all who were of that church were called by the one name "brethren," see in *Isaiah*:—

They shall bring all your brethren out of all the nations for an offering unto Jehovah, upon horses, and in chariots, and in litters, and upon mules, and upon dromedaries, to the mountain of My holiness, Jerusalem (lxvi. 20).

They who know nothing beyond the sense of the letter, as was the case with the Jews, believe that no others are signified than the posterity of Jacob; thus that they will be brought back to Jerusalem upon horses, and in chariots, and in litters, and upon mules, by those whom they call the Gentiles. But by the "brethren" are meant all who are in good; and by the "horses," "chariots," and "litters," the things which are of truth and good; and by "Jerusalem" the Lord's kingdom. [4] In *Moses*:—

> When there shall be among thee a needy one of one of thy brethren, in one of thy gates, thou shalt not harden thy heart, and shalt not shut thy hand from thy needy brother (*Deut.* xv. 7, 11).

Again:—

> From among thy brethren thou shalt set a king over thee; thou mayest not put over thee a foreigner, who is not thy brother, and his heart shall not be lifted up above his brethren (*Deut.* xvii. 15, 20).

Again:—

> A prophet from the midst of thee, of thy brethren, like unto me, Jehovah thy God will raise up unto thee; him shall ye obey (*Deut.* xviii. 15, 18).

[5] From all this it is evident that the Jews and Israelites all called one another brethren; but those united by covenant they called companions. Yet as they understood nothing beyond the historical and worldly things of the Word, they believed that they called one another brethren because they were all sons of one father, or of Abraham; yet they were not called "brethren" in the Word from this circumstance, but from the good which they represented. "Abraham" also, in the internal sense, denotes nothing else than love itself, that is, the Lord (n. 1893, 1965, 1989, 2011), whose sons, consequently those who are "brethren," are those who are in good, in fact all those who are called the neighbor; as the Lord teaches in *Matthew*:—

> One is your Master, Christ; all ye are brethren (xxiii. 8).

[6] Again:—

> Whosoever is angry with his brother without cause shall be in danger of the judgment; whosoever shall say to his brother, Raca, shall be in danger of the council. If thou offer a gift upon the altar, and there remember that thy brother hath aught against thee, leave there thy gift before the altar, and go thy way, first be reconciled to thy brother (v. 22–24).

Again:—

> Why beholdest thou the mote that is in thy brother's eye? how wilt thou say to thy brother, Let me cast out the mote out of thine eye (vii. 2–4).

Again :—

If thy brother sin against thee, go and show him his fault between thee and him alone ; if he shall hear thee, thou hast gained thy brother (xviii. 15).

Again :—

Peter coming to Him said, Lord, how oft shall my brother sin against me, and I forgive him ? (xviii. 21).

Again :—

So also will My heavenly Father do unto you, if ye from the heart forgive not every one his brother their trespasses (xviii. 35).

[7] It is clear from these teachings that all in the universe who are the neighbor are called " brethren," and this because every one ought to love his neighbor as himself, thus they are so called from love or good. And as the Lord is good itself, and regards all from good, and is Himself the Neighbor in the highest sense, He also calls them " brethren," as in *John :*—

Jesus said to Mary, Go to My brethren (xx. 17).

And in *Matthew :*—

The King answering shall say unto them, Verily I say unto you, Inasmuch as ye have done it unto one of the least of these My brethren, ye have done it unto Me (xxv. 40).

Thus it is evident that " brother" is a term of love.

2361. Verse 8. *Behold I pray I have two daughters who have not known man ; let me I pray bring them out unto you, and ye may do unto them as is good in your eyes ; only unto these men do not anything ; for therefore are they come under the shadow of my roof.* " Behold I pray I have two daughters who have not known man," signifies the affections of good and of truth; " let me I pray bring them out unto you," signifies blessedness therefrom; " and ye may do unto them as is good in your eyes," signifies enjoyment in so far as they perceived it to be from good; " only unto these men do not anything;" signifies that they should not do violence to the Lord's Divine Human and Holy proceeding; " for therefore are they come under the shadow of my roof," signifies that they are in the good of charity; the " shadow of the roof," denoting in his obscure general [perception] of it.

2362. *Behold I pray I have two daughters who have not known man.* That this signifies the affections of good and of truth, is evident from the signification of " daughters," as being affections (see n. 489–491). Their "not having known man" signifies that falsity had not contaminated them; for "man (*vir*)" signifies rational truth, as also in the opposite sense falsity (n. 265, 749, 1007). There are two affections, namely, of good and of truth (see n. 1997). The former, or the affection of good, constitutes the celestial church, and is called in the Word the "daughter of Zion," and also the "virgin daughter of Zion;" but the latter, or the affection of truth, constitutes the spiritual church, and is called in the Word the "daughter of Jerusalem." [2] As in *Isaiah :*—

The virgin daughter of Zion hath despised thee, hath mocked at thee ; after thee hath the daughter of Jerusalem shaken her head (xxxvii. 22 ; 2 *Kings* xix. 21).

In *Jeremiah :*—

What shall I liken to thee, O daughter of Jerusalem ; what shall I equal to thee, and comfort thee, O virgin daughter of Zion (*Lam.* ii. 13).

In *Micah :*—

Thou, O tower of the flock, the hill of the daughter of Zion, even to thee shall it come, and the former dominion shall come, the kingdom of the daughter of Jerusalem (iv. 8).

In *Zephaniah :*—

Shout, O daughter of Zion ; make a loud noise, O Israel ; be glad and rejoice with all thy heart, O daughter of Jerusalem (iii. 14).

In *Zechariah :*—

Rejoice greatly, O daughter of Zion ; make a loud noise, O daughter of Jerusalem ; behold, thy King shall come unto thee (ix. 9 ; *Matt.* xxi. 5 ; *John* xii. 15).

[3] That the celestial church, or the Lord's celestial kingdom, is called the "daughter of Zion" from the affection of good, that is, from love to the Lord Himself, may be seen further in *Isaiah* (x. 32 ; xvi. 1 ; lii. 2 ; lxii. 11 ; *Jer.* iv. 31 ; vi. 2, 23 ; *Lam.* i. 6 ; ii. 1, 4, 8, 10 ; *Micah* iv. 10, 13 ; *Zech.* ii. 14 ; *Ps.* ix. 14). And that the spiritual church, or the Lord's spiritual kingdom, is called the "daughter of Jerusalem" from the affection of truth, and thus from charity toward the neighbor, may

be seen in *Jeremiah* (*Lam.* ii. 15). Both of these churches and
their characteristics have been treated of many times in Part
First. [4] From the fact that the celestial church is from
love to the Lord in love toward the neighbor, it is likened especially to an unmarried daughter or virgin, and indeed is also
called a " virgin," as in *John :*—

These are they who have not been defiled with women, for they are
virgins ; these are they that follow the Lamb whithersoever He goeth,
for they are without spot before the throne of God (*Rev.* xiv. 4, 5).

That this might be represented in the Jewish Church also, it
was enjoined upon the priests that they should not take widows,
but virgins, for wives (*Lev.* xxi. 13–15; *Ezek.* xliv. 22). [5]
From the things contained in this verse it can be seen how
pure is the Word in the internal sense, although it may not so
appear in the letter; for when these words are read : " Behold
I pray I have two daughters who have not known man ; let
me I pray bring them out unto you, and ye may do unto them
as is good in your eyes, only unto these men do not anything,"
nothing but what is impure enters the ideas, especially the
ideas of those who are in a life of evil. And yet how chaste
these words are in the internal sense, is manifest from the
explication, by which it is shown that they signify the affections of good and of truth, and the blessedness which they who
do no violence to the Lord's Divine and Holy perceive from
the enjoyment of them.

2363. *Let me I pray bring them out unto you.* That this
signifies blessedness therefrom, that is, from the affections of
good and of truth, is evident from the sense of these words
when they are predicated of the affections which are here
meant by the " daughters." As regards the thing itself,
namely, that there is blessedness and happiness solely in the
affection of good and of truth, it is a matter profoundly unknown to all who are in evil and its delight. To them the
blessedness in the affection of good and of truth appears either
as something that is non-existent, or as something that is sad ;
while to some it appears as what is painful, and even deadly.
This is the case with the genii and the spirits of hell, who
think and believe that if the delight of the love of self and of
the world, consequently of the evils therein originating, were

taken away from them, nothing of life could remain to them; and when they are shown that true life with its blessedness and happiness then begins, they feel a kind of sadness from the loss of their own delight; and when they are brought among those who are in such a life, pain and torture seize upon them; and besides this, they then begin to feel in themselves something that is cadaverous and direfully infernal; so that they call heaven (which is the abode of this blessedness and happiness) their hell, and flee away, in order so far as possible to remove and hide themselves from the Lord's face. [2] That neverthless all blessedness and happiness consist in the affection of the good which is of love and charity, and also of the truth which is of faith in so far as the latter leads to the former, can be seen from the fact that heaven (that is, angelic life) consists in this blessedness, and that it affects from the inmosts those who receive it, because it flows in through the inmosts from the Lord (see n. 540, 541, 545). Then also do wisdom and intelligence enter into and fill the inmost recesses of the mind, and kindle the good with heavenly flame, and the truth with heavenly light; and this with a perception of blessedness and happiness of which no description can be given except that they are unutterable. They who are in this state perceive how dead, how sad, and how lamentable is the life of those who are in the evils of the love of self and of the world. [3] In order to obtain a clear idea of the nature of this life of the love of self and of the world (or what is the same, of a life of pride, avarice, envy, hatred, revenge, unmercifulness, adultery), let any person of talent make for himself an impersonation of some one of these evils; or if he can, let him paint it before his eyes in accordance with the ideas he is able to conceive of it from experience, knowledge, and reason; and he will then see, in proportion to the energy of his description or picture, how horrible these evils are, and that they are diabolical forms, in which there is nothing human. Forms such as these do all those become after death who perceive the delight of their life in such evils, and the greater is their delight in them, the more horrible are their own forms. [4] On the other hand, let the same person delineate for himself an impersonation of love and charity, or let him express it before his eyes under some form; and then in proportion to his power of description or portrayal he will see that the form is angelic, full of bliss and beauty, and pervaded within with what is heavenly and Divine. Can any one believe that these two forms can abide together? or that the diabolical form can be put off and be transmuted into the form of charity? and this by a faith to which the life is contrary? For after death every one's life remains; or what is the same, his affection; and in accordance with this is then all his thought, and consequently his faith, which thus manifests itself as it had been at heart.

2364. *And ye may do unto them as is good in your eyes.* That this signifies enjoyment in so far as [they perceived it to be] from good, can be seen even from the sense of the words, as well as from the series, when these words are predicated of the affections signified by the "daughters." That Lot applied himself prudently, is signified by his "going out unto them to the door" (n. 2356). This prudence is evident from the words just quoted, together with what else is contained in this verse, namely, that they should enjoy the blessedness of the affections of good and of truth, in so far as this was from good; which is signified by their "doing unto them as was good in their eyes." To enjoy in so far as this was from good, here means in so far as they knew it to be good, beyond which no one is required to go; for all are bent by the Lord to the good of life through the good of their faith, thus Gentiles otherwise than Christians, the simple otherwise than the learned, little children otherwise than adults. They who have imbued their life with evil are bent by abstaining from evil and intending good, and by doing this according to their apprehension. It is their intention or end that is regarded; and although their acts may not be good in themselves, they nevertheless derive from the end something of good, and of the derivative life, which makes their blessedness.

2365. *Only unto these men do not anything.* That this signifies that they should not do violence to the Lord's Divine Human and Holy proceeding, is evident from the signification of the "men" and the "angels," as above.

2366. *For therefore are they come under the shadow of my roof.* That this signifies that they are in the good of charity, is evident from the signification of a "house," as being good (n. 710, 2233, 2234), which is here called the "shadow of the roof" for a reason to be presently explained.

2367. As to the "shadow of the roof" denoting in an obscure general [perception], the case is this : With man, even when regenerate, the perception of good and truth is very obscure, and this is still more the case with a man who is in external worship, such as is here represented by "Lot." While a man is in corporeal things (that is, while he is living in the body), the affections, like the perceptions, are of a very general nature, and consequently are very obscure, no matter how much the man may suppose that such is not the case. There are myriads of myriads of particulars in every little affection, and even in every idea of his perception, that appear to him as all one, as of the Lord's Divine mercy will be shown hereafter, when affections and ideas are treated of. Sometimes it is possible for a man by reflection to explore and describe a few of the things that are in him, but there lie hidden innumerable other things, things without limit or measure, that never come to his knowledge, nor can come so long as he is living in the body, but which become manifest after corporeal and worldly things have been abolished—as may be sufficiently evident from the fact that when a man who has been in the good of love and of charity passes into the other life, he passes from an obscure life into a clearer one, as from a kind of night into day ; and in proportion as he passes into the Lord's heaven, in the same proportion does he pass into a light that is more and more clear, until he arrives at the light in which are the angels, a light of intelligence and wisdom that is unutterable. In comparison with this the light in which is man, is darkness. Hence it is here said that they "came under the shadow of his roof;" by which is signified that those signified by "Lot" are in their obscure general [perception]; that is, that they know but little concerning the Lord's Divine and Holy ; but that nevertheless they acknowledge and have faith in the existence of these, and that these are in the good of charity, that is, present with those who are in this good.

2368. Verse 9. *And they said, Come on. And they said, Is one come to sojourn, and shall he judge indeed ? now will we do*

*worse to thee than to them.   And they pressed upon the man,
upon Lot, exceedingly ; and drew near to break open the door.*
" And they said," signifies a reply from anger ; " Come on," signifies the threats of their anger.   And they said, " Is one come
to sojourn," signifies those who are of another doctrine and another life ; " and shall he judge indeed?" signifies, Shall they
teach us ?   " Now will we do worse to thee than to them,"
signifies that they would reject the good of charity more than
the Lord's Divine Human and Holy proceeding ; " and they
pressed upon the man," signifies that they desired to offer violence to truth ; " upon Lot exceedingly," signifies most especially to the good of charity ; " and drew near to break open
the door," signifies that they came even to the endeavor to
destroy both.

2369. *And they said.*   That this signifies a reply from
anger, is evident from what precedes and what follows, and
thus without explication.

2370. *Come on.*   That this signifies threats of anger, namely,
against the good of charity, is evident from the signification
of " Lot," as being the good of charity, to which and concerning which these things are said ; and that these are threats of
anger, is evident from the words themselves, and also from
what follows, as involving that they would altogether reject it
if he should say anything more about it, and should persuade ;
which is meant by " Come on."

2371. *And they said, Is one come to sojourn, and shall he
judge indeed?*   That this signifies those who are in another
doctrine and another life, is evident from the signification of
" sojourning," which is to be instructed and to live, thus doctrine and life (see n. 1463, 2025).   The state of the church is
here described such as it is near the last times, when there is
no longer any faith, because there is no charity, namely, that
the good of charity, because it has altogether receded from the
life, is also rejected from the doctrine.   [2] The subject here
treated of is not those who falsify the good of charity by ex-
plaining all things in their own favor, both for their own sake,
that they may be the greatest, and for the sake of the good
things of this world, that they may possess them all ; and who
arrogate to themselves the dispensation of rewards, and thereby

defile the good of charity by various arts and delusive means; but the subject treated of is those who desire to hear nothing of the goods of charity, or of good works, but only of faith separate from them; and this from reasoning that there is nothing but evil in man, and that the good which is from him is also in itself evil, in which therefore there is thus nothing of salvation; and that no one can merit heaven by any good, nor be saved by it, but only by the faith with which they acknowledge the Lord's merit.   This is the doctrine that flourishes in the last times, when the church is beginning to expire, and it is ardently taught and favorably received.   [3] But it is false to infer from these considerations that a man can have an evil life and a good faith; or that because there is nothing but evil in man, he cannot receive good from the Lord that has heaven in it because it has Him in it, and that having heaven in it has also bliss and happiness in it.   And it is certainly very false to infer that because no one can merit heaven by any good, therefore it is impossible to receive from the Lord heavenly good in which self-merit is regarded as monstrous wickedness.   In such good are all the angels, in such are all the regenerate, and in such are they who perceive delight, and even bliss, in good itself, that is, in the affection of it.   Concerning this good, that is, concerning this charity, the Lord speaks thus in *Matthew* :—

Ye have heard that it has been said, Thou shalt love thy neighbor and hate thine enemy; but I say unto you, Do good to them that hate you, and pray for them that injure you and persecute you, that ye may be sons of your Father who is in the heavens; for if ye love them that love you, what reward have ye? and if ye salute your brethren only, what do ye more [than others]? do not even the publicans so? (v. 43-48).

In like manner in *Luke*, with this addition :—

Do good, and lend, hoping for nothing again; then shall your reward be great, and ye shall be sons of the Highest (vi. 27-36).

[4] Here the good which is from the Lord is described, and that it is free from all purpose of receiving recompense; on which account they who are in it are called "sons of the Father who is in the heavens," and "sons of the Highest;" and because the Lord is in it, there is also a reward, as we read in *Luke* :—

When thou makest a dinner or a supper, call not thy friends, nor thy
brethren, nor thy kinsmen, nor thy rich neighbors; lest haply they call
thee in turn, and a recompense be made thee.   But when thou makest a
feast, call the poor, the maimed, [the lame,] and the blind; then shalt
thou be blessed, for they have not wherewith to recompense thee; but
thou shalt be recompensed in the resurrection of the just * (xiv. 12–14).

A " dinner," " supper," or " feast," denotes the good of charity,
in which there is the Lord's dwelling-place with man (n. 2341);
so that it is here described, and made clearly manifest, that
the recompense is in the good itself, because in this is the
Lord; for it is said, " thou shalt be recompensed in the resurrection of the just."   [5] Those who strive to do good of themselves, because the Lord has so commanded, are they who at
length receive this good; and who, being afterwards instructed,
acknowledge with faith that all good is from the Lord (n. 1712,
1937, 1947); and they are then so averse to self-merit that
when they merely think of it they grow sad, and perceive their
blessedness and happiness to be proportionately diminished.
[6] Quite different is it with those who do not do this, but
lead a life of evil, teaching and professing that in faith alone
there is salvation.   People of this character are not aware that
such a good is possible; and wonderful to say (as has been
given me to know from much experience) in the other life
these same people desire to merit heaven on account of whatever good deeds they recollect; because then for the first time
are they aware that in faith separated from charity there is no
salvation.   These are the people of whom the Lord says in
Matthew :—

They will say to Me in that day, Lord, Lord, have we not prophesied
by Thy name, and by Thy name cast out demons, and in Thy name done
many mighty works ?   But then will I confess unto them, I know you
not; depart from Me, ye that work iniquity (vii. 22, 23).

In the case of these same people it also becomes apparent that
they have paid no attention whatever to the things which the
Lord Himself so often taught concerning the good of love and
of charity; but that these things have been to them like passing clouds, or like things seen in the night: for example such
things as are found in *Matthew* iii. 8, 9; v. 7–48; vi. 1–20;

* *Mortuorum*, but elsewhere *justorum*, as in n. 6393.   [*Rotch ed.*]

vii. 16–20, 24–27; ix. 13; xii. 33; xiii. 8, 23; xviii. 21–23, and
to the end; xix. 19; xxii. 34–39; xxiv. 12, 13; xxv. 34 to the
end; *Mark* iv. 18–20; xi. 13, 14, 20; xii. 28–35; *Luke* iii. 8, 9;
vi. 27–39, 43 to the end; vii. 47; viii. 8, 14, 15; x. 25–28; xii.
58, 59; xiii. 6–10; *John* iii. 19, 21; v. 42; xiii. 34, 35; xiv. 14,
15, 20, 21, 23; xv. 1–8, 9–19; xxi. 15–17. Such, then, and
other such things as these, are what are signified by the men
of Sodom (that is, those who are in evil, n. 2220, 2246, 2322)
saying to Lot, " Is one come to sojourn, and shall he judge
indeed ?" that is, Shall they who are in another doctrine and
another life teach us ?

2372. *And shall he judge indeed?*   That this signifies, Shall
they teach us ? is evident from the signification of "judging,"
as being to teach.   That "righteousness" is predicated of the
practice of good, but "judgment" of the instruction of truth,
was shown above (n. 2235); hence in the internal sense to
"judge" is to instruct or teach.   To teach truth is the same
as to teach what is good, because all truth looks to good.

2373. *Now will we do worse to thee than to them.*   That this
signifies that they would reject the good of charity more than
the Lord's Divine Human and Holy proceeding, is evident
from the signification of " Lot," as being the good of charity;
for Lot represents those who are in the good of charity (n.
2324, 2351, 2371); and from the signification of the "men,"
or "angels," as being the Lord as to the Divine Human and
Holy proceeding (see above).   Hence it is evident that to " do
worse to thee than to them" has this meaning.   The reason
why they who are in evil within the church reject charity
more than they deny the Lord, is that in this way they can
favor their concupiscences by a kind of religion, and have external worship with no internal (that is, worship of the lips
and not of the heart), and the more they make this worship
to be Divine and holy, so much the greater are their dignities
and wealth, besides many other causes that are hidden and
yet are manifest.   Nevertheless the truth really is that he who
rejects the one (that is, does so in doctrine and at the same
time in life) rejects also the other (for even if he dare not do
this openly he does it in his heart); and this is here expressed
in the sense of the letter by its being said that the men of

Sodom drew near to break open the door, by which is signified that they came even to the endeavor to destroy both. But that which prevents this endeavor from bursting forth into act is by no means hidden.

2374. *They pressed upon the man.* That this signifies that they desired to offer violence to truth, is evident from the signification of a man (*vir*), as being the intellectual and rational in man, and consequently truth (see n. 158, 1007). To offer violence to truth is to pervert the things of faith; and these are perverted when they are separated from charity, and when it is denied that they lead to the good of life.

2375. *Upon Lot exceedingly.* That this signifies that they desired to offer violence especially to the good of charity, is evident from the signification of "Lot," as being the good of charity (see above, n. 2324, 2351, 2371, 2373). From the very words—that they "pressed upon the man, upon Lot exceedingly"—it is evident that one thing is signified by the "man," and another by "Lot exceedingly;" otherwise one expression would have sufficed.

2376. *And drew near to break open the door.* That this signifies that they came even to the endeavor to destroy both, is evident from the signification of "drawing near," as being to endeavor, and from the signification of a "door," as being that which introduces to good and to the Lord, and also as being good itself and the Lord Himself (n. 2356, 2357). (How this is may be seen above, n. 2373.)

2377. Verse 10. *And the men put forth their hand, and brought Lot into the house to them, and shut the door.* "The men put forth their hand," signifies the Lord's powerful aid; "and brought Lot into the house to them," signifies that the Lord protects those who are in the good of charity; "and shut the door," signifies that He also closes all access to them.

2378. *The men put forth their hand.* That this signifies the Lord's powerful aid, is evident from the signification of the "men," as being the Lord (as shown above), and from the signification of the "hand," as being power (see n. 878).

2379. *And brought Lot into the house to them.* That this signifies that the Lord protects those who are in the good of charity, is evident from the representation of Lot, as being those who are in the good of charity (spoken of above); and from the signification of "bringing into the house to them," as being to protect. To be "brought into the house" denotes to be brought into good; and they who are brought into good are brought into heaven; and they who are brought into heaven are brought to the Lord; hence they are protected from all infestation as to their souls. That the man who is in good is as to his soul in society with angels, and while living in the body is nevertheless in heaven (although at the time he is not aware of this, and is not able to perceive angelic joy in consequence of being in corporeal things and in a state of preparation), may be seen above (n. 1277).

2380. *And shut the door.* That this signifies that He also closes all access to them, is evident from the signification of a "door," as being that which introduces (n. 2356, 2357, 2376), thus access. Hence it is that to "shut the door" denotes to preclude access. In the other life access is precluded by the good being separated from the evil, so that they cannot be infested by the spheres of the persuasions of falsity and of the cupidities of evil; for the exhalation from hell cannot penetrate to heaven. In the life of the body access is precluded by the principles and persuasions of falsity being rendered powerless against those who are in good; for whenever any falsity of evil or evil of falsity is infused into them, whether in speech by an evil man, or in thought by an evil spirit or devil, the angels who are with them at once turn it aside, and bend it to something true and good in which the persons in question have been confirmed; and this however severely they may be suffering bodily trouble, for the angels esteem the body as nothing in comparison with the soul. [2] While a man remains in corporeal things, he is in such a general and obscure idea and perception (see n. 2367) that he scarcely knows whether he is in the good of charity or not; and this for the additional reason that he does not know what charity is, and what the neighbor is. But be it known who the persons in question are. All those are in the good of charity who have conscience (that is, who are unwilling to depart in any degree from what is just and fair, and good and true, and this for the very sake of what is just and fair, and good and true, for this principle is from conscience), and who from having conscience think well of the neighbor and desire his welfare, even should he be an enemy; and this without any recompense. These are they who are in the good of charity, whether they be without the church or within the church. If within the church, they adore the Lord, and willingly hear and do the things that He has taught. [3] On the other hand, they who are in evil have no conscience; for that which is just and fair they care not, except in so far as thereby they can gain the reputation of seeming to care for it. What the good and truth are that affect the spiritual life they know not, and even reject this as being no life at all. Further than this: they think evilly about the neighbor and desire his injury, and also inflict injury upon him if he does not favor them, even if a friend; and in doing this they feel delight. Should they do anything good, it is with a view to recompense. Such within the church deny the Lord in secret; and in so far as honor, gain, reputation, or life are not endangered they do so openly. [4] Be it known however that some persons think they are not in good when they are, and some that they are in good when they are not. The reason why some think they are not in good when they are, is that when they reflect upon the good in themselves, it is at once insinuated by the angels in whose society they are, that they are not in good, lest they should attribute the good to themselves, and lest their thought should be turned to their own merit, and thereby to the setting up of themselves above others. Without this guardianship they would fall into temptations. [5] As regards some supposing themselves to be in good when they are not, the cause of this is that when they reflect upon it, it is immediately insinuated by the evil genii and spirits in whose companionship they are, that they are in good (for the evil believe delight to be good), and it is suggested that whatever good they have done to others for the sake of the love of self and of the world is good that is to be recompensed even in the other life; thus that they have merit above others, whom they despise in comparison with themselves, and indeed esteem them as of no account. And, wonderful to say, if they were to think differently they would fall into temptations, in which they would yield.

2381. Verse 11. *And the men who were at the door of the house they smote with blindness, from small even to great ; and they labored to find the door.* "The men who were at the door of the house," signifies things rational and the derivative doctrinals, by which violence is offered to the good of charity ; "they smote with blindness," signifies that they were filled with falsities ; "from small even to great," signifies in particular and in general ; "and they labored to find the door," signifies so that they could not see any truth that would lead to good.

2382. *And the men who were at the door of the house.* That this signifies things rational and the derivative doctrinals, by which violence is offered to the good of charity, is evident from the signification of "men," as being things rational (see n. 158, 1007) ; from the signification of a "door," as being introduction or access, leading either to truth or to good, and thus what is doctrinal (see above, n. 2356) ; and from the signification of a "house," as being the good of charity (see above in various places). Here, because those are treated of who drew near to break open the door (that is, who attempted to destroy both the good of charity and the Divine and the Holy of the Lord, n. 2376), evil rational things are meant, and the derivative false doctrinals by which violence is inflicted on the good of charity.

2383. *They smote with blindness.* That this signifies that they were filled with falsities, is evident from the signification of "blindness." In the Word "blindness" is predicated of those who are in falsity, and also of those who are in ignorance of truth. Both are called the "blind ;" but which are meant in any special instance can be seen from the series or connection, especially in the internal sense. That they who are in falsity are called the "blind," is evident from the following passages. In *Isaiah :*—

His watchmen are blind, they are all ignorant, they are all dumb dogs, they cannot bark (lvi. 10).

"Blind watchmen," denotes those who from reasoning are in falsity. Again :—

We look for light, and behold darkness ; for brightness, but we walk in thick darkness ; we grope for the wall like the blind (lix. 9, 10).

In *Jeremiah* :—

They have wandered as the blind in the streets ; they have polluted themselves with blood ; what they cannot pollute, they touch with their garments (*Lam.* iv. 14) ;

meaning that all truths have been polluted; the " streets" denoting the truths wherein they have gone astray (n. 2336). [2] In *Zechariah* :—

In that day I will smite every horse with astonishment, and his rider with madness ; every horse of the peoples will I smite with blindness (xii. 4).

Here and elsewhere in the Word a " horse" denotes the understanding ; hence it is said that the " horse should be smitten with astonishment," and that the " horse of the peoples should be smitten with blindness," that is, should be filled with falsities. [3] In *John* :—

For judgment am I come into the world, that they that see not may see, and that they that see may become blind. They of the Pharisees heard these things, and said, Are we also blind ? Jesus said unto them, If ye were blind, ye would not have sin ; but now ye say, We see, therefore your sin remaineth (ix. 39–41).

Here the " blind" in both senses are spoken of, namely, those who are in falsity, and those who are in ignorance of truth. With those who are within the church and know what the truth is, " blindness" is falsity ; but with those who do not know what the truth is (as is the case with those who are outside the church), " blindness" is ignorance of the truth, and these are blameless. [4] Again :—

He hath blinded their eyes, and hardened their heart, that they may not see with their eyes, and understand with their heart, and I should heal them (*John* xii. 40 ; *Isa.* vi. 9–11) ;

meaning that it would be better for them to be in falsities than to be in truths, because they are in a life of evil, and if they were instructed in truths, they would not only still falsify them, but would also defile them with evils ; for the like reason that the men of Sodom were smitten with blindness, that is, the doctrinal things were filled with falsities. (Why this was done was shown above, n. 301–303, 593, 1008, 1010, 1059, 1327, 1328, 2426.) [5] As what is blind signified what is false, therefore in the representative Jewish Church it was forbidden to sacrifice anything that was blind (*Lev.* xxii. 22; *Deut.* xv. 21; *Mal.* i. 8). It was also forbidden that any one of the priests who was blind should draw near to offer upon the altar (*Lev.* xxi. 18, 21). [6] That "blindness" is predicated of ignorance of truth, such as prevails with the Gentiles, is evident in *Isaiah* :—

In that day shall the deaf hear the words of the Book, and the eyes of the blind shall see out of thick darkness and out of darkness (xxix. 18).

Here the "blind" denotes those who are in ignorance of truth, being chiefly those outside the church. Again :—

Bring forth the blind people and they shall have eyes ;* and the deaf and they shall have ears (xliii. 8) ;

where the church of the Gentiles is spoken of. Again :—

I will lead the blind in a way that they have not known ; I will make darkness light before them (xlii. 16).

[7] And again :—

I will give Thee for a light of the people, to open the blind eyes, to bring out the bound from the dungeon, and them that sit in darkness out of the prison-house (xlii. 6, 7) ;

where the Lord's advent is treated of, in that they who are in ignorance of truth should then be instructed ; for those who are in falsity do not suffer themselves to be so instructed, because they are acquainted with the truth and have confirmed themselves against it, and have turned the light into darkness, which cannot be dispelled. In *Luke* :—

The master of the house said to his servant, Go out quickly into the streets and lanes of the city, and bring in hither the poor, and the maimed, and the lame, and the blind (xiv. 21) ;

where the Lord's kingdom is treated of, and it is evident that the poor, maimed, lame, and blind are not meant, but those who are such in the spiritual sense. [8] Again :—

Jesus said that they should tell John that the blind see, the lame walk, the lepers are cleansed, the deaf hear, the dead are raised, and to the poor the gospel is preached (vii. 22).

* *Et oculi erunt ;* but *cui oculi sunt* in n. 6989. [*Rotch ed.*]

According to the sense of the letter, by the "blind," the
"lame," the "lepers," the "deaf," the "dead," the "poor,"
only these are meant; because it was actually the case that
the blind received sight, the deaf hearing, the lepers health,
the dead life; [9] but yet in the internal sense the same are
meant as in *Isaiah :—*

   Then shall the eyes of the blind be opened, and the ears of the deaf
shall be unstopped, and the lame shall leap as the hart, and the tongue of
the dumb shall sing (xxxv. 5, 6) ;

where the Lord's advent is treated of, and the new church at
that time, which is called that of the Gentiles; of whom it is
declared that they were "blind," "deaf," "lame," and "dumb;"
being so called in respect to doctrine and to life. For be it
known that all the miracles performed by the Lord always
involved, and thence signified, such things as are meant in the
internal sense by the healing of the blind, of the lame, of the
lepers, the deaf, the dead, and the poor. For this reason the
Lord's miracles were Divine, as also were those performed in
Egypt and in the wilderness, as well as all the other miracles
that are treated of in the Word. This is an arcanum.

   2384. *From small even to great.* That this signifies in particular and in general, is evident from the signification in the
internal sense of these words when predicated of rational
things and the doctrinal things thence derived, which are signified by the men who were at the door of the house; for particulars and generals are related to each other as are the small
and the great, particulars being as small things, and the generals of particulars as great ones. (What particulars are relatively to generals, and how they stand related to each other,
may be seen above, n. 920, 1040, 1316.)

   2385. *And they labored to find the door.* That this signifies
so that they could not see any truth that would lead to good,
is evident from the signification of a "door," as being introduction and access, and as being truth itself, because this introduces to good (see above, n. 2356). But here by the "door"
are signified the knowledges that introduce to truth; for the
"door" (as said above, n. 2356) was at the front of the house,
for it is said that Lot "went out to the door, and shut the door

behind him" (verse 6): hence to "labor to find the door," denotes not to see any truth that would lead to good. [2] Such do those become, especially in the last times, who by ratiocination hatch doctrinal things, and believe nothing unless they first apprehend it; for in this case the life of evil continually inflows into their rational, and a kind of fallacious light pours in from the fire of the affections of evil, and causes them to see falsities as truths; as are wont to do those who see phantoms in nocturnal light. These same things are then confirmed in many ways, and become matters of doctrine, such as are the doctrinal tenets of those who say that the life (which is of the affection) is of no efficacy, but only the faith (which is of the thought). [3] That every principle whatever, even if falsity itself, when once taken up, can be confirmed by innumerable things, and be presented in the outward form as if it were truth itself, may be known to every one. Hence come heresies; from which, when once confirmed, the man never recedes. Yet from a false principle nothing but falsities can flow; and even if truths are interlarded among them, they became truths falsified when used to confirm a false principle, because they are contaminated by its essence. [4] Very different is the case when truth itself is received as a principle, and this is confirmed, as for example that love to the Lord and charity toward the neighbor are that on which hangs all the Law, and of which all the Prophets speak, and that they are therefore the essentials of all doctrine and worship; for in this case the mind would be illuminated by innumerable things in the Word, that otherwise lie hidden in the obscurity of a false principle. Nay, in such a case heresies would be dissipated, and one church would arise out of many, no matter how greatly the doctrinal and ritual matters that flowed from or led to it might differ. [5] Such was the ancient Church, which extended through many kingdoms, namely, Assyria, Mesopotamia, Syria, Ethiopia, Arabia, Libya, Egypt, Philistia as far as Tyre and Sidon, and through the land of Canaan on both sides the Jordan. Among these the doctrinal and ritual matters differed, but still the church was one, because to them charity was the essential thing. Then was there the Lord's kingdom on earth as in the heavens, for such is heaven (see

n. 684, 690). If it were so now, all would be governed by
the Lord as one man; for they would be as the members and
organs of one body, which, although not of similar form, nor
of similar function, yet all have relation to one heart, on which
depend all and each in their several forms, that are everywhere varied. Then would each person say, in whatever doctrine and in whatever outward worship he might be, This is
my brother, I see that he worships the Lord, and is a good
man.

2386. Verse 12. *And the men said unto Lot, Hast thou yet
any one here? son-in-law, and thy sons, and thy daughters, and
whomsoever thou hast in the city, bring them out of the place.*
"And the men said unto Lot," signifies that the Lord admonishes those who are in the good of charity; "hast thou yet
any one here? son-in-law, and thy sons, and thy daughters,
and whomsoever thou hast in the city, bring them out of the
place," signifies that all who are in the good of charity, and
that all things belonging thereto, would be saved, and also
those who are in the truth of faith, provided they would recede from evil; "sons-in-law," are the truths that are associated
with the affections of good; here, that were to be associated;
"sons," are truths; "daughters," affections of good and of
truth; "whomsoever thou hast in the city," denotes whatever
derives anything from truth; the "place," is the state of evil.

2387. *And the men said unto Lot.* That this signifies that
the Lord admonishes those who are in the good of charity, is
evident from the signification of the "men," as being the Lord
(see n. 2378); from the signification of "saying," as being to
admonish; and from the representation of Lot, as being those
who are in the good of charity (see n. 2324, 2351, 2371).
Hence these words, "the men said unto Lot," signifies that
the Lord admonishes those who are in the good of charity.

2388. *Hast thou yet any one here? son-in-law, and thy sons,
and thy daughters, and whomsoever thou hast in the city, bring
them out of the place.* That this signifies that all who are in
the good of charity, and that all things belonging thereto,
would be saved, and also those who are in the truth of faith,
provided they would recede from evil, is evident from the
signification of "sons-in-law," of "sons," of "daughters," of

" city," and of " place," concerning which in what follows. [2]
As regards those being saved who are in the truth of faith,
provided they recede from evil, the case is this.   The truths
of faith are the very receiving vessels of good (n. 1900, 2063,
2261, 2269); and they receive good in so far as the man recedes from evil; for good continually flows in from the Lord,
and it is the evil of life that hinders its being received in the
truths which are with man in his memory or knowledge. Therefore in so far as a man recedes from evil, so far good enters
and applies itself to his truths; and then the truth of faith
with him becomes the good of faith. A man may indeed know
truth, may also confess it under the incitement of some worldly
cause, may even be persuaded that it is true; and yet this truth
does not live so long as he is in a life of evil. For such a man
is like a tree on which there are leaves, but no fruit; and his
truth is like light in which there is no heat, such as there is
in the time of winter when nothing grows. But when there
is heat in it, the light then becomes such as there is in the
time of spring, when all things grow. In the Word truth is
compared to light and is called "light," but heat is compared
to love, and is also called spiritual heat. In the other life
also truth manifests itself by light, and good by heat; but
truth without good by cold light, and truth with good by light
similar to that of spring. This shows what the truth of faith
is without the good of charity. Hence it is that the sons-in-
law and the sons, by whom such truths are signified, were not
saved; but only Lot with his daughters. [3] As it is here
said that those also who are in the truth of faith are saved,
provided they recede from evil, be it known that these are
they who profess faith and think nothing about charity for
the reason that they have been so instructed, and do not know
what charity is (supposing that it consists merely in the giving
of our own to others, and in pitying everybody), and who also
do not know what the neighbor is toward whom charity is to
be exercised (for they suppose that the neighbor is almost
everybody, without distinction), and yet who live in the life
of charity toward the neighbor, because in the life of good. It
does these persons no harm to profess faith along with all the
rest, for in their faith there is charity, since this means all

the good of life in general and in particular. What therefore charity is, and what the neighbor, will of the Lord's Divine mercy be told in what follows.

2389. That the "sons-in-law" are the truths that are associated with the affections of good and of truth, in this case that were to be associated, is evident from the signification of "sons-in-law." In the Word "a man" signifies truth, and a "wife" good (n. 265, 749, 915, 1007), for the reason that between truth and good there is a likeness of a marriage (n. 1432, 1904, 2173). Hence "sons-in-law" signify the knowledges of truth, with which are associated the affections of good (denoted by the "daughters"), but which here are to be associated, for it is said afterwards, in verse 14, that Lot went out and spoke to his sons-in-law that were marrying, that is, were about to marry his daughters.

2390. That the "sons" are truths, or what is the same, are they who are in truths, is evident from the signification of "sons," as being truths (see n. 489, 491, 533, 1147).

2391. That the "daughters" are affections of good, and of truth, or what is the same, are those who are in these affections, is evident from the signification of "daughters," as being these affections (see n. 2362).

2392. That "whomsoever thou hast in the city," denotes whatever derives anything from truth, is evident from the signification of a "city," as being what is doctrinal, thus truth in its complex (see n. 402, 2268).

2393. That the "place" is a state of evil, is evident from the signification of "place," as being state (see above, n. 1273 to 1275, 1377), here a state of evil, because it was Sodom, by which is signified evil in general (n. 2220, 2246, 2322).

2394. Verse 13. *For we will destroy this place, because their cry is become great before Jehovah, and Jehovah hath sent us to destroy it.* "For we will destroy this place," signifies that the state of evil in which they were would condemn them; "because their cry is become great before Jehovah," signifies because the falsity from evil is so great; "and Jehovah hath sent us to destroy it," signifies that they cannot but perish.

2395. *For we will destroy this place.* That this signifies that the state of evil in which they were would condemn them,

is evident from the meaning of " destroying," when predicated
of the Lord, as being in the internal significance to perish by
evil, that is, to be condemned; and also from the signification
of " this place," as being a state of evil (n. 2393). It is frequently said in the Word that Jehovah " destroys;" but in the
internal sense it is meant that man destroys himself; for Jehovah or the Lord destroys no one.   But as from the fact of
His seeing and regulating all things in both general and particular it appears as if the destruction came from Jehovah or
the Lord, it is so expressed in many places in the Word, to the
end that men may thereby be kept in a most general idea that
all things are under the Lord's eyes, and all things under His
auspices; for if at first they are kept in this idea, they can
afterwards be easily-instructed.   For the explications of the
Word as to the internal sense are nothing but particulars
that elucidate a general idea.   [2] Another reason why it is
so expressed is that they who are in no love are kept in fear,
and thereby stand in awe of the Lord, and flee to Him for the
sake of deliverance.   This shows that it does no harm to believe the sense of the letter, even though the internal sense
teaches something else, provided that it is done from a simple
heart.   But these things will be treated of more fully in what
follows, at verse 24 (n. 2447), where it is said that Jehovah
caused it to rain brimstone and fire upon Sodom and Gomorrah.   The angels, being in the internal sense, are so far from
thinking that Jehovah destroys any one, that they cannot endure even the idea of such a thing; and therefore when these
and other such things are read in the Word by man, the sense
of the letter is cast away as it were to the back, and at last
passes into this : that evil itself is what destroys man, and that
the Lord destroys no one (as may be seen from the example
given above in n. 1875).

2396. *Because their cry is become great before Jehovah.* That
this signifies because the falsity from evil is so great, is evident from the signification of a " cry" (n. 2240), as being predicated of falsity; and here of falsity from evil (n. 2351).

2397. *And Jehovah hath sent us to destroy it.* That this
signifies that they cannot but perish, is to be understood in
the same way as the signification given just above (n. 2395).

That " us" (that is, the " men" or " angels") denotes the Lord's Divine Human and Holy proceeding, has been shown above. Through these were the good saved, and the evil destroyed; and yet the latter by the law that evil itself destroyed them. And because they perished in this way, and this through the Lord's advent into the world, it is said according to the appearance, that they " were sent to destroy them." [2] It is sometimes said of the Lord in the Word, that He was "sent by the Father," as it is said here, " Jehovah hath sent us ;" but in the internal sense by being "sent" is everywhere signified to go forth, as in *John :*—

They have received, and have known of a truth that I came forth from Thee, and they have believed that Thou didst send Me (xvii. 8).

So in other places, as in the same :—

God sent not His Son into the world to judge the world, but that the world through Him may be saved (iii. 17).

Again :—

He that honoreth not the Son, honoreth not the Father who hath sent Him (v. 23).

Besides many other passages (as *Matt.* x. 40; xv. 24; *John* iii. 34; iv. 34; v. 30, 36–38; vi. 29, 39, 40, 44, 57; vii. 16, 18, 28, 29; viii. 16, 18, 29, 42; ix. 4; x. 36; xi. 41, 42; xii. 44, 45, 49; xiii. 20; xiv. 24; xvii. 18; xx. 21; *Luke* iv. 43; ix. 48; x. 16; *Mark* ix. 37; *Isa.* lxi. 1). [3] In the same way it is said of the Holy Spirit, that it was " sent," that is, that it goes forth from the Lord's Divine, as in *John :*—

Jesus said, When the Comforter shall come, whom I will send unto you from the Father, the Spirit of Truth which goeth forth from the Father, He shall testify of Me (xv. 26).

Again :—

If I go away, I will send the Comforter unto you (xvi. 5, 7).

Hence the prophets were said to be " sent," because the words which they spoke came forth from the Holy of the Lord's Spirit. And because all Divine Truth comes forth from Divine Good, the expression "to be sent" is properly predicated of Divine Truth. But what "to go forth" means, is also evident, namely, that he who goes forth, or that which goes forth, is of him from whom it goes forth.

2398. Verse 14. *And Lot went out and spake to his sons-in-law, that were to marry his daughters, and said, Up, get you out of this place, for Jehovah will destroy the city. And he was in the eyes of his sons-in-law as one that jested.* "Lot went out," signifies those who are in the good of charity, and also the good itself of charity; "and spake to his sons-in-law, that were to marry his daughters," signifies with those who were in truths, with which the affections of good could be adjoined; "and said, Up, get you out of this place," signifies that they should not remain in a state of evil; "for Jehovah will destroy the city," signifies that they must needs perish; "and he was in the eyes of his sons-in-law as one that jested," signifies derision.

2399. *And Lot went out.* That this signifies those who are in the good of charity, and also the good itself of charity, has been repeatedly shown before. He who represents those who are in good, also signifies that good itself in which they are.

2400. *And spake to his sons-in-law, that were to marry his daughters.* That this signifies with those who were in truths, with which the affections of good could be conjoined, is evident from the signification of "sons-in-law," as being the knowledges of truth, and consequently truths (concerning which see above, n. 2389); and from the signification of "daughters," as being the affections of good (see also above, n. 2362); and because it is said that he "spake to his sons-in-law, that were to marry his daughters," it is signified with those who were in truths with which the affections of good could be conjoined. As they could be conjoined, they are called his "sons-in-law;" but as they were not conjoined, it is said "that were to marry his daughters." [2] The subject here treated of is the third kind of men who are within the church, namely, those who know truths, yet live in evil. For there are three kinds of men within the church: first, those who live in the good of charity; these are represented by "Lot;" second, those who are altogether in falsity and evil, and reject both truth and good; these are they who are represented by the "men of Sodom;" third, those who indeed know truths, but nevertheless are in evil; these are here signified by the " sons-in-law," and are especially those who teach, but the truth which they teach has not sent down its root deeper than is wont to do the knowledge that is solely of the memory, for it is learned and vaunted merely for the sake of honor and gain. And because with such persons the ground in which the truth is sown is the love of self and the love of the world, they have no belief in the truth, except a kind of persuasive one derived from these loves, the quality of which shall of the Lord's Divine mercy be told elsewhere. Such are here described by the sons-in-law, in that they believed nothing concerning the overthrow of Sodom, but laughed at it; and such is the faith of their heart.

2401. *And said, Up, get you out of this place.* That this signifies that they should not remain in a state of evil, is evident from the signification of "rising up," and of "getting out," and also of the "place." To "rise up" often occurs in the Word, but excites little thought as to what it further signifies, because it is a familiar expression. But in the internal sense this expression involves elevation, as here, from evil to good; for the mind is elevated when it recedes from evil (n. 2388). To "get out" is to recede, or not to remain. And the "place" is a state of evil (n. 2393). Thus the signification is evident. [2] The quality of those who are in the knowledges of truth, but at the same time in a life of evil, has been repeatedly stated before, namely, that so long as they are in a life of evil they believe nothing; for to will evil and from will to do evil, and at the same time to acknowledge truth in faith, is not possible. This shows also that a man cannot be saved by thinking and speaking what is true, nor even what is good, while he wills nothing else, and from this his will does nothing else, than evil. It is the very will of man that lives after death; not so his thought, except that which flows from his will. [3] As therefore a man is such as his will is, it is evident what must be his opinion of the truths of faith he has learned, and even taught, seeing that they condemn him. So far is he then from making them the basis of his thoughts, that he feels a positive aversion for them; nay, in so far as he is permitted to do so, he, like the devil's crew, blasphemes them. They who have not been instructed concerning the life after death may suppose that it will be easy for them to receive faith when they see that the Lord governs the universe, and when they hear that heaven consists in loving the Lord and the neighbor; whereas the truth is that the evil are as far from being able to receive faith, that is, to believe from the will, as hell is from heaven, for they are wholly in evil, and in the falsity thence derived. That such persons are against the Lord and against the neighbor, and therefore against good, and consequently against truth, is known and perceived from their mere approach, or presence. There is a horrible sphere that exhales from the life of their will and of their derivative thought (n. 1048, 1053, 1316, 1504). [4] If by mere instruction in the other life it were possible that men could be brought to believe and to become good, there would not be a single person in hell; for the Lord desires to raise all without exception to Himself into heaven. For His mercy is infinite, because it is the Divine mercy itself, that is extended toward the whole human race, and therefore toward the evil as well as toward the good.

2402. *For Jehovah will destroy the city.* That this signifies that they must needs perish, is evident from the explication of nearly the same words above (n. 2395, 2397).

2403. *And he was in the eyes of his sons-in-law as one that jested.* That this signifies derision, is evident from the signification of "jesting," as being to utter as it were a joke, a fable, or trifles, thus such things as they would laugh at. "In their eyes," signifies that which was before their rational, as is evident from the signification of the "eyes" (n. 212). This shows what is the character of those who are in the truth of faith and not at the same time in the good of life.

2404. Verse 15. *And when the dawn arose the angels pressed Lot to hasten, saying, Arise, take thy wife, and thy two daughters that are found, lest thou be consumed in the iniquity of the city.* "When the dawn arose," signifies when the Lord's kingdom is approaching; "the angels pressed Lot to hasten," signifies that the Lord withheld them from evil and kept them in good; "saying, Arise, take thy wife, and thy two daughters that are found," signifies the truth of faith and the affections of truth and of good; "found," denotes that they are separated from evil; "lest thou be consumed in the iniquity of the city," signifies lest they should perish by the evils of falsity.

2405. *When the dawn arose.* That this signifies when the Lord's kingdom is approaching, is evident from the signification in the Word of the "dawn" or "morning." As in this chapter the subject treated of is the successive states of the church, that which is done in the evening is first treated of, next that which is done in the night, and there now follows that which is done in the morning twilight, and presently that which is done after the sun is gone forth. The twilight is here expressed by "when the dawn arose," and it denotes the time when the upright are being separated from the evil; which separation is treated of in this verse, and as far as verse 22, by Lot together with his wife and daughters being led out and saved. That separation precedes Judgment is evident from the Lord's words in *Matthew* :—

Before Him shall be gathered all nations, and He shall separate them one from another, as the shepherd separateth the sheep from the goats (xxv. 32).

[2] This time or state is called in the Word the "dawn," because the Lord then comes; or what is the same, His kingdom then approaches. The case is similar with the good, for at such a time there shines out with them a semblance of the morning twilight or dawn; and therefore in the Word the advent of the Lord is compared to the "morning," and is also called the "morning." As in *Hosea* :—

After two days Jehovah will revive us, on the third day He will raise us up, and we shall live before Him ; and we shall know, and we shall follow on to know Jehovah ; His going forth is as the dawn (vi. 2, 3).

"Two days" denotes the time and state which precedes; the "third day" denotes the Judgment, or the advent of the Lord, and therefore the approach of His kingdom (n. 720, 901), which advent or approach is compared to the "dawn."
[3] In *Samuel* :—

The God of Israel is as the light of the morning, the sun riseth, a morning without clouds ; from the brightness, from the rain, there is a growth from the earth (2 *Sam.* xxiii. 4).

The "God of Israel" denotes the Lord; for no other God of Israel was meant in that church, and He was represented in each and all things of it. In *Joel :*—

The day of Jehovah cometh, for it is nigh at hand ; a day of darkness and of thick darkness, a day of cloud and obscurity ; as the dawn spread upon the mountains (ii. 1, 2).

Here also the Lord's advent and His kingdom are treated of; it is said a "day of darkness and of thick darkness," because the good are then being separated from the evil, as here Lot from the men of Sodom; and after the good have been separated, the evil perish. [4] That the Lord's advent or the approach of His kingdom, is not merely compared to the "morning," but is actually called the "morning," may be seen in *Daniel :*—

A holy one said, How long shall be the vision, the continual sacrifice, and the transgression that maketh waste ? He said unto me, Until evening and morning, two thousand three hundred, then shall the holy one be justified. The vision of the evening and the morning which hath been told is truth (viii. 13, 14, 26).

"Morning" here manifestly denotes the Lord's advent. In *David :*—

Thy people are willing offerings in the day of thy strength, in honors of holiness, from the womb of the dawn thou hast the dew of thy youth* (*Ps.* cx. 3).

In this whole Psalm the subject treated of is the Lord, and His victories in temptations, which are the "day of His strength," and the "honors of His holiness;" "from the womb of the dawn," denotes Himself, thus the Divine love from which He fought. [5] In *Zephaniah :*—

Jehovah in the midst of her is righteous, He will not do perversity ; in the morning, in the morning will He give judgment for light (iii. 5).

The "morning" denotes the time and state of Judgment, which is the same as that of the Lord's advent; and this is the same as the approach of His kingdom. [6] Because the "morning" signified these things, in order that the same might be represented, it was commanded that

Aaron and his sons should light up the lamp, and should order it from evening until morning before Jehovah (*Exod.* xxvii. 21).

* *Nativitatis;* but *juventutis* elsewhere, as T. C. R. 764. [*Rotch ed.*]

The "evening" here denotes the twilight before the morning (n. 2323). In like manner it was commanded that the fire upon the altar should be kindled every morning (*Lev.* vi. 5): also that nothing of the paschal lamb and of the sanctified things of the sacrifices should be left till the morning (*Exod.* xii. 10; xxiii. 18; xxxiv. 25; *Lev.* xxii. 29, 30; *Num.* ix. 12); by which was signified that when the Lord came, sacrifices should cease.   [7] In a general sense it is called "morning" both when the dawn appears, and when the sun rises; and in this latter case "morning" denotes the Judgment as it concerns both the good and the evil, as in this chapter:—

The sun was gone forth upon the earth, and Lot came unto Zoar; and Jehovah caused it to rain upon Sodom and upon Gomorrah brimstone and fire (verses 23, 24).

In like manner in so far as regards the Judgment upon the evil; in *David*:—

In the mornings will I destroy all the wicked of the land, to cut off from the city of Jehovah all the workers of iniquity (*Ps.* ci. 8).

And in *Jeremiah*:—

Let that man be as the cities which Jehovah overthrew, and He repenteth not; and let him hear a cry in the morning (xx. 16).

As in the proper sense the "morning" signifies the Lord, His advent, and thus the approach of His kingdom, it is evident what it signifies besides, namely, the rise of a new church (for this is the Lord's kingdom on earth), and this both in general and in particular, and even in the least particular; in general, when any church on the globe is being raised up anew; in particular, when a man is being regenerated, and being made new (for then the Lord's kingdom is arising in him, and he is becoming a church); and in the least particular, whenever the good of love and faith is working in him; for in this consists the advent of the Lord.   Hence the Lord's resurrection on the third day in the morning (*Mark* xvi. 2, 9; *Luke* xxiv. 1; *John* xx. 1) involves all these things (even in the particular and the least particular) in regard to His rising again in the minds of the regenerate every day, and even every moment.

2406. *The angels pressed Lot to hasten.* That this signifies that the Lord withheld them from evil and kept them in good, is evident from the signification of "pressing" and "hastening," as being to urge; and that by these words is signified to be withheld from evil, is evident both from the internal sense of these words and from what follows. The internal sense is that when the church begins to fall away from the good of charity, its people are at that time withheld from evil by the Lord more strongly than when it is in the good of charity. The same is evident from what follows, namely, that although the angels pressed Lot to go out of the city, he still lingered; and that they then laid hold of the hands of himself, his wife, and his daughters, and led them forth, and set them without the city; by which is signified and described the character of man in that state; for it is the second state of this church that is here treated of. The first state is described in the first three verses of this chapter; which state is such that they are in the good of charity and acknowledge the Lord, and are confirmed in good by Him. The second state is described here, which is such that with the men of the church themselves evils begin to act against goods, and that they are then powerfully withheld from evils and kept in goods by the Lord; which state is treated of in this verse, and in the 15th, 16th, and 17th, that follow. [2] As regards this matter, few, if any, know that all men without exception are withheld from evils by the Lord, and this by a mightier force than man can ever believe. For the endeavor of every man is continually toward evil, and this both from what is hereditary, into which he is born, and from what is actual, which he has procured for himself; and this to such a degree that if he were not withheld by the Lord, he would rush headlong every moment toward the lowest hell. But the mercy of the Lord is so great that at every moment, even the least, the man is uplifted and held back, to prevent him from rushing thither. This is the case with the good also, but with a difference according to their life of charity and faith. Thus the Lord combats continually with man, and for man with hell, although it does not so appear to the man. That it is really so has been given me to know by much experience, which of the Lord's Divine mercy will be related elsewhere. (See also n. 929, 1581.)

2407. *Saying, Arise, take thy wife, and thy two daughters that are found.* That this signifies the truth of faith and the affections of truth and of good, and that "found" means separated [from evil], is evident from the signification of "arising," as being to be elevated from evil (n. 2401); also from the signification in this place of "wife," as being the truth of faith (respecting which see under verse 26, where it is said of Lot's wife that she was turned into a statue of salt); and also from the signification of the "two daughters," as being the affections of truth and of good (see n. 2362). That "found" denotes separated from evil, is also evident, because they were set free. By these few words is this second state of the church here described, namely, that they do not from good suffer themselves to be led to truth, as before, but through truth to good; and yet they are in an obscure affection of good; for in the proportion that truth is made the leader, good is obscure; whereas in the proportion that good is made the leader, truth is plain and evident in its own light.

2408. *Lest thou be consumed in the iniquity of the city.* That this signifies lest they should perish in the evils of falsity, is evident from the signification of "iniquity," as being evil; and from the signification of "city," as being what is doctrinal, even if it is false (see n. 402). What the evil of falsity is may be seen from what was said in Part First (n. 1212, 1679).

2409. Verse 16. *And he lingered; and the men laid hold of his hand, and of the hand of his wife, and of the hand of his two daughters, in the clemency of Jehovah upon him, and they led him forth, and set him without the city.* "And he lingered," signifies opposition arising from the nature of evil; "and the men laid hold of his hand, and of the hand of his wife, and of the hand of his two daughters," signifies that the Lord powerfully withheld them from evils, and thereby strengthened the goods and truths signified by "Lot," his "wife," and his "daughters;" "in the clemency of Jehovah upon him," signifies from grace and mercy; "and they led him forth and set him without the city," signifies his state then.

2410. *And he lingered.* That this signifies opposition arising from the nature of evil, is evident from what was said above (n. 2406); for the evil which is in man continually reacts against the good which is from the Lord. Evil from what is hereditary and from what is actual adheres to man in each of his thoughts, nay, in the least things of his thoughts. This drags him downward (but the Lord, by means of the good which he instils, withholds him, and uplifts him, so that the man is held suspended between evil and good), and the consequence of this downward tendency is that if even for the least moment the man were not withheld from evils, he would of himself rush downward; and this he would do more in the state in which is the man of the church now represented by Lot than in the former state. This state is that he is beginning to think and to act not so much from good as from truth; thus at some distance from good.

2411. *And the men laid hold of his hand, and of the hand of his wife, and of the hand of his two daughters.* That this signifies that the Lord powerfully withheld from evils, and thus strengthened the goods and truths signified by "Lot, his wife, and his daughters," is evident from the signification of the "men," as being the Lord (concerning which above); from the signification of the "hand," as being power (see n. 878); also from the signification of "Lot," as being the good of charity (see n. 2324, 2351, 2371, 2399); from the signification of "wife," as being the truth of faith (treated of in the 26th verse); from the signification of "daughters," as being the affections of good and of truth (see n. 489 to 491, 2362); and finally from what was said above (n. 2388), namely, that good and truth flow in from the Lord in the proportion that man is withheld from evil; consequently, that the goods and truths signified by "Lot, his wife, and his two daughters," are in the same proportion strengthened. [2] On reflection every man may know this from his own experience; for in proportion as he is removed from corporeal and worldly things, in the same proportion he is in a spiritual idea, that is, is uplifted toward heaven; as is the case when he is in any holy worship, when in any temptation, also when in misfortune or sickness. It is well known that corporeal and worldly things, that is, the loves of them, are then removed, the reason being as stated, namely, that what is heavenly and spiritual from the Lord continually flows in; but evil and its derivative falsity, and falsity and its derivative evil, which flow in from corporeal and worldly things, are what hinder its being received.

2412. *In the clemency of Jehovah unto him.* That this signifies from grace and mercy, is evident from the signification of the "clemency of Jehovah," which can be nothing else than grace and mercy. That man's being withheld from evil and kept in good by the Lord is of His pure mercy, may be seen above (n. 1049). The reason both grace and mercy are mentioned, is (as before explained, n. 598, 981) that they who are in truth and from truth in good implore the Lord's grace only, whereas they who are in good and from good in truth implore His mercy; and this difference results from the difference that exists in their respective states of humiliation and consequent adoration.

2413. *And they led him forth and set him without the city.* That this signifies his * state at the time, is evident from the signification of "leading forth," as being to withhold; and from the signification of "setting without the city," as being away from falsity; so that the state here referred to was that by his being withheld from evils, goods and truths from the Lord were strengthened.

2414. Verse 17. *And it came to pass when they were leading them forth abroad, that he said, Escape for thy life; look not back behind thee, and stay not in all the plain; escape to the mountain, lest thou be consumed.* "And it came to pass when they were leading them forth abroad," signifies the state when they were being withheld from falsity and evil; "that he said, Escape for thy life," signifies that he should take thought for his eternal life; "look not back behind thee," signifies that he should not look to doctrinal things; "and stay not in all the plain," signifies that he should not linger in any of these doctrinal matters; "escape to the mountain," signifies to the good of love and of charity; "lest thou be consumed," signifies that if he should do otherwise he would perish.

2415. *And it came to pass when they were leading them forth abroad.* That this signifies the state when they were being withheld from falsity and evil, is evident from what was said just above (n. 2413; as also n. 2388, 2411).

---

*In this and following numbers we have "he" and "his" in the explication, grammatically referring to Lot, when in fact those are meant who are represented by him, as occasionally explained. [*Rotch ed.*]

2416. *That he said, Escape for thy life.* That this signifies that he should take thought for his eternal life, is evident without explication. But in what way he should take thought for his life, now follows.

2417. *Look not back behind thee.* That this signifies that he should not look to doctrinal things, is evident from the signification of " looking back behind him," when the city was behind him and the mountain before him. For by " city" is signified what is doctrinal (n. 402, 2268, 2392) ; and by " mountain," love and charity (n. 795, 1430). That this is the signification will be evident in the explication at verse 26, where it is said that his wife " looked back behind him," and became a pillar of salt. Every one may know that in this expression, " looking back behind him," there is some Divine arcanum, and that it lies too deep to be seen. For in looking back behind him there appears to be nothing criminal, and yet it is a matter of importance so great that it is said he should escape for his life, that is, should take thought for his eternal life by not looking back behind him. But what it is to look to doctrinal things will be seen in what follows ; in this place we shall merely state what these doctrinal things are. [2] Doctrine is twofold : that of love and charity, and that of faith. At first, while it is still a little maid and a virgin, every church of the Lord has no other doctrine, and loves no other, than that of charity ; for this belongs to life. But successively the church turns itself away from this doctrine, until it begins to hold it cheap, and at length to reject it ; and then it acknowledges no other doctrine than that which is called the doctrine of faith ; and when it separates faith from charity, this doctrine conspires with a life of evil. [3] Such was the case with the Primitive Church, or that of the Gentiles, after the Lord's coming. In its beginning it had no other doctrine than that of love and charity, for this the Lord Himself taught (see n. 2371 at the end). But after His time, successively, as love and charity began to grow cold, there arose the doctrine of faith, and with it dissensions and heresies, which increased as men came to lay stress on this doctrine. [4] The like was the case with the Ancient Church that was after the flood, and was extended through so many kingdoms

(n. 2385): this church also in its beginning knew no other doctrine than that of charity, because this looked to and affected the life, and by so doing they had regard for their eternal welfare. And yet after some time the doctrine of faith too began to be cultivated with some, and at length to be separated from charity; but those who did this they called "Ham," because they were in a life of evil (see n. 1062, 1063, 1076). [5] The Most Ancient Church which was before the flood and which in pre-eminence to all others was called "Man," was in the very perception of love to the Lord and of charity toward the neighbor; thus it had the doctrine of love and charity inscribed on itself. But even then there were those who cultivated faith, and when they separated it from charity they were called "Cain;" for by "Cain" is signified such faith, and by "Abel," whom he killed, charity (see the explication of chapter iv.). [6] This shows that there are two doctrines, the one of charity, and the other of faith, although in themselves the two are one; for the doctrine of charity involves all things of faith. But when the doctrine comes to be from those things alone which are of faith, it is then called twofold, because faith is separated from charity. That these doctrines are separated at the present day may be seen from the fact that it is altogether unknown what charity is, and what the neighbor is. They who are solely in the doctrine of faith are not aware that charity toward the neighbor consists in anything beyond giving of their own to others, and in feeling pity for anybody who may seem to need it, because they call everybody the neighbor without distinction; and yet charity is all good whatever there is in a man: in his affection, and in his zeal, and from these in his life; and the neighbor is all the good in others by which one is affected, consequently those who are in good; and this with every possible distinction. [7] For example: that man is in charity and mercy who exercises justice and judgment by punishing the evil and rewarding the good. There is charity in punishing the evil, for to this are we impelled by our zeal to amend them, and at the same time to protect the good, lest these suffer injury at the hands of the evil. In this way does a man consult the welfare of one who is in evil, or his enemy, and express his good feeling toward him, as well as to others, and to the common weal itself ; and this from charity toward the neighbor.   The case is the same with all the other goods of life ; for the good of life is never possible unless it comes from charity toward the neighbor, because it looks to this, and involves it.   [8] Seeing then that there is obscurity so great as regards the true nature of charity and of the neighbor, it is clear that the doctrine of charity (the doctrine of faith having assumed the first place) is among the things that are lost; when yet it was this alone that was cultivated in the Ancient Church; and that to such a degree that they reduced into classes all the goods that belonged to charity toward the neighbor, that is, all those who were in good; and this with many distinctions, to which they also gave names, calling them the poor, the miserable, the oppressed, the sick, the naked, the hungry, the thirsty, captives or those in prison, strangers, orphans, and widows ; some also they called the lame, the blind, the deaf, the dumb, the maimed; besides many other names.   In the Word of the Old Testament the Lord has spoken in accordance with this doctrine, on which account such terms so often occur there ; and He himself again spoke in accordance with the same doctrine, as in *Matt.* xxv. 35, 36, 38, 39, 40, 42–45; *Luke* xiv. 13, 21 ; and in many other places.   Hence it is that in the internal sense these names have quite a different signification. In order therefore that the doctrine of charity may be restored, it will of the Lord's Divine mercy be stated in the following pages who those denoted by these names are, and what charity is, and what the neighbor is, both generally and specifically.

2418. *Stay not in all the plain.*   That this signifies that he should not linger in any of these doctrinal matters, is evident from the signification of a " plain," as being everything of a doctrinal nature, concerning which presently.   How the case stands with his not lingering in any of these doctrinal matters shall be stated at verse 26, where Lot's wife is treated of in that she looked back behind him.   That in the Word a " plain" signifies all things of a doctrinal nature, is evident in *Jeremiah :*—

He that layeth waste shall come upon every city, and no city shall escape, and the valley shall perish, and the plain shall be destroyed (xlviii. 8) ;

where "city" denotes false doctrine; and the "plain" all
things that belong to that doctrine.   In *John :*—

When the thousand years are finished, Satan shall be loosed out of
his prison, and shall go forth to seduce the nations, Gog and Magog, to
gather them together to war, the number of whom is as the sand of the
sea ; and they went up upon all the plain of the earth, and compassed
the camp of the saints about, and fire came down from God out of
heaven, and consumed them (*Rev.* xx. 7–9);

where "Gog and Magog" denote those who are in external
worship without internal, thus worship become idolatrous (n.
1151) ; the "plain of the earth," the doctrinal things of the
church, which they lay waste; the "camp of the saints," the
goods of love and of charity ; their being "consumed by fire
from God out of heaven" means the same as when this is said
of the men of Sodom and Gomorrah, in verse 24.   Again : the
doctrinal things of charity are called the "cities of the mountain," and the doctrinal things of faith the "cities of the
plain," in *Jeremiah* xxxiii. 13.

2419. *Escape to the mountain.* That this signifies to the
good of love and of charity, is evident from the signification
of a "mountain," as being love and charity (see n. 795, 1430).

2420. *Lest thou be consumed.* That this signifies that if he
should do otherwise he would perish, is evident without explication.

2421. Verses 18, 19. *And Lot said unto them, Nay I pray
my lords.   Behold I pray thy servant hath found grace in
thine eyes, and thou hast made thy mercy great which thou
hast done with me to make alive my soul ; and I cannot escape
to the mountain, lest peradventure evil cleave to me, and I die.*
"Lot said unto them, Nay I pray my lords," signifies weakness, so that he could not; "Behold I pray thy servant hath
found grace in thine eyes," signifies humiliation from the
affection of truth ; "thou hast made thy mercy great," signifies a semblance of humiliation from the affection of good;
"which thou hast done with me to make alive my soul," signifies on account of His desiring to save him; "and I cannot
escape to the mountain," signifies doubt as to his being able to
have the good of charity ; "lest peradventure evil cleave to
me, and I die," signifies that then it could not but come to

pass that he would be at the same time in evil, and thereby would be condemned.

2422. *Lot said unto them, Nay I pray my lords.* That this signifies weakness, so that he could not, is evident from the affection in the very words, as also from what follows. There is here treated of the third state of the church represented in this chapter by Lot, which is that they no longer think and act from the affection of good, but from the affection of truth; which state succeeds, when the affection of good begins to be diminished, and as it were to recede. Good is indeed present, but has withdrawn itself more toward the interiors, and therefore is in obscurity; and yet it manifests itself in a certain affection, which is called the affection of truth. (What the affection of good is, and what the affection of truth, may be seen above, n. 1997, and in what presently follows, n. 2425.) That there are these states is not apparent to man, still less what is the nature of them; but they are apparent to the angels as in clear light, for the angels are in every good affection of man; and they are apparent also to man himself when he comes into the other life. It is in accordance with these affections, and the quality of them, that the good are distinguished into societies (n. 685).

2423. That *Behold I pray thy servant hath found grace in thine eyes,* signifies humiliation from the affection of truth; and that *thou hast made thy mercy great,* signifies a semblance of humiliation from the affection of good, is evident from what has been said before concerning " grace" and " mercy" (n. 598, 981). For they who are in the affection of truth cannot humble themselves so far as to acknowledge from the heart that all things are of mercy; and therefore, instead of " mercy" they say " grace;" nay, the less of the affection of truth there is in them, the less of humiliation there is in their mention of grace; whereas on the other hand, the more of the affection of good there is in any one, the more of humiliation there is in his mention of mercy. This shows how much the adoration, and consequently the worship, that exists with those who are in the affection of truth differs from that which exists with those who are in the affection of good. For in order that there may be worship, there must be adoration; and in order that there may be adoration, there must be humiliation; and this in all things of the worship both in general and particular. What has been said will serve to show why both "grace" and "mercy" are here mentioned.

2424. *Which thou hast done with me to make alive my soul.* That this signifies on account of His desiring to save him, is evident without explication.

2425. *And I cannot escape to the mountain.* That this signifies doubt as to his being able to have the good of charity, that is, to think and act from that good, is evident from the signification of a "mountain," as being love and charity (see n. 795, 1430). [2] As regards this doubt, the case is this. Within the affection of truth of those who are in this affection there is the affection of good, but so obscurely that they do not perceive, thus do not know, what the affection of good is, and what genuine charity is. They do suppose that they know, but it is from truth, thus from memory-knowledge, and not from good itself. Nevertheless they do the goods of charity, not in order to merit anything thereby, but from obedience; and this in so far as they apprehend that it is the truth. For they suffer themselves to be led by the Lord out of their obscurity of good by means of the truth which appears to them to be truth. For example: being ignorant what the neighbor is, they do good to every one whom they suppose to be the neighbor; especially to the poor, because these call themselves poor on account of being destitute of worldly wealth; to orphans and widows, because they are so termed; to strangers, because they are such; and so on with all the rest; and this they do so long as they are ignorant what is signified by the poor, by orphans, widows, strangers, and others. Nevertheless seeing that in their affection of apparent truth there lies in obscurity the affection of good, by which the Lord leads them to such action, they are at the same time in good as to their interiors, and in this good the angels are present with them, and are delighted there with their appearances of truth by which such persons are affected. [3] But they who are in the good of charity, and from this in the affection of truth, do all things with discrimination, for they are in light; since the light of truth is from no other source than good, because the Lord flows in by means of good. These persons do not do good to the poor, to orphans, to widows, and to strangers, for the mere reason that they are so termed; for they know that those who are good, whether poor or rich, are neighbors more than all others; since by the good, good is done to others; and therefore in so far as these persons do good to the good, they do it to others through them. They also know how to make distinctions among goods, and so among good men. They call the general good itself their neighbor in a greater degree, for in this there is regarded the good of still greater numbers. As still more their neighbor to whom charity is to be done they acknowledge the Lord's kingdom on earth, which is the church; and the Lord's kingdom itself in the heavens even still more. But they who set the Lord before all these—who adore Him alone and love Him above all things—derive the neighbor in all these degrees from Him; for the Lord alone is the neighbor in the highest sense, thus all good is the neighbor in so far as it is from Him. [4] But they who are in the opposite derive the degrees of the neighbor from themselves, and acknowledge only those as neighbor who favor and serve them—calling no others brethren and friends—and this with a distinction, accordingly as they make one with them. All this shows what the neighbor is, namely, that a man is our neighbor according to the love in which he is; and that *he* is truly the neighbor who is in love to the Lord and in charity toward his neighbor, and this with every possible difference; thus it is the good itself with every one that determines the point in question.

2426. *Lest peradventure the evil cleave to me, and I die.* That this signifies that then it could not but come to pass that he would be at the same time in evil, and that thereby he would be condemned, is evident without explication. What these words involve may be known from what has been said and shown before (n. 301–303, 571, 582, 1001, 1327, 1328), namely, that the Lord constantly provides that evil should not be commingled with good; but that in so far as a man is in evil, so far is he removed from good; for it is better for a man to be altogether in evil, than in evil and at the same time in good. For if he is in evil and at the same time in good, he must needs be damned eternally.   It is the deceitful and hypocrites within the church who are most in danger of this.   Such therefore is the meaning, in the internal sense, of "lest the evil cleave to me, and I die."

2427. Verse 20. *Behold I pray this city is near to flee thither, and it is a little one; let me I pray escape thither—is it not a little one?—and my soul shall live.*   "Behold I pray this city is near to flee thither," signifies that he might be permitted [to think and act] from the truth of faith; "and it is a little one," signifies from the little truth that he had; "let me I pray escape thither," signifies that from this small amount of truth it might be permissible to have regard to good; "is it not a little one?" signifies might he not have some little truth; "and my soul may live," signifies that so perchance he might be saved.

2428. *Behold I pray this city is near to flee thither.*   That this signifies that he might be permitted [to think and act] from the truth of faith, is evident from the signification of a "city," as being what is of doctrine, thus the truth of faith (see n. 402, 2268).   It is said to be "near," because truth is nearly related to good; on which account to "flee thither" signifies that he might be permitted [to think and act] from truth, seeing that he could not do so from good (n. 2422).

2429. *It is a little one.*   That this signifies from the little truth that he had, is evident from the signification of a "city," as being truth, concerning which just above.   Its being "little" signifies that there was little of truth; here, from the little that he had, as is evident from what precedes and what follows. [2] As regards the thing itself, namely, that they who are in the affection of truth have little truth in comparison with those who are in the affection of good, this is evident from the fact that it is from the meager and obscure good appertaining to them that they regard truth.   The truth in a man is exactly according to the good that is in him.   Where there is little good, there is little truth.   They are in a like ratio and in a like degree, or, as we say, they march with even step.   This indeed may seem a paradox, but still the case is so.   Good is the very essence of truth, and truth without its essence is not truth, although it appears as if it were; it is merely a sounding brass, and is like an empty vessel. [3] In order that any one may have truth in himself, he must not only know it, but also acknowledge it, and have faith in it; he then for the first time has truth, because it then affects him, and remains. It is otherwise when he only knows truth, and does not acknowledge it, and have faith in it; for in this case he has not the truth in himself. This is the case with many who are in evil: they are able to know truths, sometimes more than other men; but still they have not the truth; nay, they have it so much the less, because at heart they deny it. [4] It is provided by the Lord that no one should have (that is, acknowledge and believe) more truth than he receives of good. Hence it is here said of the city, by which truth is signified, that it is a "little one," and again in this verse, " Is it not a little one ?" also in verse 22, that he called the name of the city " Zoar," which in the original language means "little ;" for the reason that those are here treated of who are in the affection of truth, and not so much in the affection of good.

2430. *Let me I pray escape thither.* That this signifies that from this small amount of truth it might be permissible to have regard to good, is evident from what precedes and what follows. It was said that he should "escape to the mountain," by which is signified the good of love and of charity (n. 2419); but it was answered that he could not do this, but could escape to the city, by which is signified the truth of faith (n. 2428); thus that he could regard good from truth, or what is the same, charity from faith. Moreover that city was situated at the foot of the mountain; and from it he afterwards went up and dwelt on the mountain, but in a cave (verse 30).

2431. *Is it not a little one?* That this signifies might he not have some little truth, is evident from what was said above (n. 2429), thus without further explication. This question is asked for the reason that the Lord alone knows how much good there is in the truth, and thus how much truth there is in a man.

2432. *And my soul shall live.* That this signifies that so perchance he might be saved, is likewise evident without explication. That he also was saved, because there was good in his truth, is evident from what follows, namely, from the answer, " Behold, I have accepted thy face as to this word also, that I will not overthrow the city of which thou hast spoken" (verse 21); and afterwards, " The sun was gone forth upon the earth, and Lot came unto Zoar" (verse 23); by which is meant that they who are in the affection of truth, that is, who are in faith, are saved, provided it is the faith of good.

2433. Verse 21. *And He said unto him, Behold, I have accepted thy face as to this word also, that I will not overthrow the city of which thou hast spoken.* " He said unto him, Behold, I have accepted thy face as to this word also," signifies assent, provided that the interiors in the truth derive anything from good; " that I will not overthrow the city of which thou hast spoken," signifies that thus he would not perish.

2434. *He said unto him, Behold, I have accepted thy face as to this word also.* That this signifies assent, provided that the interiors in the truth derive anything from good, is evident from the signification of " face." The term " face" is of frequent occurrence in the Word, and there signifies the interiors, as before shown (n. 358, 1999); and also that when the face is attributed to Jehovah or the Lord, it signifies Mercy, Peace, Good (n. 222, 223); so that here it signifies the good which is interiorly in truth; and therefore to " accept the face" denotes to assent, provided that the interiors in the truth derive anything from good. " As to this word," denotes as to this matter. That there is no truth unless there is good within it, may be seen above (n. 1496, 1832, 1900, 1904, 1928, 2063, 2173, 2269, 2401, 2403, 2429); and that the blessedness and happiness which a man has after death is not from truth, but from the good that is in the truth (n. 2261); and hence the more good there is in his truth, the more blessed and happy he is. That good is within truth, and causes it to be truth, is evident also from the goods and truths that exist even in worldly things. When a man learns and acknowledges that anything in these is good, then whatever favors this good he calls truth; but whatever does not favor it, he rejects and calls falsity. He may indeed say that that is true * which does not favor the

* *Verum non sit*, apparently by a slip. [*Rotch ed.*]

good in question; but he is then making a pretense, while thinking differently. And the case is the same in spiritual things.

2435. *That I will not overthrow the city of which thou hast spoken.* That this signifies that so he would not perish, namely, the man with whom there is truth within which there is good, is evident from the signification of a "city," as being truth (see n. 402, 2268, 2428). It has been disputed from the most ancient times which is the firstborn of the church, charity or faith; for the reason that man is regenerated and becomes a church by means of the truths of faith. But they who have set faith foremost and made it the firstborn, have all fallen into heresies and falsities, and at length have extinguished charity altogether; as we read of Cain, by whom such faith is signified, that at length he killed his brother Abel, by whom is signified charity; and afterwards of Reuben, the firstborn son of Jacob, by whom likewise faith is signified, that he polluted his father's couch (*Gen.* xxxv. 22; xlix. 4), and therefore was held unworthy, and the primogeniture was given to Joseph (*Gen.* xlviii. 5; 1 *Chron.* v. 1). [2] This was the source of all the contentions, and also all the laws, respecting primogeniture that are mentioned in the Word. The cause of there being such a controversy was that it was not known, as even at this day it is not known, that a man has only so much of faith as he has of charity; and that when a man is being regenerated, charity presents itself to faith, or what is the same, good presents itself to truth, and insinuates itself into it and adapts itself to it in every particular, causing faith to be faith; and thus that charity is the very firstborn of the church, although to man it appears otherwise (see also n. 352, 367). But as these things will frequently be treated of hereafter, of the Lord's Divine mercy we shall say more on the subject as the occasion arises.

2436. Verse 22. *Haste thee, escape thither, for I cannot do anything until thou be come thither. Therefore he called the name of the city Zoar.* "Haste thee, escape thither," signifies that he should remain in it, because he cannot go further; "for I cannot do anything until thou be come thither," signifies that before the Judgment upon the evil, they are to be saved who are in the affection of truth; "Therefore he called the name of the city Zoar," signifies the affection of truth.

2437. *Haste thee, escape thither.* That this signifies that he should remain in it, because he could not go further (that is to say, in the truth of faith and the affection of it, because he could not be in the very good of charity and the affection of it), is evident from what precedes.

2438. *For I cannot do anything until thou be come thither.* That this signifies that before the Judgment upon the evil they are to be saved who are in the affection of truth, is evident from the fact that the words "I cannot do anything," refer to the Judgment upon the evil, which is presently described by the overthrow of Sodom and Gomorrah; and that the words "until thou be come thither," signify that they are first to be saved who are in the affection of truth, and who are here represented by Lot; which also is what is meant by Lot's coming to Zoar (verse 23). [2] That the good and the just are saved before the evil and the unjust perish, is evident also elsewhere in the Word, as where the Last Judgment is treated of in *Matthew*, and it is said that the sheep were separated from the goats, and the sheep were told to enter into the Lord's kingdom before the goats were told to depart into eternal fire (xxv. 32, 34, 41). The like was also represented in the exodus of the sons of Israel from Egypt—that they were saved before the Egyptians were drowned in the Red Sea. [3] The same is also signified by the declarations of the Prophets, that after the faithful had been brought back from captivity, their enemies should then undergo their punishments and perish. This is continually taking place in the other life, that is, the faithful are first saved, and then the unfaithful are punished; or what is the same, the faithful are elevated into heaven by the Lord, and the unfaithful then cast themselves down into hell. The reason why these two things do not take place at the same time is that unless the good were carefully withdrawn from the wicked, they would easily perish by the cupidities of evil and the persuasions of falsity, which the wicked continually scatter around like poisons. But in general, before this comes to pass, it is provided that evils should be separated from the good, and that goods should be separated from the evil, so that the former may by means of their goods be uplifted by the Lord into heaven, and the latter by means of their evils may cast themselves down into hell; concerning which subject of the Lord's Divine mercy hereafter, at n. 2449, 2451.

2439. *Therefore he called the name of the city Zoar.* That this signifies the affection of truth, is evident from the signification of " Zoar," as being the affection of good, namely, of the good of knowledge, that is, the affection of truth (see n. 1589); and from the signification of " calling a name," as being to know the quality (see n. 144, 145, 1754, 2009); here that there was a little truth, for in the original language " Zoar" means " little," or " small." In comparison with those who are in the affection of good, they who are in the affection of truth have little truth because they have little good (see above, n. 2429). [2] Moreover that truths which are in themselves truths are with one person more true, with another less true, and with some not true at all, and even false, is evident from almost all things which in themselves are true; for they are varied in the man with whom they are, in accordance with his affections. For example, the doing of a good work or a good of charity : in itself it is a truth that this is to be done; and with one person it is a good of charity, because it proceeds from charity; with another it is a work of obedience, because it proceeds from obedience; with some it is work of self-merit, because by it they desire to merit and to obtain salvation; but with others it is hypocritical, being done in order that they may seem charitable; and so on. It is the same with all other things that are called truths of faith. And this shows that there is much truth with those who are in the affection of good, and less truth with those who are in the affection of truth; for the latter regard good as being more remote from themselves, whereas the former regard good as being present in themselves.

2440. Verse 23. *The sun was gone forth upon the earth, and Lot came to Zoar.* " The sun was gone forth upon the earth," signifies the last period, which is called the Last Judgment; " and Lot came to Zoar," signifies that those are saved who are in the affection of truth.

2441. *The sun was gone forth upon the earth.* That this signifies the last period, which is called the Last Judgment, is

evident from the signification of the " rising of the sun," when
the subject treated of is the times and states of the church.
That in the internal sense the times of the day, and also the
times of the year, signify the successive states of the church,
has been shown before (n. 2323); and that the dawn or morning signifies the Lord's advent, that is, the approach of His
kingdom (n. 2405); so that in the passage before us the rising
of the sun, that is, his " going forth upon the earth," signifies
the Lord's presence itself; and this for the reason that both
the " sun" and the " east" signify the Lord. (As to the " sun,"
see n. 31, 32, 1053, 1521, 1529–1531, 2120; as to the " east,"
n. 101.) [2] The reason why the Lord's presence is the same
as the last period, which is called the Judgment, is that His
presence separates the good from the evil, and results in the
good being elevated into heaven, and the evil casting themselves down into hell; for in the other life the Lord is the Sun
to the universal heaven (see n. 1053, 1521, 1529–1531), for
it is the Divine Celestial of His love that so appears before
their eyes and actually makes the very light of heaven. In so
far therefore as the inhabitants of the spiritual world are in
celestial love, so far are they elevated into that celestial light
which is from the Lord; but in so far as they are remote from
celestial love, so far do they cast themselves away from this
light into infernal darkness. [3] This therefore is the reason
why the " rising of the sun," by which is signified the presence
of the Lord, involves both the salvation of the good and the
damnation of the evil; and this is why it is now said for the
first time that " Lot came to Zoar," that is, that they who are
here represented by Lot were saved; and presently that " Jehovah caused it to rain upon Sodom and Gomorrah brimstone
and fire," that is, that the evil were damned. [4] To those who
are in the evils of the love of self and of the world, that is, to
those who are in hatreds against all things of love to the Lord
and of charity toward the neighbor, the light of heaven actually appears as thick darkness; on which account it is said
in the Word that to such the " sun was blackened;" by which
is signified that they rejected everything of love and charity,
and received everything that is contrary thereto. As in *Ezekiel* :—

When I shall extinguish thee, I will cover the heavens, and make the stars thereof black ; I will cover the sun with a cloud, and the moon shall not make her light to shine ; all the luminaries of light in the heavens will I make black over thee, and will set darkness upon thy land (xxxii. 7, 8).

Every one can see that by "covering the heavens," "blackening the stars," "covering the sun," and "blackening the luminaries of heaven," other things than these are signified. [5] In like manner in *Isaiah* :—

The sun shall be darkened in his going forth, and the moon shall not cause her light to shine (xiii. 10).

And in *Joel* :—

The sun and the moon are blackened, and the stars withdraw their shining (ii. 2, 10).

It is therefore evident what is signified by the Lord's words in *Matthew*, where He is speaking of the last period of the church, which is called the Judgment :—

Immediately after the affliction of those days, the sun shall be darkened, and the moon shall not give her light, and the stars shall fall from heaven (xxiv. 29) ;

where by the "sun" is not meant the sun ; nor by the "moon," the moon ; nor by the "stars," the stars ; but by the "sun" are signified love and charity ; by the "moon," the faith thence derived ; and by the "stars," the knowledges of good and truth ; which are said to be "obscured," to "lose their light," and to "fall from heaven," when there is no longer any acknowledgment of the Lord, nor any love to Him, nor any charity toward the neighbor ; and when these have become nought, the love of self with its falsities takes possession of the man ; for the one thing is a consequence of the other. [6] Hence we read also in *John* :—

The fourth angel poured out his vial upon the sun ; and it was given unto him to scorch men with fire, and men were scorched with great heat, and blasphemed the name of God (*Rev.* xvi. 8, 9) ;

where also the last times of the church are treated of, when all love and charity are being extinguished ; or, speaking according to the common mode, when there is no longer any faith. The extinction of love and charity is meant by the "pouring out of the vial upon the sun;" so that it was the love of self and its cupidities by which men were then "scorched with fire," and "scorched with great heat;" and from which came the "blaspheming of the name of God." [7] By the "sun" the Ancient Church understood nothing else than the Lord and the Divine Celestial of His love; and therefore they were accustomed to pray toward the sun-rising, while not thinking at all about the sun. But after their posterity had lost this also, together with the rest of their representatives and significatives, they began to worship the sun itself and also the moon; which worship spread to many nations, so much so that they dedicated temples to them, and set up pillars; and because the sun and the moon then took on an opposite signification, they came to signify the love of self and of the world, which are diametrically contrary to heavenly and spiritual love. Hence in the Word by the "worship of the sun and the moon" is meant the worship of self and of the world; [8] as in *Moses*:—

Lest thou lift up thine eyes unto heaven, and see the sun and the moon and the stars, all the army of the heavens, and thou be driven to bow down unto them, and serve them (*Deut.* iv. 19).

And again:—

If he have gone and served other gods, and the sun and the moon, or any of the army of the heavens, which I have not commanded, then thou shalt stone them with stones, and they shall die (*Deut.* xvii. 3, 5).

Into such idolatry was the ancient worship turned when they no longer believed that anything internal was signified by the rites of the church, but only what was external. [9] In like manner in *Jeremiah*:—

At that time shall they spread out the bones of the kings of Judah, of the princes, of the priests, of the prophets, and of the inhabitants of Jerusalem, before the sun and the moon, and all the army of the heavens, which they have loved, and which they have served (viii. 1, 2).

The "sun" here denotes the love of self and its cupidities; their "spreading out the bones" signifies the infernal things that belong to such worshipers. Again:—

He shall break the pillars of the house of the sun, which are in the land of Egypt, and the houses of the gods of Egypt shall he burn with fire (xliii. 13).

The "pillars of the house" denote the worship of self.

2442. *And Lot came to Zoar.* That this signifies that those who are in the affection of truth are saved, is evident from the signification of " Zoar," as being the affection of truth (see n. 2439). This shows that those also are saved who are in faith, provided there is good in their faith; that is, provided they are affected by the truths of faith for the sake of good, for this is from good: all the life of faith is from no other source. (That charity is the essential of faith, nay, that it is faith itself, because it is the very substance of faith, may be seen above, n. 379, 389, 654, 724, 809, 916, 1162, 1176, 1798, 1799, 1834, 1844, 2049, 2116, 2189, 2190, 2228, 2261, 2343, 2349, 2417).

2443. Verse 24. *And Jehovah caused it to rain upon Sodom and upon Gomorrah brimstone and fire from Jehovah out of heaven.* " Jehovah caused it to rain upon Sodom and upon Gomorrah brimstone and fire," signifies the hell of those who are in the evils of the love of self and the falsities thence derived; "to rain" is to be damned; "brimstone" is the hell of the love of self; "fire" is the hell of the falsities thence derived; "from Jehovah out of heaven," signifies from the laws of order as to truth, because they separate themselves from good.

2444. *Jehovah caused it to rain upon Sodom and upon Gomorrah brimstone and fire.* That this signifies the hell of those who are in the evils of the love of self and the falsities thence derived, is evident from the signification of "raining," as being to be damned; of "brimstone," as being the hell of the evils of the love of self; and of "fire," as being the hell of the falsities thence derived, concerning which presently; also from the signification of "Sodom," as being the evil of the love of self; and of "Gomorrah," as being the falsity thence derived (see n. 2220, 2246, 2322). [2] Here "Gomorrah" is also mentioned, for the first time in this chapter, for the reason that "Gomorrah" signifies the falsity that comes from the evil of the love of self. For within the church, whose last period or Judgment is here treated of, this evil is that which chiefly acts against good, and its falsity is that which acts against truth; and these two things are so conjoined that he who is in the one is also in the other, and indeed in a like ratio and a like degree. It does indeed appear otherwise, but yet is

plainly so in the other life, if not in the world. (As regards
the love of self, its nature, the vastness of the evils that come
from it, and that it is the source of the hells, see n. 693, 694,
760, 1307, 1308, 1321, 1594, 1691, 2041, 2045, 2051, 2057,
2219).

2445. That to " rain" denotes to be damned, is evident from
the signification of " rain." In the Word " rain" in the genuine sense signifies a blessing, and therefore also salvation ; but
in the opposite sense a curse, and therefore also damnation.
That it signifies a blessing and therefore salvation, is evident
from many passages ; but that in the opposite sense it signifies
a curse, and therefore damnation, is manifest from the following. In *Isaiah :*—

> There shall be a tabernacle for a shadow in the daytime from the heat,
> and for a refuge and a covert from flood, and from rain (iv. 6).

In *Ezekiel :*—

> Say to them that daub on what is untempered, that it shall fall ; there
> shall be an overflowing rain, and ye hailstones shall fall ; an overflowing
> rain shall there be in Mine anger, and hailstones in wrath unto the con-
> summation (xiii. 11, 13).

In *David :*—

> He made their rains hail, a fire of flames in their land, and He smote
> their vine and their fig-tree (*Ps.* cv. 32, 33) ;

concerning Egypt, of which we read in *Moses :*—

> Jehovah gave thunders and hail, and fire quivered upon the land ; and
> Jehovah made it rain hail upon the land of Egypt (*Exod.* ix. 23, 24).

2446. That " brimstone" denotes the hell of the evils of the
love of self, and " fire" the hell of the falsities thence derived,
is evident from the signification in the Word of " brimstone"
and the " fire" from it, as being the love of self with its cupidities and the derivative falsities, thus as being hell, for hell consists of such things. That " brimstone" and " fire" have this
signification is evident in *David :*—

> Jehovah shall rain upon the wicked snares, fire and brimstone (*Ps.*
> xi. 6).

That fire and brimstone are not here meant, but something
else that is signified by " fire and brimstone," is evident also

from its being said that Jehovah "rains snares." In *Eze-kiel :*—

I will contend against him with pestilence and with blood, and I will make it rain an overflowing rain, and hailstones, fire and brimstone, upon him, and upon his troops, and upon the many peoples that are with him (xxxviii. 22) ;

where Gog is treated of, who lays waste the land of Israel, that is, the church. (The signification of " Gog" may be seen above, n. 1151.) " Fire" denotes falsities, " brimstone" the evils thence, and at the same time the hells of those who lay waste. In *John :*—

They who adored the beast were cast into a lake of fire burning with brimstone   (*Rev.* xix. 20) ;

meaning hell. Again :—

The devil was cast into a lake of fire and brimstone, where the beast and the false prophet are ; and they shall be tormented day and night for ever and ever (*Rev.* xx. 10) ;

manifestly meaning hell. Again :—

The abominable, and murderers, and adulterers, and sorcerers, and idolaters, and all liars, shall have their part in the lake that burneth with fire and brimstone (*Rev.* xxi. 8) ;

where also " fire and brimstone" plainly denote hell. [2] That they denote the evils of the love of self and the falsities thence derived, from which come the hells—in *Isaiah :*—

The day of the vengeance of Jehovah, and the year of retributions in the controversy of Zion ; and the streams thereof shall be turned into pitch, and the dust thereof into brimstone, and the land thereof shall become burning pitch (xxxiv. 8, 9) ;

where " burning pitch," here mentioned instead of " fire," denotes dense and direful falsities ; and " brimstone" the evils from the love of self. Again :—

The pile thereof is fire and much wood ; the breath of Jehovah is like a stream of brimstone kindling in it (xxx. 33) ;

speaking of Topheth; the " stream of kindling brimstone" denoting falsities from the evils of the love of self. In *Luke :*—

In the day that Lot went out of Sodom it rained fire and brimstone from heaven and destroyed them all ; even thus shall it be in the day when the Son of man is revealed (xvii. 29, 30).

That it will not then rain fire and brimstone is obvious; but what is meant is that the falsities and cupidities of the love of self, which are signified by "fire and brimstone," and which make the hells, will then predominate. [3] That in the Word "fire" signifies cupidities, and at the same time the hells, and that in this case the "smoke" from the fire signifies the falsity thence derived, and which is in those hells, may be seen above (n. 1861); and in *John* :—

> I saw the horses in the vision, and them that sat upon them, having breastplates of fire and of brimstone ; and the heads of the horses were like the heads of lions, and out of their mouth issued fire, smoke, and brimstone : by these three were the third part of men killed, by the fire, and the smoke, and the brimstone (*Rev.* ix. 17, 18) ;

"fire, smoke, and brimstone" denote evils and falsities of every kind, of which as before said the hells consist.

2447. *From Jehovah out of heaven.* That this signifies from the laws of order as to truth, because they separate themselves from good, cannot be seen except from the internal sense, by which there is disclosed how the case stands with punishments and damnations : that they in no wise come from Jehovah, that is, from the Lord, but from the man himself, the evil spirit, and the devil; and this from the laws of order as to truth, because they separate themselves from good. [2] All order is from Jehovah, that is, from the Lord, and according to this order are all things directed by Him both in general and in particular, but in many different ways, to wit, from *Will*, from *Good-pleasure*, from *Leave*, and from *Permission*. The things that are from His will and good-pleasure are from the laws of order as to good, and so also are many of those which are from leave, and some of those which are from permission. But when a man separates himself from good he casts himself into the rule of the laws of order that are of truth separated from good, which are such that they condemn ; for all truth condemns man and casts him down into hell; whereas the Lord from good, that is, from mercy, saves him, and uplifts him into heaven. From this we see that it is man himself who condemns himself. [3] The things done from permission are mostly of this nature, as for example, that one devil punishes and torments another; and innumerable other things of this kind. These things are from the laws of order as to truth separated from good ; for the devils could not otherwise be held in bonds, and withheld from rushing upon all the well disposed and good, and eternally destroying them. It is the prevention of this which is the good the Lord has in view. The case herein is similar to that which exists on earth, where a mild and clement king, who intends and does nothing but good, must needs suffer his laws to punish the evil and the wicked (although he punishes no one, but rather grieves that they are such that their evils must punish them), for otherwise he would leave his kingdom itself a prey to them ; which would be the height of rigor and of unmercifulness. [4] This shows that Jehovah in no wise caused it to rain brimstone and fire, that is in no wise condemned to hell; but that the men themselves who were in evil and thence in falsity did this, because they had separated themselves from good, and so had cast themselves into the rule of the laws of order that come from truth alone. From all which it follows that this is the internal sense of these words. [5] That in the Word " evil," " punishing," " cursing," " damnation," and many other such things are attributed to Jehovah or the Lord, as here that He made it " rain brimstone and fire," we read in *Ezekiel* :—

I will contend against him with pestilence and with blood ; and I will rain upon him fire and brimstone (xxxviii. 22).

In *Isaiah* :—

The breath of Jehovah like a stream of brimstone doth kindle it (xxx. 33).

In *David* :—

Jehovah shall rain upon the wicked snares, fire and brimstone (*Ps.* xi. 6).

Again :—

There went up a smoke out of His nostrils, and fire out of His mouth, coals did burn from Him (*Ps.* xviii. 8).

In *Jeremiah* :—

Lest My fury go forth like fire, and burn, and there is none to quench it (xxi. 12).

In *Moses* :—

A fire is kindled in Mine anger, and shall burn unto the lowest hell (*Deut.* xxxii. 22) ;

besides similar things in many other places. The reason why
such things are attributed in the Word to Jehovah or the
Lord has been explained in Part First (n. 223, 245, 589, 592,
696, 735, 1093, 1638, 1683, 1874); for such things are as far
from coming from the Lord, as good is far from evil, or as
heaven is from hell, or what is Divine from what is diabolical.
Evil, hell, and the devil do these things; but by no means
the Lord, who is mercy itself and good itself; but because He
appears to do them, therefore for the reasons mentioned in
the numbers cited, they are attributed to Him. [6] From its
being said in this verse that Jehovah caused it to rain from
Jehovah out of heaven, it appears in the sense of the letter
as if there were two; one on earth, and one in heaven; but
the internal sense teaches how this also is to be understood,
namely, that by the Jehovah first named is meant the Lord's
Divine Human and Holy proceeding (meant in this chapter by
the "two men") and by the Jehovah named in the second
place is meant the Divine Itself that is called the "Father"
(spoken of in the preceding chapter); and that this Trine is
in the Lord, as He himself says in *John*:—

He that hath seen Me hath seen the Father; believe Me, that I am in
the Father, and the Father in Me (xiv. 9–11).

And concerning the Holy proceeding, in the same:—

The Comforter shall not speak from Himself; but He shall take of
Mine, and shall declare it unto you (xvi. 13–15).

Thus Jehovah is one, although two are here named; two
being named for the reason that all the laws of order are
from the Lord's Divine Itself, Divine Human, and Holy proceeding.

2448. Verse 25. *And He overthrew those cities, and all the
plain, and all the inhabitants of the cities, and the growth of
the ground.* " He overthrew those cities," signifies that all
truths were separated from them, in order that they might
have only falsities; "and all the plain," signifies all things
that pertained to truths; "and all the inhabitants of the
cities," signifies that all goods were separated from them, in
order that they might have nothing but evils; "and the
growth of the ground," signifies all that is of the church.

2449. *He overthrew those cities.* That this signifies that all truths were separated from them, in order that they might have only falsities, is evident from the signification of " cities," as being doctrinal things, thus truths, since these belong to doctrinal things (see n. 402, 2268, 2428); and which are said to be " overthrown" when there are falsities instead of truths, in the present case when all truths have been separated from them, as well as all goods, which are likewise treated of in this verse because the subject is the last state of those within the church who are in falsities and evils; and this is the state into which they come, concerning the nature of which a few words shall be said. [2] They who come into the other life are all brought again into a life similar to that which they had in the body; and then with the good evils and falsities are separated, in order that by means of goods and truths they may be elevated by the Lord into heaven; but with the evil, goods and truths are separated in order that by evils and falsities they may be borne into hell (see n. 2119); precisely in accordance with the Lord's words in *Matthew* :—

Whosoever hath, to him shall be given, that he may have more abundance ; but whosoever hath not, from him shall be taken away even that which he hath (xiii. 12).

And elsewhere in the same :—

Unto him that hath shall be given, that he may have abundance ; but from him that hath not, shall be taken away even that which he hath (xxv. 29 ; *Luke* viii. 18 ; xix. 24–26 ; *Mark* iv. 24, 25).

The same things are also signified by these words in *Matthew* :—

Let both grow together until the harvest ; and in the time of the harvest I will say to the reapers, Gather together first the tares, and bind them in bundles to burn them ; but gather the wheat into my barn. The harvest is the consummation of the age ; as therefore the tares are gathered and burned in the fire, so shall it be in the consummation of the age (xiii. 30, 39, 40).

The same are also signified by what is said of the net cast into the sea that gathered fishes of various kinds, the good being collected into vessels and the bad cast away ; and of its being so at the consummation of the age (verses 47 to 50). (What the " consummation" is, and that it involves like things as these in regard to the church, may be seen above, n. 1857, 2243.) The reason why evils and falsities are separated from the good is that they may not hang between evils and goods, but may be elevated by means of goods into heaven; and the reason why goods and truths are separated from the evil is that they may not by means of any goods that pertain to them seduce the upright, and also that by means of their evils they may go away among the evil who are in hell. For such is the communication in the other life, of all ideas of thought, and of all affections, that goods are communicated among the good, and evils among the evil (n. 1388–1390); so that unless the good and the evil were separated, countless mischiefs would result, and moreover all association together would be impossible; when yet all things are most exquisitely consociated, in the heavens according to all the differences of love to the Lord and of mutual love, and of the derivative faith (n. 685, 1394); and in the hells according to all the differences of cupidities and of the derivative phantasies (n. 695, 1322). Be it known however that the separation is not entire removal, for from no one is that which he has had altogether taken away.

2450. *And all the plain.* That this signifies all things that pertained to those truths, is evident from the signification of a "plain," as being everything of what is doctrinal, thus everything that pertains to truths (see n. 2418).

2451. *And all the inhabitants of the cities.* That this signifies that all goods were taken away from them, in order that they might have nothing but evils, is evident from the signification of "inhabitants," when predicated of a city, as being goods; which may be confirmed by many things in the Word. The same is also evident from the fact that when a "city" signifies truth (as already shown), an "inhabitant" denotes good; for truth is that in which good dwells; and truth in which there is no good, is like a city empty, or without an inhabitant. Moreover as regards the fact that all goods are separated from the evil, so that they may have nothing but evils, see above (n. 2449).

2452. *And the growth of the ground.* That this signifies all that is of the church, is evident from the signification of the "growth" (by which is meant both the crops and also every green thing, and that goods and truths are signified by these, is evident from the Word throughout); and also from the signification of the "ground," as being the church (see n. 566, 1068). That goods and truths are everything of the church, is well known.

2453. Verse 26. *And his wife looked back behind him, and she became a pillar of salt.* " His wife looked back behind him," signifies that truth turned itself away from good, and looked to doctrinal things ; " and she became a pillar of salt," signifies that all the good of truth was vastated.

2454. *His wife looked back behind him.* That this signifies that truth turned itself away from good, and looked to doctrinal things, is evident from the signification of "looking back behind him," and from the signification of a "wife." It has been already said (n. 2417) that to "look back behind him" is to look to doctrinal things, which are of truth, and not to a life according to doctrinal things, which is of good ; for that is said to be "behind" him, which is posterior ; and that is said to be "before" him, which is prior. It has been frequently shown that truth is posterior, and good prior ; for truth is of good, because good is the essence and life of truth ; and therefore to "look back behind him" is to look to truth, which is of doctrine, and not to good, which is of life according to doctrine. That this is the signification is very evident from the Lord's words (where also He is speaking of the last time of the church, or of the consummation of the age) in *Luke* :—

In that day he that shall be upon the house, and his vessels in the house, let him not go down to take them away ; and let him that is in the field likewise not turn back behind him : Remember Lot's wife (xvii. 31, 32).

[2] These words of the Lord are not at all intelligible without the internal sense, thus unless it is known what is signified by being upon the house, what by the vessels in the house, what by going down to take them away, and what by the field, and lastly what by turning back behind him. According to the internal sense, to be "upon the house" is to be in good (that a "house" denotes good may be seen above, n. 710, 2233,

2234). The "vessels" in a house denote the truths which are
of good (that truths are the vessels of good, may be seen above,
n. 1496, 1832, 1900, 2063, 2269). To "go down to take them
away" denotes to turn one's self away from good to truth, as
we can see; for as good is prior it is also higher; and as truth
is posterior it is lower. That a "field" denotes the church,
being so called from the seed which it receives into it, consequently that those are "fields" who are in the good of doctrine, is evident from many passages in the Word. This shows
what is signified by "turning back behind him," namely, to
turn one's self away from good, and to look to doctrinal things;
wherefore, because these things are signified by Lot's wife, it
is added, "Remember Lot's wife." It is not said that she
"looked back behind herself," but "behind him;" because
"Lot" signifies good (see n. 2324, 2351, 2370, 2399). Hence
it is that when Lot was told what to do (verse 17), it was said,
"Look not back behind thee." [3] The reason why it is said
in *Luke*, "Let him not turn back behind him," and not "to
the things that are behind him," is that the celestial are not
willing even to mention anything of a doctrinal nature (see n.
202, 337); which is the reason why nothing specific is mentioned, but it is merely said "behind him." These same things
are thus described in *Matthew* :—

When ye shall see the abomination of desolation, foretold by Daniel
the prophet, then let them that are in Judea flee into the mountains ; let
him that is upon the house not go down to take anything out of his
house ; and let him that is in the field not return back to take his garments (xxiv. 15–17) ;

[4] where the "abomination of desolation" denotes the state
of the church when there is no love and no charity, for when
these are desolated, abominable things predominate. That
"Judea" denotes the church, and indeed the celestial church,
is evident from the Word of the Old Testament throughout,
both the historic and the prophetic. That the "mountains"
into which they shall flee, denote love to the Lord and the consequent charity toward the neighbor, may be seen above (n.
795, 1430, 1691). That "he who is upon the house," denotes
the good of love, has just been stated. That to "go down to
take anything out of his house," denotes to turn one's self

away from good to truth, has also just been stated. That "they who are in the field" denote those who are in the spiritual church, is evident from the signification in the Word of a "field." That "let him not return back to take his garments," denotes that he should not turn himself away from good to the truth that is of doctrine, is because "garments" signify truths, for truths act as garments in clothing good (see n. 1073). Every one can see that very different things are meant and that arcana are involved by all that the Lord there said concerning the consummation of the age, as that they who were in Judea should flee into the mountains, that they who were upon the house should not go down to take anything out of the house, and that they who were in the field should not return back to take their garments; and in like manner by its being said that Lot should not look back behind himself (verse 17), and here that his wife did look back behind him. This is further evident from the signification of a "wife," as being truth (see n. 915, 1468); and from the signification of "Lot," as being good (see n. 2324, 2351, 2370, 2399); hence it is said "behind *him*." [5] Truth is said to turn itself away from good, and to look to doctrinal things, when the man of the church no longer has at heart what kind of a life he lives, but what kind of a doctrine he possesses; when yet it is a life according to doctrine that makes a man of the church, but not doctrine separate from life; for when doctrine is separated from life, then because good, which is of the life, is laid waste, truth, which is of doctrine, is also laid waste, that is, becomes a pillar of salt; which every one may know who looks only to doctrine and not to life, when he considers whether, although doctrine teaches them, he believes in the resurrection, in heaven, in hell, even in the Lord, and in the rest of the things that are of doctrine.

2455. *And she became a pillar of salt.* That this signifies that all the good of truth was laid waste, is evident from the signification of a "pillar," and from the signification of "salt." In the original language a "pillar" is expressed by a word which signifies a standing still, not by one that means a pillar erected for worship, or for a sign, or for a witness; so that by the "pillar of salt" is here signified that it, namely, the truth signified by Lot's wife, stood vastated (n. 2454). Truth is said to be vastated, or laid waste, when there is no longer any good in it, vastation itself being signified by "salt." [2] As most things in the Word have a double sense, namely, the genuine sense and its opposite, so also has "salt;" in the genuine sense it signifies the affection of truth; in the opposite sense, the vastation of the affection of truth, that is, of good in truth. That "salt" signifies the affection of truth may be seen in *Exod.* xxx. 35; *Lev.* ii. 13; *Matt.* v. 13; *Mark* ix. 49, 50; *Luke* xiv. 34, 35; and that it signifies the vastation of the affection of truth is evident from the following passages. In *Moses* :—

The whole land shall be brimstone and salt, a burning ; it shall not be sown, it shall not bear, neither shall any herb spring up therein ; like the overthrow of Sodom and Gomorrah, Admah and Zeboim (*Deut.* xxix. 23) ;

where "brimstone" denotes the vastation of good; and "salt" the vastation of truth : that the subject is vastation is evident from every particular. [3] In *Zephaniah* :—

Moab shall be as Sodom, and the sons of Ammon as Gomorrah ; a place that is left to the nettle, and a pit of salt, and an eternal desolation (ii. 9) ;

where a "place that is left to the nettle" denotes vastated good, and a "pit of salt" vastated truth; for the expression "place left to the nettle" refers to Sodom, by which is signified evil or vastated good, and a "pit of salt" to Gomorrah, by which is signified falsity or vastated truth, as already shown. That the subject is vastation is manifest, for it is said an "eternal desolation." In *Jeremiah* :—

He that maketh flesh his arm shall be like a bare shrub in the solitude, and shall not see when good cometh, but shall inhabit the parched places in the wilderness, a salt land, and not inhabited (xvii. 5, 6) ;

where "parched places" denote vastated goods, and a "salt land" vastated truths. [4] In *David* :—

Jehovah maketh rivers into a wilderness, and water springs into dry ground, a fruitful land into a salt one, for the wickedness of them that dwell therein (*Ps.* cvii. 33, 34) ;

a " fruitful land made into a salt one" denotes the vastation
of good in truth.   In *Ezekiel* :—

The miry places thereof and the marshes thereof shall not be healed ;
they shall be given up to salt (xlvii. 11) ;

to be " given up to salt" denotes being altogether vastated as
to truth.   As " salt" signified vastation, and " cities" the doctrinal things of truth (shown at n. 402, 2268, 2428, 2451), in
ancient times when cities were destroyed they were sown with
salt, in order to prevent their being rebuilt (*Judges* ix. 45).
The words before us therefore denote the fourth state of that
church which was represented by Lot, which state was that all
truth was vastated as to good.

2456. Verses 27–29. *And Abraham rose up early in the
morning unto the place where he had stood before Jehovah.
And he looked against the faces of Sodom and Gomorrah, and
against all the faces of the land of the plain ; and he saw and
behold the smoke of the land went up, as the smoke of a furnace.
And it came to pass when God destroyed the cities of the plain,
that God remembered Abraham, and sent Lot out of the midst
of the overthrow, when He overthrew the cities in which Lot
dwelt.*   " Abraham rose up early in the morning," signifies the
Lord's thought concerning the last time ; Abraham here as before denotes the Lord in that state ; " unto the place where
he had stood before Jehovah," signifies the state of perception
and thought in which He had been before ; " place" denotes
state.   " And he looked against the faces of Sodom and Gomorrah," signifies thought concerning their interior state in
respect to evil and falsity ; " and against all the faces of the
land of the plain," signifies all the interior states thence derived ; " and he saw and behold the smoke of the land went
up, as the smoke of a furnace," signifies a state of falsity
(which is " smoke") from a state of evil (which is the " furnace") within the church (which is the " land").   " And it
came to pass when God destroyed the cities of the plain," signifies when they perished through the falsities of evil, which
are the " cities of the plain ;" " that God remembered Abraham," signifies salvation through the unition of the Lord's
Divine Essence with His Human Essence ; " and sent Lot out

of the midst of the overthrow," signifies the salvation of those who are in good, and of those who are in truth in which is good, all of whom are here meant by " Lot ;" " when He overthrew the cities," signifies when those who were in falsities from evils perished; " in which Lot dwelt," signifies although they who were saved were also in such falsities.

2457. It is not necessary to explain these things in detail, because for the most part they have been explained in the preceding chapter, and also previously to that. They have been here added and inserted to the end that it might be evident that the good were separated from the evil, the former being saved while the latter were condemned, solely through the unition of the Lord's Divine Essence with His Human Essence; for if this had not taken place all those who are here represented by Lot would have perished together with the rest; which is meant by these words : " And it came to pass when God destroyed the cities of the plain, that God remembered Abraham, and sent Lot out of the midst of the overthrow, when He overthrew the cities in which Lot dwelt;" which in the internal sense denote that through the unition of the Lord's Divine Essence with His Human Essence, all who were in good were saved, and also those who were in truth in which there is good, here represented by Lot, while those who were in falsities from evils perished, although they who were saved were also in falsities and evils. In this way therefore are the things said in this chapter conjoined with those said in the preceding one ; namely, that Abraham (that is, the Lord in that state) interceded for those people of Sodom and Gomorrah who are signified by the " fifty," the " forty-five," the " forty," the " thirty," the " twenty," and the " ten ;" concerning whom it was there explained that these are all in their order who are in good, and also those who are in truth in which there is anything of good.

2458. Verse 30. *And Lot went up out of Zoar, and dwelt in the mountain, and his two daughters with him ; for he feared to dwell in Zoar ; and he dwelt in a cave, he and his two daughters.* " Lot went up out of Zoar," signifies when they were no longer in the affection of truth ; "and dwelt in the mountain," signifies that they then betook themselves to a kind of good; " and his two daughters with him," signifies that so did the affections thence derived; " for he feared to dwell in Zoar," signifies because they could no longer look to good from the affection of truth; "and he dwelt in a cave," signifies the good of falsity; " and his two daughters," signifies the affections thence derived, which are those of such good and such falsity.

2459. *Lot went up out of Zoar.* That this signifies when they were no longer in the affection of truth, is evident from the signification of " Zoar," as being the affection of truth (see n. 2439); and as there follows the statement that " he dwelt in the mountain because he feared to dwell in Zoar," the signification is "when they were no longer in the affection of truth," and this because all the good of truth had been vastated, as is evident from verse 26. In this verse therefore there is described the fifth state of the church which was represented by Lot, which state was that after there was no longer any affection of truth, a kind of impure good, or good of falsity, infused itself.

2460. *And dwelt in the mountain.* That this signifies that they then betook themselves to a kind of good, is evident from the signification of a "mountain," as being love in every sense, namely, celestial and spiritual love (n. 795, 1430); and also the love of self and of the world (n. 1691); and this because most things in the Word have also an opposite sense. And as all good is of some love, by the "mountain" is here signified good; but what kind of good is described in what follows, namely, that it was obscure, and became impure; for it is presently said that he "dwelt in a cave," and afterwards that profane things took place there.

2461. *And his two daughters with him.* That this signifies that so did the affections thence derived, is evident from the signification of "daughters," as being affections (see n. 489–491); but such as the good is, such are the affections that are derived from it. Even spurious and impure good has its affections, for all are affected by the things which they deem to be good, of whatever kind these may be, for they are the objects of their love.

2462. *For he feared to dwell in Zoar.* That this signifies because he could no longer regard good from the affection of

truth, is evident from the signification of "Zoar," as being the
affection of truth (n. 2439); and when this is vastated no one
can any longer have regard to good from it. There is then
also a fear of all truth, because this is opposed to the good of
an impure love.

2463. *And he dwelt in a cave.* That this signifies the good
of falsity, is evident from the signification of a "cave." A
cave is a kind of dwelling in a mountain, but a dark one; and
as all dwellings whatever, like "houses," signify goods (n.
2233, 2234), but goods of such sort as are the dwellings; here
the "cave," being a dark dwelling, signifies the good of falsity.
"Caves of mountains" are often mentioned in the Word, and
in the internal sense have such a signification, as in *Isaiah*
(ii. 19; xxxii. 14), and in the historical books, as when Elijah,
escaping from Jezebel,

> Came to a cave in Mount Horeb, and spent the night there ; and there
> the word of Jehovah came to him, and He said unto him, go forth and
> stand on the mount before Jehovah ; and he wrapped his face in his
> mantle, and went out, and stood at the entrance of the cave (1 *Kings*
> xix. 9, 13) ;

where in the internal sense by a "cave" is signified obscure
good, but such as exists in temptations; and as this could not
endure the Divine, he wrapped his face in his mantle. So too
elsewhere in the historical books, as that the sons of Israel made
for themselves caves in the mountains on account of Midian
(*Judges* vi. 2); also on account of the Philistines (1 *Sam.*
xiii. 6). These historical facts, like those now explained in the
books of *Moses*, have a different meaning in the internal sense.

2464. *And his two daughters.* That this signifies the affections thence derived, which are those of such good and such
falsity, is evident from the signification of "daughters," as
being affections (n. 2461). The good from which came these
affections, or the father from whom came these daughters, was
Lot; and the truth from which came these affections, or the
mother of the daughters, was Lot's wife; and when she was
made a pillar of salt, that is, when the good of truth was vastated, then there came forth such good as is signified by "Lot
in the cave," and such affections thence derived as are signified by the "daughters."

2465. Verses 31–36. *And the firstborn said unto the younger, Our father is old, and there is no man in the earth to come unto us according to the way of all the earth. Come, let us make our father drink wine, and let us lie with him, and let us quicken seed from our father. And they made their father drink wine that night; and the firstborn went in, and lay with her father; and he knew not when she lay down, nor when she arose. And it came to pass on the morrow, that the firstborn said unto the younger, Behold, I lay yesternight with my father; let us make him drink wine this night also, and go thou in and lie with him, and let us quicken seed from our father. And they made their father drink wine that night also; and the younger arose, and lay with him; and he knew not when she lay down, nor when she arose. And the two daughters of Lot conceived by their father.* [2] " The firstborn said unto the younger," signifies here as before the affections; the firstborn the affection of such good, the younger the affection of such falsity; " our father is old, and there is no man in the earth," signifies that it is no longer known what good is, and what truth is; " to come unto us," signifies with which they might be conjoined; " according to the way of all the earth," signifies according to doctrinal things; the " earth" is the church. " Come, let us make our father drink wine," signifies that they should imbue such good with falsities, which are the " wine;" " and let us lie with him," signifies that in this way they would be conjoined; " and let us quicken seed from our father," signifies that so there would be a newness of a sort of church. [3] " And they made their father drink wine," signifies that they imbued such good with falsities; " that night," signifies when all things were in such obscurity; " and the firstborn went in," signifies the affection of such good; " and lay with her father," signifies that thus they were brought into accordance; " and he knew not when she lay down nor when she arose," signifies that such a general kind of good knew no otherwise than that it was so. " And it came to pass on the morrow," signifies afterwards; " that the firstborn said unto the younger," signifies that the affection of such good persuaded the falsity; " Behold, I lay yesternight with my father," signifies that thus they were conjoined;

"'let us make him drink wine this night also," signifies here
as before that they imbued such good with falsities when
everything was in such obscurity; [4] " and go thou in and
lie with him," signifies that these things also should be conjoined ; " and let us quicken seed from our father," signifies
here as before that so there would be a newness of a sort of
church. " And they made their father drink wine that night
also," signifies that in that obscure state they imbued such
good with falsities ; " and the younger arose and lay with
him," signifies that the affection of falsity did in like manner,
so that falsities appeared as truths, and in this way they were
conjoined ; " and he knew not when she lay down nor when
she arose," signifies that such general good knew no otherwise
than that it was so. " And the two daughters of Lot conceived by their father," signifies that hence was the origin of
such a religion as is signified by Moab and the son of Ammon.

2466. That the things now set forth are signified in the
internal sense, can be confirmed, and indeed as to each word ;
but most of them have been confirmed before, and besides,
they are such as do violence to our ideas and give offense to
chaste ears. From the summary explication we can see that
by the things in question there is described the origin of such
a religion as is signified in the Word by " Moab" and the " son
of Ammon." The nature of this religion will be told hereafter, where Moab and the son of Ammon are treated of.
That it is adulterated good and falsified truth, is evident. The
adulterations of good and the falsifications of truth are com-
monly described in the Word by "adulteries" and "whoredoms,"
and are also so called, the reason of which is based on the fact
that good and truth form a marriage with each other (n. 1904,
2173) ; nay, incredible as it may appear to most, it is from
this marriage as from its genuine origin that there comes the
sanctity of marriages on earth, and also the laws of marriages
given in the Word. [2] For the case is this : When celestial
and spiritual things descend out of heaven into a lower sphere,
they are there turned in the most perfect manner into some
likeness of marriages, and this from the correspondence that
exists between spiritual and natural things (concerning which
correspondence of the Lord's Divine mercy elsewhere). But

when they are perverted in the lower sphere, as is done where
evil genii and evil spirits are present, the same are then
turned into such things as belong to adulteries and whoredoms. Hence it is that contaminations of good and perversions of truth are described in the Word by adulteries and
whoredoms, and are also so named, as is very evident from
the following passages in *Ezekiel :—*

Thou didst commit whoredom because of thy name, and pouredst out
thy whoredoms on every one that passed by ; thou didst take of thy garments and madest for thee high places decked with divers colors, and
didst commit whoredom upon them ; thou didst take the vessels of thy
adornment of My gold and of My silver, which I had given thee, and
madest for thee images of a male, and didst commit whoredom with
them ; thou hast taken thy sons and thy daughters, whom thou hast
borne unto Me, and these hast thou sacrificed unto them. Was there
but little of thy whoredoms ? thou hast committed whoredom with the
sons of Egypt, thy neighbors, great of flesh ; and hast multiplied thy
whoredom to provoke Me to anger ; thou hast committed whoredom
with the sons of Asshur, and hast committed whoredom with them, and
wast not satisfied ; and thou hast multiplied thy whoredom even unto
the land of traffic, unto Chaldea ; and yet thou wast not satisfied therewith (xvi. 15–17, 20, 26, 28, 29, etc.) ;

[3] where Jerusalem is treated of, by which is here signified the church perverted in respect to truths. Every one
can see that all these things have quite different meanings.
That something of the church that has been perverted is
called " whoredom" is quite evident ; the " garments" here
mentioned denote the truths that are being perverted; the
falsities thence derived, which are worshiped, are the " high
places decked with divers colors," with which there was
whoredom. (That " garments" denote truths may be seen
above, n. 1073 ; and that "high places" denote worship, n. 796.)
The " vessels of adornment of gold and silver which I had
given," denote the knowledges of good and truth from the
Word by which they confirm falsities; and when these appear as truths, they are called " images of a male" with which
whoredom was committed. (That the " vessels of adornment
of gold and silver," denote the knowledges of good and truth,
is evident from the signification of " gold," as being good, n.
113, 1551, 1552 ; and of " silver" as being truth, n. 1551,
2048 ; and that the " images of a male" signify that they ap-

pear as truths may be seen above, n. 2046.) That the "sons and daughters" which they bore and sacrificed to them denote the truths and goods which they have perverted, is evident from the signification of "sons and daughters" (see n. 489–491, 533, 2362). That to "commit whoredom with the sons of Egypt," denotes to pervert these truths and goods by means of memory-knowledges, is evident from the signification of "Egypt," as being memory-knowledge (n. 1164, 1165, 1186, 1462). That to "commit whoredom with the sons of Asshur," denotes to pervert them by reasonings, is evident from the signification of "Asshur," as being reasoning (n. 119, 1186). That to "multiply whoredom even unto the land of Chaldea," denotes to pervert them even to the profanation of truth, which is "Chaldea" (n. 1368). All this makes clear what is the nature of the internal sense of the Word in the very sense of the letter. [4] In like manner elsewhere in the same Prophet:—

Two women, the daughters of one mother, committed whoredom in Egypt; they committed whoredom in their youth; Samaria is Oholah, Jerusalem is Oholibah. Oholah committed whoredom under Me, and she doted on her lovers, the Assyrians her neighbors, she bestowed her whoredoms upon them, the choice of all the sons of Asshur; she hath not forsaken her whoredoms from Egypt, for they lay with her in her youth. Oholibah corrupted her love more than she, and her whoredoms more than the whoredoms of her sister; she doted upon the sons of Asshur; she added to her whoredoms, and saw the images of the Chaldeans, she doted upon them at the view of her eyes; the sons of Babel came to her into the bed of loves (xxiii. 2–5, 7, 8, 11, 12, 14, 16, etc.).

"Samaria" denotes the church which is in the affection of truth, and "Jerusalem" that which is in the affection of good; whose "whoredoms with the Egyptians," and "with the sons of Asshur," denote perversions of good and truth by means of memory-knowledges and reasonings, by which falsities are confirmed, as is evident from the signification of "Egypt" (n. 1164, 1165, 1186, 1462); and of "Asshur" (n. 119, 1186). That this was done even to profane worship, which in respect to truth is "Chaldea" (n. 1368); and in respect to good is the "sons of Babel" (n. 1182, 1326). [5] In *Isaiah*:—

And it shall come to pass at the end of seventy years that Jehovah will visit Tyre, and she shall return to her harlot hire, and shall commit whoredom with all the kingdoms of the earth (xxiii. 17).

It is the vaunting of what is false that is signified by the
"harlot hire" and the "whoredom" of Tyre. That "Tyre"
denotes the knowledges of truth may be seen above (n. 1201);
and also that the "kingdoms" with which the whoredom was
committed denote truths (n. 1672). [6] In *Jeremiah :*—

Thou hast committed whoredom with many companions; and return
again unto Me. Lift up thine eyes unto the hills, and see; where hast
thou not been debauched? Upon the ways hast thou sat for them as an
Arab in the wilderness, and thou hast profaned the land with thy whoredoms and with thy wickedness (iii. 1, 2).

To "commit whoredom" and to "profane the land with whoredoms" denote to pervert and falsify the truths of the church
(that the "land" denotes the church see above, n. 662, 1066,
1067). [7] Again :—

By the voice of her whoredom she hath profaned the land, she hath
committed adultery with stone and with wood (*Jer.* iii. 9);

to "commit adultery with stone and with wood," denotes to
pervert the truths and goods of external worship (that "stone"
is such truth may be seen above, n. 643, 1298; and that "wood"
is such good, n. 643). [8] Again :—

Because they have wrought folly in Israel, and have committed adultery
with the wives of their fellows, and have spoken a word in My name that
is false, which I commanded them not (*Jer.* xxix. 23);

to "commit adultery with the wives of their fellows," is to
teach falsity as from them. [9] Again :—

In the prophets of Jerusalem I have seen a horrible thing, in committing adultery and walking in falsehood (*Jer.* xxiii. 14);

where to "commit adultery" regards good which is contaminated; and to "walk in falsehood" regards truth which is perverted. Again :—

I have seen thine abominations; thine adulteries, and thy neighings,
the foulness of thy whoredom upon the hills in the field. Woe unto thee,
O Jerusalem, thou wilt not be made clean; how long shall it yet be? (*Jer.*
xiii. 27).

[10] In *Hosea :*—

Whoredom, and wine, and new wine, have taken possession of the
heart. My people inquireth of wood, and the staff thereof will declare
it; for the spirit of whoredom hath led them astray, and they have committed whoredom from under their God; they sacrifice upon the tops of

the mountains, and burn incense upon the hills, under the oak, the poplar, and the terebinth (*robore*) ; therefore your daughters commit whoredom, and your daughters-in-law commit adultery ; shall I not visit upon
your daughters because they commit whoredom, and upon your daughters-
in-law because they commit adultery ? for they divide with whores, and
sacrifice with prostitutes (iv. 11–14).

What each of these things signifies in the internal sense can
be seen from the signification of "wine," as being falsity ; of
"new wine," as being the evil thence derived ; of the "wood
that is inquired of," as being the good of the delight of some
cupidity ; of the "staff that will declare," as being the imagi-
nary power of their understanding ; also of the "mountains"
and the "hills," as being the loves of self and of the world ; of
the "oak, the poplar, and the terebinth," as being so many
gross perceptions thence derived in which they trust ; of
"daughters" and the "daughters-in-law," as being such affections ; all of which show what is here signified by "whoredoms," "adulteries," and "harlots." [11] In the same :—

O Israel, thou hast committed whoredom over thy God, thou hast
loved harlot hire upon all the corn-floors (ix. 1) ;

"harlot hire" denotes the vaunting of what is false. In
Moses :—

Lest thou make a covenant with the inhabitants of the land, and they
commit whoredom after their gods, and sacrifice unto their gods ; and
one call thee, and thou eat of his sacrifices, and thou take of his daughters for thy sons, and his daughters commit whoredom after their gods,
and make thy sons commit whoredom after their gods (*Exod.* xxxiv.
15, 16).

In the same :—

I will cut off all that commit whoredom after him, committing whoredom after Molech, from the midst of their people ; and the soul that
turneth unto them that have familiar spirits, and unto the soothsayers,
to commit whoredom after them, I will set My face against that soul,
and will cut him off from the midst of his people (*Lev.* xx. 5, 6).

In the same :—

Your sons shall be shepherds in the wilderness forty years, and shall
bear your whoredoms, until your bodies be consumed in the wilderness
(*Num.* xiv. 33).

In the same :—

Remember all the precepts of Jehovah, and do them, that ye seek not after your own heart, and your own eyes, after which ye do commit whoredom (*Num.* xv. 39).

[12] And still more plainly in *John :—*

An angel said, Come hither, I will show thee the judgment of the great harlot that sitteth upon many waters, with whom the kings of the earth have committed whoredom, and the inhabitants of the earth have been made drunk with the wine of her whoredom (*Rev.* xvii. 1, 2) ;

the "great harlot" denotes those who are in profane worship; the "many waters" upon which she sits, are knowledges (n. 28, 739); the "kings of the earth" who have committed whoredom with her, are the truths of the church (n. 1672, 2015, 2069); the "wine" with which they were made drunk, is falsity (n. 1071, 1072). Because "wine" and "drunkenness" signify these things, it is said of the daughters of Lot, that they made their father drink wine (verses 32, 33, 35). [13] In the same :—

Babylon hath made all nations drink of the wine of the fury of her whoredom, and the kings of the earth have committed whoredom with her (*Rev.* xviii. 3).

"Babylon" or "Babel" denotes a worship the externals of which appear holy, while the interiors are profane (n. 1182, 1295, 1326); the "nations that she makes to drink," are the goods which are being profaned (n. 1259, 1260, 1416, 1849); the "kings" who committed whoredom with her, are truths (n. 1672, 2015, 2069). In the same :—

True and just are the judgments of the Lord God, for He hath judged the great harlot, who corrupted the earth with her whoredom (*Rev.* xix. 2) ;

where the "earth" denotes the church (n. 566, 662, 1066, 1068, 2117, 2118). [14] As "whoredoms" signify such things, and "daughters" signify affections, it was therefore forbidden so severely that the daughter of a priest should commit whoredom ; concerning which we read in *Moses :—*

The daughter of a priest, having begun to commit whoredom, she is profaning her father, she shall be burned with fire (*Lev.* xxi. 9).

It was also commanded that they should not bring the hire of a harlot into the house of Jehovah, because it is an abomination (*Deut.* xxiii. 18). And for the same reason there was such an inquisitorial process concerning a wife whose husband had conceived a suspicion of adultery (*Num.* v. 12–31), in which instance each and all things have relation to the adulterations of good. Moreover in the Word many different kinds of adulteries and whoredoms are spoken of, and still more varieties. This kind which is here described by Lot's daughters lying with their father, is what is called "Moab" and the "son of Ammon," now to be explained.

2467. Verses 37, 38. *And the firstborn bare a son, and called his name Moab ; he is the father of Moab even unto this day. And the younger, she also bare a son, and called his name Benammi ; he is the father of the sons of Ammon even unto this day.* "The firstborn bare a son," signifies the religion of that church in respect to good ; "and called his name Moab," signifies its quality ; "he is the father of Moab even unto this day," signifies that this is the source of such persons. "And the younger she also bare a son," signifies the falsified truth of that church ; "and called his name Benammi," signifies its quality ; "he is the father of the sons of Ammon even unto this day," signifies that this is the source of such persons.

2468. These things, again, need no confirmation ; for that such things are signified is evident from the explication itself, and from what precedes and what follows. But what is the nature and quality of the religion signified by "Moab" and the "sons of Ammon," can be seen from their origin, as here described ; as well as from many passages in the Word, both historic and prophetic, where these nations are mentioned. To speak generally they denote those who are in an external worship which appears in a manner holy, but who are not in internal worship ; and who readily learn as being goods and truths the things that belong to external worship, but reject and despise those of internal worship. [2] Such worship and such religion fall to the lot of those who are in natural good, but despise others in comparison with themselves. They are not unlike fruits which in the external form are not unbeautiful, but which are mouldy or rotten within ;

and they are not unlike marble vases, within which are things impure and even foul; or not unlike women seemly enough in face, form, and manners, but diseased within, and full of impurities. For there is a general good appertaining to such which appears not ill-favored; but the particulars that enter into it are filthy. In the beginning indeed it is not so, but it gradually becomes so; for such men easily suffer themselves to be imbued with whatever things are called good, and with any falsities whatsoever that are derived from these, and which, because they confirm them, they suppose to be truths; and this because they despise the interior things of worship, for the reason that they are in the love of self. Such persons have their existence and derivation from those who are in external worship alone (represented in this chapter by Lot); and this when the good of truth has been desolated. They are described in the Word, both such as they are in the beginning, when their good has not yet become so defiled; and afterwards when it is becoming defiled; and also after this, when it has become utterly defiled; and it is shown that they reject the interior things of worship and of doctrine. [3] The character of such in the beginning when their good has not yet become so defiled, is described in *Daniel* :—

In the time of the end shall the king of the south be at variance with him; and the king of the north shall rush upon him like a storm, with chariot, and with horsemen, and with many ships, and shall come into the lands, and shall overflow, and shall pass through; and he shall come into the land of beauty, and many lands shall go to ruin : these shall be rescued out of his hand, Edom, and Moab, and the firstlings of the sons of Ammon (xi. 40, 41).

The "king of the south," denotes those who are in goods and truths; the "king of the north," those who are in evils and falsities; the "king of the north with chariot, horsemen, and and ships, coming upon the lands, overflowing, and passing through," signifies that the evils and falsities denoted by "chariots," "horsemen," and "ships," will prevail; "Edom, Moab, and the firstlings of the sons of Ammon who are to be rescued out of his hand," denote those who are in such good that is not as yet so defiled by falsities; on which account they are called the "firstlings of the sons of Ammon." [4] In *Moses* :—

We passed through by the way of the wilderness, and Jehovah said unto Moses, Distress not Moab, neither mingle thyself with them in war, for I will not give thee of his land for an inheritance, because I have given Ar unto the sons of Lot for an inheritance (*Deut.* ii. 8, 9).

And concerning the sons of Ammon :—

Jehovah spake unto Moses, saying, Thou art to pass this day over Ar the border of Moab, and thou wilt come near over against the sons of Ammon ; distress them not, nor mingle thyself with them ; for I will not give thee of the land of the sons of Ammon for an inheritance, because I have given it unto the sons of Lot for an inheritance (*Deut.* ii. 17–19) ;

" Ar" denotes such good ; " Moab" and the " sons of Ammon" denote those who are in such good, but in the beginning ; on which account it is ordered that they be not distressed. [5] Hence it is that Moab drove out the Emim, and the Rephaim who were like the Anakim ; and that the sons of Ammon also drove out the Rephaim whom they called the Zamzumim (*Deut.* ii. 9–11, 18–21). By the Emim, Rephaim, Anakim, and Zamzumim, are signified those who are imbued with persuasions of what is evil and false (see n. 581, 1673) ; by Moab and the sons of Ammon are here meant those who were not yet so imbued. These nations however when they too had become so imbued, that is, when their good was defiled by falsities, were likewise driven out (*Num.* xxi. 21–31 ; *Ezek.* xxv. 8–11). [6] Their character when their good is becoming defiled is described in *Jeremiah* :—

Unto Moab thus saith Jehovah, Woe unto Nebo, for it is laid waste ; Kiriathaim is put to shame, is taken ; Misgab is put to shame and is dismayed ; the praise of Moab is no more ; give wing to Moab, for flying she must fly away, and her cities shall become a desolation, without any to dwell therein. Leave the cities, and dwell in the rock, O inhabitants of Moab ; and be like the dove, she maketh her nest in the passages of the mouth of the pit. I know his anger, saith Jehovah, but it is not firm ; his falsities, they have not done right. Therefore will I howl over Moab, and I will cry out to all Moab. From the weeping of Jazer will I weep for thee, O vine of Sibmah ; thy shoots have passed over the sea, they reached even to the sea of Jazer ; upon thy summer fruits and upon thy vintage the spoiler is fallen. Therefore my heart is moved over Moab, like flutes. Woe unto thee, O Moab, the people of Chemosh is destroyed ; for thy sons are taken into captivity, and thy daughters into captivity. And I will bring back the captivity of Moab in the latter days (xlviii. 1, 9, 28, 30–32, 36, 46, 47).

[7] In this whole chapter the subject treated of is Moab; but through him those are treated of who are in such good, in that they suffer themselves to be imbued with falsities; on which account it is said that they should "give wing to Moab, that it may fly away, and that its cities shall become a desolation;" but that they should "leave the cities, and dwell in the rock, and make nests like the dove in the passages of the mouth of the pit," and so on, by which expressions it is signified that they are persuaded to remain in their general goods and truths; and that if they should then be seduced by the falsities of ignorance, they will be brought back from captivity in the latter days; but concerning those with whom this was not done it is said, "I will howl over Moab, and I will cry out for all Moab, and my heart is moved over Moab." The falsities with which they are imbued are signified by Nebo, Kiriathaim, Misgab, Sibmah, Jazer, Chemosh, and other names in this chapter.   [8] In *Isaiah :*—

A nest sent away shall the daughters of Moab be. Bring forth counsel, execute judgment; make thy shadow like the night * in the midst of the noonday; hide the outcasts, betray not the wanderer, let mine outcasts dwell with thee, O Moab; be thou a covert to them from the spoiler. We have heard the arrogance of Moab, he is very arrogant, his pride, and his arrogance, and his anger; his lies are not so; therefore Moab shall howl, for Moab all shall howl. Therefore my bowels shall be stirred like a harp over Moab, and mine inward part for the city of Heres. And it shall come to pass when Moab shall be seen, when he is wearied upon the high place, and shall come to his sanctuary to pray, that he shall not prevail. In three years, as if years of hire, and the praise of Moab shall become vile, in all the great multitude; and the remnant shall be very small, and not strong (xvi. 2–4, 6, 11, 12, 14).

Moab is further treated of in this whole chapter, and through him those who are in such good; and they are described there in words similar to those in *Jeremiah* (chapter xlviii); and are in like manner persuaded to remain in their general goods and truths, and not to suffer themselves to be imbued with falsities. These general goods and truths are signified by their "giving counsel," "executing judgment," "hiding the outcasts," "not betraying the wanderer," and being "a covert to the outcasts from the spoiler;" all of which things signify the

* *Totam;* but *sicut noctem* n. 9642. [*Rotch ed.*]

externals of worship. But as they suffer themselves to be imbued with falsities, it is said, "in three years, as years of hire, shall the praise of Moab become vile in all the great multitude, and the remnant shall be very small, and not strong." [9] As such persons are easily led away, Moab is called "the sending forth of the hand of the Philistines," and the sons of Ammon their "obedience," in *Isaiah* :—

The root of Jesse which standeth for an ensign of the peoples, unto Him shall the nations seek, and His rest shall be glory ; the envy of Ephraim shall depart, and the enemies of Judah shall be cut off ; Ephraim shall not envy Judah, and Judah shall not distress Ephraim ; and they shall fly upon the shoulder of the Philistines toward the sea ; together shall they spoil the sons of the east, Edom, Moab the sending forth of their hand, and the sons of Ammon their obedience (xi. 10, 13, 14) ;

the "root of Jesse" denotes the Lord; "Judah" those who are in celestial good; "Ephraim" those who are in spiritual truth; the "Philistines" those who are in the mere memory-knowledge of the knowledges of truth, and not in charity; the "sons of the east," those who are in the mere memory-knowledge of the knowledges of good, and also not in charity; and Moab is called the "sending forth of their hand," and the sons of Ammon their "obedience," because they are imbued with falsities by them. [10] But of what character become those who are called Moab and the sons of Ammon when their good has been altogether defiled by falsities, is described in *David* :—

God hath spoken in His holiness, Gilead is Mine, Manasseh is Mine, Ephraim also is the strength of My head, Judah is My lawgiver, Moab is My washpot (*Ps.* lx. 7–9, and also *Ps.* cviii. 8–10) ;

the "washpot" denotes good defiled by falsities.   [11] In *Jeremiah* :—

The praise of Moab is no more ; in Heshbon they have devised evil against him : come, let us cut him off from being a nation. Moab hath been at peace from his youth, and he hath settled on his lees, and hath not been emptied from vessel to vessel, and hath not gone into exile ; therefore his taste remaineth in him, and his odor is not changed. On all the housetops of Moab there shall be lamentation everywhere, because I have broken Moab like a vessel in which there is no pleasure (xlviii. 2, 11, 38).

The falsities with which the good denoted by Moab is defiled, are here called " lees, in which the taste and the odor remain," if he is not reformed, which is here denoted by being "emptied from vessel to vessel." This good itself is called the "vessel in which there is no pleasure," just as in *David* it is called a "washpot," in which washing is done.   In *Isaiah :*—

In this mountain the hand of Jehovah resteth, and Moab shall be trodden down under it, as chaff is trodden down in the dunghill (xxv. 10).

[12] That they who are in such good care for external things only, and despise, reject, and indeed spew out the internal things of worship and of doctrine, and that consequently they have falsities instead of truths—in *Ezekiel :*—

Son of man, set thy face toward the sons of Ammon, and prophesy against them, and say unto the sons of Ammon, Hear the word of the Lord Jehovih. Thus saith the Lord Jehovih, Because thou saidst, Aha, against My sanctuary when it was profaned, and against the land of Israel when it was made desolate, and against the house of Judah when they went into captivity, I will make Rabbah a habitation for camels, and the sons of Ammon a couching-place for the flock. Thus saith the Lord Jehovih, Because thou hast clapped the hand, and hast stamped with the foot, and hast been glad with all the contempt of thy soul against the ground of Israel, therefore behold I will stretch out My hand upon thee, and give thee for a spoil to the nations, and I will cut thee off from the peoples, and destroy thee from the lands (xxv. 2–11).

These words : " Aha, against My sanctuary when it was profaned, and against the land of Israel when it was made desolate, and against the house of Judah when they went into captivity," " thou hast clapped the hand, and hast stamped with the foot, and hast been glad with all the contempt of thy soul against the land of Israel," are expressions of contempt, derision, and rejection of the interior things of worship and of doctrine ; and when these are rejected, external things are of no avail ; but such persons are " given for a spoil to the nations," that is, they are taken possession of by evils, and are " cut off from the peoples," that is by falsities, and are " destroyed from the earth," that is they become of no church.
[13] In *Zephaniah :*—

I have heard the reproach of Moab, and the blasphemies of the sons of Ammon, who have reproached My people ; they enlarged against their border : therefore, as I live, Moab shall be as Sodom, and the sons of

Ammon as Gomorrah, a place abandoned to the nettle, and a pit of salt, and a perpetual desolation. This they have for their pride, because they reproached and enlarged against the people of Jehovah Zebaoth (ii. 8–10).

To "reproach the people," and to "enlarge against their boundary, and against the people of Jehovah Zebaoth," is to hold as vile and to reject interior truths, which are the "people of Jehovah Zebaoth." The consequence of this is that goods become evils of falsity, which are "Sodom" and a "place abandoned to the nettle;" and truths become falsities, which are "Gomorrah" and a "pit of salt." For it is from internal things that external are capable of being good and true. [**14**] In *David*:—

> Thine enemies craftily meditate a secret thing against thy people, they consult together against thy hidden ones : Come, let us cut them off from being a nation, and let the name of Israel be no more in remembrance ; for they consult together with one heart ; against thee do they cut out a covenant, the tents of Edom, and the Ishmaelites, Moab and the Hagarenes, Gebal and Ammon and Amalek, Philistia with the inhabitants of Tyre ; Asshur also is joined with them, they are an arm to the sons of Lot (*Ps.* lxxxiii. 2–8).

To "consult together against the hidden ones," to "cut them off from being a nation, that the name of Israel should be no more in remembrance," denotes to utterly reject interior things ; the "tents of Edom, the Ishmaelites, Moab, the Hagarenes, Gebal, and Ammon," denote those who are in the external things of worship and of doctrine ; "Philistia with Tyre" denote the things they say concerning internal things while not being in them ; "Asshur, who is an arm to the sons of Lot," denotes the reasoning by which they contend in favor of external things and against internal things. [**15**] In *Moses*:—

> A man shall not take his father's wife, and shall not violate his father's skirt. He that is bruised with a bruising, or is bruised in the testicle, shall not come into the congregation of Jehovah ; a Moabite and an Ammonite shall not come into the congregation of Jehovah ; even to the tenth generation, they shall not come into the congregation of Jehovah forever (*Deut.* xxii. 30 ; xxiii. 1–3).

These words show what is the character of Moab and Ammon in the "end of days," or when they have become altogether imbued with falsities (that is, those with whom good is being adulterated and truth falsified), in that they despise, reject, and at length utterly cast out all interior things. On this account they are here mentioned after mention has been made of foul adulteries, such as taking a father's wife, and violating a father's skirt; nearly as is related of Lot's daughters, from whom came Moab and Ammon; and also after the mention of those who are bruised with a bruising, and bruised in the testicle, by whom are signified those who utterly reject whatever is of love and charity. The "congregation of Jehovah" is heaven, into which they cannot come, because they have no remains, which are solely from interior goods and interior truths, and are signified by the "tenth generation" (n. 576, 1738, 2280). [16] These were also among the nations who sacrificed their sons and daughters to Molech, by which is signified in the internal sense that they extinguished truths and goods; for the god of Moab was Chemosh, and the god of the sons of Ammon was Molech and Milchom (1 *Kings* xi. 7, 33; 2 *Kings* xxiii. 13), to which they sacrificed (2 *Kings* iii. 27). That by "sons and daughters" are signified truths and goods, may be seen above (n. 489–491, 533, 1147). [17] Such then is the signification of Moab and Ammon; but as regards the various kinds of falsity by which they adulterate goods and extinguish truths, these are numerous, being thus recounted in *Jeremiah*, but merely by names :—

Judgment is come upon the land of the plain, upon Holon, upon Jahzah, and upon Mephaath ; and upon Dibon, and upon Nebo, and upon Beth-diblathaim ; and upon Kiriathaim, and upon Beth-gamul, and upon Beth-meon ; and upon Kerioth, and upon Bozrah, and upon all the cities of the land of Moab, far and near. The horn of Moab is cut off, and his arm is broken. Make him drunken, because he magnified himself against Jehovah ; and let Moab exult in his vomit (xlviii. 21–26).

These are the kinds of falsity that assemble together in those who are called Moab and Ammon; but what is the nature and quality of these various kinds of falsity can be seen from the signification of these several names in the internal sense. That in the Word names signify nothing else than actual things, has often been shown already.

CONCERNING MAN'S MEMORY WHICH REMAINS AFTER DEATH,
  AND THE RECOLLECTION OF WHAT HE HAD DONE IN THE
  LIFE OF THE BODY.

2469. Scarcely any one has yet known that every man has
two memories, one exterior and the other interior; and that
the exterior memory is proper to his body, but the interior
memory to his spirit.

2470. Man, while living in the body, can scarcely be aware
that he has an interior memory, because the interior memory
then acts almost as one with his exterior memory; for the
ideas of thought of the interior memory flow into the things
in the exterior memory as into their vessels, and the two are
there conjoined together. It is as when angels and spirits are
speaking to a man; for then the ideas of the former, by which
they converse with each other, flow into the words of the man's
language, and so conjoin themselves with them that the spirits
know no otherwise than that they are speaking the man's own
language; when yet the ideas are theirs, and the words into
which they flow are the man's; on which subject I have often
spoken with spirits.

2471. These two memories are entirely distinct from each
other. To the exterior memory, which is proper to man while
he is living in the world, pertain all the words of languages,
also the objects of the outer senses, and also the knowledges
that belong to the world. To the interior memory pertain the
ideas of the speech of spirits, which are of the inner sight, and
all rational things, from the ideas of which thought itself comes
into existence. That these two classes of things are distinct
from each other, man does not know, both because he does not
reflect upon it, and because he is in corporeal things, from
which he cannot then so far withdraw his mind.

2472. Hence it is that men while living in the body cannot
speak with each other except by means of languages distinguished into articulate sounds, that is, into words, and are
unable to understand one another unless they are acquainted
with these languages, for the reason that their speech is from
the exterior memory. Whereas spirits speak with each other

by means of a universal language distinguished into ideas such
as are of thought itself, and thus they can have converse with
any spirit whatever, of whatever language and nation he had
been while in the world, for the reason that their speech is
from the interior memory. Into this language comes every
man immediately after death, because he comes into this
memory, which, as before said, is proper to his spirit (see n.
1637, 1639, 1757, 1876).

2473. The interior memory immeasurably surpasses the
exterior, and is relatively as are some myriads to one, or as
light is to darkness; for myriads of the ideas of the interior
memory flow into a single thing of the exterior memory, and
there present a general obscure something. Hence all the
faculties of spirits, and still more those of angels, are in a
more perfect state, that is, both their sensations, and their
thoughts and perceptions. In what way the interior memory
excels the exterior, may be seen from examples. When a
man calls to rememberance any other man whose quality is
known to him from the intercourse of many years, whether a
friend or an enemy, that which he then thinks about him is
presented as one obscure thing; and this because he is thinking from the exterior memory. But when the same man has
become a spirit, and calls the other to remembrance, that
which he then thinks about him is presented as to all the
ideas which he had ever conceived concerning him; and this
because he is then thinking from the interior memory. And
so it is with everything: the thing itself about which any one
has known many things presents itself in the exterior memory
as a single general thing; but in the interior memory it presents itself as to all the particulars about which he has ever
acquired for himself an idea in respect to that thing; and this
in a wonderful form.

2474. All things whatever that a man hears and sees, and
by which he is affected, are, unknown to the man, insinuated
as to ideas and ends into his interior memory; and they remain in it, so that not anything perishes; although the same
things are obliterated in the exterior memory. Such therefore is the interior memory that there are inscribed on it all
the single, nay, the most singular things that the man has

ever thought, spoken, and done; nay, even those which have appeared to him as but a shade, with the minutest particulars, from his earliest infancy to the last of old age. The memory of all these things the man has with him when he comes into the other life, and he is successively brought into full recollection of them. This is his *Book of Life*, which is opened in the other life, and according to which he is judged. Men can scarcely believe this, but yet it is most true. All the ends, which to him have been in obscurity, and all the things he has thought; together with everything that from these he has spoken and done, down to the smallest point, are in that Book, that is, in the interior memory, and whenever the Lord grants, are made manifest before the angels as in clear day. This has several times been shown me, and has been attested by so much experience that not the least doubt remains.

2475. As yet no one knows what is the state of souls after death in respect to the memory. From much and daily experience of many years, it has been given me to know that after death a man loses nothing whatever of what has been in his memories, whether in the exterior or in the interior memory; insomuch that nothing can possibly be thought of so small or so minute that the man does not have it with him; so that after death he leaves nothing whatever behind him except his bones and flesh, which, while he lived in the world, were not animated from themselves, but from the life of his spirit, which was his purer substance annexed to the things of the body.

2476. But as regards man's exterior memory, the case is this: He has all things of it with him both in general and in particular; but he is not then allowed to use this memory, but only the interior memory. The reasons are many; the first being that which has been stated, namely, that from the interior memory one can speak and hold intercourse in the other life with all in the universe. The second is, that this memory is proper to the spirit and is adapted to the state in which it then is; for exterior things—that is, those of memory-knowledge, of the world, and of the body—are adapted to man and correspond to his state while he is in the world and the body; but interior things—that is, things rational, spiritual, and celestial—are adapted and correspond to his spirit.

2477. I once heard spirits speaking together of the fact that whatever is adopted as a principle, no matter what it may be, can be confirmed by innumerable things, until at length, to the man who has confirmed himself, it appears entirely true even though false; and that men can be more easily persuaded of a falsity than of a truth. In order that they might be convinced of this, it was proposed to them that they should think and speak together on the point as to whether it is useful to spirits to use the exterior memory (for spirits converse on such subjects in a manner far surpassing man's belief, or even conception, but each one in accordance with his affection). The spirits who were in favor of corporeal and worldly things confirmed the proposition in question by many reasons, such as that in this way they would have lost nothing, but would be men after death equally as before; that in this way they could come again into the world through man; that the delight of life is in the exterior memory; and that in no other faculty and endowment are there intelligence and wisdom; besides many other reasons by which they confirmed themselves in their principle, until it appeared to them true. [2] But others then thought and spoke from the opposite principle, knowing that what they said was true, because it was from Divine order. They said that if spirits were permitted to use the exterior memory they would then be in similar imperfection as before, when they were men; that by so doing they would be in gross and obscure ideas, in comparison with those who are in the interior memory; and thus would not only become more and more foolish, but would also descend, and not ascend; thus would not live eternally; for to immerse themselves again in worldly and corporeal things would be to give themselves again into a state of death. They said also that if spirits were permitted to use the exterior memory the human race would perish; for every man is directed by the Lord through angels and spirits; and that if spirits were to flow into man from the exterior memory, he could not think from his own memory, but only from that of the spirit; thus man would come to be no longer in the enjoyment of his own life and his own freedom, but would be obsessed (the obsessions of former times being nothing else); besides other reasons.

2478. In order that I might know how the case is as to man's not being able to think from his own memory if spirits flowed in from their exterior memory, it has been permitted two or three times that this should be done; and I then knew no otherwise than that that was mine which was not mine, but a spirit's; and that I had thought things before which I had not thought; and this I was not able to perceive until they withdrew.

2479. A certain newly arrived spirit was indignant that he did not remember many things which he knew in the life of the body, grieving on account of the delight which he had lost, and with which he had been very greatly pleased. But he was told that he had lost nothing at all, and that he knew everything he had known; but that in the other life it is not permitted to draw forth such things; and that it is sufficient that he is now able to think and speak much better and more perfectly, without immersing his rational as before in dense, obscure, material, and corporeal things which are of no use in the kingdom into which he has now come; and that the things which were in the kingdom of the world had been left behind; and that he now has whatever conduces to the use of eternal life; and that thus and not otherwise can he become blessed and happy; thus that it is a result of ignorance to believe that in the other life intelligence perishes with the disuse of the corporeal memory; when yet the case is that in so far as the mind can be withdrawn from sensuous or corporeal things, so far is it elevated to spiritual and heavenly things.

2480. Seeing that men after death are in the interior memory (which has belonged to their rational) therefore those who in the world have been pre-eminently skilled in languages, cannot call forth even one syllable of them; and they who have been pre-eminently versed in the sciences cannot call up anything of their knowledges, and are sometimes more stupid than others. But whatever they have imbibed by means of the languages, or of the sciences, this they bring forth into use, because it has formed their rational. The rational they had so procured is that from which they think and speak. He who has imbibed falsities by means of the languages and sciences, and has confirmed himself in them, reasons from nothing but,falsities; but he who has imbibed and confirmed truths, speaks from the truths. It is the affection itself which gives life—the affection of evil which gives life to falsities, and the affection of good which gives life to truths. Every one thinks from affection, and no one without affection.

2481. That men after death, that is, spirits, have lost nothing whatever of the things which belong to their external or corporeal memory; but that they retain all things of it (that is to say, they retain the whole of it), although it is not permitted to bring forth from it the particulars * of their life, has been given me to know from much experience, as may be seen from what follows. Two persons whom I had known during their life in the body, and who had been enemies to each other, met; and I heard one describing the character of the other with many circumstances, and also telling what opinion he had had of him, repeating an entire letter that he had written to him, and many other things in series which were particulars, and that belonged to the exterior memory; all of which the other acknowledged, and at which he was silent.

2482. I heard a certain one upbraiding another, in that he had kept back his property, and had not restored it; and this together with circumstances that were of the exterior memory, until the other was ashamed. I also heard the other replying, and rehearsing the reasons why he had done it; all of which were worldly particulars.

2483. A certain woman was let into the state in which she had been in the world when she had plotted a misdeed; and then all the details of her thoughts, and of her conversation with another female, came out as into clear day. A certain female belonging to the crew of the Sirens, because she persisted in denying that she had been such in the life of the body, was let into the state of her corporeal memory; and then her adulteries and shameless deeds, which while she lived had been known to scarcely any one, were laid open and were recounted in series, almost to hundreds : where she had been; with whom she had committed adultery; what she then plotted;

---

* By " particulars" Swedenborg here means such things as the words of natural languages, the names of men, and of cities, together with other similar merely external matters. See this plainly stated in the *Spiritual Diary*, n. 2285. [REVISER.]

and all these as much to the life as if in open day; thus was she convicted. Such things are brought forth when any one desires to exculpate himself from having been such; and indeed to the life, with every circumstance.

2485. A certain one was with me whom I had not known during his life in the body. When I inquired whether he knew whence he was, he did not know; but by means of the interior sight he was led by me through the cities where I had been, and at length through the city from which he was, and then through its streets and squares, all of which he recognized, and at length into the street where he had dwelt; and if I had been acquainted with the houses, and how they were situated, I should have been able to know his house.

2486. That men have with them everything of the corporeal memory, both in general and in particular, has frequently been made evident to me from those with whom I had been acquainted during their life in the body, in that when I spoke with them they recognized everything they had done while I was present, and which they had then spoken and thought. From these and many other experiences, it has been given me to know for certain that a man carries with him into the other life all things of the exterior or corporeal memory.

2487. I have been instructed that regarded in itself the exterior memory is simply something organic formed from the objects of the senses—especially those of the sight and of the hearing—in the substances which are the beginnings of the fibres; and that according to the impressions from these objects are effected variations of form, which are reproduced; and that these forms are varied and changed according to the changes of the state of the affections and persuasions. Also that the interior memory is in like manner organic, but purer and more perfect, being formed from the objects of the interior sight; which objects are disposed into regular series, in an incomprehensible order.

2488. Before I had been instructed by living experience, I had supposed, as do others, that no spirit could possibly know the things in my memory and in my thought; but that they were solely in my possession, and were hidden. But I can assert that the spirits with man know and take note of the smallest things of his memory and thoughts; and this much more clearly than the man himself; and that the angels know and take note of the ends themselves, how they bend themselves from good to evil, and from evil to good; and of many more things than the man knows; such as those which he has immersed in his delights, and thus as it were in his nature and disposition; for when this is done such things no longer appear, because he no longer reflects upon them. Let no man therefore any longer believe that his thoughts are hidden, and that he is not to render an account of his thoughts, and of his deeds according to the degree and the quality of the thoughts that have been in them; for the deeds have their quality from the thoughts, and the thoughts from the ends.

2489. The things of the interior memory manifest themselves in the other life by a certain sphere, from which the quality of spirits is known at a distance, that is, what is their affection, and what their opinions. This sphere comes forth from the activity of the things in the interior memory. (Concerning these spheres see above, n. 1048, 1053, 1316, 1504, etc.)

2490. As regards the interior memory the case is this: There are retained in it not only all and each of the things the man from his infancy has ever seen and heard, and those he has thought, spoken, and done; but also those which he sees and hears, and which he thinks, speaks, and does, in the other life. But this takes place with a difference. They who are in the persuasion of falsity and the cupidity of evil imbibe and retain all things that are in agreement therewith, for they enter in as water does into a sponge. All other things do indeed also flow thereto, but are retained so slightly that they scarcely know that they are anything. But they who are in the faith of truth and the affection of good retain all things which are true and good, and are thereby being continually perfected. Hence it is that they can be instructed, and that they are instructed in the other life.

2491. There are spirits whose origin shall of the Lord's Divine mercy be spoken of elsewhere, who relate to the interior memory. These wander about in bands, and in wonderful ways elicit whatever others know, and whatever they hear they communicate to their companions.

2492. The nature of the memories is sometimes presented to view in the other life, in forms to be seen there alone. (Many things are there presented to the sight, which in the case of men fall only into the ideas.) The exterior memory is thus presented to view as a callosity; the interior memory as a medullary substance such as is in the human brain. From this circumstance it is possible to know of what quality the spirits are. With those who in the life of the body have fostered the memory alone, and so have not cultivated their rational, the callosity appears hard, and striated within. With those who have filled the memory with falsities, it appears as if made of hair and shaggy, and this from the disorderly mass of things. With those who have fostered the memory for the sake of the love of self and of the world, it appears conglutinated and indurated. With those who have desired to penetrate into Divine arcana by things scientific, and especially by things philosophical, and who would not believe until persuaded by means of these things, it appears dark, and of such a nature as to absorb the rays of light, and turn them into darkness. With those who have been deceitful and hypocrites, it appears as if bony and of ebony,* reflecting the rays of light. But with those who have been in the good of love and the truth of faith, such a callosity does not appear; because their interior memory transmits the rays of light into the exterior memory, in the objects or ideas of which—as in their basis or as in their ground—the rays are terminated, and find there delightful receptacles. For the exterior memory is the ultimate of order, in which spiritual and heavenly things are softly terminated and reside when there are goods and truths therein.

2493. I have spoken with the angels concerning the memory of things past, and the consequent anxiety regarding things to come; and I have been instructed that the more interior and perfect the angels are, the less do they care for past things, and the less do they think of things to come; and also that from this comes their happiness. They say that the Lord gives them every moment what to think, and this with blessedness and happiness; and that they are thus free from

* *Ebena*, perhaps for *eburnea*, of ivory, as in the *Apocalypse Explained*, n. 253. [*Rotch ed.*]

cares and anxieties.   Also, that this was meant in the internal sense by the manna being received daily from heaven; and by the daily bread in the Lord's Prayer; and likewise by the instruction not to be solicitous about what they should eat and drink, and wherewithal they should be clothed.   But although the angels do not care for past things, and are not solicitous about things to come, they nevertheless have the most perfect recollection of past things, and the most perfect mental view of things to come; because in all their present there are both the past and the future.   Thus they have a more perfect memory than can ever be thought of or expressed.

2494. When men who are in love to the Lord and in charity toward the neighbor are living in the world, they have with themselves and in themselves angelic intelligence and wisdom, but stored up in the inmosts of their interior memory; which intelligence and wisdom cannot possibly appear to them until they put off corporeal things.   Then the memory of particulars (spoken of above) is put to sleep; and they are awakened into the interior memory, and successively afterwards into the angelic memory itself.

CHAPTER THE TWENTIETH.

2495. That the Word contains within it an internal sense that is not apparent in the letter has already been stated and shown in many places, and the nature of this internal sense appears from all that has thus far been unfolded, beginning with the first chapter of *Genesis*.   Nevertheless as the few who at this day believe in the Word do not know that there is such a sense, it may be well to confirm it further.   [2] The Lord describes the Consummation of the Age, or the last period of the church, as follows :—

Immediately after the affliction of those days the sun shall be darkened, and the moon shall not give her light, and the stars shall fall from heaven, and the powers of the heavens shall be shaken (*Matt.* xxiv. 29 ; *Mark* xiii. 24).

That in this passage the "sun" does not mean the sun, nor the "moon" the moon, nor the "stars" the stars; but that the

" sun" signifies love to the Lord and charity toward the neighbor; the "moon" the faith of love and charity; and the
"stars" the knowledges of good and truth, was shown above
(n. 31, 32, 1053, 1521, 1529–1531, 2120, 2441); so that by these
words of the Lord there is signified that in the consummation
of the age (or last period of the church) there will no longer
be any love, or charity, nor therefore any faith.   [3] That this
is the meaning is evident from similar words of the Lord in
the Prophets, as in *Isaiah* :—

> Behold, the day of Jehovah cometh, to make the earth a solitude ; and
> He shall destroy the sinners thereof out of it ; for the stars of the heavens
> and the constellations thereof shall not shine with their light ; the sun
> shall be darkened in his going forth, and the moon shall not cause her
> light to shine (xiii. 9, 10) ;

where also the last period of the church, or what is the same,
the consummation of the age, is treated of.   In *Joel* :—

> A day of darkness and of thick darkness, a day of cloud and obscurity,
> before Him the earth quaked, the heavens trembled, the sun and the
> moon were darkened, and the stars withdrew their shining (ii. 2, 10) ;

with a similar meaning.   Again in the same :—

> The sun shall be turned into darkness, and the moon into blood, before
> the great and terrible day of Jehovah come (ii. 31).

And again in the same :—

> The day of Jehovah is near, the sun and the moon have been darkened,
> and the stars have withdrawn their shining (iii. 14, 15).

In *Ezekiel* :—

> When I shall extinguish thee, I will cover the heavens, and make the
> stars thereof dark ; I will cover the sun with a cloud, and the moon shall
> not make her light to shine ; all the luminaries of light in the heavens
> will I make dark, and will set darkness upon thy land (xxxii. 7, 8).

So too in *John* :—

> I saw when he opened the sixth seal, and behold there was a great
> earthquake, and the sun became black as sackcloth of hair, and the moon
> became as blood, and the stars fell unto the earth (*Rev.* vi. 12, 13).

In the same :—

> The fourth angel sounded, so that the third part of the sun was smit-
> ten, and the third part of the moon, and the third part of the stars, and
> the third part of them was darkened (*Rev.* viii. 12).

[4] From these passages it is evident that the Lord's words
in the Evangelists involve much the same as His words in the
Prophets, namely, that in the last times there will be neither
charity, nor faith; and that this is the internal sense; as also
is still further evident in *Isaiah :*—

The moon shall blush, and the sun shall be ashamed, for Jehovah
Zebaoth shall reign in Mount Zion, and in Jerusalem (xxiv. 23) ;

that is to say, faith, which is the "moon," shall blush; and
charity, which is the "sun," shall be ashamed, because they
are such; for it cannot be said of the moon and the sun that
they shall blush and be ashamed.   And in *Daniel :*—

The goat's horn grew toward the south, and toward the east, and
grew even to the army of the heavens, and some of the army and of the
stars it cast down to the earth and trampled upon them (viii. 9, 10) ;

where it is plain to every one that the "army of the heavens"
does not signify an "army," nor the "stars" stars.

CHAPTER XX.

1. And Abraham journeyed thence toward the land of the
south, and dwelt between Kadesh and Shur, and he sojourned
in Gerar.

2. And Abraham said of Sarah his wife, She is my sister;
and Abimelech king of Gerar sent and took Sarah.

3. And God came to Abimelech in a dream by night, and
said to him, Behold thou wilt die because of the woman whom
thou hast taken, for she is married to a husband.

4. And Abimelech had not come near her; and he said,
Lord, wilt Thou slay also a righteous nation ?

5. Said he not himself unto me, She is my sister? and she
herself also said, He is my brother: in the uprightness of my
heart and in the blamelessness of my hands have I done this.

6. And God said unto him in the dream, Yea, I know that
in the uprightness of thy heart thou hast done this ; and I also
withheld thee from sinning against Me; therefore I did not
suffer thee to touch her.

7. And now restore the man's wife, for he is a prophet; and he shall pray for thee, and thou shalt live; and if thou restore her not, know thou that dying thou shalt die, thou and all that are thine.

8. And Abimelech rose early in the morning, and called all his servants, and spake all these words in their ears; and the men feared greatly.

9. And Abimelech called Abraham, and said unto him, What hast thou done unto us? and wherein have I sinned against thee that thou hast brought on me and on my kingdom a great sin? Thou hast done unto me deeds that ought not to be done.

10. And Abimelech said unto Abraham, What sawest thou that thou hast done this word?

11. And Abraham said, Because I said, Surely there is no fear of God in this place, and they will kill me on account of the word of my wife.

12. And moreover truly she is my sister, being the daughter of my father, but not the daughter of my mother, and she became my wife.

13. And it came to pass when God caused me to depart from my father's house that I said unto her, This is thy goodness which thou shalt do unto me; at every place whither we shall come, say of me, He is my brother.

14. And Abimelech took flock and herd, and menservants and maidservants, and gave unto Abraham; and restored to him Sarah his wife.

15. And Abimelech said, Behold my land is before thee; dwell in that which is good in thine eyes.

16. And unto Sarah he said, Behold I have given a thousand of silver to thy brother; behold it is unto thee a covering of the eyes to all that are with thee, and with all; and she was vindicated.

17. And Abraham prayed unto God, and God healed Abimelech, and his wife, and his maidservants; and they brought forth.

18. For closing Jehovah had therefore closed every womb of the house of Abimelech, because of the word of Sarah, Abraham's wife.

THE CONTENTS.

2496. In the twelfth chapter above, Abraham's sojourning in Egypt has been treated of; by which was signified the Lord's instruction in memory-knowledges while still a boy. In this chapter the subject treated of is Abraham's sojourn in Gerar, where Abimelech was; by which the Lord's instruction is in like manner signified, but in the doctrinal things of charity and faith. The subject that is especially treated of here is the doctrine of charity and faith in respect to its origin; namely, that it is spiritual from a celestial origin, but is not from the rational.

2497. The Lord's state in which He was when He first instructed Himself in the doctrinal things of charity and faith is treated of; the state itself is signified by "Kadesh and Shur;" the doctrine of faith by "Abimelech king of Gerar" (verses 1, 2). That He at first thought in regard to the rational that it should be consulted (verse 2). That still it was not consulted (verses 3, 4, 8, 9). The reasons why He so thought (verses 5, 6, 10 to 13). That the doctrine of charity and faith is spiritual from a celestial origin (verse 7). That He was so instructed; and that then all things rational, as well as all memory-knowledges, were of service to Him, being like a covering or garment (verses 14 to 16). And in this way the doctrine was perfect (verse 17). That it would have been otherwise if the doctrine had come from the rational (verse 18).

THE INTERNAL SENSE.

2498. That these historical matters, like all the other things of the Word, involve Divine arcana, is evident from the fact that Abraham now again said that his wife was his sister; for the same thing had occurred when he came into Egypt; for he then said to Sarah, "Say, I pray, thou art my sister" (*Gen.* xii. 13). And not Abraham alone, but Isaac likewise, when he came to Gerar, said that his wife Rebecca was his sister: "The men of that place asked concerning his wife, and he said, She is my sister" (*Gen.* xxvi. 6, 7); and there are other things in the same chapters that resemble each other, so that such historical matters are related three times; which, without a hidden cause in the internal sense, would by no means have been done.

2499. Verse 1. *And Abraham journeyed thence toward the land of the south, and dwelt between Kadesh and Shur, and he sojourned in Gerar.* "Abraham journeyed thence toward the land of the south," signifies the Lord's progression in the goods and truths of faith ("Abraham" is the Lord in that state); "and dwelt between Kadesh and Shur," signifies His state specifically ("Kadesh" is the affection of interior truth proceeding from things rational; "Shur" is the affection of exterior truth proceeding from memory-knowledges); "and he sojourned in Gerar," signifies instruction thence in the spiritual things of faith.

2500. *Abraham journeyed thence toward the land of the south.* That this signifies the Lord's progression in the goods and truths of faith, is evident from the signification of "journeying," as being to progress (see n. 1457); and from the signification of the "land of the south," as being the good and truth of faith (see n. 1458). It has already been stated concerning Abraham, in the twelfth chapter, that he "journeyed, going and journeying toward the south," when he went into Egypt (verses 9, 10); by which was signified in the internal sense that the Lord when a child progressed into goods and truths in respect to the memory-knowledge of knowledges (n. 1456, 1459);* and here it is said that he journeyed "toward the *land* of the south," by which there is signified a further and more interior progression, which is into goods and truths in respect to the doctrine of faith; on which account it is here said the "*land*" of the south, because "land" in its proper sense signifies the church, for the sake of which is doctrine (n. 566, 662, 1066, 2117, 2118). [2] As regards the Lord's instruction in general, the nature of it is very clear in the internal sense of

---

* That is in respect to possessing a mere memory acquaintance with the knowledges of what is good and true. [REVISER.]

this chapter; namely, that it was by continual revelations, and thus by Divine perceptions and thoughts from Himself, that is, from His Divine; which perceptions and thoughts He implanted in Divine intelligence and wisdom, and this even to the perfect union of His Human with His Divine. This way of growing wise is not possible with any man; for it flowed in from the Divine itself, which was His inmost, being of the Father, of whom He was conceived; thus from the Divine Love itself, which the Lord alone had, and which consisted in His desire to save the universal human race. [3] It is an arcanum which is as yet known to scarcely any one, that within love itself there are wisdom and intelligence; these being such as is the love. That wisdom and intelligence are within love comes from the fact that all influx takes place into the love, or what is the same, into the good, thus into man's very life. This is the source of the wisdom and intelligence of the angels, which is ineffable. It is also the source of the wisdom and intelligence of men who are in love to the Lord and in charity toward the neighbor; who, although they have no perception of it in themselves while they are living in the body, nevertheless come into it after death, for the reason that it is within this very love and charity (see n. 2494). But as regards the Lord's love, it was infinitely above the love in which the angels are, for it was the Divine love itself; and therefore He had in Himself a supereminence of all wisdom and intelligence; into which however because He was born a man, and was to progress as a man according to Divine order, He introduced Himself by successive steps, in order that He might thus unite His Human to the Divine, and make it Divine; and this by His own power.

2501. That "Abraham" is the Lord in that state, is evident from the representation of Abraham, as being the Lord; here the Lord in that state (as also before, n. 1893, 1965, 1989, 2011, 2172, 2198).

2502. *And dwelt between Kadesh and Shur.* That this signifies His state specifically, is evident from the signification of "dwelling," as being to live (see n. 1293). What precedes also indicates this, namely, that Abraham journeyed thence toward the land of the south, by which there is signified the Lord's progression into the goods and truths of faith; and as it is now said that he "dwelt between Kadesh and Shur," it follows that nothing else is signified than the Lord's state specifically, which is described by "Kadesh and Shur"—now to be explained.

2503. That "Kadesh" is the affection of interior truth that proceeds from things rational, and "Shur" the affection of exterior truth that proceeds from memory-knowledges, is evident from the signification of "Kadesh and Shur." That "Kadesh" signifies truth about which there is contention, was shown above (n. 1678), thus contention concerning truth in regard to its origin, as to whether it is from the rational; as is evident from what follows. But as with the Lord all truth was from a celestial origin, "Kadesh" here signifies the affection of truth. With every man of the church there are rational truths and truths of mere memory (*vera scientifica*), the former being more interior, and the latter more exterior. These are distinct from each other, precisely as are man's two memories (see n. 2469–2473, etc.). From this it follows that there are also two affections of truth—one more interior, as being of rational things, and the other more exterior, as being of mere memory truths. The affection of interior truth that proceeds from rational things is here signified by "Kadesh;" and the affection of exterior truth that proceeds from memory truths, by "Shur." (That "Shur" signifies this truth may be seen above, n. 1928. That names in the Word signify nothing else than actual things, has been shown above, n. 1224, 1264, 1876, 1888, and in many other places.)

2504. *And he sojourned in Gerar.* That this signifies instruction thence in the spiritual things of faith, is evident from the signification of "sojourning," as being to be instructed (see n. 1463, 2025); and from the signification of "Gerar," as being what is spiritual of faith. Gerar is named in several places in *Genesis* (as chapter x. 19; xxvi. 1, 6, 17, 20, 26); and in these it signifies faith, and this for the reason that Gerar was in Philistia; and by "Philistia" is signified the mere memory-knowledge of the knowledges of faith (see n. 1197, 1198); and it was Gerar where the king of the Philistines dwelt. Hence it is that faith itself is signified by "Gerar"

(n. 1209); and by the "king of Gerar," the truth itself of faith; for "king" in the internal sense is truth (n. 1672, 2015, 2069). Thus by "Abimelech" is signified the doctrine of faith, concerning which in what follows. [2] In general there are intellectual things of faith, rational things of faith, and memory-knowledges of faith. They thus proceed in their order from interiors to exteriors. The things of faith which are inmost are called intellectual; those which proceed from them or thence are the rational things of faith; and those which proceed again from these are the memory-knowledges of faith. They are—to use the language of the learned—as prior to posterior, or what is the same, as higher to lower, that is, as interior to exterior. It indeed appears to man as if the memory-knowledge of faith were first, and that the rational then came forth from it, and at length the intellectual; and this for the reason that man advances in this way from his childhood. Nevertheless, although man is not aware of it, the intellectual flows in continually into the rational, and this into the faculty of knowing;* but in childhood obscurely, in adult age more evidently, and at last in full light when the man has been regenerated. Then it is apparent that this is the order, and still more fully in the other life (see n. 1495). All these are called "spiritual things;" which are distinguished in this way into degrees, and succeed one another in such an order. The spiritual things of faith are all the truths which are from good, that is, from a celestial origin. Whatever is derived from the celestial is a spiritual thing of faith.

2505. Verse 2. *And Abraham said of Sarah his wife, She is my sister; and Abimelech king of Gerar sent and took Sarah.* "Abraham said," signifies the Lord's thought; "of Sarah his wife," signifies spiritual truth conjoined with the celestial; "she is my sister," signifies rational truth; "and Abimelech king of Gerar sent," signifies the doctrine of faith ("Abimelech" signifies the doctrine of faith that looks to rational things); "and took Sarah," signifies the affection of consulting the rational.

2506. *Abraham said.* That this signifies thought, is evident from the signification of "saying," in the historicals of

* See n. 1901 at the end as compared with n. 1902. [REVISER.]

the Word, as being to perceive, as well as to think (see n. 1898, 1919, 2061, 2080, 2238, 2260, 2271, 2287).

2507. *Of Sarah his wife.* That this signifies spiritual truth conjoined with the celestial, is evident from the signification of " Sarah" as a wife, as being intellectual truth conjoined with the Divine good, or what is the same, spiritual truth conjoined with the celestial (see n. 1468, 1901, 2063, 2065, 2172, 2173, 2198). What the spiritual is, and what the celestial, has often been stated before (see n. 1155, 1577, 1824, 2048, 2088). That is called Celestial, which is of good, that is, which is of love to the Lord and of charity toward the neighbor; and that Spiritual, which is of truth, that is, which is of faith derived from those loves.

2508. *She is my sister.* That this signifies rational truth, is evident from the signification of a " sister," as being rational intellectual truth (see n. 1495). That rational truth is a " sister," can be seen only from the heavenly marriage; for the things which descend from this have kinships among themselves like the relationships and connections on earth (concerning which see n. 685, 917); and this with indefinite variety. The heavenly marriage itself exists solely between the Divine good and the Divine truth. From this there are conceived in man the intellectual, the rational, and the faculty of knowing; for without conception from the heavenly marriage man cannot possibly be imbued with understanding, with reason, or with knowledge, and consequently cannot be man. In proportion therefore as he receives from the heavenly marriage, in the same proportion is he man. The heavenly marriage is in the Lord Himself, thus the Lord is this marriage itself, for He is the Divine good itself and at the same time the Divine truth. Angels and men are in the heavenly marriage in so far as they are in love to the Lord and in charity toward the neighbor, and in so far as they are thence in faith; that is, in so far as they are in the Lord's good, and thence in truth; and they are then called " daughters and sons," and in their relation to one another " sisters and brothers;" but this with differences. The reason why rational truth is called a " sister" is that it is conceived from the influx of the Divine good into the affection of rational truths; the good which is

thence in the rational is called a "brother," and the truth
which is thence, a "sister." But this will be better seen from
what is said by Abraham in verse 12 of this chapter: "and
moreover truly she is my sister; she is the daughter of my
father, but not the daughter of my mother; and she became
my wife."

2509. *And Abimelech king of Gerar sent.* That this signifies the doctrine of faith, is evident from what was said above
(n. 2504), namely, that by "Philistia" is signified the memory-
knowledge of the knowledges of faith (n. 1197, 1198); by
"Gerar," which was in Philistia, faith (n. 1209, 2504); and
by a "king," the truth itself of faith (n. 1672, 2015, 2069).
Hence by "Abimelech" is signified the doctrine of faith, but
the doctrine of faith looking to rational things; as will be
manifest from what now follows.

2510. That "Abimelech" is the doctrine of faith looking
to rational things, is evident from the fact that he looked upon
Sarah, not as Abraham's wife, but as his sister; and by Sarah
as a sister is signified rational truth (n. 2508). The same is
also manifest from what follows; for the doctrine of faith is
there treated of, as to whether it has its origin from the rational, or from the celestial. Hence "Abimelech" signifies the
doctrine of faith looking to rational things. Doctrine is said
to look to rational things when nothing is acknowledged as
truth of doctrine except what can be comprehended by the
reason, so that the consideration of all the things which are
of doctrine is from the rational. Yet that the doctrine of faith
is not from a rational but from a celestial origin, is taught in
the internal sense in what follows.

2511. *And took Sarah.* That this signifies the affection of
consulting the rational, is evident from the signification of
Sarah as a "sister," as being rational truth (see n. 2508);
and also from the signification of "taking" her, as being from
affection toward her; thus, in the internal sense, from the affection of consulting the rational. The things contained in this
verse involve the Lord's first thought respecting the doctrine
of faith, as to whether it would be well to consult the rational
or not. The reason why the first thought was of such a character is that the Lord progressed according to all Divine order;

and whatever was of the human into which He was born, and which He derived from the mother, must necessarily be put off in order that He might put on the Divine; thus also this human thought, namely, as to whether the rational was to be consulted in regard to the doctrinal things of faith.

2512. Verse 3. *And God came to Abimelech in a dream by night, and said to him, Behold, thou wilt die because of the woman whom thou hast taken, for she is married to a husband.* "God came to Abimelech," signifies the Lord's perception concerning the doctrine of faith; "in a dream by night," signifies that it was obscure; "and said to him," signifies thought thence; "Behold, thou wilt die because of the woman," signifies that the doctrine of faith would be null and void if the rational were consulted in regard to its contents; "for she is married to a husband," signifies that the doctrine of true faith, and the things therein, are conjoined with the celestial.

2513. *God came to Abimelech.* That this signifies the Lord's perception concerning the doctrine of faith, is evident from the signification of "God coming," and from the signification of "Abimelech." That "God coming" signifies to perceive, is evident, for perception is nothing else than the Divine advent or influx into the intellectual faculty. (That "Abimelech" signifies the doctrine of faith was shown above, n. 2504, 2509, 2510.)

2514. *In a dream by night.* That this signifies that the perception was obscure, is evident from the signification of a "dream," and likewise of "night." A "dream," when perception is treated of, signifies something obscure in comparison with wakefulness; and still more when it is said "a dream by night." The Lord's first perception is called obscure, because it was in the human that He was to put off, and the shades of which He was to disperse. The Lord's perception, although from the Divine, was yet in the human, which is such that it does not immediately receive the light itself, but gradually as the shades which are there are dispersed. That He brought Himself into what was less obscure in regard to the doctrine of faith, is signified by "God coming again to Abimelech in a dream," as declared in verse 6, where there is no mention of "night;" and that He afterwards came into clear perception is signified in verse 8 by the words, " Abimelech rose early in the morning."

2515. *And said to him.* That this signifies thought therefrom, namely, from the perception, is evident from the signification of " saying," as being to perceive, and also to think (as shown in n. 2506). As it is here said that there was thought from the perception, it may be well to state in a few words how the case is with thought. There are thoughts from perception; thoughts from conscience; and thoughts from no conscience. *Thoughts from perception* exist only with the celestial, that is, with those who are in love to the Lord; such thought is the most internal that exists with man; and it exists with the celestial angels in heaven, for it is perception from the Lord by which and from which their thought exists; and to think contrary to perception is impossible. *Thoughts from conscience* are lower, and exist with the spiritual, that is, with those who are in the good of charity and faith as to life and as to doctrine. Moreover with these persons to think contrary to conscience is impossible; for this would be to think against the good and truth which are dictated to them from the Lord through conscience. [2] But *thoughts from no conscience* exist with those who do not suffer themselves to be inwardly directed by what is good and true, but only by what is evil and false; that is, not by the Lord, but by themselves. Such persons believe that they inwardly think just as do those who think from conscience and perception, for the reason that they do not know what conscience is, still less perception; but the difference is as great as is that between hell and heaven. They who think without conscience think from any cupidities and phantasies whatever; thus from hell; and when it seems otherwise, it is from external decorum for the sake of reputation. But they who think from conscience think from the affections of good and truth; thus from heaven. But as regards the Lord's thought, it transcended all human understanding, for it was immediately from the Divine.

2516. *Behold, thou wilt die because of the woman.* That this signifies that the doctrine of faith would become null and void if the rational were consulted as to its contents, is evident from the signification of " Abimelech," who is here addressed, as being the doctrine of faith; from the signification of "dying," as being to become null and void; and from the signification of a "sister," who is here called "the woman," as being the rational (see n. 2508). Hence now by "Abimelech dying because of the woman" is signified that the doctrine of faith would become null and void if the rational were consulted. [2] The reason why there is no doctrine of faith from the rational, is that the rational is in appearances of good and truth, which appearances are not in themselves truths (as before shown, n. 2053, 2196, 2203, 2209). Moreover the rational has under it fallacies which are from external sensuous things confirmed by memory-knowledges, which induce obscurity in these appearances of truth. The rational for the most part is merely human, as also is evident from its birth; and this is why nothing doctrinal of faith can begin from it, and still less be constructed from it; but must be from the Lord's Divine Itself and Divine Human. This is its origin, and indeed so entirely that the Lord is doctrine itself; on which account also in the Word He is called the Word, the Truth, the Light, the Way, the Door; and (what is an arcanum) all doctrine is from the Divine good and the Divine truth, and has in itself the heavenly marriage. Doctrine that has not this in it is not the genuine doctrine of faith. Hence it is that in all the particulars of the Word (the source of doctrine) there is an image of a marriage (see n. 683, 793, 801). [3] In the literal or external sense of the Word the doctrine of faith does indeed appear as if it possessed much from the rational, and even from the natural; but this is because the Word is for man, and has been in this manner accommodated to him; but still in itself it is spiritual from a celestial origin, that is, from Divine truth conjoined with Divine good. That doctrine would become null and void if as to its contents the rational were consulted, will be illustrated by examples in what follows.

2517. *For she is married to a husband.* That this signifies that the doctrine of true faith is spiritual, and that its contents are conjoined with the celestial, is evident from the signification of being "married to a husband." "Husband," when mentioned in the Word, signifies good, and " wife" then signifies truth. It is otherwise when the husband is called the "man ;" for then "man" signifies truth, and "wife" good (see n. 915, and elsewhere). Here therefore her being "married to a husband" signifies that truth is conjoined with good, and in such a manner that the truth also is good. The same is also evident from the signification of "Sarah as a wife," as being spiritual truth, and of "Abraham," as being celestial good, both Divine (see n. 2501, 2507). And as "Sarah" signifies Divine spiritual truth, the doctrine itself of true faith is also meant by "Sarah a wife ;" for the doctrine is from truths. It is plain from this that her being "married to a husband" means that the doctrine of true faith is spiritual, and that its contents are conjoined with the celestial.

2518. Verse 4. *And Abimelech had not come near her ; and, he said, Lord, wilt Thou slay also a righteous nation?* "Abimelech had not come near her," signifies that in the doctrine of faith rational truth had not been consulted in any manner; "and he said, Lord, wilt Thou slay also a righteous nation?" signifies whether would the good and truth of doctrine be extinguished.

2519. *Abimelech had not come near her.* That this signifies that in the doctrine of faith rational truth had not been consulted in any manner, is evident from the signification of "Abimelech," as being the doctrine of faith (see n. 2504, 2509, 2510); and from the signification of "coming near her," namely to Sarah as a sister, as being to touch, or in any manner to consult rational truth, which is a "sister" (n. 1495, 2508). The reason why the rational had not been consulted in any manner, is that which has been stated before, namely, that the doctrinal things of faith are in their entirety from the Divine, which is infinitely above the human rational. It is from the Divine that the rational receives its good and its truth. The Divine can enter into the rational, but not the rational into the Divine; as the soul can enter into the body, and form it, but not the body into the soul; or as light can enter into shade, and modify it variously into colors; but not shade into light. But as it appears at first as if the rational ought to be present, because the rational is the very thing that receives the doctrine, it is here shown that the first subject of

thought was, whether it also should not be consulted at the
same time. But the Lord revealed and answered to Himself
that doctrine would thus become null and void; and therefore
the rational was not consulted; which is here signified by
" Abimelech not coming near her."

2520. *And he said, Lord, wilt Thou slay also a righteous
nation?* That this signifies whether would the good and
truth be extinguished, is evident from the signification of
"nation," as being good (see n. 1259, 1260, 1416); and as it
is predicated of the nation of Abimelech, by whom is signified
the doctrine of faith, by a " righteous nation" is here signified
both good and truth; for both are of doctrine. [**2**] That this
was said from the zeal of affection or of love toward the whole
human race, is manifest. This love directed the Lord's
thoughts while He was still in the maternal human; and
although He perceived from the Divine that the doctrine of
faith was from a celestial origin only, nevertheless in order
that the human race might be provided for, which does not
receive anything of which it cannot have some idea from its
rational, it is therefore said, " Wilt Thou slay also a righteous
nation ?" by which is signified whether would the good and
truth of doctrine be extinguished. That man does not receive
anything of which he cannot have some idea from his rational,
is evident from the ideas which man cherishes respecting
Divine arcana. Some idea from worldly things or from things
analogous to these always adheres to them, by which they are
retained in the memory, and by which they are reproduced in
the thought; for without an idea from worldly things man can
think nothing at all. If therefore truths from a Divine origin
were set forth naked, they would never be received, but would
completely transcend man's comprehension, and therefore his
belief, and most especially with those who are in external
worship. [**3**] To illustrate this take the following examples:
The Divine Itself can be in nothing but the Divine, thus in
nothing but the Lord's Divine Human, and with man through
this. If the rational were consulted it would say that the
Divine Itself can be in the human of every one. Again:
Nothing is holy which does not proceed from the Lord, thus
from the Divine, which is one. If the rational were consulted

it would say that there may be what is holy from other sources also. [4] Again: Man does not live, nor do good, nor believe truth, from himself, nay, does not even think from himself; but the good and truth are from the Lord, while the evil and falsity are from hell; and what is more, hell, that is, they who are in hell, do not think from themselves, but receive the Lord's good and truth in the manner indicated. If the rational were consulted it would reject this, because it does not comprehend it. In like manner it would reject the truth that no one is rewarded on account of doing what is good and teaching what is true; and that the external contributes nothing, but only the internal in so far as there is the affection of good in doing what is good, and in so far as there is from that the affection of truth in teaching what is true, and this not from self. And so in a thousand other instances. [5] It is because the human rational is of such a character that the Word has spoken in accordance with man's apprehension, and also in accordance with his genius. This therefore is the reason why the internal sense of the Word is different from its literal sense; which is very evident in the Word of the Old Testament, where most things have been written in accordance with the apprehension and genius of the people who then lived. On this account almost nothing is said concerning the life after death, salvation, and the internal man. For the Jewish and Israelitish people with whom the church then was, were of such a character that if these things had been disclosed they would not only not have understood them, but would also have derided them. And it would have been the same if it had been disclosed to them that the Messiah or Christ was to come to eternally save their souls: this also they would have rejected as a matter of no moment; as is also evident from the same nation at the present day; for if what is internal or spiritual is mentioned in their presence even now, and it is said that the Messiah will not be the greatest king on the earth, they deride it. [6] This is why the Lord sometimes spoke like the Prophets, and taught the rest of what He had to say by parables, as He Himself has declared in *Matthew* :—

Jesus said, I speak unto them by parables, because seeing they see not, and hearing they hear not, neither do they understand (xiii. 13).

By "those who see and hear" are meant those within the church who although they see and hear, still do not understand. Also in *John :*—

He hath blinded their eyes, and hardened their heart, lest they should see with their eyes, and understand with their heart, and should be converted, and I should heal them (xii. 40).

Their being "converted" and "healed" implies that nevertheless they would afterwards reject, and so would profane, which involves eternal condemnation (see n. 301–303, 582, 1008, 1010, 1059, 1327, 1328, 2051, 2426). Nevertheless the Lord has disclosed the interior things of the Word in many places, but only for the wise.

2521. Verse 5. *Said he not himself unto me, She is my sister? and she herself also said, He is my brother: in the uprightness of my heart and in the blamelessness of my hands have I done this.* "Said he not himself unto me," signifies exculpation for having so thought; "she is my sister," signifies that it was the rational which should be consulted; "and she herself also said, He is my brother," signifies that the rational itself so dictated that celestial good should be adjoined to it; "in the uprightness of my heart," signifies that it was so thought from innocence and simple good; "and in the blamelessness of my hands have I done this," signifies from the affection of truth, and so with all ability.

2522. *Said he not himself unto me.* That this signifies exculpation for having so thought, is evident from the particulars in this verse, as also from the signification of "saying," as being to think (see n. 2506).

2523. *She is my sister.* That this signifies that it was the rational which should be consulted (that is, that he so thought), is evident from the signification of "sister" in this chapter as being rational truth (see n. 1495, 2508). In the internal sense of the Word the Lord's whole life is described, such as it was to be in the world, even as to the perceptions and thoughts, for these were foreseen and provided because from the Divine; this being done for the additional reason that all these things might be set forth at that time as present to the angels, who perceive the Word according to the internal sense; and that so the Lord might be before them, and at the same time how by successive steps He put off the human, and put on the Divine. Unless these things had been as if present to the angels, through the Word, and also through all the rites in the Jewish Church, the Lord would have been obliged to come into the world immediately after the fall of the Most Ancient Church, which is called Man or Adam; for there was an immediate prophecy of the Lord's advent (*Gen.* iii. 15); and what is more, the human race of that time could not otherwise have been saved. [2] As regards the Lord's life itself, it was a continual progression of the Human to the Divine, even to absolute union (as already frequently stated), for in order that He might combat with the hells and overcome them, He must needs do it from the Human; for there is no combat with the hells from the Divine. It therefore pleased Him to put on the human like another man, to be an infant like another, to grow up into knowledges (*in scientias et in cognitiones*), which things are represented by Abraham's sojourning in Egypt (chapter xii.), and now in Gerar; thus it pleased Him to cultivate the rational as another man, and in this way to disperse its shade, and bring it into light, and this from His own power. That the Lord's progression from the Human to the Divine was of this nature, can be denied by no one if he only considers that He was a little child, and learned to talk like one; and so on. But there was this difference: that the Divine Itself was in Him, seeing that He was conceived of Jehovah.

2524. *And she herself also said, He is my brother.* That this signifies that the rational itself dictated that celestial good should be adjoined to it, is evident from the signification of a " sister" (here meant by " she herself") as being the rational (n. 1495, 2508); and from the signification of a " brother," as being the good of truth (n. 367, 2508). For the case herein is as follows: Divine good and Divine truth are united to each other as if by marriage; for thence comes the heavenly marriage, and thence comes marriage love also, even down to lower nature. But the good and truth of the rational are not conjoined with each other as by marriage, but by consanguinity, like brother and sister; since the rational as to truth is conceived from the influx of Divine good into the affection of knowledges (*scienti-*

arum et cognitionum) (see n. 1895, 1902, 1910); and the good of the rational, through the influx of Divine good into that truth, which then becomes the good itself of charity, which is the "brother" of faith, or what is the same, of truth (n. 367). [2] But in regard to the good and truth of the rational, the procuring of this takes place in such a way that its good is from Divine good, whereas its truth is not from Divine truth; for the truth of the rational is procured by means of knowledges (*scientias et cognitiones*), which are insinuated through the external and internal senses, thus by an external way. Hence it is that there adhere to its truths many fallacies from the senses, which cause the truths not to be truths; nevertheless when Divine good flows into them, and conceives them, they then appear as truths, and are acknowledged as truths, although they are nothing but appearances of truth. The good itself is then modified in these truths according to the shades there, and becomes in quality like the truth. This is one arcanum which lies hidden in these words, that the rational thus dictated that celestial good should be adjoined to it.

2525. *In the uprightness of my heart.* That this signifies that it was so thought from innocence and simple good, is evident from the signification of "uprightness," and of "heart." In the original tongue "uprightness" is expressed by a word which signifies also integrity and perfection, and also simplicity; moreover "heart" signifies love and charity, which are of good, as is well known. Hence it is that "from the uprightness of the heart" means from innocence and simple good.

2526. *And in the blamelessness of my hands have I done this.* That this signifies from the affection of truth, and so from all ability, is evident from the signification of "blamelessness," and also of "hands." In the original language "blamelessness" is expressed by a word which also means cleanness and purity. "Hands" are predicated of truth, and signify power, thus ability (n. 878). That "I have done this from the uprightness of my heart and the blamelessness of my hands" signifies that it was so thought from innocence and simple good, and from the affection of truth, and thus from all ability, is because good is good from innocence; and truth is truth from good; and when these are in their order, there is then all ability. That these things are involved in the words is plain; for there is not an upright, sound, or perfect heart (by which good is signified) unless innocence be in the good, as just said; from this it becomes simple good. And there are not blameless, clean, or pure hands (which are predicated of truths) unless good be in the truths, as also just said; that is, unless there be the affection of truth. When the thought is from these, it is also from all ability or power; which is likewise signified by "hands" (n. 878).

2527. Verse 6. *And God said unto him in the dream, Yea, I know that in the uprightness of thy heart thou hast done this; and I also withheld thee from sinning against Me; therefore I did not suffer thee to touch her.* "God said unto him in the dream," signifies perception less obscure; "Yea, I know that in the uprightness of thy heart thou hast done this," signifies here as before that it was so thought from innocence and from simple good; thus that there was no fault; "and I also withheld thee from sinning against Me," signifies that no harm resulted; "therefore I did not suffer thee to touch her," signifies that the rational was not at all consulted.

2528. *God said unto him in the dream.* That this signifies perception less obscure, is evident from what was said and explained above (n. 2514). The name "God" is used in this chapter, but not "Jehovah," except in the last verse, for the reason that spiritual things are treated of, that is, the doctrinal things of faith. When this is the subject He is called "God;" but when celestial things, or love and charity, are treated of, He is then called "Jehovah" (see n. 709, 732, 2001).

2529. *Yea, I know that in the uprightness of thy heart thou hast done this.* That this signifies that it was so thought from innocence and from simple good, is evident from what was said above (n. 2525, 2526), where are the same words. That it is not also said, as above, "in the blamelessness of thy hands," is for the hidden reason that in the affection of truth (which is signified by the "blamelessness of the hands") there was something of the human; for truth was insinuated into the Lord also through the human of His birth, but good from the Divine alone; as is evident from the coming forth (*existentia*) of the rational as to good and as to truth (n. 2524).

2530. *And I also withheld thee from sinning against Me.*
That this signifies that no harm resulted, that is, that in the
doctrine of faith the rational was not consulted (as also follows presently) is evident without explication.

2531. *Therefore I did not suffer thee to touch her.* That this
signifies that the rational was not at all consulted, is evident
from the signification of "suffering to touch," as being to consult (as is also meant by "coming near her" in verse 4, n.
2519); and from the signification of "Sarah as a sister," who
is here meant, as being the rational (see n. 1495, 2508). [2]
That it may be further known how the case is with the doctrine of faith, as being spiritual from a celestial origin, be it
known that it is Divine truth from Divine good, and thus
wholly Divine. What is Divine is incomprehensible, because
above all understanding, even the angelic; but still this Divine, which in itself is incomprehensible, can flow in through
the Lord's Divine Human into man's rational; and when it
flows into his rational, it is there received according to the
truths which are therein; thus variously, and not with one as
with another. In so far therefore as the truths with a man
are more genuine, so far the Divine which flows in is received
more perfectly, and so far the man's understanding is enlightened. [3] In the Lord's Word are Truths themselves; but in
its literal sense are truths which are accommodated to the apprehension of those who are in external worship; whereas in
its internal sense are truths accommodated to those who are
internal men; that is, to those who are angelic as to doctrine
and at the same time as to life. Their rational is enlightened
therefrom to such a degree that their enlightenment is compared to the brightness of the stars and the sun (*Dan.* xii. 3;
Matt. xiii. 43). Hence it is plain how important it is that interior truths be known and received. These truths may indeed
be known, but by no means received, except by those who have
love to the Lord, or faith in Him; for as the Lord is the Divine
good, so He is the Divine truth; consequently He is doctrine
itself, since whatever is in the doctrine of true faith looks to
the Lord, and looks also to the heavenly kingdom and the
church, and to all things of the heavenly kingdom and the
church. But all these are His, and are the intermediate ends

through which the last end, that is, the Lord, is regarded.
[4] That the Lord is doctrine itself as to truth and good, and
thus that it is He who alone is regarded in doctrine, He teaches
in *John* :—

> Jesus said, I am the Way, the Truth, and the Life (xiv. 6, 7) ;

where the " Way" is doctrine, the " Truth" all that is of doctrine, and the " Life" the good itself which is the life of the
truth.   And that love to Him or faith in Him is what receives,
He also teaches in *John* :—

> His own received Him not ; but as many as received Him, to them
> gave He power to be the sons of God, even to them that believe on His
> name ; who were born, not of bloods, nor of the will of the flesh, nor of
> the will of man, but of God (i. 11–13).

Those are " born of God" who are in love and thence in faith.

2532. Verse 7. *And now restore the man's wife ; for he is
a prophet, and shall pray for thee, and thou shalt live ; and if
thou restore her not, know thou that dying thou shalt die, thou
and all that are thine.*   " And now restore the man's wife," signifies that he should render up the spiritual truth of doctrine
without taint from the rational ; " for he is a prophet," signifies that thus it should be taught ; " and he shall pray for thee,"
signifies that it will thus be revealed ; " and thou shalt live,"
signifies that thus doctrine will have life ; " and if thou restore
her not," signifies here as before that if he should not render
up the spiritual truth of doctrine without taint from the rational ; " know thou that dying thou shalt die," signifies there
will be no doctrine of truth and good ; " and all that are thine,"
signifies all things that belong to it together.

2533. *And now restore the man's wife.*   That this signifies
that he should render up the spiritual truth of doctrine without taint from the rational, is evident from the signification of
" wife," as being spiritual truth (see n. 2507, 2510) ; and from
the signification of the " man," as being doctrine itself ; for
Abraham (by whom the Lord in that state is represented),
when called a " man," signifies celestial truth, which is the
same as doctrine from a celestial origin ; for in the internal
sense a " man" is the intellectual (see n. 158, 265, 749, 915,
1007, 2517).   Hence it is evident that to " restore the man's
wife" is to render up the spiritual truth of doctrine without

taint. That it means without taint from the rational, is because Abimelech, who was to restore her, signifies doctrine that has regard to rational things, or what is the same, the rational things of doctrine (n. 2510). [2] It was said above that although the doctrine of faith is in itself Divine, and therefore above all human and even angelic comprehension, it has nevertheless been dictated in the Word according to man's comprehension, in a rational manner. The case herein is the same as it is with a parent who is teaching his little boys and girls : when he is teaching, he sets forth everything in accordance with their genius, although he himself thinks from what is more interior or higher ; otherwise it would be teaching without their learning, or like casting seed upon a rock. The case is also the same with the angels who in the other life instruct the simple in heart : although these angels are in celestial and spiritual wisdom, yet they do not hold themselves above the comprehension of those whom they teach, but speak in simplicity with them, yet rising by degrees as these are instructed ; for if they were to speak from angelic wisdom, the simple would comprehend nothing at all, and thus would not be led to the truths and goods of faith. The case would be the same if the Lord had not taught in the Word in accordance with man's comprehension, in a rational manner. Nevertheless in its internal sense the Word is elevated to the angelic understanding ; and yet that sense, in its highest elevation in which it is perceived by the angels, is infinitely below the Divine. It is hence manifest what the Word is in its origin, and thus in itself ; and that it thus everywhere involves more things than the whole heaven is capable of comprehending, even as to a small part, although in the letter it appears so unimportant and so rude. [3] That the Lord is the Word, because the Word is from Him and He is in the Word, is evident in *John* :—

In the beginning was the Word, and the Word was with God, and God was the Word ; in Him was life, and the life was the light of men ; the Word was made flesh, and dwelt among us ; and we saw His glory, the glory as of the Only-begotten of the Father, full of grace and truth (i. 1, 4, 14 ; see also *Rev.* xix. 11, 13, 16).

And as the Lord is the Word, He is also doctrine ; for there is no other doctrine which is itself Divine.

2534. *For he is a prophet.* That this signifies that thus it would be taught, is evident from the signification of a "prophet." In the Word we frequently read of a "prophet;" and in the sense of the letter "prophet" signifies those to whom revelation is made, also abstractedly, revelation itself; but in the internal sense a "prophet" signifies one who teaches, and also abstractedly doctrine itself; and as the Lord (as before said) is doctrine itself, that is, the Word which teaches, He is called a "Prophet," as in *Moses :—*

A Prophet from the midst of thee, of thy brethren, like unto me, will Jehovah thy God raise up ; unto Him shall ye be obedient (*Deut.* xviii. 15, 18).

It is said "like unto me," because the Lord was represented by Moses, as well as by Abraham, Isaac, Jacob, David, and many more ; and because they expected Him it is said in *John :—*

The men, seeing the sign which Jesus did, said, This is of a truth that Prophet that should come into the world (vi. 14).

[2] It is because the Lord is the "Prophet" in the highest sense, and that " the testimony of Jesus is the spirit of prophecy" (*Rev.* xix. 10), that in the internal sense of the Word a "prophet" signifies one who teaches, and also abstractedly, doctrine; which is plainly evident from the following passages. In *Luke :—*

Thou child shalt be called the prophet of the Highest (i. 76).

This was said by Zacharias of his son John the Baptist, who himself said that he was not the prophet, but one preparing the way by teaching and preaching concerning the Lord's coming :—

They asked him, What art thou ? art thou Elias ? but he said, I am not. Art thou that prophet ? he answered, No. They said therefore unto him, Who art thou ? he said, I am the voice of one crying in the wilderness, Make straight the way of the Lord (*John* i. 21–23).

[3] In *Matthew :—*

Many will say in that day, Lord, Lord, have we not prophesied by Thy name ? (vii. 22), where it is manifest that to "prophesy" is to teach. In *John :—*

Thou must prophesy again before many peoples, and nations, and tongues, and kings (*Rev.* x. 11) ;

to "prophesy" denotes to teach ; and what " peoples, nations, tongues, and kings" mean, has been stated and shown before. In the same :—

The nations shall trample the holy city forty-two months ; but I will give to My two witnesses that they shall prophesy a thousand two hundred and sixty days clothed in sackcloth (xi. 2, 3) ;

where also to " prophesy" denotes to teach. In *Moses :—*

Jehovah said unto Moses, See, I have made thee a god to Pharaoh, and Aaron thy brother shall be thy prophet (*Exod.* vii. 1) ;

where " prophet" denotes the one who should teach or speak what Moses would say. In *Joel :—*

I will pour out My spirit upon all flesh, and your sons and your daughters shall prophesy (ii. 28) ;

" shall prophesy" denotes shall teach. [4] In *Isaiah :—*

Jehovah hath poured out upon you the spirit of deep sleep, and hath closed your eyes ; the prophets and your heads, the seers, hath He covered ; the vision of all hath become like the words of a sealed book, which they give to him that knoweth letters, saying, Read this, I pray thee ; and he saith, I cannot, for it is sealed (xxix. 10, 11) ;

where by " prophets" are meant those who teach truth ; and by " seers" those who see truth ; who are said to be " covered" when they know and see nothing of the truth. As in ancient times those who taught were called " prophets," they were therefore called also " seers," because to " see" signifies to understand (n. 2150, 2325 ; that they were called " seers" may be seen 1 *Sam.* ix. 9 ; 2 *Sam.* xxiv. 11). They were also called " men of God," from the signification of " man" (n. 158, 265, 749, 915, 1007, 2517 ; that they were called " men of God," 2 *Kings* i. 9–16 ; iv. 7, 9, 16, 21, 22, 25, 27, 40, 42 ; v. 8, 14, 20 ; xiii. 19 ; xxiii. 16, 17). [5] That in the internal sense by " prophets" are signified those who teach, is evident in *Jeremiah* in the whole of chapter xxiii., and in *Ezekiel* in the whole of chapter xiii., where " prophets" are specifically treated of ; as also in many other places where they are mentioned.

Hence also by "false prophets" are signified those who teach falsities; as in *Matthew* :—

In the consummation of the age many false prophets shall arise, and shall mislead many. There shall arise false Christs and false prophets, and shall show great signs, and shall mislead if possible even the elect (xxiv. 11, 24);

where by "false prophets" no others are signified. In like manner by the "false prophet" in *Rev.* xvi. 13; xix. 20; xx. 10. [6] This shows how greatly the internal sense of the Word is obscured by the ideas that have been formed from the representatives of the Jewish Church; for whenever a "prophet" is mentioned in the Word, there at once occurs the idea of prophets such as they were at that time; which idea is a great obstacle to perceiving what is signified by them. Yet the wiser any one is, the more easily is the idea gathered from those representatives removed; as for example where the "temple" is mentioned, they who think more wisely do not perceive the temple at Jerusalem, but the Temple of the Lord; where "Mount Zion," or "Zion," is mentioned, they do not perceive that mountain at Jerusalem, but the Lord's kingdom; and where "Jerusalem" is mentioned, they do not perceive the city that was in the tribes of Benjamin and Judah, but the holy and heavenly Jerusalem.

2535. *He shall pray for thee.* That this signifies that it will thus be revealed, is evident from the signification of "praying." Prayer, regarded in itself, is speech with God, and some internal view at the time of the matters of the prayer, to which there answers something like an influx into the perception or thought of the mind, so that there is a certain opening of the man's interiors toward God; but this with a difference according to the man's state, and according to the essence of the subject of the prayer. If the man prays from love and faith, and for only heavenly and spiritual things, there then comes forth in the prayer something like a revelation (which is manifested in the affection of him that prays) as to hope, consolation, or a certain inward joy. It is from this that to "pray" signifies in the internal sense to be revealed. Still more is this the case here, where praying is predicated of a prophet, by whom is meant the Lord, whose prayer was nothing else than internal speech with the Divine, and at the same time revelation. That there was revelation is evident in *Luke :*—

It came to pass when Jesus was baptized, and prayed, that the heaven was opened (iii. 21).

In the same :—

It came to pass that He took Peter, James, and John, and went up into the mountain to pray ; and as He prayed, the fashion of His countenance was altered, and His raiment became white and glistening (ix. 28, 29).

In *John :*—

When He prayed, saying, Father glorify Thy name, then came there a voice from heaven : I have both glorified, and will glorify again (xii. 27, 28) ;

where it is plain that the Lord's " praying" was speech with the Divine, and revelation at the same time.

2536. *And thou shalt live.* That this signifies that thus doctrine will have life, is evident without explication.

2537. *And if thou restore her not.* That this signifies that if spiritual truth were not rendered up without taint from the rational, is evident from what has been said just above (n. 2533), where are the same words.

2538. *Know thou that dying thou shalt die.* That this signifies that there will be no doctrine of truth and good, is also evident from what was said above (n. 2516); where also the words are similar. In like manner that " all that are thine" signifies all the things that are of it, namely, of the doctrine, together. That in the internal sense " all" signifies everything or all things, is because in the Word persons signify actual things ; and thus "all that belonged to Abimelech" signifies everything or all things that are of doctrine. From all this then it is evident what is the internal sense of the words in this verse ; namely, that He should render up the spiritual truth of doctrine without taint from the rational, and that thereby it would be taught and revealed to Him, and thus doctrine would have life ; but that if He should not render up spiritual truth without taint from the rational, the doctrine of truth and good would become null and void in respect to each and all things of it. [2] In regard to doctrine the case is this : In so far as there is what is human (that is, what is of sense, of memory-knowledge, and of the rational) as the ground of belief, so far the doctrine is null and void. But in so far as what is of sense, of memory-knowledge, and of the rational is removed, that is, in so far as doctrine is believed without these things, so far doctrine lives; for so far the Divine flows in. It is that which is proper to the human that hinders the influx and the reception. But it is one thing to believe from what is of the rational, of memory-knowledge, and of sense (that is, to consult such things in order to believe), and quite another thing to confirm and corroborate by means of things rational, of memory-knowledge, and of sense, that which is believed. What the difference is will be made plain in what follows; for these things also are treated of in this chapter in the internal sense.

2539. Verse 8. *And Abimelech rose early in the morning, and called all his servants, and spake all these words in their ears ; and the men feared greatly.* " Abimelech rose early in the morning," signifies clear perception, and the light of confirmation from celestial good; " and called all his servants," signifies things rational and of memory-knowledge; " and spake all these words in their ears," signifies an exhortation to the things thence derived that confirm, even until they should become obedient; " and the men feared greatly," signifies until they were also averse.

2540. *Abimelech rose early in the morning.* That this signifies clear perception, and the light of confirmation from celestial good, is evident from the signification of " rising in the morning," also of " Abimelech," and also of " early." What " morning" signifies has been shown above (n. 2333, 2405) : that it is here clear perception is manifest in itself, as well as from the series; that the perception was at first obscure (n. 2513, 2514); and that afterwards it was less obscure (n. 2528). That " Abimelech" signifies the doctrine of faith looking to rational things, may be seen above (n. 2509, 2510); and what " early" signifies is manifest from the signification of " morning." As it is here said that he " rose early in the morning," this not only signifies clear perception, but also the light of confirmation from celestial good; for it is celestial good from which comes the confirming light of truth; all of which shows that this is the signification. [2] The reason why the perception which the Lord had when in the Human, and His thought concerning what is rational in the doctrine of faith, are so much treated of in the internal sense, is that which has been stated above; as well as that it is angelic to think with distinctiveness of various things concerning the Lord's life in the world, and how He put off the human rational, and made the rational Divine from His own power; and at the same time concerning the doctrine of charity and faith, such as it is when the rational mixes itself with it; besides many more things dependent on these, which are interior things of the church and of man. To the man whose mind and heart are set upon worldly and corporeal things, these things appear as unimportant, and perchance as of no advantage to him; yet to the angels, whose minds and hearts are set upon celestial and spiritual things, these same things are precious; and their ideas and perceptions respecting them are ineffable. This shows that very many things which seem unimportant to man, because they transcend his comprehension, are held in the highest estimation by the angels, because they enter into the light of their wisdom; and on the other hand, things that are most highly esteemed by man, because they are of the world, and therefore come within his comprehension, are unimportant to the angels, for they pass outside of the light of their wisdom. And such is the case with the internal sense of the Word, relatively to angels and to men, in many places.

2541. *And called all his servants.* That this signifies rational things and memory-knowledges, is evident from the signification in the Word of "servants" (concerning which hereafter at verse 14, n. 2567). In a man who is in the Lord's kingdom, or who is the Lord's kingdom, there are celestial things, spiritual things, rational things, memory-knowledges, and things of sense; and these are in subordination to one another. Celestial and spiritual things hold the first place, and are the Lord's; to these rational things are subordinate, and are subservient; to these again memory-knowledges are subordinate and subservient; and lastly the things of sense are subordinate and subservient to these, that is to memory-knowledges. The things which are subservient, or which serve, are relatively servants, and in the Word are called " servants." That there is such a subordination, the man who thinks only from sense and memory-knowledge is ignorant; and he who knows anything of them nevertheless has a most obscure idea, because he is still in corporeal things; but the angels have a most distinct idea; for thousands, nay myriads, of ideas that to the angels are distinct, present nothing but a single obscure idea to men. For example, in regard to Abimelech calling his servants and speaking all the words in their ears, and the men fearing greatly, the angels perceive deeper arcana than man can possibly apprehend, or can even believe—namely, how the Lord reduced rational things and memory-knowledges to obedience; and indeed in such manner that He reduced to obedience not the rational things and memory-knowledges themselves, but the affections that rose up against the celestial and spiritual things of doctrine, for on the subjugation of these the rational things and memory-knowledges were reduced to obedience, and at the same time into order. To the angels, these are among the most common things; but to man they are perchance among those which are most obscure or unintelligible to him.

2542. *And spake all these words in their ears.* That this signifies an exhortation to the things thence derived that confirm, even until they should become obedient, is evident from the series in the internal sense, as well as from the signification of " ears." From the series : There are many confirmatory things that support whatever the rational acknowledges ; for it is precisely from these confirmatory things that its acknowledgment comes ; and therefore it is that when rational things are being reduced to obedience exhortation is made to the things that confirm ; for these are ever pressing in, and as it were rising up. From the signification of " ears :" In the internal sense of the Word " ears" signify obedience, by reason of the correspondence between hearing and obeying; which correspondence is moreover latent in the very word " hear," and still more in " hearken ;" the origin of which correspondence is from the other life, where they who are willing and obedient belong to the province of the ear, and indeed correspond to the hearing itself; which is an arcanum not yet known. But these things will become more clearly manifest when in what follows, of the Lord's Divine mercy, correspondence will be treated of. That " ears" have this signification is evident from many passages in the Word. For the present we may adduce a single passage from *Isaiah* :—

Make the heart of this people fat, and make their ears heavy, and shut their eyes ; lest peradventure they see with their eyes, and hear with their ears, and their heart should understand (vi. 10).

Here to " see with the eyes" is to understand ; and to " hear with the ears" is to perceive with affection, consequently to obey. And nothing else is signified where the Lord says, " He that hath an ear to hear, let him hear" (*Matt.* xi. 15 ; xiii. 9, 43 ; *Luke* viii. 8 ; xiv. 35).

2543. *The men feared greatly.* That this signifies even until they should become averse, is evident from the signification here of " fearing;" and from the signification of the " men." " Fearing," or " fear," like all other emotions, though in appearance simple, involves in itself many things, namely, in worldly matters the loss of life, of reputation, of honor, and of gain ; and in heavenly matters the loss of what is good and true, and of the life thence derived. As fear involves these things it also involves aversion to whatever endeavors to destroy them ; and this the more in proportion as the man is in the affection of what is good and true. To this very affection aversion is the opposite or contrary, and therefore by " fearing" is here signified to become averse. How great was the Lord's aversion is evident from the zeal with which the things in the next verse are said ; which zeal was for doctrine, that it might be free from contamination by anything rational or by anything of memory-knowledge. (That " men" signify rational things and memory-knowledges, or all intellectual things whatever, has been shown above, n. 158, 265, 749, 915, 1007.)

2544. Verse 9. *And Abimelech called Abraham and said unto him, What hast thou done unto us? and wherein have I sinned against thee that thou hast brought on me and on my*

*kingdom a great sin? Thou hast done unto me deeds that
ought not to be done.* "Abimelech called Abraham and said
unto him," signifies the Lord's thought from the doctrine of
faith ; "what hast thou done unto us ? and wherein have I
sinned against thee ?" signifies self-conviction for having so
thought ; "that thou hast brought on me and on my kingdom
a great sin," signifies that thereby the doctrine of faith and
all doctrinal things would be in danger ; "thou hast done unto
me deeds that ought not to be done," signifies horror.

2545. *Abimelech called Abraham and said unto him.* That
this signifies the Lord's thought from the doctrine of faith,
is evident from the representation of Abimelech, and also of
Abraham, and from the signification of "saying," which have
all been explained several times. What it is to think from
the doctrine of faith cannot be explained to the apprehension ;
for the perception of this can fall into angelic ideas only ; but
to these it is presented in a light so great, attended with
heavenly representatives, that scarcely anything of it can be
described ; as is evident when we say that the Lord's thought
was from intellectual truth, which was above that rational
which He looked upon therefrom ; but that the perception
from which He thought was from Divine truth.

2546. *What hast thou done unto us ? and wherein have I
sinned against thee ?* That this signifies self-conviction for
having so thought, is evident from the emotion and zeal in
these words (see n. 2543), on account of the faculties of reason
and memory-knowledge desiring to rise up and enter, and thus
to have some share in the doctrine of faith, which is Divine.

2547. *That thou hast brought on me and on my kingdom a
great sin.* That this signifies that thereby the doctrine of faith
and all doctrinal things would be in danger, is evident from
the signification of "Abimelech," here meant by "me," as being
the doctrine of faith ; and from the signification of "kingdom,"
as being the truth of doctrine or that which is doctrinal. That
in the internal sense "kingdom" signifies the truths of doctrine ; and in the opposite sense, falsities of doctrine, is evident from the Word ; as in *Jeremiah :*—

He is the Former of all things, and the scepter of His inheritance ;
Jehovah Zebaoth is His name. Thou art My hammer, weapons of war ;

and I will scatter nations in thee, and destroy kingdoms in thee (li. 19, 20),

where the Lord is treated of, who evidently will not scatter nations nor destroy kingdoms, but will scatter and destroy the things signified by nations and kingdoms, namely, the evils and falsities of doctrine.   [2] In *Ezekiel :*—

Behold, I will take the sons of Israel from among the nations whither they be gone, and will gather them from every side, and bring them into their own land ; I will make them one nation in the land in the mountains of Israel, and one king shall be king to them all ; and they shall no more be two nations, neither shall they any more be divided into two kingdoms (xxxvii. 21, 22) ;

here " Israel" denotes the spiritual church; and " nation" the good of that church or of doctrine.   (That " nations" denote goods may be seen above, n. 1259, 1260, 1416, 1849.)   " Kingdom" denotes its truths.   It is evident that something else than nations and kingdoms is here meant by " nations and kingdoms," for it is said of the sons of Israel or of the Israelites that they are to be " gathered and brought back into the land," the fact being that when dispersed among the nations they were transformed into Gentiles.   [3] In *Isaiah :*—

I will confound Egypt with Egypt, and they shall fight every man against his brother, and every man against his companion, city against city, kingdom against kingdom (xix. 2),

where " Egypt" denotes reasonings from memory-knowledges concerning the truths of faith (n. 1164, 1165, 1186); " city" denotes doctrine, here one that is heretical (n. 402, 2268, 2449); " kingdom" denotes the falsity of doctrine; so that " city against city, and kingdom against kingdom" denotes that heresies and falsities will fight among themselves ; in like manner as is denoted by what the Lord said in regard to the consummation of the age, in *Matthew :*—

Nation shall rise up against nation, and kingdom against kingdom (xxiv. 7) ;

denoting evils against evils, and falsities against falsities.   [4] That which Daniel prophesied in regard to the four kingdoms (chapter ii. 37–46; vii. 17 to the end); and concerning the kingdoms of Media and Persia (chapter viii. 20 to the end); and concerning the kingdoms of the king of the south and the king of the north (chapter xi.) ; and that which John prophesied in the *Revelation* concerning kings and kingdoms, have no other signification : "kingdoms" there merely mean the states of the church in respect to truths and falsities. States of monarchs and of the kingdoms of the earth in the sense of the letter, are in the internal sense states of the church and of the Lord's kingdom; in which sense there are none other than spiritual and celestial things; for regarded in itself the Lord's Word is solely spiritual and celestial; but in order that it may be read and apprehended by every man whatever, the things of heaven are set forth by such things as are on earth.

2548. *Thou hast done unto me deeds that ought not to be done.* That this signifies horror, is evident from the emotion in the words; as well as from the series, namely, that the Lord was averse (n. 2543); that He reproved Himself from zeal (n. 2546); and here that He felt horror.

2549. Verses 10, 11. *And Abimelech said unto Abraham, What sawest thou that thou hast done this word? And Abraham said, Because I said, Surely there is no fear of God in this place, and they will kill me on account of the word of my wife.* "Abimelech said unto Abraham," signifies further thought from the doctrine of faith; "what sawest thou that thou hast done this word?" signifies a looking into the cause; "Abraham said," signifies a perception which is an answer; "because I said surely there is no fear of God in this place," signifies thought thence derived : that they would have no respect for spiritual truth in the state in which they were; "and they will kill me on account of the word of my wife," signifies that the celestial things of faith would thus also perish if they were to think that spiritual truth alone could be conjoined with celestial good.

2550. *Abimelech said unto Abraham.* That this signifies further thought from the doctrine of faith, is evident from what was said above (n. 2545), where are nearly the same words. As the statement is here repeated, it signifies further thought, and indeed concerning the cause. (What thought from the doctrine of faith is may also be seen there.)

2551. *What sawest thou that thou hast done this word?* That this signifies a looking into the cause, is evident without explication; as well as from what follows, where the cause is stated. The reason of there being thus presented in regular order, in the internal sense, how the Lord perceived and thought concerning the doctrine of faith, and concerning the rational as to whether it should be consulted, is that it is angelic to think of these things in such a series. The internal sense of the Word is especially for the angels; and therefore is adapted to their perceptions and thoughts. They are in their delightful, nay, in their blessed and happy states, when they are thinking about the Lord, His Divine and His Human, and how the Human was made Divine; for they are encompassed with a celestial and spiritual sphere which is full of the Lord; so that it may be said that they are in the Lord. Hence nothing is more blessed and happy to them than to think in accordance with the things that belong to that sphere and its derivative affection. [2] At the same time moreover they are instructed and perfected, especially in this: how the Lord by degrees and of His own power, as He grew up, made Divine the human into which He was born; and thus how, by means of the knowledges that He revealed to Himself He perfected His rational, dispersed by successive steps its shadows, and introduced it into Divine light. These and innumerable other things are presented before the angels in a celestial and spiritual manner, with a thousand and a thousand representatives, in the light of life, when the Word is being read. But these things, which are so precious to the angels, are to men as of no importance, because above their comprehension, and thus in the shade of their understanding; and on the other hand, the things that are precious to men, such as those which contain within them worldly matters, are of no importance to the angels, because below their state and thus in the shade of their wisdom. Thus, wonderful to say, the things that come into shade with man, and almost into contempt, with the angels pass into light, and into their affection, as is the case with many things of the internal sense of the Word.

2552. *Abraham said.* That this signifies a perception which is an answer, is evident from the signification of "saying" in the historicals of the Word, as explained many times before (n. 1791, 1815, 1819, 1822, 1898, 1919, 2061, 2080, 2238,

2260, 2271, 2287). With regard to the Lord's thought from the doctrine of faith being signified by the words "Abimelech said to Abraham;" and the perception which was an answer being meant by "Abraham said," the case is this : Perception is a higher thing, and the Lord had it from the Divine Itself; whereas thought is a lower thing, and the Lord had it from the intellectual itself; and as it was perception from which He had the thought, so the answer of the thought was from perception. This may be illustrated by something similar with man. The celestial man cannot think except from perception, nor the spiritual man except from conscience (n. 2515). The perception of the former, like the conscience [of the latter] is from the Lord, and it is not apparent to the man himself whence it is; but his thought is from the rational, and appears to him as from himself. And so again, when a man is thinking concerning any subject from the rational, then the conclusion of the thought, or the answer, comes either from perception or from conscience ; consequently an answer is given him by the Lord in accordance with his state of life, his affection, and the truth of doctrine implanted or impressed in agreement therewith.

2553. *Because I said, Surely there is no fear of God in this place.* That this signifies the thought thence derived : that they would have no respect for spiritual truth in that state in which they were, is evident from the signification of the expression "fear of God," as being respect for Divine or spiritual truth; and from the signification of "place," as being state (see n. 1273–1275, 1377). The case herein is this : Man cannot apprehend any doctrine that is purely spiritual and celestial, that is, Divine, because it infinitely transcends his apprehension, and thus also his belief. All man's thoughts are terminated in the natural things which are connected with his senses. Whatever is not said from and according to these natural things is not comprehended, but perishes, like sight that has no bound in some ocean or universe ; and therefore if doctrinal matters were set forth before a man in any other manner, they would not be at all received, and thus no respect would be entertained for them ; as may be sufficiently evident from everything in the Word, where for this very reason purely Divine things

themselves are set forth naturally, nay, sensuously; as that
Jehovah has ears, eyes, and a face; and that He has feelings
like a man, such as anger, and so forth. [2] This need was
still greater at the time when the Lord came into the world,
for then men did not know even what the celestial and the
spiritual was, nor even that there was anything internal.
Things merely earthly and worldly, and thus external, had
full possession of their minds, as was the case with the apostles themselves, who imagined that the Lord's kingdom would
be like a kingdom of this world, and therefore asked that one
might sit on His right hand and another on His left, and who
long thought that they should sit upon twelve thrones to judge
the twelve tribes of Israel; not as yet being aware that in the
other life they would not have ability to judge even the smallest thing of one man (n. 2129, at the end). His looking into
this state of the human race was the reason of the Lord's
thinking at first whether the rational was to be consulted in
the doctrine of faith; and this from His love, which was that
the salvation of all might be provided for, and that the Word
might not perish.

2554. *They will kill me for my wife's sake.* That this signifies that thus the celestial things of faith also would perish,
if they were to think that spiritual truth alone could be conjoined with celestial good, is evident from the signification of
"killing," as being to perish; and from the signification of
"wife," as being spiritual truth conjoined with celestial good
(see n. 2507). This is another reason why the Lord thus
thought, and is as follows. The Divine good, which is here
called celestial good, is united as by a marriage to the Divine
truth, which is here called spiritual truth (n. 2508); and although the Divine good is united in this manner to the Divine
truth alone, it nevertheless flows into lower truths, and conjoins itself with them, but not as by a marriage; for it flows
into rational truths which are only appearances of truth, and
conjoins itself with them; nay, it flows into truths of sense
and of memory-knowledge, which are scarcely anything but
fallacies, and conjoins itself with these. Unless this were so,
no man could possibly have been saved (see Part First, n.
1831, 1832). That the Divine good might be conjoined with

truths of reason and of memory-knowledge, and that man might thus be saved, was the purpose of the Lord's coming into the world; for without the Lord's Human made Divine there cannot possibly be any conjunction; whereas through Him there is conjunction. [2] Besides this arcanum, there are still other arcana in the words "they will kill me for my wife's sake" (by which is signified that so the celestial things of faith would perish, if they were to think that spiritual truth alone could be conjoined with celestial good); for example, that if men were to have no regard for spiritual truth, celestial good would thereby also perish; for when the former is rejected the latter perishes; and again, that unless it were said that they should adore the Father (although there is no access to Him except through the Son, and he who sees the Son sees the Father, *John* xiv. 8–12), it would not have been received : besides other arcana.

2555. Verses 12, 13. *And moreover truly she is my sister, being the daughter of my father, but not the daughter of my mother, and she became my wife. And it came to pass when God caused me to depart from my father's house, that I said unto her, This is thy goodness which thou shalt do unto me ; at every place whither we shall come, say of me, He is my brother.* " And moreover truly she is my sister," signifies that rational truth had such an affinity ; " the daughter of my father, but not the daughter of my mother," signifies that the rational was conceived of celestial good as a father, but not of spiritual truth as a mother ; " and she became my wife," signifies that spiritual truth was conjoined with the celestial by the mediumship of rationality ; " and it came to pass when God caused me to depart from my father's house," signifies when He left what is of memory-knowledge and the appearances therefrom, together with their delights, which are here the " house of his father ;" " that I said unto her," signifies the thought at the time ; " this is thy goodness which thou shalt do unto me," signifies that He would then have therefrom this comfort ; " at every place whither we shall come," signifies all that He should afterwards conclude concerning rational truth ; " say of me, he is my brother," signifies that it should be said that rational truth had been adjoined to celestial good.

2556. *And moreover truly she is my sister.* That this signifies that rational truth had such an affinity, is evident from the representation of Sarah as a sister, as being rational truth (see n. 2508); as well as from what now follows concerning the birth of the rational, and its consequent affinity. It is to be held in general that all things in a truly rational, that is, a regenerate man—all the things of his affections, of his perceptions, and of his thoughts—are conjoined with one another as if by blood-relationship and affinity; for they have been so disposed that they mutually regard one another as do the families of one house, and this in the most distinct manner; and hence they are reproduced in accordance with these affinities. This they derive from the influx of heaven, that is, of the Lord through heaven. With the man who is truly rational, that is, regenerate, all things have been disposed into order such as exists in heaven, and this from influx. From this there is given man a faculty of thinking, concluding, judging, and reflecting so wonderful as to exceed all mere human knowledge and wisdom, and immeasurably to surpass the analyses which human industry has drawn from these sources. The reason why these things have been hitherto unknown, is that it has not been believed that all things of the affections, perceptions, and thoughts flow in (the evil from hell, and the good from heaven), thus that these have a connection with the things which are without them; when yet the truth is that man is so conjoined as to his spirit with those who are without him, that if he were deprived of this connection he would not live a single moment; as may also be known from the fact that anything unconnected is impossible, and that anything unconnected perishes in a moment.

2557. *The daughter of my father, but not the daughter of my mother.* That this signifies that the rational was conceived of celestial good as a father, but not of spiritual truth as a mother, is evident from the conception of the rational, namely, that this is effected by the influx of Divine celestial good into the affection of memory-knowledges (see n. 1895, 1902, 1910). Two arcana are contained herein; one, that man's rational is conceived of Divine celestial good as a father, and that otherwise no rational would exist; the other, that the rational is not conceived of spiritual truth as a mother. As regards the first, namely, that man's rational is conceived of Divine celestial good as a father, and that otherwise no rational would exist, this is evident from what has been said above (n. 1895, 1902, 1910), and also from what may be known to every man if he reflects. [2] For it is known that a man is born into no knowledge and into nothing of reason, but only into the faculty of receiving them; and also that he afterwards learns and imbues himself with all things by degrees, and this principally through the sensuous things of the hearing and sight; and as he learns and imbues himself with these, he so becomes rational. That these things take place by the way of the body, that is, by an external way, because through the hearing and sight, is manifest; but the reason why man has not become acquainted with this (on account of not reflecting upon it) is that there is something constantly flowing in from within that receives the things which thus enter and are insinuated from without, and disposes them into order. That which flows in and receives and disposes them, is Divine celestial good, which is from the Lord. Thence comes the life of these things, thence their order, and thence the kinships and affinities among them severally, as before said. All this shows that man's rational is from Divine celestial good as a father, in accordance with the words in this verse : " she is the daughter of my father." [3] As regards the other arcanum, namely, that the rational is not conceived of spiritual truth as a mother; this is evident from what was said above (n. 1902). For if spiritual truth were to flow in from within, as good does, man would then be born into everything of reason, and at the same time into everything of knowledge, so that he would have no need to learn anything. But as man is such that he is hereditarily in all evil, and thence in all falsity, and therefore if truths themselves also were to flow in would adulterate and falsify them, and thereby the man would eternally perish, it has been provided by the Lord that nothing of truth flows in through man's internal, but only through his external. From this it is evident that man's rational is *not* from spiritual truth as a mother, in accordance with the words in this verse : " she is not the daughter of my mother." It was the Lord's pleasure that His rational should be formed according to the same order, to the end that from His own power He might make what was human in Himself Divine, and might implant and unite Divine spiritual truth to Divine celestial good, and Divine celestial good to Divine spiritual truth.

2558. *And she became my wife.* That this signifies that spiritual truth was conjoined with the celestial by the mediumship of rationality, is evident from the representation of Sarah as Abraham's wife, as being spiritual truth conjoined with celestial good (see n. 2507); and from the representation of the same as his sister, as being rational truth (n. 2508). Hence that she became his wife, from being his sister, signifies that by rationality as a medium spiritual truth was conjoined with the celestial. (How these things are circumstanced is evident from what has been said just above, n. 2557.)

2559. *And it came to pass when God caused me to depart from my father's house.* That this signifies when He left what is of memory-knowledge, and the appearances therefrom, together with their delights, which here are the "house of his father," is evident from the signification of "departing," as being to leave; and from the signification of "house," as being good (n. 2231, 2233), here the good of the delight from the appearances of the things of memory-knowledge and of rational things; for all delight appears as good. That by the "house of his father" are here signified the delights of memory-knowledges and of rational things, consequently of their appearances, comes from the fact that they are predicated of Abraham when he departed from the house of his father; for then Abraham together with the house of his father worshiped other gods (see n. 1356, 1992). Hence it is that it is said in the plural, "God (*Elohim*) caused me to depart." It might also be rendered according to the original tongue : "the gods caused me to wander;" but as the Lord is represented by Abraham it must be rendered "God caused me to depart." As with the Lord the first memory-knowledges and the rational things derived from them were human, being imbued with what was hereditary from the mother, and thus were not purely Divine, they are therefore represented by Abraham's first state (but how far representations go, see n. 665, 1907[e], 1361, 1992).

2560. *That I said unto her.* That this signifies the thought at the time, is evident from the signification of "saying" as being to think, as explained several times before.

2561. *This is thy goodness which thou shalt do unto me.* That this signifies that He would then have therefrom this comfort, is evident from what goes before and from what follows, and thus without further explication.

2562. *At every place whither we shall come.* That this signifies all that He should afterwards conclude respecting rational truth, is evident from the signification of "place," as being state (see n. 1273–1275, 1377). The state of the thing here treated of is the state of concluding concerning rational truth (that it should be said that rational truth was adjoined to celestial good), as follows.

2563. *Say of me, He is my brother.* That this signifies that it should be said that rational truth was adjoined to celestial good, is evident from what was said above (n. 2524), where nearly the same words occur.

2564. Verse 14. *And Abimelech took flock and herd, and menservants and maidservants, and gave unto Abraham; and restored to him Sarah his wife.* "Abimelech took," signifies the doctrine of faith; "flock and herd," signifies that it was enriched with rational goods and natural goods; "and menservants and maidservants," signifies also with rational truths and natural truths, as well as with their affections; "and gave unto Abraham," signifies to the Lord; "and restored to him Sarah his wife," signifies when the Divine spiritual had been adjoined to the Divine celestial.

2565. *Abimelech took.* That this signifies the doctrine of faith, is evident from the signification of "Abimelech," as being the doctrine of faith (see n. 2504, 2509, 2510).

2566. *Flock and herd.* That this signifies that it was enriched with rational goods and natural goods, is evident from the signification of "flock and herd." Those within the church are called the "flock" who are truly rational, that is, are internal men; hence also it is that in the abstract rational or internal goods themselves are signified by "flock" (concerning which signification of "flock" see above, n. 343, 415, 1565). But those within the church are called the "herd" who are natural, that is, are external men; hence also in the abstract natural or external goods themselves are signified by "herd;" (concerning which signification of "herd" see also above, n. 2180. That such things are signified by "beasts" has been shown above, n. 45, 46, 142, 143, 246, 714, 715, 776, 1823, 2179). Its being said that "Abimelech took and gave" signifies that the doctrine of faith was enriched; for as already said by "Abimelech" is signified the doctrine of faith.

2567. *And menservants and maidservants.* That this signifies that it was enriched also with rational truths and natural truths, as well as with the affections of them, is evident from the signification of "menservants and maidservants." These are frequently mentioned in the Word, and by them are signified in the internal sense things that are relatively lower and of less value, such as are rational and natural things in comparison with spiritual and celestial things. By natural truths are meant memory-knowledges of every kind, for these are natural. That in the Word these are signified by "menservants and maidservants," is manifest from the internal sense of the words where they are mentioned, as in *Isaiah :*—

Jehovah will have compassion on Jacob, and will yet choose Israel, and will set them upon their own ground ; and the sojourner shall cleave unto them, and shall join themselves unto the house of Jacob ; and the peoples shall take them, and shall bring them to their own place ; and the house of Israel shall possess them for themselves upon the ground of Jehovah for menservants and for maidservants (xiv. 1, 2),

[2] where "Jacob" denotes the external church; "Israel," the internal; "sojourners," those who are being instructed in truths and goods (see n. 1463, 2025); "menservants and maidservants," natural and rational truths together with the affections of them, which are to serve the church meant by "Jacob and Israel." It is evident that Jacob and Israel are not meant here, nor the Jews and Israelites, for the latter when dispersed among the Gentiles became Gentiles. The Jews still cherish this prophecy and expect its fulfillment, even according to the letter, namely, that sojourners will cleave to them, that the people will bring them to their place, and will be to them for menservants and maidservants ; when yet not even the smallest thing is to be understood of the Jews and Israelites in the

prophecies of the Word where these are mentioned; as must be evident even to themselves from the fact that it is often said of Israel equally as of Judah that they shall be brought back. [3] Again in the same Prophet :—

Behold, Jehovah maketh the earth empty, and emptieth it out, and will disfigure the face of it, and scatter the inhabitants thereof ; and it shall be, as the people, so the priest ; as the servant, so his master ; as the maidservant, so her mistress (*Isa.* xxiv. 1, 2).

Here the " earth" denotes the church (n. 662, 1066, 1068, 1850), which is made empty and is emptied out, and its face is disfigured, and its inhabitants scattered, when there are no longer any interior truths and goods, which are the "people and the priest," nor any exterior truths and goods, which are the "servant" and the "maidservant," as comes to pass when external things rule over internal things. [4] Again :—

I will bring forth a seed out of Jacob and out of Judah an inheritor of My mountain, and My chosen shall possess it, and My servants shall dwell there (*Isa.* lxv. 9),

where "Jacob" denotes the external church ; "Judah," the internal celestial church ; the "chosen," its goods ; and the "servants," its truths. [5] In *Joel :—*

I will pour out My spirit upon all flesh, and your sons and your daughters shall prophesy ; also upon the servants and the maidservants will I pour out My spirit in those days (ii. 28, 29) ;

where the Lord's kingdom is treated of ; "to prophesy" denotes to teach (n. 2534); "sons," truths themselves (n. 489, 491, 533, 1147) ; "daughters," goods themselves (n. 489–491); "servants" and "maidservants," lower truths and goods, upon which the spirit is said to be poured out when they accede and confirm. That such things are signified by "menservants and maidservants" here and elsewhere, does not so appear, by reason both of the common idea respecting menservants and maidservants, and of the apparent history. [6] In *John :—*

I saw an angel standing in the sun, and he cried with a loud voice, saying to the birds that fly in the midst of heaven, Eat the flesh of kings, and the flesh of captains, and the flesh of mighty men, and the flesh of horses and of them that sit thereon, and the flesh of all, both of free and bond, both of small and great (*Rev.* xix. 17, 18).

Vol. III.—19

It is here evident that it is not the flesh of kings, of captains, of mighty men, of horses, of those who sit on them, of the free and of the bond, which they should eat; but that it is the truths of the church, both internal and external, that were made "flesh" for them. [7] That "menservants" signify truths, and "maidservants" goods, which are subservient to and thus serve spiritual and celestial truths and goods, is more clearly evident from the laws enjoined in the Representative Church in regard to menservants and maidservants; which laws all have regard to the state of the church and of the Lord's kingdom in general and in particular; and to the way in which lower truths and goods, or those which are natural and rational, are to serve those which are spiritual and celestial, and thereby those which are Divine. For example: The Hebrew manservant and the Hebrew maidservant were to be free in the seventh year, and were then to be endowed from the flock, the threshing-floor, and the wine-press (*Exod.* xxi. 2, 6; *Deut.* xv. 12–15; *Jer.* xxxiv. 9–14): The servant's wife was to be free if she entered into service with him; but if the master gave him his wife, the wife and children were to be the master's (*Exod.* xxi. 3, 4): A poor brother who had been purchased was not to serve as a bondservant, but as a hired servant and a sojourner; at the jubilee he was to go out together with his children (*Lev.* xxv. 39–43): If a brother were bought by a foreign sojourner, he might be redeemed, and was to go out in the year of the jubilee (*Lev.* xxv. 47, etc.): Menservants and maidservants might be bought of the nations around, and of the sons of foreign sojourners, and they were to be their perpetual possession, whom they might rule absolutely, but not the sons of Israel (*Lev.* xxv. 44–46): If a manservant did not desire to go out of service, his ear was to be pierced with an awl, at the door, and he was to be a perpetual servant; and the same with a maidservant (*Exod.* xxi. 6; *Deut.* xv. 16, 17): If any one smote his manservant or his maidservant with a rod, so that he died, vengeance was to be taken on him; but if he survived a day or more, he was to be free, because he was his money (*Exod.* xxi. 20, 21): If he should smite a servant's eye or tooth, he was to go forth free (*Exod.* xxi. 26, 27): If an ox should gore a manservant or a maidservant so that he died, the owner was to pay thirty shekels to his master, and the ox was to be stoned (*Exod.* xxi. 32) : A servant who had escaped from his master was not to be placed in confinement, but should dwell in the place where he chose, and was not to be afflicted (*Deut.* xxiii. 15, 16) : A servant bought with silver, and circumcised, was to eat of the Passover (*Exod.* xii. 44) : Any one's daughter that was bought was not to go out of service like the manservants ; if she were evil, her master was not to sell her to a stranger ; if she were betrothed to his son, she was to be as a daughter ; if he took another, he was not to diminish her food, her raiment, nor her duty of marriage ; if these things were not done, she was to go out of service without price (*Exod.* xxi. 7–12). [8] All these laws have their origin from the laws of truth and good in heaven, and in the internal sense have reference to them ; partly by correspondences, partly by representatives, and partly by significatives. But after the representatives and significatives of the church (which were the most external and lowest things of worship) had been abolished, the necessity for these laws ceased also. Now if these laws were to be unfolded from the laws of order of truth and good, and from representatives and significatives, it would be plain that nothing else was meant by "menservants" than rational and memory truths (*vera rationalia et scientifica*), which are lower truths, and therefore ought to serve spiritual truths ; and that by "maid-servants" were signified the goods of these, which being also lower, ought to serve indeed, but in another manner ; and therefore certain of the laws laid down respecting maidservants differ from those laid down respecting menservants ; for regarded in themselves truths are more fully servants than their goods are. [9] By the "king's right," in *Samuel*, nothing else is signified in the internal sense than the "right" of truth, and likewise the "right" of falsity when it begins to rule over truth and over good ; as is evident from the explication of the words by which this is described :—

This will be the right of the king that shall reign over you : he will take your sons and appoint them to him over his chariots and for his horsemen, and they shall run before his chariots ; he will take your daughters for perfumers, and for cooks, and for bakers ; your menservants and your maidservants and your goodliest young men and your asses will he take and put them to his work ; he will take the tenth of your flock ; and ye shall be for servants. And ye shall cry out in that day because of your king whom ye have chosen for you, and Jehovah will not answer you in that day (1 *Sam.* viii. 11, 13, 16–18).

[10] That by a "king" is signified truths, may be seen above (n. 1672, 2015, 2069) ; thus in the opposite sense things that are not true, that is, falsities. By the "sons whom he would appoint for himself over his chariots and for his horsemen," are signified the truths of doctrine, which should be subservient to principles of falsity, which are the "chariots and horsemen." By the "daughters whom he should take for perfumers, cooks, and bakers," are signified the goods of doctrine, by which those falsities would be filled with delight; and which would be made to favor the falsities. By the "menservants and maidservants, the young men, and the asses, by which he would do his work," are signified the things of reason and of memory-knowledge, by which those falsities would be confirmed. By the "flock of which he will take a tenth" are signified the remains of good that he would do violence to. And by their "being servants" is signified that it would come to pass that the celestial and spiritual things of the Word and of doctrine, instead of ruling, would be subservient to the confirmation of the falsities of his principles, and the evils of his cupidities. For there is nothing that cannot be injected into principles of falsity as confirmatory of them, either by a false application, by a wrong interpretation, by perversion, or by a rejection of those things which do not favor ; and therefore it is added : "if ye cry out in that day because of your king whom ye have chosen for you, Jehovah will not answer in that day."

2568. It has been said above in this chapter that doctrine would become null and void if the rational were consulted (n. 2516, 2538); and that it was not consulted (n. 2519, 2531). But here it is said that the doctrine of faith was enriched with goods and truths both rational and natural. At first view these statements appear as if they were adverse and contrary to each other; and yet are not so. How the case was with the Lord, has been stated; but how it is with man, remains to be told.

[2] As regards man it is one thing to regard the doctrine of faith from rational things, and altogether another to regard rational things from the doctrine of faith. To regard the doctrine of faith from rational things is not to believe in the Word, or in the doctrine thence derived, until one is persuaded from rational things that it is so; whereas to regard rational things from the doctrine of faith is first to believe in the Word, or in the doctrine therefrom, and then to confirm the same by rational things. The former is inverted order, and results in nothing being believed; whereas the latter is genuine order, and causes the man to believe the better. It is the former that is here meant by its being said that Abimelech should die because of the woman; by which is signified that the doctrine of faith would become null and void if the rational were consulted (n. 2516, 2538); but the latter is meant by its being said that Abimelech gave flock and herd, and menservants and maidservants; by which is signified that the doctrine of faith was enriched with rational and natural goods and truths. [3] These things are much treated of in the Word in its internal sense, especially where Asshur and Egypt are spoken of; for the reason that while the doctrine of faith is regarded from rational things, that is, while a man does not believe until he is persuaded from them that it is so, it then not only becomes null and void, but whatever is contained in it is also denied; whereas when rational things are regarded from the doctrine of faith, that is, when a man believes the Word, and afterwards the same things are confirmed by rational things, the doctrine is then living and whatever is contained in it is affirmed. [4] There are therefore two principles; one of which leads to all folly and insanity, and the other to all intelligence and wisdom. The former principle is to deny all things, or to say in the heart that we cannot believe them until we are convinced by what we can apprehend, or perceive by the senses; this is the principle that leads to all folly and insanity, and is to be called the negative principle. The other principle is to affirm the things which are of doctrine from the Word, or to think and believe within ourselves that they are true because the Lord has said them: this is the principle that leads to all intelligence and wisdom, and is to be called the

affirmative principle.   [5] The more they who think from the
negative principle consult things rational, the more they consult memory-knowledges, and the more they consult things
philosophical, the more do they cast and precipitate themselves into darkness, until at last they deny all things.   The
causes of this are, that no one can apprehend higher things
from lower ones, that is, spiritual and celestial things, still
less Divine things, from lower ones, because they transcend
all understanding, and moreover everything is then involved
in negatives from that principle.   On the other hand, they
who think from an affirmative principle can confirm themselves by whatever things rational, by whatever memory-knowledges, and whatever things philosophic they have at command;
for all these are to them things confirmatory, and give them a
fuller idea of the matter.   [6] Moreover there are some who
are in doubt before they deny, and there are some who are in
doubt before they affirm.   They who are in doubt before they
deny are they who incline to a life of evil; and when this life
carries them away, then in so far as they think of the matters in
question they deny them.   But they who are in doubt before
they affirm are they who incline to a life of good; and when
they suffer themselves to be bent to this by the Lord, then in
so far as they think about those things so far they affirm.
As this subject is further treated of in the verses which follow,
it is permitted of the Lord's Divine mercy to illustrate them
more fully there (see n. 2588).

2569.   *And gave unto Abraham ; and restored to him Sarah
his wife.*   That he " gave unto Abraham" signifies to the Lord,
is evident from the representation of Abraham, as being the
Lord (concerning which frequently before).   That he " restored
unto him Sarah his wife" signifies when the Divine spiritual
had been adjoined to the Divine celestial, is evident from the
signification of " Sarah a wife," as being spiritual truth adjoined to celestial good (see n. 2507).   The internal sense of
the words in this verse is manifest from what has been said,
namely, that when the Human in the Lord had been united to
the Divine, and the Divine to the Human, He then possessed
omniscience not only of Divine celestial and spiritual things,
but also of infra-celestial and infra-spiritual things, that is, of

rational and natural things; for from the Divine, as from the
Sun of all light, everything is seen as present.

2570. Verse 15. *And Abimelech said, Behold my land is*
before thee ; dwell in that which is good in thine eyes. "Abimelech said, Behold my land is before thee," signifies the Lord's
perception concerning the doctrine of love and charity; "dwell
in that which is good in thine eyes," signifies that he was in
everything where there was good.

2571. *Abimelech said, Behold my land is before thee.* That
this signifies the Lord's perception concerning the doctrine of
love and charity, is evident from the signification of "saying,"
as being to think (see n. 2506); and from the signification of
"land," as being here the doctrine of love and charity.
"Land" (or "earth") in the internal sense signifies various
things (n. 620, 636, 1066); and that which it signifies is evident from the series or connection. For it signifies the external man of the church, when "heaven" signifies the internal
(n. 82, 913, 1411, 1733); it also signifies the region where the
church is (n. 662, 1066); it signifies the church itself; also in
a universal sense the Lord's kingdom in the heavens and on
earth, since this was represented by the land of Canaan or the
holy land (n. 1437, 1585, 1607); the same being signified also
by the "new heaven and new earth" (n. 1733, 1850, 2117,
2118); and because "land" signifies the man of the church,
the church, and the Lord's kingdom, it also signifies that
which is their essential, namely, love to the Lord and charity
toward the neighbor, for on this they all hang (n. 537, 540,
547, 553, 2130); consequently it signifies the doctrine of love
and charity, which belongs to the church, and which is here
the "land of Abimelech;" for by Abimelech as a king is signified the doctrine of faith, as shown above; and by his
"land," whence and where he was, is signified the doctrine of
love and charity, whence and where faith is. [2] That the
Lord's thought hitherto had been concerning the doctrine of
faith, but now was concerning the doctrine of love and charity, comes from the fact that the Lord adjoined the Human
to the Divine by means of the truths which are of faith (although at the same time by means of Divine goods which are
of love, in the truths) according to the order by which man

also becomes spiritual and celestial; but not Divine, so as to
have life in himself, like the Lord. But when the Divine
marriage of truth and good and of good and truth in the Lord
had been effected (which is signified by Abimelech restoring
to Abraham Sarah his wife, see n. 2569), the Lord's thought
then was concerning the doctrine of love and charity, and this
also according to order; for when a man has become spiritual
and celestial he then no longer thinks from truth, but from
good; yet not from the Divine good united to the Divine
truth, as did the Lord. This is the reason why the doctrine
of love and charity is now for the first time mentioned, although regarded in itself the doctrine of faith is the same;
and the Lord's perception and thought in everything of faith
was always from the Divine Love. Hence it is that the doctrine of love and charity is the Divine doctrine itself, and is
that which was cultivated in the most ancient churches; and
because this made a one with the doctrine of faith, they cast
out those who separated them (see n. 2417).

2572. *Dwell in that which is good in thine eyes.* That this
signifies that He was in everything where there was good (in
the proximate sense, that He was in the good of doctrine)
is evident from the' signification of "eyes," as being the intellectual, which is of doctrine; and from the signification of
"dwelling," as being to live (n. 1293); here *Esse* (being), because it is predicated of the Lord. *Esse* in everything where
there is good, is *Esse* in the omniscience of all Divine, celestial, spiritual, rational, and natural things, and this from Divine love; for in the Divine Love there is omniscience of all
these things (n. 2500). [2] Moreover there are both the good
and the truth of doctrine. The good of doctrine is love and
charity, the truth of doctrine is faith. They who are in the
good of doctrine, that is, in love and charity, are in the truth of
doctrine, that is, in faith. But it is one thing to be in good, or
in love and charity, and another to be in the good of doctrine.
Little children who are in love to their parents and in charity
toward other little children are in good, but not in the good
of doctrine, consequently not in the truth of doctrine, or
faith. But they who have been regenerated by the truths of
faith are in the good of doctrine. In so far as these are in

good, so far are they in truths; that is, in so far as they are in love and charity, so far are they in faith, consequently, so far in wisdom and intelligence. [**3**] The angels, being in love to the Lord and in mutual love, are also in all truth, and thus in all wisdom and intelligence; not only in regard to celestial and spiritual things, but also in regard to rational and natural things; for from love, because from the Lord, they are in the very principles or springs of things; that is, in their ends and causes. To see from principles, or from ends and causes, is to see from heaven all things that are below, even those which are on the earth. To use a comparison, this is like one who is on a high mountain, in a watch-tower, who is able to look around for many miles upon the things below; while they who are below, especially if they are in a valley or in a forest, can scarcely see as many paces. Precisely so is it with those who are in the good of doctrine, in comparison with those who are in the truth of doctrine separated from its good; although the latter think that they see farther than the former. Nevertheless these see nothing of good, nor anything of truth except very slightly on the surface, and even this defiled by falsities. [**4**] Yet at the best the wisdom and intelligence of angels is finite, and in comparison with the Lord's Divine wisdom, most finite, and scarcely anything; as is evident from the fact that between the Infinite and the finite there is no ratio; but yet there is a communication from the Divine omnipotence; and also from the fact that the Lord is Good Itself and Love Itself, consequently the *Esse* itself of good, and the *Esse* itself of the love that exists with the angels, and thus the *Esse* itself of their wisdom and intelligence. From this we can see that the Lord is in everything in which there is good, both in heaven and on earth. They who think that the Lord is in truth separate from good are much mistaken. He is not in anything but good, and from that in truth; that is, in love and charity, and from that in faith.

2573. Verse 16. *And unto Sarah he said, Behold I have given thy brother a thousand of silver ; behold it is unto thee a covering of the eyes to all that are with thee, and with all ; and she was vindicated.* "And unto Sarah he said," signifies perception from spiritual truth; "behold I have given thy brother a thousand of silver," signifies an abundance of rational truth adjoined to celestial good; "behold it is unto thee a covering of the eyes to all that are with thee," signifies that rational truths are like a covering or clothing to spiritual truths; "and with all," signifies that so also are the derivative truths; "and she was vindicated," signifies that thus there was no fault and no harm.

2574. *And unto Sarah he said.* That this signifies perception from spiritual truth, is evident from the representation of "Sarah a wife," as being Divine spiritual truth (see n. 2507), and of the same as a "sister," as being rational truth (see n. 2508); and from the signification of "saying," as being to perceive (see n. 2506). Sarah is here addressed as a wife, and also as a sister; as a wife, inasmuch as she had been restored (n. 2569), and as a sister, inasmuch as it is said, "I have given thy brother a thousand of silver;" and that which was said by Abimelech was perceived by Sarah in the former relation; therefore by "saying to Sarah" is signified to perceive from spiritual truth.   [2] It is evident that these things involve deeper arcana than can be set forth to the apprehension; and even if they were set forth merely to some extent, it would be necessary to explain many things first that are as yet unknown; such as what spiritual truth is, and what perception from spiritual truth is; that the Lord alone had perception from spiritual truth; that as the Lord had implanted rational truth in rational good, so had He implanted spiritual truth in celestial good, thus continually the Human in the Divine, so that there might be in everything a marriage of the Human with the Divine, and of the Divine with the Human. These and many more things must come first, before the things in this verse can be unfolded to the apprehension. These things are chiefly adapted to the minds of angels who are in the understanding of such things, and for whom is the internal sense of the Word. To them these things are represented in a heavenly manner, and thereby, and by the things contained in this chapter, it is insinuated how the Lord by degrees cast out the human from the mother, until at last He was no longer her son (that He did not acknowledge her as His mother, is manifest in *Matthew* xii. 46–49; *Mark* iii. 31–35; *Luke* viii. 20, 21;

John ii. 4); also how He made the Human Divine by His own power, even until He was one with the Father, as He Himself teaches in *John* xiv. 6, 8–11, and elsewhere. [3] These things are presented by the Lord to the angels in clear light by means of myriads of ideas and representations, all ineffable. The reason as before said is that such things are adapted to their minds, and when in them they are in the blessedness of their intelligence and the happiness of their wisdom. Moreover as there are angels who when they were men had conceived an idea of the Lord's Human as of the human with another man, in order that in the other life these may be able to be with the celestial angels (for there ideas inspired by the affection of good conjoin), such things are dispersed by means of the spiritual sense of the Word, and in this way they are perfected. This shows how precious to the angels is that which is contained in the internal sense of the Word, although perchance it may appear as but of little consequence to man, who has so obscure an idea about such things that it is scarcely any idea at all.

2575. *Behold I have given to thy brother a thousand of silver.* That this signifies an infinite abundance of rational truth adjoined to good, is evident from the signification of a "thousand," as being much and countless; here infinite, or an infinite abundance, because predicated of the Lord (concerning which signification see below); from the signification of "silver," as being rational truth (see n. 1551, 2048); and from the signification of "brother," as being celestial good adjoined to rational truth, as a brother to a sister (n. 2524, 2557). From all this it is evident that "I have given to thy brother a thousand of silver" signifies an infinite abundance of rational truth adjoined to good. Its being given to good, which is the "brother," but not to truth, is because truth is from good, not good from truth. (Concerning this infinite abundance, see above, n. 2572.) [2] That in the Word a "thousand" signifies much and countless, and when predicated of the Lord what is infinite, is manifest from the following passages. In *Moses* :—

I Jehovah thy God am a jealous God, visiting the iniquity of the fathers upon the sons, upon the third and upon the fourth generation of them that hate Me, and showing mercy unto thousands of them that love Me, and keep My commandments (*Exod.* xx. 5, 6 ; xxxiv. 7 ; *Deut.* v. 9, 10).

And in *Jeremiah :*—

Jehovah showeth mercy unto thousands, and recompenseth the iniquity of the fathers into the bosom of their sons after them (xxxii. 18).

In these passages by " thousands" is not signified any definite number, but what is infinite, for the Lord's mercy is infinite, because Divine. In *David :*—

The chariots of God are two myriads, thousands upon thousands ; the Lord is among them, Sinai in holiness (*Ps.* lxviii. 17) ;

where " myriads" and " thousands" denote things innumerable. [3] In the same :—

A thousand shall fall at thy side, and a myriad at thy right hand ; it shall not come nigh thee (*Ps.* xci. 7) ;

where also a " thousand" and a " myriad" denote things innumerable ; and as it is concerning the Lord, who in the *Psalms* is meant by " David," they denote all who are His enemies. In the same :—

Our garners are full, affording all manner of food, our flocks bring forth a thousand and ten thousand in our streets (*Ps.* cxliv. 13) ;

where also a " thousand," and " ten thousand," that is, a myriad, denote things innumerable. In the same :—

A thousand years in Thine eyes are as yesterday when it is past (*Ps.* xc. 4) ;

a " thousand years" denote what is without time, and therefore eternity, which is infinity of time. In *Isaiah :*—

One thousand from before the rebuke of one, from before the rebuke of five shall ye flee, until ye be left as a mast upon the top of a mountain (xxx. 17) ;

where " one thousand" denotes many without any definite number; and " five" a few (n. 649). In *Moses :*—

Jehovah the God of your fathers make you a thousand times as many more as ye are, and bless you (*Deut.* i. 11) ;

where a " thousand times" denotes numberless, as in common speech, in which also a " thousand" is used for many ; as when it is said that a thing has been said a thousand times, or done in a thousand ways. In like manner in *Joshua :*—

One man of you shall chase a thousand, for Jehovah your God fighteth for you (xxiii. 10).

[4] As in computation a "thousand" is a definite number, it appears in the prophecies, especially when connected with history, as if a "thousand" meant simply a thousand, when yet it signifies many or innumerable, apart from any fixed number; for historical matters are of such a nature as to determine the ideas into the nearest and proper significations of the words, as also to the names given; when yet real things are signified in the Word by numbers as well as by names (as is evident from what has been shown before, n. 482, 487, 575, 647, 648, 755, 813, 1963, 1988, 2075, 2252). Hence also it is supposed by some that by the "thousand years" in the *Revelation* (chapter xx. 1–7) there are meant a thousand years or a thousand periods, for the reason as already said that things prophetic are there described under the form of history; when yet by the "thousand years" nothing is there meant except an indeterminate large amount, as elsewhere also infinity of time, or eternity.

2576. *Behold it is unto thee a covering of the eyes to all that are with thee.* That this signifies that rational truths are like a covering or clothing to spiritual truths, is evident from the signification of a "covering" (concerning which presently); and from the signification of the "eyes," as being things intellectual (as is evident from very many passages in the Word); and also from the signification of "seeing," as being to understand (n. 2150, 2325). Every one can see that in everything in this verse there are arcana which cannot be revealed except by some interior sense; such as the statement that he gave a thousand of silver, and that this is said to have been given, not to her husband, but to her brother; that it was a covering of the eyes both to her and to all that were with her, and also with all; and that thereby she was vindicated. Many historical conjectures might possibly be drawn from the sense of the letter, but without having anything spiritual in them, still less anything Divine; and yet this is what the Word is. [2] As regards rational truths being like a covering or clothing to spiritual truths, the case is this: Man's inmost things are those of his soul, and his outer things are those of his body; the former are goods and truths, from which the soul has its life, for otherwise the soul would not be a soul : the latter draw their life therefrom, and are all like a body, or what is the same, a covering or clothing. This is especially evident from the things that appear in the other life; as from angels when presented to view; for their interiors shine forth from their faces; their exteriors being represented in both their bodies and their dress; and this so fully that every one there can know their quality from their garments alone; for these are real substances, and thus essences in form. The same is the case with the angels seen and described in respect to their faces and dress in the Word, such as those seen in the Lord's sepulchre (*Matt.* xxviii. 3; *Mark* xvi. 5); and the four and twenty elders around the throne (*Rev.* iv. 4); and others. Nor is this the case with the angels only, but also with all other things that are mentioned in the Word, even those which are inanimate; in all cases their exteriors are a covering or clothing; as for example the ark of the covenant and the tent that was round about it; the ark, being the inmost, represented the Lord Himself, for therein was the Testimony; and the tent outside of it represented the Lord's kingdom. The clothing, that is, the veils and coverings, each and all represented the more exterior celestial and spiritual things in His kingdom, that is, in the three heavens; as is evident from the fact that the form of the Tent was shown to Moses on Mount Sinai (*Exod.* xxv. 9; xxvi. 30). From this it had its holiness, and not from the gold, the silver, and the carvings, that were in it. [3] Since rational truths are now treated of, as being a kind of veil or clothing to spiritual truths, and as the tent is described in *Moses* in respect to its clothing or coverings, and also in respect to its veils which were before the entrance, for the sake of illustration we may explain what was specifically signified by the veils; but what was signified by the encompassing coverings will of the Lord's Divine mercy be told elsewhere. The veils of the tent were three : the first, which made the division between the Holy and the Holy of Holies; the second, which is called the hanging for the door of the tent; and the third, which was the hanging for the gate of the court. [4] Concerning *the veil itself*, which was the first, before the ark, we read in *Moses* :—

Thou shalt make a veil of hyacinthine, and bright crimson, and double-dyed scarlet, and fine-twined linen, the work of a designer, thou shalt make it with cherubim ; and thou shalt hang it upon four pillars of shittim-wood, overlaid with gold, and their hooks of gold ; upon four bases of silver ; and thou shalt hang the veil under the clasps ; and thou shalt bring in thither, within the veil, the Ark of the Testimony ; and the veil shall divide unto you between the Holy and the Holy of Holies (*Exod.* xxvi. 31–34 ; xxxvi. 35, 36).

This veil represented the nearest and inmost appearances of rational good and truth, in which are the angels of the third heaven ; which appearances are described by the hyacinthine, the bright crimson, the double-dyed scarlet, and the fine-twined linen ; in which the red color represented the goods of love, and the white its truths. The same is true also of the gold and silver with which the pillars were overlaid, and of which the hooks and the bases were made. (That colors are representative may be seen above, n. 1042, 1043, 1053, 1624 ; that "gold" is the good of love, n. 113, 1551, 1552 ; and that "silver" is truth, n. 1551, 2048.) [5] From this we can see what is signified by the veil of the temple being rent in twain (*Matt.* xxvii. 51 ; *Mark* xv. 38 ; *Luke* xxiii. 45), namely, that the Lord entered into the Divine Itself by dispersing all appearances ; and that He at the same time opened the way to His Divine Itself through His Human made Divine. [6] Concerning the second veil, or the hanging for the door of the tent, we read in *Moses :—*

Thou shalt make a hanging for the door of the tent, of hyacinthine, and bright crimson, and double-dyed scarlet, and fine-twined linen, the work of the embroiderer ; and thou shalt make for the hanging five pillars of shittim-wood, and overlay them with gold, and their hooks shall be of gold ; and thou shalt cast for them five bases of brass (*Exod.* xxvi. 36, 37 ; xxxvi. 37, 38).

By this hanging were represented appearances of good and truth that are lower or more external than the former, that is, the middle ones of the rational, in which are the angels of the second heaven ; which appearances are described almost in the same manner as the first, with the difference however that for this hanging there were five pillars and five bases, by which number is signified what is comparatively but little ; for these appearances do not so cohere together, or are not so heavenly, as are the appearances of the inmost or third heaven. (Concerning the number five as meaning a little, see above, n. 649, 1686.) And because these appearances look to natural things, it was commanded that the bases should be cast of brass; for by brass was represented and signified natural good (n. 425, 1551). [7] Concerning the third veil, or the hanging for the gate of the court, we read in *Moses :*—

For the gate of the court shall be a hanging of twenty cubits, of hyacinthine, and bright crimson, and double-dyed scarlet, and fine-twined linen, the work of the embroiderer; their pillars four, and their bases four; all the pillars of the court round about shall be filleted with silver, their hooks of silver, but their bases of brass (*Exod.* xxvii. 16, 17; xxxviii. 18, 19).

By this hanging were represented still lower or more external appearances of good and truth, which are the lowest ones of the rational, in which are the angels of the first heaven. As these appearances correspond to interior things, they are described in a similar manner, yet with the difference that these pillars were not overlaid with gold, but filleted with silver, and that the hooks were of silver, by which are signified rational truths that derive their origin immediately from memory-knowledges; and the bases were of brass, by which are signified natural goods. All this shows that there was nothing in the Tent that was not representative of the celestial and spiritual things of the Lord's kingdom, or that all things were made according to the type of celestial and spiritual things in the three heavens; also that the veilings or coverings signified the things that are like a body or dress around or without the inmost. [8] Moreover that "veilings," "coverings," "clothing," or "garments" signify relatively lower truths, is evident from many passages in the Word, as in *Ezekiel :*—

Fine linen with broidered work from Egypt was thy spread of sail; hyacinthine and bright crimson from the isles of Elishah was thy covering (xxvii. 7);

where Tyre is treated of, by which are signified interior knowledges of celestial and spiritual things, and consequently those who are in them (n. 1201); "broidered work from Egypt" denotes what is of memory-knowledge (that "Egypt" denotes this may be seen above, n. 1164, 1165, 1186, 1462); "hyacinthine

and bright crimson from the isles of Elishah, which was the
covering," denote the rituals that correspond to internal worship (n. 1156).   [9] In the same :—

All the princes of the sea shall come down from their thrones, and lay
aside their robes, and put off their broidered garments ; they shall be
clothed with tremblings, they shall sit upon the earth (xxvi. 16) ;

also speaking of Tyre ; "robes" and "broidered garments"
denote knowledges derived from the contents of the memory
(*cognitionibus ex scientificis*), and thus lower truths.   [10] In
the same : —

I clothed thee with broidered work, and shod thee with badger, and
girded thee about with fine linen, and covered thee with silk ; I decked
thee also with ornaments, and put bracelets upon thy hands, and a neck-
lace upon thy throat.   Thou didst take of thy garments, and madest for
thee high places with divers colors, and didst commit whoredom upon
them ; thou tookest thy broidered garments, and coveredst them (xvi.
10, 11, 16, 18) ;

speaking of Jerusalem, which is the spiritual church, described
as it was of old, and such as it was afterwards, when perverted : its lower spiritual things and its doctrinal matters are
the "garments of broidered work, fine linen, and silk."   [11]
In *Isaiah* :—

The Lord Jehovih Zebaoth doth take away from Jerusalem the whole
staff of bread and the staff of water.   Then shall a man take hold of his
brother, of the house of his father—Thou hast a garment, be thou our
prince.   In that day he shall lift up his voice, saying, I will not be a
binder up, and in my house there is neither bread, nor garment ; ye shall
not make me a prince of the people.   The Lord will smite with a scab the
crown of the head of the daughters of Zion ; and in that day the Lord
will take away the bravery of their anklets, and their network, and cres-
cents, and their collars, and chains, and plates ; and the headtires, and
the ankle chains, and the sashes, and the soul houses, and the ear-drops ;
the rings, and the nose jewels, the festival garments, and the mantles,
and the robes, and the satchels, the mirrors, and the fine linen, and the
turbans, and the cloaks (iii. 1, 6, 7, 17–24).

"Jerusalem" denotes the spiritual church ; "Judah" the celestial church ; the "staff of bread and the staff of water, which
will be removed," denote good and truth ; the "garment which
the prince should have," the truths which are of doctrine ;
the clothing and various ornaments of the daughters of Zion,
which are enumerated, all and each, the kinds and varieties of

good and truth, of which they would be deprived. Unless
everything here mentioned signified something peculiar to the
church, they would not be of the Word, in every expression
of which there is what is Divine; but they are predicated
of the daughters of Zion, and by these are signified the things
of the church, as may be seen above (n. 2362). [12] In the
same :—

Awake! awake! put on thy strength, O Zion; put on the garments of
thy beauty, O Jerusalem, the city of holiness; for henceforth there shall
no more come into thee the uncircumcised and the unclean (*Isa.* lii. 1, 2);

"Zion" denotes the celestial church; "Jerusalem" the spiritual church; and "garments of beauty" the holy things of
faith. In the same :—

Their webs shall not become a garment, neither shall they cover themselves with their works; their works are works of iniquity (*Isa.* lix. 6);

"webs" denote fictitious truths that do not become a garment;
a "garment" denotes the exterior truths of doctrine and of
worship; hence it is said, "neither shall they cover themselves
with their works." [13] In the same :—

Rejoicing I will rejoice in Jehovah, my soul shall exult in my God;
for He hath clothed me with the garments of salvation, He hath covered
me with the robe of righteousness (*Isa.* lxi. 10);

the "garments of salvation" denote the truths of faith; and
the "robe of righteousness" the good of charity. In *John :—*

Thou hast a few names even in Sardis that have not defiled their garments; and they shall walk with Me in white, for they are worthy; he
that overcometh shall be clothed in white raiment (*Rev.* iii. 4, 5).

In the same :—

Blessed is he that watcheth, and keepeth his garments, lest he walk
naked (*Rev.* xvi. 15).

In the same :—

Upon the thrones I saw four and twenty elders sitting, clothed in white
garments (*Rev.* iv. 4);

where it is manifest that the "garments" are not garments,
but the spiritual things of truth. [14] So where the Lord
said in reference to the consummation of the age that they
should not return back to take their garments (*Matt.* xxiv. 18;

Mark xiii. 16), where that "garments" are truths may be seen above (n. 2454). Also in regard to the one not clothed in a wedding garment (*Matt.* xxii. 11, 12). And concerning *John* :—

What went ye out to see ? a man clothed in bright * garments ? Behold they that wear bright * garments are in kings' houses (*Matt.* xi. 8 ; *Luke* vii. 25) ;

meaning that they were not in the externals of doctrine and worship, but in the internals ; on which account He adds :—

What went ye out to see ? a prophet ? yea, I say unto you and more than a prophet (*Matt.* xi. 9) ;

a "prophet" denotes the externals of doctrine and of worship. [15] As "garments" signified truths of every kind, it was commanded that the sons of Israel on going out of Egypt should borrow gold and silver, and garments, and put them upon their sons (*Exod.* iii. 22 ; xii. 35, 36) ; also that garments of various kinds, or mixed garments, should not be worn (*Lev.* xix. 19 ; *Deut.* xxii. 11) ; and that they should make for themselves fringes on the borders of their garments, and should put a blue thread there, and that when they saw it they should call to mind the commandments, and do them (*Num.* xv. 38–40). [16] Formerly also they rent their garments (as is seen in *Josh.* vii. 6 ; *Judges* xi. 35 ; 1 *Sam.* iv. 12 ; 2 *Sam.* i. 2, 11, 12 ; iii. 31 ; xiii. 30, 31 ; xv. 32 ; 1 *Kings* xxi. 27 ; 2 *Kings* v. 7, 8 ; vi. 30 ; xxii. 11, 14, 19 ; *Isa.* xxxvi. 22 ; xxxvii. 1) ; by which was signified zeal for doctrine and truth, which was thus torn to pieces ; and also humiliation, because there was nothing appertaining to them that is signified by the adornment of garments. [17] That such things are signified by "veilings," "coverings," "clothing," or "garments," is also manifest from the prophecy of Jacob, then Israel :—

He shall bind his foal to the vine, and his ass's colt unto the choice vine ; he shall wash his garments in wine, and his clothes in the blood of grapes (*Gen.* xlix. 11) ;

what these words signify can be known to none except from the internal sense ; namely a "vine," a "choice vine," a "foal," an "ass's colt," "wine," the "blood of grapes," "garments,"

---

* *Splendidis* and *splendida ;* but *mollibus* and *mollia* in n. 9372. [*Rotch ed.*]

and "clothes;" but it is evident that they are predicated of the Lord, who is here called "Shiloh." The subject spoken of is Judah, by whom is represented the Lord's Divine celestial; and by the "garments he should wash in wine," and "the vesture he should wash in the blood of grapes," are signified the Lord's rational and natural, which He should make Divine.   [18] In like manner in *Isaiah :*—

Who is this that cometh from Edom, with dyed garments from Bozrah? this that is glorious in His apparel, marching in the multitude of His strength? Wherefore art Thou red in Thine apparel, and Thy garment like him that treadeth in the wine-vat? I have trodden the winepress alone, and of the peoples there was none with Me; their victory is sprinkled upon My garments, and I have stained all My raiment (lxiii. 1–3);

where also "garments" and "raiment" denote the Lord's Human which of His own power He made Divine by combats of temptations and by victories; on which account it is said, "I have trodden the winepress alone, and of the peoples there was none with Me." Isaac's smelling the smell of Esau's garments, and so blessing him (*Gen.* xxvii. 27), involved the same.   [19] The Holy itself of the Lord's Divine Human was also a garment which appeared as the light, and as white and glistening, when He was transfigured, concerning which we read in *Matthew :*—

When Jesus was transfigured, His face did shine as the sun, and His garments became as the light (xvii. 2).

In *Luke :*—

When Jesus prayed, the appearance of His countenance was changed, and His raiment became white and glistening (ix. 29).

And in *Mark :*—

When Jesus was transfigured, His garments became shining, exceeding white like snow, so as no fuller on earth can white them (ix. 3).

The garments of holiness with which Aaron was clothed when he entered within the veil, and which were of linen, had a similar representation (*Lev.* xvi. 2, 4): likewise the garments of holiness that were for glory and for beauty; and those of his ministry (*Exod.* xxviii. 2 to the end, and xxxix. 1 to the end) : for in these there was not one whit that was not representative.

2577. *And with all.* That this signifies that so also are the derivative truths, namely, those of memory and of the senses, is evident from what has been said above, and from the series itself; for it is said just above, " behold it shall be unto thee a veiling of the eyes unto all who are with thee;" by which are signified rational truths, which are like a veil to spiritual truths; and it is now said again, " with all;" by which are therefore signified still lower truths which are derived from rational truths; these being no other than what are called memory truths and sensuous truths. That these truths are derived from rational truths is evident from the order of influx. Interior things flow into exterior things; or what is the same, higher things into lower; but not the reverse. It indeed appears otherwise, namely, that man becomes rational by means of the things of sense and of memory, but this is a fallacy. Good from the Lord is constantly flowing in through man's rational faculty, and it meets and adopts to itself the knowledges in the memory; and in so far as it can do this, and dispose them in due order, so far the man becomes rational. The case herein is the same as with the good and truths which are called those of faith : good from the Lord flows into truths, and adopts them, and in so far as it can do this the man becomes spiritual; although it appears as if truths, called the truths of faith, flow in, and render the man spiritual. It is also owing to this appearance that the truth of faith is so much cultivated at this day, while the good of charity is not thought of.

2578. *And she was vindicated.* That this signifies that thus there was no fault and no harm, is evident from all that precedes, of which this is a brief conclusion.

2579. Verse 17. *And Abraham prayed unto God, and God healed Abimelech, and his wife, and his maidservants; and they brought forth.* " Abraham prayed unto God," signifies a revelation ; " and God healed Abimelech," signifies soundness of the doctrine in respect to good; "and his wife," signifies in respect to truth; "and his maidservants," signifies in respect to the affections of doctrinal things ; "and they brought forth," signifies their fruitfulness.

2580. *Abraham prayed unto God.* That this signifies revelation, is evident from the signification of "praying" when

predicated of the Lord, as being to be revealed (see n. 2535);
and from the representation of Abraham, as being the Lord—
often shown above.   Here in the sense of the letter there are
two, namely, one who prayed, and another to whom he
prayed; for it is said, "Abraham prayed unto God."   But in
the internal sense there are not two, but one; for it was God
or Jehovah in the Lord who made the revelation, because He
was conceived of Jehovah; yet in so far as He had that which
belonged to the maternal human, so far He was another.
How the case is herein can with difficulty fall into the ideas
so as to be understood.   These things can indeed fall into
angelic ideas, which are presented in the light of heaven; but
not so well into human ideas, which do not perceive unless
illuminated by things that are of the light of the world; still
less can they fall into the ideas of those to whom everything
that is of the light of heaven is thick darkness, so as to be
nothing at all.

2581. *And God healed Abimelech.*   That this signifies the
soundness of the doctrine in respect to good, is evident from
the signification of "healing," as being to make sound; and
from the representation of Abimelech, as being the doctrine of
faith looking to rational things (n. 2510).   That it is in respect to *good* is evident from the fact that his wife also is said
to be healed, by which is meant the soundness of the doctrine
in respect to truth; for when in the Word a husband is called
"husband," and also when he is called by name, he then signifies good, and his wife truth; but when a husband is called
a "man," he then signifies truth, and his wife good (see also n.
915, 1468, 2517).

2582. *And his wife.*   That this signifies in respect to truth,
is evident from the signification of a "wife," as being truth
(see just above, n. 2581).

2583. *And his maidservants.*   That this signifies in respect
to the affections of the derivative doctrinal things, is evident
from the signification of "maidservants," as being the affections of the things of the reason and of the memory (see n.
1895, 2567); here of doctrinal things, because they are predicated of the doctrine of faith (for they belonged to Abimelech,
by whom is signified the doctrine of faith, n. 2509, 2510); for

the signification of everything is determined by what is being treated of.

2584. *And they brought forth.* That this signifies fruitfulness, is evident from the signification of "bringing forth" and of "birth." In the internal sense of the Word none but spiritual and celestial things are signified; on which account where mention is made of "conception" or of "conceiving;" of "bearing" or of "bringing forth;" of "birth" or of "being born;" of "generation" or of "generating," as well as of those who beget, as "father and mother;" and of those who are begotten, as "sons and daughters," all these are meant in none but a spiritual sense, for in itself the Word is spiritual and celestial; and such is the case here in regard to "bringing forth," by which is signified fruitfulness in respect to the things of doctrine. [2] That in the Word "birth" means no other kind of birth than this, is evident from the passages that follow. In *Samuel :—*

The full have hired out themselves for bread, and the hungry have ceased, until the barren hath borne seven, and she that hath many children hath languished ; Jehovah killeth and maketh alive. He causeth to go down into hell, and bringeth up (1 *Sam.* ii. 5, 6).

In *Jeremiah :—*

She that hath borne seven languisheth, she breatheth out her soul ; her sun is gone down while it is yet day (xv. 9).

In *Isaiah :—*

Sing, O barren, that did not bear ; break forth into singing and cry aloud, that did not travail with child ; for more are the sons of the desolate than the sons of the married wife, saith Jehovah (liv. 1).

In *David :—*

The voice of Jehovah maketh the hinds to calve, and strippeth the forests ; and in His temple every one speaketh glory (*Ps.* xxix. 9).

In *Isaiah :—*

Blush O Zidon, for the sea hath spoken, the stronghold of the sea, saying, I have not travailed, nor brought forth, neither have I brought up young men, nor caused maids to grow up ; as with the report of Egypt, they shall travail according to the report of Tyre (xxiii. 4, 5).

In the same :—

Before she travailed she brought forth, and before her pain came she was delivered of a man child. Who hath heard such a thing ? who hath

seen such things ? Does the earth travail in one day, and shall I not
cause to bring forth ? saith Jehovah ; shall I cause to bring forth, and
close up ? said thy God (lxvi. 7–9).

In *Jeremiah* :—

Ask I pray and see whether a man bringeth forth ; wherefore have I
seen every man with his hands on his loins, as one that bringeth forth
(xxx. 6).

In *Ezekiel* :—

I will set a fire in Egypt, and Sin travailing shall travail, and No may
be . . . (xxx. 16).

In *Hosea* :—

Ephraim, their glory shall fly away like a bird, from the birth, and
from the womb, and from conception (ix. 11).

In the same :—

The pains of one that travaileth came upon Ephraim ; he is an unwise
son, for at the time he will not stand in the place of the breaking forth
of sons (xiii. 13).

In *John* :—

A woman clothed with the sun, and the moon under her feet, and upon
her head a crown of twelve stars ; and she being with child cried, travailing, and pained to bring forth. The dragon stood before the woman who
was about to bring forth, that when she brought forth her son, he might
devour him. And she brought forth a man child, who was to pasture all
nations with a rod of iron ; but the child was caught up unto God and to
His throne (*Rev.* xii. 1–5).

[3] Who cannot see from all these passages that no other con-
ceptions and births are signified than those which are of the
church ?   And the same is the case with what is here said
concerning Abimelech, that " God healed Abimelech, and his
wife, and his maidservants, and they brought forth;" and that
" Jehovah closing had closed up every womb of the house of
Abimelech, because of the word of Sarah, Abraham's wife."
What is signified by these things in the internal sense is evident from the explication of the same, namely, the quality of
the doctrine of faith when regarded from Divine truths, and
when regarded from the rational : when it is regarded from
Divine truths, that is, from the Word, then each and all things,
of both reason and memory, confirm it; but this is not the case

when it is regarded from human things, that is, from reason and memory-knowledges; for then nothing of good and nothing of truth is conceived; for to regard it from the Word is to regard it from the Lord, whereas to regard it from reason and memory-knowledge is to regard it from man. From the former comes all intelligence and wisdom; from the latter all insanity and folly.

2585. Verse 18. *For closing Jehovah had therefore closed every womb of the house of Abimelech, because of the word of Sarah, Abraham's wife.* "For closing Jehovah had therefore closed every womb of the house of Abimelech," signifies the barrenness of the doctrine; "because of the word of Sarah," signifies by reason of the rational, if it had conjoined itself; "Abraham's wife," signifies that spiritual truth might be conjoined with celestial good.

2586. *For closing Jehovah had therefore closed every womb of the house of Abimelech.* That this signifies barrenness, namely, of doctrine, is evident from the signification of "closing to close up the womb," as being to prevent conception itself; and from the signification of "the house of Abimelech," as being the good of the doctrine of faith, which shows that barrenness is signified. That up to this point in this chapter "God" is mentioned, but here for the first time "Jehovah," is because "God" is mentioned where the subject is truth, but "Jehovah" where the subject is good. All the conception of doctrine is from good as a father, but its birth is by means of truth as a mother, as occasionally stated before. Here the conception of doctrine is treated of, and as this is from good, "Jehovah" is mentioned; whereas above its birth is treated of, and as this takes place by means of truth, "God" is mentioned, as in the verse preceding: "God healed Abimelech, and his wife, and his maidservants, and they brought forth." [2] The case is the same elsewhere in the Word where conception is treated of, as in *Isaiah:*— .

Jehovah hath called me from the womb. Thus saith Jehovah that formed me from the womb; then shall I be precious to Jehovah; and my God shall be my strength (xlix. 1, 5);

"strength" is predicated of truth, and therefore "God" is mentioned. In the same :—

Thus saith Jehovah thy Maker, and thy Former from the womb (xliv. 2, 24, and elsewhere).

For the same reason it is said "the house of Abimelech," by which is signified the good of the doctrine of faith (that a "house" denotes good may be seen above, n. 2048, 2233, 2234; and that "Abimelech" denotes the doctrine of faith, n. 2509, 2510). That there is a Divine arcanum in the fact that they brought forth, and that the wombs of the house of Abimelech were shut on account of Sarah, is manifest; and this arcanum cannot possibly be disclosed except by the internal sense.

2587. *Because of the word of Sarah.* That this signifies by reason of the rational if it had conjoined itself, is evident from the representation of "Sarah" as a sister, as being rational truth (see n. 2508). The "word of Sarah" signifies the whole transaction, namely, that she was called a sister, and that Abimelech took her, but that he did not come near her. What these things signify further will be told in what follows.

2588. *Abraham's wife.* That this signifies in order that spiritual truth might be conjoined with celestial good, is evident from the representation of Sarah as a wife, as being spiritual truth conjoined with celestial good (see n. 1468, 1901, 2063, 2065, 2172, 2173, 2198, 2507); and from the representation of Abraham, as being celestial good conjoined with spiritual truth (see n. 2011, 2172, 2198, 2501). Whether we say "spiritual truth and celestial good," or "the Lord," it is the same; because the Lord is truth itself and good itself, and is the very marriage itself of truth and good, and of good and truth. How the case herein is can indeed be seen from the explication; but as these matters are among those which are obscure at this day, we may so far as possible illustrate them. The subject here treated of is the doctrine of faith, concerning which the Lord thought in His childhood, namely, whether it was allowable to enter into it by means of rational things, and thus form for one's self ideas concerning it. His so thinking came from His love and consideration for the human race, who are such as not to believe what they do not comprehend in a rational manner. But He perceived from the Divine that this ought not to be done; and He therefore revealed the doctrine to Himself from the Divine, and thereby at the same time all things in the universe that are subordinate, namely, all things of the rational and of the natural. [2] How the case is with the doctrinal things of faith among men has been stated above (n. 2568), namely, that there are two principles from which they think, a negative and an affirmative; and that those think from the negative principle, who believe nothing unless they are convinced by what is of reason and memory-knowledge; nay, by what is of sense; but those think from the affirmative who believe that things are true because the Lord has said so in the Word, thus who have faith in the Lord. They who are in the negative in regard to a thing being true because it is in the Word, say at heart that they will believe when they are persuaded by things rational and memory-knowledges. But the fact is that they never believe; and indeed they would not believe if they were to be convinced by the bodily senses of sight, hearing, and touch; for they would always form new reasonings against such things, and would thus end by completely extinguishing all faith, and at the same time turning the light of the rational into darkness, because into falsities. But those who are in the affirmative, that is, who believe that things are true because the Lord has said so, are continually being confirmed, and their ideas enlightened and strengthened, by what is of reason and memory-knowledge, and even by what is of sense; for man has light from no other source than by means of the things of reason and memory, and such is the way with every one. With these the doctrine thus "living lives;" and of them it is said, that they "are healed," and "bring forth;" whereas with those who are in the negative the doctrine "dying dies;" and it is said of them that "the womb closing is closed." All this shows what it is to enter into the doctrine of faith by means of rational things, and what to enter into rational things by means of the doctrine of faith; but let this be illustrated by examples. [3] It is from the doctrine of the Word, that the first and principal thing of doctrine is love to the Lord and charity toward the neighbor. They who are in the affirmative in regard to this can enter into whatever things of reason and of memory, and even of sense, they please, every one according to his gift,

his knowledge, and his experience. Nay, the more they enter
in, the more they are confirmed; for universal nature is full
of confirmation. But they who deny this first and principal
thing of doctrine, and who desire to be first convinced of anything true by means of the things of reason and memory,
never suffer themselves to be convinced, because at heart they
deny, and all the time take their stand in favor of some other
principle which they believe to be essential; and finally, by
confirmations of their principle they so blind themselves that
they cannot even know what love to the Lord and love to the
neighbor are. And as they confirm themselves in what is
contrary, they at length confirm themselves in the notion that
no other love is possible that has any delight in it except the
love of self and of the world; and this to such a degree (if
not in doctrine, yet in life) that they embrace infernal love in
place of heavenly love. But with those who are not in the
negative nor as yet in the affirmative, but are in doubt before
they deny or affirm, the case is as above stated (n. 2568),
namely that they who incline to a life of evil fall into the
negative, but they who incline to a life of good are brought into
the affirmative. [4] Take another example : It is among
the primary things of the doctrine of faith that all good is
from the Lord, and all evil from man, that is, from one's self.
They who are in the affirmative that it is so, can confirm themselves by many things of reason and of memory-knowledge,
such as that no good can possibly flow in except from good
itself, that is, from the Fountain of Good, thus from the
Lord; and that the beginning or principle of good can be from
no other source; finding illustration in all things that are
truly good, in themselves, in others, in the community, and
also in the created universe. But they who are in the negative confirm themselves in what is contrary by everything
they think of, insomuch that at last they do not know what
good is; and dispute among themselves as to what is the
highest good, being deeply ignorant of the fact that it is the
celestial and spiritual good from the Lord, by which all lower
good is made alive, and that the delight therefrom is truly delight. Some also think that unless good is from themselves,
it cannot possibly come from any other source. [5] Take as

another example the truth that they who are in love to the
Lord and charity toward the neighbor can receive the truths
of doctrine and have faith in the Word, but not they who are
in the life of the love of self and the world; or what is the
same, that they who are in good can believe, but not they who
are in evil.   They who are in the affirmative can confirm this
by numberless things of reason and memory.   From reason
they can confirm it on the ground that truth and good agree,
but not truth and evil; and that as all falsity is *in* evil, so it
is *from* evil; and that if any who are in evil nevertheless have
truth, it is on the lips, and not in the heart; and from their
memory-knowledge they can confirm by many things that
truths shun evils, and that evils spew out truths.   But they
who are in the negative confirm themselves by alleging that
every one, of whatever character, is able to believe just as
well as others, even though he lives in continual hatred, in
the delights of revenge, and in deceit; and this even while
they themselves altogether reject from their doctrine the good
of life, after the rejection of which they do not believe anything.   [6] That it may be still more manifest how the case
herein is, let us take this example: They who are in the affirmative that the Word has been so written as to possess an
internal sense which does not appear in the letter, can confirm
themselves therein by many rational considerations; as that
by the Word man has connection with heaven; that there are
correspondences of natural things with spiritual, in which the
spiritual are not seen; that the ideas of interior thought are
altogether different from the material ideas which fall into the
words of language; that man, being born for both lives, can,
while in the world, be also in heaven, by means of the Word
which is for both worlds; that with some persons a certain Divine light flows into the things of the understanding, and also
into the affections, when the Word is read; that it is of necessity that there should be something written that has come down
from heaven, and that therefore the Word cannot be such in its
origin as it is in the letter; and that it can be holy only from
a certain holiness that it has within it.   He can also confirm
himself by means of memory-knowledges; as that men were
formerly in representatives, and that the writings of the An-

cient Church were of this nature; also that the writings of
many among the Gentiles had this origin; and that it is on this
account that in the churches such a style has been revered as
holy, and among the Gentiles as learned, as examples of which
the books of many authors might be mentioned. But they
who are in the negative, if they do not deny all these things,
still do not believe them, and persuade themselves that the
Word is such as it is in the letter, appearing indeed worldly,
while yet being spiritual (as to where the spiritual is hidden
within it they care little, but for manifold reasons are willing
to let it be so), and this they can confirm by many things.
[7] In order to present the subject to the apprehension of the
simple, take as an example the following matter of knowledge. They who are in the affirmative that sight is not of
the eye, but of the spirit, which sees the things that are in
the world through the eye as an organ of its body, can confirm
themselves by many things; as from our hearing things said
by others; in that they refer themselves to a certain interior
sight, into which they are changed; which would be impossible unless there were an interior sight; also that whatever is
thought of is seen by an interior sight, by some more clearly,
by others more obscurely; and again, that things we imagine
present themselves not unlike objects of sight; and also that
unless it were the spirit within the body that saw the objects
which fall within the ken of the eye as the organ of sight,
the spirit could see nothing in the other life, when yet it cannot but be that it will see innumerable and amazing things
that cannot possibly be seen with the bodily eye. Then again
we may reflect that in dreams, especially those of the prophets,
many things have been seen although not with the eyes.
And finally, should any one be skilled in philosophy, he may
confirm himself by considering that outer things cannot enter
into inner things, just as compounds cannot into simples; and
therefore that things of the body cannot enter into those of
the spirit, but only the reverse; not to mention a host of
other proofs, until at last the man is persuaded that the spirit
has sight, and not the eye, except from the spirit. But they
who are in the negative call every consideration of this kind
either a matter of nature or one of fancy, and when they are

told that a spirit possesses and enjoys much more perfect sight than a man in the body, they ridicule the idea, and reject it as an idle tale, believing that if deprived of the sight of the bodily eye they would live in the dark; although the very opposite is the truth, for they are then in the light. [8] From these examples we may see what it is to enter into the things of reason and memory-knowledge from truths, and what it is to enter into truths from the things of reason and memory-knowledge; and that the former is according to order, but the latter contrary to order; and that when we do that which is according to order we are enlightened; but when we do that which is contrary to order, we are made blind. All of which shows of how great concern it is that truths should be known and believed; for man is enlightened by truths, but is made blind by falsities. By truths there is opened to the rational an immense and almost unbounded field; but by falsities comparatively none at all, although this does not appear to be so. It is because the angels are in truths that they enjoy wisdom so great; for truth is the very light of heaven. [9] They who have blinded themselves by not being willing to believe anything which they do not apprehend by the senses, until at length they have come to believe nothing, were in old times called " serpents of the tree of knowledge ;" for such reasoned much from sensuous things and their fallacies, which easily fall into man's apprehension and belief, and thereby they seduced many (see n. 195, 196). In the other life such are readily distinguished from other spirits by the fact that in regard to all things of faith they reason whether it be so; and if they are shown a thousand and a thousand times that it is so, still they advance negative doubts against every proof that is offered ; and this they would go on doing to all eternity. So blind are they on this account that they have not common sense, that is, they cannot comprehend what good and truth are ; and yet every one of them thinks himself wiser than all in the universe; making wisdom to consist in being able to invalidate what is Divine, and deduce it from what is natural. Many who in this world have been esteemed wise, are pre-eminently of this character; for the more any one is endowed with talent and knowledge, and is in the negative, the more insane he is, beyond all others; whereas the more any one is endowed with talent and knowledge, and is in the affirmative, the wiser he is able to be. It is by no means denied man to cultivate the rational faculty by means of memory-knowledges; but that which is forbidden is to harden ourselves against the truths of faith which belong to the Word. [**10**] These things are much treated of in the internal sen$\text{\v{s}}$e of the Word, especially in that of the prophetic Word, where Asshur (or Assyria) and Egypt are treated of; for reasoning is signified by "Asshur" (n. 119, 1186); and memory-knowledge by "Egypt" (n. 1164, 1165, 1186, 1462). Concerning those who desire to enter into doctrinal and Divine things by means of memory-knowledges and rational things, we read in *Isaiah* :—

I will confound Egypt in Egypt, and they shall fight every man against his brother, and every man against his companion, city against city, and kingdom against kingdom ; and the spirit of Egypt shall be made void in the midst of it, and I will swallow up the counsel thereof ; the waters shall fail from the sea, and the river shall be dried up and shall become totally dry ; and the streams shall vanish, the rivers of Egypt shall be minished and dried up ; the reed and the flag shall wither away ; and all the seed of the river shall become dry. Jehovah hath mingled a spirit of perversities in the midst of her, and they have caused Egypt to go astray in every work thereof, as a drunken man strayeth in his vomit (xix. 2, 3, 5–7, 14).

In the same :—

Woe to the rebellious sons, who walk to go down into Egypt, but have not asked at My mouth, to strengthen themselves in the strength of Pharaoh, and to trust in the shadow of Egypt. And the strength of Pharaoh shall be unto you for a shame, and the trust in the shadow of Egypt for a reproach (xxx. 1–3).

In the same :—

Woe to them that go down into Egypt for help, and stay upon horses, and trust in chariots, because they are many ; but they look not unto the Holy One of Israel, and seek not Jehovah. And when Jehovah shall stretch out His hand, he that helpeth shall stumble, and he that is helped shall fall, and they shall all be consumed together. And Asshur shall fall by the sword not of man, and the sword not of man shall devour him (xxxi. 1, 3, 8).

In *Jeremiah* :—

My people have committed two evils ; they have forsaken Me, the fountain of living waters, to hew them out pits, broken pits, which can hold no water. Is Israel a servant? If he was born of the house, why is he become a prey? Dost thou not do this unto thyself, in that thou hast forsaken Jehovah thy God in the time when He led thee in the way? And now what hast thou to do with the way to Egypt to drink the waters of Shihor? or what hast thou to do with the way of Asshur to drink the waters of the river? O generation, see ye the Word of Jehovah : have I been a wilderness unto Israel? a land of darkness? wherefore said My people, We will rule, we will come no more unto Thee? why goest thou away so much to change thy way? thou shalt be ashamed from Egypt also, as thou wast ashamed from Asshur (ii. 13, 14, 17, 18, 31, 36).

In the same :—

Hear ye the word of Jehovah, O remnant of Judah ; thus saith Jehovah Zebaoth the God of Israel, If setting ye set your faces to come into Egypt, and ye come to sojourn there ; then it shall come to pass that the sword which ye were fearing for yourselves shall overtake you there in the land of Egypt, and the famine whereof ye were afraid shall cleave unto you there in Egypt, that ye die there. So shall it be with all the men who set their faces to come into Egypt, to sojourn there ; they shall die by the sword, by the famine, and by the pestilence ; and none of them shall remain or escape from the evil that I will bring upon you (xlii. 15–17, etc.).

In *Ezekiel :*—

And all the inhabitants of Egypt shall know that I am Jehovah ; because they have been a staff of reed to the house of Israel ; in their taking thee by thy hand thou didst break, and didst rend for them every shoulder, and in their leaning upon thee thou breakest, and makest all their loins to be at a stand ; therefore thus said the Lord Jehovih, Behold I will bring a sword upon thee, and will cut off from thee man and beast, and the land of Egypt shall be a desolation and a waste, and they shall know that I am Jehovah ; because he hath said, The river is mine, and I have made it (xxix. 6–9, etc.).

In *Hosea :*—

Ephraim was like a silly dove ; they called unto Egypt, they went unto Asshur ; when they shall go, I will spread out My net upon them ; woe unto them because they have wandered away from Me (vii. 11–13).

In the same :—

Ephraim feedeth on wind, and followeth after the east wind ; every day he multiplieth a lie and a waste, and they make a covenant with Asshur, and oil is carried down into Egypt (xii. 1).

In the same :—

Israel hath committed whoredom under her god ; thou hast loved hire upon all the corn-floors ; Ephraim shall return into Egypt, and they shall

eat what is unclean in Asshur; for lo they are gone away from devastation, Egypt shall gather them up, Moph shall bury them, the thorn shall
possess their desirable things of silver, the thistle shall be in their tents.
Ephraim is smitten, their root is dried up, they shall bear no fruit ; yea,
though they bring forth yet will I slay the desired fruit of their womb ;
my God will cast them out, because they did not hearken unto Him, and
they shall be wanderers among the nations (ix. 1, 3, 6, 16, 17).

In *Isaiah :—*

Woe to Asshur, the rod of Mine anger, and he is the staff in their hand
of Mine indignation ; he thinketh not right, neither doth his heart medi-
tate right ; for it is in his heart to destroy and to cut off nations not a
few ; for he saith, Are not my princes all of them kings ? I will visit
upon the fruit of the elation of heart of the king of Asshur, for he hath
said, In the strength of my hand I have done it, and in my wisdom, for I
am intelligent ; and I will remove the bounds of the peoples, and will
plunder their treasures, and will cast down as a mighty one the inhabitants. Therefore shall the Lord of lords Zebaoth send among his fat ones
leanness ; and instead of his glory, kindling there shall be kindled a burning of fire (x. 5, 7, 8, 12, 13, 16).

[11] In all these passages, by "Asshur" as before shown is
signified reasoning; by "Egypt" and "Pharaoh" memory-
knowledge; by "Ephraim" the intellectual; and there is described in these and in many other places of what quality
man's rational becomes when it reasons concerning the truths
of faith from the negative principle. The like is involved in
Isaiah (chapters xxxvi. and xxxvii.), where we read that when
Rabshakeh, sent by the king of Asshur, spake against Jerusalem and king Hezekiah, the angel of Jehovah smote a hundred
and eighty-five thousand in the camp of the king of Asshur;
by which is signified what an overthrow of man's reasonings
takes place when he reasons against Divine things, however
much the man may then appear to himself to be wise. [12]
This reasoning is also in various places called "whoredom with
the sons of Egypt and with the sons of Asshur." As in
Ezekiel :—

Thou hast committed whoredom with the sons of Egypt, thy neighbors, great of flesh, and hast multiplied thy whoredom ; and hast committed whoredom with the sons of Asshur, and yet thou wast not satisfied
(xvi. 26, 28 ; xxiii. 3, 5-21 ; see n. 2466).

[13] Concerning those who enter into rational things and
memory-knowledges from the doctrine of faith, and thence are
wise. In *Isaiah :—*

In that day shall there be an altar to Jehovah in the midst of the land of Egypt, and a pillar at the border thereof to Jehovah ; and it shall be for a sign and for a witness unto Jehovah Zebaoth in the land of Egypt ; for they shall cry unto Jehovah because of the oppressors, and He shall send them a Saviour and a Prince, and He shall deliver them ; and Jehovah shall be known to Egypt, and the Egyptians shall know Jehovah in that day ; and they shall offer sacrifice and meat-offering, and shall vow a vow unto Jehovah, and shall perform it (xix. 19–21).

In the same :—

In that day there shall be a highway from Egypt to Asshur, and Asshur shall come into Egypt, and the Egyptians shall serve Asshur. In that day shall Israel be the third with Egypt and with Asshur, a blessing in the midst of the land, which Jehovah Zebaoth shall bless, saying, Blessed be Egypt My people, and Asshur the work of My hands, and Israel Mine inheritance (xix. 23–25) ;

where the spiritual church is treated of, of which the spiritual is " Israel," the rational is " Asshur," and the faculty of knowing is " Egypt ;" which three constitute the intellectual things of that church, which thus follow in order ; on which account it is said, " In that day shall Israel be the third with Egypt and with Asshur," and " Blessed be Egypt My people, and Asshur the work of My hands, and Israel Mine inheritance." [14] In the same :—

It shall come to pass in that day that the great trumpet shall be blown, and they shall come which were ready to perish in the land of Asshur, and they that were outcasts in the land of Egypt, and they shall bow themselves down to Jehovah in the mountain of holiness at Jerusalem (*Isa.* xxvii. 13).

In the same :—

Thus saith Jehovah, The labor of Egypt, and the merchandise of Cush and of the Sabeans, men of stature, shall come over unto thee, and they shall be thine ; they shall go after thee, and shall bow themselves down to thee, they shall make supplication unto thee. In thee only is God, and there is no God else besides (*Isa.* xlv. 14) ;

" Cush and the Sabeans" are knowledges (n. 117, 1171). In *Zechariah :*—

Egypt shall go up to Jerusalem, to worship the King Jehovah Zebaoth (xiv. 17, 18).

In *Micah :*—

I look unto Jehovah, I wait for the God of my salvation ; my God will hear me ; a day for building thy walls, in this day, and they shall come even unto thee thence from Asshur, and the cities of Egypt, and thence from Egypt even to the river (vii. 7, 11, 12).

[15] In *Ezekiel :—*

Thus saith the Lord Jehovih, At the end of forty years will I gather Egypt from the peoples whither they were scattered, and I will bring again the captivity of Egypt (xxix. 13, 14).

In the same :—

Behold, Asshur was a cedar in Lebanon with fair branches and a shadowing forest, and lofty in height, and its branch was among the tangled boughs ; the waters made it grow, going with her streams round about her plantation, and she sent out her canals unto all the trees of the field ; therefore its height was exalted above all the trees of the field, and its boughs were multiplied, and its branches became long by reason of many waters ; all the birds of the heavens made their nests in its boughs, and under its branches all the beasts of the field brought forth, and under its shadow dwelt all great nations. And it became fair in its greatness, in the length of its branches, for its root was by many waters ; the cedars in the garden of God did not hide it, the firs were not like its boughs, nor was any tree in the garden of God like unto it in its beauty. I made it fair by the multitude of its branches, and all the trees of Eden that were in the garden of God, envied it (xxxi. 3–8).

The Most Ancient Church, which was celestial, is here described in regard to the quality of its rational, and thereby its wisdom and intelligence, because that church looked at things below from Divine things, thus at truths from goods themselves, and thence at things that are subordinate. " Asshur" and the " cedar" are the rational ; the " tangled boughs among which were its branches" are memory-knowledges ; the " rivers and waters" are spiritual goods, among which was its root ; the "height and length of its branches" are its extension ; the " garden of God" is the spiritual church ; the " trees of Eden" are perceptions. From this and from all that goes before we can see what is the quality of man's rational, and what is the quality of his faculty of knowing, when they are subordinated to Divine truths, and serve them by confirming them. [16] That rational things and memory-knowledges are of service to those who are in the affirmative as means of being wise, was represented and signified by its being commanded the sons of Israel to borrow from the Egyptians vessels of gold, and vessels of silver, and garments (*Exod.* iii. 22 ; xi. 2 ; xii. 35, 36).

The like is meant by its being said in various passages of the Word that they should possess the goods, houses, vineyards, and oliveyards, and other things, of the nations; and also that the very gold and silver taken from the nations should become holy. As in *Isaiah :—*

Jehovah will visit Tyre, and she shall return to her harlot hire, and shall commit whoredom with all the kingdoms of the earth upon the face of the ground, and her merchandise and her harlot hire shall be holiness to Jehovah; it shall not be stored up nor laid away, for to them that dwell before Jehovah her merchandise shall be for eating till satisfied, and for an ancient covering (xxiii. 17, 18) ;

"the merchandise of Tyre" denotes knowledges (n. 1201), which to those who are in the negative are as harlot hire; but to those who are in the affirmative are as what is holy. The like is also meant by the Lord's words :—

Make to yourselves friends by means of the mammon of unrighteousness, that when ye fail they may receive you into eternal habitations; if ye have not become faithful in the unrighteous mammon, who will intrust you with the true? (Luke xvi. 9, 11).

CONCERNING THE STATE AND LOT IN THE OTHER LIFE OF THE NATIONS AND PEOPLES BORN OUTSIDE OF THE CHURCH.

2589. It is the common opinion that they who are born out of the church, and who are called Pagans and Gentiles, cannot be saved, because they have not the Word, and thus are ignorant of the Lord, without whom there is no salvation. But that these also are saved, may be known from the following considerations : that the Lord's mercy is universal, that is, toward every one; that these are born men equally with those who are within the church, who are comparatively few; and that it is not their fault that they are ignorant of the Lord. Consequently, their state and lot in the other life, have of the Lord's Divine mercy been shown me.

2590. I have been instructed in many ways that Gentiles who have led a moral life, and have been obedient, and have lived in mutual charity, and have received some sort of conscience according to their religion, are accepted in the other life, and are there instructed by angels with anxious care in the goods and truths of faith. While receiving instruction they conduct themselves modestly, intelligently, and wisely, and easily receive and become imbued with the instruction; for they have formed for themselves no principles contrary to the truths of faith that have to be dispersed, still less stumbling-blocks against the Lord; as have many Christians who have led a life of evil. Moreover such do not hate others, nor avenge injuries, nor plot artifices and deceits. Nay, they wish well to Christians; although on the other hand Christians despise them and even do them violence so far as they can; but they are withdrawn by the Lord from their unmercifulness, and are protected. [2] For the case of Christians and Gentiles in the other life is such that Christians who have acknowledged the truths of faith, and have at the same time led a life of good, are received in preference to Gentiles; although at the present day such are few; but Gentiles who have lived in obedience and mutual charity are received in preference to Christians who have not led so good a life. For in the wide world all those who have lived in good are of the Lord's mercy received and saved; for good is that which receives truth. The good of life is the very ground for the seed, that is, for the truth. Evil of life cannot possibly receive it, for although such as are in evil be instructed in a thousand ways, nay, even if they become most fully instructed, nevertheless the truths of faith enter no further with them than into the memory, and do not penetrate to the affection which is of the heart; and therefore in the other life their truths of memory are dissipated, and become null and void.

2591. Among the Gentiles however, just as among Christians, there are both the wise and the simple. In order that I might be instructed as to the quality of these, it has been granted me to speak with both wise and simple, sometimes for hours and days. But of the wise there are scarcely any at this day, whereas in ancient times there were very many, especially in the Ancient Church, from which wisdom emanated to many nations. In order that I might know of what quality these were, I have been allowed to hold familiar converse with some

of them ; so that the nature of their wisdom, and its superiority
to that of the present day may be seen from what follows.

2592. There was present with me a certain person * who
was formerly among the more wise, and was thereby well known
in the learned world. I conversed with him on various subjects, and as I knew that he had been a wise man, I spoke with
him concerning wisdom, intelligence, order, the Word, and
finally concerning the Lord. Concerning wisdom he said that
there is no other wisdom than that which is of life, and that
wisdom can be predicated of nothing else. Concerning intelligence he said that it was from wisdom. Concerning order he
said that it is from the Supreme God, and that to live in that
order is to be wise and intelligent. [2] As regards the Word,
when I read to him something from the prophecies, he was
very greatly delighted, especially from the fact that each of
the names and each of the words signified interior things, won-
dering greatly that the learned of this day are not delighted
with such a study. I plainly perceived that the interiors of
his thought or mind had been opened, and at the same time
that those of certain Christians who were present had been
closed ; for ill-will against him prevailed with them, and also
unbelief that the Word is of this nature. Nay, when I went
on reading the Word he said that he could not be present, because he perceived it to be too holy for him to endure, so interiorly was he affected. The Christians on the other hand
said aloud that they could be present ; and this was because
their interiors had been closed, and therefore the holy things
did not affect them. [3] At length I talked with him about
the Lord ; that He was born a man, but was conceived of God ;
that He had put off the human and had put on the Divine ;
and that it is He who governs the universe. To this he made
answer that he knew many things about the Lord, and had perceived in his own way that it could not have been done otherwise if the human race was to be saved. Meantime certain
wicked Christians injected various difficulties, for which he did
not care, saying that it was not surprising, because they had
become imbued in the life of the body with unbecoming ideas
respecting these things, and that until such ideas were dis-

* Probably Cicero ; see *Heaven and Hell*, n. 322. [REVISER.]

persed they could not admit things confirmatory, as could those who are ignorant. This man was a Gentile.

2593. I have also been permitted to speak with others who lived in ancient times and who were then among the more wise. They were at first seen in front at a distance, and were there able to perceive the interiors of my thoughts, thus many things in a thorough manner. From one idea of the thought they could know the entire series, and fill it with delightful things of wisdom together with pleasing representations, which showed me that they were among the more wise, and I was told that they were from the Ancients. So they drew nearer, and when I read to them something from the Word they were most highly delighted. It was granted me to perceive their very delight and enjoyment, which arose chiefly from the fact that all the things they heard from the Word were both in general and in particular representative and significative of heavenly and spiritual things. They said that in their time when they lived in the world their mode of thinking and speaking, and also of writing, was of this nature, and that this was their wisdom's study.

2594. But as regards the Gentiles who are on earth at this day, they are not so wise, but are for the most part simple in heart; and yet those of them who have lived in mutual charity receive wisdom in the other life—concerning whom I may relate what follows.

2595. I heard the sound of a certain gyre,* but coarser than usual, and from the sound I at once knew that they were from the Gentiles. I was told by the angels that they were Gentiles who had been raised up three or four days before. The gyre or choir was heard for several hours, and it was perceived that even during the short time in which it was heard they were being perfected more and more. When I wondered at this I was told that these can be initiated into choirs, and thus into harmony, in one night; while most Christians barely can in thirty years. Gyres or choirs exist when many speak together, all as one, and each as all; but concerning gyres or choirs, of the Lord's Divine mercy elsewhere.

---

* That is, a revolving circle, or gyration. See *Arcana Coelestia*, n. 4041, 5182, etc. [REVISER.]

2596. One morning there was a choir at a distance from me, and it was given me to know from the representations of the choir that they were Chinese; for they presented a kind of woolly goat, a cake of millet, and an ivory spoon, as also the idea of a floating city. They desired to come nearer to me; and when they had applied themselves they said that they desired to be alone with me, that they might open their thoughts. But they were told that they were not alone, and that there were others who were indignant at their desiring to be alone, when yet they were guests. When they perceived the indignation of the others, they began to think whether they had trespassed against the neighbor, and whether they had claimed anything for themselves that belonged to others. (In the other life all thoughts are communicated.) I was permitted to perceive their trouble: it was that of an acknowledgment that perhaps they had wronged the others, and of shame on that account, and of other good affections at the same time, from which it was known that they were endued with charity. Presently I spoke with them, and at length about the Lord. When I called Him Christ, a kind of repugnance was perceived in them; but the cause was discovered to be that they brought this repugnance from the world, from their having known Christians to live worse than they did themselves, and in no charity. But when I simply called Him the Lord, they were inwardly moved. They were afterwards instructed by the angels that beyond every other doctrine in the whole world the Christian doctrine prescribes love and charity, but that there are but few persons who live in accordance with it.

2597. There are Gentiles who when they lived in the world had known from social intercourse and report that Christians lead the very worst life—in adulteries, in hatreds and quarrels, in drunkenness, and the like things—at which they are affected with horror, because such things are contrary to their laws, their morals, and their religion. In the other life these are more timid than others in receiving the truths of faith; but they are instructed by the angels that the Christian doctrine, and the faith itself, teach the very opposite, but that Christians live less in accordance with their doctrine than do the Gen-

tiles.   When they perceive this they receive the truths of faith
and adore the Lord, but more tardily.

2598. When I read the 17th and 18th chapters of *Judges*,
concerning Micah, how the sons of Dan took away his graven
image, the teraphim, and the Levite, there was present a spirit
from the Gentiles, who in the life of the body had adored a
carved image.   While he listened attentively to what was done
to Micah, and in what grief he was on account of his graven
image that the Danites took away, he too was overcome with
grief, and was affected to such a degree that he scarcely knew
what to think for inward grief.   I perceived his grief, and at
the same time perceived the innocence in each of his affections.   Christian spirits were also present and observed it, and
wondered that a worshiper of a graven image should be moved
by so strong an affection of mercy and innocence.   Afterwards
good spirits spoke to him, saying that a graven image ought
not to be adored, and that he could understand this because
he was a human being; but that he ought to think beyond the
graven image of God the Creator and Governor of the universal heaven and earth; and that this God is the Lord.
When these things were said I was permitted to perceive the
interior emotion of his adoration, which was communicated to
me, and was much more holy than that with Christians; from
which it could be seen that Gentiles come into heaven more
easily than Christians at this day who are not so affected (according to the Lord's words in *Luke* xiii. 29, 30); for in the
state in which he was he could be imbued with all things of
faith, and could receive them with interior affection.   There
was in him the mercy that is of love, and in his ignorance there
was innocence; and when these are present, all things of faith
are received as it were spontaneously, and with joy.   He was
afterwards received among the angels.

2599. There was also another among the Gentiles, who had
lived in the good of charity.   When he heard Christian spirits
reasoning about things to be believed (spirits reason with one
another much more fully and much more acutely than men,
especially about goods and truths, because these belong to the
other life), he marveled that they should dispute so, and said
that he did not want to hear such things, because they were

reasoning from fallacies, and he gave them the following instruction : If I am good, I can know from good itself what is true, and what I do not know, I can receive.

2600. Well-disposed Gentiles are instructed in the other life, for the most part, and so far as possible, in accordance with their states of life and in accordance with their religion, thus in various ways. I may here describe only three.

2601. Some are reduced into a state of tranquillity, as it were a kind of sleep; and they then seem to themselves to be building small cities, and in the midst of them to hide some secret thing which they wish to preserve from violence. They give these cities to others, with entreaties not to do violence to the secret thing in the midst of them. Innocence is thus insinuated into them, and also charity, together with the idea that the secret thing is concerning the Lord. They are kept in this state a considerable time. It is a state of ignorance in which there is innocence. They are guarded by little children, lest any one should do them harm. I have spoken with them, and have been much affected by their state of innocence and charity, and also by the solicitude with which they hide the secret, and by the holy fear lest it should be violated.

2602. There is one nation (I was told that it is from the Indies) which makes it their religion to worship the Greatest God with the following rite. When they are adoring Him they first magnify themselves, but soon prostrate themselves as worms; and at the same time they hold, that above the universe, which they believe to be whirling around, is that Greatest God, looking down on what they are doing. As they have had such religious observances, in the other life they are brought back into them; and I have spoken with them while they imagined such things. They are for the most part modest, obedient, and simple in heart. They are by successive steps freed by the angels from this phantasy ; for they are instructed, in accordance with their religion, that the Greatest God is the Lord; and that they can indeed magnify themselves on account of their being able to adore Him; and that nevertheless they are like little worms ; and that the Lord from on high sees each and all things. In this manner, by means of their own religion, they are brought into the knowledges of good and truth.

2603. There are some Gentiles from those regions where they are black, who bring with them from their life in the world a wish to be treated severely; believing that no one can come into heaven except through punishments and afflictions, and that they will afterwards receive more gladsome things, which they call paradisal. As they have such ideas from their religion they are at first treated severely in the other life by some whom they call devils, and are afterwards taken to the paradises already described (n. 1622). But they are instructed by the angels that their punishments and afflictions are turned by the Lord into what is good for them, as with those who are in temptations; also that paradisal things are not heaven, but that heaven is the affection of the celestial and spiritual things that are in them; and that they have been in a certain way of truth, although in the shade of ignorance. They spoke with me a long time. While in their state of affliction their speech was attended with a kind of collision; thus was distinct from that of others; but after their afflictions were over, and they were taken up to the paradises, they no longer had such a speech, but one that was almost angelic. From their religion they have that they believe, and desire to have interior things. They said that whenever they are treated severely they are black; but that they shortly put off the blackness, and put on whiteness; knowing that their souls are white, but their bodies black.

2604. It is usual for Gentiles who adore any god under an image or statue, or any carved thing, to be introduced, on coming into the other life, to certain ones who are in the place of their gods or idols, in order that they may put away their phantasies; and when they have been with these for some days, they are taken away from such persons. They who have adored men are also sometimes introduced to them, or to others in their stead; as many of the Jews are to Abraham, Jacob, Moses, and David; but when they perceive that these have the same kind of human nature as others have, and can afford them no help, they become ashamed, and are taken to their own places in accordance with their life. Among the Gentiles in the other life the Africans are the most beloved, because they receive the goods and truths of heaven more easily than others. They especially desire to be called the obedient, but not the faithful. They say that Christians can be called faithful, because they have the doctrine of faith; but not they, unless they receive it, or as they say, are able to receive it.

2605. I have spoken with some who were in the Ancient Church, and who then knew concerning the Lord that He was to come, and who had been imbued with the goods of faith, but yet fell away and became idolaters. They were in front, toward the left, in a darksome place, and in a miserable state. Their speech was like the sound of a fife, of one tone, almost devoid of rationality of thought. They said that they had been there for many ages, and that they are sometimes taken out thence to serve others for some uses, which are vile. From these it was given me to think about many Christians, who are idolaters not exteriorly but interiorly, and who at heart deny the Lord, and thereby also the truths of faith; and to reflect upon what kind of a lot must await them in the other life.

CHAPTER THE TWENTY–FIRST.

2606. The Word of the Old Testament was formerly called the " Law and the Prophets." By the " Law" were meant all the historical books, which are the five books of *Moses,* and those of *Joshua, Judges, Samuel,* and *Kings :* by the "Prophets" were meant all the prophetical books, which are those of *Isaiah, Jeremiah, Ezekiel, Daniel, Hosea, Joel, Amos, Obadiah, Jonah, Micah, Nahum, Habakkuk, Zephaniah, Haggai, Zechariah, Malachi ;* and also the *Psalms of David.* The historical books of the Word are also called " Moses ;" hence it is occasionally said, " Moses and the Prophets," instead of the " Law and the Prophets ;" and the prophetical books are called " Elias" (see the preface to the eighteenth chapter of *Genesis*).

2607. As regards the historicals they are all historically true, except those in the first chapters of *Genesis,* which are

made up history, as shown in Part First.   Yet although they
are historically true, they nevertheless have an internal sense;
and in that sense, like the propheticals, treat solely of the
Lord.   They do indeed treat of heaven and the church, and
of what belongs to heaven and the church, but as these are
of the Lord, through these the historicals look to the Lord,
and therefore are the Word.   The historic events are all representative, and every word by which they are described is
significative.   That the historic events are representative is
evident from what has been unfolded thus far concerning
Abraham, and will be further evident from what of the Lord's
Divine mercy is to be explained concerning Isaac, Jacob, and
his twelve sons; concerning Egypt, the sojourning of the people in the wilderness, their entrance into the land of Canaan,
etc.   [2] That every word by which these historicals are described is significative, is also evident from what has been
shown for instance in regard to the names as signifying actual
things; thus "Egypt" signifies memory-knowledge, "Asshur"
the rational, "Ephraim" the intellectual, "Tyre" knowledges,
"Zion" the celestial church, "Jerusalem" the spiritual church,
and so on.   The same has been shown in regard to the words;
as that "king" signifies truth, "priest" good, and that all other
words have their respective internal significance; such as "kingdom," "city," "house," "nation," "people," "garden," "vineyard," "oliveyard," "gold," "silver," "brass," "iron," "birds,"
"beasts," "bread," "wine," "oil," "morning," "day," "light;"
and this uniformly in both the historical and the prophetical
books, although they were written by various individuals, and
at different times—a uniformity that would not be possible
unless the Word had come down from heaven.   From this it
may be known that there is an internal sense in the Word;
as well as from the fact that the Divine Word cannot treat of
mere men, such as Abraham, Isaac, Jacob, and their posterity
(which was the worst of nations); of their kings, their wives,
sons, and daughters; of harlots, plunderings, and such things,
which, considered in themselves, are not worthy to be even
mentioned in the Word, unless by them are represented and
signified such things as are in the Lord's kingdom: it is these
things that are worthy of the Word.

2608. Similar to these also are very many things in the Prophets, such as those adduced above (n. 1888); and also the following in *Isaiah :*—

Moab shall howl, all Moab shall howl, for the foundations of Kir-hareseth shall ye mourn howbeit ye have been bruised; for the fields of Heshbon have failed, the vine of Sibmah; the lords of the nations break down the shoots, they reached even unto Jazer, they wandered in the wilderness, her offshoots have been torn away; they have passed over the sea. Therefore with weeping will I weep for Jazer, for the vine of Sibmah; I will water thee with my tears, O Heshbon and Elealeh; for upon thy vintage and upon thy harvest the shout is fallen (xvi. 7–9).

In *Jeremiah :*—

The voice of a cry from Horonaim, wasting and great destruction, Moab is broken to pieces, her little ones have caused a cry to be heard; for by the ascent of Luhith with weeping a weeping goeth up; for in the going down of Horonaim the enemies have heard a cry of a breaking to pieces. Judgment is come unto the land of the plain, unto Holon, and unto Jahzah, and unto Mephaath, and upon Dibon, and upon Nebo, and upon Beth-diblathaim, and upon Kiriathaim, and upon Beth-gamul, and upon Beth-meon, and upon Kerioth, and upon Bozrah (xlviii. 3, 4, 5, 21–24).

Such in very many places is the character of the propheticals of the Word, which would be of no use unless they had an internal sense; and yet the Word, being Divine, must needs contain within itself the laws of that Heavenly Kingdom into which man is to come.

2609. But as regards the Precepts of Life, such as all things in the decalogue, and many in the Law and the Prophets—these, being of service to man's very life, are of use in both senses, both the literal and the internal. The things contained in the literal sense were for the people and peoples of that period, who did not apprehend internal things; and the things contained in the internal sense were for the angels, who have no care for external things. Unless the precepts of the decalogue contained internal things also, they would never have been promulgated on Mount Sinai with so great a miracle; for such things as it contains, such as that parents are to be honored, that men must not steal, must not kill, must not commit adultery, must not covet what is another's, are things which the Gentiles also know and have prescribed in their laws; and which the sons of Israel as men must have been well acquainted with, without such a promulgation. But as those precepts were for the service of life, in both senses, and were as external forms produced from internal, that corresponded to each other,—this was the reason why they came down out of heaven upon Mount Sinai with so great a miracle, and in their internal sense were uttered and heard in heaven, while in their external sense they were uttered and heard on earth. [2] Take as an example the promise that they who honor their parents shall have their days prolonged upon the land: by "parents" the angels in heaven perceived the Lord; by the "land," His kingdom, which those who worship Him from love and faith should eternally possess as sons and heirs; whereas by "parents" men on earth understood parents; by "land," the land of Canaan; by the "prolongation of their days," the years of their life. Take again the precept that men must not steal: by this the angels who were in heaven perceived that they should take nothing away from the Lord, and should not claim anything of righteousness and merit for themselves; whereas men on earth understood that they must not steal; from which we can see that these precepts are true in both senses. Take again the precept that men must not kill: by this the angels in heaven perceived that they should not hate any one, and should not extinguish anything of good and truth with any one; whereas men on earth understood that their friends must not be killed. The case is the same with all the other precepts.

CHAPTER XXI

1. And Jehovah visited Sarah, as He had said; and Jehovah did unto Sarah as He had spoken.

2. And Sarah conceived and bare Abraham a son in his old age, at the appointed time, as God had spoken with him.

3. And Abraham called the name of his son that was born unto him, whom Sarah bare to him, Isaac.

4. And Abraham circumcised Isaac his son, a son of eight days, as God had commanded him.

5. And Abraham was a son of a hundred years when Isaac his son was born unto him.

6. And Sarah said, God hath made laughter for me, every one that heareth will laugh with me.

7. And she said, Who would have said unto Abraham, Sarah shall suckle sons ? for I have borne a son to his old age.

8. And the child grew, and was weaned ; and Abraham made a great feast, on the day when he weaned Isaac.

9. And Sarah saw the son of Hagar the Egyptian, whom she had borne unto Abraham, mocking.

10. And she said unto Abraham, Cast out this handmaid and her son; for the son of this handmaid shall not inherit with my son, with Isaac.

11. And the word was evil exceedingly in the eyes of Abraham, on account of his son.

12. And God said unto Abraham, Let it not be evil in thine eyes because of the boy, and because of thine handmaid; all that Sarah saith unto thee, hearken unto her voice, for in Isaac shall thy seed be called.

*   *   *   *   *   *   *   *   *

13. And also the son of the handmaid I will make a nation, because he is thy seed.

14. And Abraham rose early in the morning, and took bread, and a bottle of water, and gave to Hagar, and put them on her shoulder, and the child, and sent her away; and she went and wandered in the wilderness of Beer-sheba.

15. And the water was spent out of the bottle, and she cast the child under one of the shrubs.

16. And she went and sat by herself over against him, withdrawing about a bowshot; for she said, Let me not see the death of the child; and she sat over against him; and she lifted up her voice, and wept.

17. And God heard the voice of the child, and the angel of God called to Hagar out of heaven, and said unto her, What aileth thee, Hagar ? fear not, for God hath heard the voice of the child where he is.

VOL. III.—22

18. Arise, lift up the child, and strengthen thy hand in him, for I will make him a great nation.

19. And God opened her eyes, and she saw a well of water, and she went and filled the bottle with water, and gave the child drink.

20. And God was with the child, and he grew, and he dwelt in the wilderness, and became a shooter of the bow.

21. And he dwelt in the wilderness of Paran; and his mother took him a wife out of the land of Egypt.

*   *   *   *   *   *   *   *   *

22. And it came to pass at that time, that Abimelech and Phicol the captain of his army said unto Abraham, saying, God is with thee in all that thou doest.

23. And now swear unto me here by God, that thou wilt not be false to me, nor to my son, nor to my son's son; according to the kindness that I have done unto thee, thou shalt do unto me, and to the land wherein thou hast sojourned.

24. And Abraham said, I will swear.

25. And Abraham reproved Abimelech, because of the well of water which Abimelech's servants had taken away.

26. And Abimelech said, I know not who hath done this word, neither didst thou tell me, neither heard I of it, but to-day.

27. And Abraham took flock and herd, and gave to Abimelech, and they two struck a covenant.

28. And Abraham set seven ewe lambs of the flock by themselves.

29. And Abimelech said unto Abraham, What are these seven ewe lambs which thou hast set by themselves?

30. And he said, Because these seven ewe lambs thou shalt take from my hand, that it may be a witness unto me that I have digged this well.

31. Therefore he called that place Beer-sheba, because there they sware both of them.

32. And they struck a covenant at Beer-sheba; and Abimelech rose up, and Phicol the captain of his army, and they returned into the land of the Philistines.

33. And he planted a grove in Beer-sheba, and called there on the name of the God of eternity.

34. And Abraham sojourned in the land of the Philistines many days.

THE CONTENTS.

THE INTERNAL SENSE.

2615. Verse 1. *And Jehovah visited Sarah, as He had said ; and Jehovah did unto Sarah as He had spoken.* "Jehovah visited Sarah," signifies the presence of the Divine celestial in the Divine spiritual; "as He had said," signifies as He had perceived; "and Jehovah did unto Sarah," signifies the state of unition; "as He had spoken," signifies as He had thought.

2616. *Jehovah visited Sarah.* That this signifies the presence of the Divine celestial in the Divine spiritual, is evident from the signification of "Jehovah," as being the Divine celestial, that is, the Divine Good, or *Esse* (Being) itself, which, because it is of love and mercy, is Good itself; from the significiation of "visiting," as meaning to be present; and from the signification of " Sarah," as being the Divine spiritual, that is, Divine Truth (see n. 1468, 1901, 2063, 2065, 2507).

2617. *As He had said.* That this signifies as He had perceived, is evident from the signification in the historical parts of the Word of " saying," as meaning to perceive (see n. 2238, 2260, 2552).

2618. *And Jehovah did unto Sarah.* That this signifies the state of unition, namely, of the Lord's Divine spiritual in His Divine celestial, is evident from the signification of " doing," when predicated of the Lord's Divine, as being the sum total of the effect, consequently the state; and from the signification of " Jehovah," and also of " Sarah" (concerning which see above, n. 2616). As regards the state of unition of the Lord's Divine spiritual in His Divine celestial, this is the very marriage itself of good and truth, from which comes the heavenly marriage; and this marriage is the Lord's kingdom in the heavens and on earth. For this reason the Lord's kingdom is so frequently in the Word called a " marriage," and is compared to a marriage. The reason (a secret one) is that all conjugial love (and through this all celestial and spiritual love) comes from the marriage of Divine good and truth, and of Divine truth and good, in the Lord. What further arcana are enfolded in these words : that " Jehovah visited Sarah as He had said," and that " Jehovah did unto Sarah as He had spoken," cannot be declared, because they are inexpressible; for they comprise the very state itself of the unition of the Lord's Divine with His Human. Appearances of this are presented by the Lord before the angels by means of heavenly lights, and are illustrated by means of ineffable representations; but they cannot be presented before men, because it would have to be done by means of such things as belong to the light of the world, into which such arcana do not fall; nay, by a description based on such things they become more obscure.

2619. *As He had spoken.* That this signifies as He had thought, is evident from the signification of "speaking," as being to think (see n. 2271, 2287). The perception which is

signified by "Jehovah said" was from the Divine celestial; but
the thought which is signified by "Jehovah spake" was from
the Divine celestial through the Divine spiritual; and there is
therefore an apparent repetition in the sense of the letter,
namely, "as He said," and "as He spake." But what it is to
perceive from the Divine celestial and to think from the Divine
celestial through the Divine spiritual, does not fall into even
the most enlightened apprehension by means of things that
belong to the light of the world. This shows how infinite the
rest of the Word may be. (That thought is from perception
may be seen above, n. 1919, 2515.) With man the case is
this: it is good from which he perceives, but it is truth by
means of which he thinks. Good is of love and its affections,
consequently from it is perception; but truth is of faith, consequently this is of thought. The former is signified in the
historic parts of the Word by "saying," but the latter by
"speaking." But when "saying" is found alone, it then sometimes signifies perceiving, and sometimes thinking; because
"saying" involves both.

2620. Verse 2. *And Sarah conceived and bare Abraham a
son in his old age, at the appointed time, as God had spoken
with him.* She "conceived and bare," signifies that it was and
came forth; "Sarah bare Abraham," signifies from the unition
of the Lord's Divine spiritual with His Divine celestial; "a
son" signifies the Divine rational; "in his old age," signifies
when the days were fulfilled that He should put off the human;
"at the appointed time," signifies when the rational was such
as to receive; "as God had spoken with him," signifies as He
had willed.

2621. That "conceived and bare" signifies that it Was and
Came forth, namely (as follows) the Divine rational, from the
unition of the Lord's Divine spiritual with His Divine celestial, is evident from the signification of "conceiving and bearing." That in the internal sense of the Word no other con-
ceptions and bearings are meant than those which are spiritual
and celestial, may be seen above (n. 2584); but here those
which were Divine, because the subject here treated of is the
Lord's rational made Divine; and of Him, namely, the Lord,
Being and Coming forth (*Esse et Existere*) are chiefly predi-

cated; for He alone Is and Comes forth. As regards Being
and Coming forth (*Esse et Existere*) we may add that they
seem as if they were nearly the same, but are not the same.
Every person and every thing, has its Being from conception,
but its Coming forth from birth; and thus, as conception is
prior to birth, so Being is prior to Coming forth. [2] The
soul is the Being itself of man, and the sensitive or corporeal
faculty is its Coming forth, for the former comes forth in the
latter. Celestial and spiritual love are the very Being of the
man who is being regenerated; and the rational and sensitive
faculties, when imbued with that love, are his Coming forth.
And so it is with each and all things in the universe; for there
is nothing whatever which has not its conception that it may
Be, and its birth that it may Come forth; which may also be
illustrated in the terms of philosophy by saying that every
effect has its cause, and every cause has its end. The end
is the Being of the cause, and the cause is the Coming forth
of the end. In the same way, the cause is the Being of the
effect, and the effect is the Coming forth of the cause.

2622. *Sarah to Abraham.* That this signifies from the unition of the Divine spiritual with the Divine celestial, is evident
from the representation of Sarah, as being the Divine spiritual,
or Divine Truth (see n. 1468, 1901, 2063, 2065, 2172, 2173,
2198, 2507); and from the representation of Abraham, as
being the Divine celestial, or Divine Good (see n. 1989, 2011,
2172, 2198, 2501). (Concerning the unition of the Divine
spiritual with the Divine celestial, see what was said above, n.
2618.)

2623. *A son.* That this signifies the Divine rational, is evident from the signification of a "son." In the internal sense
of the Word a "son" signifies truth (n. 489, 491, 533); and
as truth is the chief thing in the rational (n. 2072, 2189),
the rational is also signified by a "son;" but here the Divine
rational, in which principally there is good, which Isaac, who
is the "son," also represents (concerning which hereafter).

2624. *In his old age.* That this signifies when the days
were fulfilled that the human should be put off, is evident
from the signification of "old age," as being the state when
the human should be put off and the Divine put on (see n.

2198); for Abraham was at that time a hundred years old; and by this number is signified a full state of unition, as will be seen in the explication at verse 5.

2625. *At the appointed time.* That this signifies when the rational was such as to receive, is evident from the signification of "time." There are two things which while man lives in the world appear to be essential, because they are proper to nature, namely, space and time. Hence to live in space and time is to live in the world or in nature. But in the other life these two things are of no consequence. In the world of spirits indeed they do appear to be of some consequence, for the reason that spirits fresh from the body still retain the idea of natural things; yet it is not long before they perceive that there is no space and time there, but state instead; and that in the other life states correspond to spaces and times in nature; to spaces states as to Being (*esse*), and to times states as to Coming forth (*existere*). (In regard to space or place see above, n. 1274, 1379, 1380, 1382.) [2] From this any one can see what kind of an idea a man may have, while in the world or in nature, respecting the things of the other life and many arcana of faith; namely, that he is not willing to believe them until he apprehends them by means of the things in the world, nay, by sensuous things; for he must needs suppose that if he were to put off the idea of space and time, and still more space and time themselves, he would become absolutely nothing; and thus that he would have nothing left from which he could feel and think, except something confused and incomprehensible; when yet the case is exactly the reverse. Angelic life is of such a nature as to be the wisest and happiest of all. [3] This is the reason why in the Word "ages" in the internal sense do not signify ages, but states; so that in this verse "old age" does not mean old age. And in the same way the numbers do not signify numbers, but some specific state, as for instance the number a hundred years, concerning which hereafter. From this we can now see that by the "appointed time" is signified the state when the rational was such as to receive. [4] In regard to the specific matter here treated of, namely, that the Divine rational was and came forth from the unition of the Divine spiritual with the Divine celestial of the

Lord, when the days were fulfilled for the human to be put off, and when the rational was such as to receive (all of which is signified in the internal sense by Sarah's conceiving and bearing to Abraham a son to his old age at the appointed time), be it known that the human begins in the inmost of the rational (see n. 2106, 2194); and that the Lord advanced successively to the union of the Human Essence with the Divine Essence, and of the Divine Essence with the Human Essence (n. 1864, 2033, 2523); and this by His own power (n. 1921, 2025, 2026, 2083), by continual temptations and victories (n. 1737, 1813, 1690), and by continual revelations from His Divine (n. 1616, 2500); and this until at length He had expelled all the maternal human (n. 1414, 1444, 2574); and thus had made His Human Divine in respect to the rational, according to the things contained in this verse. Hence it is manifest what is to be understood by the days being fulfilled for the human to be put off, and by the rational being such as to receive. [5] Some idea of this may be formed from what takes place in those who are being regenerated. The celestial things of love and the spiritual things of faith are not at once implanted in them by the Lord, but successively; and when by means of them the man's rational has become such that it can receive, then for the first time is he becoming regenerate, for the most part by means of temptations in which he conquers. When these things take place, the days are fulfilled for him to put off the old man, and to put on the new. (Concerning man's regeneration, see above, n. 677, 679, 711, 848, 986, 1555, 2475.)

2626. *As God had spoken with him.* That this signifies as He had willed, is evident from the signification of "speaking," as being to think (see n. 2271, 2287, 2619); but that here it means to will is because it is said, "as God had spoken;" since for the Divine to think is to will.

2627. Verse 3. *And Abraham called the name of his son, that was born unto him, whom Sarah bare to him, Isaac.* "Abraham called the name of his son that was born unto him," signifies the quality of the rational as being Divine; "whom Sarah bare to him," signifies that it was and came forth from the Divine spiritual united to the Divine celestial; "Isaac" signifies the Divine rational.

2628. *Abraham called the name of his son that was born unto him.* That this signifies the quality of the rational as being Divine, is evident from the representation of Abraham, as being the Lord as to the Divine celestial, or the Divine Good, treated of many times before; and from the signification of "calling a name," as being the quality (see n. 144, 145, 1754, 1896, 2009); and from the signification of his "son," as being the rational (see n. 2623); and also from the signification of his being "born unto him," as being to come forth from the Divine. Hence it is evident that "Abraham called the name of his son that was born unto him," signifies the quality of the rational as being Divine. From these few words three arcana shine forth for those who are in the internal sense:— First, that the Lord's Divine Human came forth (*exstiterit*) from the Divine Itself; which is further treated of in this verse. Second, that the Lord's Divine Human was not only conceived, but also born, of Jehovah, and hence the Lord as to His Divine Human is called the "Son of God," and the "Only-begotten" (*John* i. 14, 18, 50; iii. 16, 18, 35, 36; v. 19–27; vi. 69; ix. 35; x. 36; xi. 27; xiv. 13, 14; xvii. 1; xx. 31; and in like manner in the other Evangelists). Third, that the Lord's Divine Human is the "name" of Jehovah, that is, His quality (see *John* xii. 28).

2629. *Whom Sarah bare to him.* That this signifies being and coming forth from the Divine spiritual united to the Divine celestial is evident from the signification of "bearing," as being to come forth (*existere*) (see n. 2621); and as birth involves conception, and the birth or coming forth is from the Divine spiritual, and the conception, or being, from the Divine celestial, which two have now been united, hence "bearing" here signifies both being and coming forth; and also from the representation of Sarah, as being the Divine spiritual united to the Divine celestial (see n. 1468, 1901, 2063, 2065, 2172, 2173, 2198, 2507). These things are arcana too deep to be described, or indeed to be illustrated by anything in this world. They are for angelic minds, to whom they are presented in the light of heaven by means of things ineffable.

2630. *Isaac.* That this signifies the Divine Rational, is evident from what has been said before concerning Abraham,

Isaac, and Jacob (n. 1893, 2066, 2083), namely, that Abraham represents the supreme Divine, Isaac the Divine rational, and Jacob His Divine natural; as will also be seen hereafter, where Isaac is treated of.

2631. Verse 4. *And Abraham circumcised Isaac his son, a son of eight days, as God had commanded him.* "Abraham circumcised Isaac his son," signifies the purification of the rational; "a son of eight days," signifies a beginning and continuance; "as God had commanded him," signifies according to Divine order.

2632. *Abraham circumcised Isaac his son.* That this signifies the purification of the rational, is evident from the signification of "being circumcised," which is to be purified (see n. 2039); and from the representation of "Isaac," as being the Divine rational (see n. 2630). [2] That the Lord's first rational was born as with others, namely, by means of knowledges (*scientifica et cognitiones*), has been stated before, where Ishmael was treated of, by whom that rational is represented. As this was born by means of knowledges, thus by the external way, which is that of the senses, and as with others, it could not but have in itself many things from the outward world, for from them are the ideas of the rational procured; and this the more because it had its hereditary from the mother. It was these worldly things and this hereditary which the Lord successively expelled from His rational, and this until it was such as to be able to receive the Divine (n. 2624, 2625). The Lord's Divine rational was then born, which is represented by Isaac (n. 2630); not however by the external way, which is that of the senses, as the former rational was; but by the internal way from the Divine Itself (n. 2628, 2629). As this was not done at once, but successively (n. 1690, 2033), it was purified, and this continually; which is signified by "Abraham's circumcising his son, a son of eight days." That the Lord made His rational Divine by successive steps, and continually purified it, is evident also in *John* :—

Jesus said, Father, glorify Thy name. Then came there a voice from heaven : I have both glorified, and will glorify again (xii. 28).

That to "glorify" is to make Divine, may be seen above (n. 1603, 1999). [3] In the Ancient Church nothing else was represented and signified by circumcision than that a man should be purified from the loves of self and of the world, and this also by successive steps and continually (see n. 2039, 2046 at the end, 2049, 2056) ; especially when he has been born a new man, that is, when he has been regenerated ; for the Lord then flows in by the internal way, that is, by the good of conscience, and successively and continually separates the things which adhere both from hereditary and from actual evil.

2633. *A son of eight days.* That this signifies a beginning and continuance, is evident from the signification of the " eighth day," on which they were circumcised, as being any beginning, and thus continuance (see n. 2044).

2634. *As God had commanded him.* That this signifies according to Divine order, is evident from the signification of " God commanding," or of His precepts. God's precepts, or the things which God has commanded, are all things that are of Divine order both in general and in particular; so that Divine order is nothing but the perpetual precept of God ; and therefore to live according to the precepts of God, and to live in the precepts of God, is to live according to Divine order and in Divine order. Hence it is that by "as God commanded," is signified according to Divine order. It was according to Divine order that every male should be circumcised on the eighth day from his birth ; not that circumcision was of any avail, or that they who were circumcised would enter into the kingdom of God before the uncircumcised ; but because in the representative church such a rite corresponded to the purification of the heart ; which correspondence will of the Lord's Divine mercy be spoken of elsewhere. It is of Divine order that the heart, that is, man's interiors, should be purified gradually and continually from the evils of cupidities, and from the falsities of the phantasies thence derived. The precepts relating to the purification of the heart are all things of Divine order both in general and in particular. In so far therefore as a man lives in those precepts, so far he lives in Divine order ; and in so far as he lives in this, so far all things in him, both of reason and memory, are disposed by the Lord according to the order which is from Him in the heavens. Hence the man becomes a little heaven corresponding to the greatest.

2635. Verse 5. *And Abraham was a son of a hundred years when Isaac his son was born unto him.* " Abraham was a son of a hundred years," signifies a full state of unition; "when Isaac his son was born unto him," signifies when the Lord's rational was made Divine.

2636. *Abraham was a son of a hundred years.* That this signifies a full state of unition, is evident from the signification of a "hundred," as being what is full (concerning which presently); and from the signification of "years," as being state (see n. 482, 487, 488, 493, 893); here, a state of unition. What a full state of unition of the Lord's Divine with His Human is, or what is the same, with His rational (for the human begins in the inmost of the rational, n. 2106, 2194), cannot so well be told to the apprehension, but still can be illustrated by what is called with man a full state when he is being reformed and regenerated. [2] It is known that a man cannot be regenerated until adult age, because he then for the first time has the full exercise of reason and judgment, and thus can receive good and truth from the Lord. Before he comes into this state he is being prepared by the Lord by such things being insinuated into him as may serve him as ground for receiving the seeds of good and truth; which are the many states of innocence and charity, and also the knowledges of good and truth, and the thoughts derived from them. This preparation is going on for some years before his regeneration commences. When the man has been imbued with these things, and is thus prepared, his state is then said to be full; for his interiors are then disposed for receiving. All those things with which a man is endowed by the Lord before regeneration, and by means of which he is regenerated, are called remains, which are signified in the Word by the number "ten" (n. 576, 1738, 2284); and also by a "hundred," when the state for regeneration is full (n. 1988). [3] These things may serve for illustration as to what is signified by a full state of unition of the Human with the Divine in the Lord, namely, when from His own power, by means of the combats of temptations and by victories, and by the powers of the Divine wisdom and intelligence, He had procured to Himself so much of the Divine in His Human, that is, in His rational, as to be able to unite the

Divine Itself to the Divine acquired in the rational. That this state might be represented, it was brought to pass that, although Abraham had dwelt for many years in the land of Canaan, Isaac was not born to him until he was a hundred years old. These are the arcana contained in the number a "hundred years," which was Abraham's age. [4] That the number a "hundred" signifies what is full, is evident from other passages in the Word, as in *Isaiah :*—

There shall be no more thence an infant of days, nor an old man that hath not filled his days ; for the child shall die a son of a hundred years, and the sinner a son of a hundred years shall be accursed (lxv. 20) ;

where a "hundred" manifestly denotes what is full; for it is said, there shall be no more an infant of days, nor an old man that hath not filled his days, and a child and a sinner of a hundred years; that is, when his state is full. [5] In *Matthew :*—

Every one that hath left houses, or brethren, or sisters, or father, or mother, or wife, or children, or lands, for My name's sake, shall receive a hundredfold, and shall inherit eternal life (xix. 29 ; *Mark* x. 29, 30) ;

where a "hundredfold" denotes what is full; or "good measure, pressed down, shaken together, running over" (*Luke* vi. 38). [6] And in *Luke :*—

And other seed fell upon the good earth ; and having sprung up it brought forth fruit a hundredfold (viii. 8 ; *Matt.* xiii. 8, 23 ; *Mark* iv. 20) ;

where also a "hundred" denotes what is full, which number would not have been mentioned unless it had signified that. The same is true where the Lord speaks by parable concerning the debtors, that one owed "a hundred baths of oil," and the other "a hundred cors of wheat" (*Luke* xvi. 5–7). So also in other places where a "hundred" is mentioned. The case is similar with a "thousand," respecting which number, see above (n. 2575).

2637. *When Isaac his son was born unto him.* That this signifies when the Lord's rational was made Divine, is evident from the signification of "being born," which is to come forth (*existere*) (see n. 2584, 2621, 2629) ; and from the representation of "Isaac," as being the Divine rational (see n. 2630). This is said to be "born to Abraham," when made

Divine; as also above, verse 3: "Abraham called the name of
his son that was born unto him" (see n. 2628).

2638. Verses 6, 7. *And Sarah said, God hath made laugh-*
ter for me ; every one that heareth will laugh with me. And
she said, Who would have said unto Abraham, Sarah shall
suckle sons? for I have borne a son to his old age. "Sarah said,"
signifies perception from the Divine spiritual; "God hath
made laughter for me," signifies the affection of celestial
truth; "every one that heareth will laugh with me," signifies
that all things in it will have this affection; "and she said,"
signifies thought; "who would have said unto Abraham,
Sarah shall suckle sons?" signifies that the Lord implanted
the Human in the Divine by His own power; "for I have
borne a son to his old age," signifies that this was done when
the days were fulfilled.

2639. *Sarah said.* That this signifies perception from the
Divine spiritual, is evident from the signification of "saying,"
as being to perceive (as has been often shown); and from the
representation of Sarah, as being the Divine spiritual, or Divine
truth (see n. 2622).

2640. *God hath made laughter for me.* That this signifies
the affection of celestial truth, is evident from the signification of "laughter," as being the affection of truth (see n. 2072,
2216); and from the expression "God making," as denoting
the celestial from which it is.

2641. *Every one that heareth will laugh with me.* That
this signifies that all things in it will have this affection, is
evident from the signification of "hearing" and "laughing."
In the Word to "hear" is predicated of what is of affection, but
to "see" of what is of thought; which is evident from a great
many passages in the Word, as also from the correspondences
(see n. 2542). As the affection of celestial truth is here
treated of, it is said, "Every one that heareth," by which are
signified all things that are of affection. (That to "laugh"
denotes to be affected by truth, that is, to have the affection of
truth, see above, n. 2072, 2216, 2640.)

2642. *And she said.* That this signifies thought, is evident
from the signification of "saying," as being to perceive, and also
to think (as explained very often, see n. 2619 at the end).

2643. *Who would have said unto Abraham, Sarah shall suckle sons?* That this signifies that the Lord implanted the Human in the Divine by His own power, is evident from the representation of Abraham, and also of Sarah, and from the signification of "suckling" and of "sons." That Abraham represents Divine good, and Sarah Divine truth, has been shown before. That "milk" denotes what is spiritual from a celestial origin, or truth from good, may be seen above (n. 2184); and thus to "suckle" is to implant it. That "sons" are truths, here those that are in the rational, is evident from the signification of "sons" (n. 489, 490, 491, 533). That these things signify in the internal sense that the Lord implanted the Human in the Divine by His own power, is because the Divine truth is the same as the Divine Human; and when it is said of this that it "suckles sons to Abraham," the signification is that it has implanted the Human in the Divine; and as it was the Human, He did it from His own power. But these things can with difficulty be explained more clearly to the understanding. If many words be used, the sense will become still more obscure; for these are Divine things, which can only be presented before angels by things celestial and spiritual; and if they were presented before man in any more elevated style, they would fall into the material and corporeal ideas which man has. [2] It is further to be known that the Lord's Divine rational is described as to its quality when it was first born in the words, "God hath made laughter for me; every one that heareth will laugh with me; and she said, Who would have said unto Abraham, Sarah shall suckle sons?" For it was according to ancient custom, that when a child was born, a name was given significative of the state; and that the state also was then described; as when Cain was born to Eve and Adam (*Gen.* iv. 1); when Sheth was born to them (*Gen.* iv. 25); when Noah was born to Lamech (*Gen.* v. 29); when Esau and Jacob were born to Isaac (*Gen.* xxv. 25, 26); when the twelve sons were born to Jacob (*Gen.* xxix. 32–35; xxx. 6, 8, 11, 13, 18, 20, 24; xxxv. 18); when Perez and Zerah were born to Tamar (*Gen.* xxxviii. 29, 30); when Manasseh and Ephraim were born to Joseph (*Gen.* xli. 51, 52); when Gershom and Eliezer were born to Moses (*Exod.*

ii. 22; xviii. 4). What all these represent, and what they signify in the internal sense, was involved in the descriptions added to the names which were given; thus here what Isaac represents. What is involved is manifest in some degree from this brief explication, but deeper arcana yet are hidden within; for they are Divine things, which can be expressed by no forms or formulas of expression.

2644. *For I have borne a son to his old age.* That this signifies that this was done when the days were fulfilled, is evident from the explication of nearly the same words in the second verse (as to which see n. 2621–2624).

2645. Verse 8. *And the child grew, and was weaned; and Abraham made a great feast on the day when he weaned Isaac.* " The child grew," signifies the further perfecting of the Lord's rational; "and was weaned," signifies the separation of the merely human rational; " Abraham made a great feast," signifies dwelling together and union; " on the day when he weaned Isaac," signifies the state of separation.

2646. *The child grew.* That this signifies the further perfecting of the Lord's rational, is evident from the signification of " growing," as being to be perfected; and from the signification of the " child" or " son," as being the Lord's Divine rational (see n. 2623).

2647. *And was weaned.* That this signifies the separation of the merely human rational, is evident from the signification of " being weaned," as being to be separated, like infants from their mothers' breasts. That the merely human rational was separated, is further described in this chapter, and is represented by Hagar's son, in his being cast out of the house.

2648. *Abraham made a great feast.* That this signifies dwelling together and union, is evident from the signification of a " feast," as being a dwelling together (see n. 2341); here union also, because the Lord is treated of, whose Human was united to His Divine, and the Divine to the Human; and because this union is treated of, it is said a " great feast."

2649. *On the day when he weaned Isaac.* That this signifies the state of separation, is evident from the signification of " day," as being state (see n. 23, 487, 488, 493, 893); and from the signification of " being weaned," as being to be separated (see n. 2647). From the first verse of this chapter the uniting of the Lord's Divine Essence with His Human Essence has been treated of, in this order: The presence of the Divine in the Human for the sake of unition (verse 1). The presence of the Human in the Divine, and thus a reciprocal unition (see n. 2004) (verse 2). From this unition the Human was made Divine (verse 3). And this successively and continually while the Lord lived in the world (verse 4). And this commenced when the rational was in a state to receive (verse 5). The state of the unition is described as to its quality, with its arcana (verses 6, 7). Now follows the separation of the maternal human, and this is continued down to verse 12; which separation is signified in this verse by the weaning of Isaac, and is represented in the following verses by Hagar's son being sent away out of the house. And as the union of the Lord's Divine with His Human and of His Human with His Divine is the very marriage of good and truth, and from it is the heavenly marriage, which is the same as the Lord's kingdom, therefore a great feast is mentioned which Abraham made when he weaned Isaac, by which the beginning of marriage or the first union is signified; which feast and weaning, but for the signification, would never have been mentioned. [2] As the separation of the first human, which the Lord had from the mother, now follows, and at length the full removal of it, it is to be known that the Lord gradually and continually, even to the last of His life when He was glorified, separated from Himself and put off that which was merely human, namely, that which He derived from the mother, until at length He was no longer her son, but the Son of God, not only as to conception but also as to birth, and thus was one with the Father, and was Jehovah Himself. That He separated from Himself and put off all the human from the mother, so that He was no longer her son, is manifest from His words in *John*:—

When the wine failed, the mother of Jesus said unto Him, They have no wine. Jesus saith unto her, Woman, what [belongs] to Me and to thee ? (ii. 3, 4).

In *Matthew*:—

One said, Behold, Thy mother and Thy brethren stand without, seeking to speak to Thee. But Jesus answering said unto him that told Him,

Who is My mother? and who are My brethren? And stretching forth
His hand toward His disciples, He said, Behold My mother, and My
brethren; for whosoever shall do the will of My Father who is in the
heavens, the same is My brother, and sister, and mother (xii. 47–50;
Mark iii 32–35; *Luke* viii. 20, 21).

In *Luke :—*

A certain woman out of the multitude lifting up her voice, said unto
Him, Blessed is the womb that bare Thee, and the breasts which Thou
didst suck. But Jesus said, Blessed are they that hear the Word of God,
and keep it (xi. 27, 28).

[**3**] Here, when the woman spoke of His mother, the Lord
spoke of those described above, namely, " Whoever shall do the
will of My Father, the same is My brother, and sister, and
mother;" which is the same as this, " Blessed are they that
hear the Word of God, and keep it." In *John :—*

Jesus seeing His mother and the disciple whom He loved standing by,
said unto His mother, Woman, behold thy son. Then said He to the disciple, Behold thy mother. Therefore from that hour the disciple took her
to his own home (xix. 26, 27).

From these words it is manifest that the Lord spoke to her
according to her thought when she saw Him on the cross, and
even then not calling her mother, but " woman;" and that He
transferred the name of mother to those who are signified by
the disciple; on which account He said to the disciple, " Behold thy mother." Still more manifest is this from the Lord's
own words, in *Matthew :—*

Jesus asked the Pharisees, saying, What think ye of Christ? whose son
is He? They say unto Him, David's. He saith unto them, How then
doth David in the spirit call Him Lord, saying, The Lord said unto my
Lord, Sit Thou on My right hand until I make Thine enemies Thy footstool? If David therefore call Him Lord, how is He his Son? And no
one was able to answer Him a word (xxii. 41–46; *Mark* xii. 35–37; *Luke*
xx. 42–44).

Thus He was no longer the Son of David as to the flesh. [**4**]
And further, in regard to the separation and putting off of the
maternal human—those do not comprehend this who have
merely corporeal ideas respecting the Lord's Human, and think
of it as of the human of any other man; hence to such these
things are stumbling-blocks. They do not know that such as

the life is such is the man, and that the Divine *Esse* (Being) of life, or Jehovah, was in the Lord from conception, and that a similar *Esse* of life came forth in His Human by means of the union.

2650. Verse 9. *And Sarah saw the son of Hagar the Egyptian, whom she had borne unto Abraham, mocking.* "Sarah saw," signifies the Lord's insight from the Divine spiritual; "the son of Hagar the Egyptian," signifies into the merely human rational; "Hagar the Egyptian" is the affection of memory-knowledges, of which as a mother that rational was born; "whom she had borne unto Abraham," signifies that it came forth from the Divine celestial as a father; "mocking" signifies not in agreement with or favoring the Divine rational.

2651. *And Sarah saw.* That this signifies the Lord's insight from the Divine spiritual, is evident from the signification of "seeing," as being to understand (see n. 897, 2150, 2325), which is the same as to look into, from the mind's sight; also from the representation of Sarah, as being the Divine spiritual, or Divine truth (see n. 2622). "Sarah saw," means that the Divine spiritual had insight, which is the same as to say that the Lord had it from the Divine spiritual.

2652. *The son of Hagar the Egyptian.* That this signifies into the merely human rational, and that "Hagar the Egyptian" is the affection of memory-knowledges, of which that rational was born as a mother, is evident from the signification of the "son," namely Ishmael, as being the first rational which the Lord had—treated of in the sixteenth chapter of *Genesis*, where Hagar and Ishmael are the subject—also from his representation, and that of Hagar the Egyptian, his mother, explained under that chapter. (That the first or merely human rational in the Lord was conceived from the Divine celestial as a father, and born of the affection of memory-knowledges as a mother, may be seen above, n. 1895, 1896, 1902, 1910.)

2653. *Whom she had borne unto Abraham.* That this signifies that it came forth from the Divine celestial as a father, is evident from the signification of "bearing," as being to come forth (*existere*) (see n. 2621, 2629); and from the representation of Abraham, as being the Divine celestial (see n. 1989, 2011, 2172, 2198, 2501). (That the first rational came forth from the Divine celestial as a father, may be seen above, n. 1895, 1896, 1902, 1910.)

2654. *Mocking.* That this signifies not in agreement with or favoring the Divine rational, is evident from the signification of "mocking," as being that which comes of an affection contrary to what does not agree with and favor one's self. In the preceding verse it was said that the child grew, and was weaned, and that Abraham made a great feast when he weaned Isaac; by which is signified that when the Lord's rational was made Divine, the former rational was separated. Therefore there now immediately follows that which concerns the son of Hagar the Egyptian, by whom this rational is meant, as was shown in the explication at the sixteenth chapter, where Ishmael and Hagar are treated of. From this it is likewise manifest that the things which are in the internal sense follow together in a continuous series. [2] But in regard to the Lord's first rational, seeing that it was born as with another man, namely, by means of knowledges (*per scientias et cognitiones*), it could not but be in appearances of truth, which are not truths in themselves, as is evident from what has been shown before (n. 1911, 1936, 2196, 2203, 2209, 2519); and as it was in appearances of truth, truths without appearances, such as Divine truths are, could not agree with it or favor it, both because this rational does not comprehend them, and because they oppose it. But take examples for illustration. [3] The human rational—that namely which has its birth * from worldly things through impressions of sense, and afterwards from analogies of worldly things by means of knowledges (*per scientifica et cognitiones*)—is ready to laugh and mock if told that it does not live of itself, but only appears to live so; and that one lives the more, that is, the more wisely and intelligently, and the more blissfully and happily, the less he believes that he lives of himself; and that this is the life of angels, especially of those who are celestial, and inmost, or nearest to the Lord; for they know that no one lives of himself except Jehovah alone, that is, the Lord. [4] This rational would mock also if it were told that it has nothing of its own, and that its having anything of its own is a fallacy or an

---

* *Natura*, probably a misprint for *natum*. [*Rotch ed.*]

appearance; and still more would it mock if told that the more
it is in the fallacy that it has anything of its own, the less it
has; and the converse. So too would it mock if told that
whatever it thinks and does from what is its own is evil,
although it were good; and that it is not wise until it believes
and perceives that all evil is from hell, and all good from the
Lord. In this belief, and even in this perception, are all the
angels; who nevertheless have what is their own more abundantly than all others; but they know and perceive that this
is from the Lord, although it altogether appears as theirs.
[5] Again: this rational would mock if it were said that in
heaven the greatest are they who are least, the wisest they
who believe and perceive themselves to be the least wise, and
the happiest they who desire others to be the most happy, and
themselves the least so; that it is heaven to wish to be below
all, but hell to wish to be above all; consequently that in the
glory of heaven there is absolutely nothing the same as in the
glory of the world. [6] In the same way would that rational
mock, if it were said that in the other life there is nothing of
space and time, but that there are states, according to which
there are appearances of space and time; and that life is the
more heavenly the further it is from what is of space and time,
and the nearer it is to what is eternal; in which, namely, in
what is eternal, there is nothing at all from the idea of time,
nor from anything analogous to it: and so with numberless
other things. [7] That there were such things in the merely
human rational, and that therefore this rational mocked at
Divine things, the Lord saw, and indeed from the Divine spiritual (which is signified by Sarah's seeing the son of Hagar
the Egyptian, n. 2651, 2652). That man is able to look from
within into the things in himself which are below, is known
by experience to those who are in perception, and even to those
who are in conscience; for they see so far as to reprove their
very thoughts. Hence the regenerate can see what is the
quality of the rational which they had before regeneration.
With man such perception is from the Lord; but the Lord's
was from Himself.

2655. Verse 10. *And she said unto Abraham, Cast out this
handmaid and her son ; for the son of this handmaid shall not*

inherit with my son, with Isaac. " She said unto Abraham," signifies perception from the Divine ; " cast out this handmaid and her son," signifies that the things of the merely human rational should be banished ;" for the son of this handmaid shall not inherit with my son, with Isaac," signifies that the merely human rational could not have a common life with the Divine rational itself, either as to truth or as to good.

2656. *She said unto Abraham.* That this signifies perception from the Divine, is evident from the signification of " saying" in the historic parts of the Word, which is to perceive (as stated often before) ; and from the representation of Abraham, as being the Divine celestial, or the Divine good (see n. 2622).

2657. *Cast out this handmaid and her son.* That this signifies that the things of the merely human rational should be banished, is evident from the signification of " casting out," as being to banish ; from the signification of a " handmaid," as being the affection of rational things and memory-knowledges, thus as being the good of them (see n. 2567) ; and from the signification of her " son," as being the truth of that rational (see n. 264, 489, 533, 1147). But it is apparent good and truth which are predicated of this first or merely human rational. Hence it is that " cast out this handmaid and her son," signifies that the things of the merely human rational were to be banished. How this is, namely, that the first rational was banished when the Divine rational took its place, has been stated and shown several times before ; but as it is here treated of specifically, it must be still further explained in a few words. [2] With every man who is being regenerated there are two rationals, one before regeneration, the other after regeneration. The first, which is before regeneration, is procured through the experience of the senses, by reflections upon things of civic life and of moral life, and by means of the sciences and the reasonings derived from them and by means of them, also by means of the knowledges of spiritual things from the doctrine of faith or from the Word. But these go no further at that time than a little above the ideas of the corporeal memory, which comparatively are quite material. Whatever therefore it then thinks is from such things ; or, in order that what it thinks may be comprehended at the same time by interior or intellectual sight, the semblances of such things are presented by comparison, or analogically. Of this kind is the first rational, or that which is before regeneration. [3] But the rational after regeneration is formed by the Lord through the affections of spiritual truth and good, which affections are implanted by the Lord in a wonderful manner in the truths of the former rational; and those things in it which are in agreement and which favor, are thus vivified; but the rest are separated from it as of no use; until at length spiritual goods and truths are collected together as it were into bundles, the incongruous things which cannot be vivified being rejected to the circumference, and this by successive steps, as spiritual goods and truths grow, together with the life of the affections of them. From this it appears what the second rational is. [4] How the case is with these things may be illustrated by comparison with the fruit of trees. The first rational, in the beginning, is like unripe fruit, which gradually matures till it forms seeds within itself, and when it is of such age as to begin to separate itself from the tree, its state is then full (see above, n. 2636). But the second rational, with which one is gifted by the Lord when he is being regenerated, is like the same fruit in good ground, in which those things which are round about the seeds decay, and the seeds push forth from their inmost parts, and send out a root, and then a shoot above the ground, which grows into a new tree, and unfolds itself at length even into new fruits, and then into gardens and paradises, according to the affections of good and truth which it receives (see *Matt.* xiii. 31, 32; *John* xii. 24). [5] But as examples aid conviction, take as an example that which is man's own before regeneration, and that which is his own after it. From the first rational, which he has procured to himself by the means described above, the man believes that he thinks truth and does good from himself, and thus from what is his own. This first rational cannot apprehend otherwise, even if it has been instructed that all the good of love and all the truth of faith are from the Lord. But when man is being regenerated, which takes place in adult age, then from the other rational with which he is gifted by the Lord he begins to think that the good and truth are not from himself, or from what is his own, but from the Lord (but that nevertheless he does good and thinks truth as from himself, may be seen above, n. 1937, 1947). The more he is then confirmed in this, the more is he led into the light of truth respecting these things, till at last he believes that all good and all truth are from the Lord. The Own that belongs to the former rational is then successively separated, and the man is gifted by the Lord with a heavenly Own, which becomes that of his new rational. [6] Take another example. The first rational, in the beginning, knows no other love than that of self and the world ; and although it hears that heavenly love is altogether of another character, it nevertheless does not comprehend it. But then, when the man does any good, he perceives no other delight from it than that he may seem to himself to merit the favor of another, or may hear himself called a Christian, or may obtain from it the joy of eternal life. The second rational however, with which he is gifted by the Lord through regeneration, begins to feel some delight in good and truth itself, and to be affected by this, not for the sake of anything of his own, but for the sake of the good and truth ; and when he is led by this delight, he disclaims merit, till at length he rejects it as an enormity. This delight grows with him step by step, and becomes blessed ; and in the other life it becomes happiness, and is itself his heaven. Hence it is now evident how it is with each rational in the man who is being regenerated. [7] But be it known that although a man is being regenerated, still each and all things of the first rational remain with him, and are merely separated from the second rational, and this in a most wonderful manner by the Lord. But the Lord wholly banished His first rational, so that nothing of it remained ; for what is merely human cannot be together with the Divine. Hence He was no longer the son of Mary, but was Jehovah as to each Essence.

2658. *For the son of this handmaid shall not inherit with my son, with Isaac.* That this signifies that the merely human rational could not have a life in common with the Divine rational itself, either as to good or as to truth, is evident from the signification of "inheriting," as being to have another's life (to be explained presently); from the signification of the "son of the handmaid," as being the merely human rational as to truth and as to good (see n. 2657); from the signification of "my son Isaac," as being the Divine rational as to truth (which is "my son"), and as to good (which is "Isaac"), concerning which see n. 2623, 2630. That "Isaac" is the Divine rational as to good, is evident from the signification of "laughter," from which he was named, as being the affection of truth, or the good of truth, in the sixth and seventh verses (2640, 2641, 2643). Hence it is manifest that "the son of this handmaid shall not inherit with my son, with Isaac," denotes that the merely human rational cannot have a life in common with the Divine rational, either as to truth or as to good. That it cannot have a life in common, is evident from the mere fact that the Divine is Life itself, and thus has life in Itself; whereas the merely human is an organ of life, and thus has not life in itself. [2] When the Lord's Human was made Divine it was no longer an organ of life, or a recipient of life, but was Life itself, such as is that of Jehovah Himself. It had this at first from its very conception from Jehovah, as is clearly manifest from the Lord's own words in *John* :—

As the Father hath life in Himself, so hath He given to the Son to have life in Himself (v. 26) ;

the Divine Human is what is here called the "Son" (n. 1729, 2159, 2628). In the same :—

In Him was life, and the life was the light of men (i. 4).

In the same :—

Jesus said, I am the way, the truth, and the life (xiv. 6).

In the same :—

Jesus said, I am the resurrection and the life, he that believeth in Me, though he die, yet shall he live (xi. 25).

In the same :—

The bread of God is He that cometh down from heaven, and giveth life unto the world (vi. 33).

But that man is not life, but an organ or recipient of life, may be seen above (n. 2021, and occasionally elsewhere). From all this it is evident that when the Lord was made Jehovah even as to His Human, that which was not life in itself, that is, that which was merely human, was banished. This is signified by its being said that the son of the handmaid could not inherit with the son Isaac. [3] That to "inherit," in the internal sense, when predicated of the Lord, is to have the Father's life, thus to have life in Himself; and when predicated of men, it is to have the Lord's life, that is, to receive life from the Lord, is evident from many passages in the Word. To have life in Himself is the *Esse* itself of life, that is, Jehovah; whereas to have the Lord's life, or to receive life from the Lord, is to receive the Lord in love and faith; and as those who so receive Him are in the Lord, and are the Lord's, they are called His "heirs," and His "sons." [4] In the Word of the Old Testament "inheriting" is predicated not only of what is celestial, or of good, but also of what is spiritual, or of truth, but still the one is expressed by a different word from the other: the word that is predicated of good may be rendered "to possess by inheritance;" and the word that is predicated of truth, "to inherit." The former word also in the original language involves possession, but the latter, derivation from something else, as is the case with the spiritual in relation to the celestial, or with truth in relation to good. In this verse, where the Lord's Divine rational, or His Divine Human, is represented by Isaac, the word denoting possession by hereditary right is used, because the Lord's Divine Human is the sole heir-possessor, as He also teaches in the parable (*Matt.* xxi. 33, 37, 38; *Mark* xii. 7; *Luke* xx. 14); and He declares in several places that all things of the Father are His. [5] That to "possess by inheritance" and to "inherit," in the Word, when predicated of men, signify to receive life from the Lord, consequently eternal life or heaven (for they alone receive heaven who receive the Lord's life), is evident in *John*:—

He that overcometh shall inherit all things, and I will be his God, and he shall be My son (*Rev.* xxi. 7).

In *Matthew*:—

Every one that hath left houses, or brethren, or sisters, for My name's sake, shall receive a hundredfold, and shall inherit eternal life (xix. 29; xxv. 34; *Mark* x. 17; *Luke* xviii. 18).

Here heaven is called "eternal life," elsewhere simply "life" (as in *Matt.* xviii. 8, 9; xix. 17; *John* iii. 36; v. 24, 29), for the reason that the Lord is Life itself, and he who receives His life is in heaven. [6] In *David :—*

God will save Zion, and build the cities of Judah, and they shall dwell there, and possess it by inheritance, the seed also of His servants shall inherit it, and they that love His name shall dwell therein (*Ps.* lxix. 35, 36) ;

where to "possess by inheritance" is predicated of those who are in celestial love, and to "inherit" of those who are in spiritual love. In *Isaiah :—*

He that putteth his trust in Me shall inherit the land, and shall possess by inheritance the mountain of My holiness (lvii. 13).

[7] In like manner in *Moses :—*

I will bring you unto the land concerning which I lifted up My hand to give it to Abraham, to Isaac, and to Jacob, and I will give it to you for an hereditary possession (*Exod.* vi. 8).

In the sense of the letter these words signify that the land of Canaan should be given to them for an hereditary possession, which also was done ; but in the internal sense they signify that heaven should be given to those who are in love to the Lord and faith in Him ; for as the Lord is represented by Abraham, Isaac, and Jacob, so love itself and faith itself are signified, consequently those who are in love and faith, and thus those who are in the Lord. The same are also signified by Abraham, Isaac, and Jacob, with whom many shall sit down in the kingdom of the heavens, as we read in *Matthew* viii. 11 ; for in heaven Abraham, Isaac, and Jacob are not known at all ; but it is only known what is represented and signified by them, as also what is signified by sitting down or eating with them. For that all names in the Word signify actual things may be seen above (n. 1224, 1264, 1876, 1888) ; also that the "land of Canaan" is the heavenly Canaan or heaven (n. 1585, 1607, 1866), which is called simply the "land" (n. 1413, 1607, 1733, 2571). So too in *Matthew :—*

Blessed are the meek, for they shall inherit the earth (v. 5).

2659. Verse 11. *And the word was evil exceedingly in the eyes of Abraham, on account of his son.* "The word was evil exceedingly in the eyes of Abraham," signifies the Lord's state when He first thought of that rational being separated from Himself; "on account of his son," signifies on this account, that He loved it.

2660. *The word was evil exceedingly in the eyes of Abraham.* That this signifies the Lord's state at first when He thought of that rational being separated from Himself, namely, that it was a state of grief from love, is evident without explication.

2661. *On account of his son.* That this signifies on this account, that He loved it, namely, the first rational, is evident from the signification of the "son," namely, that of the hand-maid, as being the merely human or first rational, described before. Although the cause of this grief is not told, it is evident from what follows. That the cause is the love is plain enough, for it is said "on account of his son;" and the same son is treated of in what follows, from verse 13 to verse 21. Nevertheless in order that it may be known why there was this grief, or on what account it is said that the word was very evil in Abraham's eyes on account of his son; take these few things by way of illustration. [2] The Lord did not come into the world to save the celestial, but the spiritual. The Most Ancient Church, called "Man," was celestial; and if this church had remained in its integrity, the Lord would have had no need to be born a man. But as soon as this church began to decline, the Lord foresaw that the celestial church would wholly perish from the world; and on that account the prediction was then made concerning the Lord's coming into the world (*Gen.* iii. 15). After the time of that church there was no longer a celestial church, but a spiritual church; for the Ancient Church which was after the flood (spoken of many times in the first Part) was a spiritual church; and this church, that is, those who were of the spiritual church, could not have been saved unless the Lord had come into the world. This is meant by the Lord's words in *Matthew:*—

They that are well have no need of a physician, but they that are sick; I came not to call the righteous, but sinners to repentance (ix. 12, 13).

Also by these words in *John:*—

And other sheep I have which are not of this fold; them also I must bring, and they shall hear My voice, and there shall be one flock and one shepherd (x. 16).

Also by the parable of the hundred sheep, in *Matthew* xviii.
11–13. [3] Now as by Isaac is represented the Lord's Divine
rational, and as by him are also signified the celestial who are
called "heirs;" and as by Ishmael is represented the Lord's
merely human rational, and as by him are also signified the
spiritual who are called "sons" (as is manifest from what was
said above, n. 2658), this was the reason why the Lord felt
grief from Divine love, as shown in the words of this verse;
and also in those which follow from verse 13 to verse 21,
where by Hagar's son and the mother of that son is represented the spiritual church; and the state of this church, that
is, the state of those who were of this church, is treated of (n.
2612).   These arcana cannot as yet be set forth more fully;
it may simply be said that with the Lord when in the world all
the states of the church were represented, and also in what
manner those who belonged to the church were to be saved by
Him; and for this reason the same states of the church are
likewise signified by these same names.

2662. Verse 12. *And God said unto Abraham, Let it not
be evil in thine eyes because of the child, and because of thine
handmaid; all that Sarah saith unto thee, hearken unto her
voice; for in Isaac shall thy seed be called.* "God said unto
Abraham," signifies the Lord's perception from the Divine;
"let it not be evil in thine eyes because of the child, and
because of thine handmaid," signifies a change of state toward
that rational; "all that Sarah saith unto thee, hearken unto
her voice," signifies that He should act according to spiritual
truth; "for in Isaac shall thy seed be called," signifies that
from the Lord's Divine Human is all salvation for those who
are in good.

2663. *God said unto Abraham.* That this signifies the
Lord's perception from the Divine, is evident from the signification of "saying" in the historic parts of the Word, as being
to perceive (explained very often before); and because it was
from the Divine it is said that "God said to Abraham." By
both names "God" and "Abraham," is meant the Lord; which
shows that the historic statements which are the sense of the
letter, divide the ideas; but that the internal sense unites
them; for in the historic sense of the letter there are two

(namely, God and Abraham) who speak to each other; but in the internal sense there is one, namely, the Lord in respect to the Divine. This also shows that they who are three in the sense of the letter are one in the internal sense; as the Father, the Son, and the Holy Spirit, who are not three gods, but one; and that all the Trinity is complete in the Lord; namely, that in Him is the Father, as He says; and that from Him is the Holy Spirit, as He also says.

2664. *Let it not be evil in thine eyes because of the child, and because of thine handmaid.* That this signifies a change of state toward that rational, is evident. In the internal sense nearest the words, the meaning is that He should not grieve at having to separate the merely human rational from Himself; and also that He did not grieve; for it belonged to His perception from the Divine that it was necessary that it should be separated; because in no other manner could the human race be saved. This is the change of state that is signified.

2665. *All that Sarah saith unto thee, hearken unto her voice.* That this signifies that He should act according to spiritual truth, is evident from the representation of Sarah, as being the Divine spiritual, or Divine truth (see n. 2622); and from the signification of "hearkening to the voice," as being to act according to it (see n. 2542). What it is to act according to spiritual truth cannot be unfolded to the apprehension in the fullness in which it can be perceived by those who are in the internal sense; and therefore if we were to state what it is according to their perception, it would scarcely be acknowledged; and there is the further reason that more arcana are first to be unfolded, nay, believed, before the matter when unfolded can enter into the ideas of men's belief. What it signifies in a general way can be told in some small degree, namely, that the Lord formed a conclusion from the Human Divine, and acted according to it, and thus from His own power: for Divine truth was that by means of which He united the Human to the Divine; and Divine good that by means of which He united the Divine to the Human; which unition was reciprocal (see n. 2004).

2666. *In Isaac shall thy seed be called.* That this signifies that from the Lord's Divine Human is all salvation for those

who are in good, is evident from the representation of Isaac,
as being the Divine rational (as shown before), thus the
Divine Human (for the human commences in the inmost of
the rational, n. 2106); and from the signification of "seed,"
which is predicated of Isaac, as being the celestial rational, or
what is the same, those who are celestial (see n. 2085, 2661).
Thus that "thy seed shall be called" signifies that they will
be heirs, consequently that they will have salvation. The
spiritual also are " seed," but from the son of the handmaid,
as is said in the following verse :—" and also the son of the
handmaid, I will make him a nation, because he is thy seed;"
and therefore the spiritual also have salvation if they are in
good, as will appear from the internal sense of these words.
The Lord also teaches the same in many places, and plainly in
John :—

> As many as received Him, to them gave He power to become the sons
> of God, to them that believe in His name ; who were born, not of bloods,
> nor of the will of the flesh, nor of the will of man, but of God (i. 12, 13).

2667. From the first verse of this chapter to the seventh,
the unition of the Lord's Human with His Divine, and of His
Divine with His Human, has been treated of ; and it has been
shown that from that unition the Lord's Human was made
Divine. The contents of the several verses may be seen above
(n. 2649). From that point the merely human rational has
been treated of, as being separated (verse 8) ; because it was
not in agreement with the Divine Rational (verse 9) ; nor could
it have a life in common with it, either as to truth or as to
good (verse 10) ; that the separation was at first a grief to the
Lord (verse 11) ; but that He perceived from the Divine that
the human race could be saved in no other manner (verse 12).
There now follows the subject of those who were of the spiritual church, who are signified by Hagar's son after he was sent
away.

*   *   *   *   *   *   *   *   *

2668. Verse 13. *And also the son of the handmaid I will
make a nation, because he is thy seed.* " The son of the handmaid I will make a nation," signifies the spiritual church which
was to receive the good of faith ; "because he is thy seed."

signifies that they also shall have salvation from the Lord's Divine Human.

2669. *Also the son of the handmaid I will make a nation.* That this signifies the spiritual church which was to receive the good of faith, is evident from the signification of the "son of the handmaid," and also of a "nation." The son of the handmaid, or Ishmael, when he was in Abraham's house, or with Abraham, represented the Lord's first rational, as shown above (n. 2652, 2653, 2657, 2658); but now, when separated, he puts on another representation, namely, that of the spiritual church (n. 2666); in the same manner as did Lot before, who while with Abraham represented the Lord's external man (n. 1428, 1429, 1434, 1547, 1597, 1598, 1698); but when separated from Abraham represented the external church, and the many states of that church (n. 2324, 2371, 2399, 2422, 2459; and in the whole of the nineteenth chapter of *Genesis*). That a "nation" signifies good may be seen above (n. 1159, 1258-1260, 1416, 1849); here the good of faith, because it is predicated of the spiritual church. Hence now "also the son of the handmaid I will make a nation" signifies the spiritual church which was to receive the good of faith, that is, charity. [2] The Lord's kingdom in the heavens and on earth is celestial and spiritual; and the angels are therefore distinguished into celestial and spiritual (see n. 202, 337). To the celestial angels the Lord appears as a Sun, and to the spiritual as a Moon (n. 1053, 1521, 1529-1531). In the same manner are men distinguished into celestial and spiritual. They who were of the Most Ancient Church, which was before the flood, were celestial (treated of n. 607, 608, 780, 895, 920, 1114-1125); but they who were of the Ancient Church, which was after the flood, were spiritual (treated of n. 609, 640, 641, 765). What the difference between these churches was, may be seen above (n. 597, 607); also what the difference is between what is celestial and what is spiritual (n. 81, 1155, 1577, 1824, 2048, 2069, 2088, 2227, 2507). [3] The celestial are they of whom the Lord says:—

He calleth His own sheep by name, and leadeth them out; and when He hath led out His own sheep, He goeth before them, and the sheep follow Him, for they know His voice.

But the spiritual are they of whom He says :—

And other sheep I have which are not of this fold ; them also I must bring, and they shall hear My voice, and there shall be one flock, and one shepherd (*John* x. 3, 4, 16).

The good of love is what makes the celestial church, but the good of faith is what makes the spiritual church. The truth of faith does not make, but introduces.

2670. *Because he is thy seed.* That this signifies that they also have salvation from the Lord's Divine Human, is evident from what was said above (n. 2666). That "seed" is faith, but the faith of charity, may be seen above (n. 255, 880, 1025, 1447, 1610, 1940).

2671. From this thirteenth verse to the twenty-first, the Lord's spiritual kingdom is treated of in general, and specifically those who become spiritual; and this in order from the first state of their reformation to the last. Their state before reformation, as being one of wandering in the doctrinal things of faith (verse 14). That they are reduced even to ignorance, so as to know nothing of truth (verse 15). That they have grief from it (verse 16). And then comfort and help from the Lord (verse 17). And enlightenment (verse 18). And instruction from the Word (verse 19). That still their state after reformation, in comparison with the celestial, is obscure (verse 20). But that they have light from the Lord's Divine Human in their affection of memory-knowledges and of appearances of truths (verse 21).

2672. Verse 14. *And Abraham rose early in the morning, and took bread and a bottle of water, and gave to Hagar, and put them on her shoulder, and the child, and sent her away, and she went and wandered in the wilderness of Beer-sheba.* "Abraham rose early in the morning," signifies the Lord's clear perception from the Divine ; "and took bread and a bottle of water," signifies good and truth ; "and gave to Hagar," signifies implantation in its life ; "and put them on her shoulder," signifies as much as it could receive ; "and the child," signifies spiritual truth ; "and sent her away," signifies that he left it in what is their own ; "and she went and wandered in the wilderness of Beer-sheba," signifies a state of wandering in the doctrinal things of faith.

VOL. III.—24

2673. *Abraham rose early in the morning.* That this signifies the Lord's clear perception from the Divine, is evident from the signification of "morning," and of "rising early," as being to perceive clearly (see above, n. 2540, where the same words occur); and from the representation of Abraham, as being the Lord's Divine (shown often before). The Lord had a clear perception from the Divine concerning the state of His spiritual kingdom; namely, what they who are of that kingdom or of that church are in the beginning, what they are successively, and what they at length become; for all their state is accurately and fully described in the internal sense, from verse 13 to verse 21 of this chapter.

2674. *And he took bread and a bottle of water.* That this signifies good and truth, is evident from the signification of "bread," as being what is celestial, or good (see n. 276, 680, 2165); and from the signification of "water," as being what is spiritual, or truth (see n. 28, 680, 739). It is said a "bottle of water," because it is very little truth with which they are gifted in the beginning; as much that is to say as they are able to receive, which is signified by his "putting it on her shoulder" (n. 2676). Every one can see that these historic statements involve arcana, from the fact that Abraham, who was rich in flock and herd, and also in gold and silver, sent away in this manner his handmaid by whom he had a son, and the boy Ishmael whom he much loved, giving them only bread [and water]. He could also foresee that when these were consumed they would die; and this would have come to pass if they had not received help from the angel. And besides, these things respecting the bread and the bottle of water, and their being put on her shoulder, are not of so much importance as to be narrated. But still it was so done, and was related because these things involve and signify the first state of those who are becoming spiritual—to whom in the beginning something of good and something of truth, and indeed but little, is imparted—and afterwards that the water fails them, and they then receive help from the Lord.

2675. *And gave to Hagar.* That this signifies implantation in its life, is evident from the signification of "Hagar," as being the life of the exterior man (see n. 1896, 1909). The life of the exterior man is the affection of memory-knowledges, which is specifically signified by "Hagar the Egyptian." With those who are becoming spiritual, good and truth are implanted by the Lord in the affection of memory-knowledges; and this so that they desire to know and to learn what is good and true for the purpose and use of becoming rational and of becoming spiritual; for the affection of memory-knowledges is the mother through whom is born the rational in which is the spiritual (n. 1895, 1896, 1902, 1910). The like does indeed flow in from the Lord with all, but no others receive it for that end and that use except those who can be reformed; the rest do it for other ends and other uses, which are innumerable, and have regard to themselves and the world.

2676. *Put it on her shoulder.* That this signifies as much as it could receive, is evident from the signification of the "shoulder," as being all power (see n. 1085); thus as much of good and truth as one can receive.

2677. *And the child.* That this signifies the spiritual, is evident from the signification of a "child," here as being that which is called the spiritual; for Ishmael or the son of the handmaid here represents the man of the spiritual church; and because he here represents the beginning of it, he is called a "child."

2678. *And sent her away.* That this signifies that He left it in what is their own, is evident from the signification of "sending away," when done by Abraham, who represents the Lord; and also from the first state of those who are being reformed and are becoming spiritual. Their first state is that they suppose they do good and think truth from themselves, thus from what is their own, nor do they then know otherwise; and when told that all good and truth are from the Lord they do not indeed reject it, but do not acknowledge it at heart, because they do not feel it, nor interiorly perceive that anything flows in from any other source than themselves. As all who are being reformed are in such a state at first, they are therefore left by the Lord in what is their own; nevertheless they are led by means of this without knowing it.

2679. *And she went and wandered in the wilderness of Beersheba.* That this signifies a state of wandering at that time in the doctrinal things of faith, is evident from the signification of " going and wandering in the wilderness," as being a wandering state; and from the signification of " Beer-sheba," as being the doctrine of faith (treated of at the end of this chapter, where it is said that Abraham and Abimelech made a covenant in Beer-sheba, verse 32; and that Abraham planted a grove in Beer-sheba, verse 33). In this verse is described what the quality of the state of those who are reformed is in the beginning, namely, that they are carried away into various wanderings; for it is given them by the Lord to think much about eternal life, and thus much about the truths of faith; but because from what is their own (as just stated) they cannot do otherwise than wander hither and thither, both in doctrine and in life, seizing as truth that which has been inseminated from their infancy, or is impressed upon them by others, or is thought out by themselves—besides their being led away by various affections of which they are not conscious—they are like fruits as yet unripe, on which shape, beauty, and savor cannot be induced in a moment; or like tender blades which cannot in a moment grow up into bloom and ear. But the things which enter in at that time, though for the most part erroneous, are still such as are serviceable for promoting growth; and afterwards, when the men are being reformed, these are partly separated, and are partly conducive to introducing nourishment and as it were juices into the subsequent life—which again can afterwards be partly adapted to the implanting of goods and truths by the Lord, and partly to being serviceable to spiritual things as ultimate planes; and thus as continual means to reformation, which means follow on in perpetual connection and order; for all things even the least with man are foreseen by the Lord, and are provided for his future state to eternity; and this for his good in so far as is in any wise possible, and as he suffers himself to be led by the Lord.

2680. Verse 15. *And the water was spent out of the bottle, and she cast the child under one of the shrubs.* " The water was spent out of the bottle," signifies the desolation of truth; "and she cast the child under one of the shrubs," signifies despair that nothing of truth and good was perceived.

2681. *The water was spent out of the bottle.* That this signifies the desolation of truth, is evident from the signification of being "spent," as being desolated; and from the signification of "water," as being truth (see n. 28, 680, 739).

2682. *And she cast the child under one of the shrubs.* That this signifies despair that nothing of truth and good was perceived, is evident from the signification of the "child," as being spiritual truth (see n. 2669, 2677); and from the signification of a "shrub" or "bush," as being perception, but so little as to be scarcely anything; on which account it is also said "under one of the shrubs"—having the same signification as trees, but in a less degree; and that "trees" signify perceptions may be seen above (n. 103, 2163): also from the feeling there was in the act, which was one of despair; all which shows that by her casting the child under one of the shrubs is signified despair that nothing of truth and good was perceived. That being "cast under one of the shrubs" denotes to be desolated as to truth and good even to despair, is manifest in *Job :—*

Alone in want and famine ; they flee to the drought, yesternight desolation and wasteness ; they pluck mallows upon the shrub ; to dwell in the cleft of the valleys, in holes of the dust and of the rocks ; among the shrubs they were groaning, under the thistle they were joined together (xxx. 3, 4, 6, 7) ;

where the desolation of truth is treated of, which is described by forms of expression in common use in the Ancient Church (for the book of *Job* is a book of the Ancient Church), such as to be alone, in want and in famine, to flee to the drought, yesternight desolation and wasteness ; to dwell in the clefts of the valleys and of the rocks ; also to pluck mallows upon the shrub, and to groan among the shrubs. So too in *Isaiah :—*

They shall come and shall rest all of them in the rivers of desolations, in the clefts of the rocks, and in all shrubs, and in all watercourses (vii. 19) ;

where also desolation is treated of, which is described by similar forms of expression, that is to say, by resting in the rivers of desolations, in the clefts of the rocks, and in the shrubs. [2] In this verse the second state of those who are being reformed is treated of, which is that they are reduced to ignorance till they know nothing of truth, and this even to despair. The cause of their being reduced to such ignorance is that persuasive light may be extinguished, which is of such a nature as to illuminate falsities equally as well as truths, and to induce a belief in falsity by means of truths, and a belief in truth by means of falsities, and at the same time trust in themselves; also that they may be led by experience itself to a knowledge of the fact that nothing of good and nothing of truth is of self or of man's own, but from the Lord. They who are being reformed are reduced into ignorance even to despair, and then they have comfort and enlightenment, as is evident from what follows; for the light of truth from the Lord cannot flow into the persuasive which is from man's own; for this is of such a nature as to extinguish that light. In the other life that which is persuasive appears like the light of winter; but at the approach of the light of heaven, instead of that light there comes darkness, in which there is ignorance of all truth. With those who are being reformed this state is called the state of desolation of truth, and this also is much treated of in the internal sense of the Word. [3] But of this state few have any knowledge, because few at this day are being regenerated. To those who are not being regenerated it makes no difference whether they know the truth, or do not; nor whether what they do know be truth or not, provided they can palm a thing off for truth. But they who are being regenerated think much about doctrine and life, because they think much about eternal salvation; and therefore if truth be deficient with them, as it is the subject of their thought and affection, they grieve at heart. The state of the one and of the other may be seen from this: While a man is in the body he is living as to his spirit in heaven, and as to his body in the world; for he is born into both, and has been so created that as to his spirit he can be actually with the angels, and at the same time with men by means of what is of the body. But as there are few who believe that they have a spirit which is to live after death, there are few who are being regenerated. To those who believe it, the other life is the whole of their thought and affection, and the world is nothing in comparison; but to those who do not believe it, the world is the whole of their thought and affection, and the other life is in comparison nothing. The former are they who can be regenerated, but the latter are they who cannot.

2683. Verse 16. *And she went and sat by herself over against him, withdrawing about a bowshot ; for she said, Let me not see the death of the child ; and she sat over against him ; and she lifted up her voice and wept.* " She went and sat by herself over against him," signifies a state of thought ; " withdrawing about a bowshot," signifies how far that state was from the doctrine of truth (a " bow" is the doctrine of truth) ; " for she said, Let me not see the death of the child," signifies grief that it should thus perish ; " and she sat over against him," signifies a state of thought ; " and she lifted up her voice and wept," signifies a further degree of grief.

2684. *And she went and sat by herself over against him.* That this signifies a state of thought, is evident from the signification of " going," and also of " sitting by herself," and this over against, as applied to the things that precede and that follow. To " go," here to go away from the child, signifies removal from spiritual truth ; which is further expressed and determined by her withdrawing about a bowshot. To " sit by one's self," signifies a solitary state, such as is that of thought in grief and despair ; " over against," signifies that she might not look on, and yet might look on ; that to " look on" means to think, see above (n. 2245) ; this is also further expressed and determined by her saying, " Let me not see the death of the child ; and she sat over against." There is thus involved in these words the state of thought of those who are in desolation of truth, and in the consequent despair.

2685. *Withdrawing about a bowshot.* That this signifies how distant the state was from the doctrine of truth, is evident from the signification of " withdrawing," as being to be distant ; and from the signification of a " bow," as being the doctrine of truth (concerning which presently) ; a " shot" signifies as far distant as possible, since it was as far as an arrow could be sent by a bow. It is here said a " bowshot," because a " bow" is predicated of the spiritual man, and he is a shooter of the bow—as is said of him in the 20th verse following :— " and he dwelt in the wilderness, and became a shooter of the bow."

2686. That a "bow" here denotes the doctrine of truth, is evident from its signification. Wherever wars are treated of in the Word, and wherever they are mentioned, no other wars are signified than spiritual ones (n. 1664). There were books also in the Ancient Word that were entitled "The Wars of Jehovah;" as is evident in Moses (*Num.* xxi. 14–16); which, being written in the prophetic style, had an internal sense, and treated of the combats and temptations of the Lord, and also of those of the church, and of the men of the church. This is manifest from the fact that some things were taken from these books by Moses; and also from other books of that church called "The Books of the Prophetic Enunciators" (respecting which see *Num.* xxi. 27–30), in which almost the same words are found as in *Jeremiah* (compare *Num.* xxi. 28, and *Jer.* xlviii. 45). From this it may also be concluded that the Ancient Church had writings both historic and prophetic that were Divine and inspired, and that in their internal sense treated of the Lord and His kingdom; and that these were the Word to them, as are to us those historic and prophetic books which in the sense of the letter treat of the Jews and Israelites, but in their internal sense of the Lord, and of the things which are His. [2] As in the Word, and also in the books of the Ancient Church, "war" signified spiritual war, so all arms, such as sword, spear, buckler, shield, darts, bow, and arrows, signified special things belonging to war as understood in the spiritual sense. What the several kinds of arms specifically signify, will of the Lord's Divine mercy be told elsewhere. Here it will now be shown what a "bow" signifies, namely, the doctrine of truth; and this from the darts, arrows, or other missiles, which denote the doctrinal things from which and with which those in especial fight who are spiritual, and who were thence formerly called "shooters with the bow." [3] That a "bow" signifies the doctrine of truth is evident from the following passages. In *Isaiah :*—

Jehovah's arrows are sharp, and all His bows are bent, the hoofs of His horses are counted as rock, and His wheels as the whirlwind (v. 28).

Here the truths of doctrine are treated of; "arrows" are spiritual truths; "bows" are doctrine; the "horses' hoofs" are natural truths; the "wheels" are their doctrine; and as these things have such a signification they are attributed to Jehovah, to whom they cannot be attributed except in a spiritual sense; for otherwise they would be empty words and unbecoming.   In *Jeremiah* :—

The Lord hath bent His bow like an enemy, He hath stood with His right hand as an adversary, and hath slain all that were pleasant to the eye in the tent of the daughter of Zion, He hath poured out His fury like fire (*Lam.* ii. 4).

Here "bow" denotes the doctrine of truth, which appears to those who are in falsities as an enemy and as hostile; no other bow can be predicated of the Lord.   In *Habakkuk* :—

O Jehovah, Thou ridest upon Thy horses, Thy chariots of salvation, Thy bow will be made quite bare (iii. 8, 9).

Here also the "bow" is the doctrine of good and truth.   In *Moses* :—

They grieved him, and shot at him, the archers hated him, his bow abode in strength, and the arms of his hands were made strong by the hands of the Mighty One of Jacob; from thence is the Shepherd, the Stone of Israel (*Gen.* xlix. 23, 24) ;

where Joseph is spoken of.   His "bow" denotes the doctrine of good and truth.   [4] In *John* :—

I saw and behold a white horse, and he that sat thereon had a bow, and there was given unto him a crown (*Rev.* vi. 2).

The "white horse" denotes wisdom; "he that sat thereon," the Word, as is said plainly in chapter xix. 13, where the white horse is again treated of; and as he that sat thereon was the Word, it is evident that the "bow" is the doctrine of truth. In *Isaiah* :—

Who hath raised up righteousness from the east, and called him to his footsteps ? he hath given nations before him, and made him to rule over kings; he gave them as dust to his sword, as the driven stubble to his bow (xli. 2) ;

where the Lord is treated of; the "sword" denotes truth; the "bow," doctrine from Him.   In the same : —

I will set a sign among them, and I will send such as escape of them unto the nations, to Tarshish, Pul, and Lud, that draw the bow, to Tubal and Javan (lxvi. 19).

They that "draw the bow" denote those who teach doctrine. The signification of "Tarshish" may be seen above (n. 1156); that of "Lud" (n. 1195, 1231), that of "Tubal" (n. 1151), and that of "Javan" (1152, 1153, 1155). [5] In *Jeremiah :*—

> For the voice of the horseman and of him that shooteth the bow, the whole city fleeth ; they have entered into clouds, and climbed up upon the rocks, the whole city is forsaken (iv. 29).

The "horseman" denotes those who declare truth ; the "bow," the doctrine of truth, which they who are in falsities flee from or fear.   In the same :—

> Set yourselves in array against Babel round about ; all ye that bend the bow shoot at her, spare not with the arrow, for she hath sinned against Jehovah (l. 14, 29 ; li. 2, 3) ;

where "they that shoot, and bend the bow" denote those who declare and teach the doctrine of truth.   [6] In *Zechariah :*—

> I will cut off the chariot from Ephraim, and the horse from Jerusalem ; and the battle bow shall be cut off, and He shall speak peace unto the nations (ix. 10).

"Ephraim" denotes the understanding of truth in the church ; the "bow," doctrine.   In *Samuel :*—

> David lamented with this lamentation over Saul, and over Jonathan his son, and he said it to teach the sons of Judah the bow (2 *Sam.* i. 17, 18).

where the "bow" is not the subject, but the doctrinal things of faith.   In *Ezekiel :*—

> Said the Lord Jehovih, This is the day whereof I have spoken ; and they that dwell in the cities of Israel shall go forth, and shall set on fire and burn up the weapons, the shield and the buckler, the bow and the arrows, and the hand staff and the spear, and they shall kindle fire in them seven years (xxxix. 8, 9).

The arms here named are all arms of spiritual war ; the "bow with the arrows" denote doctrine and its truths.   In the other life truths themselves when separated from good and represented to the sight, appear like arrows.   [7] As a "bow" signifies the doctrine of truth, in the opposite sense it signifies the doctrine of falsity.   The same things in the Word have usually an opposite sense, as has been said and shown in several places ; thus in *Jeremiah :*—

Behold a people cometh from the north country, and a great nation shall be stirred up from the sides of the earth ; they lay hold on bow and spear ; they are cruel, and shall not have compassion ; their voice shall roar like the sea, they shall ride upon horses set in array as a man for battle, against thee, O daughter of Zion (vi. 22, 23) ;

where " bow" denotes the doctrine of falsity.   In the same :—

Behold a people cometh from the north, and a great nation, and many kings shall be stirred up from the sides of the earth, they lay hold on bow and spear, they are cruel, and have no compassion (l. 41, 42) ;

where the meaning is similar.   In the same :—

They bend their tongue ; their bow is a lie, and not for truth, they are grown strong in the land ; for they have gone forth from evil to evil, and have not known Me (ix. 3).

[8] That the " bow" is the doctrine of falsity is plainly manifest, for it is said, " they bend their tongue ; their bow is a lie, and not for truth."   In the same :—

Jehovah Zebaoth said, Behold I will break the bow of Elam, the chief of his might (xlix. 35).

In *David* :—

Come, behold the works of Jehovah, who hath made desolations in the earth ; He maketh wars to cease unto the end of the earth, He breaketh the bow, He cutteth the spear in sunder, He burneth the chariots in the fire (*Ps.* xlvi. 9).

In the same :—

In Judah is God known, His name is great in Israel ; in Salem also shall be His tabernacle, and His dwelling-place in Zion ; there brake He the fiery shafts of the bow, the shield and the sword, and the war (*Ps.* lxxvi. 1–3).

In the same :—

Lo the wicked bend the bow, they make ready their arrows upon the string, to shoot in darkness at the upright in heart (*Ps.* xi. 2).

Here the " bow and arrows" plainly denote doctrinal things of falsity.

2687. *For she said, Let me not see the death of the child.* That this signifies grief that it should so perish, is evident from the signification of " seeing the death," as being to perish ; and from the signification of the " child," as being spiritual truth—explained above.   Hence, and from the feeling of despair on account of the desolation of truth, it is manifest that it is interior grief that is within these words.

2688. *And she sat over against him.* That this signifies a state of thought, is evident from what was said above (n. 2684), where are the same words. The reason that this is said again in this verse is that the state of thought was increased and aggravated even to the last degree of grief, as is manifest from what just precedes : "let me not see the death of the child;" and from what next follows : "she lifted up her voice and wept."

2689. *And she lifted up her voice and wept.* That this signifies a further degree of grief, is evident from the signification of "lifting up the voice and weeping," as being the last degree of grief; for weeping with a loud voice is nothing else. The state of desolation of truth, and also of removal from truths, with those who are becoming spiritual, is described in this verse. How these things are to be understood shall be briefly told. Those who cannot be reformed do not at all know what it is to grieve on account of being deprived of truths; for they suppose that no one can feel in the least anxious about such a thing. The only anxiety they believe to be possible is on account of being deprived of the goods of the body and the world; such as health, honors, reputation, wealth, and life. But they who can be reformed believe altogether differently : these are kept by the Lord in the affection of good and in the thought of truth; and therefore they come into anxiety when deprived of this thought and affection. [2] It is known that all anxiety and grief arise from being deprived of the things with which we are affected, or which we love. They who are affected only with corporeal and worldly things, or who love such things only, grieve when they are deprived of them; but they who are affected with spiritual goods and truths and love them, grieve when they are deprived of them. Every one's life is nothing but affection or love. Hence it is evident what is the state of those who are desolated as to the goods and truths with which they are affected, or which they love, namely, that their state of grief is more severe, because more internal; and in the deprivation of good and truth they do not regard the death of the body, for which they do not care, but eternal death. It is their state which is here described. [3] That it may be known who those are that can be kept by the Lord in the affection of good and truth, and thus be reformed and become spiritual, and who those are that cannot, we will briefly state that during childhood, while being for the first time imbued with goods and truths, every one is kept by the Lord in the affirmative idea that what he is told and taught by his parents and masters is true. With those who can become spiritual men this affirmative is confirmed by means of knowledges (*scientifica et cognitiones*); for whatever they afterwards learn that has an affinity with it, insinuates itself into this affirmative, and corroborates it; and this more and more, even to affection. These are they who become spiritual men in accordance with the essence of the truth in which they have faith, and who conquer in temptations. But it is otherwise with those who cannot become spiritual men. Although during their childhood these are in the affirmative, yet in the age that follows they admit doubts, and thus trench upon the affirmative of good and truth; and when they come to adult age, they admit negatives, even to the affection of falsity. If these should be brought into temptations, they would wholly yield; and on this account they are exempted from them. [4] But the real cause of their admitting doubts, and afterwards negatives, is to be found in their life of evil. They who are in a life of evil cannot possibly do otherwise; for as before said the life of every one is his affection or love; and such as is the affection or love, such is the thought. The affection of evil and the thought of truth never conjoin themselves together. With those in whom there is an appearance of this conjunction, there is really no such conjunction, but only the thought of truth without the affection of it; and therefore with such persons truth is not truth, but only something of sound, or of the mouth, from which the heart is absent. Such truth even the worst can know, and sometimes better than others. With some also there is found a persuasion of truth, of such a nature that no one can know but that it is genuine; and yet it is not so if there is no life of good : it is an affection of the love of self or of the world, which induces such a persuasion that they defend it even with the vehemence of apparent zeal, nay, they will even go so far as to condemn those who do not receive it, or believe in the same way. But this truth is of such a quality as is the principle with each person from which it starts, being strong in proportion as the love of self or of the world is strong. It indeed attaches itself to evil, but does not conjoin itself with it, and is therefore extirpated in the other life. Very different is it with those who are in the life of good. With these truth itself has its own ground and heart, and has its life from the Lord.

2690. Verse 17. *And God heard the voice of the child; and the angel of God called to Hagar out of heaven, and said unto her, What aileth thee, Hagar? fear not, for God hath heard the voice of the child where he is.* "God heard the voice of the child," signifies help at that time; "and the angel of God called to Hagar out of heaven," signifies consolation; "and said unto her, What aileth thee Hagar?" signifies perception concerning one's state; "fear not, for God hath heard the voice of the child where he is," signifies the hope of help.

2691. *God heard the voice of the child.* That this signifies help at that time, is evident from the signification of "God hearing a voice," said in the historic sense, as being in the internal sense to bring help; and from the signification of the "child," as being spiritual truth—explained before; here it is the state in which the spiritual was as to truth; for it is said that He heard the voice of the child, and again in this verse, that He heard the voice of the child where he was, that is, in what state; and in what precedes it was shown that it was in a state of the greatest grief on account of the privation of truth. The voice of the child, and not Hagar's, is said to have been heard, because the state of the spiritual man is treated of. By the child, or Ishmael, is represented the man of the spiritual church; by his mother Hagar, the affection of the knowledges of truth, which is that which had grief. Man's rational is born of the affection of memory-knowledges as a mother (n. 1895, 1896, 1902, 1910, 2094, 2524); but his spiritual is born of the affection of the knowledges of truth from doctrine, especially from the Word. The spiritual itself is here the "child;" and the affection of the knowledges of truth is "Hagar."

2692. *And the angel of God called to Hagar out of heaven.*
That this signifies consolation, is evident from the signification of "calling out of heaven," and also of the "angel of
God," as well as of "Hagar." To "call out of heaven," signifies influx; the "angel of God," signifies the Lord (n. 1925,
2319); and "Hagar," the affection of the knowledges of truth
(n. 2691). The influx of the Lord into the affection of truth,
when this is in deepest grief on account of the deprivation, is
consolation. That which flows in with man from the Lord is
said to be "called out of heaven," because it is through heaven,
and is there manifest; but in man's perception and thought it
is obscure, manifesting itself only by a change of the state of
his affection; as here by its receiving consolation.

2693. *And said unto her, What aileth thee, Hagar?* That
this signifies perception concerning its state, is evident from
the signification of "saying" in the historic parts of the Word,
as being to perceive—explained before; and from the signification of "What aileth thee, Hagar?" as being the state in
which it was: here it signifies that the Lord thoroughly knew
its state, although she was questioned, and it is said, What
aileth thee, Hagar? In the sense of the letter it is interrogation from the Lord, but in the internal sense it is infinite
perception of all things. We read here and there in the
Word that men are questioned as to their state; but the reason is that man believes that no one knows his thoughts, still
less the state of his affection. A further reason is that men
may have consolation from being able to express their feelings,
which often proves a relief (see n. 1701, 1931).

2694. *Fear not, for God hath heard the voice of the child
where he is.* That this signifies the hope of help, is evident
from the signification of "fear not," as being not to despair;
for when fear is taken away, hope is present; and from the
signification of "hearing the voice of the child," as being help
(see above, n. 2691, where the words are similar). In the
verses which precede, the state of desolation in which those
are who are being reformed and are becoming spiritual, is
treated of; now the subject is their being restored, and here
their comfort and hope of help. [2] That they who are being
reformed are reduced into ignorance of truth, or desolation,

even to grief and despair, and that they then for the first time
have comfort and help from the Lord, is unknown at this day,
for the reason that few are reformed. They who are such
that they can be reformed are brought into this state, if not in
the life of the body, nevertheless in the other life, where this
state is well known, and is called vastation or desolation, concerning which there has been some mention in the first Part
(where also see n. 1109). They who are in such vastation or
desolation are reduced even to despair; and when they are in
this state they then receive comfort and help from the Lord,
and are at length taken away into heaven, where they are instructed among the angels as it were anew in the goods and
truths of faith. The reason of this vastation and desolation
is chiefly that the persuasive which they have conceived from
what is their own may be broken (see n. 2682); and that they
may also receive the perception of good and truth, which they
cannot receive until the persuasive which is from their own
has been as it were softened. This is effected by the state
of anxiety and grief even to despair. What is good, nay,
what is blessed and happy, no one can perceive with an ex-
quisite sense unless he has been in a state of what is not
good, not blessed, and not happy. From this he acquires a
sphere of perception, and this in the degree in which he has
been in the opposite state. The sphere of perception and the
extension of its limits arise from the realizing of contrasts.
These are causes of vastation or desolation, besides many
others. [3] But take examples for illustration. If to those
who ascribe all things to their own prudence and little or
nothing to Divine Providence, it be proved by thousands of
reasons that the Divine Providence is universal, and this because it is in the most minute particulars; and that not even
a hair falls from the head (that is, nothing happens however
small) which is not foreseen and provided accordingly, nevertheless their state of thought about their own prudence is not
changed by it, except at the very moment when they find
themselves convinced by the reasons. Nay, if the same thing
were attested to them by living experiences; just at the moment when they see the experiences, or are in them, they may
confess that it is so; but after the lapse of a few moments

they return to their former state of opinion. Such things have some momentary effect upon the thought, but not upon the affection; and unless the affection is broken, the thought remains in its own state; for the thought has its belief and its life from the affection. But when anxiety and grief are induced upon them by the fact of their own helplessness, and this even to despair, their persuasive is broken, and their state is changed; and then they can be led into the belief that they can do nothing of themselves, but that all power, prudence, intelligence, and wisdom are from the Lord. The case is similar with those who believe that faith is from themselves, and that good is from themselves. [4] Take another example for illustration : If to those who have conceived the persuasion that when justified there is no longer any evil in them, but it is completely wiped away and blotted out, and thus they are pure—if to these it be made clear by thousands of reasons that nothing is wiped away or blotted out, but that they are kept back from evil and held in good by the Lord (that is to say those who are of such a character that from the life of good in which they had been in the world this is possible to them); and if moreover they be convinced by experience that of themselves they are nothing but evil, and indeed are most impure heaps of evils,—after all they will not recede from the belief of their opinion. But when they are reduced to such a state that they perceive hell in themselves, and this to such a degree as to despair of ever being able to be saved, then for the first time that persuasive is broken, and with it their pride, and their contempt of others in comparison with themselves, and also the arrogance that they are the only ones who are saved; and they can be led into the true confession of faith, not only that all good is from the Lord, but also that all things are of His mercy ; and at length into humiliation of heart before the Lord, which is not possible without the acknowledgment of the true character of self. Hence now it is manifest why they who are being reformed, or are becoming spiritual, are reduced into the state of vastation or desolation treated of in the verses which precede ; and that when they are in that state even to despair, they then for the first time receive comfort and help from the Lord.

2695. Verse 18. *Arise, lift up the child, and strengthen thy hand in him, for I will make him a great nation.* "Arise," signifies elevation of mind; "lift up the child," signifies the spiritual as to truth; "and strengthen thy hand in him," signifies support therefrom; "for I will make him a great nation," signifies the spiritual church.

2696. *Arise.* That this signifies elevation of mind, is evident from the signification in the Word of "arising," as involving where mentioned some kind of elevation (see n. 2401); here elevation of mind, because enlightenment—and in the following verse instruction—in truths.

2697. *Lift up the child.* That this signifies the spiritual as to truth, is evident from the signification of the "child," as being the spiritual especially as to truth (see n. 2677, 2687); for the man of the spiritual church seems to be regenerated by means of the truths of faith, but does not know that it is by means of the good of truth; for this is not apparent, and only manifests itself in the affection of truth, and then in life according to truth. Never can any one be regenerated by means of truth, except when in the truth there is good; for truth without good has no life; and therefore by truth separate from good there does not come any new life; which however a man possesses by regeneration.

2698. *And strengthen thy hand in him.* That this signifies support from it, is evident from the signification of "being strengthened," as meaning to be supported; and from the signification of the "hand," as being power (see n. 878), which relates to support. "In him," that is, in the child, means from it, that is, from the spiritual as to truth. They who are in internal grief, and in despair from the privation of truth, are elevated and sustained solely by truth, because it is for this that they have grief and despair. With those who are in the affection of good, their good desires good as one hungers for bread; but with those who are in the affection of truth, their good desires truth, as one thirsts for water. What "strengthening the hand in him" here means, will not be understood by any one except from the internal sense.

2699. *For I will make him a great nation.* That this signifies the spiritual church, is evident from the signification of

a " great nation," as being the spiritual church, which will receive the good of faith (see above, n. 2669).   It is said a " great
nation," because the spiritual kingdom is the Lord's second
kingdom (spoken of also in the same number).   As the man of
the spiritual church is represented by Ishmael, so also is the
spiritual church itself represented by him, and also the Lord's
spiritual kingdom in the heavens; for the image and likeness
of the one is in the other.   The first state after desolation was
described in the preceeding verse, which was a state of consolation and of the hope of help.   Their second state after desolation is described in this verse, which is a state of enlightenment and of refreshment therefrom.   [2] As these states are
unknown in the world, for the reason as before said that at
this day few are being regenerated, we may describe the state
of those who are being regenerated in the other life, where it
is most fully known.   Those who have been in vastation or
desolation there, after being comforted by the hope of help,
are elevated by the Lord into heaven, thus from a state of
shade which is a state of ignorance, into a state of light which
is a state of enlightenment and of the refreshment therefrom,
thus into a joy that affects their inmosts.   It is actually light
into which they come, of such a quality as to enlighten not
only their sight, but also their understanding at the same time;
and how much this light refreshes them may be seen from the
opposite state, from which they have been delivered.   Some
who had been of an infantile disposition and of simple faith,
then appear to themselves in white and shining garments;
some with crowns; some are taken around to various angelic
societies, and are everywhere received with charity as brethren;
and whatever of good is gratifying to their new life is shown
them : to some it is given to see the immensity of heaven, or
of the Lord's kingdom, and at the same time to perceive the
blessedness of those who are there; besides innumerable other
things which cannot be described.   Such is the state of the first
enlightenment, and of the refreshment therefrom with those
who come out of desolation.

2700. Verse 19. *And God opened her eyes, and she saw a
well of water ; and she went, and filled the bottle with water,
and gave the child drink.*   " God opened her eyes," signifies

intelligence; "and she saw a well of water," signifies the Lord's Word from which are truths; "and she filled the bottle with water," signifies truths from the Word; "and she gave the child drink," signifies instruction in spiritual things.

2701. *God opened her eyes.* That this signifies intelligence, is evident from the signification of "opening"—and of "God opening," and also of "eyes"—as being to give intelligence (that "eyes" signify the understanding may be seen above, n. 212, in like manner as "sight" or "seeing," n. 2150, 2325). It is said that "God opens the eyes" when He opens the interior sight or understanding; which is effected by an influx into man's rational, or rather into the spiritual of his rational. This is done by the way of the soul, or the internal way, unknown to the man. This influx is his state of enlightenment, in which the truths which he hears or reads are confirmed to him by a kind of perception interiorly within his intellectual. This the man believes to be innate in him, and to proceed from his own intellectual faculty; but in this he is very much mistaken; for it is an influx through heaven from the Lord into what is obscure, fallacious, and seeming with the man, which by means of the good therein causes the things which he believes to be similar to truth. But they only who are spiritual are blessed with enlightenment in the spiritual things of faith. It is this which is signified by "God opening the eyes." [2] That the "eye" signifies the understanding is because the sight of the body corresponds to the sight of its spirit, which is the understanding; and because it corresponds, in the Word the understanding is signified by the "eye" in almost every place where it is mentioned, even where it is believed to be otherwise; as where the Lord says in *Matthew:*—

The light of the body is the eye; if therefore thine eye be single, thy whole body shall be full of light; but if thine eye be evil, thy whole body shall be full of darkness; if therefore the light that is in thee be darkness, how great is that darkness (vi. 22, 23; *Luke* xi. 34).

Here the "eye" is the understanding, the spiritual of which is faith, as also is evident from the explication:—"if therefore the light that is in thee be darkness, how great is that darkness." So too in the same:—

If thy right eye causeth thee to stumble, pluck it out, and cast it from thee (v. 29 ; xviii. 9).

The "left eye" is the intellectual, but the "right eye" is its affection : that the right eye is to be plucked out means that the affection is to be subdued if it causes stumbling. [3] In the same :—

Blessed are your eyes for they see, and your ears for they hear (xiii. 16) ;

and in *Luke :*—

Jesus said to the disciples, Blessed are the eyes which see the things which ye see (x. 23).

Here by the "eyes which see," intelligence and faith are signified ; for their seeing the Lord, and also His miracles and works, did not make them blessed ; but comprehending them with the understanding and having faith, which is "seeing with the eyes ;" and obeying, which is "hearing with the ears." That to "see with the eyes" is to understand, and also to have faith, may be seen above (n. 897, 2325) ; for the understanding is the spiritual of the sight, and faith is the spiritual of the understanding. The sight of the eye is from the light of the world, but the sight of faith is from the light of heaven. Hence it is common to speak of seeing with the understanding, and of seeing by faith. (That to "hear with the ear" is to obey, may be seen above, n. 2542.) [4] Also in *Mark :*—

Jesus said to the disciples, Do ye not yet perceive, neither understand ? have ye your heart yet hardened ? having eyes see ye not ? and having ears hear ye not ? (viii. 17, 18) ;

where it is manifest that not to be willing to understand and not to believe, is to "have eyes and not see." In *Luke :*—

Jesus said of the city, If thou hadst known the things that belong unto thy peace ; but now it is hid from thine eyes (xix. 41, 42).

And in *Mark :*—

This is the Lord's doing, and it is marvelous in our eyes (xii. 11) ;

where to be "hid from the eyes," and to be "marvelous in the eyes," means to be so to the understanding, as is known to every one from the signification of the eye even in the common use of language.

2702. *And she saw a well of water.* That this signifies the
Lord's Word from which are truths, is evident from the signification of a "well of water," and of a "fountain," as being the
Word, and also doctrine from the Word, consequently also
truth itself; and from the signification of "water," as being
truth. That a "well in which there is water," and a "fountain," denote the Lord's Word, and also doctrine from the
Word, consequently also truth itself, may be seen from very
many passages. A "well," and not a "fountain," is spoken
of here, because the spiritual church is treated of, as also in
the following verses of this chapter :—

Abraham reproved Abimelech because of the well which the servants
of Abimelech had taken away (verse 25).

So too in the twenty-sixth chapter :—

All the wells which the servants of Isaac's father digged in the days
of Abraham his father, the Philistines had stopped up. And Isaac returned, and digged the wells of water which they had digged in the days
of Abraham his father, and the Philistines had stopped them up after
the death of Abraham. And Isaac's servants digged in the valley, and
found there a well of living water. And they digged another well, and
for that they strove not. And it came to pass in that day that Isaac's
servants came and told him concerning the well which they had digged,
and said unto him, We have found water (verses 15, 18, 19, 20, 21, 22,
25, 32).

Here by "wells" nothing else is signified than doctrinal matters
about which they contended, and those about which they did
not contend. Otherwise their digging wells and contending
so many times about them would not be of so much importance as to be worthy of mention in the Divine Word. [2]
The "well" spoken of by Moses signifies in like manner the
Word, or doctrine :—

They journeyed to Beer ; this is the well whereof Jehovah said unto
Moses, Gather the people together, and I will give them water. Then
sang Israel this song : Spring up, O well ; answer ye from it. The princes
digged the well, the willing of the people digged it, in the law-giver, with
their staves (*Num.* xxi. 16–18).

As a "well" signified these things, there was therefore this
prophetic song in Israel, in which the doctrine of truth is
treated of, as is evident from every particular in the internal
sense. Hence came the name "Beer" (a "well"), and hence

the name "Beer-sheba," and its signification in the internal sense, as being doctrine itself. [3] But doctrine in which there are no truths is called a "pit," or a "well in which there is no water," as in *Jeremiah* :—

Their nobles have sent their little ones to the water ; they came to the pits, they found no water ; they returned with their vessels empty (xiv. 3) ;

where "waters" denote truths ; and "pits where they found no water," doctrine in which there is no truth. In the same :—

My people have committed two evils : they have forsaken Me the fountain of living waters, to hew them out pits, broken pits, that can hold no waters (ii. 13) ;

where "pits" in like manner denote doctrines that are not true ; and "broken pits," fabricated doctrines. [4] That a "fountain" is the Word, and also doctrine, consequently truth, may be seen in *Isaiah* :—

The afflicted and the needy seek waters, and there are none ; their tongue faileth for thirst. I Jehovah will hear them, the God of Israel will not forsake them ; I will open rivers upon the hillsides, and fountains in the midst of the valleys ; I will make the wilderness a pool of waters, and the dry land springs of waters (xli. 17, 18) ;

where the desolation of truth is treated of, which is signified by the afflicted and needy seeking for waters when there are none, and by their tongue failing for thirst ; and then their consolation, refreshment, and instruction after desolation are treated of (as in the verses about Hagar now being explained), signified by Jehovah opening rivers upon the hillsides, making fountains in the midst of the valleys, and the wilderness into a pool of waters, and the dry land into springs of waters ; all which things relate to the doctrine of truth, and to the affection thence derived. [5] In *Moses* :—

Israel dwelt securely alone at the fountain of Jacob, in a land of corn and new wine ; yea, his heavens drop down dew (*Deut.* xxxiii. 28).

The "fountain of Jacob" denotes the Word and the doctrine of truth therefrom. Because the "fountain of Jacob" signified the Word and the doctrine of truth therefrom, when the Lord came to the fountain of Jacob, He spoke with the woman of Samaria, and taught what is signified by a "fountain" and by "water," as described in *John* :—

Jesus came to a city of Samaria called Sychar, and Jacob's fountain was there ; Jesus therefore being wearied with His journey, sat thus by the fountain. There cometh a woman of Samaria to draw water. Jesus saith unto her, Give Me to drink : Jesus said, If thou knewest the gift of God, and who it is that saith unto thee, Give Me to drink, thou wouldst ask of Him that He should give thee living water. Every one that drinketh of this water shall thirst again ; but whosoever drinketh of the water that I shall give him shall never thirst, but the water that I shall give him shall become in him a fountain of water springing up unto eternal life (iv. 5, 6, 7, 10, 13, 14).

As "Jacob's fountain" signified the Word, the "water" truth, and "Samaria" the spiritual church (as is frequently the case in the Word), the Lord spoke with the woman of Samaria, and taught that the doctrine of truth is from Him; and that when it is from Him, or what is the same, from His Word, it is a fountain of water springing up unto eternal life; and that truth itself is living water. [6] Again in the same :—

Jesus said, If any man thirst, let him come unto Me, and drink ; whosoever believeth in Me, as the Scripture saith, out of his belly shall flow rivers of living water (vii. 37, 38).

And in the same :—

The Lamb that is in the midst of the throne shall feed them, and shall lead them unto living fountains of waters ; and God shall wipe away all tears from their eyes (*Rev.* vii. 17).

In the same :—

I will give unto him that is athirst of the fountain of the water of life freely (*Rev.* xxi. 6) ;

"rivers of living water," and "living fountains of waters," denote truths that are from the Lord, or from His Word; for the Lord is the Word. The good of love and of charity, which is solely from the Lord, is the life of truth. He is said to be "athirst" who is in the love and affection of truth; no other can "thirst." [7] These truths are also called "fountains of salvation" in *Isaiah :—*

With joy shall ye draw waters out of the fountains of salvation ; and in that day shall ye say, Confess to Jehovah, call upon His name (xii. 3, 4).

That a "fountain" is the Word, or doctrine from it, is plain also in *Joel :—*

It shall come to pass in that day that the mountains shall drop down
new wine, and the hills shall flow with milk, and all the streams of Judah
shall flow with waters, and a fountain shall go forth out of the house of
Jehovah, and shall water the stream of Shittim (iii. 18) ;

where " waters" denote truths; and a " fountain out of the
house of Jehovah," the Lord's Word.   [8] In *Jeremiah :—*

Behold I will bring them from the north country, and gather them
from the sides of the earth ; and among them the blind and the lame ;
they shall come with weeping, and with supplications will I bring them
unto fountains of waters in a straight way, wherein they shall not stumble (xxxi. 8, 9) ;

" fountains of waters in a straight way" manifestly denote the
doctrinal things of truth; the " north country," ignorance or
desolation of truth; " weeping" and " supplications," their
state of grief and despair; and to be " brought to the fountains
of waters," refreshment and instruction in truths (as here,
where Hagar and her son are treated of).   [9] The same
things are also thus described in *Isaiah :—*

The wilderness and the parched land shall be glad for them, and the
desert shall rejoice and blossom as the rose ; budding it shall bud, and
shall rejoice even with rejoicing and singing ; the glory of Lebanon has
been given unto it, the honor of Carmel and Sharon ; they shall see the
glory of Jehovah, the honor of our God.   Make ye firm the enfeebled
hands, and strengthen the tottering knees.   The eyes of the blind shall
be opened, and the ears of the deaf shall be unstopped ; in the wilderness
shall waters break out, and streams in the desert ; and the dry place shall
become a pool, and the thirsty ground springs of waters (xxxv. 1-3, 5-7) ;

where the " wilderness" denotes the desolation of truth ;
" waters," " streams," " lakes," and " springs of waters," the
truths that are a refreshment and joy to those who have been
in vastation, whose joys are there described with many words.
[10] In *David :—*

Jehovah sendeth forth fountains into the valleys, they shall run among
the mountains ; they shall give drink to every wild beast of the field, the
wild asses shall quench their thirst.   He watereth the mountains from His
chambers (*Ps.* civ. 10, 11, 13) ;

" fountains" denote truths ; " mountains," the love of good and
truth ; to " give drink," instructing ; " wild beasts of the field,"
those who live from this (see n. 774, 841, 908); " wild asses,"

those who are solely in rational truth (n. 1949–1951).   **[11]**
In *Moses* :—

Joseph is the son of a fruitful one, the son of a fruitful one by a fountain (*Gen.* xlix. 22) ;

a "fountain" denotes doctrine from the Lord.   In the same :—

Jehovah thy God bringeth thee into a good land, a land of rivers, of waters, of fountains, and of depths going forth in valley and in mountain (*Deut.* viii. 7) ;

the "land" denotes the Lord's kingdom and church (n. 662, 1066, 1067, 1262, 1413, 2571); which is called "good" from the good of love and charity; "rivers," "waters," "fountains," and "depths," denote the truths thence derived.   In the same :—

The land of Canaan, a land of mountains and valleys, that drinketh water of the rain of heaven (*Deut.* xi. 11).

[12] That "waters" are truths, both spiritual and rational, and also those of memory-knowledge, is manifest from these passages in *Isaiah* :—

Behold the Lord Jehovih Zebaoth doth take away from Jerusalem and from Judah the whole staff of bread, and the whole staff of water (iii. 1).

In the same :—

Bring ye waters to him that is thirsty ; meet the fugitive with his bread (xxi. 14).

In the same :—

Blessed are ye that sow beside all waters (xxxii. 20).

In the same :—

He that walketh in righteousnesses, and speaketh uprightnesses, shall dwell on high ; his bread shall be given, his waters shall be faithful (xxxiii. 15, 16).

In the same :—

Then shall they not thirst, He shall lead them in the desert, He shall cause the waters to flow out of the rock for them ; He cleaveth the rock also, and the waters flow out (xlviii. 21 ; *Exod.* xvii. 1–8 ; *Num.* xx. 11, 13).

[13] In *David* :—

He clave the rocks in the wilderness, and gave them to drink abundantly as out of the deeps. He brought streams out of the rock, and caused waters to run down like a river (*Ps.* lxxviii. 15, 16) ;

where the "rock" denotes the Lord; "waters," "rivers," and "deeps" from it, denote truths from Him.   In the same :—

Jehovah maketh rivers into a wilderness, and water-springs into dry ground ; He maketh a wilderness into a pool of waters, and a dry land into water-springs (*Ps.* cvii. 33, 35).

In the same :—

The voice of Jehovah is upon the waters; Jehovah is upon many waters (*Ps.* xxix. 3).

In the same :—

A river, the streams whereof shall make glad the city of God, the holy place of the tabernacles of the Most High (*Ps.* xlvi. 4).

In the same :—

By the Word of Jehovah were the heavens made, and all the army of them by the breath of His mouth ; He gathereth the waters of the sea together as a heap, He layeth up the deeps in storehouses (*Ps.* xxxiii. 6, 7).

In the same :—

Thou dost visit the earth, and delightest in it greatly ; thou enrichest it, the river of God is full of waters (*Ps.* lxv. 9).

In the same :—

The waters saw Thee, O God, the waters saw Thee, the deeps also trembled ; the clouds poured out waters ; Thy way was in the sea, and Thy path in many waters (*Ps.* lxxvii. 16, 17, 19).

It is manifest to every one that the " waters" here do not signify waters, and that it is not meant that the deeps trembled, nor that the way of Jehovah was in the sea, and His path in the waters; but that spiritual waters are meant, that is, spiritual things which are of truth; otherwise this would be a heap of empty words.   In *Isaiah* :—

Ho every one that thirsteth, come ye to the waters ; and he that hath no silver, come ye, buy (lv. 1).

In *Zechariah* :—

It shall come to pass in that day that living waters shall go out from Jerusalem, half of them toward the eastern sea, and half of them toward the western sea (xiv. 8).

[14] Moreover where the church is treated of in the Word as about to be planted and as having been planted, and where it

is described by a paradise, a garden, a grove, or by trees, it is usual for it to be also described by waters or rivers which irrigate; by which either spiritual, rational, or memory things (which are of truth) are signified—as in the description of Paradise in *Genesis* (ii. 8, 9); which is also described by the rivers there (verses 10 to 14), signifying the things of wisdom and intelligence (see n. 107–121). The same is true in many other places in the Word, as in *Moses :*—

As valleys are they planted, as gardens by the river, as sandal-wood trees which Jehovah hath planted, as cedars beside the waters; waters shall flow from his buckets, and his seed shall be in many waters (*Num.* xxiv. 6, 7).

In *Ezekiel :*—

He took of the seed of the land, and planted it in a field of sowing, he placed it beside many waters; it budded, and became a luxuriant vine (xvii. 5, 6) ;

that a " vine" and a " vineyard" signify the spiritual church may be seen above (n. 1069). In the same :—

Thy mother was like a vine in thy likeness, planted by the waters ; she became fruitful and full of branches by reason of many waters (xix. 10).

In the same :—

Behold Asshur was a cedar in Lebanon ; the waters nourished him, the deep made him high, going with her rivers round about his plant ; and she sent out her canals unto all the trees of the field (xxxi. 4).

[15] In the same :—

Behold upon the bank of the river were very many trees on this side and on that. He said unto me, These waters issue forth toward the eastern border, and shall go down into the plain, and shall go toward the sea ; and being sent into the sea the waters are healed. And it shall be that every living soul that creepeth, in every place whither the two rivers come, shall live ; and there shall be a very great multitude of fish, because these waters are come thither ; and they shall be healed, so that everything whithersoever the river cometh shall live. The miry places thereof and the marshes thereof shall not be healed ; they shall be given up to salt (xlvii. 7, 8, 9, 11).

Here the New Jerusalem, or the Lord's spiritual kingdom, is described : the " waters going forth to the eastern border," signify spiritual things from celestial things, which are truths from a celestial origin ; that is, faith from love and charity (n.

101, 1250). To "go down into the plain," signifies doctrinal things which are of the rational (n. 2418, 2450). To "go toward the sea," signifies to memory-knowledges; the "sea" is the collection of them (n. 28); the "living soul which creepeth," signifies their delights (n. 746, 909, 994); which will "live from the waters of the river," that is, from spiritual things from a celestial origin. "Much fish" denotes an abundance of appliable memory-knowledges (n. 40, 991). The "miry places and the marshes" denote things not appliable and impure; being "given up to salt," denotes being vastated (n. 2455). In *Jeremiah* :—

Blessed is the man that trusteth in Jehovah; he shall be like a tree planted by the waters, and that sendeth forth its roots by the river (xvii. 7, 8).

In *David* :—

He shall be like a tree planted by the rivers of water, that bringeth forth its fruit in its season (*Ps.* i. 3).

In *John* :—

He showed me a pure river of water of life, bright as crystal, proceeding out of the throne of God and of the Lamb; in the midst of the street of it, and on this side of the river and on that was the tree of life bearing twelve fruits (*Rev.* xxii. 1, 2).

[16] Seeing that in the internal sense of the Word "waters" signify truths, therefore in the Jewish Church, for the sake of representation before the angels with whom the rituals were viewed spiritually, it was commanded that the priests and Levites should wash themselves with water when they came near to minister, and indeed out of the laver between the tent and the altar; and later, out of the brazen sea and the other lavers around the temple, which were in place of a fountain. So too for the sake of the representation was the institution of the water of sin or of purgation that was to be sprinkled upon the Levites (*Num.* viii. 7); also that of the water of separation, from the ashes of the red heifer (*Num.* xix. 2–19); and that the spoils from the Midianites should be cleansed by water (*Num.* xxxi. 19–25). [17] The waters which were given out of the rock (*Exod.* xvii. 1–8; *Num.* xx. 1–13; *Deut.* viii. 15) represented and signified an abundance of spiritual things

or truths of faith from the Lord. The bitter waters which were healed by the wood (*Exod.* xv. 23–25), represented and signified that the truths which are not pleasing become acceptable and grateful from good, that is, from the affection of it. (That " wood" signifies good which is of affection, or of the will, may be seen above, n. 643.) From all this it may now be known what " water" denotes in the Word, and hence what the water in baptism denotes, of which the Lord speaks thus in *John :—*

Except a man be born of water and of the spirit, he cannot enter into the kingdom of God (iii. 5) ;

namely, that " water" is the spiritual of faith, and the " spirit" the celestial of it; thus that baptism is the symbol of the regeneration of man by the Lord by means of the truths and goods of faith. Not that regeneration is effected by baptism, but by the life signified in baptism, into which life Christians who have the truths of faith, because they have the Word, must come.

2703. *And she filled the bottle with water.* That this signifies truths therefrom, is evident from the signification of " water," as being truth—treated of just above.

2704. *And gave the child drink.* That this signifies instruction in spiritual things, is evident from the signification of " giving to drink," as being to instruct in truths; and from the signification of the " child," as being the spiritual as to truth (see n. 2697). This state, which is that of instruction, treated of in this verse, is the third state of those who are coming out of vastation or desolation; for when they come into a state of enlightenment or of heavenly light (treated of in the preceding verse 18, see n. 2699), they are then in the affection of knowing and learning truths; and when they are in this affection, they are easily and as it were spontaneously imbued with truths : those who are on earth, from the Lord's Word or from doctrine; but those who are in heaven, from the angels, who perceive nothing more blessed and happy than to teach novitiate brethren, and imbue them with the truths and goods which are of heavenly order, and thus lead to the Lord.

2705. Verse 20. *And God was with the child, and he grew, and he dwelt in the wilderness, and became a shooter of the bow.* "God was with the child," signifies the Lord's presence with the spiritual; "and he grew," signifies increase; "and he dwelt in the wilderness," signifies obscurity, relatively; "and became a shooter of the bow," signifies the man of the spiritual church.

2706. *God was with the child.* That this signifies the Lord's presence with the spiritual, is evident from the signification of "God being with" any one, and from the signification of the "child." That "God being with" any one signifies the Lord's presence, is evident without explication. The Lord is indeed present with every one; for life is from no other source, and He governs the most minute things of it, even with the worst of men, and in hell itself; but in various ways according to the reception of life. With those who receive the life of the love of His good and truth in a wrong manner, and pervert it into loves of evil and falsity, the Lord is present, and overrules their ends as far as possible for good; but His presence with them is called absence, and indeed in the same degree in which evil is distant from good, and falsity from truth. But with those who receive the life of the love of the Lord's good and truth, He is said to be present, and indeed according to the degree of reception. It is with the Lord's presence as with that of the sun, which is present with its heat and light in the vegetation of the world also according to the reception. That the "child" signifies the spiritual as to truth, has been said above; but here he signifies those who are spiritual because he represents the man of the spiritual church, and also the spiritual church itself, and in the universal sense the Lord's spiritual kingdom; for when it is said that any one signifies what is spiritual, as here that "the child" signifies the spiritual as to truth, it involves that those are signified who are spiritual; for there is no spiritual without a subject. It is the same with all other things said in an abstract sense.

2707. *And he grew.* That this signifies increase, is evident without explication.

2708. *And he dwelt in the wilderness.* That this signifies in what is relatively obscure, is evident from the signification of "dwelling," as being to live (see n. 2451); and from the signification of "wilderness," as being that which has little vitality (see n. 1927); here what is obscure, but relatively. By what is relatively obscure is meant the state of the spiritual church relatively to the state of the celestial church, or the state of those who are spiritual relatively to that of those who are celestial. The celestial are in the affection of good, the spiritual in the affection of truth; the celestial have perception, but the spiritual a dictate of conscience; to the celestial the Lord appears as a Sun, but to the spiritual as a Moon (n. 1521, 1530, 1531, 2495). The former have light from the Lord, but giving both sight and the perception of good and truth, like the light of day from the sun; but the latter have light from the Lord like the light of night from the moon, and thus they are in relative obscurity. The reason is that the celestial are in love to the Lord, and thus in the Lord's life itself; but the spiritual are in charity toward the neighbor and in faith, and thus in the Lord's life indeed, but more obscurely. Hence it is that the celestial never reason about faith and its truths, but being in perception of truth from good, they say that it is so; whereas the spiritual speak and reason concerning the truths of faith, because they are in the conscience of good from truth; and also because with the celestial the good of love has been implanted in their will part, wherein is the chief life of man, but with the spiritual in their intellectual part, wherein is the secondary life of man; this is the reason why the spiritual are in what is relatively obscure (see n. 81, 202, 337, 765, 784, 895, 1114–1125, 1155, 1577, 1824, 2048, 2088, 2227, 2454, 2507). [2] This comparative obscurity is here called a "wilderness." In the Word a "wilderness" signifies what is little inhabited and cultivated, and also signifies what is not at all inhabited and cultivated, and is thus used in a twofold sense. Where it signifies what is little inhabited and cultivated, or where there are few habitations, folds of flocks, pastures, and waters, it signifies what has relatively little life and light—as what is spiritual, or those who are spiritual, in comparison with what is celestial, or those who are celestial. But where it signifies what is not inhabited or cultivated at all, or where there are no habitations, folds of flocks, pastures, or waters, it signifies those who are in vastation as to good and in desolation as to truth. [3] That a "wilderness" signifies what is comparatively little inhabited and cultivated, or where there are few habitations, folds of flocks, pastures, and waters, is evident from the following passages. In *Isaiah :*—

Sing unto Jehovah a new song ; and His praise from the end of the earth ; ye that go down to the sea, and the fullness thereof, the isles and the inhabitants thereof ; let the wilderness and the cities thereof lift up, the villages* that Kedar doth inhabit ; let the inhabitants of the rock sing, let them shout from the top of the mountains (xlii. 10, 11).

In *Ezekiel :*—

I will make with them a covenant of peace, and will cause the evil wild beast to cease out of the land, and they shall dwell securely in the wilderness, and sleep in the woods ; and I will make them and the places round about My hill a blessing ; the tree of the field shall yield its fruit, and the earth shall yield her fruit (xxxiv. 25–27) ;

here the spiritual are treated of. In *Hosea :*—

I will bring her into the wilderness, and will speak to her heart ; and I will give her her vineyards from thence (ii. 14, 15) ;

where the desolation of truth, and consolation afterwards, are treated of. In *David :*—

The folds of the wilderness do drop, and the hills are girded with rejoicing ; the pastures are clothed with flocks, the valleys also are covered over with corn (*Ps.* lxv. 12, 13).

[4] In *Isaiah :*—

I will make the wilderness a pool of waters, and the dry land springs of waters. I will plant in the wilderness the cedar of Shittim, and the myrtle, and the oil-tree ; I will set in the desert the fir-tree ; that they may see, and know, and consider, and understand together, that the hand of Jehovah hath done this, and the Holy One of Israel hath created it (xli. 18–20) ;

where the regeneration of those who are in ignorance of truth, or the Gentiles, and the enlightenment and instruction of those who are in desolation, are treated of; the "wilderness" is predicated of these ; the "cedar, myrtle, and oil-tree" denote the truths and goods of the interior man ; the "fir-tree" denotes those of the exterior. In *David :*—

* *Atria habitabit,* but *villæ quas habitat,* n. 3268. [*Rotch ed.*]

Jehovah maketh rivers into a wilderness, and water-springs into dry ground ; He maketh a wilderness into a pool of waters, and a dry land into water-springs (*Ps.* cvii. 33, 35) ;

where the meaning is the same.   In *Isaiah* :—

The wilderness and the parched land shall be glad for them, and the desert shall rejoice, and blossom as the rose ; budding it shall bud ; in the wilderness shall waters break out,* and streams in the desert (xxxv. 1, 2, 6).

In the same :—

Thou shalt be like a watered garden, and like a spring of water whose waters do not fail ; and they that be of thee shall build the deserts of old (lviii. 11, 12).

In the same :—

Until the spirit be poured upon us from on high, and the wilderness become Carmel, and Carmel be counted for a forest ; and judgment shall dwell in the wilderness, and righteousness in Carmel (xxxii. 15, 16) ;

where the spiritual church is treated of, which though inhabited and cultivated is called relatively a " wilderness ;" for it is said, " judgment shall dwell in the wilderness and righteousness in Carmel."   That a " wilderness" denotes a comparatively obscure state, is plain from these passages by its being called a " wilderness" and also a " forest ;" and very evidently so in *Jeremiah* :—

O generation, see ye the Word of Jehovah.   Have I been a wilderness unto Israel ? or a land of darkness ? (ii. 31).

[5] That a " wilderness" signifies what is not at all inhabited or cultivated, or where there are no habitations, folds of flocks, pastures, and waters, and thus those who are in vastation as to good and in desolation as to truth, is also evident from the Word.   This kind of " wilderness" is predicated in a double sense, namely, of those who are afterwards reformed, and of those who cannot be reformed.   Concerning those who are afterwards reformed (as here in regard to Hagar and her son) we read in *Jeremiah* :—

Thus saith Jehovah, I remember for thee the mercy of thy youth, thy going after Me in the wilderness, in a land that was not sown (ii. 2) ;

---

* *Effusæ sunt*, but *erumpent*, n. 6988.   [*Rotch ed.*]

where Jerusalem is treated of, which here is the Ancient Church that was spiritual. In *Moses :*—

Jehovah's portion is His people, Jacob is the line of His inheritance ; He found him in a desert land, and in a waste howling wilderness ; He led him about, He made him understand, He kept him as the pupil of His eye (*Deut.* xxxii. 9, 10).

In *David :*—

They wandered in the wilderness in a solitary way, they found no city of habitation (*Ps.* cvii. 4) ;

where those who have been in desolation of truth and are being reformed are treated of. In *Ezekiel :*—

I will bring you to the wilderness of the peoples, and I will judge with you there, as I judged with your fathers in the wilderness of the land of Egypt (xx. 35, 36) ;

where in like manner the vastation and desolation of those who are being reformed are treated of.   [6] The journeyings and wanderings of the people of Israel in the wilderness represented nothing but the vastation and desolation of believers before reformation ; consequently their temptation, if indeed they are in vastation and desolation when they are in spiritual temptations ; as may also be seen from the following passages in *Moses :*—

Jehovah bare them in the wilderness as a man beareth his son, in the way, even unto this place (*Deut.* i. 31).

And in another place :—

Thou shalt remember all the way which Jehovah thy God led thee these forty years in the wilderness, to afflict thee, to tempt thee, and to know what is in thy heart ; whether thou wouldest keep His commandments or no. He afflicted thee, He suffered thee to hunger, He made thee to eat manna, which thou knewest not, neither did thy fathers know ; that thou mightest know that man doth not live by bread only, but by everything that proceedeth out of the mouth of Jehovah doth man live (*Deut.* viii. 2, 3).

And again in the same chapter :—

Lest thou forget that Jehovah led thee in the great and terrible wilderness, where were serpents, fiery serpents, and scorpions ; a thirsty land where was no water ; who brought thee forth water out of the rock of flint ; He fed thee in the wilderness with manna, which thy fathers knew not, that He might afflict thee, and might tempt thee, to do thee good at thy latter end (verses 15, 16).

Here the " wilderness" denotes vastation and desolation, such as those are in who are in temptations.　By their journeyings and wanderings in the wilderness forty years, all the state of the combating church is described—how of itself it yields, but conquers from the Lord.　[7] By the " woman who fled into the wilderness," in *John*, nothing else is signified than the temptation of the church, thus described :—

The woman who brought forth a son, a man child, fled into the wilderness, where she hath a place prepared of God ; there were given unto the woman two wings of a great eagle, that she might fly into the wilderness, into her place ; and the serpent cast out of his mouth after the woman water as a flood, that he might cause her to be carried away of the flood.　But the earth helped the woman ; for the earth opened her mouth, and swallowed up the flood which the dragon cast out of his mouth (*Rev.* xii. 6, 14–16).

[8] That " wilderness" is predicated of a church altogether vastated, and of those who are altogether vastated as to good and truth, who cannot be reformed, is thus shown in *Isaiah* :—

I make the rivers a wilderness ; their fish stink because there is no water, and die for thirst ; I clothe the heavens with thick darkness (l. 2, 3).

In the same :—

Thy holy cities were become a wilderness, Zion was become a wilderness, Jerusalem a desolation (lxiv. 10).

In *Jeremiah* :—

I beheld and lo Carmel was a wilderness, and all her cities were broken down at the presence of Jehovah (iv. 26).

In the same :—

Many shepherds have destroyed My vineyard, they have trodden My portion under foot ; they have made My pleasant portion a wilderness of desolation, they have made it a desolation, it hath mourned unto Me, being desolate ; the whole land is made desolate, because no man layeth it to heart.　Spoilers are come upon all the hillsides in the wilderness (xii. 10–12).

In *Joel* :—

The fire hath devoured the folds of the wilderness, and the flame hath burned all the trees of the field, the water brooks are dried up, the fire hath devoured the folds of the wilderness (i. 19, 20).

In *Isaiah :—*

He made the world as a wilderness, and overthrew the cities thereof (xiv. 17) ;

where Lucifer is spoken of.   In the same :—

The prophecy of the wilderness of the sea. As whirlwinds in the south, it cometh from the wilderness, from a terrible land (xxi. 1, and following verses).

The "wilderness of the sea" denotes truth vastated by memory-knowledges and the reasonings from them.   [9] From all this it may be seen what is signified by the following concerning John the Baptist :—

It was said by Isaiah, The voice of one crying in the wilderness, Prepare ye the way for the Lord, make His paths straight (*Matt.* iii. 3 ; *Mark* i. 3 ; *Luke* iii. 4 ; *John* i. 23 ; *Isa.* xl. 3) ;

which means that the church was then altogether vastated, so that there was no longer any good, nor any truth; which is plainly manifest from the fact, that then no one knew that man had any internal, nor that there was any internal in the Word, and thus that no one knew that the Messiah or Christ was to come to eternally save them.   Hence it is also manifest what is signified by John being in the wilderness until the days of his appearing to Israel (*Luke* i. 80); and by his preaching in the wilderness of Judea (*Matt.* iii. 1, and following verses); and by his baptizing in the wilderness (*Mark* i. 4); for by that he also represented the state of the church.   From the signification of a "wilderness" it may also be seen why the Lord so often withdrew into the wilderness (see for examples *Matt.* iv. 1 ; xv. 32 to the end; *Mark* i. 12, 13, 35–40, 45 ; vi. 31–36 ; *Luke* iv. 1 ; v. 16 ; ix. 10 and following verses; *John* xi. 54). From the signification of a "mountain" also it is manifest why the Lord withdrew into the mountains (as in *Matt.* xiv. 23 ; xv. 29–31; xvii. 1 and following verses; xxviii. 16, 17 ; *Mark* iii. 13, 14 ; vi. 46 ; ix. 2–9 ; *Luke* vi. 12, 13 ; ix. 28 ; *John* vi. 15).

2709. *And he became a shooter of the bow.* That this signifies the man of the spiritual church, is evident from the signification of a "shaft," "dart," or "arrow," as being truth ; and from the signification of a "bow," as being doctrine (see

above, n. 2686). The man of the spiritual church was formerly called a "shooter of the bow," because he defended himself by truths, and disputed about truths; differently from the
man of the celestial church, who is secure by means of good,
and does not dispute about truths (see above, n. 2708). The
truths by which the man of the spiritual church defends himself, and respecting which he disputes, are from the doctrine
which he acknowledges. [2] That the spiritual man was in
old time called a "shooter" and an "archer," and that doctrine was called a "bow" and a "quiver," and that the truths
of doctrine, or rather doctrinal matters, were called "darts,"
"shafts," and "arrows," is further evident in *David :*—

The sons of Ephraim being armed, shooters of the bow, turned back
in the day of battle (*Ps.* lxxviii. 9).

"Ephraim" denotes the intellectual of the church. In the
book of *Judges :*—

Consider, ye that ride on white asses, ye that sit upon carpets, and ye
that walk by the way; because of the voice of archers among them that
draw water, there shall they rehearse the righteousnesses of Jehovah, the
righteousnesses toward His villages in Israel (v. 10, 11).

In *Isaiah :*—

Jehovah hath called me from the womb, from the bowels of my
mother hath He made mention of my name, and He hath made my
mouth like a sharp sword; in the shadow of His hand hath He hid me,
and He hath made me a polished arrow, in His quiver hath He hid me;
and He said unto me, Thou art My servant; Israel, in whom I will be
glorified* (xlix. 1–3).

"Israel" denotes the spiritual church. [3] In *David :*—

As arrows are in the hand of a mighty man, so are the children of the
youth; happy is the man that hath filled his quiver with them (*Ps.*
cxxvii. 4);

a "quiver" denotes the doctrine of good and truth. In *Habakkuk :*—

The sun and moon stood still in their seat; at the light of Thine arrows
shall they go, at the shining of the lightning of Thy spear (iii. 11).

That Joash king of Israel shot an arrow from a bow through
the window, at the command of Elisha, while Elisha said, "The

Quia in te gloriabor; but *in quo gloriosus reddar*, n. 3441. [*Rotch ed.*]

arrow of the salvation of Jehovah, the arrow of the salvation of Jehovah against the Syrian" (2 *Kings* xiii. 16 to 18), signifies arcana concerning the doctrine of good and truth.   [4] As most of the things in the Word have also an opposite sense, so likewise have "shafts," "darts," "arrows," "bows," and a "shooter;" and they signify falsities, the doctrine of falsity, and those who are in falsity.   Thus in *Moses :*—

Joseph is the son of a fruitful one, the son of a fruitful one by a fountain, of a daughter, she marcheth upon the wall ; they grieved him, and shot at him, and the archers hated him (*Gen.* xlix. 22, 23).

In *Jeremiah :*—

They have shot out their tongue, their bow is a lie, and not for truth ; their tongue is a lengthened arrow, it speaketh deceit (ix. 3, 8).

In *David :*—

They have sharpened their tongue like a sword, they have aimed their arrow, a bitter word, to shoot in secret places at the perfect ; suddenly will they shoot at him, and will not fear. They will make strong for themselves an evil word, they will tell of the hiding of snares (*Ps.* lxiv. 4–6).

In the same :—

Lo, the wicked bend the bow, they make ready their arrow upon the string, to shoot in the darkness at the upright in heart (*Ps.* xi. 2).

In the same :—

His truth is a shield and buckler ; thou shalt not be afraid for the terror by night, for the arrow that flieth by day (*Ps.* xci. 4, 5).

2710. In the verse before us the state of the spiritual church is described, as being obscure in comparison with the state of the celestial church, and as being combative, for the reason that the man of the spiritual church knows truth only from doctrine, and not from good itself, as does the man of the celestial church.

2711. Verse 21. *And he dwelt in the wilderness of Paran ; and his mother took him a wife out of the land of Egypt.* "He dwelt in the wilderness of Paran," signifies the life of the spiritual man as to good; the "wilderness" here as before is what is relatively obscure ; "Paran" is illumination from the Lord's Divine Human ; "and his mother took him," signifies the affection of truth ; "a wife out of the land of Egypt," sig-

nifies the affection of memory-knowledges which the man of
the spiritual church has.

2712. *He dwelt in the wilderness of Paran.* That this signifies the life of the spiritual man as to good, is evident from
the signification of " dwelling," as being predicated of the good
of truth, or of spiritual good, that is, of the good of the spiritual
man. What its quality is, is described by his "dwelling in
the wilderness of Paran," which is to be treated of presently.
That "to dwell" is predicated of the good, that is, of the affection, of truth, is evident from many passages in the Word
where cities are treated of, by which truths are signified, and
as being without an inhabitant, by whom good is signified (n.
2268, 2450, 2451); for truths are inhabited by good; and
truths without good are like a city in which there is no one
dwelling. So in *Zephaniah :—*

> I have made their streets waste, that none passeth by ; their cities are
> desolated, so that there is no inhabitant (iii. 6).

[2] In *Jeremiah :—*

> Jehovah led us through the wilderness, where no man passed through,
> and where no man dwelt ; they had made his land a waste, his cities are
> burned up, so that there is no inhabitant (ii. 6, 15).

In the same :—

> Every city is forsaken, and no one dwelleth therein (iv. 29).

In the same :—

> In the streets of Jerusalem that are desolate, without man, and with-
> out inhabitant, and without beast (xxxiii. 10) ;

"streets" denote truths (n. 2336); "without man" denotes no
celestial good ; "without inhabitant," no spiritual good; and
"without beast," no natural good. In the same :—

> The cities of Moab shall become a desolation, without any to dwell
> therein (xlviii. 9).

[3] In the Prophets in every expression there is the marriage
of truth and good ; and therefore where a city is said to be
desolate, it is also added that there is no inhabitant in it; for
the reason that the city signifies truths, and the inhabitant
good ; otherwise it would be superfluous to say that there was
no inhabitant, when it has been said that the city was deso-

late. So likewise the expressions are constant that signify the things of celestial good, those of spiritual good, and those of truth; as in *Isaiah* :—

Thy seed shall possess the nations, and they shall dwell in the desolate cities (liv. 3) ;

where to "possess" is predicated of celestial goods; and to "dwell in," of spiritual good. In the same :—

Mine elect shall possess it, and my servants shall dwell there (lxv. 9) ;

where the signification is the same. [4] In *David* :—

God will save Zion, and will build the cities of Judah ; and they shall dwell there, and shall possess it ; the seed also of His servants shall inherit it, and they that love His name shall dwell therein (*Ps.* lxix. 36, 37) ;

"dwelling" and at the same time "possessing," is predicated of celestial good; but "dwelling," of spiritual good. In *Isaiah* :—

Saying to Jerusalem, Thou shalt be inhabited, and to the cities of Judah, ye shall be built (xliv. 26) ;

where "dwelling," or "inhabiting," is predicated of the good of the spiritual church, which is "Jerusalem." To such a degree are the expressions in the Word predicated of their own goods and their own truths, that merely from a knowledge of the predication of these expressions it can be known what subject in general is treated of.

2713. That a "wilderness" here signifies what is relatively obscure, is evident from the signification of a "wilderness," when predicated of the spiritual man, as being what is obscure in comparison with the celestial man (see above, n. 2708).

2714. That "Paran" is illumination from the Lord's Divine Human, is evident from the signification of "Paran," as being the Lord's Divine Human, which is manifest from the passages in the Word where it is named, as in the prophet *Habakkuk* :—

O Jehovah, I have heard Thy fame, I was afraid ; O Jehovah, revive Thy work in the midst of the years, in the midst of the years make known, in zeal remember mercy. God will come from Teman, and the Holy One from Mount Paran ; Selah : His honor covered the heavens, and the earth is full of His praise ; and His brightness shall be as the light. He had horns going out from His hand, and there was the hiding of His strength (iii. 2–4) ;

where the Lord's advent is plainly treated of, which is signified by "reviving in the midst of the years," and by "making
known in the midst of the years." His Divine Human is described by "God coming from Teman, and the Holy One from
Mount Paran." He is said to "come from Teman" as to celestial love, and "from Mount Paran" as to spiritual love; and
that illumination and power are from these is signified by saying that there shall be "brightness and light," and by His
having "horns going out from His hand;" the "brightness
and light" are illumination, and the "horns" are power. [2]
In *Moses*:—

Jehovah came from Sinai, and rose from Seir unto them; He shone
forth from Mount Paran, and He came from the ten thousands of holiness; from His right hand was a fire of law unto them; yea, He loveth
the peoples; all His saints are in thy hand, and they were gathered
together at thy foot, and he shall receive of thy words (*Deut.* xxxiii.
2, 3).

Here also the Lord is treated of, whose Divine Human is
described by His "rising from Seir, and shining forth from
Mount Paran"—from "Seir" as to celestial love, and from
"Mount Paran" as to spiritual love. The spiritual are signified by the "peoples whom He loves," and by their being
"gathered together at His foot." The "foot" signifies what
is lower, and thus more obscure, in the Lord's kingdom. [3]
In the same:—

Chedorlaomer and the kings that were with him smote the Horites in
their Mount Seir, unto El-paran, which is in the wilderness (*Gen.* xiv.
5, 6);

that the Lord's Divine Human is here signified by "Mount
Seir," and by "El-paran," may be seen above (n. 1675, 1676).
In the same:—

It came to pass in the second year, in the second month, in the twentieth day of the month, that the cloud was taken up from over the tabernacle of the testimony; and the sons of Israel set forward according to
their journeys, out of the wilderness of Sinai; and the cloud abode in the
wilderness of Paran (*Num.* x. 11, 12).

[4] That the journeys of the people in the wilderness all signify
the state of a combating church and its temptations, in which
man yields but the Lord conquers for him—consequently the

very temptations and victories of the Lord—will of the Lord's
Divine mercy be shown elsewhere; and because the Lord from
His Divine Human sustained temptations, the Lord's Divine
Human is here signified in like manner by the "wilderness of
Paran." And so again by these words in the same:—

The people afterwards journeyed from Hazeroth, and pitched their
camp in the wilderness of Paran. And Jehovah spake unto Moses, saying, Send thou men, and let them explore the land of Canaan, which I
give unto the sons of Israel; and Moses sent them from the wilderness of
Paran, according to the command of Jehovah. And they returned, and
came to Moses, and to Aaron, and to all the congregation of the sons of
Israel, unto the wilderness of Paran to Kadesh; and brought back word
unto them, and showed them the fruit of the land (*Num.* xii. 16; xiii.
1–3, 26).

[5] By their setting out from the wilderness of Paran and ex-
ploring the land of Canaan, is signified that through the Lord's
Divine Human the sons of Israel, that is, the spiritual, have
the heavenly kingdom, which is signified by the land of Canaan;
but their also succumbing at that time signifies their weakness,
and that the Lord therefore fulfilled all things in the Law,
and endured temptations, and conquered; and that they who
are in the faith of charity, as also they who are in temptations in which the Lord conquers, have salvation from His
Divine Human. On which account also, when the Lord was
tempted, He was in the wilderness (*Matt.* iv. 1; *Mark* i. 12,
13; *Luke* iv. 1; see above, n. 2708).

2715. There are two arcana here, one, that the good of the
spiritual man is comparatively obscure; and the other, that
this obscurity is illuminated by the Lord's Divine Human.
As regards the first, that good with the spiritual man is comparatively obscure, this is evident from what was said above
concerning the state of the spiritual man in comparison with
the state of the celestial man (n. 2708); for by comparing
these states the fact becomes manifest. With the celestial,
good itself is implanted in their will part, and light comes
therefrom into their intellectual part; but with the spiritual
all the will part has been destroyed, so that they have nothing
of good from it; and therefore good is implanted by the Lord
in their intellectual part (see n. 863, 875, 895, 927, 928, 1023,
1043, 1044, 2124, 2256). The will part is what chiefly lives

in man, while the intellectual lives from it. As therefore the will part has •been so destroyed with the spiritual man as to be nothing but evil, and yet evil flows in from it perpetually and continually into his intellectual part, that is, into his thought, it is evident that the good there is comparatively obscured. [2] Hence it is that the spiritual have not love to the Lord, as have the celestial, and consequently they have not the humiliation which is essential in all worship, and by means of which good can flow in from the Lord; for an elated heart does not receive at all, but a humble heart. Neither have the spiritual love toward the neighbor, as the celestial have; for the love of self and the world continually flows in from their will part, and obscures the good of that love; as must also be evident to every one if he reflects, by considering that when he does good to any one it is for the sake of an end in the world; and that therefore, although he is not doing so consciously, still he is thinking of a recompense, either from those to whom he does good, or from the Lord in the other life; thus that his good is defiled by the idea of merit,—as also by considering that when he has done any good, if he can make it known and thus set himself above others, he is in the delight of his life. But the celestial love the neighbor more than themselves; nor do they think at all of recompense, nor in any manner set themselves up above others. [3] Moreover the good that is with the spiritual has been obscured by persuasions from various principles arising also from the love of self and of the world. The quality of their persuasion even of faith may be seen above (n. 2682, 2689 at the end); this likewise is from the influx of evil from their will part. [4] Moreover that the good with the spiritual man is obscure in comparison, is evident from the fact that he does not know what is true from any perception, as the celestial do, but from instruction from parents and masters, and also from the doctrine into which he was born; and when he superadds anything from himself and from his thought, then for the most part the sensuous and its fallacies, and the rational and its appearances, prevail, and cause him to be scarcely able to acknowledge any pure truth, such as the celestial acknowledge. Nevertheless in those seeming truths the Lord implants good, even if the truths are fallacious, or appearances of truth; but the good becomes obscure from them, being qualified by the truths with which it is conjoined. The case with this is as with the light of the sun flowing into objects. The quality of the objects which receive it causes the light to appear there under the aspect of color, beautiful if the quality of the form and of the reception is becoming and correspondent, but unbeautiful if the quality of the form and of the reception is not becoming, and thus not correspondent. In this manner the good itself is qualified according to the truth. [5] The same is also manifest from the fact that the spiritual man does not know what evil is. He scarcely believes any other things to be evil than those which are contrary to the precepts of the Decalogue, and is not aware of the evils of affection and thought, which are innumerable; nor does he reflect upon them, nor call them evils. All delights whatever of cupidities and pleasures he regards no otherwise than as good; and the very delights of the love of self he both seeks after, and approves, and excuses, being ignorant that such things affect his spirit, and that he becomes altogether such in the other life. [6] From this it is in like manner evident that though scarcely anything else is treated of in the whole Word than the good of love to the Lord and of love toward the neighbor, still the spiritual man does not know that good is the essential of faith, nor even what love and charity are in their essence; and that as to what he has learned of faith, which he makes essential, he nevertheless discusses whether it be so, unless he has been confirmed by much experience of life. This the celestial never do, for they know and perceive that it is so. Hence it is said by the Lord in *Matthew* :—

Let your speech be, Yea, yea; Nay, nay; what is more than these is of evil (v. 37).

For the celestial are in the truth itself respecting which the spiritual dispute whether it be so; hence, as the celestial are in the truth itself, they can see from it endless things which belong to that truth, and thus from light see as it were the whole heaven. But as the spiritual dispute whether it be so, they cannot, so long as they do this, come to the first boundary of the light of the celestial, still less look at anything from their light.

2716. As regards the second arcanum, namely, that the obscurity with the spiritual is illuminated by the Lord's Divine Human, it is one which cannot be explained to the comprehension, for it is the influx of the Divine that would have to be described. But some idea of it may be obtained by considering that if the Supreme Divine Itself were to flow into such a good as has been described, defiled by so many evils and falsities, it could not be received; and if anything were received by the man who had such good, he would feel infernal torture and would thus perish. But the Lord's Divine Human can flow in with such men and can illuminate such good, as the sun shines into the dense clouds and transforms them in the early morning into the glories of the dawn; and yet the Lord cannot appear before them as the light of the sun, but as the light of the moon. Hence it is evident that the cause of the Lord's coming into the world was that the spiritual might be saved (see n. 2661).

2717. *And his mother took him.* That this signifies the affection of truth, is evident from the signification of "mother," as being the church (see n. 289); and because the spiritual church that is here represented is in the affection of truth, and is a church by virtue of the affection of truth, this affection is here signified by "mother."

2718. *A wife out of the land of Egypt.* That this signifies the affection of memory-knowledges belonging to the man of the spiritual church, is evident from the signification of a "wife," as being affection or good (see n. 915, 2517); and from the signification of "Egypt," as being memory-knowledge (see n. 1164, 1165, 1186, 1462). In this verse the man of the spiritual church is described in regard to his quality as to good, that is, as to the essence of his life, namely, that the good that is with him is obscure, but is illuminated by the Lord's Divine Human; from which illumination there comes forth in his rational the affection of truth, and in his natural the affection of memory-knowledges. The reason why the affection of good cannot come forth with the spiritual man such as it is with the celestial, but in place of it the affection of truth, is that the good which is in him is implanted in his intellectual part, and is comparatively obscure (as was shown, n. 2715), from

which no other affection can be produced and derived in his
rational than the affection of truth, and thereby in his natural
the affection of memory-knowledges. By truth here no other
truth is meant than such as he believes to be true, though it
be not true in itself ; and by memory-knowledges are not meant
such as the learned have, but everything of knowledge with
which one can be imbued from experience and by hearing, from
civic life, from doctrine, and from the Word. The man of the
spiritual church is in the affection of such things. [2] That
it may be known what it is to be in the affection of truth, and
what to be in the affection of good, we will briefly state that
they who are in the affection of truth, think, search out, and
discuss whether a thing be true, or whether it be so; and when
they are confirmed that it is true, or that it is so, they think,
search out, and discuss what it is, and thus stick fast at the
first threshold ; nor can they be admitted into wisdom until
they are free from doubt. But they who are in the affection
of good, from the good itself in which they are, know and perceive that the thing is so; and thus are not at the first threshold, but are in the inner chamber, being admitted into wisdom. [3] Take as an example that it is celestial to think and
act from the affection of good, or from good: They who are in
the affection of truth discuss whether this be so, whether it be
possible, and what it is; and so long as they are occupied with
doubts about it they cannot be admitted ; but they who are in
the affection of good do not discuss, nor busy themselves with
doubts, but affirm that it is so, and are therefore admitted; for
they who are in the affection of good, that is, who are celestial,
begin where they who are in the affection of truth, that is, who
are spiritual, stop; so that the furthest boundary of the latter
is the first of the former. For this reason it is given to them
to know, to recognize, and to perceive that there are innumerable affections of good (as many, in fact, as there are societies
in heaven) ; and that they are all conjoined by the Lord into
a heavenly form, so as to constitute as it were one man ; and
it is also given them to distinguish by perception the kind and
variety of each affection. [4] Or take this example: That all
delight, blessedness, and happiness, are solely of love; and
that such as the love is, such is the delight, the blessedness,

and the happiness. The spiritual man keeps his natural mind
fixed on the question whether it be so, and whether the happiness be not from some other source, as from social intercourse,
conversation, meditation, and learning, or from possessions and
the honor, reputation, and glory of them; not confirming himself in the fact that these effect nothing, but only the affection
of love such as there is in them. But the celestial man does
not stick in these preliminaries, but affirms that it is so, and
is therefore in the end itself and the use, that is, in the very
affections of the love, which are innumerable, and in every
one of which there are ineffable things—and this with varia-
tion of delight, blessedness, and happiness, to eternity. [5]
Take also as an example that the neighbor is to be loved for
the good that is in him : They who are in the affection of truth,
think, search out, and discuss whether this be true, or whether
it be so; what the neighbor is, and what good is ; nor do they
go any further, and therefore they close to themselves the gate
to wisdom ; but they who are in the affection of good affirm
that it is so, and therefore do not close that gate to themselves,
but enter in, and know, and recognize, and perceive, from good,
who is more the neighbor than another, also in what degree he
is the neighbor, and that all are neighbors in different degrees;
and thus they perceive ineffable things beyond those who are
only in the affection of truth. [6] Take further this example :
That he who loves his neighbor for the good that is in him,
loves the Lord. They who are in the affection of truth examine carefully whether it be so; and if they are told that he
who loves his neighbor for the good that is in him, loves the
good, and that—as all good is from the Lord and the Lord is
in the good—when any one loves good he also loves Him from
whom it is and in which He is, they examine whether it be so;
also what good is, and whether the Lord is in good more than
in truth ; and so long as they stick in such things they cannot
see wisdom even at a distance. But they who are in the affection of good know from perception that it is so; and they immediately see the field of wisdom, leading even to the Lord.
[7] From all this we can see why they who are in the affection
of truth (that is, the spiritual) have obscurity in comparison
with those who are in the affection of good (that is, the celes-

tial). Nevertheless the spiritual can come from obscurity into light, provided they are willing to be in the affirmative that all good is of love to the Lord and of charity toward the neighbor; and that love and charity are spiritual conjunction; and that all blessedness and happiness are from these; and thus that heavenly life is in the good of love from the Lord, but not in the truth of faith separate from it.

*   *   *   *   *   *   *   *   *

2719. In this chapter the Lord's rational has first been treated of, as being made Divine, which rational is "Isaac;" then the merely human rational, as being separated, which is the "son of Hagar the Egyptian;" and afterwards the spiritual church, which was saved by the Lord's Divine Human, which church is "Hagar" and her "child." Now the doctrine of faith is treated of, which is to be serviceable to that church; namely, that human reasonings from memory-knowledges are adjoined to it, which are "Abimelech" and "Phicol." This conjunction is signified by the "covenant" which Abraham made with them. These reasonings are appearances, not from a Divine but from a human origin, which are adjoined for the reason that without them the spiritual church would not comprehend doctrine, and thus would not receive it. For, as was shown above (n. 2715), the man of the spiritual church is relatively in obscurity; and doctrine is therefore to be clothed with such appearances as are of human thought and affection, and is not to be in discrepancy to such a degree that the Divine good cannot have in them some kind of receptacle. As Abimelech is again treated of in the following twenty-sixth chapter, and also a covenant (but with Isaac); and in the internal sense, the reasonings and memory-knowledges added to the doctrine of faith a second time, only a summary may here be given of the things contained in the internal sense, which will become clearer by the explication of that chapter.

2720. Verse 22. *And it came to pass at that time, that Abimelech, and Phicol the captain of his army, said unto Abraham, saying, God is with thee in all that thou doest.* Verse 23. *And now swear unto me here by God, that thou wilt not be false to me, nor to my son, nor to my son's son ; according to the kind-*

ness that I have done unto thee, thou shalt do unto me, and to the land wherein thou hast sojourned. Verse 24. *And Abraham said, I will swear.* Verse 25. *And Abraham reproved Abimelech, because of the well of water which Abimelech's servants had taken away.* Verse 26. *And Abimelech said, I know not who hath done this word, neither didst thou tell me, neither heard I of it but to-day.* Verse 27. *And Abraham took flock and herd, and gave to Abimelech, and they two struck a covenant.* Verse 28. *And Abraham set seven ewe lambs of the flock by themselves.* Verse 29. *And Abimelech said unto Abraham, What are these seven ewe lambs which thou hast set by themselves?* Verse 30. *And he said, Because these seven ewe lambs shalt thou take of my hand, that it may be a witness unto me that I have digged this well.* Verse 31. *Therefore he called that place Beer-sheba, because there they sware, both of them.* Verse 32. *And they struck a covenant at Beer-sheba; and Abimelech rose up, and Phicol the captain of his army; and they returned into the land of the Philistines.* [2] "It came to pass at that time," signifies the state in which the Lord was when His rational was made Divine; "and Abimelech, and Phicol the captain of his army, said unto Abraham," signifies the human rational things from memory-knowledges that were to be adjoined to the doctrine of faith, which in itself is Divine; "saying, God is with thee in all that thou doest," signifies that it was Divine as to all things both in general and in particular; [3] "and now swear unto me here by God," signifies affirmation; "that thou wilt not be false to me," signifies without a doubt; "nor to my son, nor to my son's son," signifies concerning the things of faith; "according to the kindness that I have done unto thee," signifies the rational things in which the Lord had been previously instructed; "thou shalt do unto me and to the land wherein thou hast sojourned," signifies what is reciprocal. [4] "And Abraham said, I will swear," signifies all that is affirmative. "And Abraham reproved Abimelech," signifies the Lord's indignation; "because of the well of water which Abimelech's servants had taken away," signifies as to the doctrine of faith, that the memory-knowledges desired to attribute it to themselves. [5] "And Abimelech said," signifies a reply. "I know not who hath done this word," signifies that the rational dictated something different; "neither didst thou tell me," signifies that it was not from the Divine; "neither heard I of it but to-day," signifies that it was now first disclosed. [6] "And Abraham took flock and herd, and gave to Abimelech," signifies the Divine goods implanted in the rational things of doctrine signified by "Abimelech;" "and they two struck a covenant," signifies conjunction thus. "And Abraham set seven ewe lambs of the flock by themselves," signifies the holiness of innocence. [7] "And Abimelech said unto Abraham, What are these seven ewe lambs which thou hast set by themselves," signifies that he should be instructed and would acknowledge. "And he said, Because these seven ewe lambs shalt thou take of my hand," signifies that the holiness of innocence is from the Divine; "that it may be a witness unto me," signifies certainty; "that I have digged this well," signifies that the doctrine was from the Divine. "Therefore he called that place Beer-sheba," signifies the state and quality of the doctrine; "because there they sware both of them," signifies from the conjunction. [8] "And they struck a covenant in Beer-sheba," signifies that human rational things were adjoined to the doctrine of faith; "and Abimelech rose up, and Phicol the captain of his army, and they returned into the land of the Philistines," signifies that nevertheless these things had no part in the doctrine.

2721. Verse 33. *And he planted a grove in Beer-sheba; and he called there on the name of the God of eternity.* "He planted a grove in Beer-sheba," signifies doctrine with its knowledges and its quality; "and he called on the name of the God of eternity," signifies worship from it.

2722. *He planted a grove in Beer-sheba.* That this signifies doctrine thence with its knowledges and its quality, is evident from the signification of a "grove," and from the signification of "Beer-sheba." As regards groves:—In the Ancient Church holy worship was performed on mountains and in groves; on mountains, because mountains signified the celestial things of worship; and in groves, because groves signified its spiritual things. So long as that church, namely, the Ancient, was in its simplicity, their worship at that time on mountains and in groves was holy, for the reason that celestial things, which

are those of love and charity, were represented by things high
and lofty, such as mountains and hills; and spiritual things,
which are therefrom, by things fruitful and leafy, such as
gardens and groves; but after representatives and significatives began to be made idolatrous, by the worship of external
things without internal, that holy worship became profane;
and they were therefore forbidden to worship on mountains
and in groves. [2] That the ancients held holy worship on
mountains is evident from the twelfth chapter of *Genesis*,
where we read of Abraham :—

He removed thence unto a mountain on the east of Bethel, and
pitched his tent, having Bethel on the sea, and Ai on the east; and there
he built an altar, and called on the name of Jehovah (verse 8, n. 1449–
1455);

and also from the signification of a " mountain," as being the
celestial of love (n. 795, 796, 1430). That they also held holy
worship in groves is evident from what is stated in this verse :
" Abraham planted a grove in Beer-sheba, and called there on
the name of the God of eternity ;" and also from the signification of a " garden," as being intelligence (n. 100, 108, 1588);
and of " trees," as being perceptions (n. 103, 2163). That this
was forbidden is evident from the following passages. In
Moses :—

Thou shalt not plant thee a grove of any tree beside the altar of Jehovah thy God which thou shalt make thee, and thou shalt not set thee
up a pillar; which Jehovah thy God hateth (*Deut.* xvi. 21, 22).

In the same :—

The altars of the nations shall ye break down, and dash in pieces their
pillars, and cut down their groves (*Exod.* xxxiv. 13);

and they were commanded to burn the groves of the nations
with fire (*Deut.* xii. 3). [3] And as the Jews and Israelites,
among whom the representative ritual of the Ancient Church
was introduced, were solely in externals, and at heart were
nothing but idolaters, neither knowing nor wishing to know
what anything internal was, nor the life after death, nor even
that the Messiah's kingdom was a heavenly one, therefore
whenever they were in freedom they held profane worship on
mountains and hills, and also in groves and forests; and like-

wise in place of mountains and hills they made for themselves high places, and in place of groves carved representations of a grove, as is evident from many passages in the Word. As in the book of *Judges :*—

The sons of Israel served Baalim and the groves (iii. 7).

In the book of *Kings :*—

Israel made groves provoking Jehovah (1 *Kings* xiv. 15).

And in another place :—

Judah built them high places, and pillars, and groves, upon every high hill, and under every green tree (1 *Kings* xiv. 23).

And again :—

Israel built them high places in all their cities, and set up pillars and groves upon every high hill, and under every green tree (2 *Kings* xvii. 9, 10).

And again :—

Manasseh king of Judah reared up altars for Baal, and made a grove, as did Ahab king of Israel, and set the carved image of the grove which he had made in the house of God (2 *Kings* xxi. 3, 7) ;

from which it is manifest that they also made for themselves carved images of a grove. That these were destroyed by king Josiah may be seen in the same book :—

Josiah caused all the vessels that were made for Baal and for the grove, and for the sun and the moon, and for all the army of the heavens, to be brought out of the temple of Jehovah, and he burnt them without Jerusalem, and the houses which the women had woven there for the grove.

He also cut down the groves which Solomon had made, and likewise the grove in Bethel which Jeroboam had made (2 *Kings* xxiii. 4, 6, 7, 13–15). That king Hezekiah also demolished such things may be seen in the same book :—

Hezekiah king of Judah removed the high places, and brake the pillars, and cut down the grove, and brake in pieces the brazen serpent which Moses had made (2 *Kings* xviii. 4).

[4] That the brazen serpent was holy in the time of Moses is evident; but when the external was worshiped it became profane, and was broken in pieces, for the same reason that worship on mountains and in groves was forbidden. These things are still more evident in the Prophets. In *Isaiah:*—

Inflaming yourselves with gods under every green tree ; sacrificing the children in the rivers under the crags of the rocks ; thou hast also poured out a drink-offering to the rivers, thou hast offered a gift ; upon a high and lofty mountain hast thou set thy habitation, and thither wentest thou up * to offer sacrifice (lvii. 5–7).

In the same :—

In that day shall a man look unto his Maker, and his eyes shall see the Holy One of Israel ; and he shall not look to the altars the work of his hands, neither shall he see that which his fingers have made, and the groves and the sun-images (xvii. 7, 8).

In *Micah* :—

I will cut off thy graven images and thy pillars out of the midst of thee, and thou shalt no more bow thyself down to the work of thy hands ; and I will pluck up thy groves out of the midst of thee, and I will destroy thy cities (v. 13, 14).

In *Ezekiel* :—

That their slain may be among their idols, round about their altars, upon every high hill, on all the tops of the mountains, and under every green tree, and under every tangled oak, the place where they did offer an odor of rest to all their idols (vi. 13).

[5] From all this it is now manifest from what origin idola-trous worship came, namely, the worship of objects that were representative and significative. The most ancient people who were before the flood saw in each and everything—in mountains, hills, plains, and valleys, gardens, groves, and for-ests, rivers and waters, fields and plantations, trees and ani-mals of every kind, and the luminaries of heaven—something representative and significative of the Lord's kingdom ; but they never dwelt with their eyes, still less with their minds, on these objects ; but these things served them as means for think-ing about the celestial and spiritual things in the Lord's king-dom ; and this to such a degree that there was nothing at all in universal nature that did not serve them as such means. The real fact is that everything in nature is representative, which is an arcanum at this day and scarcely believed by any one. But after the celestial which is of love to the Lord had perished, the human race was then no longer in that state— namely, that from objects as means they could see the celestial

* *Ibi obtulisti*, but *eo ascendisti, Apocalypse Explained* 405.   [*Rotch ed.*]

and spiritual things of the Lord's kingdom. [6] Yet the ancients after the flood knew, from traditions, and from collections made by certain persons, that these things had such a signification; and as they were significative they esteemed them holy. Hence came the representative worship of the Ancient Church; which church, being spiritual, was not in the perception that a thing was so, but was in the knowledge of the fact; for it was relatively in obscurity (n. 2715). Nevertheless they did not worship outward things, but by means of outward things they called to mind inward things; and hence when they were in those representatives and significatives, they were in holiness of worship. They were able to be so because they were in spiritual love, that is, in charity, which they made an essential of worship; and therefore holiness from the Lord could flow into their worship. But when the state of the human race had become so changed and perverted that they removed themselves from the good of charity, and thus no longer believed that there was any heavenly kingdom, or any life after death, but that men were in a similar condition with animals, save only that they could think (as is also believed at this day), then the holy representative worship was turned into idolatry, and the outward things were worshiped. Hence with many Gentiles at that time, and also with the Jews and Israelites, the worship was not representative, but was a worship of the representatives and significatives; that is, of the outward things without the inward. [7] As regards groves in particular, among the ancients they were of various signification, and indeed according to the kinds of trees in them. Groves of olive-trees signified the celestial things of worship; groves of vines signified the spiritual things of worship; but groves of fig-trees, cedars, fir-trees, poplars, and oaks, signified various things relating to what is celestial and spiritual. In the passage before us mention is made simply of a grove or plantation of trees; and this signifies the things of reason that were adjoined to doctrine and its knowledges; for trees in general signify perceptions (n. 103, 2163), but when they are predicated of the spiritual church they signify knowledges, for the reason that the man of the spiritual church has no other perceptions than those which come through knowledges from doctrine or the Word; for these become of his faith, and thus of conscience, from which he has perception.

2723. But in regard to Beer-sheba—"Beer-sheba" signifies the state and quality of the doctrine, namely, that it is Divine and to which what is of human reason is adjoined—as is evident from the series of things treated of from verse 22 to this verse (see n. 2613, 2614); and also from the signification of the word itself in the original language, which is "the well of the oath," and "of seven." That a "well" is the doctrine of faith may be seen above (n. 2702, 2720); that an "oath" is conjunction (n. 2720); and that a "covenant made by an oath," has the same meaning (n. 1996, 2003, 2021, 2037); and that "seven" denotes what is holy and thus Divine (n. 395, 433, 716, 881); from all which it is evident that "Beer-sheba" signifies doctrine which is in itself Divine together with things of human reason or appearances adjoined. [2] That the name Beer-sheba comes from all this is manifest from Abraham's words :—

Because these seven ewe lambs shalt thou take from my hand, that it may be a witness unto me that I have digged this well; therefore he called that place Beer-sheba, because there they sware both of them; and they struck a covenant in Beer-sheba (verses 30–32).

In like manner from Isaac's words in chapter xxvi. :—

It came to pass on that day that Isaac's servants came and told him concerning the well which they had digged, and said unto him, We have found water; and he called it Shibah (an "oath" and "seven"); therefore the name of the city is Beer-sheba unto this day (verses 32, 33).

There also wells are spoken of about which there was contention with Abimelech, and a covenant with him is treated of; and by "Beer-sheba" are signified the things of human reason again adjoined to the doctrine of faith; and because they are again adjoined, and the doctrine thus became adapted to human comprehension, it is called a "city" (that a "city" signifies doctrine in its complex may be seen above, n. 402, 2268, 2450, 2451). Moreover Beer-sheba is mentioned with a similar signification as to the internal sense in other places (*Gen.* xxii. 19; xxvi. 22, 23; xxviii. 10; xlvi. 1, 5; *Josh.* xv. 28; xix. 1, 2; 1 *Sam.* viii. 2; 1 *Kings* xix. 3; and also in the op-

posite sense, *Amos* v. 5; viii. 13, 14). [3] The extension of
the celestial and spiritual things belonging to doctrine is signified in the internal sense, where the extent of the land of
Canaan is described by the expression "from Dan even to
Beer-sheba;" for by the land of Canaan is signified the Lord's
kingdom, and also His church, consequently the celestial and
spiritual things of doctrine; as in the book of *Judges :*—

All the sons of Israel went out, and the congregation was assembled
as one man from Dan even to Beer-sheba (xx. 1).

In the book of *Samuel :*—

All Israel from Dan even to Beer-sheba (1 *Sam.* iii. 20).

And again :—

To transfer the kingdom from the house of Saul, and to set up the
throne of David over Israel and over Judah, from Dan even to Beer-
sheba (2 *Sam.* iii. 10).

And again :—

Hushai said to Absalom, Let all Israel be gathered together, from Dan
even unto Beer-sheba (2 *Sam.* xvii. 11).

And again :—

David told Joab to go through all the tribes of Israel from Dan even to
Beer-sheba (2 *Sam.* xxiv. 2, 7).

And again :—

There died of the people from Dan even to Beer-sheba seventy thousand men (2 *Sam.* xxiv. 15).

In the book of *Kings :*—

Judah dwelt under his vine and under his fig-tree, from Dan even to
Beer-sheba, all the days of Solomon (1 *Kings* iv. 25).

2724. *And called there on the name of the God of eternity.*
That this signifies worship therefrom, is evident from the signification of "calling upon the name of God," as being worship (see n. 440). They who were of the Ancient Church
did not by a name understand the name, but all the quality (see
n. 144, 145, 440, 768, 1754, 1896, 2009); and thus by the "name
of God" all that in one complex by which God was worshiped,
consequently everything of love and faith; but when the internal of worship perished, and only the external remained,

they then began to understand by the name of God nothing else than the name, so much so that they worshiped the name itself, feeling no care about the love and the faith from which they worshiped. On this account the nations began to distinguish themselves by the names of their gods ; and the Jews and Israelites set themselves up above the rest, because they worshiped Jehovah, placing the essential of worship in uttering the name and invoking it, when in truth the worship of a name only is no worship, and may also be found among the worst of men, who thereby profane the more. [2] But as by the "name of God" everything of worship is signified, that is, everything of love and faith from which He is worshiped, it is therefore evident what is meant by "hallowed be Thy Name," in the Lord's Prayer (*Matt.* vi. 9) ; also by what the Lord said :—

Ye shall be hated for My name's sake (*Matt.* x. 22).

If two shall agree on earth as touching anything that they shall ask, it shall be done for them by My Father who is in the heavens ; for where two or three are gathered together in My name, there am I in the midst of them (*Matt.* xviii. 19, 20).

Every one that hath left houses, or brethren, or sisters, or father, or mother, or wife, or children, or lands, for My name's sake, shall receive a hundredfold, and shall inherit eternal life (*Matt.* xix. 29).

Hosanna to the Son of David ! blessed is He that cometh in the name of the Lord (*Matt.* xxi. 9).

Jesus said, Ye shall not see Me henceforth till ye shall say, Blessed is He that cometh in the name of the Lord (*Matt.* xxiii. 39).

Ye shall be hated of all nations for My name's sake ; and then shall many be offended, and shall betray one another, and shall hate one another (*Matt.* xxiv. 9, 10).

As many as received Him, to them gave He power to become the sons of God, to them that believe on His name (*John* i. 12).

He that believeth not is judged already, because he hath not believed on the name of the only begotten Son of God (*John* iii. 18).

Jesus said, Whatsoever ye shall ask in My name, that will I do (*John* xiv. 14, 15 ; xv. 16 ; xvi. 23, 24, 26, 27).

Jesus said, I have manifested Thy name unto the men (*John* xvii. 6).

Holy Father, keep them in Thy name whom Thou hast given Me, that they may be one, as We are (*John* xvii. 11, 12).

I have made known unto them Thy name, and will make it known ; that the love wherewith Thou hast loved Me may be in them, and I in them (*John* xvii. 26).

That ye may believe that Jesus is the Christ, the Son of God ; and that believing ye may have life in His name (*John* xx. 31).

Besides very many passages in the Old Testament, in which
by the "name" of Jehovah and of God the name is not meant,
but everything of love and faith from which is worship. [3]
But they who worship a name only, without love and faith,
are thus spoken of in *Matthew* :—

Many will say to Me in that day, Lord, Lord, have we not prophesied
by Thy name, and by Thy name have cast out demons, and in Thy name
done many mighty works? But I will confess unto them, I know you
not; depart from Me ye that work iniquity (vii. 22, 23).

When as before said the men of the church became external,
from being internal, and began to place worship in a name
alone, they then no longer acknowledged one God, but many.
For it was a common thing for the ancients to add something
to the name of Jehovah, and thereby call to mind some benefit
or attribute of His, as in the passage before us, "he called
upon the name of the God of eternity;" and in the following
chapter (xxii.), "Abraham called the name of that place, Je-
hovah-jireh," that is, "Jehovah shall see" (verse 14). "Moses
built an altar, and called the name of it Jehovah-nissi," that
is, "Jehovah my banner" (*Exod.* xvii. 15); "Gideon built an
altar there unto Jehovah, and called it Jehovah-shalom" that
is, "Jehovah of peace" (*Judges* vi. 24); besides other places.
From this it came to pass that they who placed worship in a
name only, acknowledged so many gods; and also that among
the Gentiles, especially in Greece and at Rome, so many gods
were acknowledged and worshiped; whereas the Ancient
Church, from which the epithets emanated, never worshiped
but one God, reverenced under so many names, because by the
"name" they understood the quality.

2725. Verse 34. *And Abraham sojourned in the land of the
Philistines many days.* "Abraham sojourned in the land of
the Philistines many days," signifies that the Lord adjoined
to the doctrine of faith very many things from the memory-
knowledge of human knowledges (*ex scientia cognitionum hu-
manarum*).

2726. *Abraham sojourned in the land of the Philistines
many days.* That this signifies that the Lord adjoined to the
doctrine of faith very many things from the memory-knowledge of human knowledges, is evident from the signification of

"sojourning," as being to instruct (see n. 1463, 2025); from the representation of Abraham, as being the Lord (see n. 1965, 1989, 2011, 2501); from the signification of the "land of the Philistines," or Philistia, as being the memory-knowledge of knowledges (see n. 1197, 1198); and from the signification of "days," as being the state of the thing which is treated of (n. 23, 487, 488, 493, 893); here, because knowledges from the things of memory and reason are treated of, and it is said "many days," it signifies relatively very many things. Thus far, from verse 22, rational things from human memory-knowledges, added to the doctrine of faith, are treated of, as is manifest from the explication; and here is the conclusion of them. As regards the subject itself·; as in itself it is deep, and as much is said about it in chapter xxvi., it may be well at present to defer further explication.

CONCERNING MARRIAGES, HOW THEY ARE REGARDED IN THE
HEAVENS; AND CONCERNING ADULTERIES.

2727. What genuine conjugial love is, and whence its origin, few at this day know, for the reason that few are in it. Almost all believe that it is inborn, and so flows from a kind of natural instinct, as they say, and this the more, because something of marriage exists also among animals; whereas the difference between conjugial love among human beings and what is of marriage among animals is such as is that between the state of a human being and the state of a brute animal.

2728. And because, as was said, few at this day know what genuine conjugial love is, it shall be described from what has been discovered to me. Conjugial love takes its origin from the Divine marriage of good and truth, and thus from the Lord Himself. That conjugial love is from this, is not apparent to sense nor to apprehension; but still it may be seen from influx and from correspondence, as well as from the Word. From influx, inasmuch as heaven, from the union of good and truth, which inflows from the Lord, is compared to a marriage, and is called a marriage: from correspondence, since, when good united to truth flows down into a lower sphere, it forms a union of minds; and when into one still lower, it forms a marriage: wherefore union of minds from good united to truth from the Lord, is conjugial love itself.

2729. That genuine conjugial love is from this, may be seen from the fact that no one can be in it unless he is in the good of truth and the truth of good from the Lord; also from the fact that heavenly blessedness and happiness is in that love; and they who are in it all come into heaven, or into the heavenly marriage. Also from the fact that when angels are conversing about the union of good and truth, there is then presented among good spirits in the lower sphere a representative of marriage; but among evil spirits a representative of adultery. Hence it is that in the Word the union of good and truth is called "marriage;" but the adulteration of good and the falsification of truth, "adultery" and "whoredom" (see n. 2466).

2730. The people of the Most Ancient Church above all on this earth lived in genuine conjugial love, because they were celestial, were in truth from good, and were in the Lord's kingdom together with the angels; and in that love they had heaven. But their posterity, with whom the church declined, began to love their children, and not their consorts; for children can be loved by the evil, but a consort can be loved only by the good.

2731. From those most ancient people it has been heard that conjugial love is of such a nature as to desire to be altogether the other's, and this reciprocally; and that when this is experienced mutually and reciprocally they are in heavenly happiness: also, that the conjunction of minds is of such a nature that this mutuality and reciprocity is in everything of their life, that is, in everything of their affection, and in everything of their thought. On this account it has been instituted by the Lord that wives should be affections of good which are of the will, and husbands thoughts of truth which are of the understanding; and that from this there should be a marriage such as there is between the will and the understanding, and between all things thereof with one who is in the good of truth and the truth of good.

2732. I have spoken with angels as to the nature of this mutuality and reciprocity, and they said that there is the image and likeness of the one in the mind of the other, and that they thus dwell together not only in the particulars, but also in the inmosts of life; and that into such a *one* the Lord's love and mercy can flow with blessedness and happiness. They said also that they who have lived in such conjugial love in the life of the body are together and dwell together in heaven as angels, sometimes with their children also; but that very few from Christendom at this day have so lived, though all so lived from the Most Ancient Church, which was celestial, and many from the Ancient Church, which was spiritual. But that they who have lived in marriage, joined together not by conjugial love, but by lascivious love, are separated in the other life, because nothing of lasciviousness is tolerated in heaven; and that still more are those separated who have lived in mutual aversion, and more still they who have hated each other. When both first come into the other life, they for the most part meet again, but after much suffering are separated.

2733. There were certain spirits who from practice in the life of the body infested me with peculiar adroitness, and this by a somewhat gentle influx, like a wave, such as that of upright spirits is wont to be; but it was perceived that there was in it craftiness and the like, to captivate and deceive. I at length spoke with one of them who I was told had been in the world the commander of an army. And as I perceived that in the ideas of his thought there was lasciviousness, I spoke with him about marriage. The speech of spirits is illustrated by representatives, which fully express the sense, and many things in a moment of time. [2] He said that in the life of the body he thought nothing of adulteries. But it was given to tell him that adulteries are horribly wicked—though to such men they do not appear to be so, but even allowable, owing to the delight they take in them, and the persuasion therefrom—which he might also know from the fact that marriages are the nurseries of the human race, and hence also the nurseries of the heavenly kingdom, and on that account are in no wise to be violated, but to be kept holy; as well as from

the consideration that being in the other life and in a state of
perception he ought to be aware that conjugial love comes down
through heaven from the Lord; and that from that love, as
from a parent, is derived mutual love, which is the basis of
heaven; and also from the fact that when adulterers merely
approach heavenly societies they become sensible of their own
stench, and cast themselves down toward hell. Further, he
might at least know that to violate marriages is contrary to
the Divine laws, and contrary to the civil laws of all, and also
contrary to the genuine light of reason, because contrary to
order both Divine and human; and much more besides. [3]
But he answered that he had never known such things in the
life of the body, nor had thought of them. He wished to
reason whether they were so; but was told that in the other
life truth does not admit of reasonings, for these favor one's
delights, and thus his evils and falsities; and that he ought
first to think of the things that had been said, because they
were true. Or he ought also to think from the principle most
fully known in the world, that one must not do to another
what he is not willing that the other should do to him: and
thus, if any one had in such a manner beguiled his wife, whom
he loved—as every one does in the beginning of marriage—
would he not himself also at that time, when in a state of
wrath about it, if he spoke from that state, have detested
adulteries? and at the same time, as he was of superior talent,
would he not have confirmed himself against them more than
others, even to condemning them to hell? and thus he might
have judged himself from himself.

2734. They who in the life of the body have had happiness
in marriages from genuine conjugial love, have happiness also
in the other life; so that with them the happiness of the one
life is continued into that of the other, and becomes there a
union of minds, in which is heaven. I have been told that
the kinds of celestial and spiritual happiness from it, even only
the most universal, cannot be numbered.

2735. Genuine conjugial love is the image of heaven, and
when it is represented in the other life this is done by the
most beautiful things that can ever be seen by the eyes, or
conceived by the mind. It is represented by a virgin of inex-

pressible beauty, encompassed by a bright cloud, so that it may be said to be beauty itself in essence and form. It has been said that all beauty in the other life is from conjugial love. Its affections and thoughts are represented by diamond-like auras, sparkling as it were with rubies and carbuncles, and these things are attended with delights which affect the inmosts of the mind; but as soon as anything of lasciviousness enters in, they disappear.

2736. I have been instructed that genuine conjugial love is innocence itself, which dwells in wisdom. Those who have lived in conjugial love are in wisdom more than all others in heaven; and yet when viewed by others they appear like little children, in the age of bloom and spring; and whatever then befalls is joy and happiness to them. They are in the inmost heaven, which is called the heaven of innocence. Through this heaven the Lord flows into conjugial love, and angels from that heaven are present with those who live in that love. They are also present with little children in their earliest age.

2737. With those who live in conjugial love, the interiors of their minds are open through heaven even to the Lord; for this love flows in from the Lord through a man's inmost. From this they have the Lord's kingdom in themselves, and from this they have genuine love toward little children for the sake of the Lord's kingdom; and from this they are receptive of heavenly loves above others, and are in mutual love more than others; for this comes from that source as a stream from its fountain.

2738. Mutual love, such as there is in heaven, is not like conjugial love. Conjugial love consists in desiring to be in the other's life as a one; but mutual love consists in wishing better to another than to one's self, as is the case with the love of parents toward their children, and as is the love of those who are in the love of doing good, not for their own sake, but because this is a joy to them. Such angelic love is derived from conjugial love, and is born from it as a child from its parent; and for this reason it exists with parents toward their children. This love is preserved by the Lord with parents, even if they are not in conjugial love, in order that the human race may not perish.

2739. From the marriage of good and truth in the heavens descend all loves, which are such as the love of parents toward their children, the love of brothers for one another, and the love for relatives, and so on, according to their degrees in their order. According to these loves, which are solely from good and truth, that is, from love to the Lord and faith in Him, are formed all the heavenly societies; which are so joined together by the Lord as to represent one man, and therefore heaven is also called the Grand Man. There are unutterable varieties, all of which take their origin and are derived from the union of good and truth from the Lord, which union is the heavenly marriage. Hence it is that the origin of all consanguinities and relationships on earth is derived from marriages, and that loves were derived in like manner according to their degrees mutually among themselves; but as there is no conjugial love at this day, consanguinities and relationships are indeed reckoned from marriage, but there are no consanguinities and relationships of love. In the Most Ancient Church the derivations of love were of this nature, and therefore they dwell together in the heavens distinguished as it were into nations, families, and houses, all of which acknowledge the Lord as their only Parent.

2740. Genuine conjugial love is not possible except between two consorts, that is, in the marriage of one man with one wife, and by no means with more than one at the same time; for the reason that conjugial love is mutual and reciprocal, and is the alternate life of the one in the other, so that they are as it were a one. Such a union is possible between two, but not among more: more tear that love asunder. The men of the Most Ancient Church, who were celestial and in the perception of good and truth, like the angels, had but one wife. They said that with one wife they perceived heavenly delights and happiness, and that when marriage with more was merely mentioned, they were filled with horror; for as before said the marriage of one husband and one wife comes down from the marriage of good and truth, or from the heavenly marriage, which is of this nature, as is very evident from the Lord's words in *Matthew* :—

Jesus said, have ye not read that He who made them from the beginning made them male and female, and said, For this cause shall a man leave father and mother, and shall cleave to his wife, and they twain shall be one flesh ? Wherefore they are no more twain, but one flesh ; what therefore God hath joined together, let not man put asunder. Moses, for the hardness of your heart, permitted you to put away your wives ; but from the beginning it was not so. All cannot receive this word, save they to whom it is given (xix. 3–12).

2741. Good and truth are continually flowing in from the Lord with all, and consequently so is genuine conjugial love; but it is received in various ways; and as it is received, such it becomes. With the lascivious it is turned into lasciviousness, with adulterers into adulteries, its heavenly happiness into unclean delight, thus heaven into hell. The case with this is as with the light of the sun flowing into objects, which is received according to the nature of the objects, and becomes blue, red, yellow, green, dark, and even black, according to the reception.

2742. A certain semblance of conjugial love is found with some, but is not really that unless they are in the love of good and truth. It is a love appearing like conjugial love, but it is for the sake of the love of the world or of self, namely, to be served at home, or to be in security or at ease, or to be ministered to when ill and when growing old; or for the sake of the care of their children whom they love. With some this seeming love is induced from fear of the consort, or for one's reputation, or fear of misfortunes; and with some from lascivious love. This appears in the first period as if it were conjugial love; for at that time they behave with something like innocence, they sport like little children, they have a perception of joy as of something from heaven; but with the progress of time they do not become united more and more closely, like those who are in conjugial love, but are being separated. Conjugial love also differs with the consorts; with the one it may be more or less, with the other little or nothing; and because of this difference there may be heaven for the one, but hell for the other. The affection and the reception determine this.

2743. A great dog like Cerberus was seen by me, and I asked what it signified, and was told that by such a dog is signified a guard lest any one should pass in conjugial love from heavenly delight to infernal delight, or the reverse; for they who are in genuine conjugial love are in heavenly delight;

but they who are in adulteries are also in a delight which appears to them as heavenly, but is infernal.   By the dog is thus represented that those opposite delights must not communicate.

2744. It was shown me how the delights from conjugial love advance, on the one side to heaven, and on the other to hell.   The advancement of the delights toward heaven was into blessedness and happiness continually more and more, even to what was beyond number or description; and the more interior, the more innumerable and ineffable, even to the very celestial happiness of the inmost heaven, or of the heaven of innocence; and this with the greatest freedom, for all freedom is from love; and thus the greatest freedom is from conjugial love, and is heavenly freedom itself.   It was then shown how the delights of conjugial love descend toward hell—that they remove themselves little by little away from heaven, and this likewise with apparent freedom, till at last scarcely anything human remains in them.   The deadly and infernal end to which they come has been seen, but cannot be described.   A certain spirit who was then with me, and likewise saw these things, ran hastily forward to some sirens, of this character, declaring that he would show them the quality of their delight, and at first having the idea of delight; but as by little and little he came more in front, his idea was continued on, like the progress of the delight, to hell; and at length it ended in such horror.   Sirens are women who have been in the persuasion that it is honorable to commit whoredom and adultery, and have also been valued by others for being so disposed, and for being in the elegancies of life.   Most of them come into the other life from Christendom.   They are treated of above (n. 831, 959, 1515, 1983, 2484).

2745. There are women who do not love their husbands, but hold them in contempt, and at length esteem them as of no account.   Their quality was represented to me by a cock, a wild cat, and a tiger of a dark color.   It was said that such begin by talking much, and then proceed to scolding, and at length put on the nature of the tiger.   It was said by some that such still love their children; but it was answered that such love is not human, and that it flows equally into the evil, and even into animals of whatever kind, to such a degree that these also love their offspring more than themselves. It was added that with such persons there is nothing of conjugial love.

2746. There was a certain spirit in middle altitude above the head, who in the life of the body had lived wantonly, delighted with variety, so that he loved no one constantly, but passed his time in brothels, and thus had scortated with many, every one of whom he had afterwards rejected. It hence came to pass that he had beguiled many, and had thereby extinguished the desire for marriage, even for the procreation of children, and thus had contracted an unnatural nature. All these things were disclosed, and he was miserably punished, and this in the sight of the angels; and afterwards he was cast into hell. (Concerning the hells of adulterers, see Part First, n. 824–830.)

2747. As adulteries are contrary to conjugial love, adulterers cannot be in heaven with the angels; for the reason also that they are in what is contrary to good and truth, and thus are not in the heavenly marriage; and also because they have none but filthy ideas respecting marriage. When marriage is merely mentioned, or the idea of it occurs, instantly in their ideas are things lascivious, obscene, nay, unmentionable. It is the same when the angels are speaking about good and truth: such persons then think things that are opposite; for all affections and the derivative thoughts remain with a man after death, such as they had been in the world. Adulterers are in the desire of destroying society; many of them are cruel (n. 824), and thus in heart they are opposed to charity and mercy; laughing at the miseries of others; wishing to take away from every one what is his; and doing this as far as they dare. Their delight is to destroy friendships, and to bring about enmities. Their religious profession is that they acknowledge a Creator of the universe and a Providence—but only a universal one— and salvation by faith, and believe that nothing worse can be done to them than to others. But when they are examined as to what they are at heart, which is done in the other life, they do not believe even what they have professed; but instead of the Creator of the universe they think of nature; instead of a universal Providence, they think of none; and they think nothing of faith. All this is so, because adulteries are wholly contrary to good and truth. Judge then how such can be in heaven.

2748. Some spirits who in the world had lived a life of adultery, came and spoke to me. I perceived that they had not been long in the other life, for they did not know that they were there, thinking that they were still in the world, and reflection as to where they were, being taken away from them. It was given to tell them that they were in the other life; but soon forgetting it, they asked where there were houses into which they might get introduced. But they were asked whether they had no respect for spiritual things, namely, for conjugial love, which is broken up by such allurements; and they were told that such things are contrary to heavenly order. But to this they paid no attention, neither did they understand what was said. I inquired further whether they did not fear the laws, and punishments according to the laws; but these things they held in contempt. But when I said that perhaps they would be severely beaten by the servants, this alone they feared. It was afterwards given to perceive their thoughts, which are communicated in the other life. They were so filthy and obscene that the well disposed could not but be struck with horror; and yet they are made manifest as to each and every particular before spirits and angels in the other life. From all this it is evident that such cannot be in heaven.

2749. With those who have by adulteries conceived a loathing and nausea for marriages, when any delight, blessedness, and happiness from the heaven of the angels reaches them, it is turned into what is loathsome and nauseous, and then into what is painful, and at length into an offensive stench, until they cast themselves down from thence into hell.

2750. I have been instructed by angels that when any one commits adultery on earth, heaven is then immediately closed to him, and he afterwards lives only in worldly and corporeal things; and although he then hears of the things of love and faith, they nevertheless do not penetrate to his interiors; and what he says about them himself does not come from his interiors, but only from the memory and the mouth, being called forth by pride or the love of gain; for his interiors are closed up, and cannot be opened except by serious repentance.

2751. Above in front before the left eye were massed together such as in the life of the body had in secret and with great craftiness plotted against others.   They were adulterers, and were still in the world of spirits, as they were among the new-comers.   Their custom was to send forth from their troop this way and that some to plot intrigues, not only against conjugial love, but also against good and truth, and most of all against the Lord.   They who are thus sent out return to them, and relate what they have heard; and so they take counsel.   They also sent one to me, supposing that I was a spirit, because I spoke with the speech of spirits.   When that emissary spoke, he uttered scandalous things, mostly against the Lord; so that he was as it were made up of mere scandals.   But I answered that he should abstain from such things, as I knew from what band and what refuse he was; and that as regards the Lord, I knew beyond all doubt that He is one with the Father; that the universal heaven is His; that all innocence, peace, love, charity, and mercy are from Him, and all conjugial love also; and that from Him are all good and truth; all of which things are Divine; and that Moses and the Prophets, that is, all and everything in the Word, in the internal sense, treats of Him; and that all the rites of the Jewish Church represented Him; and as I was so certain of these things that I had no doubt, what more did he want? On hearing these things he withdrew with shame.   These things were said, that he might tell them to the adulterers who constituted that wicked troop from which he was sent.

2752. In the other life they who have been eaten up with adulteries desire more than others to obsess men, and thus through them to return into the world; but they are kept back in hell by the Lord, lest they should come among the spirits who are with men.   The most who are such are from the Christian world; rarely from elsewhere.

2753. There are some in the world who are carried away by the lust of seducing virgins to whoredom, wherever they may be: in nunneries, in families, or with their parents, and also wives; and they insinuate themselves by crafty modes and with flatteries.   As they are accustomed to such things, and have formed their nature from them, they retain in the other life the ability to insinuate themselves into societies by flatteries and simulations; but as their thoughts lie plainly open, they are rejected. They thus pass from one society to another, but are everywhere rejected: they are also treated with severity, for they study to steal away the delights and blessedness of others. At length they are admitted into no societies, but after having endured severe punishments, are associated with their like in hell.

2754. The most deceitful sometimes appear high above the head, but their hell is deep under the heel of the foot. They are the modern antediluvians. They ensnare by pretense of innocence, of pity, and of various good affections, with persuasion. When they lived in the world they were adulterers beyond others. Where there was a wife beautiful and young, there they entered without conscience and by such means seduced her. They are invisible and are unwilling to be discovered, as they act in secret. They are also cruel, having cared for themselves alone, and reckoning it as nothing even if the whole world should perish for them. There are great numbers of such spirits at this day, and it was said that they are from Christendom. Their hell is the most grievous of all.

2755. The hells of adulterers are many. There they love nothing more than filth and excrement, in which they now find delight. This may also be evident from many of that sort in the life of the body, to whom it is delightful to think and talk of filthy things, abstaining only for decorum's sake. The delight of adultery is turned into such things in the other life. It is as when the heat of the sun, even that of spring, flows into excrement or into carrion.

2756. There are those who have held as a principle community of wives. These in the other life speak as if they were good, but they are malignant and deceitful. Their punishment is horrible. They are bound together as if into a bundle, and by representation a serpent appears wound around them, which binds them all as it were into a great ball, and thus they are cast out.

2757. When I was being conducted through several abodes, I came to one where heat seized my feet and loins, and it was said that those were there who have indulged in pleasures, but still have not extinguished the natural desire of procreating offspring.

2758. That genuine conjugial love is heaven, is represented in the kingdoms of nature; for there is nothing in all nature that does not in some way represent the Lord's kingdom in general, since the natural kingdom derives all its origin from the spiritual. What is without an origin prior to itself is nothing. Nothing exists that is unconnected with a cause, and thus with an end. What is unconnected falls away in a moment, and becomes nothing; from this then are the representatives of the Lord's kingdom in the kingdoms of nature. That conjugial love is heaven, is manifest from the transformation of little worms into nymphs and chrysalides, and thus into winged insects; for when their time of nuptials comes— which is when they put off their earthly form, or their worm-like form, and are embellished with wings and become flying creatures—they are then elevated into the air, which is their heaven; and there they sport with each other, perform their marriage rites, lay eggs, and nourish themselves on the juices of flowers. They are then also in their beauty; for they have wings decorated with golden, silver, and other elegantly marked colors. Such things does the marriage principle produce among such vile little worms.

2759. On the right side there rose up from the lower earth as it were a roll; and it was said that they were many spirits from the lower class of people, untaught but not depraved. They were peasants and other simple people. I spoke with them, and they said that they know the Lord, to whose name they commend themselves. Further than this they knew little of faith and its mysteries. Afterwards others rose up who knew some little more. It was perceived that their interiors were capable of being opened; for in the other life this can be manifestly perceived. They had conscience, which was communicated to me, that I might know it; and it was said that they lived in conjugial love in simplicity. They said that they loved their consorts and abstained from adulteries. That this was from conscience was evident from their saying that they could not do otherwise, because it was contrary to their will. Such persons are instructed in the other life and are perfected in the good of love and truth of faith, and are at length received among the angels.

PREFACE (TO PART III.).

How greatly they are deluded who remain in the sense of the letter alone, and do not search out the internal sense from other passages in the Word in which it is explained, is very evident from the many heresies, every one of which proves its dogmas from the literal sense of the Word: especially is this manifest from that great heresy which the insane and infernal love of self and the world has drawn from the Lord's words to Peter :—

I say unto thee that thou art Peter, and upon this rock I will build My church, and the gates of hell shall not prevail against it; and I will give unto thee the keys of the kingdom of the heavens, and whatsoever thou shalt bind upon earth shall be bound in the heavens, and whatsoever thou shalt loose upon earth shall be loosed in the heavens (*Matt.* xvi. 15-19).

[2] They who press the sense of the letter think that these things were said of Peter, and that power so great was given him; although they are fully aware that Peter was a very simple man, and that he by no means exercised such power; and that to exercise it is contrary to the Divine. Nevertheless, as owing to the insane and infernal love of self and the world they desire to arrogate to themselves the highest power on earth and in heaven, and to make themselves gods, they explain this according to the letter, and vehemently defend it; whereas the internal sense of these words is, that Faith itself in the Lord, which exists solely with those who are in love to the Lord and in charity toward the neighbor, has that power; and yet not faith, but the Lord from whom faith is. By "Peter" there is meant that faith, as everywhere else in the Word. Upon this is the Church built, and against it the gates of hell do not prevail. This faith has the keys of the kingdom of the heavens, and it shuts heaven lest evils and falsities should enter in, and opens heaven for goods and truths. This is the internal sense of these words. [3] The twelve apostles, like the twelve tribes of Israel, represented nothing else than all the things of such faith (n. 577, 2089,

2129, 2130 at the end). Peter represented faith itself, James charity, and John the goods of charity (see the preface to *Gen.* xviii.); in like manner as did Reuben, Simeon, and Levi, the firstborn sons of Jacob, in the representative Jewish and Israelitish Church, which is plain from a thousand passages in the Word. And as Peter represented faith, the words in question were said to him. From this it is manifest into what darkness those cast themselves, and others with them, who explain all things according to the letter; as those who so explain these words to Peter, by which they derogate from the Lord and arrogate to themselves the power of saving the human race.

CHAPTER THE TWENTY-SECOND.

2760. The Word as to its internal sense is thus described by John in the *Apocalypse :*—

I saw heaven opened, and behold a white horse, and He who sat upon him was called faithful and true ; and in righteousness He doth judge and make war. His eyes were a flame of fire ; and upon His head were many diadems ; and He had a name written which no one knew but He Himself ; and He was clothed in a garment dipped in blood ; and His name is called The Word of God. And the armies which are in heaven followed Him upon white horses, clothed in fine linen white and clean. And He hath upon His garment and upon His thigh a name written, King of kings, and Lord of lords (xix. 11–14, 16).

What each of these things involves no one can know except from the internal sense. It is manifest that every one of them is something representative and significative, as, that heaven was opened, that the horse was white, that He that sat upon him was faithful and true, and judgeth and maketh war in righteousness ; that His eyes were a flame of fire, that upon His head were many diadems, that He had a name written which no one knew but He Himself, that He was clothed in a garment dipped in blood, that the armies which are in heaven followed Him upon white horses, that they were clothed in fine linen white and clean, and that He had upon His garment and upon His thigh a name written. It is said in plain words that it is the

Word which is meant, and that it is the Lord who is the Word;
for it is said, "His name is called the Word of God," and then,
"He hath upon His garment and upon His thigh a name written, King of kings, and Lord of lords." [2] From the interpretation of each of the words it is manifest that the Word
is here described as to its internal sense. "Heaven being
opened," represents and signifies that the internal sense of
the Word is not seen except in heaven, and by those to whom
heaven is opened, that is, who are in love to the Lord and
thence in faith in Him. The "horse which was white" represents and signifies the understanding of the Word as to its
interiors; that a "white horse" is this will be manifest from
what follows. That "He who sat upon him" is the Word,
and the Lord who is the Word, is evident. He is called
"faithful and judging from righteousness" on account of
good, and "true and making war from righteousness" on
account of truth. His "having upon His head many diadems," signifies all things of faith. His "having a name
written which no one knew but He Himself," signifies that no
one sees what the Word is in its internal sense but Himself,
and he to whom He reveals it. "His being clothed in a garment dipped in blood," signifies the Word in the letter. The
"armies in the heavens which followed Him upon white
horses," signify those who are in the understanding of the
Word as to its interiors. "Clothed in fine linen white and
clean," signifies the same in love and thence in faith. The
"name written upon His garment and upon His thigh," signifies truth and good. From all this, and from what there precedes and follows, it is manifest that toward the last period
the internal sense of the Word will be opened; but what will
then come to pass is also described there (verses 17–21).

2761. That the "white horse" is the understanding of the
Word as to its interiors, or what is the same, the internal
sense of the Word, is evident from the signification of a
"horse," as being the intellectual faculty. In the prophetic
parts of the Word a horse and a rider are often named; but
no one has hitherto known that a "horse" signifies the faculty
of understanding, and a "rider" one who is intelligent—as in
the prophecy of Jacob, then Israel, respecting Dan:—

Dan shall be a serpent upon the way, an arrow-snake upon the path, biting the horse's heels, and his rider shall fall backward. I wait for Thy salvation, O Jehovah (*Gen.* xlix. 17, 18).

That a "serpent" is one who reasons concerning Divine arcana from the senses and from memory-knowledges, may be seen above (n. 195); also that a "way" and a "path" are truth (n. 627, 2333); and that the "heel" is the lowest of the natural (n. 259); a "horse" is the understanding of the Word; and a "rider" he that teaches. Hence it is manifest what these prophetic words signify, namely, that one who reasons concerning the truths of faith from the senses and from memory-knowledges, sticks fast in the lowest things of nature only, and thus believes nothing, which is to "fall backward;" wherefore it is added, "I wait for Thy salvation, O Jehovah." [2] In *Habakkuk* :—

O God, Thou dost ride upon Thy horses, Thy chariots are salvation ; Thou hast made Thy horses to tread in the sea (iii. 8, 15) ;

where "horses" denote the Divine truths which are in the Word; "chariots," doctrine from them; the "sea," knowledges (n. 28, 2120); and because these are of the understanding of the Word from God, it is said, "Thou hast made Thy horses to tread in the sea." Horses are here attributed to God, as in the *Apocalypse*, above; to whom they cannot be attributed unless they signify such things. [3] In *David* :—

Sing unto God, sing praises to His name, extol Him that rideth upon the clouds, by His name Jah (*Ps.* lxviii. 4) ;

to "ride upon the clouds" denotes the understanding of the Word as to its interiors, or in its internal sense. That a "cloud" is the Word in the letter, in which is the internal sense, may be seen in the Preface to *Genesis* xviii., where it is explained what is signified when it is said that the Lord will come in the clouds of heaven with power and glory. [4] In the same :—

Jehovah bowed the heavens, and came down, and thick darkness was under His feet; and He rode upon a cherub (*Ps.* xviii. 9, 10) ;

"thick darkness" here denotes clouds; to "ride upon a cherub" represents the Lord's providence lest man should of himself enter into the mysteries of faith which are in the Word (n. 308). In *Zechariah :*—

In that day shall there be upon the bells of the horses, Holiness unto Jehovah (xiv. 20) ;

the "bells of the horses" denote the understanding of the spiritual things of the Word, which are holy.   [5] In *Jeremiah :*—

There shall enter in by the gates of this city kings and princes, sitting upon the throne of David, riding in chariot and on horses, they, and their princes, the men of Judah, and the inhabitants of Jerusalem, and this city shall be inhabited forever (xvii. 25, 26 ; xxii. 4) ;

the "city Jerusalem" denotes the Lord's spiritual kingdom and church; "kings," truths (n. 1672, 2015, 2069); "princes," the primary precepts of truth (n. 1482, 2089); "David," the Lord (n. 1888); the "men of Judah and the inhabitants of Jerusalem," those who are in the good of love, of charity, and of faith (n. 2268, 2451, 2712); thus to "ride upon a chariot and upon horses" means to be instructed in the doctrine of truth from the internal understanding of the Word.   [6] In *Isaiah :*—

Then shalt thou delight thyself in Jehovah, and I will make thee to ride upon the high places of the earth, and I will feed thee with the heritage of Jacob (lviii. 14) ;

to "ride upon the high places of the earth" denotes intelligence.   In *David :*—

A song of loves : Gird Thy sword upon Thy thigh, O mighty one, Thy glory and Thy majesty ; and in Thy majesty go forward, ride upon the word of truth, and of the gentleness of righteousness, and Thy right hand shall teach Thee wonderful things (*Ps.* xlv. Title, 3, 4) ;

to "ride upon the word of truth" manifestly denotes the understanding of truth; and "upon the word of the gentleness of righteousness," the wisdom of good.   [7] In *Zechariah :*—

In that day, saith Jehovah, I will smite every horse with astonishment, and his rider with madness ; and I will open Mine eyes upon the house of Judah, and will smite every horse of the peoples with blindness (xii. 4, 5) ;

where also the "horse" manifestly denotes the understanding, which would be smitten with astonishment and blindness ; and the "rider" him that understands, who would be smitten with madness.   In *Hosea :*—

Take away all iniquity, and accept that which is good, and we will render the bullocks of our lips. Asshur shall not save us; we will not ride upon horses; and we will no more say to the work of our hands, Thou art our god (xiv. 2, 3) ;

"Asshur" denotes reasoning (n. 119, 1186); the "horse" one's own intelligence. Besides these there are many other passages.

2762. That a "horse" signifies the faculty of understanding is from no other source than the representatives in the other life. Often there, in the world of spirits, horses are seen, and this with great variety, and those also that sit on them; and whenever they are seen they signify the faculty of understanding. There are such representatives continually with spirits. It is from the representation of the horse, as being the understanding, that when horses are mentioned in the Word, the spirits and angels with man at once know that the understanding is what is treated of. It is also from this that when spirits from a certain distant world on being imbued with intelligence and wisdom are taken up from the world of spirits into heaven, there appear to them horses shining as with fire; which also I have seen when they were taken up. [2] From this I could see what is signified by the chariot of fire and horses of fire seen by Elisha when Elijah went up by a whirlwind into heaven; as also what is signified by the exclamation of Elisha then : "My Father, my Father, the chariot of Israel and the horsemen thereof" (2 *Kings* ii. 11, 12); and by Joash king of Israel saying the same to Elisha when he was dying: "My Father, my Father, the chariot of Israel and the horsemen thereof" (2 *Kings* xiii. 14). That by Elijah and Elisha was represented the Lord as to the Word, will of the Lord's Divine mercy be told elsewhere; the doctrine of love and charity from the Word being meant by the "chariot of fire," and the doctrine of faith therefrom by the "horses of fire." The doctrine of faith is the same as the understanding of the Word as to its interiors, or as to its internal sense. [3] That chariots and horses are seen in the heavens with spirits and angels, is evident from the fact of their being seen by the prophets, as by Zechariah (chapter i. 8–10; vi. 3–7), and by others, and also by Elisha's servant, as thus described in the book of *Kings:*—

Jehovah opened the eyes of Elisha's boy, and he saw ; and behold the mountain was full of horses and chariots of fire round about Elisha (2 *Kings* vi. 17).

Moreover, where the abode of the intelligent and wise is, in the world of spirits, chariots and horses appear continually; for the reason as said that by chariots and horses are represented the things of wisdom and of intelligence. Resuscitated persons after death, who are entering into the other life, see represented to them a young man sitting upon a horse, and then alighting from the horse; and by this is signified that they are to be instructed in the knowledge of good and truth before they can come into heaven (see Part First, n. 187, 188). [4] That chariots and horses signified these things, was well known in the Ancient Church, as also is evident from the book of *Job*, which is a book of that Church, where are these words :—

God hath made her to forget wisdom, and hath not imparted to her intelligence ; what time she lifteth up herself on high she scorneth the horse and his rider (xxxix. 17–19).

From the Ancient Church the signification of the horse, as being the faculty of understanding, was extended to the wise round about, even into Greece. From this it came to pass that when they described the sun (by which was signified love, n. 2441, 2495), they placed in it the god of their wisdom and intelligence, and gave him a chariot and four horses of fire; and that when they described the god of the sea, because by the sea were signified knowledges in general (n. 28, 2120), they gave horses also to him; and that when they described the rise of knowledges from the understanding, they represented a flying horse which with his hoof broke open a fountain, where dwelt the virgins that were the sciences; and by the Trojan horse nothing else was signified than a contrivance of their understanding for destroying city walls. Even at this day the intellect is often described, according to the custom received from those ancient people, under the figure of a flying horse, or Pegasus ; and learning is described as a fountain; but scarcely any one knows that a horse, in the mystic sense, signifies the understanding, and a fountain truth; still less that these significatives were handed down to the Gentiles from the Ancient Church.

2763. From all this it is now manifest whence come the representatives and significatives in the Word, namely, from the representatives that exist in the other life. From this source they came to the men of the Most Ancient Church, who were celestial, and were in company with spirits and angels while living on earth. From them the representatives passed to their posterity, and at length to those who merely knew that they had such a signification; but because the representatives came from the most ancient times, and were in their Divine worship, they were venerated and held sacred. [2] Besides representatives, there are also correspondences which suggest and also signify something altogether different in the spiritual world from what they do in the natural world; as the heart, the affection of good; the eyes, the understanding; the ears, obedience; the hands, power; besides innumerable other correspondences. These are not represented in this way in the world of spirits; but they correspond, as what is natural to what is spiritual. Hence it is that every word, even to the smallest iota of all, in the Word, involves spiritual and heavenly things; and that the Word is in this manner inspired, so that when it is read by man, spirits and angels immediately perceive it spiritually according to the representations and correspondences. But this knowledge, which was so much cultivated and esteemed by the ancients after the flood, and by means of which they were able to think with spirits and angels, is at this day altogether obliterated, so much so that scarcely any one is willing to believe that it exists; and they who believe in it merely call it a kind of mystical thing, of no use; and this for the reason that man has become altogether worldly and corporeal; to such a degree that when what is spiritual and heavenly is mentioned, he feels a repugnance, and sometimes a loathing, or even nausea. What then will he do in the other life, which lasts forever, and where there is nothing worldly and corporeal, but only what is spiritual and heavenly, which makes the life in heaven?

CHAPTER XXII.

1. And it came to pass after these words, that God did tempt Abraham, and said unto him, Abraham; and he said, Here am I.

2. And He said, Take I pray thy son, thine only one, whom thou lovest, even Isaac, and get thee to the land of Moriah, and offer him there for a burnt-offering upon one of the mountains which I will tell thee of.

3. And Abraham rose early in the morning, and saddled his ass, and took two of his boys with him, and Isaac his son; and he clave the wood for the burnt-offering, and rose up, and went unto the place of which God told him.

4. On the third day, and Abraham lifted up his eyes, and saw the place afar off.

5. And Abraham said unto his boys, Abide ye here with the ass, and I and the boy will go yonder, and we will bow ourselves down, and will come again to you.

6. And Abraham took the wood of the burnt-offering, and laid it upon Isaac his son; and he took in his hand the fire and the knife; and they went both of them together.

7. And Isaac said unto Abraham his father; and he said, My father; and he said, Here am I, my son. And he said, Behold the fire and the wood; and where is the lamb for a burnt-offering?

8. And Abraham said, God will see for Himself the lamb for a burnt-offering, my son: and they went both of them together.

9. And they came to the place which God told him of; and Abraham built there the altar, and laid the wood in order, and bound Isaac his son, and laid him on the altar upon the wood.

10. And Abraham put forth his hand, and took the knife to slay his son.

11. And the angel of Jehovah called unto him out of heaven, and said, Abraham, Abraham; and he said, Here am I.

12. And He said, Put not forth thine hand upon the boy, and do not anything unto him; for now I know that thou

fearest God, and thou hast not withheld thy son, thine only one, from Me.

13. And Abraham lifted up his eyes, and saw, and behold a ram behind, caught in a thicket by his horns; and Abraham went, and took the ram, and offered him up for a burnt-offering in the stead of his son.

14. And Abraham called the name of that place, Jehovah-will-see, as it is said to this day, In the mountain Jehovah will see.

15. And the angel of Jehovah called unto Abraham a second time out of heaven.

16. And said, By Myself have I sworn, saith Jehovah, because thou hast done this thing, and hast not withheld thy son, thine only one,

17. That in blessing I will bless thee, and in multiplying I will multiply thy seed, as the stars of the heavens, and as the sand which is upon the sea shore; and thy seed shall inherit the gate of thine enemies.

18. And in thy seed shall all the nations of the earth be blessed, because thou hast hearkened to My voice.

19. And Abraham returned unto his boys; and they rose up, and went together to Beer-sheba; and Abraham dwelt in Beer-sheba.

20. And it came to pass after these words that it was told Abraham, saying, Behold, Milcah, she also hath borne children unto Nahor thy brother:

21. Uz his firstborn, and Buz his brother, and Kemuel the father of Aram;

22. And Chesed, and Hazo, and Pildash, and Jidlaph, and Bethuel.

23. And Bethuel begat Rebekah; these eight did Milcah bear to Nahor, Abraham's brother.

24. And his concubine, whose name was Reumah, she also bare Tebah, and Gaham, and Tahash, and Maacah.

THE CONTENTS.

2764. In this chapter in the internal sense the Lord's most grievous and inmost temptations are treated of, by which He united His Human Essence to His Divine Essence; and also the salvation by this union of those who constitute the Lord's spiritual church.

2765. The Lord's most grievous and inmost temptations are treated of (verses 1, 3, 4, 5, 6, 9, 10, 11). Concerning the union of His Human Essence with His Divine Essence, or His glorification, by means of them (verses 2, 11, 12, 16). Concerning the salvation by the Lord's Divine Human of the spiritual, of those who are in charity and faith, within the church (verses 2, 7, 8, 13, 14, 15, 16, 17, 18, 19). And concerning the salvation of those who are in good, outside the church (verses 20, 21, 22, 23, 24).

THE INTERNAL SENSE.

2766. Verse 1. *And it came to pass after these words that God did tempt Abraham, and said unto him, Abraham ; and he said, Here am I.* " It came to pass after these words," signifies after the things just accomplished; "that God did tempt Abraham," signifies the Lord's most grievous and inmost temptations ; "and said unto him, Abraham," signifies the Lord's perception from Divine truth; "and he said, Here am I," signifies thought and reflection.

2767. *It came to pass after these words.* That this signifies after the things just accomplished, is evident without explication. The things which have been treated of are those respecting Abimelech and Abraham, that they made a covenant in Beer-sheba, and lastly that Abraham raised up a grove in Beer-sheba, by which was signified that human rational things were adjoined to the doctrine of faith, which is in itself Divine. Here now the Lord's temptation as to the rational, which is signified by Isaac, is treated of; for by temptations the Lord made His Human Divine, and thus His rational, in which the human commences (n. 2106, 2194), by chastising and expelling all in the rational that was merely human, or the maternal human. This is the connection of the things of the preceding chapter with those in this chapter; whence it is said, " It came to pass after these things that God did tempt Abraham."

2768. *That God did tempt Abraham.* That this signifies the Lord's most grievous and inmost temptations, is evident from what follows. That in the internal sense by " Abraham" is represented and meant the Lord, is manifest from all that precedes where Abraham is treated of. That the Lord suffered most grievous and inmost temptations, which are described in this chapter in the internal sense, will be made evident. But its being said that " God did tempt," is according to the sense of the letter, in which temptations and many other things are attributed to God; but it is according to the internal sense that God tempts no one; but in the time of temptations is continually liberating from them, as far as possible, or as far as the liberation does not do harm, and is continually looking to the good into which He is leading him who is in the temptations; for God never takes part in temptations in any other manner; and though it is predicated of Him that He permits, still it is not according to the idea which man has of permission, namely, that by permitting He concurs. Man cannot comprehend it in any other manner than that he who permits is also willing; but it is the evil within the man which causes, and even leads into the temptation; and no cause of this is in God—as the cause is not in the king or in the judge, when a man does evil and suffers punishment therefor. For he who separates himself from the laws of Divine order, all of which are the laws of good and thence of truth, casts himself into the laws that are opposite to Divine order, which are those of evil and falsity, and thence of punishments and torments.

2769. *And said unto him, Abraham.* That this signifies the Lord's perception from Divine truth, is evident from the signification of " saying" in the historical statements of the Word, as being to perceive (see n. 1898, 1919, 2080, 2619); and from the representation of Abraham, as being the Lord. That the perception was from Divine truth, may be seen from the fact that "God" is named, and not "Jehovah;" for where truth is treated of in the Word, there "God" is named; but where good is treated of, there "Jehovah" is named (see n. 2586). Hence it is that it is said "God" in this verse and also in those which follow, to verse 11, for the reason that temptation is there treated of. And that it is said "Jehovah" in verse 11 and those that follow, is because liberation is then treated of; for all temptation and condemnation is from truth, but all liberation and salvation is from good. (That truth condemns and good saves may be seen above, n. 1685, 2258, 2335.)

2770. *And he said, Here am I.* That this signifies thought and reflection, is evident from the signification of "saying," as being to perceive (n. 2769), but here to think and reflect, because they are the words of an answer; for all thought and the reflection therefrom comes from perception (n. 1919, 2515, 2552).

2771. Verse 2. *And He said, Take I pray thy son, thine only one, whom thou lovest, even Isaac, and get thee to the land of Moriah, and offer him there for a burnt-offering upon one of the mountains which I will tell thee of.* "He said, Take I pray thy son," signifies the Divine rational begotten by Him; "thine only one, whom thou lovest," signifies the sole one in the universe by which He was to save the human race; "even Isaac," signifies its quality; "and get thee to the land of Moriah," signifies a place and state of temptation; "and offer him there for a burnt-offering," signifies that He should sanctify Himself to the Divine; "upon one of the mountains," signifies the Divine Love; "which I will tell thee of," signifies as He should perceive.

2772. *He said, Take I pray thy son.* That this signifies the Divine rational begotten by Him, is evident from the signification of a "son," as being the rational (see n. 2623); here the Divine rational, because by the son is meant Isaac; and that he represents the Lord's Divine rational has been shown above (n. 1893, 2066, 2083, 2630). And as the Lord made His rational Divine by His own power, as has been often said, by "thy son" is also signified that it was begotten by Him (see n. 1893, 2093, 2625).

2773. *Thine only one, whom thou lovest.* That this signifies the only one in the universe by which He was to save the human race, is evident from the signification of the "only one," as being the sole and indeed the only one in the universe, because the Lord is treated of, who alone as to all His Human became God, or Divine.

2774. *Even Isaac.* That this signifies the quality of the rational, namely, as being the good of truth and the truth of good, that is, the Divine marriage as to the Lord's Human, is evident from the naming of Isaac (see the preceding chapter, xxi., verses 6, 7).

2775. *And get thee to the land of Moriah.* That this signifies a place and state of temptation, may be seen from the signification of the "land of Moriah." That the "land of Moriah" means a place of temptation, is manifest from Abraham's being commanded to go thither and offer up his son as a burnt-offering, and thus to undergo the extremity of temptation. That Jerusalem, where the Lord Himself endured the extremity of temptation, was in the same land, is evident from the fact that an altar was built by David on Mount Moriah, and afterwards the temple by Solomon; as is manifest from the book of *Chronicles :—*

Solomon began to build the house of Jehovah in Jerusalem, on Mount Moriah, which was seen by David his father, in the place which David prepared in the threshing-floor of Ornan (Araunah) the Jebusite (2 *Chron.* iii. 1 ; compare 1 *Chron.* xxi. 16–28 with 2 *Sam.* xxiv. 16–25).

From this it is sufficiently evident that these things which are said respecting the sacrificing of Isaac are representative of the Lord; otherwise this might have been done where Abraham was then tarrying; and he would not have been commanded to proceed from thence a journey of nearly three days.

2776. *And offer him there for a burnt-offering.* That this signifies that He should sanctify Himself to the Divine, is evident from the representation of a burnt-offering among the Hebrew nation and in the Jewish Church, as being the most holy thing of their worship. There were burnt-offerings and there were sacrifices, and what these represented may be seen above (n. 922, 923, 1823, 2180). Their sanctifications were made by means of them, and hence it is that by "offering up

for a burnt-offering" is here signified to be sanctified to the
Divine, for the Lord Himself sanctified Himself to the Divine,
that is, united His Human to His Divine by the combats and
victories of temptations (see n. 1663, 1690, 1691 at the end,
1692, 1737, 1787, 1812, 1813, 1820). [2] It is a common
belief at this day that the burnt-offerings and sacrifices signified the Lord's passion, and that by this the Lord made expiation for the iniquities of all; indeed, that He took them upon
Himself, and thus bore them; and that those who believe are
in this manner justified and saved, provided they think, even
though it were in the last hour before death, that the Lord
suffered for them, no matter how they may have lived during
the whole course of their life. But the case is not really so:
the passion of the cross was the extremity of the Lord's temptation, by which He fully united His Human to His Divine and
His Divine to His Human, and thus glorified Himself. This
very union is the means by which those who have the faith
in Him which is the faith of charity, can be saved. For the
Supreme Divine Itself could no longer reach to the human
race, which had removed itself so far from the celestial things
of love and the spiritual things of faith, that men no longer
even acknowledged them, and still less perceived them. In
order therefore that the Supreme Divine might be able to
come down to man in such a state, the Lord came into the
world and united His Human to the Divine in Himself; which
union could not be effected otherwise than by the most grievous combats of temptations and by victories, and at length by
the last, which was that of the cross. [3] Hence it is that
the Lord can from His Divine Human illumine minds, even
those far removed from the celestial things of love, provided
they are in the faith of charity. For the Lord in the other life
appears to the celestial angels as a Sun, and to the spiritual as
a Moon (n. 1053, 1521, 1529, 1530, 2441, 2495), whence comes
all the light of heaven. This light of heaven is of such a
nature that when it illumines the sight of spirits and angels, it
also illumines their understanding at the same time. This is
inherent in that light, so that in heaven so much as any one
has of external light, so much has he of internal light, that is,
so much of understanding; which shows wherein the light of

heaven differs from the light of the world. It is the Lord's
Divine Human which illuminates both the sight and the understanding of the spiritual; which would not take place if
the Lord had not united His Human Essence to His Divine
Essence; and if He had not united them, man in the world
would no longer have had any capacity of understanding and
perceiving what is good and true, nor indeed would a spiritual
angel in heaven have had any; so that they would have had
nothing of blessedness and happiness, consequently nothing of
salvation. From this we can see that the human race could not
have been saved unless the Lord had assumed the Human and
glorified it. [4] Hence then any one may infer what truth
there is in the idea that men are saved if they only think from
a kind of interior emotion that the Lord suffered for them,
and took away their sins, however they may have lived;
whereas the light of heaven from the Lord's Divine Human
cannot reach to any but those who live in the good of faith, that
is, in charity; or what is the same, those who have conscience.
The very plane into which that light can operate, or the receptacle of that light, is the good of faith, or charity, and thus conscience. (That the spiritual have salvation from the Lord's
Divine Human, may be seen above, n. 1043, 2661, 2716, 2718.)

2777. *Upon one of the mountains.* That this signifies the
Divine Love, is evident from the signification of a "mountain," as being love (see n. 795, 796, 1430); here, the Divine
Love, because it is predicated of the Lord; and what the
quality of this love is, may be seen above (n. 1690, 1691 at the
end, 1789, 1812, 1820, 2077, 2253, 2500, 2572). As it was the
Divine Love from which the Lord fought in temptations and
conquered, and by which He sanctified and glorified Himself,
it is here said to Abraham that he should offer up Isaac for a
burnt-offering upon one of the mountains in the land of Moriah. This representative is elucidated by the fact that an
altar was built by David, and the temple was built by Solomon, upon the mountain of Moriah (n. 2775); for the altar
upon which burnt-offerings and sacrifices were offered, was the
principal representative of the Lord, as was afterwards the
temple. That the altar was so may be seen above (n. 921);
and it is evident in *David :—*

Let them bring me to the mountain of Thy holiness, and to Thy tabernacles ; and I will go unto the altar of God, unto God, the gladness of
my joy (*Ps.* xliii. 3, 4).

That the temple was so too, is evident in *John* :—

Jesus said, Destroy this temple, and in three days I will raise it up.
He spake of the temple of His body (ii. 19, 21).

2778. *Which I will tell thee of.* That this signifies as He
should perceive, is evident from the signification of "saying,"
as being to perceive (see above, n. 2769).

2779. Verse 3. *And Abraham rose early in the morning, and
saddled his ass, and took two of his boys with him, and Isaac
his son ; and he clave the wood for the burnt-offering, and rose
up, and went unto the place of which God told him.* "And
Abraham rose early in the morning," signifies a state of peace
and innocence ; "and saddled his ass," signifies the natural
man which He prepared ; "and took two of his boys," signifies the former rational which He had adjoined ; "and Isaac
his son," signifies the Divine rational begotten by Himself ;
"and he clave the wood for the burnt-offering," signifies the
merit of righteousness ; "and rose up," signifies elevation ;
"and went unto the place of which God told him," signifies
the state at that time according to perception.

2780. *And Abraham rose early in the morning.* That this
signifies a state of peace and innocence, is evident from the
signification of "morning," and also of "rising early," when
predicated of the Lord, who here is "Abraham." "Morning"
in the universal sense signifies the Lord, and hence His kingdom ; consequently the celestial of love in general and in particular (as was shown n. 2333) ; and as it signifies these, it
signifies the state itself in which they are, which state is that
of peace and innocence. The state of peace in the heavens is
like that of the dawn on earth. In the state of peace in the
heavens come forth all celestial and spiritual things, and derive therefrom all that is auspicious, blessed, and happy in
them, as in the time of dawn on earth all things come forth
before man as things of delight and gladness ; for all the singulars derive their quality from the general affection (see n. 920,
2384). The case is the same with the state of innocence : this
comes forth in the state of peace, and is a general thing affect-

ing all the things of love and faith. Unless these have innocence in them, they lack their essential. Hence it is that no
one can come into heaven unless he have something of innocence (see *Mark* x. 15). It is plain from this what "morning"
signifies in the internal sense, and still more when it is said
that he "rose early in the morning;" and as in the highest
sense "morning" is the Lord, and as the state is from Him
which effects and affects all things in His kingdom, "morning"
and "rising in the morning" signify many other things which
come forth in that state; and this as related to the things
which follow in the internal sense.

2781. *And saddled his ass.* That this signifies the natural
man which He prepared, is evident from the signification of
an "ass," as explained in what now follows. There are in man
things of the will and things of the understanding; to the
former class belong the things of good, to the latter those of
truth. There are various kinds of beasts by which the things
of the will, or those of good, are signified; such as lambs,
sheep, kids, goats, bullocks, oxen (see n. 1823, 2179, 2180);
and there are likewise beasts by which intellectual things, or
those of truth, are signified, namely, horses, mules, wild-asses,
camels, asses, and also birds. That the intellectual faculty is
signified by the "horse," has been shown above (n. 2761, 2762).
That by the "wild-ass" truth separate from good is signified,
see above (n. 1949). That by the "camel" there is signified
memory-knowledge in general, and by the "ass" memory-knowledge in particular, may be seen above (n. 1486). [2] There
are two things which constitute the natural with man, or what
is the same, which constitute the natural man, namely, natural
good and natural truth. Natural good is the delight flowing
forth from charity and faith; natural truth is the memory-
knowledge of them. That natural truth is what is signified
by the "ass," and rational truth by the "mule," may be seen
from the following passages. In *Isaiah :—*

The prophecy of the beasts of the south. In a land of straitness and
distress; the lion and the old lion,* and from them the viper and the
flying fire-serpent; they carry their riches upon the shoulder of young
asses, and their treasures upon the hump of camels, to a people that

* *Tigris;* but *leo vetus,* n. 3048. [*Rotch ed.*]

shall not profit; and the Egyptians shall help in vain and to no purpose (xxx. 6, 7);

those are called the "beasts of the south" who are in the knowledges of good and truth, but who make them not of the life but of memory; of whom it is said that "they shall bring their riches upon the shoulder of young asses, and their treasures upon the hump of camels," for the reason that "young asses" signify memory-knowledges in particular, and "camels" memory-knowledges in general: that the "Egyptians" are memory-knowledges, may be seen above (n. 1164, 1165, 1186); of whom it is said that "they shall help in vain and to no purpose." That this prophecy has an internal sense, without which it is understood by nobody, is plain to every one; for without the internal sense it cannot be known what the prophecy of the beasts of the south is, the lion and the old lion, the viper and the flying fire-serpent; and what is meant by these beasts bringing their riches upon the shoulder of young asses, and their treasures upon the hump of camels, and why it immediately follows that the Egyptians shall help in vain and to no purpose. The like is meant by the "ass" in the prophecy of Israel respecting Issachar, in *Moses :—*

Issachar is a bony ass, lying down between the burdens (*Gen.* xlix. 14).

[3] In *Zechariah :—*

This shall be the plague wherewith Jehovah will smite all the peoples that shall fight against Jerusalem; there shall be the plague of the horse, of the mule, of the camel, and of the ass, and of every beast (xiv. 12, 15);

that by the "horse," "mule," "camel," and "ass," are signified things of the understanding in man, which will be affected by the plague, is evident from all that precedes and follows there; for the plagues which precede the last judgment or consummation of the age are treated of, a subject also much treated of by John in the *Apocalypse*, and by the rest of the prophets in many places. By these animals are meant those who will then fight against Jerusalem, that is, against the Lord's spiritual church and its truths, and who will be affected by such plagues as to the things of their understanding. [4] In *Isaiah :—*

Blessed are ye that sow beside all waters, that send forth the foot of the ox and the ass (xxxii. 20) ;

"they that sow beside all waters" denote those who suffer themselves to be instructed in spiritual things. (That "waters" are spiritual things, thus intellectual things of truth, may be seen above, n. 680, 739, 2702.) " They that send forth the foot of the ox and the ass" denote natural things which are to do service. The " ox" is the natural as to good (see n. 2180, 2566). The " ass" is the natural as to truth. [5] In *Moses :—*

Binding his young ass unto the vine, and his ass's colt unto the choice vine ; he hath washed his garments in wine, and his vesture in the blood of grapes (*Gen.* xlix. 11) ;

this is the prophecy of Jacob, at that time Israel, concerning the Lord; the " vine" and the " choice vine" denote the spiritual church external and internal (n. 1069); the " young ass" denotes natural truth ; the " ass's colt" rational truth. The reason an " ass's colt" denotes rational truth is that a " she-ass" signifies the affection of natural truth (n. 1486), the son of which is rational truth, as may be seen above (n. 1895, 1896, 1902, 1910). [6] In old times a judge rode upon a she-ass, and his sons upon young asses ; for the reason that the judges represented the goods of the church, and their sons the truths thence derived. But a king rode upon a she-mule, and his sons upon mules, by reason that kings and their sons represented the truths of the church (see n. 1672, 1728, 2015, 2069). That a judge rode upon a she-ass, is evident in the book of *Judges :—*

My heart is toward the lawgivers of Israel, that offered themselves willingly among the people ; bless ye Jehovah, ye that ride upon white she-asses, ye that sit upon carpets (v. 9, 10).

That the sons of the judges rode upon young asses :—

Jair the judge over Israel had thirty sons, that rode on thirty young asses (*Judges* x. 3, 4 ; and in other places). Abdon the judge of Israel had forty sons, and thirty sons' sons, that rode on seventy young asses (*Judges* xii. 14).

That a king rode upon a she-mule :—

David said unto them, Take with you the servants of your lord, and cause Solomon my son to ride upon the she-mule which is mine. And they caused Solomon to ride upon king David's she-mule, and Zadok the priest and Nathan the prophet anointed him king in Gihon (1 *Kings* i. 33, 38, 44, 45).

That the sons of a king rode upon he-mules :—

All the sons of king David rose up, and rode each one upon his mule, and fled, because of Absalom (2 *Sam.* xiii. 29).

[7] Hence it is manifest that to ride on a she-ass was the badge of a judge, and to ride on a she-mule, the badge of a king; and that to ride on a young ass was the badge of a judge's sons, and to ride on a mule was the badge of a king's sons; for the reason as already said that a she-ass represented and signified the affection of natural good and truth, a she-mule the affection of rational truth, an ass or a young ass natural truth itself, and a mule and also the son of a she-ass rational truth.   Hence it is plain what is meant by the prophecy concerning the Lord in *Zechariah* :—

Rejoice, O daughter of Zion ; shout, O daughter of Jerusalem ; behold, thy King cometh unto thee.   He is just and having salvation, lowly and riding upon an ass, and upon a young ass the son of she-asses.   His dominion shall be from sea to sea, and from the river to the ends of the earth (ix. 9, 10).

That the Lord, when He came to Jerusalem, willed to ride upon these animals, is known from the Evangelists, as in *Matthew* :—

Jesus sent two disciples, saying unto them, Go into the village that is over against you, and straightway ye shall find a she-ass tied, and a colt with her ; loose them, and bring them unto Me.   This was done that it might be fulfilled which was spoken by the prophet, saying, Tell ye the daughter of Zion, Behold thy King cometh unto thee, meek, sitting upon a she-ass, and upon a colt the son of a beast of burden.   And they brought the she-ass and the colt, and put their garments upon them, and set Him thereon (xxi. 1, 2, 4, 5, 7) ;

[8] to " ride upon an ass" was a sign that the natural was made subordinate ; and to " ride upon a colt the son of a she-ass" was a sign that the rational was made subordinate. (That the " son of a she-ass" signified the same as a " mule," has been shown above, at the passage from *Gen.* xlix. 11.) From this their signification, and because it belonged to the highest judge and to a king to ride upon them, and at the

same time that the representatives of the church might be fulfilled, it pleased the Lord to do this : as is thus described in *John* :—

On the next day a great multitude that had come to the feast, when they heard that Jesus was coming to Jerusalem, took branches of palmtrees, and went forth to meet Him, and cried, Hosanna, Blessed is He that cometh in the name of the Lord, even the King of Israel. And Jesus, having found a young ass, sat thereon ; as it is written, Fear not, daughter of Zion ; behold thy King cometh sitting on the colt of a sheass. These things understood not His disciples at the first ; but when Jesus was glorified, then remembered they that these things were written of Him, and that they had done these things unto Him (xii. 12–16 ; *Mark* xi. 1–12 ; *Luke* xix. 28–41).

[**9**] From all this it is now evident that all and everything in the church of that period was representative of the Lord, and therefore of the celestial and spiritual things that are in His kingdom—even to the she-ass and the colt of a she-ass, by which the natural man as to good and truth was represented. The reason of the representation was that the natural man ought to serve the rational, and this the spiritual, this the celestial, and this the Lord : such is the order of subordination.   [**10**] Since by an "ox and an ass" the natural man as to good and truth is signified, many laws were therefore given in which oxen and asses are mentioned, which laws at first sight do not appear to be worthy of mention in the Divine Word ; but when unfolded as to their internal sense, the spiritual meaning in them appears to be of great moment—as the following in *Moses* :—

If a man shall open a pit, or if a man shall dig a pit, and not cover it, and an ox or an ass fall into it, the owner of the pit shall give money to the owner, and the dead shall be his (*Exod.* xxi. 33, 34).

If thou meet thine enemy's ox or his ass going astray, thou shalt surely bring it back to him again. If thou see the ass of him that hateth thee lying under his burden, and wouldest forbear to remove it, removing thou shalt remove it from him (*Exod.* xxiii. 4, 5 ; *Deut.* xxii. 1, 3).

Thou shalt not see thy brother's ass or his ox falling down in the way, and hide thyself from them ; lifting thou shalt lift them up again (*Deut.* xxii. 4).

Thou shalt not plow with an ox and an ass together. Thou shalt not wear a mixed web of wool and linen together (*Deut.* xxii. 10, 11).

Six days thou shalt do thy works, and on the seventh day thou shalt rest, that thine ox and thine ass may rest also, and the son of thy handmaid, and the sojourner (*Exod.* xxiii. 12).

Here the " ox and ass" signify nothing else in the spiritual sense than natural good and truth.

2782. *And took two of his boys.* That this signifies the former rational which He had adjoined, is evident from the signification of " boys." A " boy" and " boys" signify various things in the Word; because these terms are applied not only to the sons of the house but also to the sons of the stranger, and to servants also; here to servants. (That man's natural things which are to serve the rational are signified by " servants" also in the Word, may be seen above, n. 1486, 1713, 2541, 2567.) As however they are not here called " servants," but " boys," the former or merely human rational, which was to serve the Divine rational, is signified; as may also be seen from the very series of the things.

2783. *And Isaac his son.* That this signifies the Divine rational begotten by Himself, is evident from the representation of Isaac, as being the Lord's Divine rational, often spoken of before. That it was begotten by Him is meant by its being called his " son" (as above, n. 2772).

2784. *And he clave the wood for the burnt-offering.* That this signifies the merit of righteousness, is evident from the signification of " wood" and of " cleaving wood." That " wood" signifies the goods that are of works, and of righteousness; and that " cleaving wood" signifies the placing of merit in the goods that are of works, but " cleaving wood for a burnt-offering" the merit of righteousness, appears too remote to be known without revelation. That " cleaving wood" denotes placing merit in the goods that are of works, was made clear to me by what I have seen and have described in Part First (n. 1110) respecting the hewers of wood, as being those who had desired to merit salvation by the goods which they had done. Moreover there are others also, in front, above, a little to the right, from a certain world, who in the same way had claimed all good to themselves, and appear in like manner to cut and cleave wood. When these seem to themselves to be laboring, they sometimes shine in the face from a kind of fatuous fire, which is the good of merit that they attribute to themselves. The reason of its appearing so is that wood is a representative of good; as was all the wood in the ark and in the temple, and also all the wood upon the altar when the burnt-offerings and sacrifices were made. But they who attribute good to themselves, and make it self-meritorious, these also are said in the Word to "worship wood," or a "graven image" of wood.

2785. *And he rose up.* That this signifies elevation, is evident from the signification of "rising up," as meaning where it occurs in the Word some elevation.

2786. *And went unto the place of which God told him.* That this signifies His state at that time according to perception, is evident from the signification of "place," as being state (see n. 1273–1277, 1376–1381, 2625); and from the signification of "God saying," as being to perceive from the Divine (n. 2769, 2778). As regards the state itself, it is described in this verse, that is, the state which the Lord assumed when He underwent temptations, and here that which He assumed when He underwent the most grievous and inmost temptations. His first preparation for that state was that He entered into a state of peace and innocence, and that He prepared the natural man in Himself, as also the rational, so that they should serve the Divine rational, and that He adjoined the merit of righteousness, and in this manner elevated Himself. These things cannot be explained at all to the comprehension, or be presented to the idea, of any one who does not know that many states exist together, and these distinct from one another; and who does not also know what a state of peace and innocence is, what the natural man is, what the rational man, and also what the merit of righteousness is; for he must first have a distinct idea of all these, and must also know that the Lord from His Divine could induce upon Himself whatever states He pleased, and that He prepared Himself for temptations by inducing many states. Although these things are in obscurity as of night with men, they are nevertheless in clearness as of day with the angels, who being in the light of heaven from the Lord, see in these and similar things innumerable things distinctly, and from the affection flowing in at the time perceive ineffable joy. Hence it is evident how far human understanding and perception fall short of angelic understanding and perception.

2787. Verse 4. *On the third day, and Abraham lifted up his eyes, and saw the place afar off.* " On the third day," signifies completeness, and the beginning of sanctification ; "and Abraham lifted up his eyes and saw," signifies thought and view from the Divine ; "the place afar off," signifies the state which He foresaw.

2788. *On the third day.* That this signifies completeness, and the beginning of sanctification, is evident from the signification of the "third day." "Day" in the Word signifies state (n. 23, 487, 488, 493, 893) ; as also does "year," and in general all periods of time ; as an "hour," a "day," a "week," a "month," a "year," an "age ;" as also "morning," "noon," "evening," and "night ;" and "spring," "summer," "autumn," and "winter ;" and when "third" is added to these, they signify the end of that state, and at the same time the beginning of the following state. As the Lord's sanctification is here treated of, which was effected by temptations, the "third day" signifies completeness, and at the same time the beginning of sanctification, as also follows from what has been already said. The reason of this signification is that when the Lord had fulfilled all things He would rise again on the third day ; for the things that were done, or that would be done by the Lord when He lived in the world, were in the representatives of the church as if already done (as also they were in the internal sense of the Word) ; for in God to be and to become are the same ; indeed all eternity is present to Him. [2] Hence the number "three" was representative, not only in the Ancient Church and in the Jewish, but also among various nations. (See what is said concerning this number above, n. 720, 901, 1825.) That this was the origin of the signification of "three," is evident in *Hosea :—*

Let us return unto Jehovah, for He hath wounded, and He will heal us ; He hath smitten, and He will bind us up ; after two days He will revive us, on the third day He will raise us up, that we may live before Him (vi. 1, 2) ;

where the "third day" denotes the Lord's coming, and His resurrection. And from Jonah, that he "was in the belly of the fish three days and three nights" (*Jonah* i. 17) ; concerning which the Lord thus speaks in *Matthew :—*

As Jonah was in the whale's belly three days and three nights, so shall the Son of man be three days and three nights in the heart of the earth (xii. 40).

[3] Be it known that in the internal sense of the Word " three days" and the " third day" signify the same, as also do " three" and " third" in the passages which now follow. In *John* :—

Jesus said to the Jews, Destroy this temple, and in three days I will raise it up ; He spake of the temple of His body (ii. 19-21 ; *Matt.* xxvi. 61 ; *Mark* xiv. 58 ; xv. 29).

[4] That the Lord rose again on the third day is known. For the same reason the Lord distinguished the periods of His life into three, as stated in *Luke* :—

Go ye and tell that fox, Behold I cast out demons, and perform cures to-day and to-morrow, and the third day I am perfected (xiii. 32).

His last temptation also, that of the cross, the Lord endured at the " third hour" of the day (*Mark* xv. 25) ; and after three hours there came darkness over the whole land, or at the " sixth hour" (*Luke* xxiii. 44) ; and after three hours, or at the " ninth hour," the end (*Mark* xv. 33, 34, 37).   But on the morning of the " third day" He rose again (*Mark* xvi. 1-4 ; *Luke* xxiv. 7) ; (see *Matt.* xvi. 21 ; xvii. 22, 23 ; xx. 18, 19 ; *Mark* viii. 31 ; ix. 31 ; x. 33, 34 ; *Luke* xviii. 33 ; xxiv. 46).   From all this, and especially from the Lord's resurrection on the third day, the number " three" was representative and significative, as may be seen from the following passages in the Word :—

When Jehovah came down upon Mount Sinai, He told Moses to sanctify the people to-day and to-morrow, and that they should wash their garments, and be ready against the third day, for on the third day Jehovah would descend (*Exod.* xix. 10, 11, 15, 16).

When they set forth from the mount of Jehovah on a journey of three days, the ark of Jehovah went before them a three days' journey to seek out a resting place for them (*Num.* x. 33).

There was thick darkness in all the land of Egypt three days, and they saw not one another for three days, but the sons of Israel had light (*Exod.* x. 22, 23).

[5] The flesh of the sacrifice of a vow, or of a free-will offering, was to be eaten on the first and second day ; nothing was to be left to the third day, but the remainder was to be burnt, because it was an abomination.

So too with the flesh of the peace-offering ; and if it should be eaten on the third day it would not propitiate, but the soul should carry its iniquity (*Lev.* vii. 16–18 ; xix. 6, 7).

He that touched one dead was to purify himself on the third day, and on the seventh day he should be clean ; otherwise that soul should be cut off from Israel ; and one that was clean should sprinkle water upon him that was unclean on the third day and on the seventh day (*Num.* xix. 12, 13, 19).

They who slew a person in battle, or touched one that was slain, were to purify themselves on the third day, and on the seventh day (*Num.* xxxi. 19).

[6] When they came into the land of Canaan the fruit was to be uncircumcised three years, and was not to be eaten (*Lev.* xix. 23).

At the end of three years they were to bring all the tithes of their increase in that year and lay it up in their gates, that the Levite, the sojourner, the orphan, and the widow might eat (*Deut.* xiv. 28, 29 ; xxiv. 12).

Three times in the year they were to keep a feast to Jehovah, and three times in the year every male was to appear before the face of the Lord Jehovih (*Exod.* xxiii. 14, 17 ; *Deut.* xvi. 16).

Joshua told the people that in three days they should pass over the Jordan and inherit the land (*Josh.* i. 11 ; iii. 2).

[7] Jehovah called to Samuel three times, and he answered the third time (1 *Sam.* iii. 8).

When Saul wished to kill David, David hid himself in the field till the third evening.   Jonathan said to David that he would sound his father on the third day.   Jonathan shot three arrows by the side of the stone, and David then fell upon his face to the earth before Jonathan and bowed himself down three times (1 *Sam.* xx. 5, 12, 19, 20, 35, 36, 41).

David was to choose one of three things : seven years of famine in the land ; or that he should flee before his enemies three months ; or a pestilence in the land three days (2 *Sam.* xxiv. 12, 13).

[8] There was a famine in the days of David three years, year after year (2 *Sam.* xxi. 1).

Elijah stretched himself upon the dead child three times and brought him to life (1 *Kings* xvii. 21).

When Elijah had built the altar to Jehovah, he told them to pour water upon the burnt-offering and upon the wood three times (1 *Kings* xviii. 34).

The fire twice consumed the commanders over fifty, sent to Elijah, but not him that was sent the third time (2 *Kings* i. 13).

It was a sign to king Hezekiah that they should eat that year what sprung up spontaneously, in the second year the after-growth, but in the third year they should sow, reap, plant vineyards, and eat the fruit of them (2 *Kings* xix. 29).

[9] Daniel entered into his house and had the windows open in his chamber toward Jerusalem, and here three times a day he blessed upon his knees and prayed (*Dan.* vi. 11, 14).

Daniel mourned three weeks of days, eating no pleasant bread, nor drinking wine, nor anointing himself, until the three weeks of days were fulfilled (*Dan.* x. 2, 3).

Isaiah went naked and barefoot three years, for a sign and a wonder upon Egypt and upon Cush (*Isa.* xx. 3).

Out of the candlestick went forth three branches on each side, and three almond-shaped cups on each branch (*Exod.* xxv. 32, 33).

In the Urim and Thummim there were three precious stones in each row (*Exod.* xxviii. 17–19).

[**10**] In the new temple there were to be three chambers of the gate on this side and three on that side, and they three should have one measure ; at the porch of the house the breadth of the gate should be three cubits on this side and three cubits on that side (*Ezek.* xl. 10, 21, 48).

In the New Jerusalem there were to be three gates to the north, three to the east, three to the south, and three to the west (*Ezek.* xlviii. 31–34 ; *Rev.* xxi. 13).

So in the following passages :—

Peter denied Jesus thrice (*Matt.* xxvi. 34, 69 and following verses).

The Lord said to Peter three times, " Lovest thou Me ?" (*John* xxi. 17).

Also in the parable, the man who planted the vineyard sent servants three times, and at length his son (*Luke* xx. 12 ; *Mark* xii. 2, 4–6).

They who labored in the vineyard were hired at the third hour, the sixth hour, the ninth hour, and the eleventh hour (*Matt.* xx. 1–17).

Because the fig-tree did not bear fruit for three years, it was to be cut down (*Luke* xiii. 6, 7).

[**11**] As a trine and a third were representative, so also was a third part ; as that in the meat-offering of fine flour two tenths were mixed with a third part of a hin of oil ; and the wine for a libation was a third part of a hin (*Num.* xv. 6, 7 ; *Ezek.* xlvi. 14).

The prophet Ezekiel was to pass a razor upon his head, and upon his beard, and then divide the hair and burn a third part in the fire, and smite a third with the sword, about it (the city), and scatter a third to the wind (*Ezek.* v. 1, 2, 11).

In the whole land, two parts were to be cut off and the third was to be left ; but the third was to be brought through the fire and proved (*Zech.* xiii. 8, 9).

[**12**] When the first angel sounded there came hail and fire mingled with blood, and it fell upon the earth so that a third part of the trees were burnt up. The second angel sounded, and as it were a great mountain burning with fire was cast into the sea, and a third part of the sea became blood ; because of which a third part of the creatures in the sea having souls, died, and a third part of the ships were destroyed. The third angel sounded, and there fell a great star from heaven burning like a lamp, and it fell upon a third part of the rivers ; the name of the star was Wormwood. The fourth angel sounded, and a third part of the sun was smitten, and a third part of the moon, and a third part of the stars,

so that a third part of them was darkened, and the day shone not for a third part of it, and the night in like manner (*Rev.* viii. 7–12).

[**13**] The four angels were loosed to kill a third part of men (*Rev.* ix. 15).

By these three were the third part of men killed, by the fire, and the smoke, and the brimstone, which proceeded out of the mouth of the horses (*Rev.* ix. 18).

The dragon drew with his tail a third part of the stars of heaven and cast them to the earth (*Rev.* xii. 4).

A " third part," however, signifies some, and what is not yet complete; but the " third," and a " trine," what is complete; and this, of evil to the evil, and of good to the good.

2789. *And Abraham lifted up his eyes and saw.* That this signifies thought and mental view from the Divine, is evident from the signification of the " eyes," as being intelligence (see n. 2701); hence to " lift up the eyes" denotes to elevate the intelligence, thus to think; and from the signification of " seeing," as being to view from the Divine, because it is predicated of the Lord.

2790. *The place afar off.* That this signifies into the state which He foresaw, is evident from the signification of " place," as being state (see n. 1273–1277, 1376–1381, 2625); and from the signification of " seeing afar off," as being to foresee.

2791. Verse 5. *And Abraham said unto his boys, Abide ye here with the ass, and I and the boy will go yonder, and we will bow ourselves down, and will come again to you.* " Abraham said unto his boys, Abide ye here with the ass," signifies the separation of the former rational together with the natural at that time; "and I and the boy will go yonder," signifies the Divine rational in a state of truth prepared for the most grievous and inmost combats of temptations; the " boy" is the Divine rational in such a state; "and we will bow ourselves down," signifies submission; " and will come again to you," signifies conjunction afterwards.

2792. *Abraham said unto his boys, Abide ye here with the ass.* That this signifies the separation of the former rational together with the natural at that time, is evident from the signification of " abiding here," as being to be separated so long; from the signification of the " boys," as being the former rational (explained above, n. 2782); and from the signification of the "ass," as being the natural man, or the natural (also explained above, n. 2781).

2793. *And I and the boy will go yonder.* That this signifies the Divine rational in a state of truth prepared for the most grievous and inmost combats of temptations, is evident; and that the " boy" is the Divine rational in such a state, is evident from the representation of Isaac, as being the Divine rational; but as he is not here called " Isaac," nor " my son," as before, but " the boy," it denotes the Divine rational in such a state, concerning which presently.

2794. *And we will bow ourselves down.* That this signifies submission, is evident without explication.

2795. *And will come again to you.* That this signifies conjunction afterwards, is also evident without explication. As the Lord's most grievous and inmost temptations are treated of in this chapter, all the states that He assumed when He underwent these temptations are described. The first state is described in the third verse, the second state in this verse, the third state in the verse next following, and the rest afterwards. But these states cannot be expounded to the common apprehension unless many things are first known, not only respecting the Lord's Divine, as here represented by Abraham, but also respecting His Divine Human as represented by Isaac, and respecting the state of this rational when He engaged in and underwent the combats of temptation (this being the " boy"); and also what and of what quality the former rational was, and also the natural which it had; and likewise what the state was when the one was adjoined to the other, and what the state was when they were more or less separated. Moreover many things concerning temptations must be known, as what exterior and interior temptations are, and hence what were the inmost and most grievous temptations the Lord had, and which are treated of in this chapter. So long as these things are unknown, the things contained in this verse cannot possibly be described to the comprehension ; and if they should be described, even most clearly, they would still appear obscure. To the angels, who are in the light of heaven from the Lord, all these things are manifest and clear, indeed blessed, because they are most heavenly. [2] Here we will merely say that the Lord could not be tempted at all when He was in the Divine Itself, for the Divine is infinitely above all temptation; but He could be tempted as to His human. This is the reason why when He was to undergo the most grievous and inmost temptations, He adjoined to Himself the prior human, that is, the rational and the natural of it, as described in verse 3; and why He afterwards separated Himself from these, as is said in this verse; but nevertheless retaining something by means of which He could be tempted; which is the reason why it is not here said, "Isaac my son," but "the boy," by whom is meant the Divine rational in such a state, namely, in a state of truth, prepared for the most grievous and inmost combats of temptations (see n. 2793). That neither the Divine Itself nor the Divine Human could be tempted, must be evident to every one simply from the fact that not even the angels can approach the Divine, much less the spirits who induce temptations, and still less the hells. Hence it is manifest why the Lord came into the world, and put on the human state itself with its infirmity; for thus He could be tempted as to the human, and by means of the temptations subjugate the hells, and reduce each and all things to obedience and into order, and save the human race which had removed itself so far away from the supreme Divine.

2796. As regards the putting on of the various states by the Lord which is here treated of, they cannot but be unknown to man, because he never reflects on his changes of state; which are nevertheless going on continually, both as to what is of the understanding or the thoughts, and as to what is of the will or the affections. The reason of his not reflecting upon them is that he believes that all things in him follow in natural order, and that there is nothing higher which directs; whereas the case is that all things are disposed by means of the spirits and angels with him; and all his states and changes of states are therefrom, and are thus to eternity directed by the Lord to ends which the Lord alone foresees. That the reality is so, has become most fully known to me now by the experience of many years. It has also been given to know and observe what spirits and angels were with me, and what states they induced; and this I can solemnly assert—that all states, even to the least particulars, come from this source and are thereby directed by the Lord. It has also been given to know and observe that in every state there are a great many others, which do not appear, and which together appear as one general state; and that these states are disposed in relation to the states which follow in order in their series. With a man these things are done by the Lord; but with the Lord Himself, when He lived in the world, they were done by Himself; because He was Divine, and the very being of His life was Jehovah. [2] The changes of state with man as to what is of the understanding and as to what is of the will, and the order in which they follow on, as also the series through which they pass, and thus how they are bent by the Lord as far as possible to good, it belongs to the angels to know. The wisdom of the angels is such that they perceive all these things most minutely. Hence it is that these things which are revealed in the internal sense concerning the changes of state with the Lord, are clearly and distinctly perceivable by the angels, because they are in the light of heaven from the Lord; and they are also in some degree intelligible to a man who lives in simple good; but they are merely obscure and as nothing to those who are in evil, and also to those who are in the deliriums of wisdom; for these have obscured and extinguished their natural and rational light by many things which have induced darkness, however much they may believe that they are pre-eminently in light.

2797. Verse 6. *And Abraham took the wood of the burnt-offering, and laid it upon Isaac his son; and he took in his hand the fire and the knife; and they went both of them together.* " Abraham took the wood of the burnt-offering," signifies the merit of righteousness; "and laid it upon Isaac," signifies that it was adjoined to the Divine rational; "and he took in his hand the fire and the knife," signifies the good of love and the truth of faith; "and they went both of them together," signifies unition as far as possible.

2798. *Abraham took the wood of the burnt-offering, and laid it upon Isaac his son.* That this signifies the merit of righteousness, is evident from what was said and shown above (n. 2784), thus without further explication. That he " laid it upon Isaac" signifies that the merit of righteousness was adjoined to the Divine rational, is evident from the representation of Isaac, as being the Lord's Divine rational (often shown before); and from the signification of "laying upon him," as being to adjoin. He is called his "son," because the Lord's Divine Human was not only conceived, but was also born of Jehovah. That the Lord was conceived of Jehovah is most fully known from the Word of the Lord; hence He is called the "Son of the Highest," the "Son of God," and the "Only-begotten of the Father," in many places (*Matt.* ii. 15; iii. 16, 17; xvi. 13–17; xvii. 5; xxvii. 43, 54; *Mark* i. 10; ix. 7, 9; xiv. 61, 62; *Luke* i. 31, 32, 35; iii. 21, 22; ix. 35; x. 22; *John* i. 14, 18, 50; iii. 13, 16–18; v. 20–27; vi. 69; ix. 34, 35, 38; x. 35, 36; xx. 30, 31), and in many other places He calls Jehovah His "Father." [2] That He was born of the virgin Mary is known, yet as another man; but when He was born again, or became Divine, it was from Jehovah who was in Him, and who was Himself as to the very being of life. The unition of the Divine and the Human Essence was effected mutually and reciprocally, so that He united the Divine Essence to the Human and the Human to the Divine (see n. 1921, 1999, 2004, 2005, 2018, 2025, 2083, 2508, 2523, 2618, 2628, 2632, 2728, 2729). Hence it is evident that the Lord made the Human in Himself Divine by His own power, and thus became righteousness. The merit of righteousness was what was adjoined to the Divine rational when He underwent inmost temptations, and from it He then fought, and against this the evil genii fought, until He glorified this also. These are the things meant in the internal sense by Abraham laying the wood of the burnt-offering upon Isaac his son, and these are what are perceived by the angels when the words are read.

2799. *And he took in his hand the fire and the knife.* That this signifies the good of love and the truth of faith, is evident from the signification of "fire," as being the good of love (see n. 934); and from the signification of a "knife," as being the truth of faith. That the knife used upon the victims in the sacrifices signified the truth of faith, may be seen from the signification of a "sword" or "little sword" in the Word; for instead of "knife" it is said "little sword." Both have the same signification, but with the difference that the knife used for sacrifices signified the truth of faith, but a sword truth combating; and as a knife is rarely mentioned in the Word, for a secret reason to be mentioned presently, we may show what a "sword" signifies. A "sword" in the internal sense signifies the truth of faith combating, and also the vastation of truth; and in the opposite sense falsity combating, and the punishment of falsity. [2] I. That a "sword" signifies the truth of faith combating, may be seen from the following passages. In *David :*—

Gird Thy sword upon Thy thigh, O mighty One, prosper in Thy glory and Thy majesty, ride upon the word of truth, and Thy right hand shall teach Thee wonderful things (*Ps.* xlv. 3, 4) ;

where the Lord is treated of, the "sword" denoting truth combating. In the same :—

Let the merciful exult in glory, let them sing upon their beds ; let the high praises of God be in their throat, and a two-edged sword in their hand (*Ps.* cxlix. 5, 6).

In *Isaiah :*—

Jehovah hath called Me from the womb ; from the bowels of My mother hath He made mention of My name, and He hath made My mouth like a sharp sword, and hath made Me a polished arrow (xlix. 1, 2) ;

a "sharp sword" denotes truth combating; and a "polished arrow," the truth of doctrine (see n. 2686, 2709). In the same :—

Asshur shall fall by the sword not of a man ; and the sword not of man shall devour him ; and he shall flee before the sword, and his young men shall become tributary (xxxi. 8) ;

"Asshur" denotes reasoning in Divine things (n. 119, 1186); the "sword not of a man, and not of man," falsity; the "sword before which he shall flee," truth combating. [3] In *Zechariah :*—

Turn you to the stronghold ye prisoners of hope ; even to-day do I declare that I will render double unto thee ; I who have bent Judah for Me as a bow, I have filled Ephraim, and have stirred up thy sons, O Zion, against thy sons, O Javan, and I will make thee as the sword of a mighty man, and Jehovah shall be seen over them, and His arrows shall go forth as the lightning (ix. 12–14) ;

the "sword of a mighty man" denotes truth combating. In *John* :—

In the midst of the seven candlesticks was one like unto the Son of man ; He had in His right hand seven stars ; out of His mouth proceeded a sharp two-edged sword, and His countenance was as the sun shining in his strength (*Rev.* i. 13, 16).

Again :—

These things saith He that hath the sharp two-edged sword; I will come unto thee quickly, and will fight against them with the sword of My mouth (*Rev.* ii. 12, 16) ;

the "sharp two-edged sword" manifestly denotes truth combating, which was therefore represented as a "sword going out of the mouth." [4] In the same :—

Out of the mouth of Him that sat upon the white horse proceeded a sharp sword, that with it He should smite the nations ; and they were slain by the sword of Him that sat upon the horse, which came forth out of His mouth (*Rev.* xix. 15, 21) ;

where it is manifest that the "sword out of His mouth" is truth combating. (That He who sat upon the white horse is the Word, and thus the Lord who is the Word, may be seen above, n. 2760–2763.)   Hence it is that the Lord says in *Matthew* :—

Think not that I came to send peace on the earth ; I came not to send peace, but a sword (x. 34).

Also in *Luke:*—

Now he that hath a purse, let him take it, and likewise a wallet ; and he that hath none, let him sell his garment, and buy a sword ; they said, Lord, behold here are two swords ; and Jesus said, It is enough (xxii. 36–38) ;

where nothing else is meant by a "sword" than the truth from which and for which they would combat. [5] In *Hosea :*—

In that day will I make a covenant for them with the wild beast of the field, and with the fowl of the heavens, and with the creeping thing of the ground ; and I will break the bow, and the sword, and the war out of the land ; and will make them to lie down securely (ii. 18) ;

where the Lord's kingdom is treated of ; by "breaking the bow, the sword, and the war," is signified that there is no combat there respecting doctrine and truth. In *Joshua :*—

Joshua lifted up his eyes and looked, and behold there stood a man over against him, and his sword drawn in his hand ; and he said to Joshua, I am prince of the army of Jehovah ; and Joshua fell on his face to the earth (v. 13, 14).

This was when Joshua entered with the sons of Israel into the land of Canaan, by which is meant the entrance of the faithful into the Lord's kingdom. Truth combating, which is of the church, is the " drawn sword in the hand of the prince of the army of Jehovah." [6] But that by " little swords" or " knives" is signified the truth of faith, may be seen from the fact that they were used not only in the sacrifices, but also in circumcision. For use in circumcision they were of stone, and were called " little swords of flint," as is manifest in *Joshua* :—

Jehovah said unto Joshua, Make thee little swords of flint, and circumcise again the sons of Israel the second time. And Joshua made him little swords of flint, and circumcised the sons of Israel at the hill of the foreskins (v. 2, 3).

That circumcision was a representative of purification from the love of self and the world, may be seen above (n. 2039, 2632) ; and as this purification is effected by the truths of faith, therefore little swords of flint were used (n. 2039 at the end, 2046 at the end). [7] II. That a " sword" signifies the vastation of truth, is evident from the following passages. In *Isaiah* :—

These two things are befallen thee ; who shall bemoan thee ? desolation and destruction, and the famine and the sword ; who will comfort thee ? Thy sons have fainted, they lie at the head of all the streets (li. 19, 20) ;

" famine" denotes the vastation of good ; and the " sword" the vastation of truth ; to " lie at the head of all the streets," is to be deprived of all truth. (That a " street" is truth may be seen above, n. 2336 ; and what vastation is, at n. 301–304, 407, 408, 410, 411.) In the same :—

I will number you to the sword, and ye shall all bow down to the slaughter ; because I called, and ye did not answer ; I spake, and ye did not hear (lxv. 12).

[8] In the same :—

By fire and by the sword will Jehovah judge all flesh, and the slain of Jehovah shall be many (lxvi. 16) ;

the "slain of Jehovah" denote those who are vastated. In *Jeremiah* :—

Spoilers are come upon all the hillsides in the wilderness, for the sword of Jehovah devoureth from the one end of the land even to the other end of the land ; no flesh hath peace ; they have sown wheat, and have reaped thorns (xii. 12, 13) ;

the " sword of Jehovah" plainly denotes the vastation of truth. In the same :—

They have lied against Jehovah, and said, It is not He, neither shall evil come upon us, neither shall we see sword nor famine ; and the prophets shall become wind, and the word is not in them (v. 12, 13).

[9] In the same :—

I will visit upon them ; the young men shall die by the sword, their sons and their daughters shall die by famine (xi. 22).

In the same :—

When they offer burnt-offering and meat-offering I will not accept them ; for I will consume them by the sword, and by the famine, and by the pestilence. And I said, Ah, Lord Jehovih, behold the prophets say unto them, Ye shall not see the sword, and ye shall not have famine (xiv. 12, 13).

In the same :—

The city is given into the hand of the Chaldeans that fight against it, because of the sword, and of the famine, and of the pestilence (xxxii. 24, 36).

In the same :—

I will send the sword, the famine, and the pestilence among them, until they be consumed from off the land that I gave unto them and to their fathers (xxiv. 10).

[10] In these passages by " the sword, the famine, and the pestilence" vastation is described ; by the " sword" the vastation of truth, by the " famine" the vastation of good, and by the " pestilence" a wasting away even to consumption. In *Ezekiel* :—

Son of man, take thee a sharp sword, a barber's razor shalt thou take it unto thee, and shalt cause it to pass upon thy head, and upon thy beard ; and take thee balances to weigh, and divide them. A third part shalt thou burn with fire in the midst of the city ; a third part thou shalt smite with the sword round about it ; and a third part thou shalt scatter to the wind ; and I will draw out a sword after them. A third part shall die with the pestilence, and with famine shall they be consumed in the midst of thee ; and a third part shall fall by the sword round about thee ; and a third part I will scatter to every wind, and I will draw out a sword after them (v. 1, 2, 12, 17).

Here the vastation of natural truth is treated of, which is thus described. In the same :—

The sword is without, and the pestilence and the famine within ; he that is in the field shall die by the sword, and he that is in the city, famine and pestilence shall devour him (vii. 15).

[11] In the same :—

Say to the land of Israel, Thus said Jehovah, Behold I am against thee, and will draw forth My sword out of its sheath, and will cut off from thee the just and the wicked. Because I will cut off from thee the just and the wicked, therefore shall My sword go forth out of its sheath, it shall not return any more. The word of Jehovah came unto me, saying, Son of man, prophesy and say, Thus said Jehovah, Say a sword, a sword, it is sharpened and also furbished ; it is sharpened to slaughter a slaughter ; it is furbished that it may be as lightning. Son of man, prophesy and say, Thus said the Lord Jehovih to the sons of Ammon, and to their reproach ; and say thou, A sword, a sword is drawn for the slaughter, it is furbished to devour because of the lightning, whiles they see vanity unto thee, whiles they divine a lie unto thee (xxi. 3–5, 8–10, 28, 29).

Nothing else is here signified by the "sword" than vastation, as is manifest from the particulars in the internal sense. [12] In the same :—

The king of Babel shall break down thy towers with his swords ; by reason of the abundance of his horses their dust shall cover thee ; by reason of the noise of the rider, and of the wheel, and of the chariot, thy walls shall shake ; with the hoofs of his horses shall he tread down all thy streets (xxvi. 9–11).

What Babel is, may be seen above (n. 1326) ; and that it vastates (n. 1327). In *David* :—

If he turn not, God will whet His sword, He will bend His bow, and make it ready (*Ps.* vii. 12).

In *Jeremiah* :—

I said, Ah Lord Jehovih surely deceiving Thou hast deceived this people and Jerusalem, saying, Ye shall have peace ; and the sword hath reached even to the soul (iv. 10).

[13] In the same :—

Declare ye in Egypt, and make it to be heard in Migdol, Stand forth and prepare thee, for the sword shall devour round about thee (xlvi. 14).

In the same :—

A sword is upon the Chaldeans, and upon the inhabitants of Babel, and upon her princes, and upon her wise men ; a sword is upon her boasters, and they shall be foolish ; a sword is upon her mighty men, and they shall be dismayed ; a sword is upon her horses, and upon her chariots, and upon all the mixed multitude that is in the midst of her, and they shall become as women ; a sword is upon her treasures, and they shall be robbed ; a drought is upon her waters, and they shall be dried up (l. 35 38) ;

a "sword" manifestly denotes the vastation of truth, for it is said, "a sword is upon the wise men, upon the boasters, upon the mighty men, upon the horses and the chariot, and upon the treasures," and that "drought is upon the waters, and they shall be dried up." **[14]** In the same :—

We have given the hand to Egypt, to Asshur, to be satisfied with bread. Servants have ruled over us, there is none to deliver us out of their hand ; we gat our bread with our lives, because of the sword of the wilderness (*Lam.* v. 6, 8, 9).

In *Hosea :*—

He shall not return into the land of Egypt, and Asshur he shall be his king, because they refused to return to Me, and the sword shall hang over his cities, and shall consume his bars, and shall devour them, because of their counsels (xi. 5, 6).

In *Amos :*—

I have sent among you the pestilence in the way of Egypt, I have slain your young men with the sword, with the captivity of your horses (iv. 10) ;

"in the way of Egypt" denotes the memory-knowledges which vastate, when they reason from them on Divine things; the "captivity of the horses" denotes the intellectual faculty deprived of its endowment. **[15]** III. That a "sword" in the opposite sense signifies falsity combating, may be seen in *David :*—

My soul lieth in the midst of lions, the sons of men are set on fire ; their teeth are spears and arrows, and their tongue a sharp sword (*Ps.* lvii. 4).

In the same :—

Behold they belch out with their mouth, swords are in their lips, for who doth hear ? (lix. 7).

In *Isaiah :*—

Thou art cast forth out of thy sepulchre as an abominable branch, as the raiment of the slain, that are thrust through with the sword, that go down to the stones of the pit, as a carcase trodden under foot (xiv. 19) ;

where Lucifer is treated of.　In *Jeremiah :*—

In vain have I smitten your sons, they received no correction ; your own sword hath devoured your prophets, like a destroying lion.　O generation, see ye the word of Jehovah : have I been a wilderness unto Israel ? (ii. 30, 31).

[16] In the same :—

Go not forth into the field, and walk not in the way, for there is the sword of the enemy, terror is on every side (vi. 25, 26).

In the same :—

Take the cup of the wine of fury, and cause all the nations to whom I send thee to drink it ; and they shall drink, and reel, and be mad because of the sword that I will send among you.　Drink ye and be drunken, and spue and fall, and rise no more because of the sword (xxv. 15, 16, 27).

In the same :—

Go up, ye horses ; and rage, ye chariots ; let the mighty men go forth : Cush and Put that handle the shield, and the Ludim that handle and bend the bow.　For that is a day of the Lord Jehovih of Armies, a day of vengeance ; and the sword shall devour, and be satisfied, and shall be drunken with their blood (xlvi. 9, 10).

[17] In *Ezekiel :*—

They shall strip thee of thy garments, and take the jewels of thy glory, and shall leave thee naked and bare ; and they shall bring up an assembly against thee ; and they shall stone thee with stones, and thrust thee through with their swords (xvi. 39, 40) ;

where the abominations of Jerusalem are treated of.　In *Zechariah :*—

Woe to the worthless shepherd that leaveth the flock ; the sword shall be upon his arm, and upon his right eye ; his arm shall be clean dried up, and his right eye shall be utterly darkened (xi. 17).

In *Hosea :*—

Against me have they thought evil; their princes shall fall by the sword, because of the rage of their tongue ; this shall be their derision in the land of Egypt (vii. 15, 16).

[18] In *Luke :*—

There shall be great distress upon the land, and wrath unto this people ; for they shall fall by the edge of the sword, and be led captive among all the nations ; and at length Jerusalem shall be trodden down by the nations (xxi. 23, 24) ;

where the Lord is speaking of the consummation of the age; and in the sense of the letter, of the dispersion of the Jews and the destruction of Jerusalem; but in the internal sense, of the last state of the church. By "falling by the edge of the sword," is signified that there is no longer any truth, but mere falsity; by "all nations" are signified evils of every kind, among which they should be led captive; that "nations" are evils may be seen above (n. 1259, 1260, 1849, 1868); also that "Jerusalem" is the church (n. 2117), which is thus "trodden down." [19] IV. That a "sword" also signifies the punishment of falsity, is evident in *Isaiah :*—

In that day Jehovah with His hard, and great, and strong sword, will visit upon leviathan the long serpent, and upon leviathan the crooked serpent, and will slay the whales that are in the sea (xxvii. 1) ;

where those are treated of who by reasonings from sensuous things and from memory-knowledges enter into the mysteries of faith; the "hard and great and strong sword" denotes the punishments of the falsity therefrom. [20] Where we read that they were "given over to the edge of the sword and slain by it," sometimes both man and woman, boy and old man, ox and herd, and ass, in the internal sense the punishment of the condemnation of falsity is signified (as in *Josh.* vi. 21; viii. 24, 25; x. 28, 30, 37, 39; xi. 10–12, 14; xiii. 22; xix. 47; *Judges* i. 8, 25; iv. 15, 16; xviii. 27; xx. 37; 1 *Sam.* xv. 8, 11.; 2 *Kings* x. 25; and other places). Hence it was commanded that a city which should worship other gods should be smitten with the sword, be utterly destroyed, and be burnt up with fire, and be a heap forever (*Deut.* xiii. 13, 15–17) ; the "sword" denoting the punishment of falsity; and "fire" the punishment of evil. The angel of Jehovah standing in the way against Balaam with a drawn sword (*Num.* xxii. 31) signified the truth which resisted the falsity in which Balaam was; and for that reason also he was killed with a sword (*Num.* xxxi. 8). [**21**] That a "sword" in the genuine sense signifies truth combating, and in the opposite sense falsity combating, also the vastation of truth, and the punishment of falsity, has its origin from the representatives in the other life; for when any one there speaks what he knows to be false, there then immediately come down over his head as it were little swords, and strike terror; and besides, truth combating is represented by things that have a point, like swords; for indeed truth without good is of this nature, but when together with good it has a rounded form and is gentle. From this origin it comes to pass that whenever a "knife," or "spear," or "little sword," or "sword" is mentioned in the Word, to the angels there is suggested truth combating. [**22**] But the reason that a knife is seldom mentioned in the Word, is that there are evil spirits in the other life who are called "knifers," at whose side there appear knives hanging; for the reason that they have such a brutal nature that they wish to cut every one's throat with the knife. Hence it is that "knives" are not mentioned, but "little swords" or "swords;" for as these are used in combats, they suggest the idea of war, and thus of truth combating. [**23**] As it was known to the ancients that a little sword, a little lance, and a knife signify truth, the nations to whom this came by tradition were accustomed to pierce and lacerate themselves with little swords, little lances, or knives, at the time of their sacrifices, even to blood; as we read of the priests of Baal:—

> The priests of Baal cried with a loud voice, and cut themselves after their manner with swords and little lances, even till the blood gushed out (1 *Kings* xviii. 28).

That all the weapons of war in the Word signify things which belong to spiritual combat, and each one something specific, may be seen above (n. 2686).

2800. *And they went both of them together.* That this signifies unition as far as possible, is evident without explication.

2801. Verse 7. *And Isaac said unto Abraham his father; and he said, My father; and he said, Here am I, my son. And he said, Behold the fire and the wood; and where is the lamb for a burnt-offering?* "Isaac said unto Abraham his father; and he said, My father; and he said, Here am I, my son," signifies a conference of the Lord from love—of the Divine Truth with the Divine Good; the Divine Truth is the "son," and the Divine Good is the "father;" "and he said, Behold the fire and the wood," signifies that love and righteousness are present; "where is the lamb for a burnt-offering?" signifies where are they of the human race who are to be sanctified?

2802. *Isaac said unto Abraham his father; and he said, My father; and he said, Here am I, my son.* That this signifies the Lord's conference from love—of the Divine Truth with the Divine Good—is evident from the signification of "Isaac the son," as being the Divine Truth; and from the signification of "Abraham the father," as being the Divine Good; which are treated of in what presently follows; and from the affection that is in these words, as being from love on both sides. Hence it is manifest that it is a conference of the Lord with His Father. That more arcana lie hid in these words than can come to human perception, is evident from the fact that the words "he said" occur four times in this verse. It is usual in the Word, when any new thing is begun, to say, "and he said" (see n. 2061, 2238, 2260). The same is evident from the fact that the words are words of love; and when such come to the perception of the celestial angels who are in the inmost sense, they form for themselves from them most celestial ideas; for they form for themselves luminous ideas from the affections in the Word, whereas the spiritual angels do so from the significations of the words and of the things (n. 2157, 2275); and thus from these words, in which there are four distinct periods and affections of love, the celestial angels form such things as can in no wise come down to human apprehension, nor can be put into words; and this with ineffable abundance and variety. Hence we can see what the quality of the Word is in its internal sense, even where it appears simple in the letter, as in this verse.

2803. That the Divine Truth is the "son," and the Divine Good the "father," is evident from the signification of a "son," as being truth (see n. 489, 491, 533, 1147, 2633); and of a "father," as being good; and also from the conception and birth of truth, which is from good. Truth cannot be and come forth (*existere*) from any other source than good, as has been shown many times. That the "son" here is the Divine Truth, and the "father" the Divine Good, is because the union of the Divine Essence with the Human, and of the Human Essence with the Divine, is the Divine marriage of Good with Truth, and of Truth with Good, from which comes the heavenly marriage; for in Jehovah or the Lord there is nothing but what is infinite; and because infinite, it cannot be apprehended by any idea, except that it is the being and the coming forth (*esse et existere*) of all good and truth, or is Good itself and Truth itself. Good itself is the "Father," and Truth itself is the "Son." But because as before said there is a Divine marriage of Good and Truth, and of Truth and Good, the Father is in the Son, and the Son is in the Father, as the Lord Himself teaches in *John :*—

Jesus saith unto Philip, Believest thou not that I am in the Father and the Father in Me? Believe Me that I am in the Father and the Father in Me (xiv. 10, 11).

And again in the same Evangelist :—

Jesus said to the Jews, Though ye believe not Me, believe the works; that ye may know and believe that the Father is in Me, and I in the Father (x. 36, 38).

And again :—

I pray for them; for all Mine are Thine, and Thine are Mine; and that they all may be one, as Thou Father art in Me, and I in Thee (xvii. 9, 10, 21).

And again :—

Now is the Son of man glorified, and God is glorified in Him; if God be glorified in Him, God shall also glorify Him in Himself. Father, glorify Thy Son, that Thy Son also may glorify Thee (xiii. 31, 32; xvii. 1).

[2] From this may be seen the nature of the union of the Divine and the Human in the Lord; namely, that it is mutual and alternate, or reciprocal; which union is that which is called

the Divine Marriage, from which descends the heavenly marriage, which is the Lord's kingdom itself in the heavens—thus spoken of in *John* :—

In that day ye shall know that I am in My Father, and ye in Me, and I in you (xiv. 20).

And again :—

I pray for them, that they all may be one, as Thou Father art in Me and I in Thee, that they also may be one in us, I in them and Thou in Me ; that the love wherewith Thou hast loved Me may be in them, and I in them (xvii. 21–23, 26).

That this heavenly marriage is that of good and truth, and of truth and good, may be seen above (n. 2508, 2618, 2728, 2729 and following numbers). [3] And because the Divine Good cannot be and come forth without the Divine Truth, nor the Divine Truth without the Divine Good, but the one in the other mutually and reciprocally, it is therefore manifest that the Divine Marriage was from eternity ; that is, the Son in the Father, and the Father in the Son, as the Lord Himself teaches in *John* :—

And now O Father, glorify Thou Me with Thyself, with the glory which I had with Thee before the world was (xvii. 5, 24).

But the Divine Human which was born from eternity was also born in time ; and what was born in time, and glorified, is the same.   Hence it is that the Lord so often said that He was going to the Father who sent Him ; that is, that He was returning to the Father.   And in *John* :—

In the beginning was the Word (the " Word" is the Divine Truth itself), and the Word was with God, and the Word was God ; the same was in the beginning with God.   All things were made by Him, and without Him was not anything made that was made.   And the Word was made flesh, and dwelt among us, and we saw His glory, the glory as of the Only-begotten of the Father, full of grace and truth (i. 1–3, 14 ; see also *John* iii. 13 ; vi. 62).

2804. *And he said, Behold the fire and the wood.*   That this signifies that love and righteousness were present, is evident from the signification of "fire," as being love (see n. 934) ; and from the signification of " wood for a burnt-offering," as being the merit of righteousness (see n. 2784).

2805. *Where is the lamb* (pecus) *for a burnt-offering?* That this signifies, Where are they from the human race who are to be sanctified? is evident from the representation of sacrifices, especially of burnt-offerings. That burnt-offerings and sacrifices were representative of internal worship, may be seen above (n. 922, 923); that they were made from the flock and from the herd; that when made from the flock, they consisted of lambs, sheep, she-goats, kids, rams, he-goats, and when from the herd, of oxen, bullocks, or calves; and that these signified various kinds of celestial and spiritual things (n. 922, 1823, 2180); also that by means of them sanctifications were to be effected (n. 2776). It may be seen from this, that by Isaac's inquiry, "Where is the lamb for a burnt-offering?" is signified, Where are they from the human race who are to be sanctified? which is more plainly manifest from what follows, that is, from the answer of Abraham his father, "God will see for Himself the lamb for a burnt-offering" (verse 8); by which is signified that the Divine Human will provide those who are to be sanctified. This is also evident from the fact that a ram was afterwards seen behind them, held by the horns in a thicket, which was offered for a burnt-offering (verse 13), by which are signified those of the human race who are of the Lord's spiritual church. And the same is evident from what follows in verses 14 to 17.

2806. Verse 8. *And Abraham said, God will see for Himself the lamb for a burnt-offering, my son: and they went both of them together.* "Abraham said, God will see for Himself the lamb for a burnt-offering, my son," signifies the reply, that the Divine Human will provide those who are to be sanctified; "and they went both of them together," signifies unition still closer as far as possible.

2807. *Abraham said, God will see for Himself the lamb for a burnt-offering, my son.* That this signifies the reply that the Divine Human will provide those who are to be sanctified, is evident from the signification of "seeing for Himself," when predicated of God, as being to foresee and provide; for "seeing," in the proximate internal sense, is to understand (n. 2150, 2325); in a still more internal sense it is having faith (n. 897, 2325); but in the supreme sense it is foreseeing and providing; and also from the signification of the "lamb for a burnt-offer-

ing," as being those from the human race who are to be sanctified (see just above, n. 2805). That the spiritual are here
meant by the "lamb for a burnt-offering," is manifest from
what follows. The beasts for the burnt-offering and sacrifice
signified various things : a lamb one thing, a sheep another, a
kid and a she-goat another, a ram and a he-goat another; so
also an ox, a bullock, and a calf, and the young of doves, and
turtle-doves. That each signified a different thing is plainly
evident from its being expressly defined which kind should be
sacrificed on the several days, and at each festival; as at expiations, cleansings, inaugurations, and at other times. These
kinds would by no means have been so expressly pointed out,
unless each one had a special signification. [2] It is manifest
that all the rites or external kinds of worship that existed in
the Ancient Church, and afterwards in the Jewish, represented
the Lord, and especially the burnt-offerings and sacrifices, because among the Hebrew nation these were the principal things
of worship. And because they represented the Lord, they at
the same time also represented those things which are the
Lord's with men, namely, the celestial things of love and the
spiritual things of faith, consequently the men themselves who
are celestial or spiritual, or who ought to be. Hence it is that
by the "lamb" here are signified the spiritual, that is, they
who are of the Lord's spiritual church. That by "God will
see for Himself the lamb for a burnt-offering, my son," is signified that the Divine Human will provide, is evident from the
fact that it is not here said that "Jehovah" will see, but that
"God" will see. When both are named, as in this chapter, by
"Jehovah" is then meant the same as by the "Father," and
by "God" the same as by the "Son," and thus here the Divine Human; and this because the spiritual man is treated of,
who has salvation from the Divine Human, as may be seen
above (n. 2661, 2716).

2808. *They went both of them together.* That this signifies
union still closer as far as possible, is evident without explication. A closer union is signified because it is said a second time.

2809. Verse 9. *And they came to the place which God told
him of ; and Abraham built there the altar, and laid the wood
in order, and bound Isaac his son, and laid him on the altar*

upon the wood. "They came to the place which God told him of," signifies the state at that time according to perception from Divine Truth; "and Abraham built there the altar," signifies the preparation of the Lord's Human Divine; "and laid the wood in order," signifies the righteousness that was adjoined to it; "and bound Isaac his son," signifies the state of the Divine rational which was thus, as to truth, about to undergo the last degrees of temptation; "and laid him on the altar upon the wood," signifies in the Human Divine to which the righteousness belonged.

2810. *They came to the place which God told him of.* That this signifies the state at that time according to perception from Divine Truth, is evident from the signification of "place," as being state (see above, n. 2786); and from the signification of "saying," in the historical parts of the Word, as being to perceive—explained often before. Here "God saying" denotes perceiving from Divine Truth, because it is said "God," and not "Jehovah" (n. 2586, 2807 at the end).

2811. *And Abraham built there the altar.* That this signifies the preparation of the Lord's Human Divine, is evident from the signification of an "altar," and of "building an altar." "Altars" signified all worship in general, because they were the primary things of the worship of the representative church (n. 921); and as they signified all worship in general, they signified the Lord's Divine Human, for the Lord's Divine Human is all worship and all doctrine; so much so as to be worship itself and doctrine itself; as may be seen also from the Holy Supper, which succeeded to altars, or to burnt-offerings and sacrifices (n. 2165, 2187, 2343, 2359), and which is the primary thing of external worship, because it is the Lord's Divine Human which is there given. That to "build an altar" is to prepare the Human Divine, is evident from the above, and thus without explication. The final preparation of the Lord's Human Divine for undergoing the last degrees of temptation is treated of in this verse, and is described by Abraham laying the wood in order, binding Isaac his son, and placing him on the altar upon the wood.

2812. *And he laid the wood in order.* That this signifies the righteousness which was adjoined to it, is evident from the signification of the "wood of a burnt-offering," as being the merit of righteousness (see above, n. 2784, 2798); and from the signification of "laying the wood in order upon the altar," as being to adjoin that righteousness to the Human Divine. The merit of righteousness is adjoined when it is there, and when there is confidence from truth that it belongs to Him.

2813. *And bound Isaac his son.* That this signifies the state of the Divine rational thus about to undergo as to truth the last degrees of temptation, is evident from the signification of "binding," and also of "Isaac his son." That to "bind" is to put on the state for undergoing the last degrees of temptation, is evident from the fact that he who is in a state of temptation is no otherwise than as bound or chained. That "Isaac the son" is the Lord's Divine rational, here as to truth, may be seen above (n. 2802, 2803). All the genuine rational consists of good and truth. The Lord's Divine rational as to good could not suffer, or undergo temptations; for no genius or spirit inducing temptations can come near to Good Divine, as it is above all attempt at temptation. But Truth Divine bound was what could be tempted; for there are fallacies, and still more falsities, which break in upon and thus tempt it; for concerning Truth Divine some idea can be formed, but not concerning Good Divine except by those who have perception, and are celestial angels. It was Truth Divine which was no longer acknowledged when the Lord came into the world, and therefore it was that from which the Lord underwent and endured temptations. Truth Divine in the Lord is what is called the "Son of man," but Good Divine is what is called the "Son of God." Of the "Son of man" the Lord says many times that He was to suffer, but never of the Son of God. That He says this of the Son of man, or of Truth Divine, is evident in *Matthew :*—

Behold we go up to Jerusalem, and the Son of man shall be delivered unto the chief priests and scribes, and they shall condemn Him, and shall deliver Him unto the Gentiles to mock and to scourge, and to crucify (xx. 18, 19).

In the same :—

Jesus said to His disciples, Behold the hour is at hand, and the Son of man is delivered into the hands of sinners (xxvi. 45).

In *Mark :*—

Jesus began to teach them˙that the Son of man must suffer many
things, and be rejected by the elders, and the chief priests, and the
scribes, and be killed, and after three days rise again (viii. 31).

In the same :—

It is written of the Son of man, that He shall suffer many things, and
be set at nought. And the Son of man shall be delivered into the hands
of men, and they shall kill Him ; but when He is killed He shall rise
again on the third day (ix. 12, 31).

In the same :—

Behold we go up to Jerusalem, and the Son of man shall be delivered
unto the chief priests and the scribes, and they shall condemn Him to
death, and shall deliver Him unto the Gentiles, and they shall mock Him,
and shall spit upon Him, and shall kill Him, and the third day He shall
rise again (x. 33, 34).

In the same :—

The hour is come ; behold the Son of man is betrayed into the hands
of sinners (xiv. 41).

In *Luke :*—

The Son of man must suffer many things, and be rejected of the elders
and chief priests and scribes, and be killed, and the third day rise again
(ix. 22, 44).

In the same :—

We go up to Jerusalem, where all the things that are written by the
prophets concerning the Son of man shall be accomplished : He shall be
delivered up unto the Gentiles, and shall be mocked, and shamefully entreated, and spit upon, and they shall scourge and kill Him, and the third
day He shall rise again (xviii. 31–33).

In the same :—

The angel said to the women, Remember what He spake unto you
when He was yet in Galilee, saying that the Son of man must be delivered up into the hands of sinful men, and be crucified, and the third
day rise again (xxiv. 6, 7).

[2] In all these places by the " Son of man" is meant the Lord
as to Truth Divine, or as to the Word in its internal sense,
which was rejected by the chief priests and scribes, was shamefully entreated, scourged, spit upon, and crucified, as may be
clearly evident from the fact that the Jews applied and arro-

gated everything to themselves according to the letter, and were not willing to know anything about the spiritual sense of the Word, and about the heavenly kingdom, believing that the Messiah was to come to raise up their kingdom above all the kingdoms of the earth, as they also believe at this day. Hence it is manifest that it was Truth Divine which was rejected by them, shamefully treated, scourged, and crucified. Whether you say Truth Divine, or the Lord as to Truth Divine, it is the same; for the Lord is the Truth itself, as He is the Word itself (n. 2011, 2016, 2533 at the end).   [3] The Lord's rising again on the third day also involves that Truth Divine, or the Word as to the internal sense, as it was understood by the Ancient Church, will be revived in the consummation of the age, which is also the "third day" (n. 1825, 2788); on which account it is said that the Son of man (that is, Truth Divine) will then appear (*Matt.* xxiv. 30, 37, 39, 44; *Mark* xiii. 26; *Luke* xvii. 22, 24–26, 30; xxi. 27, 36).   [4] That the "Son of man" is the Lord as to Truth Divine, is evident from the passages adduced, and further from the following.   In *Matthew*:—

He that soweth the good seed is the Son of man, the field is the world. In the consummation of the age the Son of man shall send forth His angels, and they shall gather out of His kingdom all things that offend (xiii. 37, 41, 42) ;

where the "good seed" is the truth; the "world" is men; "He that soweth the seed" is the Son of man; and the "things that offend" are falsities.   In *John*:—

The multitude said, We have heard out of the Law that the Christ abideth forever ; and how sayest Thou that the Son of man must be lifted up ? who is this Son of man ?   Jesus answered them, A little while is the Light with you ; walk while ye have the Light, that darkness overtake you not ; for he that walketh in the darkness knoweth not whither he goeth.   While ye have the Light, believe in the Light, that ye may become the sons of Light (xii. 34, 35) ;

where, when they asked who the Son of man is, Jesus answered concerning the Light, which is the Truth, and that He is the Light or Truth in which they should believe.   (As regards the Light which is from the Lord, and which is the Divine Truth, see above, n. 1053, 1521, 1529–1531, 1619–1632.)   [5] But that the Son of God, or the Lord as to Good in His Human Divine,

could not be tempted, as was said above, this is manifest also
from the Lord's answer to the tempter, in the Evangelists :—

The tempter said, If Thou art the Son of God cast Thyself down ; for
it is written, He shall give His angels charge concerning Thee, lest haply
Thou dash Thy foot against a stone.   Jesus said unto him, It is written
again, Thou shalt not tempt the Lord thy God (*Matt.* iv. 6, 7 ; *Luke* iv.
9–12).

2814. *And laid him on the altar upon the wood.*   That this
signifies in the Human Divine to which righteousness belongs,
is evident from the signification of an " altar," as being the
Lord's Divine Human (see just above, n. 2811) ; and from the
signification of the " wood of a burnt-offering," as being the
merit of righteousness (see n. 2784, 2798, 2812).   The Truth
Divine in the Lord's Human Divine, which underwent the
temptations, and which has been treated of, is not the Divine
Truth itself, for this is above all temptation ; but it is rational
truth, such as the angels have, consisting in the appearances
of truth, and is what is called the " Son of man," but before
the glorification.   But the Divine Truth in the Lord's glorified
Divine Human is above appearances, nor can it possibly come
to any understanding, and still less to the apprehension of
man, nor even to that of angels, and thus not at all to anything
of temptation.   It appears in the heavens as light which is
from the Lord.   Concerning this Divine Truth, or the Son of
man glorified, it is thus written in *John :*—

Jesus said, Now is the Son of man glorified, and God is glorified in
Him : if God is glorified in Him, God shall also glorify Him in Himself,
and shall straightway glorify Him (xiii. 31, 32).

That a distinct idea may be had of this very deep arcanum,
we may call the Truth with the Lord which could be tempted,
and which underwent temptations, Truth Divine in the Lord's
Human Divine ; but the Truth which could not be tempted, or
undergo any temptation, because it was glorified, the Divine
Truth in the Lord's Divine Human ; this distinction has also
been observed here and there in what goes before.

2815. Verse 10. *And Abraham put forth his hand, and took
the knife to slay his son.*   " Abraham put forth his hand," signifies temptation even to the utmost of power ; " and took the

knife," signifies as to truth; "to slay his son," signifies until whatever was from the merely human was dead.

2816. *Abraham put forth his hand.* That this signifies temptation even to the utmost of power, is evident from the series of things; for the Lord's most grievous and inmost temptations are treated of. The verses which precede treat of the preparation of the Human Divine for admitting and enduring them: here the act is treated of, which is expressed in the sense of the letter by "Abraham put forth his hand." That power is signified by the "hand" may be seen above (n. 878); here the utmost of power, because nothing but the act was wanting. It is according to the internal sense, that the Lord's Divine led His Human into the most grievous temptations (for by "Abraham" is meant the Lord as to His Divine), and this even to the utmost of power. The truth is that the Lord admitted temptations into Himself in order that He might expel thence all that was merely human, and this until nothing but the Divine remained. [2] That the Lord admitted temptations into Himself, even the last, which was that of the cross, may be seen from the words of the Lord Himself, in *Matthew*:—

Jesus began to show the disciples that He must suffer many things, and be killed. Then Peter took Him, and began to rebuke Him, saying, Spare Thyself, Lord; let this not be done unto Thee. But He turned and said unto Peter, Get thee behind Me, Satan; thou art an offense unto Me; for thou savorest not the things that are of God, but those that are of men (xvi. 21–23).

And more manifestly in *John*:—

No one taketh My life from Me, but I lay it down of Myself. I have power to lay it down, and I have power to take it again (x. 18).

And in *Luke*:—

Behooved it not the Christ to suffer these things, and to enter into His glory? (xxiv. 26).

2817. *And took the knife.* That this signifies as to truth, is evident from the signification of a "knife," as being the truth of faith (explained above, n. 2799); and that the Lord's temptation was as to Truth Divine, see above (n. 2813, 2814).

2818. *To slay his son.* That this signifies until whatever was from the merely human was dead, is evident from the in-

ternal sense of these words; for they signify the Lord's most
grievous and inmost temptations, the last of which was that
of the cross, in which it is evident that what was merely
human also died. This could not be represented by Abraham's son or Isaac, because to sacrifice sons was an abomination; but it was represented so far as it could be, namely,
even to the attempt, but not to the act. Hence it is evident
that by these words, " Abraham took the knife to slay his son,"
is signified until all that was merely human was dead. [2]
That it was known from the most ancient time that the Lord
was to come into the world, and was to suffer death, is evident
from the fact that the custom prevailed among the Gentiles of
sacrificing their sons, believing that they were thus purified,
and propitiated to God; in which abominable custom they
could not have placed their most important religious observance, unless they had learned from the ancients that the Son
of God was to come, who would, as they believed, be made a
sacrifice. To this abomination even the sons of Israel were
inclined, and Abraham also; for no one is tempted except by
that to which he is inclined. That the sons of Jacob were so
inclined is evident in the Prophets; but lest they should rush
into that abomination, it was permitted to institute burnt-
offerings and sacrifices (see n. 922, 1128, 1241, 1343, 2180).

   2819. As regards the Lord's temptations in general, some
were more external and some more internal; and the more internal they were, the more grievous. The inmost ones are described by the Evangelists (*Matt.* xxvi. 37–39, 42, 44; xxvii.
46; *Mark* xiv. 33–36; xv. 34; *Luke* xxii. 42–44); but see
what has been said before respecting the Lord's temptations,
namely: That the Lord first contended from goods and truths
which appeared as goods and truths (n. 1661): That He contended against the evils of the love of self and the world from
Divine Love toward the whole human race (n. 1690, 1691 at
the end, 1789, 1812, 1813, 1820): That He alone contended
from the Divine Love (n. 1812, 1813): That all the hells
fought against the Lord's love, which was for the salvation of
the whole human race (n. 1820): That the Lord endured the
most grievous temptations of all (n. 1663, 1668, 1787): That
the Lord became righteousness from His own power by means

of temptations and victories (n. 1813, 2025): That the union
of His Human Essence with His Divine Essence was effected
by the Lord by means of temptations and victories (n. 1737,
1813, 1921, 2025, 2026). See also what has been said before
concerning temptations in general (n. 59, 63, 227, 847): That
temptation is a combat concerning power, as to whether good
or evil, truth or falsity, is to reign supreme (n. 1923): That in
temptations there are indignations, and many other affections
(n. 1917): That temptations are celestial, spiritual, and natural (n. 847): That in temptations the evil genii and spirits
assail the things of the love, and thus the things of the man's
life (n. 847, 1820): What temptations effect (n. 1692 at the
beginning, 1717, 1740): That temptation is for the purpose
that corporeal things may be subdued (n. 857): That the evils
and falsities in a man who is being regenerated are subdued by
temptations, not abolished (n. 868): That truth has the first
place in combat (n. 1685): That man combats from the goods
and truths which he has acquired by knowledges, though they
be not in themselves goods and truths (n. 1661): That evil
spirits and genii excite the falsities and evils in a man, and
hence come temptations (n. 741, 751, 761): That in temptations
man thinks that the Lord is absent, whereas He is then more
present (n. 840): That man can by no means sustain the combats of temptations of himself, because they are against all the
hells (n. 1692 at the end): That the Lord alone combats in man
(n. 1661, 1692): That by means of temptations evil genii and
spirits are deprived of the power of doing evil and inspiring
falsity in man (n. 1695, 1717): That temptations come with
those who have conscience, and more acute ones with those
who have perception (n. 1668): That temptations rarely exist
at this day, but in their place anxieties, which are of another
character and from another source (n. 762): That men spiritually dead cannot sustain the combats of temptations (n.
270): That all temptations are attended with despair respecting the end (n. 1787, 1820): That after temptations there is
fluctuation (n. 848, 857): That the good learn by temptations
that they are nothing but evil, and that all things are of
mercy (n. 2334): That by temptations goods are conjoined
more closely with truths (n. 2272): That men are not saved

by temptations if they yield in them, nor if they think that
they have merited by them (n. 2273) : That in every temptation
there is freedom, and stronger than out of temptations (n.
1937).

2820. Verse 11. *And the angel of Jehovah called unto him
out of heaven, and said, Abraham, Abraham; and he said,
Here am I.* " The angel of Jehovah called unto him out of
heaven," signifies consolation at that time from the Divine Itself ; "and said, Abraham, Abraham; and he said, Here am
I," signifies a perception of consolation in the Divine Good of   ·
the rational after temptation.

2821. *The angel of Jehovah called unto him out of heaven.*
That this signifies consolation from the Divine Itself at that
time, is evident from the signification of " calling out of
heaven," as being to console; as is also manifest from what
immediately precedes and what next follows; and also from
the signification of the " angel of Jehovah." (That when
angels are mentioned in the Word, by them is meant something in the Lord, and that it appears from the series *what* of
the Lord is meant, may be seen above, n. 1925.) We read in
like manner concerning the Lord, that when He sustained the
most grievous temptation in Gethsemane, an angel from heaven
was seen by Him strengthening Him (Luke xxii. 43). By
the " angel from heaven" here also in the internal sense is
meant the Divine which was in Him.

2822. *And said, Abraham, Abraham; and he said, Here
am I.* That this signifies a perception of consolation in the
Divine Good of the rational after temptation, is evident from
the signification of " saying" in the historical parts of the
Word, as being to perceive—explained often before. That it is
here perception in the Divine Good of the rational, is because
the Divine Good of the rational of the Lord's Human is here
signified by " Abraham." What perception in the Divine
Good of the rational is, cannot be unfolded to the apprehension; for before it is unfolded, an idea of the Lord's Divine
Human must have been formed from knowledge of many
things; and before this has been formed, all things belonging
to the explication would fall into empty and obscure ideas,
which would either pervert the truths or bring them into

things incongruous. In this verse the Lord's first state after temptation is treated of, which is a state of consolation; on which account it is now no longer said "God," but "Jehovah;" for "God" is named when truth is treated of, but "Jehovah" when good is treated of, from which comes consolation (n. 2769). All consolation after temptation is insinuated into good, for from good is all joy; and from the good it passes into truth. On this account by "Abraham" is here signified the Divine good of the rational, as in other places also, and also whenever "Jehovah" is named in the same verse.

2823. Verse 12. *And He said, Put not forth thine hand upon the boy, and do not anything unto him; for now I know that thou fearest God, and thou hast not withheld thy son, thine only one, from Me.* "He said, Put not forth thine hand upon the boy," signifies that He should admit the temptation no further into the Truth Divine which belonged to the rational; "and do not anything unto him," signifies liberation; "for now I know that thou fearest God," signifies glorification from the Divine love; "and hast not withheld thy son, thine only one, from Me," signifies the unition of the Human with the Divine by means of the last of temptation.

2824. *And He said, Put not forth thine hand upon the boy.* That this signifies that He should admit the temptation no further into the Truth Divine which belonged to the rational, is evident from the signification of "putting forth the hand," as being temptation even to the utmost of power—explained just above (n. 2816); and from the signification of the "boy," that is, of Isaac, as being the rational as to Truth Divine, into which the temptations were admitted (see n. 2803, 2813, 2814, 2817).

2825. *And do not anything unto him.* That this signifies liberation, is evident without explication; for when it is said that he should do nothing to him, it means that the act should be interrupted, and thus that he will be liberated.

2826. *For now I know that thou fearest God.* That this signifies glorification from the Divine love, is evident from the signification of "knowing," when predicated of the Lord's Divine, as being nothing else than to be united, or what is the same, to be glorified; for it was being united to the Human

Divine by means of temptations (n. 1737, 1813); and from the
signification of "fearing God," or of the "fear of God," as
being here the Divine love. And because this is predicated
of the Lord's Divine rational as to truth, it is here said to fear
"God," and not "Jehovah;" for when truth is treated of, it is
said "God;" but when good, "Jehovah" (n. 2586, 2769, 2822).
That the Divine love is that by which the Lord united His
Human Essence to His Divine Essence, and the Divine Essence
to the Human, or what is the same, glorified Himself, may be
seen above (n. 1812, 1813, 2253). What "fearing God" signifies in the Word, may be seen from a great many passages
when understood as to the internal sense. The "fear of God"
there signifies worship, and indeed worship either from fear,
or from the good of faith, or from the good of love; worship
from fear when the non-regenerate, worship from the good of
faith when the spiritual regenerate, and worship from the good
of love when the celestial regenerate are treated of. [2] I.
That the "fear of God" in general signifies worship, is manifest in the book of *Kings :*—

> The sons of Israel feared other gods, and walked in the statutes of the
> nations. The nations sent into Samaria feared not Jehovah in the begin-
> ning, therefore Jehovah sent lions among them ; and one of the priests
> whom they had carried away from Samaria came and dwelt in Bethel,
> and taught them how they should fear Jehovah. Jehovah made a cove-
> nant with the sons of Israel and commanded them, Ye shall not fear
> other gods, nor bow yourselves to them, nor serve them, nor sacrifice to
> them ; but ye shall fear Jehovah, and bow yourselves down unto Him,
> and sacrifice to Him (2 *Kings* xvii. 7, 8, 24, 25, 28, 32, 33, 35–37, 41);

here "fearing" manifestly denotes worshiping. In *Isaiah :*—

> Because this people have drawn nigh unto Me with their mouth, and
> have honored Me with their lips, and their heart hath removed itself far
> from Me, and their fear of Me is a commandment of men which hath
> been taught (xxix. 13) ;

where their " fear of Me" denotes worship in general; for it is
said that the fear was a commandment of men. In *Luke :*—

> There was in a city a judge who feared not God and regarded not man
> (xviii. 2) ;

"fearing not God" means not worshiping Him. [3] II. That
the "fear of God" signifies worship from fear when the non-

regenerate are treated of, is manifest from the following passages in *Moses :*—

When the Law was promulgated upon Mount Sinai, the people said unto Moses, Speak thou with us, and we will hear ; but let not God speak with us, lest we die.   And Moses said unto the people, God is come to prove you, and that His fear may be before you, that ye sin not (*Exod.* xx. 19, 20).

And again :—

Now why shall we die ? for this great fire will consume us ; if we hear the voice of Jehovah our God any more, then we shall die.   Go thou near, and hear all that Jehovah our God shall say ; and speak thou unto us all that Jehovah our God shall say unto thee ; and we will hear it, and do it. And Jehovah said unto Moses, Who will give them to have such a heart as this, to fear Me, and keep all My commandments always (*Deut.* v. 25, 27–29) ;

here the "fear of God before you that ye sin not, and a heart to fear Me, and keep all My commandments," signifies worship from fear, in respect to them, because such was their quality ; for they who are in external worship, and not in internal, are driven to the observance of the law and to obedience by fear ; but still they do not come into internal worship or into holy fear (*timor sanctus*) unless they are in the good of life, and know what is internal, and believe it.   In the same :—

If thou wilt not observe to do all the words of this law that are written in this book, to fear this glorious and fearful name, Jehovah thy God, Jehovah will make thy plagues wonderful, and the plagues of thy seed, plagues great and sure, and sore diseases and sure, and He will bring upon thee again all the sickness of Egypt, which thou wast afraid of, and they shall cleave unto thee (*Deut.* xxviii. 58–60) ;

here also to "fear the glorious and fearful name of Jehovah God" is to worship from fear; and that this might exist among those of such a character, all evils even to cursings were attributed to Jehovah (n. 592, 2335, 2395, 2447).   In *Jeremiah :*—

Thine own wickedness shall correct thee, and thy backslidings shall reprove thee ; know therefore and see that it is an evil thing and a bitter that thou hast forsaken Jehovah thy God, and that My fear is not in thee (ii. 19).

In *Luke :*—

I say unto you, Be not afraid of them that kill the body, but after that have no more that they can do ; but I will warn you whom ye shall fear ;

fear Him who after He hath killed, hath power to cast into hell ; yea, I say unto you, fear Him (xii. 4, 5 ; *Matt.* x. 28) ;

here also "fearing God" involves worshiping from some fear, because fear drove them to obedience, as before said. [4] III. That to "fear God" or "Jehovah" signifies worship from the good of faith, where the spiritual regenerate are treated of, is manifest from the following passages. In *Moses:*—

The king shall write for himself a copy of this law in a book before the priests the Levites, and it shall be with him, and he shall read therein all the days of his life, that he may learn to fear Jehovah his God, to keep all the words of this law, and these statutes, to do them (*Deut.* xvii. 18, 19).

In the internal sense "king" denotes the truth of faith; for royalty represented the Lord's spiritual kingdom (n. 1672, 1728, 2015, 2069). Hence to "fear Jehovah his God," is to worship Him from the truth of faith; and because this is inseparable from the good of charity, it is described by "keeping the words of the law and the statutes to do them." In *Samuel:*—

Behold Jehovah hath set a king over you. If ye will fear Jehovah and serve Him, and hearken unto His voice, then shall both ye and the king that reigneth over you be followers of Jehovah your God (1 *Sam.* xii. 13, 14) ;

here also in the internal sense "fearing Jehovah" denotes worshiping from the good and truth of faith, as before, because a king or royalty is treated of. [5] In *Joshua:*—

Now fear Jehovah, and serve Him in integrity and in truth, and put away the gods which your fathers served (xxiv. 14) ;

where also to "fear Jehovah" denotes worshiping from good and truth, which is of the spiritual man; for "integrity" is predicated of the good of faith (n. 612), and "truth" of the truth of faith. In *Jeremiah:*—

They shall be My people, and I will be their God ; and I will give them one heart, and one way, that they may fear Me forever, for the good of them and of their children after them ; and I will make an everlasting covenant with them, that I will not turn away from them, to do them good ; and I will put My fear in their heart, that they shall not depart from Me (xxxii. 38–40) ;

that "fearing God" here is worshiping from the good and truth of faith, is evident from the series, and from the use of the words "people" and " God." (That those are called " people" who are in truth, may be seen above, n. 1259, 1260; and that "God" is named where truth is treated of, n. 2586, 2769, 2807 at the end.) In *Isaiah :—*

The strong people shall honor Thee, the city of the mighty nations shall fear Thee (xxv. 3) ;

where "fearing God" also denotes worshiping from spiritual truth, for it is predicated of " people" and " city." (That a " city" is doctrinal truth may be seen above, n. 402, 2268, 2450, 2451.) [6] In *David :—*

What man is he that feareth Jehovah ? him shall He teach the way that He shall choose (*Ps.* xxv. 12) ;

where the " man that feareth Jehovah" denotes him who worships Him ; and that this is said of the spiritual man is manifest from its being said, "him shall He teach the way." (That a " way" is truth, may be seen above, n. 627, 2333.) And again with similar meaning :—

Blessed is every one that feareth Jehovah, that walketh in His ways (*Ps.* cxxviii. 1).

In the same :—

They that fear Jehovah shall glorify Him ; all the seed of Jacob shall glorify Him, and all the seed of Israel shall stand in awe of Him (*Ps.* xxii. 23) ;

here to "stand in awe of Him" means to worship from the truth of faith ; for the " seed of Israel" is the spiritual of the church, or the good and truth of faith (n. 1025, 1447, 1610). In *Moses :—*

Now Israel, what doth Jehovah thy God require of thee, but to fear Jehovah thy God, to walk in all His ways, and to love Him, and to serve Jehovah thy God, with all thy heart, and with all thy soul, to keep the commandments of Jehovah, and His statutes (*Deut.* x. 12, 13).

Here is described what it is to " fear God," with the spiritual man, that is, " Israel ;" namely, that it is to walk in the ways of Jehovah, to love Him, to serve Him, and to keep His precepts and His statutes. In *John :—*

I saw an angel flying in the midst of heaven, having the everlasting Gospel, saying with a great voice, Fear God, and give glory to Him, for the hour of His judgment is come (*Rev.* xiv. 6, 7) ;

here to "fear God" denotes holy worship from the good and truth of faith. In *Luke*:—

Jesus said to him that was palsied, Arise, take up thy couch, and go unto thy house ; and amazement took hold upon them all ; and they glorified God, and they were filled with fear (v. 24–26) ;

where "fear" denotes holy fear, such as is that of those who are being initiated into the good of love by the truth of faith. [7] IV. That to "fear God" or "Jehovah" signifies worship from the good of love, when the celestial regenerate are treated of. In *Malachi*:—

My covenant was with Levi, of lives and peace ; and I gave them to him that he might fear, and he feared Me, and for My name was he broken. The law of truth was in his mouth, and unrighteousness was not in his lips ; he walked with Me in peace and uprightness (ii. 5, 6) ;

where the Lord is treated of, who here in the internal sense is "Levi ;" "Levi" signifies the priesthood, and signifies love ; "fear" here denotes the good of Divine love ; the "law of truth," truth ; and "peace and uprightness," both. [8] In *Isaiah* :—

There shall come forth a shoot out of the stock of Jesse, and a branch shall grow out of his roots ; and the spirit of Jehovah shall rest upon Him, the spirit of wisdom and understanding, the spirit of counsel and might, the spirit of knowledge and of the fear of Jehovah, and of His scent in the fear of Jehovah (xi. 1–3) ;

where also the Lord is treated of. The "spirit of knowledge and of the fear of Jehovah" denotes the Divine love of truth ; and His "scent in the fear of Jehovah," the Divine love of good. [9] In *David*:—

The precepts of Jehovah are right, rejoicing the heart ; the commandment of Jehovah is pure, enlightening the eyes ; the fear of Jehovah is clean, standing forever ; the judgments of Jehovah are truth, made righteous together (*Ps.* xix. 8, 9) ;

where "the fear of Jehovah is clean" denotes love ; and "the judgments of Jehovah are truth" denotes faith. (That "righteousness" is predicated of the good of love, and "judgment" of the truth of faith, may be seen above, n. 2235) ; and these are said to be "made righteous together," when truth becomes good, or when faith becomes charity. [10] In the same :—

Behold the eye of Jehovah is upon them that fear Him, upon them
that wait for His mercy (*Ps.* xxxiii. 18).

And again :—

Jehovah delighteth not in the strength of the horse, He taketh not
pleasure in the legs of a man. Jehovah taketh pleasure in them that fear
Him, in those that wait for His mercy (*Ps.* cxlvii. 10, 11) ;

the "strength of the horse" denotes one's own power of
thinking truth (that a "horse" denotes the intellectual faculty,
may be seen above, 2760–2762); the "legs of a man" denote
one's own power of doing good; "they that fear Jehovah" denote those who worship Him from the love of truth; and "they
that wait for His mercy," those who worship from the love of
good. Where good is spoken of in the Prophets, so also is
truth; and where truth is spoken of, so also is good, on account of the heavenly marriage of good and truth in everything (see n. 683, 793, 801, 2516, 2712, 2713). [11] In the
same :—

Jehovah will bless the house of Israel, He will bless the house of
Aaron, He will bless them that fear Jehovah, both small and great (*Ps.*
cxv. 12, 13) ;

here "they that fear Jehovah" denote those who worship from
the good of faith, which is the "house of Israel," and from
the good of love, which is the "house of Aaron;" they are
both named on account of the heavenly marriage, as said above,
in everything in the Word. [12] In *Isaiah :*—

The truth of thy times shall be strength of salvations, wisdom, and
knowledge ; the fear of Jehovah itself a treasure (xxxiii. 6) ;

where "wisdom and knowledge" denote the good of faith conjoined with its truth; and the "fear of Jehovah," the good
of love. In the same :—

Who is among you that feareth Jehovah, hearkening to the voice of
His servant (l. 10) ;

"he that feareth Jehovah" denotes him that worships from
love; "he that hearkeneth to the voice of His servant," him
that worships from faith. When the one is of the other, then
there is the heavenly marriage. [13] From the passages which
have been adduced from the Word it is evident that the "fear
of God" is worship, either from fear, or from the good of faith,

or from the good of love. But the more there is of fear in the worship, the less there is of faith, and the less still of love; and on the other hand, the more of faith there is in the worship, and especially the more there is of love, the less there is of fear. There is indeed a fear within all worship, but under another appearance and another condition, and this is *holy fear*. But holy fear is not so much the fear of hell and of damnation, as it is of doing or thinking anything against the Lord and against the neighbor, and thus anything against the good of love and the truth of faith. It is an aversion, which is the boundary of the holy of love and the holy of faith on the one side; and as it is not a fear of hell and damnation, as before said, those have it who are in the good of faith; but those have less of it who are in the good of love, that is, who are in the Lord. [**14**] V. Therefore to "fear" signifies also to distrust, or not to have faith and love, as in *Isaiah* :—

Thus saith thy Creator, O Jacob, and thy Former, O Israel, Fear not, for I have redeemed thee ; I have called thee by thy name, thou art Mine (xliii. 1, 5 ; xliv. 8).

In *Luke* :—

The oath which He sware to our father Abraham, that He would grant unto us, that we being delivered out of the hand of our enemies, might serve Him without fear, in holiness and righteousness before Him (i. 73, 74).

In the same :—

Fear not, little flock, for it is your Father's good pleasure to give you the kingdom (xii. 32).

In *Mark* :—

Jesus said unto the ruler of the synagogue, Fear not, only believe (v. 36 ; *Luke* viii. 49, 50).

In the same :—

Jesus said, Why are ye so fearful ? how is it that ye have no faith ? (iv. 40).

In *Luke* :—

The hairs of your head are all numbered ; fear not therefore, ye are of more value than many sparrows (xii. 7).

In these passages to "fear" is to distrust, or not to have faith and love.

2827. *And thou hast not withheld thy son, thine only one, from Me.* That this signifies the unition of the Human with the Divine by the utmost of temptation, is evident from the signification of "thy son," namely, Isaac, as being the Divine rational (explained before), or the Divine Human, for this begins in the rational (n. 2106, 2194); which is called the "only one," because it was the only-begotten (see n. 2772); and from the signification of "not withholding from Me," as being to cause it to be united, namely, to the Divine Itself. That the unition was effected by the utmost of temptation, is manifest from all that precedes.

2828. Verse 13. *And Abraham lifted up his eyes, and saw, and behold a ram behind, caught in a thicket by his horns; and Abraham went, and took the ram, and offered him up for a burnt-offering in the stead of his son.* "Abraham lifted up his eyes, and saw," signifies the Lord's thought and mental view from the Divine; "and behold a ram," signifies the spiritual from the human race; "behind, caught in a thicket," signifies entangled in natural knowledge; "by his horns," signifies with all power as to the truths of faith. "And Abraham went, and took the ram," signifies their liberation by the Lord's Divine Human; "and offered him up for a burnt-offering in the stead of his son," signifies their sanctification and adoption.

2829. *Abraham lifted up his eyes, and saw.* That this signifies the Lord's thought and mental view from the Divine, may be seen above (n. 2789), where are the same words. The thought and mental view from the Divine is concerning all and each of the things that will take place to eternity, with the Divine Providence.

2830. *And behold a ram.* That this signifies the spiritual from the human race, is evident from the signification of a "ram," as explained in what follows. It is known within the church that the burnt-offerings and sacrifices in the representative Jewish and Israelitish Church signified the Lord's Divine Human; but the burnt-offerings and sacrifices from lambs signified one thing, those from sheep and she-goats another, and those also from kids, rams, and he-goats, and from oxen, bullocks, and calves, and from turtle-doves and the young of pigeons, other things; and in like manner the meat-offerings and libations. In general they signified the Divine celestial, Divine spiritual, and Divine natural things which belong to the Lord; and hence they signified the celestial, spiritual, and natural things which are from Him in His kingdom, consequently in every one who is a kingdom of the Lord; which may also be seen from the Holy Supper, which succeeded the burnt-offerings and sacrifices. The bread and wine therein signify the Lord's Divine Human; the bread His Divine celestial, and the wine His Divine spiritual; they consequently signify His love toward the universal human race; and on the other hand the love of the human race to the Lord (n. 2343, 2359). Hence it is manifest that the burnt-offerings and sacrifices involved celestial worship from love to the Lord, and spiritual worship from charity toward the neighbor and the derivative faith in the Lord (n. 922, 923, 1823, 2180). What the celestial is, and what the spiritual, or what are the celestial and the spiritual in the Lord's kingdom or in His church, has been frequently stated (see n. 1155, 1577, 1824, 2048, 2088, 2184, 2227, 2669, 2708, 2715). [2] That a "ram" therefore signifies the Lord's Divine spiritual, and consequently the spiritual with man, or what is the same, those of the human race who are spiritual, may be seen from the burnt-offerings and sacrifices made from rams; in that when Aaron and his sons were sanctified to perform the ministry, that is, when they were inaugurated, they were to offer one bullock for sin, the blood of which was to be sprinkled upon the horns of the altar, and the rest poured at the bottom of it; also that one ram was to be killed, and his blood sprinkled round the altar, and then the whole ram was to be burnt for a burnt-offering; and that the blood of the other ram that was killed was to be sprinkled upon the tip of Aaron's ear, and upon the thumb of his hand and the great toe of his foot; and that after it was waved, it was to be burnt upon the burnt-offering (*Exod.* xxix. 1–35; *Lev.* viii. 1 to the end; ix. 2 to the end). That all these rites were holy is evident; but they were holy from their representing and signifying holy things. Otherwise to

slaughter a bullock and to sprinkle his blood upon the horns
of the altar and pour the rest at its base, and to slaughter one
ram and sprinkle his blood round the altar and then to burn
him, and to sprinkle the blood of the other ram upon the tip
of Aaron's ear and the thumb of his hand and the great toe
of his foot, also to wave it, and to burn it upon the burnt-
offering—all these things would have had no holiness and
thus would have effected no worship unless they had represented holy things.   But what each particular represented can
be evident to no one except from the internal sense.   That
the bullock which was for sin signified the Lord's Divine natural, and the ram His Divine spiritual, and that it signified
also those who are spiritual of the human race, may be seen
from the signification of a "bullock" and a "ram" in the
Word.   Inaugurations into the priesthood were made by spiritual things, for by spiritual things a man is introduced into
celestial things; or what is the same, by the truths of faith
into the good of love.   In like manner when Aaron entered
into the holy place, he was to offer a bullock for sin, and a
ram for a burnt-offering (*Lev.* xvi. 2, 3).   [**3**] That the Nazirite,
when the days of his Naziriteship were fulfilled, was to offer
a whole lamb a son of a year, for a burnt-offering, and one
ewe-lamb a daughter of a year, entire, for sin, and one whole
ram for peace-offerings (*Num.* vi. 13–17), was because the
Nazirite represented the celestial man, who is a likeness of the
Lord (n. 51, 52, 1013).   The celestial man is such that he is
in celestial love, that is, in love to the Lord, and thence in
celestial truth (n. 202, 337, 2069, 2715, 2718); he was therefore to sacrifice a lamb and a ewe-lamb, by which the celestial
was signified; and also a ram, by which the spiritual was signified.   At the festivals, bullocks, rams, and lambs were sacrificed—as on the first day of the feast of the unleavened bread,
two bullocks, one ram, and seven lambs, with their meat-offering, for a burnt-offering (*Num.* xxviii. 18–20).   On the day of
the firstfruits also, two bullocks, one ram, and seven lambs,
with their meat-offering, for a burnt-offering (*Num.* xxviii.
26–28).   On the new moons, two bullocks, one ram, and seven
lambs, with their meat-offering, for a burnt-offering (*Num.*
xxviii. 11, 12).   In the seventh month, on the first of the

month, one bullock, one ram, and seven lambs, with their meat-offering. On the fifteenth day of the seventh month, thirteen bullocks, two rams, and fourteen lambs. (See also *Num.* xxix. 1, 2, 12–14, 17, 18, 20–22, 24, 26–36.) The "bullocks" and the "rams" signified spiritual things, but the "lambs" celestial things; for at the feasts they had to be sanctified and introduced by spiritual things. [4] As "rams" signified the Divine spiritual of the Lord's Divine Human, as also the spiritual things with man, therefore where the new temple and New Jerusalem, that is, the Lord's spiritual kingdom, is spoken of, it is said in *Ezekiel,* that when they had made an end of cleansing the altar there, they were to offer a bullock for a sin-offering, and a ram for a burnt-offering, and were to offer the goat of the sin-offering every day for seven days, and a bullock and a ram (xliii. 23–25); and that on this day the prince should prepare the bullock of the sin-offering for all the people, and on the seven days of the feast seven bullocks, and seven rams, with the meat-offering, for a burnt-offering (xlv. 22–24); and that on the day of the sabbath he should prepare six lambs and a ram (xlvi. 4, 6). [5] That by the new temple and the New Jerusalem in the universal sense is signified the Lord's kingdom, may be seen above (n. 402, 940); in particular the New Church (n. 2117). That there are not burnt-offerings and sacrifices there, may be known to every one, which shows that by these are signified the celestial things of love, and the spiritual things of faith; for these are of the Lord's kingdom; and thus such things are here signified by "bullocks," "rams," and "lambs." That "bullocks" and "rams" signify spiritual things, is evident from the several particulars in the internal sense; in general from this, that by the "new temple" and the "New Jerusalem" the Lord's spiritual kingdom is specifically signified, but by "Zion" the celestial kingdom. [6] That a "ram" signifies that which is spiritual, or what is the same, those who are spiritual, is plain also in *Daniel;* in that a ram was seen by him standing before the river, which had two horns; afterwards a he-goat of the goats, which smote him, broke his horns, and trampled him down (viii. 3, 4, and the following verses); where nothing else is meant by the "ram" than the spiritual church,

and by the "he-goat of the goats" than those who are in
faith separated from charity, or in truth separate from good,
who by successive steps uplift themselves against good, and
at length against the Lord—which is also described. In
Samuel :—

Samuel said to Saul, Hath Jehovah as great pleasure in burnt-offerings and sacrifices as in hearkening to the voice of Jehovah ? behold to
hearken is better than sacrifice, and to obey than the fat of rams (1 *Sam.*
xv. 22) ;

where because obedience is treated of, so is truth, which is
spiritual; and these words were said to the king, by whom
also is signified truth (n. 1672, 2015, 2069). It is not therefore said, " better than the fat of oxen," or of " lambs," but
"better than the fat of rams." [7] In *David :—*

When Israel went out of Egypt, the house of Jacob from a people of
strange language, Judah became His sanctuary, Israel His dominion.
The sea saw it, and fled, and the Jordan turned back ; the mountains
leaped like rams, the hills like the sons of the flock. What aileth thee,
O thou sea, that thou fleest ? thou Jordan, that thou turnest back ? ye
mountains, that ye skip like rams ? ye hills, like the sons of the flock ?
Thou travailest, O earth, at the presence of the Lord, at the presence of
the God of Jacob ; who turned the rock into a pool of waters, and the flint
into a fountain of waters (*Ps.* cxiv. 1 to the end);

here in the internal sense the subject treated of is spiritual
good after regeneration, and it is described in respect to its
quality ; its celestial spiritual by the " mountains leaping like
rams ;" and its celestial natural by the " hills like the sons of
the flock." (That " mountains" are the celestial things of
love, may be seen above, n. 795, 1430.) Every one may know
that in these, as in the rest of the words of David, there are
holy things, but in the internal sense ; and that something
is signified by the mountains skipping like rams, and the
hills like the sons of the flock, and by the earth travailing at
the presence of the Lord ; which things, without the internal
sense, are words of no meaning. [8] So with these words in
Moses :—

He maketh him ride on the high places of the earth, and to eat the increase of the earth, and He maketh him to suck honey out of the rock,
and oil out of the flint of the rock ; butter of kine and milk of the flock,
with fat of lambs, and of rams the sons of Bashan, and he-goats with the

fat of kidneys of wheat ; and of the blood of grapes thou shalt drink unmixed wine (*Deut.* xxxii. 13, 14) ;

" rams the sons of Bashan" denotes celestial spiritual things
(what celestial spiritual things are, may be seen above, n.
1824). In *David :*—

I will offer unto Thee burnt-offerings of fatlings with the incense of
rams, I will offer bullocks with goats (*Ps.* lxvi. 15) ;

" burnt-offerings of fatlings" denotes the celestial things of
love ; and the " incense of rams," the spiritual things of faith.
[9] In *Ezekiel :*—

Arabia and all the princes of Kedar were the merchants of thy hand ;
in lambs, in rams, and he-goats (xxvii. 21) ;

where Tyre is treated of, by which those are signified who
are in the knowledges of good and truth (n. 1201) ; " Arabia"
denotes their wisdom ; the " princes of Kedar," their intelligence ; " lambs," celestial things ; " rams," spiritual things ;
and " he-goats," natural things, which follow in order. In
Isaiah :—

All the flock of Kedar shall be gathered together unto Thee, the rams
of Nebaioth shall minister unto Thee ; they shall come up with accept-
ance on Mine altar, and I will adorn the house of My adornment (lx. 7) ;

here the Lord's Divine Human is treated of ; the " flock of
Kedar" denotes Divine celestial things ; and the " rams of
Nebaioth," Divine spiritual things. From all this it is now
evident that a " ram" in the internal sense signifies the Lord's
Divine spiritual, and hence the spiritual in men, or what is
the same, those of the human race who are spiritual.

2831. *Behind, caught in a thicket.* That this signifies entangled in natural knowledge, is evident from the signification
of being " caught," as here being entangled ; and from the signification of a " thicket" or " tangle," as being memory-knowledge—explained in what follows. That the spiritual are held
entangled in natural knowledge in regard to the truths of faith,
is as follows. The spiritual have not perception of good and
truth, as the celestial have, but instead of it conscience formed
from the goods and truths of faith which they have imbibed
from infancy from their parents and masters, and afterwards
from the doctrine of faith into which they were born. They

who have no perception of good and truth have to be confirmed by knowledges. Every one forms for himself some idea respecting the things he has learned, and also respecting the goods and truths of faith; for without an idea, nothing remains in the memory otherwise than as an empty thing. Confirmatory things are added thereto, and fill up the idea of the thing, from other knowledges, even from memory-knowledges. The confirmation of the idea itself by many things causes not only that it sticks in the memory, so that it can be called forth into the thought, but also that faith can be insinuated into it. [2] As regards perception in general, since few know what perception is, this must be declared. There is perception of what is good and true in celestial and spiritual things; there is perception of what is just and equitable in civil life; and there is perception of what is honorable in moral life. As regards the perception of what is good and true in celestial and spiritual things, the interior angels have this perception from the Lord, the men of the Most Ancient Church had it, and the celestial, who are in love to the Lord, have it. These know at once, from a kind of internal observation, whether a thing is good and whether it is true; for this is insinuated by the Lord, because they are conjoined with Him by love. Spiritual men however have no such perception of good and truth in celestial and spiritual things, but instead of it have conscience which dictates; but as before said, this conscience is formed from the knowledges of good and truth which they have imbibed from their parents and masters, and afterwards from their own study in doctrine and in the Word; and in these, even though not entirely good and true, they put their faith. Hence it is that men can have conscience from any doctrine whatever; even the Gentiles have something not unlike conscience from their religion. [3] That the spiritual have no perception of the good and truth of faith, but say and believe that to be true which they have learned and apprehended, is sufficiently evident from the fact that every one says that his own dogma is true, heretics more than others; and that they are not able to see the truth itself, still less to acknowledge it, although thousands of things should declare it. Let every one explore himself and see if he is able to perceive from any other source whether a thing is true; and if when a thing most true is made manifest to him he still does not fail to acknowledge it. As for example, one who makes faith the essential of salvation, and not love: even if all should be read before him which the Lord spoke concerning love and charity (see n. 2373), and if he should know from the Word that all the Law and the Prophets hang upon love to the Lord and charity toward the neighbor, he will nevertheless remain in the idea of faith, and will say that this alone saves. It is otherwise with those who are in celestial and spiritual perception. [4] As regards the perception of what is just and equitable in civil life however, those in the world who are rational have this, and also the perception of what is honorable in moral life. These two perceptions distinguish one man from another, but by no means do such men for this reason have the perception of the good and truth of faith, because this perception is higher or more internal, and flows in from the Lord through the inmost of the rational. [5] The reason also why the spiritual have no perception of the good and truth of faith, is that good and truth are not implanted in their will part, as with celestial men, but in their intellectual part (see n. 863, 875, 927, 1023, 1043, 1044, 2256). Hence it is that the spiritual cannot arrive at the first degree of the light in which the celestial are (n. 2718), but have what is obscure in comparison (n. 1043, 2708 at the beginning, 2715). That the spiritual are entangled in natural memory-knowledge in respect to the truths of faith, follows from this. [6] That a "thicket" or "tangle" in the internal sense signifies natural memory-knowledge, that is, that knowledge which sticks fast in the exterior memory, may also be seen from other passages in the Word. In *Ezekiel :*—

Behold, Asshur was a cedar in Lebanon, with beautiful foliage, and a shady grove, and lofty in height, and his branch was among the tangled boughs (xxxi. 3) ;

where Egypt, which is memory-knowledge, is treated of (n. 1164, 1165, 1186, 1462); "Asshur" denotes the rational (n. 119, 1186); which is also the " cedar," and also " Lebanon," in the Word ; " among the tangled boughs" means among memory-knowledges, for the human rational is founded on its memory-knowledges. [7] In the same :—

Thus saith the Lord Jehovih, Because thou art exalted in stature, and he hath set his branch among the tangled boughs, and his heart is lifted up in its height, strangers, the violent of the nations, shall cut him down, and cast him out (xxxi. 10, 12) ;

concerning Egypt; to "set the branch among the tangled boughs" denotes sticking fast in memory-knowledges, and regarding spiritual, celestial, and Divine things from them. In the same :—

To the end that none of all the trees by the waters exalt themselves in their stature, neither set their branch among the tangled boughs, nor that all that drink waters stand over them in their height, for they shall all be delivered unto death, to the lower earth in the midst of the sons of man, to them that go down to the pit (xxxi. 14) ;

here those are treated of who by reasonings from memory-knowledges desire to enter into the mysteries of faith (that they are made altogether blind, may be seen above, n. 215, 232, 233, 1072, 1911, 2196, 2203, 2568, 2588). To reason from memory-knowledges is to "set the branch among the tangled boughs." In the same :—

She had plants of strength for the scepters of them that bare rule, and her height was exalted among the tangled boughs (xix. 11) ;

this has a similar meaning. [8] In the same :—

The slain of Israel shall be among their idols, round about their altars, and under every green tree, and under every tangled oak (vi. 13) ;

this treats of the worship which those form to themselves who have faith in themselves, and thus in the things which they hatch out from their memory-knowledges; the "tangled oak" denotes the memory-knowledges in such a state. (That "oaks" are apperceptions from memory-knowledges may be seen above, n. 1442, 1443, 2144.) The like is found elsewhere in the same Prophet :—

They saw every high hill, and every tangled tree, and there they sacrificed their sacrifices (xx. 28) ;

a "tangled tree" denotes the things which are dictated not by the Word, but by one's own memory-knowledge. (That worship was performed in groves, and was significative according to the qualities of the trees, may be seen above, n. 2722.) [9] In *Isaiah* :—

Wickedness burneth as the fire ; it devoureth the briars and thorns, and kindleth in the thickets of the forest (ix. 18) ;

the "briars and thorns" denote falsity and cupidity; the "thickets of the forest," memory-knowledges. In the same :—

Jehovah Zebaoth shall cut down the thickets of the forest with iron, and Lebanon shall fall by a mighty one (x. 34) ;

the "thickets of the forest" denote memory-knowledges; and "Lebanon," things rational. In *Jeremiah :—*

Set up a standard toward Zion, for I will bring evil from the north, and a great destruction ; a lion is gone up from his thicket, and a destroyer of nations ; he is on his way, he is gone forth from his place, to make thy land a waste ; thy cities shall be destroyed, without inhabitant (iv. 6, 7) ;

" from his thicket" denotes from memory-knowledge ; and that which ascends into Divine arcana from this makes the "land a waste," that is, lays waste the church. [**10**] The reason why in the Word memory-knowledges are called "thickets," is that they are comparatively of such a character, especially when the cupidities of the love of self and of the world, and the principles of falsity, seek for them. Celestial and spiritual love is that which disposes into order the knowledges which are of the exterior memory ; and the love of self and of the world is that which perverts the order, and disturbs all things in it. These things the man does not take notice of, because he places order in perverted order, good in evil, and truth in falsity. On this account these things are in entanglement; and also on this, that the things of the exterior memory, where these knowledges are, compared with those in the interior memory, where rational things are, are as in a thicket, or as in a dark forest. How shady, opaque, and dark it is there in comparison, a man cannot know so long as he is living in the body ; for he then supposes that all wisdom and intelligence are from this source ; but he will know in the other life, when he comes into the things of his interior memory. That in the exterior memory, which is proper to man while he is living in the world, nothing is less to be found than the light of intelligence and wisdom ; but that all is relatively dark, disorderly, and entangled there, may be seen above (n. 2469–2494).

2832. *By his horns.* That this signifies with all power in regard to the truths of faith, is evident from the signification of "horns." "Horns" are mentioned in many places in the Word; and there signify the power of truth from good; and in the opposite sense the power of falsity from evil; here the meaning is that the spiritual who are signified by the "ram" are entangled in natural memory-knowledge with all their might in regard to truth, and hence that they are deprived of the power of perceiving truths. For the more any one consults natural memory-knowledges, and sticks fast in them in his *animus* and mind in regard to the things which are truths of faith, the more does he lose the light of truth, and with the light, the life of truth. Every one may know this from experience, if he attends and reflects, from those who say that they can believe nothing unless they comprehend that it is so by means of the things of sense, or of memory-knowledge. If you explore their quality, you will find that they believe nothing; and moreover that nothing seems to them more wise than to ascribe everything to nature. There are many also who say that they believe although they do not comprehend; when nevertheless, in secret with themselves, they reason equally as others do from the things of sense and memory-knowledge concerning the truths of faith, as to whether a thing is so. These either have a kind of persuasion breathed in from the love of self and the world, or they do not believe at all. Their quality is manifest from their life. Both classes are indeed in the Lord's spiritual church, but they are not of the church. They who are of the church are in a life of good, and have faith in truths; but the spiritual have faith in other truths besides those which have been impressed on them from infancy, and which they have afterwards confirmed to themselves from doctrine or from some other source. Such is the state of the spiritual, which state is here described by the "ram caught in the thicket by his horns" (see just above, n. 2831). [2] That a "horn" signifies the power of truth from good, is evident from the following passages. In *David* :—

Thou art the glory of their strength, and in Thy good pleasure wilt Thou exalt our horn; for our shield belongeth unto Jehovah, and our king to the Holy One of Israel. My truth and My mercy shall be with him, and in My name shall his horn be exalted; I will set his hand also in the sea, and his right hand in the rivers (*Ps.* lxxxix. 17, 18, 24, 25);

where "our horn" and "his horn" manifestly denote the power of truth. The Lord's spiritual kingdom is there treated of; "our king belongs to the Holy One of Israel" denotes that Divine truth belongs to the Lord. (That a "king" is truth, and that the Lord's royalty is the Divine Truth, may be seen above, n. 1672, 1728, 2015, 2069); to "put his hand in the sea, and his right hand in the rivers" denotes that strength is in the memory-knowledges and the knowledges of truth. (That the "hand" and the "right hand" denote strength, see above, n. 878; and also that the "sea" and the "rivers" denote memory-knowledges and knowledges, n. 28, 2702.) In the same :—

I will love Thee, O Jehovah, my strength; Jehovah is my rock, and my fortress, and my deliverer, my God, my strong rock in whom I trust, my shield, and the horn of my salvation (*Ps.* xviii. 1, 2; 2 *Sam.* xxii. 2, 3);

the "horn of salvation" denotes truth as to power; in this passage "strength," "rock," "fortress," "God," "strong rock," and "shield," are all significative of the power of truth. [3] In the same :—

In Zion will I make a horn to bud unto David, I will prepare a lamp for Mine anointed; His enemies will I clothe with shame (*Ps.* cxxxii. 17, 18);

where the Lord is treated of, who is "David" (n. 1888); a "horn" denotes the power of truth; a "lamp," the light of truth. In *Samuel*:—

My heart hath exulted in Jehovah, my horn is exalted in Jehovah, my mouth is enlarged against mine enemies, because I have been glad in Thy salvation. Jehovah will give strength unto His king, and will exalt the horn of His anointed (1 *Sam.* ii. 1, 10);

this is the prophecy of Hannah; the "horn" denotes the power of truth. [4] In *Moses :*—

The firstling of his ox, honor is his, and his horns are the horns of the unicorn; with them shall he push the peoples all of them, to the ends of the earth (*Deut.* xxxiii. 17);

this is the prophecy of Moses concerning Joseph, where the "horns of the unicorn" denote the great power of truth, as is

manifest also from its being said that he shall "push the peoples with them to the ends of the earth." So too in *David :—*

My horn shalt Thou exalt like the unicorn's (*Ps.* xcii. 10).

And in the same :—

O Jehovah, save me from the mouth of the lion, and answer me from
the horns of the unicorn (*Ps.* xxii. 21) ;

Divine truths, from their height, are called the "horns of uni-
corns ;" hence the "horn" is so often said to be "exalted,"
for exaltation signifies power from the interior. (That what
is internal is represented by what is high, may be seen above,
n. 1735, 2148.)   [5] In *Jeremiah :—*

The Lord hath cut off in fierce anger all the horn of Israel, He hath
drawn back His right hand from before the enemy (*Lam.* ii. 3) ;

to "cut off all the horn of Israel" denotes to deprive of truth
which has power, which is also to "draw back the right hand
from before the enemy." In *Ezekiel :—*

In that day will I make a horn to grow for the house of Israel, and I
will give thee the opening of the mouth in the midst of them (xxix. 21) ;

to "make the horn to grow for the house of Israel," denotes to
multiply the truths of the spiritual church, which is "Israel ;"
the "opening of the mouth" denotes the confession of them.
[6] In *Habakkuk :—*

God will come from Teman, and the Holy One from Mount Paran ;
His honor covered the heavens, and the earth was full of His praise ; and
His brightness shall be as the light ; He had horns out of His hand, and
there was the hiding of His strength (iii. 3, 4) ;

where the Lord is treated of; that "He had horns out of His
hand, and there was the hiding of His strength," plainly denotes the power of truth; that "Mount Paran" is the Divine
Spiritual or the Divine Truth of the Lord's Human, may be
seen above (n. 2714), which also is the "brightness" and the
"light." [7] The Divine Truth of the Lord's Human is thus
described in *John :—*

I saw and behold in the midst of the throne, and of the four animals,
a Lamb standing as if slain, having seven horns, which are the seven spirits
of God sent forth into all the earth (*Rev.* v. 6) ;

the "seven horns" denote holy or Divine truths. (That "seven" means holy, may be seen above, n. 716, 881.) The "seven spirits sent forth into all the earth," are the holy preachings of the same truths. [8] The "horns of the altars" signified nothing else than truth in which is power. Of these it is said in *Moses* :—

Thou shalt make horns upon the four corners of the altar ; out of it shall its horns be (*Exod.* xxvii. 2 ; xxxviii. 2).

So too upon the altar of incense, out of which were to be horns (*Exod.* xxx. 2 ; xxxvii. 25). (That the altar was a principal representative of the Lord and of His worship, may be seen above, n. 921.) The altar was a representative of His Divine Good ; the horns were the representatives of His Divine Truth ; that truth was from good was represented by the horns being out of it, or out of the altar. (That there is no other truth than that which is from good, may be seen above, n. 654, 1162, 1176, 1608, 2063, 2261, 2429.) It is manifest from this that "horns" in the genuine sense signify the power of truth which is from good. [9] That Aaron and his sons when initiated in the ministry, took of the blood of the bullock, and put it upon the horns of the altar with the finger (*Exod.* xxix. 12 ; *Lev.* viii. 15) ; and that Aaron made expiation upon the horns of the altar once in the year (*Exod.* xxx. 10) ; and that when a priest sinned, he offered a bullock, and put of the blood upon the horns of the altar of incense (*Lev.* iv. 3, 7) ; also that when a prince sinned, he offered a burnt-offering, and the blood was sprinkled upon the horns of the altar of burnt-offering (*Lev.* iv. 22, 25) ; and that it was the same when a soul sinned (verses 27, 30, 34, of the same chapter) ; as also when the altar was expiated (*Lev.* xvi. 18, 19)—all these things signified truths from good ; for all sanctifications, inaugurations, and expiations were made by truths, because truths introduce to good (n. 2830). That the "horns of the altar" signified truths which are from good, may also be seen in *John* :—

The sixth angel sounded, and I heard a voice from the four horns of the golden altar which is before God (*Rev.* ix. 13) ;

the "horns of the golden altar" manifestly denote truths from good, for thence came the voice (that "gold" is good may be seen above, n. 113, 1551, 1552; and still more the "golden altar"). **[10]** In *Amos :*—

In the day that I shall visit the transgressions of Israel upon him, I will visit upon the altars of Bethel, and the horns of the altar shall be cut off, and shall fall to the ground (iii. 14) ;

that the "horns of the altar were to be cut off," was because truth from good was no longer represented there; "Bethel" is the Divine Good, and is therefore called the "king's sanctuary," and the "house of the kingdom" (*Amos* vii. 13). The kings being "anointed with oil from a horn" (1 *Sam.* xvi. 1, 13; 1 *Kings* i. 39) represented in like manner truth from good. (The "oil" was good, n. 886; but the "horn," truth; the "royalty" itself in the internal sense is such truth, n. 1728, 2015, in which is power.) **[11]** That a "horn" in the opposite sense signifies the power of falsity which is from evil, is evident from the following passages. In *Amos :*—

Ye who rejoice in a thing of naught, who say, Have we not taken to us horns by our own strength ? (vi. 13) ;

"horns" here denote the power of falsity. In *Zechariah :*—

I lifted up mine eyes and saw, and behold four horns ; and I said unto the angel that talked with me, What are these? And he said to me, These are the horns which have scattered Judah, Israel, and Jerusalem. And Jehovah showed me four smiths ; and I said, What come these to do ? and He said, saying, These are the horns which scattered Judah, so that no man doth lift up his head ; and these are come to terrify them, to cast down the horns of the nations, which lifted up their horn against the land of Judah, to scatter it (i. 18–21) ;

the "horns" denote the power of falsity, which vastates the church. In *Ezekiel :*—

Ye thrust with side and with shoulder, and push all the diseased with your horns, till ye have scattered them abroad (xxxiv. 21) ;

here the shepherds who seduce by falsities are treated of; the "horns" denote the power of falsity; the "shoulder," all power (n. 1085). In *Jeremiah :*—

Jehovah hath destroyed, and hath not pitied, and He hath caused the enemy to rejoice over thee ; He hath exalted the horn of thine adversaries (*Lam.* ii. 17).

In the same :—

The horn of Moab is cut off, and his arm is broken (*Jer.* xlviii. 25) ;

" horn" here denotes powerful falsity.   [**12**] In *David :*—

I said to them that were glorying, Glory ye not, and to the wicked,
Lift not up the horn ; lift not up your horn on high, speak not with a
stiff neck.   All the horns of the wicked will I cut off, the horns of the
righteous shall be lifted up (*Ps.* lxxv. 4, 5, 10) ;

the " horns of the wicked" denote the power of falsity from
evil ; the " horns of the righteous," the power of truth from
good.   [**13**] In *Daniel :*—

A fourth beast was seen, terrible and powerful and strong exceedingly,
and it had iron teeth ; it devoured and brake in pieces, and stamped the
residue with his feet, and it had ten horns.   I considered the horns, and
behold another little horn came up among them, and three of the first
horns were rooted up before it ; and behold in this horn were eyes like
the eyes of a man, and a mouth speaking great things.   I beheld then
because of the voice of the great words which the horn spake ; I desired
certitude concerning the fourth beast, and concerning the ten horns that
were on his head, and concerning the other which came up, and three
fell before it ; and concerning the same horn that had eyes, and a mouth
speaking great things ; I beheld, and the same horn made war with the
saints.   And he said, As for the fourth beast, it shall be a fourth kingdom upon earth, which shall be diverse from all the kingdoms, and shall
devour the whole earth, and shall tread it down, and break it in pieces.
And as for the ten horns, out of this kingdom shall ten kings arise, and
another shall arise after them, and he shall be diverse from the former
ones, and he shall humble three kings ; he shall speak words against the
Most High, and shall wear out the saints ; afterwards the judgment
shall sit (vii. 7, 8, 11, 19–26).

Here in the internal sense the perverted state of the church is
treated of.   The things which were here seen by Daniel, as
the beast, the teeth of iron, the horn in which were eyes, and
the horns that spoke, and those which made war with the
saints, and that which spoke against the Most High, signify
the state of falsity and of heresies within the church.   That
" horns" signify falsity powerful and prevailing, is evident
from the mere fact that eyes are attributed to them, that is,
understanding (n. 2701); and that they spoke, even against
the Most High.   By the " kingdoms" and " kings" are not signified kingdoms and kings, but doctrinal things of falsity ; as
may be seen from their signification in the Word as being
doctrinal things of truth, and in the opposite sense of falsity
(see n. 1672, 2015, 2069, 2547).   [**14**] Again in *Daniel :*—

A ram was seen by him standing before the river, which had two horns ; and the horns were high, but one was higher than the other, and the higher came up last. I saw the ram pushing with his horn westward, and northward, and southward, so that no beasts could stand before him, neither was there any that could deliver out of his hand ; but he did according to his will, and magnified himself. As I was considering, behold a he-goat of the goats came from the west over the face of the whole earth ; this he-goat had a horn between his two eyes ; he came to the ram the lord of the horns, and ran upon him in the fury of his power, and smote him, and brake his two horns ; and there was no power in the ram to stand before him. Afterwards the he-goat of the goats magnified himself exceedingly ; and when he was strong, his great horn was broken, and there came up four horns in place of it. Soon out of one of them went forth a little horn, and grew exceedingly toward the south, and toward the east, and toward beauty ; and it grew even to the army of the heavens, and some of the army and of the stars it cast down to the earth, and trampled upon them. The ram with the two horns, they are the kings of Media and Persia ; the he-goat is the king of Greece ; the four horns in place of one are four kingdoms out of the nation (viii. 1 to the end).

Here in the spiritual sense the state of the spiritual church is treated of, which is the " ram" (n. 2830) ; and the state of that church is described, how it gradually declines and is perverted. The " he-goat of the goats" denotes those who are in faith separate from charity, or in truth separate from good, who begin to uplift themselves against good, and at length against the Lord. The " horns of the ram" are the truths of the spiritual church both internal and external ; the " horns of the he-goat of the goats" are truths which have gradually degenerated into falsities ; and by the " kingdoms" and " kings" here mentioned are not signified kingdoms and kings, but truths and falsities, as already said ; for the Lord's Word in its essence does not treat of worldly and earthly, but of spiritual and heavenly things.   [15] In *John :*—

And there was seen another sign in heaven ; and behold a great red dragon, having seven heads, and ten horns, and upon his heads seven diadems ; his tail drew a third part of the stars of heaven, and cast them to the earth (*Rev.* xii. 3, 4).

And again :—

I saw a beast coming up out of the sea, having seven heads and ten horns, and on his horns ten diadems, and upon his heads names of blasphemy. It was given unto him to make war with the saints, and to overcome them. And then I saw another beast coming up out of the earth, and he had two horns like a lamb (*Rev.* xiii. 1, 2, 7, 11).

Again in the same :—

I saw a woman sitting upon a scarlet-colored beast, full of names of blasphemy ; having seven heads and ten horns ; it was the great Babylon. The seven heads are seven mountains, on which the woman sitteth ; and they are seven kings ; the ten horns are ten kings (*Rev.* xvii. 3, 5, 7, 9, 12, 13).

That by the " horns " here in like manner as in *Daniel* are signified the powers of falsity, is evident.

2833. *And Abraham went, and took the ram.* That this signifies their liberation by the Lord's Divine Human, is evident from the representation of Abraham, as being here the Lord as to His Divine Human (for when Jehovah, or the angel of Jehovah, speaks with Abraham, then " Jehovah," or the " angel of Jehovah," is the Divine Itself, and " Abraham " is the Divine Human) ; and also from the signification of a " ram," as being the spiritual (n. 2830). It is hence manifest that Abraham's going and taking the ram caught in the thicket by his horns, signifies the liberation of the spiritual by the Lord's Divine Human. (That without the Lord's coming into the world the spiritual could not possibly have been saved, may be seen above, n. 2661, 2716 ; and that they have salvation and liberation by the Lord's Divine Human, n. 2716.)

2834. *And offered him up for a burnt-offering in the stead of his son.* That this signifies their sanctification and adoption, is evident from the signification of " offering for a burnt-offering," as being to be sanctified (see n. 2776) ; and from the signification of " in the stead of his son," as being adoption, namely, by the Lord's Divine Human, which here is " Abraham " (n. 2833). The adoption of the spiritual is described in *John* :—

Jesus said, I am the vine, ye are the branches ; he that abideth in Me, and I in him, the same bringeth forth much fruit ; for without Me ye can do nothing (xv. 5).

(That a " vine " is the spiritual church may be seen above, n. 1069.)

2835. Verse 14. *And Abraham called the name of that place, Jehovah-will-see, as it is said to this day, In the moun-*

tain Jehovah will see. "And Abraham called the name of that place," signifies the quality of their state from the Lord's Divine Human ; "Jehovah-will-see," signifies the Lord's providence; "as it is said to this day," signifies what is perpetual; "in the mountain Jehovah will see," signifies charity, by means of which it was provided by the Lord that they should be saved.

2836. *Abraham called the name of that place.* That this signifies the quality of their state (namely, of the spiritual) from the Lord's Divine Human, is evident from the signification of "calling a name," as being to know what the thing is, that is, its quality (see n. 144, 145, 1754, 1896, 2009); from the signification of "place," as being state (see n. 1273–1277, 1376–1381, 2625); and from the representation of Abraham, as being the Lord as to His Divine Human (see n. 2833). Hence it is manifest that "Abraham called the name of that place," signifies the quality of the state of the spiritual from the Lord's Divine Human. That the spiritual are saved by the Lord's coming into the world, was shown above (n. 2661, 2716); also that they have illumination from the Lord's Divine. Human (n. 2716); and that it is provided that those should be saved who are in the faith of charity, that is, in charity, follows in this verse. This is the state which is signified by these words.

2837. *Jehovah-will-see.* That this signifies the Lord's providence, is evident from the signification of "seeing," when predicated of Jehovah or the Lord, as being to foresee and provide (see n. 2807). (That "Jehovah" is the Lord, may be seen above, n. 1343, 1736, 2156, 2329.) In the literal sense this is the naming of a place, but in the internal sense it is the quality of a state which is described; for times and spaces are merely of nature; and therefore when the sense of the letter of the Word passes from nature into heaven, the natural idea of those things altogether perishes, and becomes the spiritual idea that corresponds to them.

2838. *As it is said to this day.* That this signifies what is perpetual, is evident from the signification of "to-day" in the Word—explained in what follows. We read in several places in the Word, "Even to this day," or "to to-day;" as in what goes before, " He is the father of Moab even unto this day; and the father of Ammon unto this day" (*Gen.* xix. 37, 38); and later in the same book, " The name of the city is Beer-sheba, even to this day" (*Gen.* xxvi. 33). Also this, "The sons of Israel eat not the sinew of the part put out of place, which is upon the hollow of the thigh, even to this day" (*Gen.* xxxii. 32). And also this, " This is the pillar of Rachel's grave even unto this day" (*Gen.* xxxv. 20). " Joseph made it a statute even to this day" (*Gen.* xlvii. 26). In the historical sense these things regard the time when Moses lived; but in the internal sense by " this day," and by " to-day," there is signified perpetuity and eternity of state. That " day" is state may be seen above (n. 23, 487, 488, 493, 893); and thus "to-day" also, which is time present. That which is of time in the world, is eternal in heaven. That this might be signified, "to-day" is added, or " to this day," although it appears to those who are in the historical sense as if it involved nothing further. The like is said elsewhere in the Word (as *Josh.* iv. 9; vi. 25; vii. 26; *Judges* i. 21, 26; and in other places). [2] That " to-day" signifies perpetuity and eternity may be seen in *David :—*

I will tell of the decree : Jehovah hath said unto Me, Thou art My Son, this day have I begotten Thee (*Ps.* ii. 7) ;

where " this day" manifestly denotes what is eternal. In the same :—

Forever O Jehovah Thy Word is settled in the heavens, Thy truth is unto generation and generation ; Thou hast established the earth, and it abideth ; they abide this day according to Thy judgments (*Ps.* cxix. 89–91) ;

where also " this day" manifestly denotes what is eternal. In *Jeremiah :—*

Before I formed Thee in the belly, I knew Thee ; and before Thou camest forth out of the womb, I sanctified Thee ; I gave Thee for a prophet unto the nations ; I have set Thee this day over the nations and over the kingdoms, and I have made Thee this day a defenced city, and an iron pillar, and walls of brass (i. 5, 10, 18) ;

here in the sense of the letter Jeremiah is treated of, but in the internal sense the Lord is meant; " I have set Thee this day, or to-day, over the nations and over the kingdoms, and I